Risk Analytics

The 2022 World Economic Forum surveyed 1,000 experts and leaders who indicated their risk perception that the earth's conditions for humans are a main concern in the next 10 years. This means environmental risks are a priority to study in a formal way. At the same time, innovation risks are present in the minds of leaders, new knowledge brings new risk, and the adaptation and adoption of risk knowledge is required to better understand the causes and effects can have on technological risks. These opportunities require not only adopting new ways of managing and controlling emerging processes for society and business, but also adapting organizations to changes and managing new risks.

Risk Analytics: Data-Driven Decisions Under Uncertainty introduces a way to analyze and design a risk analytics system (RAS) that integrates multiple approaches to risk analytics to deal with diverse types of data and problems. A risk analytics system is a hybrid system where human and artificial intelligence interact with a data gathering and selection process that uses multiple sources to the delivery of guidelines to make decisions that include humans and machines. The RAS system is an integration of components, such as data architecture with diverse data, and a risk analytics process and modeling process to obtain knowledge and then determine actions through the new knowledge that was obtained. The use of data analytics is not only connected to risk modeling and its implementation, but also to the development of the actionable knowledge that can be represented by text in documents to define and share explicit knowledge and guidelines in the organization for strategy implementation.

This book moves from a review of data to the concepts of a RAS. It reviews RAS system components required to support the creation of competitive advantage in organizations through risk analytics. Written for executives, analytics professionals, risk management professionals, strategy professionals, and postgraduate students, this book shows a way to implement the analytics process to develop a risk management practice that creates an adaptive competitive advantage under uncertainty.

Risk Analytics
Data-Driven Decisions under Uncertainty

Eduardo Rodriguez, PhD

Founder and Principal, IQAnalytics Inc.

University of Ottawa and Wenzhou Kean University

CRC Press
Taylor & Francis Group
Boca Raton London New York

CRC Press is an imprint of the
Taylor & Francis Group, an **informa** business
AN AUERBACH BOOK

First edition published 2024
by CRC Press
2385 Executive Center Drive, Suite 320, Boca Raton FL 33431

and by CRC Press
4 Park Square, Milton Park, Abingdon, Oxon, OX14 4RN

CRC Press is an imprint of Taylor & Francis Group, LLC

© 2024 Taylor & Francis Group, LLC

ISBN: 978-0-367-35961-4 (hbk)
ISBN: 978-1-032-50778-1 (pbk)
ISBN: 978-0-429-34289-9 (ebk)

DOI: 10.1201/9780429342899

Typeset in Times
by MPS Limited, Dehradun

Dedication

To my wife Zhouping Huang who is always taking
wonderful care of our family

Contents

Author

Eduardo Rodriguez, PhD, is a member of the advisory board of the new Finance, Innovation and Technology Certificate from the Fields Institute of Mathematics, University of Toronto in Toronto, Ontario, Canada. He is an assistant professor in the School of the Mathematical Sciences at Wenzhou-Kean University in Wenzhou, China. He is the founder and leader of the Risk Analytics Lab at Wenzhou Kean University. Lately, he has been active participant in the creation and development of the Data Science Program at the Inter-American University of Puerto Rico and keynote speaker in the CSAE International Conference on Computer Science and Application Engineering 2021 and 2022. Moreover, he is an analytics adjunct professor at Telfer School of Management at University of Ottawa, Ontario, Canada. He is the founder and principal at IQAnalytics Inc. Research Centre and Consulting Firm in Ottawa, Ontario, Canada.

Eduardo was the first Sentry Endowed chair in Business Analytics University of Wisconsin-Stevens Point. He has been corporate faculty of the MSc in analytics at Harrisburg University of Science and Technology Pennsylvania USA, senior associate faculty of the Center for Dynamic Leadership Models in Global Business at The Leadership Alliance Inc. Toronto, Ontario, Canada, and in his work, he has created and developed the Analytics Stream of the MBA at the University of Fredericton, Frederiction, New Brunswick, Canada. He has been a visiting scholar at the Chongqing University, China and EAFIT University for the Master of Risk Management.

Eduardo has extensive experience in analytics, knowledge, and risk management, mainly in the insurance and banking industry. He has been the knowledge management advisor and quantitative analyst at EDC Export Development Canada in Ottawa, regional director of PRMIA (Professional Risk Managers International Association) in Ottawa, and executive vice president and vice president of marketing and planning for insurance companies and banks in Colombia. Moreover, he has worked as a part-time professor at Andes University and CESA in Colombia, is an author of six books in analytics, and a reviewer of several journals and with publications in peer-reviewed journals and conferences. He created and chaired the Analytics Think-Tank, organized and chaired of the International Conference in Analytics ICAS, is a member of academic committees for conferences in knowledge management, and is an international lecturer in the analytics field.

Eduardo holds a PhD from Aston Business School, Aston University in the United Kingdom, an MSc. in mathematics Concordia University, Montreal, Quebec, Canada, certification of the Advanced Management Program from McGill University, Montreal, Quebec, Canada, and an MBA and bachelor's in mathematics from Los Andes University, Colombia. His main research interest is in the field of strategic risk, risk analytics, strategic intelligence development, and knowledge management applied to enterprise risk management.

Introduction

The world Economic Forum in the 2022 report of a survey to 1,000 experts and leaders indicated in their risk perception that the condition of the earth for humans is a main concern in the next 10 years. This means environmental risks are a priority to study in a formal way, using the adequate methods and techniques, obtaining data and creating multidisciplinary groups doing data analytics applied to risk management. At the same time innovation risks are present in the minds of leaders, new knowledge brings new risks and the adaptation and adoption of risk knowledge is required to understand more what causes and effects can have the technological risks. Innovation is a means to progress and to create value in a society. Artificial intelligence and digital evolution in the society are opening wonderful opportunities for new generations. These opportunities in most of the cases require not only to adopt new ways to manage and control emerging processes for the society and businesses, but also to adapt organizations to changes and manage new risks.

The innovation risks emerge from multiple dimensions; in particular, they are associated with human and machine interactions to perform tasks, solve problems, and make decisions. Moreover, risk is a factor in organizations that require an ongoing observation, assessment, and monitoring to properly create and sustain competitive advantages. From the risk management point of view, the purpose of this review is to reflect on what organizations and people are perceiving about innovation risk, such as how new knowledge creates new risks that require human intervention to mitigate and discover their consequences. The use of data science, artificial intelligence, digitalization, and application of new knowledge to several domains and problems in the society is moving very fast with an incremental need to review risk-related issues such as ethical principles, regulation, limits of actions, consequences of certain decisions, bias, wrong experiment designs, etc.

Innovation risk analysis should be part of the mindset and actions of new data and computer scientists to create solutions in support of humans' well-being and in the design of the future. The future is not a fact or result of the predictive analytics models; however, model outcomes are possible results to evaluate potential futures and actions to perform. Data Science-AI has a crucial role in the creation of new knowledge that generates inevitable new risks, and at the same time in mitigating risk of innovation. At the end of this review, the reader will have the capacity to collaborate in the creation of a mindset in data and computer scientists that proactively contributes to the understanding and control of innovation risk. Their contribution can guide and simulate possible futures and orientation to select the future that could be better and worth having for societies.

The points above indicate that risk analytics knowledge obtained in the financial sector can be a valuable support to enhance actionable knowledge in areas of risk that are less explored and with more demanding needs to mitigate the impact of possible adverse events. Thus, in this book, the reader will find the presentation of the analytics process (Rodriguez, 2017) applied to the risk management processes and the pillars for developing a risk analytics system (RAS). Additionally, the book develops the concepts related to management under uncertainty and risk and how risk analytics creates knowledge to mitigate and control risk in organizations and society development. This book is an introduction to the most important aspects for adapting risk analytics to any socio-economic sector. The application is not only to the financial organizations but also to manufacturing, service, government, and not-for-profit organizations. The concepts in this book are all with one main driver to support organizations to build adaptive and sustainable competitive advantages in organizations through risk analytics. The assumption is that some risks are possible to evaluate and prevent; some are going to have events realization

DOI: 10.1201/9780429342899-1

and the risk will be in addition about controlling the impact (losses) of those events and finally to identify how continue on track in the business.

Risk analytics is about the capacity to use data analytics/science before, during and after the risk events. In a current situation, COVID-19 modified several aspects of the socio-economic world. The Ukraine crisis generated modifications in business and families. The supply-chain risk (see Section 4.8 for exposure understanding of supply-chain risk illustration) is converted into one of the fundamental risks to understand and to find a way to assess, mitigate, and control.

Reeves and Deimler (2011) expressed, "We live in an era of risk and instability. Globalization, new technologies, and greater transparency have combined to upend the business environment and give many CEOs a deep sense of unease. Just look at the numbers. Since 1980 the volatility of business operating margins, largely static since the 1950s, has more than doubled, as has the size of the gap between winners (companies with high operating margins) and losers (those with low ones)." These points open the space for risk analytics as a means to support the adaptation of organizations in the way that data analytics is converted into the source and engine to identify possible outcomes and resources required to take the best roads to keep the business in good performance. Regarding this aspect of adaptive competitive advantages, Esser (2021) indicated that adaptability is a matter of trust and a state that is ongoing in organizations. Organizations evolution brings results that are not deterministic. Strategies are changing based on what is required to drive decisions and actions. "The key lies in achieving a permanent state of adaptability. Every business leader knows that their company needs to adapt in order to survive long term. However, the real issue is not successfully transforming your organization on a one-time basis—it's writing the ability to adapt and transform into the company's DNA. It's developing a mechanism or reflex for dealing with whatever crisis comes along, be it financial, technological, environmental, or health related." In this book, the concepts of a RAS system have purposes of monitoring, evaluating, and providing actionable knowledge through methods/techniques and mindsets to guide and support organizations' adaptation and transformation.

Some risks are continuously appearing in organizations' operation not only because they were previously known or identified but also because they were dormant and because new knowledge emerges and brings new risks. An example, among many, is the misinformation and wrong knowledge risk because of AI development, if in fractions of seconds machines change sources of knowledge information and create confusion in society. The mitigation for these disruptive risks can be different, such as the redefinition of AI as a new capacity that has to be created for the benefit of humans and as a supplement of their development more than a problem of optimization of the emulation of the human mind. The new risks with limited knowledge to deal with them are growing, as it is the case with liabilities coming from earth-related risks – climate change and its effect on societies. Or, in the case of having the interaction of humans with machines, the risk is highly unknown and simulations performed are limited. Experimentation can be a way to mitigate risks of reactions to live with intelligent holograms of people who are or not existing in the reality.

In the chapters ahead, this book introduces the way to analyze and design a risk analytics system (RAS) that integrates the components of what risk analytics does in separated settings using multiple approaches to deal with a diverse type of data and problems to solve. A risk analytics system is a hybrid system where humans and artificial intelligence/machines are interacting from a data gathering/selection process that uses data from multiple sources to the delivery of guidelines to make decisions that include humans and machines. A good example is a lending process that traditionally uses organized data of financial statements, customer data in the bank, or insurance or retail company (online or not), but when data is not available from those sources the AI component of the RAS systems needs to search for data that describe the potential risk units/users such as transactions in daily life, use of services/utilities, use of transportation, family aspects, etc. to input that data to the models and means to create risk analytics knowledge (more information to read about Ant Financial, ZestAI, AIBank-Baidu).

The models will be built based on data available; the human power will evaluate risks that are under nonstandard conditions and will control the calibration and adjustments of models and methods/rules used to guide decisions.

The RAS system is an integration of components such as data architecture with diverse data, and a risk analytics process/modeling process to obtain knowledge and then going to the stage of creation capacity for actions through the new knowledge that is obtained. Modeling outcomes are at a minimum if stakeholders do not understand what they can do with those outcomes and how to deal with them for improving operational information systems. An example is risk classification, which can have high in accuracy in modeling, but the new knowledge will require translation of these outcomes to policies, operation manuals, documents, and how people in the front, middle, and back office can improve their results of dealing with the categories of risk.

The use of data analytics is not only connected to risk modeling and its implementation but also to the development of the actionable knowledge that can be represented by text in documents to define and share explicit knowledge and guidelines in the organization for strategy implementation. There are several products in a company portfolio, the same as many stakeholders, and all of them have potential risk relationships because of transactions and operations. The support for organizations to deal with risks from known and unknown sources that can create unknown effects is the RAS for connecting the actions before, in, and after the risk events to mitigate and control losses. Models existing in organizations can be sophisticated in risk management but that is not enough to create winning and adaptive strategies; risk management requires an integral view, a system to deal with many capabilities that organizations have for risk management, and an integral risk analytics process to provide value to the organization.

The concept of risk analytics in this book is defined as the analytics process developed in the creation and use of analytics techniques, methods, and development of measurement systems to support decision making and problem solutions under uncertainty and risk. This book is not a mathematics book, but there is a presentation of how mathematical/quantitative concepts can be adopted to deal with uncertainty and risk in organizations. There are several computational tools, methods, algorithms, and techniques to solve problems with an affordable computational capacity to use them. However, there is a crucial aspect to enhance, and that is how to develop systems to be used in a proper way that is powerful and the best arsenal of possible means to solve problems and support the decision-making process. This means answering the question of how risk analytics is adding value to organizations and producing actions and operational capacity to achieve a high performance in an industry, government, or social organizations.

Figure I.1 indicates the scope of risk analytics represented by product maintenance and development, processes, and markets. The main idea is that organizations produce an offer to a market using certain process/technologies and in each component, there are risks emerging. Monitoring risk needs to be related to variables such as the needs of stakeholders, creation of portfolios, defining revenues policies and strategies, and product design. Nowadays, for example, several changes in product design can modify risk mitigation actions. For example, peer-to-peer financial transactions, use of networks to provide solutions to customers/user, blockchain changing organizations' offers and transactions in health care, insurance, banking, etc.; online transactions are changing retail commerce, work, and education; development of products is more and more based on data products; services are more on self-service and activities in organizations have higher levels of automation and digital transformation. Those changes are connected to the process to manage risk associated with profiles, transactions, and operations, the same as planning and execution processes. Moreover, what is happening in markets is part of the influencing factors that can modify the conditions of risks in organizations in this book, a market that is containing socio-economic factors that can modify the conditions of the organization's performance.

In Figures I.2 and I.3, there is a summary of the meaning of RAS in this book. The backbone of the system follows the sequence of strategic definition and alignment in all steps forward for

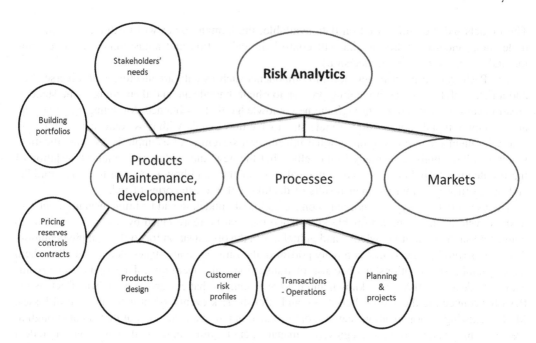

FIGURE I.1 Risk analytics in at least three areas of product development and maintenance, process and markets, from pure and applied mathematics models to statistical – ML-AI modeling.

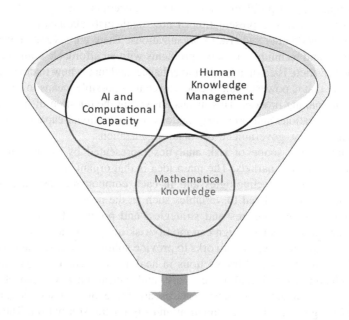

Risk Analytics System (RAS)

FIGURE I.2 The RAS combines human and artificial intelligence with computational and mathematical capacity to create value before, in, and after risk events.

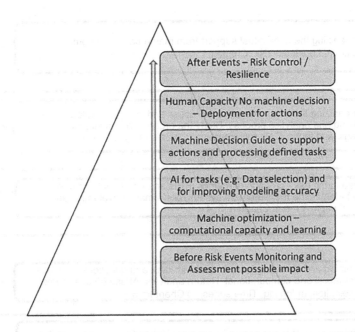

FIGURE I.3 The RAS system is moving from monitoring and follow-up to the support of actions of control and development of after risk event activities, creating the learning process.

implementing what organizations are required to do and desire to achieve. The goals/metrics to achieve need data that has to be organized and prepared for use in the analytics process, moving from EDA to modeling for providing results or new knowledge that will be shared, stored, and accessed by stakeholders. The new knowledge, data, and knowledge transferring components of the RAS system are under an ongoing process for monitoring and creation of the means for updating the operational/actionable required knowledge as it is a document or its equivalent (voice messages, wikies, tweets, or any network communication entity that transfers knowledge). Documents in the RAS are live objects that are updated according to results of the risk analytics process.

This book is divided into nine chapters (Figure I.4) that will introduce the data organization to use techniques and algorithms to solve risk analytics problems. The topics are combined with risk analytics examples that have multiple grades of mathematics/statistics/machine learning involved, but that indicate the value of having the quantitative approach mixed with qualitative combination. Regarding the concepts in this book, there is a presentation of general topics under the assumption that all companies require risk analytics and the observation of the evolution of risk analytics in monitoring the good and bad practices of risk management in organizations.

The chapters of this book are presented in a sequence that moves from a review of data to the concepts of a RAS. The topics of the chapters are linked by the main driver of the book, which is to review the RAS components required to support the creation of competitive advantage in organizations through risk analytics. The chapters are organized as follows:

- Chapter 1 provides the fundamentals of risk management, mathematics, traditional models in finance, and the basis of analysis and design of information systems, for a better understanding of the examples and concepts used across the next chapters.
- Chapter 2 is about risk management, modeling, and the data analytics process. The chapter is a presentation of risk modeling as a common subprocess to the whole risk

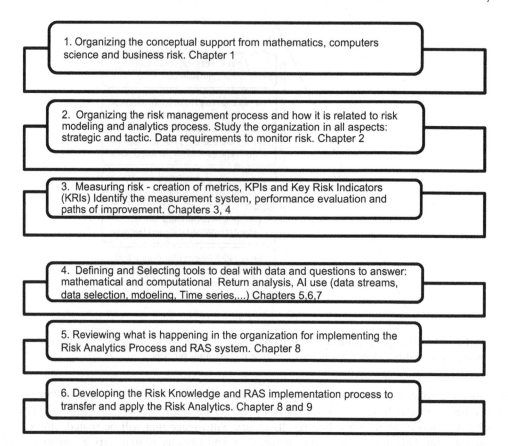

FIGURE I.4 Components of RAS and chapters in the book.

management process. There is an introduction to the data analytics process that is based on the ongoing feedback in every step that is performed from transforming data into actions based on analytics. In this regard, for example, data to use in organization will depend on the organizations' goals and problems to solve will be connected to the models used. The models' explanation starts with exploratory data analysis (EDA) to the creation of estimators for parameters for models based on the data available and usable. The chapter includes a risk analytics road map as the connection of all steps in analytics and risk management processes. The whole presentation is oriented to create understanding from data for making decisions and define paths of actions.

- Chapter 3 is related to decision making under risk and its analytics support: In risk management, there are many decisions to make (limits, exposure, etc.) and in organizations most of the decisions are under risk and uncertainty. However, all these decisions will be pointed to the organizations' goals and in this chapter, there is a presentation of descriptive analytics leading to developing a benchmarking system of risk indicators. At the same time, the chapter illustrates the use of analytics techniques like clusters or linear programming in dealing with decisions and risk. One of the aspects to consider in this chapter is the creation indicators through time in order to develop new means to evaluate the risk management results.

- Chapter 4 presents how risk management and analytics are acting in organizations: This chapter is a guide to deal with several aspects in risk analytics application to solve problems. The main points are associated with measurement systems and creation of metrics. Metrics can be related to exposure management, potential loss prediction, and creation of metrics for organizations risk control.

- Chapter 5 is dedicated to exploring tools for risk management: analytics and non-analytics based. The context is that tools are used in prevention, resilience, and prediction stages of risk management before, in, and after events that appear. The chapter is mainly on understanding the value of assets and return of individual or portfolio investments. In this chapter, there is a presentation of the capabilities that are required in risk management through the development of qualitative and quantitative models for return understanding and how to organize products created to deal with risk through hedging. The main idea is to show how conceptualization in the modeling process is led by the definition of strategic definitions.
- Chapter 6 introduces techniques in data analytics and risk management using structured and unstructured data: This chapter presents the approaches of supplementing the use of structured and unstructured data to support data analytics and decision making. The chapter starts by indicating the difference of storing and accessing traditional structured data and the diversity of data that is possible to use in risk management in current and future business environments. Structured and unstructured data complement one another and techniques to deal with them require computational capacity and algorithms that can be different as well.
- Chapter 7 explains the basic concepts of techniques in machine and statistical learning in risk analytics. In this chapter, there are examples of model construction from data gathering to model selection and development of solutions and actions. Models' explanations are looking for the understanding of the type of problem and type of data that is possible to use, depending on the problems/questions that are being required to answer.
- Chapter 8 indicates how risk analytics provide support to monitoring risks, dealing with bias, implementation barriers, and assumptions in the risk analytics process. In this chapter, the main purpose is to introduce factors affecting risk analytics implementation and development. The chapter takes into account not only the modeling process but also the risk analytics thinking culture with an enterprise-wide view. The chapter indicates the components of the RAS and how knowledge created from risk analytics can be organized in actions.
- Chapter 9 is about creation of actions and value: This chapter is concentrated on the guide to analyze and design a RAS to implement analytics solutions in the organization. In the chapter, LGD is presented and reviewed for understanding the loss distribution, with examples of combining structural analysis of organizations and possible risk combinations.

The content of the chapters is possible for use for financial and nonfinancial organizations, analytics professionals, risk management professionals, strategy professionals, and students at the postgraduate level in risk management, analytics, and strategy. The aim of the book is to indicate a way to implement the analytics process to develop a risk management practice that creates adaptive competitive advantages under the uncertainty that organizations have in the current and future times. Organizations use data based on the definition of metrics (risk indicators), business and goals definition, according to internal and external observations of organization's performance in a market or industry. All processes of risk management require risk analytics. Risk analytics is the ends to a means to manage variability of what the expected results could be for a society or organization (expected values that are weighted averages of potential results). Risk analytics is about the understanding how to control areas of exposure, losses given the occurrence of adverse events, review of what is quantitative and how to connect qualitative and quantitative risk analysis, use of techniques that are coming from data mining, and from risk management practice. Multiple techniques are used, including mathematics-based models (return or valuation of certain assets) and some statistical and machine learning approaches of solutions that are in a classification time series, prediction, etc. The purpose of risk analytics is to embed all the analytics arsenal of solutions in operational and risk management systems that support tactics and strategies using a strong risk monitoring process.

There are several metrics and technologies related to risk management that are beyond the goals of this book and they will be presented without details; however, the structure of the risk analytics process will be discussed, and it will be a key piece to support any new advances in risk analytics and quantitative finance/financial engineering and risk management in organizations that are not only financial institutions.

1 Fundamental Concepts

This chapter is about the concepts that are required to build a risk analytics system (RAS). The concepts are a combination of finance, linear algebra, multivariate statistics, probability, and risk management theory. Everything is about learning in an organization in the sense of creating knowledge to mitigate risk. The main idea is that business learning is connected with statistical and machine learning. The way to create knowledge from data is about using data analytics, but the use and implementation of solutions is about business learning. As everything in this book, the idea is that the concepts are across industries and processes. The nature of risk analytics is that techniques and processes are applicable to any type of organization. It is a matter of adaptation of the concepts based on the evolution of organizations to deal with uncertainty and risk. The learning process of risk analytics is associated with the organization's development to solve problems and put the solutions in the hands of stakeholders. As Mayer-Schönberger V. and Ramge T. (2022) pointed-out, "For many innovators exploiting digital technologies—especially AI and machine learning—great ideas need to be paired with relevant data to create a viable product. Without mountains of suitable training data, safe and reliable autonomous vehicles will remain a pipe dream."

1.1 ALL ORGANIZATIONS REQUIRE RISK ANALYTICS

Organizations are looking at implementing data-driven decision-making processes, business process improvement, and methods for advancing faster in innovation, to be smarter, reduce variance of expected results, and to keep a successful business in good performance. The assessment, prediction, analysis, and control of the variation of organizations' results are crucial tasks to generate competitive, dynamic, and adaptive advantages for organizations. As Beinhocker (1999) expressed, "Strategy development inherently requires managers to make a prediction about the future. Based on this prediction, managers make big decisions about company focus, the investment of resources, and how to coordinate activities across the company." Risk analytics creates knowledge to develop intelligence and intelligence is a capacity to adapt the organization to the no deterministic world; this means to deal with uncertainty. If risk analytics is not leading actions for adaptation the value of risk analytics is reduced, it will be great exercise of mathematics or computing data science but not to improve competitive positions in markets. The value of risk analytics in dealing with risk (Figure 1.1) is because of the capacity of data analytics to create knowledge to reduce uncertainty and it is transformed into risk in order to use the new and previous knowledge to mitigate risk.

Measuring and monitoring risk is a priority in today's organizations. There is a fundamental need for a firmwide understanding of risk exposure and its control. In its implementation, risk analytics faces important challenges, such as data management, dealing with assumptions, the modeling process, the standards and metrics building process, the evaluation process, and communication among stakeholders. In this book, the focus is on the understanding of how the analytics process is possible to embed in the risk management and strategy formulation and implementation processes. Organizations are in search of creating capacity and capabilities to deal with risk using the human, data, and intelligent machine assets to keep the business in good shape. As Traykov et al. (2015) pointed out, the interest in organizations is to promote the use of new assets: "Investors can eliminate specific risk by diversifying their companies to include many different assets. Some risks can be avoided through diversification, but exposure to these types of risk will be rewarded in the market. Instead, investors should hold a combination of non-risk assets and marketing portfolio, the exact combination depends on investors' appetite for risk."

DOI: 10.1201/9780429342899-2

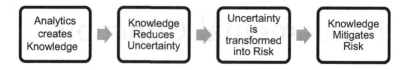

FIGURE 1.1   The value of analytics in dealing with risk.

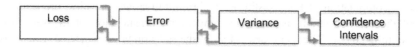

FIGURE 1.2   Basic description of risk evaluation.

Organizations are risk and knowledge entities that participate in markets in the search of value creation for their stakeholders, improving control on risks affecting performance at all levels including financial, social, employees, processes, customer, supplier, etc. In that direction of defining organizations, computational and analytic capacities produce outcomes in risk analysis that require business interpretation/contextualization to provide value to the organizations. Nowadays, risk-related disciplines are the same as analytics and are crucial to strengthen organizations' operation, marketing, finance, and stakeholders networks.

The conception of managing risk knowledge leads to many questions in all organizations to answer about risk analytics; some of them are general and basic to develop risk analytics capabilities that support organizations. For example:

- how to use the analytics process to create an integrative view of analytics for assessing and controlling risks
- how to define the data requirements for developing the appropriate risk assessment and controls
- how to add value to organizations through data analytics applied to risk management
- how to connect the steps of risk analytics to a performance measurement system
- how to provide insights for managing exposure, loss analysis, and predictive and prescriptive methods/actions in risk management
- how to use different types of analytics tools in risk management

These questions are general in organizations of all types and Figure 1.2 indicates how the concept of risk evaluation is translated to the loss concept/error/variance/confidence intervals and terms used in risk management and analytics. Loss functions are measuring errors, variation regarding expected results, and the evaluation of parameters/metrics is associated with confidence intervals. A loss function in machine learning is about errors between predicted values and actual values; the loss function in return is the distribution of returns or a loss function in insurance claims is related to the difference between revenue/premium, recoveries, and claims, and so on. These concepts are embedded in the design of measurement processes that create metrics to evaluate the "distance" between reality and prediction/inference through data analytics.

1.2   EVOLUTION OF RISK ANALYTICS

The risk analytics process is based on the incorporation of analytics approaches/methods/techniques to deal with risk-related data. In particular, structured and unstructured financial data can affect a risk management practice. This book concentrates on the principles of applying analytics techniques that can be improved by new emerging algorithms and mathematical/statistical and computational capacity. The structure and techniques are in continuous development. New models and techniques are continuously discovered, and organization of data and the process to work with it will be durable and based on the risk analytics knowledge acquired by organizations' employees.

Topics related to using data analytics have been part of the practice in risk-related areas for many years; techniques have been used in several cases for many years as well. There is, in the current socio-economic environment, more computational capacity, data is less expensive, and there are approaches through machine learning supplementing the statistical methods leading research in AI and data science use. The speed of advances in data science is high and the acceleration of knowledge creation is not well understood. A reflection about the advances can be done based on what some decades ago was observed and what is happening now. Currently, the speed of knowledge creation is at a different rate as it is imagined in the times of operations' research infancy. The capacity of solving problems, working in real time, and using software capabilities is very robust and accessible. Organizations and professional have access to more opportunities to use analytics capabilities. For example, currently there is a high possibility to use by most people several algorithms and methods of solving problems that were developed years ago; some because of computing capacity improvement, some because of algorithm implementations are handier, and some because more education and consciousness of the value of data analytics is in organizations.

Historically, the analytics capabilities have evolved and consolidated the pillars of what currently data analytics is and what is in the future possible to use: statistical test, optimization methods, statistical models, machine learning algorithms, etc. It is possible to observe this evolution through examples in the following paragraphs. Bursk and Chapman (1963) expressed, "In the years since the mid 1950s a trend toward a new and more scientific approach to the solution of business problems has been developing. It stems from methods first suggested by the advocates of 'operations research.' But it is already apparent that by drawing in depth both on mathematics and on social sciences, and by utilizing intensively the high-speed electronic computer, researchers are beginning to give to the decision-making process a scientific base akin to the established methods which have long provided the bases for research in physics, biology, and chemistry."

This note seems written now. The differences regarding the current time are associated with access to the means for solving the problems, the communities developing open-source software that provide access to what data analytics is requiring, the improvement of computational capacity, advances in data administration and use, etc. Of course, the most important is the increment of users and interest of people in what data analytics can to do to help decision-making and problem-solving processes. Models can be used in more advanced ways to solve more complex problems and concentrate on error minimization. Norbert Wiener (1961) wrote, "The theory of linear prediction and of non-linear prediction both involve some criteria of the goodness of the fit of the prediction. The simplest criterion, although by no means the only usable one, is that of minimizing the mean square of the error. This is used in a particular form in connection with the functionals of the Brownian motion which I employ for the construction of non-linear apparatus, ..."

The development of analytics work and in particular risk analytics is centered in what Raiffa (1968) indicated that decisions under uncertainty proceed by a construction of a list of viable options available, list of events that can occur, consider time horizon, evaluate possible results of the options, put some measure of uncertainty, and select a strategy. Simon (1977) noted that a decision-making process comprises intelligence (problem/opportunity definition), design (model formulation and validation), choice (selection solution to model), and implementation. Different models/DSS (decision support systems) can be designed according to the decision-making process. One big constraint for creating support systems and decision systems is in organizing and training people/users/analysts to do more with the tools that are available.

Creation of models will be a challenge by today's and future organizations. Organizations are looking for understanding reality and predicting events to be proactive and less reactive to possible events that can affect organizations' performance. Changes and variations of expected results are part of the reality. The search for understanding the variability is a way to identify what paths an organization can take based on the knowledge and observation of causes and effects of variation in variables or factors that describe events in nature and organizations. As Mosterin (1978) pointed out, the world is not structured in a unique way, but the structure is based on the projection of people's concepts on the world. The creation of models are concepts based and they are not limited to the mathematical structure. It requires the computational capacity for learning and using that knowledge in business learning improvement. It is crucial to keep in mind what Goldratt and Cox (1986) indicated with regard to the orientation of scientific approach to know: "I view science as nothing more than an understanding of the way the world is and why it is that way. At any given time our scientific knowledge is simply the current state of the art of our understanding. I do not believe in absolute truths. I fear such beliefs because they block the search for better understanding ... Knowledge should be pursued, I believe, to make our world better-to make life more fulfilling." The adoption of a view as Goldratt's is what organizations' management is looking for through data analytics.

These previous fundamentals of risk analytics are indication that data analytics have been around organizations for many years. Currently, there are new methodologies to solve problems and support decisions-making processes, similar to several techniques available to tackle problems of and access to data resources at affordable cost. What is changing very fast is the capacity to organize the process of obtaining-creating knowledge from data in a more systematic way, as Baesens et al. indicated in 2009: "Data mining involves extracting interesting patterns from data and can be found at the heart of operational research (OR), as its aim is to create and enhance decision support systems. Even in the early days, some data mining approaches relied on traditional OR methods such as linear programming and forecasting, and modern data mining methods are based on a wide variety of OR methods including linear and quadratic optimization, genetic algorithms and concepts based on artificial ant colonies."

At the same time, the creation of more and better road maps to implement analytics are advancing with a clear vision of where to go, as Saxena and Srinivasan (2013) pointed out: "In our view, analytics is the rational way to get from ideas to execution." Or, as Sheikh (2013) indicated, "We will use two different perspectives to lay out the characteristics of analytics: one is related to how business value is achieved and the other regards how it is implemented ... the business perspective of the analytics definition deals with future action and any technology, product, or service that contributes towards the action can qualify to be part of analytics solutions ... The technical implementation perspective describes the characteristics of analytics in terms of the techniques used to implement the analytics solution."

Risk analytics, on the one hand, helps to support the reasoning process and to create knowledge to mitigate risk. Buchanan and O'Connell (2006) emphasize that in organizations, management uses both reason and intuition and risk analytics needs to develop both. "Of course the gut/brain dichotomy is largely false. Few decision makers ignore good information when they can get it. And most accept that there will be times they can't get it and so will have to rely on instinct. Fortunately, the intellect informs both intuition and analysis, and research shows that people's instincts are often quite good. Guts may even be trainable, suggest John Hammond, Ralph Keeney, Howard Raiffa, and Max Bazerman, among others. In *The Fifth Discipline*, Peter Senge elegantly sums up the holistic approach: "People with high levels of personal mastery ... cannot afford to choose between reason and intuition, or head and heart, any more than they would choose to walk on one leg or see with one eye." A blink, after all, is easier when you use both eyes. And so is a long, penetrating stare."

On the other hand, risk analytics is influenced in its creation and implementation by the factor of understanding that every area of an organization needs risk management in all activities and projects. Equally, organizations as a whole require the consolidation of enterprise risk management, studying all dimensions of an organization that are acting together and under several types of corporate risks. However, risk analytics is a process that has to be implemented across the organization and it does find management without preparation for creating and bringing to management not only to the awareness but also to the ways to structure risk mitigation and control. Bazerman and Chugh (2006) expressed, "Bounded awareness can occur at various points in the decision-making process. First, executives may fail to see or seek out key information needed to make a sound decision. Second, they may fail to use the information that they do see because they aren't aware of its relevance. Finally, executives may fail to share information with others, thereby bounding the organization's awareness."

Organizations would like to be more intelligent. To achieve this goal of being more intelligent organizations requires preparation. The concept of intelligence in organizations have been around business environment for many years, as Davenport (2006) indicates: "The term intelligence has been used by researchers in artificial intelligence since the 1950s. Business intelligence became a popular term in the business and IT communities only in the 1990s. In the late 2000s, business analytics was introduced to represent the key analytical component in BI." Organizations possibly are not prepared to develop new assets based on data analytics because in the practice they are not following the advances of management, or as Cascio (2007) indicated: "Why Don't Practitioners Know about Research That Academics Think Is Very Important? Managers need not be exposed to scientific knowledge about management to practice their craft." capital analytics is a means to support the decision-making process and at the same time the creation of systems, as it is a RAS, that will produce opportunities to deal with uncertainty in the sense that Analytics in general as Davenport (2010) says. "The goal for analytics is to make better decisions. However, while many organizations collect data and some organizations engage in analytics, few organizations link their analytics activities to their decision making."

Moreover, the conditions for businesses are changing. There are several opportunities in creating assets based on data analytics, but organizations require preparation and implementation. Chen et al. (2012) showed these new business circumstances, saying: "More recently big data and big data analytics have been used to describe the data sets and analytical techniques in applications that are so large (from terabytes to exabytes) and complex (from sensor to social media data) that they require advanced and unique data storage, management, analysis, and visualization technologies. In this article we use business intelligence and analytics (BI&A) as a unified term and treat big data analytics as a related field that offers new directions for BI&A research."

Organizations are evolving to be more productive by using data analytics capabilities; the path is designed, but in some cases the speed to move to a data-driven organization to generate intelligence has not been as expected because there are steps that have not been performed. Barton and Court (2012) commented: "In our work with dozens of companies in six data rich industries, we have found that fully exploiting data and analytics requires three mutually supportive capabilities … First, companies must be able to identify, combine, and manage multiple sources of data. Second, they need the capability to build advanced analytics models for predicting and optimizing outcomes. Third, and most critical, management must possess the muscle to transform the organization so that the data and models actually yield better decisions." This extract provides insights to move organizations in the direction of creation of data assets and assets based on analytics knowledge; one of the assets is associated with the risk analytics structure and organization given the important impact that risk can have across organizations. Alpaydin (2014) supplemented the previous points, showing that organizations need to develop capabilities in modeling and developing methods and techniques to create knowledge from data. Analytics is the data science outcome: "Almost all of science is fitting models to data. Scientists design experiments and make observations and collect data. They then try to extract knowledge by finding out simple models that explain the data they observed. This is called *induction* and is the process of extracting general rules from a set of particular cases. We are now at a point that such analysis of data can no longer be done by people, both because the amount of data is huge and because people who can do such analysis are rare and manual analysis is costly. There is thus a growing interest in computer models that can analyze data and extract information automatically from them, that is, learn."

The molecule model is based on the Perpetual chain for analytics learning and use to manage uncertainty

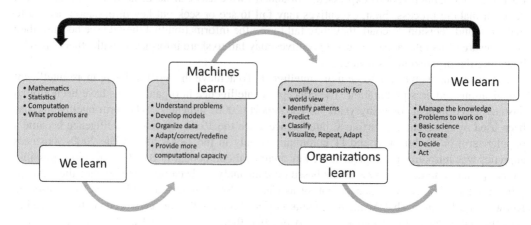

FIGURE 1.3 Illustration of the continuous chain of learning from data. People in organizations and machines.

Risk analytics Knowledge to reduce uncertainty

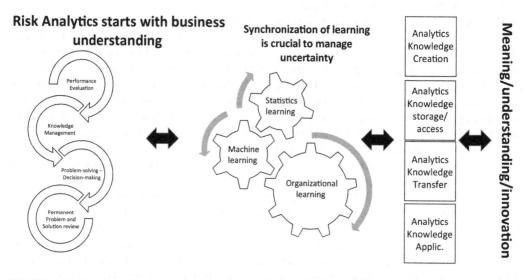

FIGURE 1.4 Creation of the risk analytics bases through the analytics knowledge processes.

At this point, the combination of business learning, statistical learning, and machine learning are connected in the purpose of creating more intelligent organizations (Figures 1.3, 1.4, 1.5) and, in particular, more strategic intelligent organizations. Strategic intelligence is the joint creation of value through business intelligence, competitive intelligence, and artificial intelligence.

Through learning, the accumulation of knowledge is a tool to manage uncertainty (Figure 1.4) when risk is considered as a variation of results and knowledge as a means to reduce uncertainty. When analytics knowledge is oriented to deal with the variation of organizations' results is when analytics is moving in the risk analytics setting. The risk analytics work is based on the analytics knowledge management processes: analytics knowledge creation, analytics knowledge storage, analytics knowledge access, analytics knowledge transfer, and analytics knowledge application.

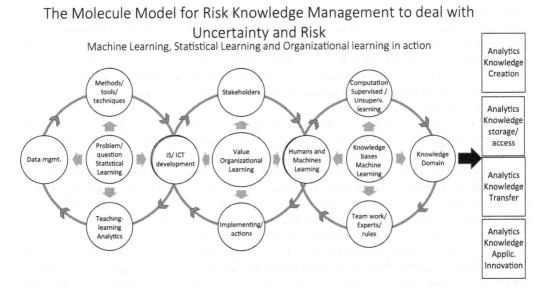

FIGURE 1.5 The learning molecule model indicating the cycles that are connected to create value.

The molecule conceptual model (Figure 1.5) illustrates the connection of three different types of learning that are converging in an organization to create value in an uncertain business environment. The atoms of the "chemical bond" are technology machines and human capabilities. Each atom of learning includes the activities proper for the learning process in machine learning, in business learning, and statistical learning.

In this section, there was a brief presentation of work done in conceptualizing data analytics and using it in several fields. In particular, all that experience is valuable to create the risk analytics system and guide the orientation to develop risk analytics in practice. Thus, the section is ending with the quote from Frees (2020), where it indicates the connection of concepts around analytics and risk. Those concepts are in the open book of the *Actuarial Community Loss Data Analytics*: "In any data-driven industry, analytics is a key to deriving and extracting information from data. But what is analytics? Making data-driven business decisions has been described as business analytics, business intelligence, and data science. These terms, among others, are sometimes used interchangeably and sometimes refer to distinct applications. *Business intelligence* may focus on processes of collecting data, often through databases and data warehouses, whereas *business analytics* utilizes tools and methods for statistical analyses of data. In contrast to these two terms that emphasize business applications, the term *data science* can encompass broader data related applications in many scientific domains. For our purposes, we use the term *analytics* to refer to the process of using data to make decisions. This process involves gathering data, understanding concepts and models of uncertainty, making general inferences, and communicating results." Loss Data Analytics (ewfrees.github.io)

1.3 RISK ANALYTICS IS A CRUCIAL CONCEPT IN RISK MANAGEMENT PROCESSES

The concepts used in risk analytics comprise discrete and continuous variables that are the same as deterministic and stochastic events, methods, and techniques for finding the means to deal with risk in organizations. In 1996, Stultz wrote, "This paper presents a theory of risk management that attempts to go beyond the "variance minimization" model that dominates most academic discussions of corporate risk management. I argue that the primary goal of risk management is to eliminate the probability of costly lower-tail outcomes—those that would cause financial distress or make a company unable to carry out its investment strategy. (In this sense, risk management can be viewed as the purchase of well-out-of-the-money put options designed to limit downside risk.)" This means that the variation of results is part of the problem to solve in risk analytics and the impact of events is a component of the problem to solve is strategic to sustaining continuing in the business. It is not only about prediction of adverse events or valuation of the adverse event or variation of results; it is additionally the capacity to deal with post-events and to continue operating and having good performance.

For many years and mainly after the financial crisis between 2008–2010, people asked themselves about the possibility of measuring risk. A value of risk management and its processes is in providing insights to prepare organizations to deal with uncertain events and circumstances that can modify the bottom line of the organization. The analytics arsenal is supporting the creation of those insights to provide orientation to certain decisions based on what the data is showing. It does not mean that the results of the risk analytics process will be 100% certain (in the case that we could convert the world into a deterministic world), but the better risk classification, risk assessment, risk monitoring, and estimation the better the awareness and orientation of the efforts of the organization to compete. Knowledge is a risk mitigant and analytics is a knowledge creation process. The risk analytics knowledge management through the risk knowledge creation, transfer, storage, access, and application provide structure to the company's management. Fraud detection, identification of factors influencing defaults, identifying opportunities of investments, etc. are risk management endeavors that analytics can handle and help management to make decisions and solve problems. Hubbard (2009) states, "The ultimate common mode failure would be a failure of risk management itself. A weak risk management approach is effectively the biggest risk in the organization." And in his presentation of how to fix risk management he pointed out: "Most of the key problems with risk management are focused primarily on the problems with risk analysis." In his terms, the process of risk analysis should concentrate on enhancing the simulation capabilities, managing the quality of the risk management process itself, managing the model risk as a piece of control method, and improving the risk management knowledge and practice of the members of teams across the organization, the same as in risk management areas.

As in the analytics process, the rational and intuitive approaches are acting together to develop decision-making and control systems. Artificial intelligence based on the analytics process can liberate human resources to study events and possible adverse conditions with special attributes (possible outliers of patterns) that can modify the course of actions of the organizations and that are not part of the identifiable patterns of event realizations. Risk analytics in the following chapters comprises the following: first, understanding of the risk analytics process including the interaction of risk and business concepts. Second, the basic concepts of risk analytics used for risk modeling. Third the use of analytic methods to support risk modeling and creation of solutions for improving risk management processes. Fourth, the steps of implementation with the review of barriers and opportunities to implement risk analytics.

Risk analytics has multiple dimensions that require various quantitative and qualitative methods to discover and implement solutions. These methods include the use of statistics, machine learning, and optimization tools with an appropriate understanding of data analytics management. In particular, risk analytics involves the review of governance needs in usable data creation, reporting, portfolio overview, analytics support, and the review of risk management strategies. The concepts of descriptive analytics, predictive analytics, and prescriptive analytics are in the whole content of the book presented with a general perspective of analytics for managerial and strategic responsibilities.

In risk analytics, it is crucial to identify not only the steps for the analytics process but also the type of methods, techniques, and models that are used. Risk analytics reviews the construction of models with different structures, such as:

- Logic and conceptual models that allow the description and visualization of the relationships of the variables and steps of the risk analysis.

- Models in spreadsheets: these provide structures of relationships among variables through the definition of formulas using data and mathematical/statistical models to determine outcomes. In the following link, you can find examples of good and bad practices in spreadsheet modeling: http://www.eusprig.org/about.htm
- Mathematical models refer to the mathematical representation of the variable relationships describing phenomena.
- Statistical models: In this regard, the important concept is that the structure of the model, for example a multiple regression, can be used in many analyses and several different evaluations of relationships among variables. However, the final model is when the parameters are estimated and the variables to use are selected.
- Machine learning models that are represented through computational algorithms and the solution to risk management problems such as classification.

Another important aspect in the development of risk analytics is that the "model risk" is real and there are several aspects from the administration of risk that need to keep the standards of development and implementation of risk model design and policy creation based on created models. One of the aspects that was mentioned before is the risk knowledge transfer. In Rodriguez and Edwards (2019), there are identified several issues in creation of value – impact in the organization because of lack of understanding of the outcomes of risk analysis and the issues in the implementation and deployment of risk systems.

Chapters ahead include the use of different tools for data analytics. In this book, there is a mix of tools used to solve risk management problems with the view that analytics tools can provide opportunities to develop solutions. The tools used in the book are SAS, KNIME, ModelRisk, Python, R, ExcelMiner, and Excel. The purpose of using different tools is to illustrate the concepts and how to deal with the problems and outcomes coming from multiple tools. The purpose is not to provide the learning means of the tools but to indicate how the daily risk analytics work the means for dealing with data can come from different tools that will feed risk management information systems. The deployment of risk analytics solutions will require support and joint work with information technology departments to implement solutions.

The individual risk studies are what, in most of the cases, is the practice and the separation of risk by activities. The main issue in general is the organization of a system where any component is influencing the performance of the system as a whole. This means that risk management by individual risk is the start, but the goal is to go to the holistic view of risk across the organization, understand it, and then go back to the individual risk analysis. The challenge is immense, mainly for identifying relationships, correlations, joint distributions, and models that can be used and the structure to understand these relationships and cause and effect (causal inference) connection among variables.

1.4 ENTERPRISE RISK MANAGEMENT (ERM)

The importance of considering risk as the core of a business or thinking about risk as the name of the game that management has to play, is the basic concept to maintain the focus on the integral view of risk management. What organizations do in business administration is managing the organization's risk. As it was mentioned before, organizations use analytics to create knowledge and knowledge to mitigate, monitor, and control risks. Risk control supports strategy formulation and strategy implementation. Organizations are exposed to events that can affect their development. Organizations need to identify – assess – quantify risks as a whole. Organizations need to create understanding of risk with models-results interpretation and define course of actions. Organizations need an integral view to manage the traditional silo approach. The concept of risk has several aspects to review from a basic definition; such as included in the Concise Oxford

Dictionary (2008), risk is "hazard, a chance of bad consequences, loss or exposure mischance". Or as McNeil et al. (2005), risk is "any event or action that may adversely affect an organisation's ability to achieve its objective and execute its strategies." Or in particular, in a quantitative view, risk is "the quantifiable likelihood of loss or less-than-expected returns" (McNeil et al., 2005).

Sax and Andersen (2019), in their study of a mix of industries beyond financial services, pointed out: "In conclusion, the results suggest that adherence to ERM practices in conjunction with strategic planning is a useful combination for harvesting the risk management potential." And they continue, saying in conclusion that the strategic planning process and ERM are complementary: "This study indicates that ERM practices and strategic planning are complementary processes, where strategic planning mediates and generates the positive effects of ERM practices on improved profitability and lower financial leverage." Bohnert et al. (2019) in a particular insurance industry indicates: "Results show a significant positive impact of ERM on firm value for the case of European insurers. In particular, we find that insurers with a high quality risk management (RM) system exhibit a Tobin's Q that on average is about 6.5% higher than for insurers with less high quality RM after controlling for covariates and endogeneity bias."

Digging deeper in risk analytics and the ERM approach there is an orientation to connect operations management and the decision-making process with risk theory that are related to randomness and uncertainty. It is part of the risk analytics process to move from different kinds of events to identify to multiple types of risks to assess and mitigate becuase they are affecting decisions. Risk in financial institutions is related to the exposure, according to financial service activities. According to Ong (200g), Van Greuning and Brajovic (2003), and Crouhy et al. (2001), a classification of risks mainly refers to financial institutions and related to market risk, credit risk, and business risk, such as an operational risk. Risks that are not financially related are classified as event risks, such as political risks, and these are shown by Harms (2000). In general, Bischoff (2008) presented several risks affecting the current society, such as health care, community risks, and global risks. Each classification can involve probability laws that describe each type of risk that affects a financial institution and society. A risk classification process will be presented in Chapter 7, and it should not be confused with the concept above of classification of risks for labeling a type of risk in an organization. The risk classification process refers to the methods and techniques to identify and assign risk profiles to classes/groups of risks in general. For example, classification in credit risk to have a good or bad prospect or identifying of having or not an earthquake.

ERM follows the risk management (RM) process for the organization's risk as a whole. This means to apply to the total what Spedding and Rose (2007) defined as: "Risk management is the process of identifying, measuring and assessing risk and developing strategies to manage them. Strategies include transferring the risk to another party; avoiding the risk; reducing the negative effect of the risk; and accepting some or all of the consequences of a particular risk." Risk management is part of the strategic management process (Meulbroek, 2002; Sharman, 2002; Liebenberg and Hoyt, 2003; Banham, 2004). To create value using risk management is an aspect that has been studied (Brown, 2001; Froot et al., 1994; Banham, 2004) in order to understand how to create competitive advantage (Galloway and Funston, 2000). Risk management has a purpose, as Buehler et al. (2008) indicate: "executives in all companies can incorporate risk into their strategic decision making." RM is a process itself: "transferring risk does not mean eliminating risk" (Buehler et al. 2008a). In 1996, Bernstein in the article "The New Religion of Risk Management" commented that "Our lives teem with numbers, but numbers are only tools and have no soul." Brown (2001) presents the subprocesses of risk management as risk identification, measurement, monitoring, control, and application. In general, authors coincide in subprocesses (see Table 1.1) to perform risk assessment, evaluation, and identification as processes to evaluate potential losses of adverse events.

TABLE 1.1

Risk Management Processes from Different Authors

Risk Management Processes	References
• Governance • Line management • Portfolio management • Risk transfer • Risk analysis • Data technology resources • Shareholder management	Lam (2000)
• Risk identification • Risk measure • Risk monitoring • Risk control	Brown, 2001
• Strategy design • Structure design • Portfolio analysis and optimization • Measuring and monitoring	Sharman, 2002
• Analyze risk • Risk strategy design • Implementing risk strategy • Monitor risk strategy	Bowling and Rieger, 2005
The review is given by layers, where activities of identification, assessment, reporting, planning, and negotiation are performed. The layers are • Comply jurisdiction layer • Strategy layer • Deployment layer • Operation layer • Events layer	Abrams et al., 2007
• Objective setting • Event identification • Risk assessment • Risk response • Control activities • Information and communication • Monitoring	COSO 2004
Description of the CRO and ERM team activities: • Risk identification • Risk assessment • Advising solutions for dealing with risks • Reporting • Management support	Liebenberg and Hoyt, 2003
Based on best practices, identify some experiences in the following steps: • Establish risk framework • Identify risk events • Assess risks • Plan risk response strategy • Monitor and control risk	Francis and Paladino, 2008
• Differentiate the financial and operational risks • Classify and prioritize strategic and manageable risks • Model the risks	Rao and Marie, 2007

(Continued)

TABLE 1.1 (Continued)

Risk Management Processes from Different Authors

Risk Management Processes	References
• Assess the impact of risk on key performance indicators • Manage ERM change (leadership, communication, involvement, measurement) • Risk identification • Risk analysis • Risk planning • Risk tracking • Risk control • Communication	Williams, Walker and Dorofee, 1997

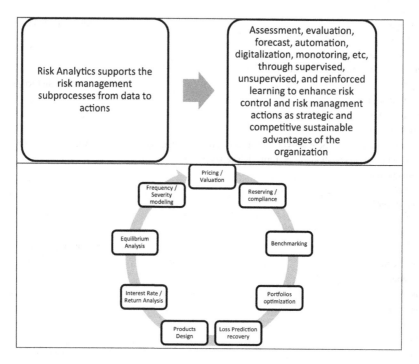

FIGURE 1.6 Creation of value in organizations through risk analytics and data analytics in specific risk management actions.

Risk analytics (see Figure 1.6) contributes to improve the risk management processes that Brown's (2001) identified:

- Risk identification: classify and map risks
- Risk measurement: quantification and assessment of risk
- Risk monitoring: capacity to follow-up risks
- Risk control: evaluate and to assure the benefit of RM actions
- Risk application: policies and solutions to control risk

From the above points, an integral view of all risks follows what Dickinson (2001) said to define ERM as: "a systematic and integrated approach to the management of the total risks that a company faces." The main purpose of ERM is to study enterprise risk (ER); thus, ERM is just the process to manage the ER aligned to shareholders' objectives. Additionally, Dickinson (2001) differentiate between insurable and financial risks. The approaches to study risk have been developed following different approaches in the analytics approaches. Nevertheless, the purpose of insuring and hedging is the reduction of potential losses or failures of the strategy and to evaluate the capacity of the organization to mitigate and control risks.

Moreover, the ERM development requires in addition to traditional information systems, analytics systems and AI support to provide value to the organization. Several years ago, Crouhy et al. (2001) expressed: "The risk management information system needs to be supported by an information technology architecture that is employed in all of the company's information processing." In particular, for banking, Crouhy et al. (2001) said: "Banks have many business units, which are engaged in different activities and support different products." And in particular, Crouhy et al. (2001) indicated: "A risk management system approach is not simply an aggregate of applications, data, and organisation; instead, it is born out of an IT vision" and "[t]he risk management system should be designed to support the transport and integration of risk information from a variety of technology platforms, as well as from multiple internal and external legacy systems around the world." One of the purposes of risk analytics is to support the development of the risk management systems that can handle different types of data (structured and unstructured), human and machine interaction, models of different levels of sophistication, and possibilities of sharing and creating decision-support systems that are updated and with predictive and prescriptive capacities. The purpose is to support management and strategic analytics based on risk knowledge/ understanding.

1.5   MEASURING, METRICS, AND BUSINESS CONCEPTS

As mentioned in the previous Section 1.3, the link between risk analytics and the risk management process includes learning that is revealed through a measurement process. All the possibilities to connect the risk analytics process and the risk management process require several concepts from mathematics, statistics, and computer science as it is in general in data science. What is different in risk analytics is that actuarial science, risk management, quantitative/mathematical finance, AI, machine learning, etc. are developing in an accelerated way with independent knowledge domains that are required to study convergence of using the techniques/methods to get clues about uncertainty – risk, because not only are the changes are in products (based on technology) but also the customers' habits change. The presentation of the topics in the next chapters has a set of backbone concepts that are exposed ahead in the next sections and start with reviewing concepts associated with data.

The concept of uncertainty is about the lack of knowledge of the possible events or course of actions that nature and organizations can have. The concept of risk is when there is a way to associate probabilities of events and the evaluation of effects that events can have in nature or activities in organizations. There is a differentiation in the concept of the events that affect the business definition (intersection of markets, solutions to customer's needs-products-offers and technology used) as the opportunity to achieve and the enterprise as the means to achieve that opportunity. Risks appear in any of the three axes of a business definition: market, products and technology; the same as in the operation, management and development of the organization to run the business. It is important to keep on mind that in this book the concept of control is used in diverse topics. The idea is that risk analytics contributes to creating knowledge to support risk control. However, it is understood that the search is for approaches that can help organizations to be closer to where the organization wants to be; it does not mean that a full control is possible or that the randomness of results will be converted into deterministic results of organizations. The use of randomness for modeling is a way to understand the reality but several assumptions can be used, and the analysis of results have to be based on the assumptions and possible results that can appear.

In a Monte Carlo Simulation, for example, the random numbers used are pseudo-random numbers that are generated by a mathematical definition of an algorithm.

The critics to the risk management identified that the problem to deal with was wrongly defined. This means risk management the organization is looking to be better in using the resources to be closer to what a goal could be a expected value but it does not mean that the search is for the goal as a fact or deterministic result, it is more on confidence intervals, and management dispersion from the goals. This means the search of answers is based on reducing an error level of that is expected to be or to be achieved. What is required is that the allocation of resources and the orientation and alignment of the organization efforts be in the direction where positive results could be and better probability of achieving the goals.

Strategic, managerial, and operational strategies are linked with risk as a way to differentiate in what a vision of organizations can be achieved or not. Strategy is how to achieve goals, goals that are at different levels in the organization. Hopefully, the goals are aligned; however, the goals depend on each of the components of the operation. Strategic risk is, for example, about market reputation and the effect of on the price of stock in a market. The price of the stock is a result; it is not a strategy, it is something that the organization is looking for but the strategy is about all the capabilities that the organization is using to do what it needs to do to achieve the goal, innovation, people, process, technology, and so on. Risk is going to appear in the variation of the results at each level of operation. The aggregated variation of goals will be reflected in the final variation of market value. The risk in this book is not understood only as adverse events; it is about the lack of answers to explain variations. If the results were better, it is important to answer why and if the results were not as good as expected, the answer to why is needed to fix where potential results can be better. Risk analytics helps to guide the search of possible causes, possible solutions, and possible results to move in the direction that can be the best for achieving the goals and the opportunity that a market presents.

As a supplement of Section 1.3 to connect risk management and data analytics as a process, the first step is to define the problem to work on, and then to search for data and gather data to find techniques/methods to create knowledge from that data and then to go to actions, implement a definition, and creation of operational information systems and artificial intelligence solutions. Analytics does not stop when the models or the tools are applied to data; the results have to be converted into the feed of business processes to create value. Models mean representation of the reality in the context of risk analytics and they are in nature as the following:

- Mathematical, statistical, simulation models
- Computational spreadsheet models
- Machine learning models
- Statistical learning models
- Conceptual models

The connection of data analytics and risk management makes problem definition a priority and the use of a variety of concepts of multiple disciplines, but in common everything starts with the vision of a measurement system. A measurement process is a way of guiding the understanding of risk analytics discovery of knowledge to mitigate/control risk. The risk analytics process creates metrics or means to evaluate and to provide means to compare results and to identify levels of variation of values that variables can take. The key performance indicators have key risk indicators associated with them (see Chapter 8). There are several factors in risk measurement to examine, to review, to evaluate, and to create maps to guide actions to achieve organizational goals. Those factors are included in the process of measuring in risk analytics that will be performed without reduction of information or knowledge. However, the selection and slicing and dicing process will require an appropriate volume of data, with the possibility to evaluate groups, separate the subsets that can indicate possible different results, clarify dependency of variables and correlations, indicate the possibility of prediction, search for analysis in a univariate and multivariate level, move to the level of creating and testing hypotheses, maintain observation and ongoing review, and calibration of the measurement/metrics creation process.

The measurement process principles follow a structure:

- Start from the goals of the organization information and knowledge management systems and start from what the organization wants to measure; in particular the RAS system.
- Review the business processes and the way that they are related to the goals.
- Make the measurement process part of the management control systems.
- Keep understanding of the metrics along the organization as key driver.
- Maintaining data alignment/availability is a crucial step to feed the metrics production. Nothing is valuable if a great metric is planned/created but no data exists to evaluate it. Metrics can be very good but not feasible or understandable. Keep the metrics as simple as possible, with the possibility of repeatable capacity. Metrics creation requires a deterministic view and then a stochastic approach. Metrics can have assumptions that are key to understand correctly. For example VaR.
- Metrics could be considered in groups: deterministic, current and facts, forecasts, and at random (in any case there is change between past and future values). In the chapters ahead, the concept of coherent metrics will be explained in cases that the metrics require certain levels of calculations.
- Metrics have to be kept and organized as new data; for example, time series analysis is expected of the results of the metrics. The analysis of metrics will be the same as other data. The metrics are created data; parameters in models are results of data analytics processes and they are going to be new data for further analysis. For example, probabilities of events are going to be the input to scale definitions for thresholds that guide actions/prescriptive analytics. The interpretation in many cases will be related to variability. Variability in metrics is a way to express risk magnitude.
- Review the business process steps and their partial results that contribute to the final result that is identified asadapting the organization to compete and perform well.
- Organize the final values of metrics as part of the cause-effect search and relationships of business process steps.
- Include dimensions to the metrics and connection to goals. This means a metric cannot be just a number; it is a piece of business knowledge. Dimension means, for example, that we can measure sales, but how often? Every second, every year, multiple periods, etc.
- Move from univariate to multivariate metrics and analysis.
- Calibrate the metrics and maintain the possibility to compare them through time, consistency in definitions, among multiple factors. Documentation of the definition of the variables and metrics is fundamental for the use of the metrics.
- Maintain metrics, planning, and reporting as a connected system.
- Search for expressing the same kind of event/activity/phenomena in different and equivalent ways. For example, a ratio can have as numerator income, and it can express income in many ways as income separated by producs, by regions and keeping the same denominator.
- Split metrics in pieces/factors/terms.

Examples of metrics appear throughout the book, risk indicators from ratios, values in financial statements, or more elaborated on the return distribution of the results/investments of the organization; for instance, numbers describing the level of risk exposure. A metric is expected to have properties as follows:

1. $m(X + Y) \leq m(X) + m(Y)$
2. $if\ X \leq Y\ then\ m(X) \leq m(Y)$
3. $m(cX) = cm(X)\ and\ m(X + a) = m(X) + a$

VaR$_\alpha$X, for example, is not following the number 1 property. VaR$_\alpha$X is for a random variable X, e.g., losses because of risk, $\alpha \in$ [0, 1] is the perc = 100 $*$ α percentile of the variable X for $\alpha \in$ [F(perc approached from bottom), F(perc)]. TVaR is the average of the VaR values above the value p used for the VaR definition; or the expected value of X given that X is greater than VarX. CVaR, AVaR, and Expected Shortfall are names given to the TVaR.

1.6 UNDERSTANDING DATA, SCALES, AND DATA ARRAYS

A risk analytics process requires data organization. In general, data is organized as a matrix and matrices theory will be used to understand properties of what is possible to do with the arrays in order to create new knowledge from the data. Multivariate data analysis is based on linear algebra results and linear algebra results are used in tools for analysis and creation of data structures, data frames and data tables, or transformation of unstructured data to structured data (text to frequencies of words matrix).

The raw input to multivariate statistics procedures is usually an $n \times p$ (n rows by p columns) rectangular array of real numbers called a data matrix. The data matrix summarizes observations made on n risk units. Each of the n units is characterized with respect to p variables (attributes). The values are the data or realization values of the variables may represent the measurement of a quantity, or a numerical code for a classification definition. A data matrix is an $n \times p$ matrix X, and the column vectors of the matrix will be identified by X_1, X_2, ..., X_p for the p variables. The entrances or elements of X are denoted by X_{ij}, with $i = 1, 2, ..., n$ and $j = 1, 2, ..., p$.

	Variable 1	Variable 2	...	Variable p
Record 1	x_{11}	x_{12}		X_{1p}
Record 2	x_{21}	x_{22}		X_{2p}
$\vdots$	$\vdots$	$\vdots$	$\vdots$	$\vdots$
Record n	X_{n1}	X_{n2}		x_{np}

That array is represented by

$$X = \begin{bmatrix} x_{11} & \cdots & x_{1p} \\ \vdots & \ddots & \vdots \\ x_{n1} & \cdots & x_{np} \end{bmatrix}$$

Using this notation, metrics will be defined in this book such as variance-covariance and the properties will appear from the mathematics of these arrays, where each variable will be a mean and variance and then the comparison among variables to study possible influence-effects in the connection among the different variables. For example, variation is defined as:

$$s_{ik} = \frac{1}{n} \sum_{j=1}^{n} \left(x_{ji} - \overline{x_i} \right)\left(x_{jk} - \overline{x_k} \right) with \ \ i = 1, 2, ..., p \ \ and \ \ 1, 2, ..., p$$

And the correlation as

$$r_{ik} = \frac{s_{ik}}{\sqrt{s_{ii}} \ \sqrt{s_{kk}}}$$

Those metrics in matrix notation for the statistical purpose has the following form for a set of x_i variables with i from 1 to p.

Sample means $\bar{x} = \begin{bmatrix} \overline{x_1} \\ \cdots \\ \overline{x_p} \end{bmatrix}$

Sample variances and covariances $\begin{bmatrix} s_{11} & \cdots & s_{1p} \\ \vdots & \ddots & \vdots \\ s_{p1} & \cdots & s_{pp} \end{bmatrix}$

Sample correlations $\begin{bmatrix} 1 & \cdots & r_{1p} \\ \vdots & \ddots & \vdots \\ r_{p1} & \cdots & 1 \end{bmatrix}$

The data treatment of risk analytics requires keeping the variable classification as quantitative or qualitative (see Section 1.10 for more details of matrix and linear algebra) and, as mentioned above, for using method-techniques for working these types of variables. The main point is that qualitative data will be transformed in a quantitative representation as it is the case of text, pictures, etc. with the purpose of using the mathematics behind matrix representation. In any case of variables, a scale definition, comparison structure, or identification of attributes to input other metrics is going to be part of risk analytics. A quantitative variable is one in which the values are numbers representing realizations of the variables, or according to the previous paragraphs are the values of metrics, measures of the variables, e.g., income, age, weight, GDP, etc. A qualitative variable is one in which the variables differ in categories, classes, labels, and types, such as social status, sex, nationality, eye color, etc. The quantitative variables use scales for identifying the measurement values and can be normalized to have evaluations according to the same unit that, for example, can be expressed as a number of standard deviations (z-scores are examples x-mu/sigma). The scales can be in real number intervals with the possibility of taking any real numbers in the interval as it is in a continuous case; in the other case the variables are only possible to take some values (countable values), for example integers and in that case the variable will be discrete.

In summary, in this book the use of terms of a measurement process will be:

- Metric is a unit of measurement that provides a way to objectively quantify what is measured in the experiment, such as performance, speed, etc.
- Measurement is the act of obtaining data associated with a metric.
- Measures are the numerical values associated with a metric.

A measurement process uses the values that variables take. In that regard, data as realization values of the variables requires revision for usability. Variables in the experiments, studies, and research are converted into data with multiple attributes, such as:

1. It can be a number, a category, a url, etc (Figure 1.7)
2. It can be deterministic=fixed value=facts or it could be random values
3. It could be affected by time
4. It can be affected by volume/size/structure
5. It can be affected by the way they are input/obtained
6. It can be used for static analysis, such as a picture, where the observation is only in a window of time, data, state, or interval. Models are used to study data behavior, changes, meaning, etc. through time or not and considering relationships with external factors.

The variety of data types leads to work more in the definition of data treatment. Ladley (2016) indicated that the following aspects are fundamental for data use:

- Granularity: The level of detail required to support the answers/solutions (applies mostly to measurements and dimensions).

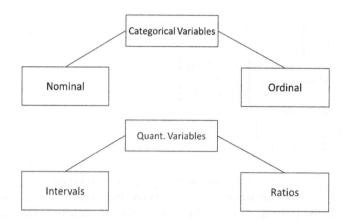

FIGURE 1.7   Part of data types/variable types that are part of risk analytics.

- Fact Volatility: The frequency at which new data is added or updated for usage.
- Dimensional Complexity: The relative nature of how extensive and/or abstract the various reporting dimensions are.
- Dimensional Volatility: The frequency at which dimensions change are added to or updated for data analytics uses.
- Algorithm Complexity: Statement of the relative sophistication of the algorithm that is applied as part of the metric.
- Style of Use: Classification of how the questions/inquiries are used.
- Historicity: Inquiry for time-related data, follow-up, relationship of data and time.
- Latency: Time of gathering and use the data.
- Cross Functionality/Distribution: Different areas and multiple problems across the organization.
- Size: Levels of details that the data analysis requires.
- Sensitivity: Access and use limitation of data because regulation, confidentiality, etc.
- Source Complexity: How the data is obtained, multiple sources, types.
- Content Variety: Data with different attributes.
- Frequency: Times of data access, use, production, reports, etc.
- Response Time: in case of requirements for reaction or prevention, the time it takes for using outcomes and results.
- Follow-up time: Once the values are known, what is the time to react and monitor.
- Data Quality: Degree of possibility to use data and level of cleanness.
- Availability: Where and when data is possible to use.
- Persistence: Possibility to continue using the data.
- Access Type: Possible means to use the data and outputs.

Hair et al. (2010) provide several recommendations to keep in mind developing data analysis: Identify what type of data is missing, by variables by records or risk units, what is the volume, is the data missing following any pattern, is it at random? If it is possible, look for imputation methods or select variables and records that are complete if they are not going to create bias in the study (randomness is the answer). The number of missing points will affect the experiment according to a volume and the technique used. More than 10% that is not available can not be good data to use or review how the technique used can be affected because of missing data points.

In the example of the happiness data (see Section 2.4), the possibility to use the original data was reduced to a third part of countries and it was not possible to use all variables. The conclusions are only based on complete data, and it is not possible to maintain as generalizable results for the world and for all possible factors; only for the observed data set. Depending on how the missing data is in the data set, for example completely at random (MCAR), missing at random (MAR) and not missing at random (NMAR), the methods of imputation can be different but the data analyst has the final definition of what is possible or not to use.

The list of issues with data is significant, as Cady F. (2017) indicates:

- Duplication in data entries
- Finding multiple entries for a single object and realization
- Finding missing entries (we already saw how to deal with missing data)
- Appearances of nulls and what is a zero
- Inconsistencies in data definitions
- Outliers; we already talked about them
- Time-related issues – out-of-date
- Wrong definition of variables – inconsistent definition of variables when you merge data from different sources
- Aggregated data issues
- Spacing or delimitation of data
- Type of characters used – invalid and non-consistent
- Dates and their formats
- Versions of tools used
- Structure of the syntax in some languages
- Issues in the definition of the variables or the newly created data
- Irregular capitalization
- Inconsistent delimiters
- Irregular NULL format
- Invalid characters
- Weird or incompatible datetimes
- Operating system incompatibilities
- Wrong software versions

In summary, data use starts with having good capabilities within the organization to deal with the complexity of data quality control and maintenance.

1.7 BASIC PROBABILITY CONCEPTS USEFUL IN RISK ANALYTICS

Assuming that there is an organization in a planning process, it needs analytics work. The organization is in the processed food sector and in the strategic plan they want to identify objectives and actions to compete through pricing, product mix, distribution channels, productivity/production, financial control/investment, etc. The organization has data for all processes and marketing relationships. They do not know what the best way is to use the data available. Data will be the source to discover the behavior of the variables in a process that will be represented by probability distributions. The company wants to use the mathematical properties of the probability distributions to get answers to many questions. Data will be the means to estimate the parameters of the probability distributions. In that process, it is needed to organize data in a mathematical structure and for that purpose, the probability concepts will support the description of variable behavior and the interpretation in the organization context. The answer to several questions will be based on the use of random variables to describe the phenomena. In the same experiment, observations would be used to answer different questions.

Data can come from a survey to customers to get answers to many questions about their behavior, desires, motivation, or any transaction involvement. The same data can be used for segmentation or prediction. The organization can manage data that is related to financials or

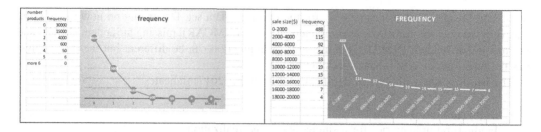

FIGURE 1.8 Using graphics and tables to describe variable behavior and sales, for example in risk terms the analysis will be about sales variation. Data can be by units or aggregated by intervals or sets.

operations or marketing or a mix of them. For example, if an organization wants to develop a management control system, the organization would like to have a good pro-forma building method for financial statements such as the projected income statement is required to take income and expenses all as random variables. Thus, the benefit or the bottom line will be a random variable as well. The question that emerges is how to manage variable relationships to get answers, mainly when there are many random variables.

A first point to analyze in the organization is, for example, how the customers are buying the products in a period of time or how they are behaving in a promotion time or how they are buying a mix of products or how they are using the phone/web to buy etc. The analysis of data and risk related is a mix of marketing understanding, customer knowledge, and capacity to predict behavior that can affect, for example, cash flow. The source of data or the areas of analysis can start discovering distribution of sales and analyzing data conditional to seasons, promotions, volume, regions, direct marketing, etc. For example, sales data can be as shown in Figure 1.8.

At the same time, an organization wants to find how much people were spending in the promotion. Remember, in some cases, people can purchase things in small quantities but with high value or to buy many with small values. What appears in these two graphs is similar behavior, but the difference is that the previous one is a discrete variable; meanwhile, the second one is continuous. From the probability point of view, risk analytics will apply different approaches depending on the variable type. The organization needs to describe the phenomena with a model and to use it for further investigation.

Now, to understand that based on the theory of conditional events, it is possible to get new results about events. For example, if the hypothetical company is in the business of processed food production, it would like to get the probability that a customer buys ice cream given that they bought chocolates or fish or potatoes. If there are only five types of products in the product portfolio and the company is interested in a market segment (there are seven market segments), the company could get answers to the strategy questions such as: What is the probability that people buy product 1 if it is known what purchases are by the segments? What is the probability that a person buys product 1 given that is part of the segment A? Or what is the probability that a person belongs to the segment A if that person is buying product 1? For these answers, the company needs to understand models – theoretical distributions in terms of what they are showing/describing to use later in these distributions and the estimated parameters in decision making.

Bernoulli distribution is one the models when there are only two possible results, 1 or 0, black and white, true or false, or very often these days grow or not grow, increase or not increase the performance indicators, etc. This distribution is useful for decision models, for risk management models, and to describe binary relationships among variables. Once there is repetition of the Bernoulli experiment of only two results appears the Binomial model that is interested in the number of cases with one of the Bernoulli results when there are several independent trials. The binomial distribution describes the number of successes (the event result to appear in the experiment). The distribution has two parameters: n is the number of trials and p is the probability of a success. From the Binomial distribution, it is possible to describe the Bernoulli results because a Binomial (1, p) is a Bernoulli one.

In probability, the way to build new distributions or to find the mathematical relationships have been allowed to create new models to describe phenomena. For example, if in the binomial distribution when p is small and n is large, the Poisson distribution appears. The Poisson distribution has one parameter that is λ that can be approached by np or the expected value or the number of events (average rate) that appear in the period of time. The Poisson distribution describes phenomena that rarely occur. It is a model to describe the number (counts) of the events in an experiment. In a marketing case, the question can be how many ice cream units were sold in a particular distribution channel per day. Now, these events are discrete, and the results can be counted. The events can be more complex and the random variables describe more situations. For example, to review the marketing situation assuming that a person buys the product 1 with probability p, and there is a promotion to give a gift to the first person who buys the product 1 in one store. In this case, the purpose is to find the number of buyers that buy something in the store up to the first person buying product 1. Product 1 only is bought with probability p. When the first person buys, a signal appears to give the gift to that person. This is a kind of event that is modeled by the geometric (Pascal) distribution $P(X = n) = (1 - p)^{n-1}p$, this means $n - 1$ people did not buy product 1.

Another option to a similar situation is when the promotion is running up to a number r of buyers of the product 1. In that case, the total number of buyers is n. This is a way to present what is called the negative binomial distribution.

$$P(X = n) = \binom{n - 1}{r - 1} p^r (1 - p)^{n-r}$$

In the case that the results are not countable, for example the total amount of sales, the models can use a continuous random variable and their corresponding distributions. The first case is when all the possible results have the same probability of occurring. This is the case where a uniform distribution appears. In a company, it could be the description of sales that are not affected by time and each event is with the same probability. Every day, every minute sales can appear with the same probability. However, this possibly is not true and there is a need to use other models. Sometimes the distribution could be a mix of discrete and continuous variables depending on where the values are analyzed. In general, the process to identify the best model describing data is based on the best fitting to a theoretical distribution function.

Interpretation of the continuous distribution is based on where the distributions are deducted from; for example, they are grouped by families (discrete indicating groups as well). Parameter changes produce some of the other distributions. Or, some approaches are possible as is the case of the binomial approach to the normal distribution. In general, several steps will be explained in the next chapters related to examining with more detail how the distribution changes because of the changes in the parameters; reviewing the distributions when there are functions of the random variables; managing questions about the sums of random variables or combination of them; extending the way to identify the distributions using methods that support approaches of the distributions based on the parameter estimations/moments analysis (means and variances); identifying how not only the distributions will be the way to describe data, but also the use of models to describe a behavior based on the underlying random variable behaviors and to consider the randomness of the parameters of the distributions. They will create known distributions, but with very particular structures according to the probability distribution of the parameters.

The risk analytics process starts creating a general model. First without the issues of dealing with probability estimations/calculations. Then, understanding data, describing it, visualizing it. Keeping in mind that the purpose is to estimate parameters, metrics, and a person with analytics thinking uses a probabilistic approach. For example, to study the best probability distribution (the best fit) for the variables used in income statement, estimate the parameters for those distributions and generate thousands of possible results in order to identify what is happening to the bottom line of a business/organization. Once the bottom line (For example NPV as a metric to study the distribution) is identified with a distribution, that distribution can be used for getting results (sample points) for managing/controlling the income in the organization.

To develop the probabilistic analysis requires understanding that probability theory is based on three axioms:

- $P(S) = 1$, S is the sample space or the set of all possible results
- $P(A \cup B) = P(A) + P(B) - P(A \cap B)$
- $0 \le P(A) \le 1$

A function P that has these properties is a probability function. The ratio of number of cases that are from interest to the number of cases that are possible in the experiment is used for defining P(A). This is (*number* of elements (results) in A)/(*number* of elements(results) in S) and this ratio works as a probability function. The denominator can be a subset B in the case that are conditional events. Set theory is used to get the correct numbers for probability calculations according to the event definitions. Several properties appear from the use of the set algebra. For example:

- $P(A^c) = 1 - P(A)$
- If A is a subset of B then $P(A) \le P(B)$
- $P(A \cap B^c) = P(A) - P(A \cap B)$

The main rule to find probabilities is to always decompose the events in other events with known probabilities. It is like counting the number of elements in sets using Venn diagrams. For example, what is the number of elements only in a set B? It is possible to obtain when from B the intersections with other events are deduced. From the analysis of events/sets, the theory grows based on the definition of random variables that are functions that assign to events real numbers. A cumulative distribution function (cdf), also called the distribution function, and usually denoted $F_x(x)$ or $F(x)$, has properties as follows:

- For a random variable X, $F_X(x)$ is the probability that X is less than or equal to a given number x. That is, $F_X(x) = \Pr(X \le x)$. The abbreviation cdf is often used.
- $0 \le F(x) \le 1$ for all x. $F(x)$ is nondecreasing. $F(x)$ is right-continuous.
- $\lim_{x \to -\infty} F(x) = 0$ and $\lim_{x \to \infty} F(x) = 1$

An empirical distribution function is defined as $F_n(x) = \frac{number\ of\ observations \le x}{n}$ with n as the number observations and there are new functions that can be defined, such as the survival function denoted $S_X(x)$ or $S(x)$, for a random variable X is the probability that X is greater than a given number. That is, $S_X(x) = \Pr(X > x) = 1 - F_X(x)$.

The probability density function, also called the density function and usually denoted $f_x(x)$ or $f(x)$, is the derivative of the distribution function (cdf). Let X be a random variable with probability distribution $f(x)$. The mean, or expected value, of X is $\mu_X = E(X) = \sum_{i=1}^{n} x_i f(x_i)$ if X is discrete, and $\mu_X = E(X) = \int_{-\infty}^{\infty} x f(x) dx$ if X is continuous. Let X be a random variable with probability distribution $f(x)$. The expected value of the random variable $g(X)$ is $\mu_{g(X)} = E[g(X)] = \sum_{i=1}^{n} g(x_i) f(x_i)$ if X is discrete, and $\mu_{g(X)} = E[g(X)] = \int_{-\infty}^{\infty} g(x) f(x) dx$ if X is continuous. Let X and Y be random variables with joint probability distribution $f(x, y)$. The mean, or expected value, of the random variable $g(X, Y)$ is $\mu_{g(X,Y)} = E[g(X, Y)] = \sum_{i=1}^{n} \sum_{i=1}^{m} g(x_i, y_i) f(x_i, y_i)$ if X and Y are discrete, and $\mu_{g(X,Y)} = E[g(X, Y)] = \int_{-\infty}^{\infty} \int_{-\infty}^{\infty} g(x, y) f(x, y) dx dy$ if X and Y are continuous.

Let X be a random variable with probability distribution $f(x)$ and mean μ. The variance of X is $\sigma^2 = E[(X - \mu)^2] = \sum_{i=1}^{n}(x_i - \mu)^2 f(x_i)$, if X is discrete, and $\sigma^2 = E[(X - \mu)^2] = \int_{-\infty}^{\infty}\int_{-\infty}^{\infty}(x - \mu)^2 f(x)dx$, if X is continuous. The positive square root of the variance, σ, is called the standard deviation of X. Now, let X be a random variable with probability distribution $f(x)$. The variance of the random variable $g(X)$ is $\sigma^2_{g(X)} = E\{[g(X) - \mu_{g(X)}]^2\}$. Let X and Y be random variables with joint probability distribution $f(x, y)$. The covariance of X and Y is $\sigma_{XY} = E[(X - \mu_X)(Y - \mu_Y)]$ and the covariance of two random variables X and Y with means μ_X and μ_Y, respectively, is given by $\sigma_{XY} = E(XY) - \mu_X\mu_Y$. The expected value of the sum or difference of two or more functions of a random variable X is the sum or difference of the expected values of the functions. That is, $E[g(X) \pm h(X)] = E[g(X)] \pm E[h(X)]$.

The expected value of the sum or difference of two or more functions of the random variables X and Y is the sum or difference of the expected values of the functions. That is, $E[g(X, Y) \pm h(X, Y)] = E[g(X, Y)] \pm E[h(X, Y)]$. Let X and Y be random variables with covariance σ_{XY} and standard deviations σ_X and σ_Y, respectively. The correlation coefficient of X and Y is $\rho_{XY} = \sigma_{XY}/\sigma_X\sigma_Y$. Let X and Y be two independent random variables; then $E(XY) = E(X)E(Y)$. Let X and Y be two independent random variables; then $\sigma_{XY} = 0$.

If X and Y are random variables with joint probability distribution $f(x, y)$ and a, b, and c are constants, then $\sigma^2_{aX+bY+c} = a^2\sigma^2_X + b^2\sigma^2_Y + 2ab\sigma_{XY}$.

A property to keep in mind for metrics estimation and understanding is Chebyshev's Theorem: The probability that any random variable X will assume a value within k standard deviations of the mean is at least $1 - 1/k^2$. That is, $P(\mu - k\sigma < X < \mu + k\sigma) \geq 1 - 1/k^2$.

The use of functions of random variables is very common in risk analytics and the linear combination of random variables is part of the analysis of aggregated risks. In the discrete case, if there is an one-to-one function u such that $Y = u(X)$, then the probability distribution of Y is $g(y) = f[w(y)]$ where $x = w(y)$ is unique because of one-to-one condition. In the case of two variables, X_1 and X_2, with one-to-one functions $Y_1 = u_1(X_1, X_2)$ and $Y_2 = u_2(X_1, X_2)$ the joint probability distribution of Y_1 and Y_2 is $g(y_1, y_2) = f[w_1(y_1, y_2), w_2(y_1, y_2)]$, with $x_1 = w_1(y_1,y_2)$ and $x_2 = w_2(y_1,y_2)$. Now a linear combination, for example, of X_1 and X_2 being two independent random variables having Poisson distributions with parameters λ_1 and λ_2, respectively, the sum $X_1 + X_2$ is Poisson with parameter $\lambda_1 + \lambda_2$. In the continuous case, the probability distribution of Y is $g(y) = f[w(y)]|J|$, where $J = \frac{dx}{dy}$ and is called the Jacobian of the transform. In the case of two variables:

$$g(y_1, y_2) = f(w_1, w_2)\begin{vmatrix} \frac{\partial x_1}{\partial y_1} & \frac{\partial x_1}{\partial y_2} \\ \frac{\partial x_2}{\partial y_1} & \frac{\partial x_2}{\partial y_2} \end{vmatrix}$$

Events appear as a result of the outcomes of other events. Conditional probability and metrics developed based on the existence of the previous result is fundamental in risk analytics. The conditional distribution when X and Y have joint distribution $f(x,y)$ is X given Y for all the points where the marginal $f_Y(y) = \int_{-\infty}^{\infty} f(x, y)dx$ is defined, and expressed as $f(x|y) = \frac{f(x,y)}{f_Y(y)}$. The conditional expected value in the discrete case is

$$E(X|Y = y) = \sum_{x} xP(X = x|Y = y)$$

And the continuous case $E(X|Y = y) = \int_{-\infty}^{\infty} x\frac{f(x,y)}{f_Y(y)}dx$ and some properties are

$$E[X] = E[E[X|Y]]; \quad E(XY) = E[E[XY|Y]]; \quad var[X|Y] = E[(X - E(X|Y))^2|Y]$$
$$= E(X^2|Y)) - E^2(X|Y) \text{ and}$$
$$Var(X) = E(E^2(X|Y)) - E^2(X) \text{ or } Var(X) = E(Var(X|Y) + Var(E(X|Y))$$

The functions of random variables lead the definition of the moment, generating functions and probability generating functions that are very useful to discover attributes of probability distributions from data. The function $M(t) = E(e^{tX})$ is the moment-generating function and $E(X) = M'(0)$ first derivative evaluated in zero, and the *n-th* derivative is $M^n(0) = E(X^n)$ that gives the possibility to calculate variance, kurtosis, and skewness. The reason is that the k-th central moment of a random variable is calculated as the expected value of $(X - \mu)^k$ and it is the basis for the calculation of the other metrics: the variance is $E((X - \mu)^2)$ and σ the standard deviation is the square root. The coefficient of variation is the standard deviation divided by the mean; the skewness is $E((X - \mu)^3)/\sigma^3$ and the kurtosis is $E((X - \mu)^4)/\sigma^4$.

In particular, it is possible to work with the sum of independent random variables because of $M_{X+Y}(t) = M_X(t)M_Y(t)$ and in the risk analytics setting it appears very often that the sum of independent variables is with a random number of terms N and in that case

If $Y = \sum_{i=1}^{N} X_i$ then $E(e^{tY}|N) = (M_X(t))^N$
Or $M_Y(t) = E(M_X(t)^N)$

In the discrete case, it is possible to use the probability generating function or the random variable X that is $E(t^X)$ for all t for which the series converges.

The limit theorems of probability in risk analytics help to simplify calculations, for example, the Central Limit Theorem says that if $\overline{X}$ is the mean of a random sample of size n taken from a population with mean μ and finite variance σ^2, then the limit of the distribution of $Z = \frac{X-\mu}{\frac{\sigma}{\sqrt{n}}}$, when n → ∞, is N(0,1).

The weak law of large numbers says that if $X_1, X_2, \ldots$ is a sequence of *(i.i.d)* independent and identically distributed random variables, each having finite mean $E[X_i] = \mu$ $(i = 1$ to $n)$. Then, for any $\varepsilon > 0$, $P(|\overline{X} - \mu| \geq \varepsilon) \to 0$ when n goes to infinite. And the strong law of large numbers says that if $X_1, X_2, \ldots$ are *i.i.d* random variables with a finite mean $\mu = E[X_i]$. Then, with probability 1, $\overline{X} \to \mu$ as n→∞.

Now the importance of having several random variables in the risk analytics process is supported by stochastic processes. The stochastic process is defined as follows: Let T be a subset of $[0, \infty)$. A family of random variables $\{X_t\}$ with $t \in T$, indexed by T, is called a stochastic (or random) process. When $T = N$, $\{X_t\}$ $t \in T$ is said to be a discrete-time process, and when $T = [0, \infty)$, it is called a continuous-time process.

1.8   EXAMPLES OF STOCHASTIC PROCESSES

In the following paragraphs, there is a presentation of some stochastic processes used in risk analytics. Starting with a random walk: A random process that is consisting of a sequence of discrete steps of fixed length. Let $\{X_k\}$ k = 1 … ∞ be a sequence of independent, identically distributed discrete random variables. For each positive integer n, we let S_n denote the sum $X_1 + X_2 + \cdots + X_n$. The sequence $\{S_n\}$ n = 1 … ∞ is called a random walk. If the common range of the X_k's is R^m, then we say that $\{S_n\}$ is a random walk in R^m.

Brownian process standard: A standard Brownian motion is a random process $X = \{X_t : t \in [0, \infty)\}$ with state space **R** that satisfies the following properties:

- $X_0=0$ with probability 1.
- X has stationary increments. That is, for $s,t \in [0, \infty)$ with $s < t$, the distribution of $X_t - X_s$ is the same as the distribution of X_{t-s}
- X has independent increments. That is, for $t_1, t_2, \ldots, t_n \in [0, \infty)$ with $t_1 < t_2 < \cdots < t_n$, the random variables $X_{t1}, X_{t2} - X_{t1}, \ldots, X_{tn} - X_{tn-1}$ are independent.
- X_t is normally distributed with mean 0 and variance t for each $t \in (0, \infty)$.
- With probability 1, $t \mapsto X_t$ is continuous on $[0, \infty)$.

And a geometric Brownian process: A stochastic process S_t is said to follow a geometric Brownian motion if it satisfies the following stochastic differential equation:

$$\delta S_t = u S_t \delta t + \sigma S_t \delta W_t.$$

where W_t is a Wiener process (Brownian motion) and u, σ are constants. The Wiener process is a continuous-time stochastic process W_t for $t \geq 0$ with $W_0 = 0$ and such that the increment $W_t - W_s$ is Gaussian distributed with mean 0 and variance t-s for any $0 \leq s < t$, and increments for non-overlapping time intervals are independent. Brownian motion (i.e., random walk with random step sizes) is the most common example of a Wiener process.

Markov process: A random process whose future probabilities are determined by its most recent values. A stochastic process $x(t)$ is called Markov if for every n and $t_1 < t_2 \ldots < t_n$, and it has the property

$$P\left(x(t_n) <= x_n | x(t_{(n-1)}), \ldots, x(t_1)\right) = P\left(x(t_n) <= x_n | x(t_{(n-1)})\right)$$

Martingales: A sequence of random variates $X_0, X_1, \ldots$ with finite means such that the conditional expectation of X_{n+1} given $X_0, X_1, X_2, \ldots, X_n$ is equal to X_n, i.e., $E(X_{n+1}|X_0, \ldots, X_n) = X_n$ Martingale is the name coming from games and pointing to the concept of fair game, where the bets are reduced to half or double depending on the losses or winning. Levy and Doob developed this area of stochastic processes. A one-dimensional random walk with steps equally likely in either direction ($p = q = 1/2$) is an example of a Martingale.

1.9 COMPOUND POISSON DISTRIBUTION

Description of the insurance portfolio: Let N be the number of claims a random variable in a portfolio of insurance policies in a defined period. Suppose X_1 is the amount of the first claim, X_2 is the amount of the second claim, and so on. Then, $Y = X_1 + X_2 + \ldots + X_N$ represents the total aggregate claims in a portfolio of policies in a time period. Assumptions:

- $X_1, X_2, \ldots$ are independent and identically distributed random variables
- Each X_i is independent of the number of claims N
- When the claim frequency N follows a Poisson distribution with a constant parameter λ, the aggregate claims Y is said to have a compound Poisson distribution.

1.9.1 DISTRIBUTION FUNCTION

$$F_Y(y) = \sum_{n=0}^{\infty} F^{*n}(y) \frac{\lambda^n e^{-\lambda}}{n!}$$

where $\lambda = E[N]$ is the common distribution function of X_i and F^{*n} is the n-fold convolution of F.

The calculations of the mean and variance are given by:

$$E[Y] = E[N]E[X] = \lambda E[X]$$
$$Var[Y] = \lambda E[X^2]$$

The moment-generating function and cumulant-generating function are given by:

$$M_Y(t) = e^{\lambda(M_X(t)-1)}$$
$$\Psi_Y(t) = ln M_Y(t) = \lambda(M_X(t) - 1)$$

Note that the moment-generating function of the Poisson N is $M_N(t) = e^{\lambda(e^t-1)}$. For a compound distribution Y in general, $M_Y(t) = M_N[lnM_X(t)]$

Properties: Skewness

$$E\left[(Y - \mu_Y)^3\right] = \Psi_Y^{(3)}(0) = \lambda E[X^3]$$

$$\gamma Y = \frac{E\left[(Y-\mu_Y)^3\right]}{Var[Y]^{\frac{3}{2}}} = \frac{1}{\sqrt{\lambda}}\frac{E[X^3]}{E[X^2]^{\frac{3}{2}}}$$

If $Y_1, Y_2, \ldots, Y_k$ are independent random variables such that each Y_i has a compound Poisson distribution with λ_i being the Poisson parameter for the number of claim variable and Fi being the distribution function for the individual claim amount. Then, $Y = Y_1 + Y_2 + \ldots + Y_k$ has a compound Poisson distribution with:

$$\text{the Poisson parameter:} \quad \lambda = \sum_{i=1}^{k} \lambda_i$$

$$\text{the distribution function:} \quad F_Y(y) = \sum_{i=1}^{k} \frac{\lambda_i}{\lambda} F_i(y)$$

Suppose there are k independent groups of insurance policies such that the aggregate claims Y_i for the i_{th} group has a compound Poisson distribution. Then, $Y = Y_1 + Y_2 + \ldots + Y_k$ is the aggregate claims for the combined group during the fixed policy period and also has a compound Poisson distribution with the parameters defined as in the previous paragraphs. To get a further intuitive understanding about the parameters of the combined group, consider N_i as the Poisson number of claims in the i_{th} group of insurance policies. The independent sum of Poisson variables is also a Poisson random variable. Thus, the total number of claims in the combined block is $N = N_1 + N_2 + \ldots + N_k$ and has a Poisson distribution with parameter $\lambda = \lambda_1 + \ldots + \lambda_k$.

For example, suppose that an insurance company acquired two portfolios of insurance policies and combined them into a single group. For each portfolio, the aggregate claims variable has a compound Poisson distribution. For one of the portfolios, the Poisson parameter is λ_1 and the individual claim amount has an exponential distribution with parameter δ_1. The corresponding Poisson and exponential parameters for the other portfolio are λ_2 and δ_2, respectively. The aggregate claim Y of the combined portfolio has a compound Poisson distribution with Poisson parameter $\lambda = \lambda_1 + \lambda_2$. The amount of a random claim X in the combined portfolio has the following distribution function and density function:

$$F_X(x) = \frac{\lambda_1}{\lambda}(1 - e^{-\delta_1 x}) + \frac{\lambda_2}{\lambda}(1 - e^{-\delta_2 x})$$
$$f_X(x) = \frac{\lambda_1}{\lambda}(\delta_1 e^{-\delta_1 x}) + \frac{\lambda_2}{\lambda}(\delta_2 e^{-\delta_2 x})$$

1.9.2 DISTRIBUTION FUNCTION

As in the general case,

$$F_Y(y) = \sum_{n=0}^{\infty} F^{*n}(y)\frac{\lambda^n e^{-\lambda}}{n!}$$

where $\lambda = \lambda_1 + \lambda_2$ here $F = F_X$ and F^{*n} is the n-fold convolution of F.

1.9.3   Mean and Variance

$$E[Y] = \frac{\lambda_1}{\delta_1} + \frac{\lambda_2}{\delta_2}$$

$$Var[Y] = \frac{2\lambda_1}{\delta_1^2} + \frac{2\lambda_2}{\delta_2^2}$$

Moment-generating function (mgf) and cumulant-generating function

To obtain the mgf and cgf of the aggregate claims Y, consider $\lambda[M_X(t) - 1]$. Note that $M_X(t)$ is the weighted average of the two exponential mgfs of the two portfolios of insurance policies. Thus, we have:

$$M_X(t) = \frac{\lambda_1}{\lambda}\frac{\delta_1}{\delta_1 - t} + \frac{\lambda_2}{\lambda}\frac{\delta_2}{\delta_2 - t}$$

$$\lambda[M_X(t) - 1] = \frac{\lambda_1 t}{\delta_1 - t} + \frac{\lambda_2 t}{\delta_2 - t}$$

$$M_Y(t) = e^{\lambda(M_X(t)-1)} = e^{\frac{\lambda_1 t}{\delta_1 - t} + \frac{\lambda_2 t}{\delta_2 - t}}$$

$$\Psi_Y(t) = \frac{\lambda_1 t}{\delta_1 - t} + \frac{\lambda_2 t}{\delta_2 - t}$$

In the case of considering randomness in the parameters of distributions-compounding – mix distributions are the concepts in the fitting process consider the fit for parameter distributions and the main random variable. The identification of the probability distributions consider randomness in the parameters in risk analytics provide a better approach to the modeling process as it is in using credibility for premium adjustment in actuarial work.

In general, the idea is to have the analysis of the distribution of variable X as a conditional distribution to a parameter θ and this means $f(x|\theta)$ and the definition of $g(x)$ is:

$g(x) = \int_\theta r(\theta)f(x|\theta)d\theta$ in a continuous case of θ and the discrete is a sum.

For example:

A Poisson distribution with a parameter that has a gamma distribution with parameters α and θ is a negative binomial:

$$\int_0^\infty \left[\frac{\theta^\alpha}{\Gamma(\alpha)}\lambda^{\alpha-1}e^{-\lambda\theta}\right]\left[\frac{\lambda^x e^{-\lambda}}{x!}\right]d\lambda = \frac{\theta^\alpha}{\Gamma(\alpha)x!}\int_0^\infty \lambda^{\alpha+x-1}e^{-\lambda(1+\theta)}d\lambda$$

The expression in the integral can be written as $\frac{\Gamma(\alpha+x)\theta^\alpha}{\Gamma(\alpha)x!(1+\theta)^{\alpha+x}}$ that when $\alpha = r > 0$ and with $\theta = \frac{p}{1-p}$ for p between 0 and 1 the expression is negative binomial distribution for X having $\frac{(r+x-1)!}{(r-1)!x!}p^r(1-p)^x$ with r success where each success has probability p.

A normal distribution with normal mean is normal distributed, but if the mean is exponential, the distribution is exponential modified normal distribution.

1.10   UNDERSTANDING LINEAR ALGEBRA

As the supplement of understanding data in general, the way to deal with arrays – data organization is through linear algebra and linear algebra is the core of several approaches for model development that includes concepts like distance definition and metrics creation will appear in multiple instead of several sections in the book, e.g., clustering definition, risk indicators creation, etc. In this section, there is an introduction to concepts that come from linear algebra results that are crucial to the analysis of deterministic and random data sets. Now, taking the variables as random variables, the matrix A

will be the array of the values (data) that the random variables are taking (realizations). Each row – record is a point of coordinates (realizations) $(x_1, x_2, ..., x_p)$. The columns will be the random vectors. A vector with nonnegative entries that add up to 1 is called a probability vector. A stochastic matrix is a square matrix whose columns are probability vectors.

Furthermore, there are properties used in data science to describe the behavior of vectors in data matrix A. This is the case of eigenvectors and eigenvalues. An eigenvector of an $n \times n$ matrix A is a nonzero vector x such that $Ax = \lambda x$ for some λ scalar. A scalar is called an eigenvalue of A if there is a nontrivial solution x of $Ax = \lambda x$; such an x is called an eigenvector corresponding to λ. A scalar λ is an eigenvalue of an n × n matrix A if and only if satisfies the characteristic equation $\det(A - \lambda I) = 0$; this equation comes from the definition of an eigenvector that is the solution to the equation $Ax = \lambda x$ for a scalar (real number λ). This means the search for a vector that is parallel to the image of x by a linear transformation is represented by Ax.

Operations in the set of matrices are used to obtain new properties in the spaces of the problems. Several operations are related to the combination of vectors, matrices, and real numbers. One of these operations is the dot product between vectors that provides the calculation of the length of a vector and the distance between two vectors u and v is $dist(u,v) = \|u - v\|$ when both vectors are in R^n.

With $\|x\| = \sqrt{x \cdot x} = \sqrt{x_1^2 + ... + x_n^2}$ and $x = (x_1, x_2, ..., x_n)$

In the development of solutions with linear models to the problems in risk analytics, the concept of orthogonal projection and the least squares solutions is fundamental. Remember that a subspace in $\mathbf{R}^n$ is subset of $\mathbf{R}^n$ with the properties of including 0, being close to the sum and the scalar product. If S is a subspace of $\mathbf{R}^n$ and for a vector y of $\mathbf{R}^n$ the orthogonal projection of y onto S, $\hat{y}$ is the closest point in S to y and the least squares solution of a system $Ax = b$ is given by $\hat{x}$ such as

$$\|y - \hat{y}\| \leq \|y - v\| \text{ for all } v \text{ in } S \text{ different from } \hat{y}$$

And with $\mathbf{A}$ $m \times n$ matrix and $b \in R^n$ and $\hat{x}$

$\|b - A\hat{x}\| \leq \|b - Ax\|$ for any x in $\mathbf{R}^n$

The vector $\hat{x} = (A^T A)^{-1} A^T b$ is the unique least squares solution when the columns of A are linearly independent and equivalently when $(A^T A)^{-1}$ exists. The matrix A is symmetric $(\mathbf{A} = \mathbf{A}^T)$ and the square matrix will be positive definite (the quadratic form $\mathbf{x}^T \mathbf{A} \mathbf{x}$ is positive for all $\mathbf{x}$, $\mathbf{x}^T \mathbf{A} \mathbf{x}$ represent the distance from the origin to the random vector) when all eigenvalues are positive or nonnegative definite if the eigenvalues are positive and including zero. The standard deviation for the vector $\mathbf{x}$ is the distance from the point to the origin. In terms of points in a regular geometric space, distance can have units such as centimeters between two points. In risk analytics, the evaluation of distance of vectors representing for example the means is based on the number of standard deviation that those mean vectors are. The distance in terms of the risk analytics process is based not only on variances but also into covariances to understand that the mean vectors can have changes in different directions. The Mahalanobis distance is the distance used in multivariate analytics to take into consideration the covariances or to include the possible correlations. In simple terms, the correction of the Euclidean distance to the use of the Mahalanobis distance is to take into consideration variations in observations. The concept of a square matrix that is positive definite is when the matrix is symmetric, and the eigenvalues are positive; in particular, the $\mathbf{S}$ matrix. The inverse of $\mathbf{S}$ means the standardized matrix.

Factorization in matrices can help in many ways to discover properties to use in calculations, in particular to improve time efficiency. Diagonalization is required to get one of these factorization results and simplification for operations calculations. A square matrix that is symmetric is orthogonally diagonalizable this means exist an orthogonal matrix P (this is orthonormal columns and $\mathbf{P}^{-1} = \mathbf{P}^T$) and a diagonal matrix D such that a matrix A $m \times m$, $A = PDP^T = PDP^{-1}$ and refreshing the memory, P is with the eigenvectors in the columns and D is defined as a matrix with a main diagonal with the eigenvalues and the rest of entries equal zero. A positive-definite matrix is possible to diagonalize. In general, the matrix A can be written in terms of the eigenvalues and eigenvectors in what is the spectral decomposition $A = \sum_{i=1}^{m} \lambda_i u_i u_i^T$ where the u_i are the orthonormal eigenvectors and it is possible to define $A^{1/2}$ the square root of A that $A^{\frac{1}{2}} = PD^{\frac{1}{2}}P^T$. Where $D^{1/2}$ is the diagonal matrix with square root of the eigenvalues in the diagonal.

Not all matrices are diagonalizable but all matrices are possible to write as $A = QD^* P^{-1} = QD^* P^T$ using the singular value decomposition result for a $m \times n$ matrix of rank r there is $m \times n$ matrix $D^* = \begin{bmatrix} D & 0 \\ 0 & 0 \end{bmatrix}$ where the entries of D are the r ordered, in descendent way, singular values of A, Q is an $m \times m$ orthogonal matrix, and P an $n \times n$ orthogonal matrix. The diagonal entries of D^* are the singular values of A with Q and P not unique. The squared roots of the eigenvalues of $A^T A$ are the singular values. These singular values are the lengths of the vectors $Ax_1, \dots Ax_n$.

In general, for two vectors y_1 and y_2 with **S** as the sample covariance matrix

$$d^2 = (y_1 - y_2)^T S^{-1}(y_1 - y_2)$$

That in terms of the mean can be written as

$$d^2 = (\hat{y} - \mu)^T S^{-1}(\hat{y} - \mu)$$

or the same expression with differences of means. The $E(X)$, the expected value of a random matrix nxm, is the matrix of expected values of each of the entries (random variables in position x_{ij} for $0 \leq i \leq n$ and $0 \leq j \leq m$).

Now some properties of the matrix calculus that are important to remember: If the matrix **A** does not depend on **x** and $y = Ax$, $\frac{\delta y}{\delta x} = A$; A is nxm and **x** is mx1 and **y** is nx1, in case that x depends on z, the derivative is $\frac{\delta y}{\delta z} = A \frac{\delta x}{\delta z}$ in the case of quadratic forms $Q(x) = x^T Ax$ where **A** is $n \times n$ the derivative is $\frac{\delta Q(x)}{\delta x} = x^T (A + A^T)$ that in the case of **A** symmetric the result is $\frac{\delta Q(x)}{\delta x} = 2x^T A$.

In linear models, the representation is $y = X\beta + \varepsilon$ that has a $\hat{\beta}$ least-squares solution as the solution of the normal equations $X^T X\beta = X^T y$. On a last point, in terms of risk analytics, the concept of principal components is about the unit eigenvectors of the variance-covariance matrix of the data after they have been ordered in descendent way. The first principal component is the eigenvector of the highest eigenvalue the second principal component will be the eigenvector of the second-highest eigenvalue, and the process continues selecting eigen-values and eigenvectors.

1.11 TRADITIONAL MODELS IN FINANCE

The other important component to build risk analytics is the finance theory, mainly in what is related to return. Organization development is based on creating value and value could be a measure in the contribution to increase the desire results using resources available. Return on investments in financial assets is an example. The parameters used in the market for creating wealth and studied by finance are an area of risk analytics. Risk will be related to the variation of the expected returns and many activities in finance will be centered around the search of understanding of how to control returns. In this chapter, the concepts are related to the market behavior in general and what portfolio could be when different risk units with different probability distribution can be combined. See the example in insurance and multiple coverage, as it is presented at the end of this section, where there is a presentation of specific products and interest/return models understanding.

To start, the first aspect to review is interest and market behavior (see Chapter 5 for more details about return analysis). In this setting, the beginning is with the use of nominal interest rate and relationships to the growth rate of the money (R). Real interest rate: growth rate of the purchasing power (r) and i is the inflation rate $1 + r = (1 + R)/(1 + i)$. The expected rate of return is the probability weighted average of the rates of return in all scenarios $E(r) = \Sigma_k p(k)r(k)$, where k represents the scenario index. In the book, the terms related to interest rates/returns (see Chapter 5) are multiple and some appear as follows:

Risk free rate = rate that is possible to gain in free risk assets T-Bills
Risk premium = difference between the holding period return (HPR) on an index stock fund and the risk free rate
Hedging = investment in an asset in order to reduce the risk of a portfolio
Diversification = is a means to control portfolio investing in a wide variety of assets

Covariance and correlation in portfolio analysis: Covariance indicates how much the return of risky assets are variating one against the other/all together and the correlation is the measure put in the scale of −1 to 1. Variance for current return (R_a) and expected return (R_e), $Var(R_a) = E(R_a - R_e)^2$ and standard deviation $\sqrt{Var(R_a)}$. It is important to analyze correlation and covariance and in a first approach, a portfolio variability is made with variance analysis and historical data review. Diversification reduces variability for a unique risk, but market risk cannot be avoided with diversification.

Creation of metrics in finance is a good example of measurement process that in risk analytics is required. In Chapter 5, there are several additional metrics to review regarding bonds or other assets, such as the Greeks (theta, vega, delta, and gamma). Metrics are used for specific assets and some of the concepts can be used across them because several of the metrics are related to the simultaneous use of variables that represent risk-related measurements. In some cases, the purpose is to use calculus tools such as areas (integrals) or derivatives to identify intensity of risk or conditions to control based on changes of markets, transactions, etc. Once the function to analyze is defined, it is as in physics the definition of distance and then velocity and acceleration or in the case of the moments of the probability distributions based on the derivatives of the moment-generating functions.

An approach, for example, to estimate the changes in portfolios/prices of assets is based on volatility (standard deviation) or partial derivative related to σ (Vega = $\frac{\partial P}{\partial \sigma}$), or changes because of time (Theta = $\frac{\partial P}{\partial t}$), or in options because of the changes in the underlying asset price (Delta = $\frac{\partial P}{\partial p}$) or the double derivative-based changes of delta (Gamma = $\frac{\partial^2 P}{\partial p^2}$) because of the underlying asset, changes because of changes in interest rates (Rho = $\frac{\partial P}{\partial i}$).

The measurement process uses the basic mathematical principles and models as in the CAPM model, where the main model concept used is regression and the slopes are the support of metrics to work for decision making. In general, the metrics are not used in isolation; they need to be used as a supplement of data observation to see how the phenomena can be described. In physics, the speed says something and the acceleration says another important thing to evaluate the impact of two objects. The same in finance; several measures are based on circumstances and possible impact of risk, for example for a wealthy company a loss of 10,000 USD cannot be big, but for a new start-up it can represent a limitation to grow or for a project, the same with the effects of different factors or conditions of operation, transactions, possibilities of increasing the losses, and so on.

In the CAPM model, the purpose is to identify the impact on the financial resources of the conditions of financial markets. The purpose is to measure the relationship between risk and expected return. There are multiple assumptions for simplifying the model and to use the results. This is particularly important in the risk analytics process. Assumptions are based on what is possible to deal with in terms of variables and their relationships to be described by a model. The purpose of the model is to provide knowledge that is possible to use based on the understanding of the constraints, limitations, and assumptions of what the model is using. Most common issues are related to the problem of having factors that are not controllable by investors or actors in the market (systemic risk, or changes in the conditions of market transactions). It is possible to say in a simplified way: total risk = *Diversification risk* + *Market risk*. The risk of a security/asset is equal to the risk premium plus the risk free. Taking beta β = Contribution of an individual security, risk of the diversified portfolio related to market risk. This indicator is the measure of changes because of systemic risk.

σ_{im} = Covariance between stock return i and market return
σ_m^2 = Variance of the market return
β = contribution to the portfolio risk

$$\beta = \frac{\sigma_{im}}{\sigma_m^2}$$

The risk premium is proportional to β and according to that, the following points are observed:

- Investors prefer a high expected return with low standard deviation.
- It is important to evaluate the stock contribution to the portfolio.
- The sensibility of a portfolio to the market portfolio variation is beta (β).
- If the investors can get loans to borrow with free risk interest rate, they should have a contribution of the investments risk free and in a stock portfolio.
- In equilibrium, no asset is under market line. Investors, instead of buying A_1 shares, would prefer to borrow and use the balance in the market portfolio. If A_2 investor would prefer debt and invest in the market portfolio.
- Higher the risk, higher the expected return.
- The most complex risks to manage are the ones that are not able to be controlled by diversification.
- The risk premium should be on the market line. The dot line shows the risk premium for different β.
- Portfolios with higher β generate higher average returns.

The CAPM assumes each stock return depends on economic influences or negative factors and noise. This means an expression such as: *Return* = a + b_1 ($R_{factor1}$) + b_2 ($R_{factor2}$) + ... + *noise*. For each stock return, there are risk factors and activities:

- Factors that are not eliminated with diversification.
- Events that are identified with the company.
- The expected risk premium is affected by the factor influencing the market
- Expected risk premium calculation = b_1 ($R_{factor1} - R_{riskfree}$) + b_2 ($R_{factor2} - R_{riskfree}$) + ...
- Presence of macroeconomic factors.
- Estimation of the premium risk of each factor.
- Estimation the factor sensibility.
- Common factors are: Industrial activity level inflation rate.
- Difference between short- and long-term interest rates.

The expected return that can be an estimator of the cost of equity and the expression of return is $R = R_{riskfree}$ + (β of the asset/security) ($R_{market} - R_{riskfree}$). β is the slope of the company's return versus market return. As any regression model, the most important is to evaluate the residuals, the p-value of the variables used, the adjusted r-square, and the confidence intervals where the values of the parameters will be according to the selected level of confidence.

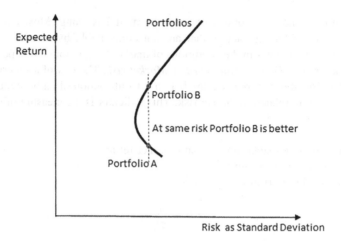

FIGURE 1.9   Efficient frontier illustration.

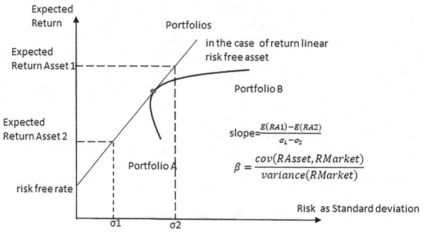

FIGURE 1.10   The intersection of efficient frontier and the difference between loans and debt.

Figures 1.9, 1.10, and 1.11 indicate properties of using the CAPM models to compare the efficient frontier. In Figure 1.9, the comparison is about expected returns versus the standard deviation a metric of risk. The meaning is that at the same standard deviation it can be possible to find two expected results in portfolios. The portfolio selection will be according to the best expected return. In Figures 1.10 and 1.11, there is representation of the portfolio that includes a risk-free asset that is represented as a linear model of the capital market line. The market portfolio is the unique intersection between the efficient frontier and the capital market line or staying at the point standard deviation of the market and its expected return of the market.

As a way to understand the CAPM as a process, Figure 1.12 indicates the definition of what is wealth as a combination of modeling, dealing with uncertainty/risk and portfolio creation, and use of models that describe the market.

The CAPM model (see Figure 1.13) as an estimator of the cost of capital can be compared to the calculation as weighted average of resources, own capital, and external funds. Capital cost = Expected

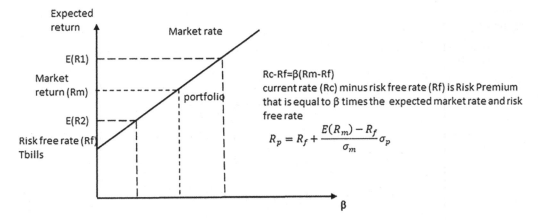

FIGURE 1.11   The concept of risk premium and risk free rate.

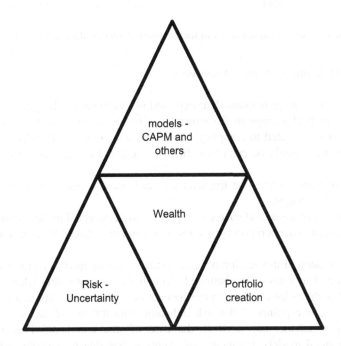

FIGURE 1.12   The CAPM model helps to define strategies to deal with risk and wealth creation.

return of assets or opportunity cost of the company's assets. Using R as return in the debt and own capital expression as follows:

$$\frac{debt}{debt + own\ capital}R\ of\ the\ debt + \frac{own\ capital}{debt + own\ capital}R\ of\ the\ own\ capital$$

Then:

$$Bassets = \frac{Debt}{Debt + Capital}\beta\ Debt + \frac{Capital}{Debt + Capital}\beta\ Capital$$

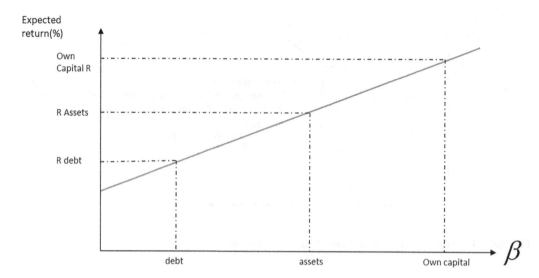

FIGURE 1.13 The structure of capital starts in the decision of mixing debt and own resources.

Some final remarks in this summary of concepts:

- The capital cost is more relevant than expected return in capital budget decisions.
- This is the weighted average of the return for debt and shares issued by the company.
- The capital cost is related to company's asset and not to the stockholder.
- The β of the asset might be calculated like the weighted average of the betas for other securities.
- When the company changes the financial leverage, the risk and expected return of individual securities change.
- The composition of assets and sources of revenues are connected to the use of resources to leverage the company operation cycles. Financial and operational leverages increase beta.

An additional observation of this section of basic finance is about insurance practice as an example of risk combination. The analysis is illustrated through the understanding what is happening for multiple risks and with the introduction to the concept of Monte Carlo simulation. Simulation is a means to identify sample points of the risk indicators and the use of the model that consider frequency/severity simultaneously as it in the case of the compound Poisson process (see Section 1.9 the general model). Frequency of events is possible to describe using a Bernoulli process with parameter probability of a claim (e.g., 7%), or using the binomial distribution or other distributions that count, such as Poisson distribution or negative binomial distribution. The calculation of the aggregation of the claims is based on the whole exposure; for example, it can be any number of units of risk (people, cars, homes). The Poisson distribution use is better when the number of claims in a period of time is possible to be more than one. Severity can be approached by Log normal with parameters for example 3,000 USD and standard deviation of 2,000 USD.

The issue appears when the combination of frequency (claim event appears or not) and severity because it is not possible to multiply the number of claims that a binomial will indicate with parameters the number of policies and the probability of 7%, times the severity of the claims or average value of the claims. This situation is because each individual claim realization can have a different severity value. Saying it in another way, the severity cannot be assumed identical for all claim events. In case that the sample is big enough it is possible to use the Central Limit Theorem to approach the aggregation using the inverse of the Poisson distribution of estimate the number of

TABLE 1.2

Join Analysis if Several Risks, Different Frequencies, and Severities as Individual Risks and Different as Combinations

Year	PrivLiability	PrivPhysicaldamage	Comliability	Comphysical	Total
2004	56,317,831	34,239,353	10,809,661	3,355,650	104,722,495
2005	57,188,070	36,762,455	10,373,070	3,508,189	107,831,784
2006	56,042,557	36,151,913	10,746,727	3,583,802	106,524,999
2007	59,760,630	37,541,418	10,079,010	3,523,677	110,904,735
2008	60,806,847	39,189,255	9,956,316	3,498,383	113,450,801
2009	63,448,211	36,497,330	9,345,288	3,005,162	112,295,991
2010	64,110,267	36,454,102	8,798,119	2,911,013	112,273,501
2011	64,310,776	40,589,159	9,363,647	3,164,880	117,428,462
2012	65,135,976	41,275,620	10,515,806	3,250,740	120,178,142
2013	67,879,783	41,754,861	11,305,714	3,255,570	124,195,928
2014	72,050,778	45,308,112	11,939,881	3,645,335	132,944,106
2015	79,098,617	48,564,511	13,587,152	3,902,124	145,152,404
2016	88,249,238	55,738,221	14,987,073	4,279,414	163,253,946
2017	90,495,835	57,052,411	15,528,570	4,874,748	167,951,564
2018	91,736,331	58,766,743	17,810,709	4,999,100	173,312,883
2019	96,191,310	62,638,267	20,435,099	5,407,130	184,671,806
2020	81,618,462	54,683,622	19,313,224	4,813,211	160,428,519

claims (one risk unit can have more than one claim) and the inverse of the normal distribution to estimate severity, using the parameters of the population mean and the standard deviation divided by the square root of the n exposure. After the multiplication of the claims number (Frequency of events) by severity of the losses will produce the estimation of the aggregated losses.

In the case that the calculations are related to several risks, the correlations have to be included in the calculations. The calculations are obtained with the help of ModelRisk tool.

With risk separated and with results on the same risk unit, the table shows:

This data (Tables 1.2, 1.3) indicates:

- Data for all combined limits. Data are for paid claims.
- Exclusion of Massachusetts and most states with no-fault automobile insurance laws.
- Excludes Massachusetts, Michigan, and New Jersey.
- Claim frequency is claims per 100 earned car years. A car year is equal to 365 days of insured coverage for a single vehicle.
- Claim severity is the size of the loss, measured by the average amount paid for each claim.
- Includes loss adjustment expenses.
- Excludes Massachusetts, Michigan, and New Jersey. Based on coverage with a $500 deductible.
- Excludes wind and water losses.

Finally, in this section, a comment about traditional models that can be performed on one variable or one risk. This is the case of Monte Carlo simulation that can be used to understand the NPV of a cash flow that is calculated using other random variables (accounts in financial statement). Figures 1.14 and 1.15 represent the simulations of the combination of variables and

TABLE 1.3
Four Different Risks, Individual and Combined with Frequency and Severity

	Liability				Physical damage (7)			
	Bodily Injury (2)		Property Damage (3)		Collision		Comprehensive (8)	
	Claim		Claim		Claim		Claim	
Year	frequency (4)	severity (5), (6)	frequency (4)	severity (5)	frequency (4)	severity (5)	frequency (4)	severity (5)
1999	1.23	9,646	4	2,294	5.73	2,352	2.8	1,116
2000	1.2	9,807	3.98	2,393	5.61	2,480	2.89	1,125
2001	1.16	10,149	3.97	2,471	5.53	2,525	3.11	1,152
2002	1.15	10,400	3.92	2,552	5.48	2,728	2.91	1,250
2003	1.12	11,135	3.84	2,558	5.13	2,921	2.76	1,324
2004	1.11	11,613	3.76	2,582	4.85	3,080	2.46	1,417
2005	1.07	11,983	3.63	2,657	5.04	3,067	2.38	1,457
2006	1.02	12,426	3.44	2,783	4.87	3,194	2.4	1,528
2007	0.95	12,712	3.48	2,830	5.13	3,139	2.47	1,519
2008	0.91	14,067	3.42	2,903	5.35	3,005	2.57	1,551
2009	0.89	13,891	3.49	2,869	5.48	2,869	2.75	1,389
2010	0.91	14,406	3.53	2,881	5.69	2,778	2.62	1,476
2011	0.92	14,848	3.56	2,958	5.75	2,861	2.79	1,490
2012	0.95	14,690	3.5	3,073	5.57	2,950	2.62	1,585
2013	0.95	15,441	3.55	3,231	5.71	3,144	2.57	1,621
2014	0.97	15,384	3.41	3,516	5.93	3,169	2.79	1,572
2015	0.89	17,014	3.45	3,628	6.01	3,377	2.72	1,679
2016	0.95	16,913	3.45	3,843	6.13	3,442	2.76	1,747
2017	1	16,761	3.45	3,933	6.14	3,423	2.86	1,811
2018	1.02	17,596	3.33	4,165	6.13	3,578	3.02	1,832
2019	1.01	18,680	3.27	4,331	6.07	3,752	3.23	1,777
2020	0.85	20,235	2.48	4,711	4.63	3,588	2.94	1,995

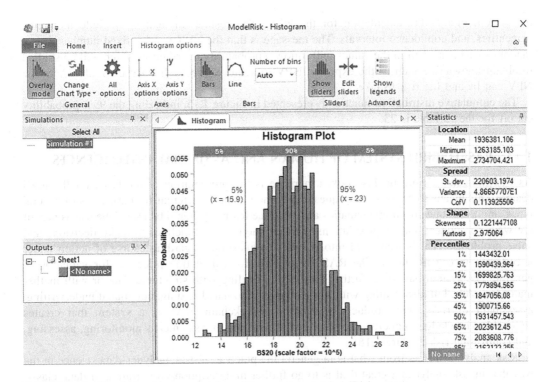

FIGURE 1.14   Simulation histogram and confidence interval. ModelRisk output.

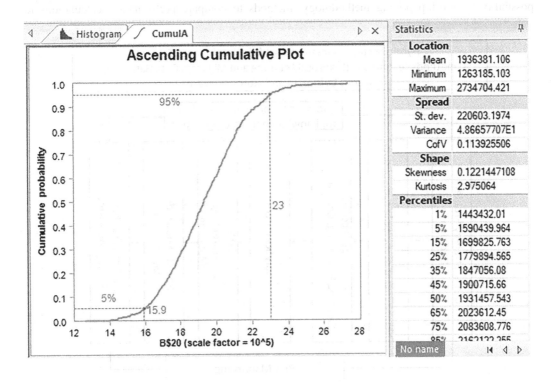

FIGURE 1.15   Accumulative probability function.

the bottom line of the calculation for the NPV. The results for analysis include moments, percentiles, and confidence intervals. The message is that the NPV is not a fixed number; it is a random variable as well in the values will follow a probability distribution which will be studied to obtain knowledge such as the expected NPV to achieve, the confidence intervals where the NPV can be and the risk to take.

The cumulative distribution function is presented in Figure 1.15, indicating the 95% probability cut off for the variable is 23.

1.12   RAS: HYBRID SYSTEM OF HUMAN AND ARTIFICIAL INTELLIGENCES

As was indicated before in this book, a purpose is the presentation of the basis for the RAS design. This means to answer many questions in how data in different formats, tools of several types, and techniques from mathematics and machine learning should be used. The use as part of the ways to connect and align solutions with production of guidelines to make decisions and solve problems. That is translated into answers to questions regarding course of action under uncertainty in organizations. The RAS is not only for calculating prices or for valuation in general. The system has to go further not only in dealing with structured data or with mathematical models, but also dealing with, for example, automated trading, automated underwriting, assessment of risks, and products development/blockchain. RAS is a system that creates actionable knowledge to operate the business; taking care of risks means monitoring, assessing, and controlling risk (Figure 1.16).

Risk analytics differs from what is in general the practice of data analytics-data science in the way that in risk analytics a great deal is to go further in description/visualization of data, classification, and basic ideas of optimization. In risk analytics, the data analysis processes include the possibility to develop pricing methodology, methods to compare performance, calculations to

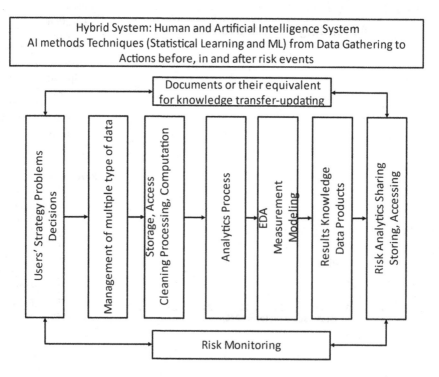

FIGURE 1.16   RAS includes all steps from data to actions based on risk measurement/modeling/monitoring, with all types of data used. Documents and risk knowledge transfer, access, use, are part of the system.

understand if organizations have the funds/reserve to answer the demand of customers, and regulators to properly operate. In addition, there is a clear development of designing products and its evaluation, understanding how financial models can be improved by using statistical and machine learning tools, etc. In general, the subprocesses of the risk management process requires data analytics in each step and in several cases the application can be different types of models or techniques; for example, in Chapter 5 the presentation will show how return analysis and its own variables/contract relationships require from deterministic to stochastic models to understand how to hedge, offer investment opportunities or even to define policies to guide society's decision.

In that order of ideas, the analysis and design of the risk analytics system comprises:

- Understanding of the business, indicating the kind of activities and processes using systems and operation of the WHO, WHAT, and HOW of the business definition. Identification of problems from general to specific, defining the problem in smaller problems; the same as thinking in smaller systems involved to build the complete RAS architecture – structure.
- Identification sources of software, information systems to solve multiple problems, individual and in connection to multiple populations/variables. For example, the use of data from many sources could require special systems to read and write structured and unstructured data. RAS design is a continuous project. The RAS requires project planning under an agile approach given the ongoing adaptation that is required in organizations to different circumstances. Modification in the business environment can introduce changes in the operation of the organization. Agile manifesto proposes focusing on adaptation, on people who are the solutions creators, and producing a more self-adaptive process according to the partial solutions creation.
- Testing as a continuous process. For example, solutions in the modeling process are going to be under ongoing testing, calibration, and deployment processes according to changes in models or artificial intelligence outcomes. The interaction among users and creators of solutions is a continuous process; the same as analysis and design is a cycle repeated multiple times in steps to solve the problems. It is the case of a model that can be reused or a model that requires several steps to be used and each step generates pieces of the system, or saying there is a dynamic cycle of development. The merge of the steps of analysis and data use with the production of answers is part of the need to maintain an organization that is updated and competitive.
- The conceptual data modeling affects the modeling process, access, and computation capacity the same as the way that is possible to reuse results; this is converting outcomes in some process as inputs for the next processes or steps (e.g., time series analysis of risk indicators). Interfaces can be different according to the users. In several cases, the interfaces are more about the organization of results, models, or visualization. In some users, the outcomes require more the connection to the process of obtaining results and creation of data products (e.g., dynamic, shareable, and interactive reports).

The RAS (Figure 1.17) design and life cycle require identification of the system components (as it was presented in the introduction), relationship of those components, what is limiting or defining boundaries, objectives, type of process environment, inputs, outputs, and interfaces. In a RAS, input (data) will come from multiple sources and formats; in general big data attributes will be the rule, and the outputs are not static. They will be dynamic and related to automation and AI development. The system environment is about multiple operations from risk metrics control to automated decisions in actions, such as approving transactions.

Continuous AI and Human interaction in the RAS System to organize and process data for inputting in the risks analytics process that is before, in and after the risk events	AI and Humans to deal with data that is structured and unstructured, streamed data, data that is in multiple repositories (data for use of services, utilities, retail transactions), documents and so on.
	AI and Humans to use data from multiples sources and variety of data, to build models, to create knowledge
	AI and Humans to put the risk analytics knowledge in the hands of the operation/production to provide valuable actions to the organization
	AI and Humans to control, follow up and monitoring the factors affecting risk analytics process in the organization, generating new data to feed and improve learning process (e.g. transferring means of risk knowledge) and creation of data products

FIGURE 1.17 A RAS architecture includes the AI support of solving problems from data gathering to data analytics and the interaction of humans and machines.

The RAS, as it will be presented ahead in the book, has data of all types and the subsystems coexist with structured and unstructured ad stream data. The variety of data implies subsystems with specific solutions (see Exhibit 1.1).

These examples and ideas around the basics to create risk analytics practice and design a RAS show the interaction of multiple disciplines and that core of the process based on the problem to solve. The most important is to clarify where the questions are and explore/discover possible ways to tackle the problem. Risk analytics is a process that provides answers with risk knowledge creation to mitigate risks. The constraint is that the approach identifies possible futures, because there is no meaning of searching only one future. One future only cannot exist for an organization; there are possible/feasible/ideal futures. One future is a deterministic approach where possibly everyone in a market would like to be or, better, must to be because there are no more options.

In risk analytics, the assumption is to keep a no deterministic approach of the nature and to develop intelligence based on adaptive processes to changes in the environment. The search of futures is about the search of the best possible control capacity to adapt organizations to new circumstances and maintain appropriate outcomes in the organizations' processes, good performance, and value for stakeholders. For the risk analytics process development, the concepts related to the risk management process are combined and connected to the risk modeling process. Finally, in terms of the data analytics process, if organizations have access to equivalent data and will use similar techniques the can arrive to similar predictions.This means competitors-member of a market potentially will lead/behave using similar strategies and tactics. This can be inconvenient because the future will not be as the expected value or estimation is, given that organizations will act in different strategic and tactic ways. The paradox is finding the best product or the best solution or the best strategy that will be the same for everyone. Will be not anymore good, possibly the worst, prices can fall, all drivers in congested roads will move to the uncongested roads and thus the congested road will be the predicted uncongested road. Strategy design and implementation is human based and machine supported, but with the

---

EXHIBIT 1.1 OVERVIEW OF RAS COMPONENTS THAT ARE COMBINING INTERFACES, DATA, AND SUBSYSTEMS

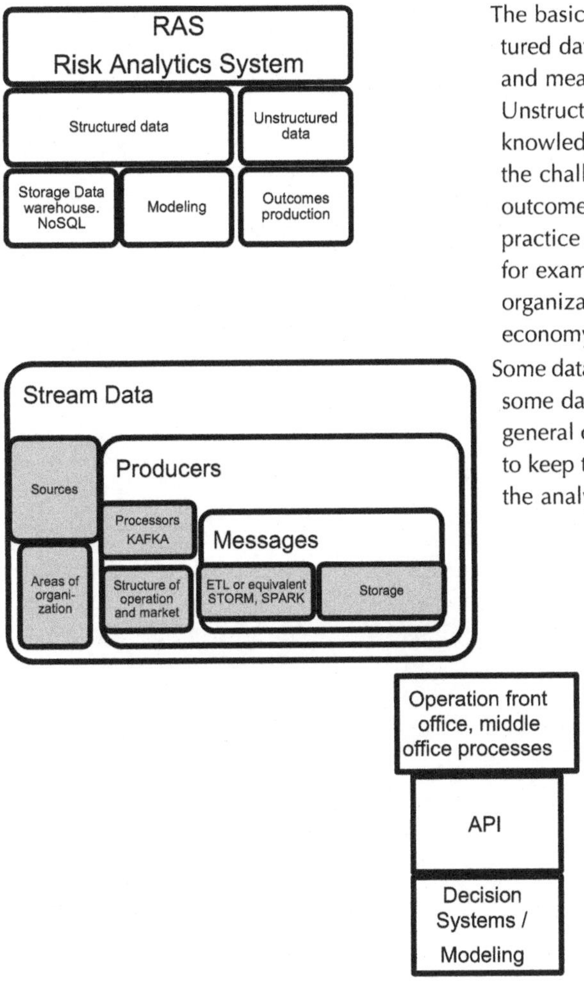

The basic architecture starts dealing with structured data and modeling; producing metrics and means to use them for operations. Unstructured data appears to supplement the knowledge obtained from structured data and the challenge is to combine both data and outcomes, or to develop risk classification practice using appropriate classifiers combining for example, sentiment analysis regarding an organization brand-name, or a sector in the economy.

Some data in risk analytics is in discrete form and some data is streamed in nature. Time series in general can be analyzed with batches of data or to keep the stream of data of prices and provide the analytics (e.g., KAFKA capabilities).

---

purpose of finding paths of differentiation and better performance among markets, actions, solutions in risk related problems.

The next chapter introduces similarities, differences, and orientation to use what it is possible from each process knowledge to answer questions related to risk, changes of factors affecting decisions, and possible outcomes of decisions. The chapters ahead describe the processes and components that use multiple techniques that converge in RAS. The assumption is that each step in the analysis and design has broken the system into subsystems that can be integrated, with all required components and outcomes. For instance, a risk indicator as it is VaR requires the subsystem to calculate it and it has to be connected to decisions related to risk management, compliance subsystem, management information system, etc.

2 Risk Management, Modeling, and Analytics Processes

In the previous chapter, it was presented as a way to connect the risk management and risk analytics processes, the measurement process and it was indicated as asset to have the tools from mathematics that in the book are used. In this chapter, there is a review of the steps in the risk management process, the risk modeling process, and the way to create a risk analytics road map. Through the book, the link concept for all the topics is the creation of a risk analytics system (RAS), as mentioned in Chapter 1. Risk analytics methods/techniques and results are used and developed under the premise of having a system that is an ongoing and alive system producing results to improve performance in the organizations; it is not about stand-alone solution creation as happens in organizations that build a model today and it is not under the umbrella of being a component of a system that supports operations of several areas and in the current and future endeavors.

The topics of the chapter are interconnected with principles of risk management to avoid issues in risk analytics that can lead to applications that with errors are in place and used for supporting the society. The risk model is clearly present and the ethical risk are part of innovation as Blackman R., 2022, indicated: "In 2019 a study published in the journal Science found that artificial intelligence from Optum, which many health systems were using to spot high-risk patients who should receive follow-up care, was prompting medical professionals to pay more attention to white people than to Black people. Only 18% of the people identified by the AI were Black, while 82% were white. After reviewing data on the patients who were actually the sickest, the researchers calculated that the numbers should have been about 46% and 53%, respectively. The impact was far-reaching: The researchers estimated that the AI had been applied to at least 100 million patients."

The above example shows errors in sampling, data selection, experiment design, etc. In risk analytics, data is fundamental of course but the definition of what is really to search for, answers to get, and how to use the answers in risk control is the key to succeed. In general, in risk analytics, descriptive analytics, predictive analytics, and prescriptive analytics are combined and used in data analytics practice. The additional part is that analytics work requires the mathematics work in specific areas that are in the core of the risk management process: pricing analytics, reserving analytics, benchmarking analytics, product analytics, customer analytics, and so on. These areas are using mathematics/statistics and computational capacity to solve the problems under the risk-uncertainty perspective for pricing, having the resources to answer the customer needs and compliance with regulation, knowing where to be to operate under controlled risk conditions, etc. In Chapters 3, 4, 5, and 6, the book illustrates how risk analytics processes are used in benchmarking, product design for hedging, and tools for dealing with models that include statistical and machine learning capabilities.

A risk analytics road map needs the creation of a risk analytics system (RAS) as the combination of the risk management and analytics processes. In Chapter 6, there is a presentation of the classification of data as structured and unstructured data to emphasize the different relationships of data and model creation. The RAS components are described throughout the book with special attention to the risk monitoring process that is presented in Chapter 9. This chapter concentrates on basic aspects of modeling for maintaining in operation the risk analytics process as a core subprocess to develop the RAS. At the same time, there is an introduction to develop steps to create meaning from data and to explain the required work in risk analytics. With the fast evolution of analytics tools, the learning of them is an ongoing process. Today, there are languages and platforms that are key ones, but they

DOI: 10.1201/9780429342899-3

are in continuous evolution, such as the R, Python, Julia, Scala, etc. Languages that are now with a high level of use are in stages of continuous review. Languages and tools for risk analytics platforms require adaptation to theoretical and practical changes to be adopted in organizations and complying regulation.

The new development of computational capacity and ways to approach and solve problems is not static; this means a skill of risk analytics people is to be lifelong learners to keep them relevant, adopting what is possible to use, adapt to new paradigms that last a short time, and deal with the complexity of multiple possible ways to tackle problems and the selection of the most appropriate tools according to the business environment. The selection of roads to solve problems requires more skills in deciding what is a good model to use or to monitor or to calibrate them than the creation of the model itself. This chapter introduces the risk modeling and analytics processes, EDA exploratory data analysis as a way to understand more the problem, and to find meaning of results of the modeling process, inference, and indication of a risk analytics map illustrated with a combination of marketing and credit risk or better to say the insurance to credit transactions.

2.1   RISK MANAGEMENT AND MODELING PROCESSES

In Chapter 1, risk, risk management, and ERM concepts were generally described. In this and the following chapters, the emphasis on the quantitative aspects of risk and its management. At the end of the chapter, an example is presented to illustrate aspects of the described process. Risk is in this book is "the uncertainty about the world and uncertainty expressed by probabilities related to the observable quantities (Performance Measures)" (Aven, 2003). Risk analytics is oriented to the study of the variance of the expected results conditioned to previous knowledge. Risk management (RM) should not be confused with risk measurement. The reason is that (Cumming and Hirtle, 2001) risk measurement "entails the quantification of risk exposures" and risk management comprises the identification of risks in organizations, the assessment, measurement, and quantifications, looking for means to control and to convert risk process into means for strategy and sustainable advantages to compete.

One of the processes in risk management is the risk modeling process which is a mathematical and conceptual process that is a key component of risk analytics and risk measurement in particular. A risk modeling process plays a crucial role in the risk analytics road map design. A road map requires understanding of business areas and their pain points, data to use, precision, algorithms, embedding, and speed. Thus, risk modeling is part of the risk measurement process providing support to the role of RM in the strategic management development (Meulbroek, 2002; Sharman, 2002; Liebenberg and Hoyt, 2003; Banham, 2004). Risk modeling keeps the importance of RM in having the capacity of creating value from an integral view of risk (Brown, 2001; Froot et al., 1994; Banham, 2004) in order to develop a competitive advantage (Galloway and Funston, 2000).

However, risk modeling cannot be the only way to create value through risk management. An adaptive competitive advantage of the organization can be limited because of potential losses. Modeling losses is the backbone of risk analytics, because loss is what it is required to minimize in the practice of risk management and in the development of models (loss as the difference between actual – real values and model outcomes). For example, in risk analytics, it is important to go through causes of loss analysis. The financial losses according to Simmons (1999) have causes such as expansion, cultural pressures, reduced controls, communication of business values, learning systems, and concentration on information. These causes are influenced by an increment of the business complexity, transaction creation, lack of control, information management, and the use of cost as the only important factor to manage. Business complexity and the cost of knowledge show the need for providing more meaning to the information and better knowledge management (Sutcliffe and Weber, 2003) in order to build actionable answers to risk threats. Risk modeling knowledge can provide meaning to information, create knowledge, and support actions but it needs to find means for a better use of outcomes and their understanding.

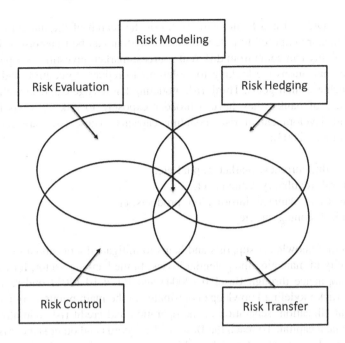

FIGURE 2.1 Risk modeling is a common process in risk management processes.

Given the business environment pressures around potential losses, organizations have transformed a reactive RM into a strategic discipline, which adds value through the learning, risk analytics (risk modeling development), and solutions as part of the day-to-day business (Meulbroek, 2002; Sharman, 2002; Liebenberg and Hoyt, 2003; Banham, 2004). However, the exposure to more risks and the losses in previous years introduced doubts about the RM practice (Degagne et al., 2004). These doubts are related to the influence of the work coordination and organization capacity to transfer and use risk knowledge, in particular risk modeling knowledge. Thus, in fact, the RM concept has evolved to enterprise risk management for gaining understanding of the holistic view of risk in the organization in "a systematic and integrated approach to the management of the total risks that a company faces" (Dickinson, 2001).

Figure 2.1 shows the risk management processes (see Chapter 1 for details) indicating that all processes create models to investigate the phenomena. There is a possibility of using similar knowledge, techniques, and tools to solve various risk problems. Risk modeling knowledge process is composed of the following seven pieces:

1. Answering the questions related to the strategy and strategic planning in an organization.
2. Identifying the enablers to transfer risk knowledge from tacit to explicit knowledge and vice versa.
3. Understanding of flows of information to produce knowledge.
4. Understanding risk knowledge organization.
5. Searching for data analytics/knowledge management technologies and techniques.
6. Designing the RAS (risk analytics system) to support risk modeling.
7. Connecting organizational performance metrics and risk modeling process.

The review of some of these pieces of risk modeling indicates that first, risk modeling knowledge can provide meaning to information "Risk Management is frequently not a problem of a lack of information, but rather a lack of knowledge with which to interpret its meaning" (Marshal and Prusak, 1996). Second, risk modeling knowledge is based on the measure of variability. RM is important because (Oldfield and Santomero, 1997) of the search of the maximization of the expected profits, which are exposed to potential variability that can be transformed into losses. The causes of the variability can come from different sources: market, investments, operation, strategy, and so on. The organizations are looking for solutions to reduce, to control, and to mitigate the risks in order to achieve their goals. Third, risk modeling knowledge can deal with different kinds of risk. In the case of banks, they have a broader exposure to risk demands requiring better understanding and development of risk modeling capacity. These risks are classified as (Van Greuning and Brajovic, 2003):

- Financial: credit, currency, market, capital etc.
- Business: legal, regulatory, country, etc.
- Operational: fraud, damage, information, products, etc.
- Event: political, contagion, etc.

Fourth, risk modeling knowledge supports and helps to mitigate doubts about the integral view of risk and the capacity of managing the potential losses. In the banking sector, for example, there is regulation for compliance through Basel II (2004) and Basel III (2011 and reviewed versions) Capital Accords. Risk modeling knowledge contributes to the main points or pillars considered in the accord: capital allocation, separation of the operation and credit risk, and alignment of regulatory and economical capital. To reach the Basel II, III accords and other standards, risk modeling knowledge transfer plays an important role and in particular thinking in banks as information and knowledge-based businesses (Fourie and Shilawa, 2004) where once a new risk is identified it implies that new knowledge is required (Shaw, 2005). Knowledge in general is coming from the use of risk modeling. The steps of risk modeling knowledge transfer and use are connected by activities described as follows.

A first activity is to get answers to questions: What resources does the organization need? What does the organization want? What does the organization measure? What is the impact? What has been the experience? What are the errors? Where is the failure is based on lack of knowledge management? This start of the risk modeling process is based on the needs of the stakeholders, their value definition, and the strategy planning process. The risk modeling process is in agreement with the "design approach to planning" introduced by Ackoff (1981) following his five proposed phases: formulating the systems of problems, identifying ideals, objectives and goals, means planning, resource planning, and design of implementation and control. In summary, the risk modeling process starts with the recognition of the strategic context and contribution that it will make to the strategic process.

A second activity refers to the creation of enablers of risk analytics knowledge transfer studying traps, errors, and constraints of the process of using models to get answers. Transferring risk modeling knowledge in both directions, tacit to explicit and vice versa, starts with the identification of traps in the decision-making process (Hammond et al., 2006) that affect a modeling process. The risk modeling process needs knowledge transfer understanding of risk knowledge to tune up people's efforts and to reduce wrong application and interpretation of concepts and relationships among risks and results of risk control/mitigation. These traps are (Hammond et al., 2006):

- "The mind gives disproportionate weight to the first information it receives"
- "Decision makers display, for example, a strong bias toward alternatives that perpetuate the status quo"
- "... is to make choices in a way that justifies past choices ..."
- "The bias leads us to seek out information that supports our existing instinct or point of view while avoiding information that contradicts it"
- "The way a problem is framed can profoundly influence the choices you make"
- "While managers continually make such estimates and forecasts, they rarely get clear feedback about their accuracy"

It is necessary to clarify whether the models will be used for decision automation or for getting insights to problem solving only. For example, the automation of quantitative solutions in a trading operation can produce issues in a market if everyone is using the same strategy. As Avery (2007) commented: "The report suggests that many of the quantitative portfolio construction techniques are based on the same historical data, such as value premium, size premium, earnings surprise, etc., and that there is a widespread use of standardized factor risk models that would explain why quant funds act in unison." Additionally, the risk modeling process can be affected by a lack of the process of transferring knowledge producing risky exposures. Some examples of the financial practice shows the influence of lack of risk knowledge transfer in creation of losses as mentioned above (Simmonds, 1999):

- Expansion: Growth affected the operations at American Express. Expansion ran faster than growth of capacity. The knowledge support was minimal (Simons, 1999).
- Culture: The Banker Trust expansion reduced the quality of the product presentation to the clients. The reason was: cultural pressures. There was a lack of information flow and the products were not well understood. The culture of avoiding bad news reduced the possibility of finding solutions to errors (Simons, 1999).
- Controls: Barings Bank's failure is related to the creation of early warning systems and the relationship to a work environment of rewards and recognition. A short-term performance view and internal competition contributed to the bad results (Simons, 1999).
- Lack of understanding: What is happening, the complexity increment, transaction creation, lack of control, information management, and cost as the only important factor to manage, reducing the capability to react in difficult and opportunity times. This complexity and the cost of knowledge show the need of managing the understanding and use of information rather than information itself (Sutcliffe and Weber, 2003).
- Lack of communication of business values in an understandable way that people can embrace. Possibly the identification of off-limits actions was not clear (Simons, 1999).
- Reduced stimulation of a learning system in order to review processes and to discuss the results and adequate diagnostic control systems (Simons, 1999).

Moreover, to take into consideration that there are additional factors supplementing the previous list; new, different workers' mentality open to technology and with different communication means, in some cases a silo culture, are living at the same time with a larger desire of understanding and searching for solution of doubts; new problems with higher complexity and demanding transformation of organization to solve problems that require enterprise-wide answers with the appropriate technological support.

The third activity of the process relates to the understanding of flows of information to produce risk knowledge and how to use these flows in risk modeling. This means analyzing experiences of risk knowledge management processes, methods and technologies used in risk management problems resolution in order to develop risk knowledge management capacity. The fourth activity consists of understanding the organization of risk modeling knowledge. Risk modeling is following the mathematical modeling process and it can be organized as a collaborative work and application of knowledge from different sources and disciplines. In the practice, there are techniques and tasks to develop in building risk analytics, such as

- Application of prediction and classification models (Burstein et al., 2002) such as financial service technology and knowledge development of the organization.
- Data mining practice as a means to support the customer focus, risk classification, and loss estimation (Hormozi and Gilles, 2004; Dzinkowski, 2002). The emphasis is put on cost of integrating risk analyses, control, and risk policy creation, deployment, and application (Cumming and Hirtle, 2001).

- The emphasis on acquiring knowledge and problem solving or on increasing the orientation to people and processes (Edwards et al., 2002).
- Search of a solution of sliced risk management data (McKibben, 2004) and the development of solutions to control risk exposure and data structures to share them with different areas in the problem-solving process.
- Orientation to new technology for data and information management, and for the modeling process (Shaw, 2005).

The assumptions behind the decisions in hedging or investment can be different according to time, regions, markets, and the lack of risk knowledge sharing can create issues in the RM processes and the controls may not be enough. The search of the truth outside of the isolation is something important in order to get better answers. Lack of risk knowledge access can create failures. Weak means for transferring risk knowledge can provide insufficient knowledge of the operation, poor assessments of the lessons learned, and poor understanding of the present and forecasts through risk knowledge.

This lack of risk knowledge can emerge because of interruption in the flow of information, which is a component of the modeling work that is complemented and used properly by the expert. As an example of influence of the expert in risk analytics, Goovaerts et al. (1984) wrote that only incomplete information that is available and it is the actuary (risk analyst) who decides the principles and distributions to use. Information use, with interpretation and context content, or better to say knowledge, is part of the risk modeling process as a common area of risk management processes for analysis of market risk, operational risk, strategic risk, credit risk, and actions of risk mitigation, risk transfer, and risk capacity evaluation.

2.2   RISK MODELING AND RISK KNOWLEDGE DEVELOPMENT

The previous section introduced risk modeling as a common component of the risk management processes. Risk analytics and in particular the risk modeling knowledge process is associated with interdisciplinary work and interdepartmental work controlling the whole process from problem definition to solutions evaluation. Davenport and Harris (2007) said that there is a need to align the organization to the age of the automated decision systems applying codified knowledge and providing decisions plus a knowledge-sharing environment. The human intervention is identified as a means to confirm decisions and to analyze particular cases, which means the use of knowledge for a risk solution. An organization needs to develop capacity to solve problems and to provide support for the modeling process under the premises of (Mladenic et al., 2003):

- Decisions come from humans and machines. Machines include decision systems and humans use some theory frameworks and decision support systems.
- People-centric or people's mind management world – Management is about knowledge and knowledge management is about people, processes, technology, and organizational structure.
- The old computing is about what computers can do and the new computing is about what people can do. New computing is about intelligence creation, reliability, comprehensibility, universality, and harmony with human needs.
- The power is not in having knowledge. The power is in sharing knowledge and using it to add value and to create a sustainable competitive advantage, similarly, going beyond of analyzing business processes and information systems.
- Technology is more than software or hardware is the answer to HOW to solve …? For example, the modeling process capacity is a competitive capacity (Davenport, 2006).

Development of risk modeling knowledge can follow the steps of the creation of mathematical–scientific groups such as the group Bourbaki and the Cambridge Club 1930. In both cases, the scientific work was based on common interest and the organization was formed by volunteer members working for a better development of the science. The group Bourbaki was composed originally of Henri Cartan, Claude Chevalley, Jean Coulomb, Jean Delsarte, Jean Dieudonné, Charles Ehresmann, René de Possel, Szolem Mandelbrojt, and André Weil. The group was created in 1935 with the purpose of writing a comprehensive text of mathematics based on set theory and axiomatic foundation. There were meetings to review the content, to identify the production logic, and to decide the structures and mathematical development. The main point was to create forums for discussion and ideas development based on formalism and axioms as Hilbert proposed.

Another means of knowledge collaboration was the one described by Foster (1985), who wrote about what he called the Cambridge Club 1930, "These four men did not comprise a school since they did not appear to have a common objective, but they knew each other and influenced each other and so might be called a club." Foster referred to Sir Arthur Eddington, Sir James Jeans, Bertrand Russell, and A.N. Whitehead all of whom were working at Cambridge at the end of 1930. The difference with the Bourbaki group was the regularity of meetings and the specific objective. In both cases, the knowledge transfer was fundamental to contributing to the mathematics formalization and to the new mathematical physics that was emerging with the relativity, quantum theory, and the uncertainty principle.

Risk analytics takes knowledge from several areas of mathematics, computer science, finance, etc. There are some examples of theories coming from general stochastic processes analysis, compound Poisson process, and Brownian motion (see details in Karlin and Taylor, 1998), or from other observations, abstraction, and reference theories, such as fractal geometry and symmetry analysis of the nature, which represent knowledge transfer from other disciplines to risk management. The Brownian motion theory coming from biology and physics is basic for financial mathematics or as the application of the general stochastic process martingales and compound Poisson processes are to the financial models and loss distribution modeling. The symmetry study through group theory is an example of starting from the observation of geometric figures to apply concepts to many different mathematical branches and practical problem solutions in many disciplines.

Risk modeling knowledge follows steps in the building models process that facilitate the identification of tasks and subprocesses that are based on knowledge and can be oriented and used in different problems. The identification of the subprocesses is based on the work of Carnap (1966), Raiffa (1968), and Leonard (1998). Carnap introduced the idea of a law in science as statements expressing regularities in the world. He identified that not all the laws are universal but, as he called them, statistical laws.

The risk modeling process belongs to the search of statistical laws and, as Carnap said, the process starts with direct observations of facts that in risk management are called claims, losses, and exposures. Additionally, these laws are used to "explain facts already known, and they are used to predict facts not yet known." A modeling creation subprocess includes the search of understanding, interpretation, and possible application to a variety of problems of the risk models. Raiffa (1968) introduced the decision analysis, and he identified the value of the outcome of the models based on the relevance in a real-world problem. He said, "In these lectures I have indicated how a decision maker's preferences for consequences, attitudes towards risk, and judgments about uncertain events can be scaled in terms of subjective utilities and probabilities and how these can be incorporated into formal analysis. By these means it may be possible in some circumstances to reduce the judgmental gap and to bring the output of the model closer to the demands of the real-world problem; the model will then have more a chance to pass the test of relevance."

Moreover, Leonard's model (1998), called "knowledge creating and diffusing activities," considers a cycle where core capabilities for shared problem solving in the present are connected to implementing and integrating, experimenting and prototyping and importing and absorbing knowledge. The core capabilities have to reduce the core rigidity that is coming from skills and knowledge, managerial systems, physical systems, and values. Subprocesses in risk modeling processes are looking for a better knowledge development in order to use knowledge to tackle different problems.

Through the comparison of what is performed in risk modeling, it is possible to identify communalities with the risk analytics process in general (Table 2.1). The examples are typical in

TABLE 2.1

First Group of Subprocesses Describing the Modeling Process of Problem Definition and Data for Three Different Problems

Risk Analytics and the Risk Modeling process: three examples			
Process	Risk Classification	Loss Distribution Compound Poisson Process	Markov Process for Credit Analysis
Problem Definition			
Problem definition: understanding the phenomenon	Meaning of customer classification, attributes available, timing, groups, etc.	Concept of loss, claim process, cost associated, income associated, reinsurance, recoveries	Classification procedure, identification of units and amounts of credit, differences, trends, sectors, markets
Search for general models/theoretical support/mathematics	New theory for parameter estimation, testing new models, decision trees, regression trees, neural networks ... GLM	New approaches for numerical and analytical solutions of the stochastic processes	New approach for transition. Time series review, comparison, GLM, Markov chains discrete, continue, absorbent, etc.
Moving from Data to Modeling			
Reducing the core rigidity: People coordination/project development	Expert identification, blueprint, maps, plans. blocks & steps definition, capacity, and roles identification	Expert identification, blueprint, maps, plans. Blocks & Steps definition, capacity, and roles identification	Expert identification, blueprint, maps, plans. Blocks & Steps definition, capacity, and roles identification
Data gathering	Data experience, profile variables, default definition, claims data, exposure set definition, clustering for outliers	Claims data, recoveries, reinsurance, investment, clustering outliers identification	Classification of loans, default definition, identification of age groups. Clustering outliers identification
Data store	Data mart creation/access, record selection, variables-fields selection	Data mart creation/access, record selection, variables-fields selection	Data mart creation/access, record selection, variables-fields selection
Data selection/ preparation	Learning set, out of time, out of sample	Different periods of time, simulation points, empirical distribution, descriptive statistics	Data from different groups in different period of time, comparison of results
Data for control	Selection of the samples, out of time and out of sample	Different periods of time, simulation points, filters	Using automated process, discretization, programming the portfolio
Programming/ specialized software	Testing assumptions, normality ..., modeling, categorization, regression process, models identification, models preparation	Histograms, ways to estimate parameters, distributions simple and mixed. Tail analysis	Matrix definitions, develop test of absorbing states, properties of Markov matrices. Discretization process

risk analytics: use of the compound Poisson for loss distribution modeling, risk classification modeling, and a modeling Markov process for credit risk evaluation and credit behavior prediction. From the review of these three examples, it is possible to identify four main components in a risk modeling process: data and information management, mathematical work, experimenting and prototyping, and communicating. These four components of the modeling process are going from data gathering up to application of the theoretical concepts to different kinds of problems.

Table 2.1 shows subprocesses from problem definition up to data manipulation. The process comparison presents the way to pass from discovering relationships and modeling initiation up to getting the solution applicable to other kinds of problems. This means application of the risk knowledge gained to get new solutions, possibly with different data and variable relationships. Table 2.2 indicates the similarities in modeling for three different analyses.

Generalization of a risk model can depend on the assumptions, theory, time, and data available. For example, time is a factor affecting whether the model is discrete or continuous on time. This has a big impact in risk management modeling. In all these steps, risk knowledge is a component to organize and to promote in order to achieve answers and to identify how to improve assumptions and methods.

In risk modeling development, a required capacity for building a RAS is how people learn to work independently and how to work simultaneously with others and with machines, coordinating and looking at the forest and not just the trees. The challenge is that organizations need to coordinate resources under the understanding that they have knowledge workers and problem solvers and not workers and jobs. Furthermore, the organizations have problems to solve and not just tasks to do, which implies that organizations have managers and analytics professionals living together and this requires organization of risk modeling knowledge and ability to use common knowledge in mathematical modeling.

A risk analytics system (RAS) design is crucial to support the risk modeling process (see Chapter 1 and 8 for RAS basic principles) and to integrate the risk knowledge management processes. Davenport et al. (2005) presented that analytics is a strategic capacity that the organization can have and develop for competing. Risk analytics work requires information systems support. However, risk management information is based on a context; it requires interpretation, and this means to design and to develop a RAS without including the use of knowledge of the context could be dangerous. Risk management does not have just a problem with information; it has problems with interpretation and communication of meaning.

Moreover, the RAS design needs the incorporation of the general knowledge management (KM) processes applied to risk management looking for answering how to support the use of common knowledge of risk management processes in mathematical modeling and its use. The risk modeling process needs to mobilize information flows to produce risk knowledge to consolidate, integrate, and organize the risk knowledge across organization and risk-related problems to solve. This can happen in the following way: risk knowledge creation where risk knowledge is represented by risk assessment; risk knowledge storage and retrieval through the data support for external and internal users; risk knowledge transfer using the experience of many people in known cases; and risk knowledge application to discover business processes opportunities. These KM processes in a risk modeling process are described in detail as follows.

2.2.1 Risk Knowledge Creation

This means to identify assumptions, conceptualization process, identification and selection of techniques to use, selection of processes, development collaboration, methods of solution, prototyping models, and testing. Risk knowledge is in developing new models, replacing existing models, promoting new solutions, participating in problem solving, organizing product development, and risk evaluation for innovation. From the technology side, risk knowledge is created for providing access to models and results, for managing technological support as intranet, developing

TABLE 2.2

Second Group of Modeling Subprocesses from Modeling Tests up to the Search of New Model Applications

Process/Subprocess	Risk Classification	Loss Distribution Compound Poisson Process	Markov Process for Credit Analysis
		Prototyping	
Prototyping: Model/program Testing definition of structure and relationships/model structure selection	Input data to different models	Input data to different models	Input data to different models, identification transition matrices multiple steps, absorption, properties of the matrix type
Parameters estimation and solutions of relationships-equations	Testing different methods	Testing different methods	Testing different methods
Model performance evaluation	ROC, classification tests, Kolmogorov-Smirnov	Fit tests, Kolmogorov-Smirnov, chi-square, normality …	Testing assumptions Markov property, normality …
Model improvements	Identification of different set of variables, parsimonious metrics, testing more variables	Identification of special cases	Time forecast, continue and discrete
Reporting	Problem solved, scope, model specifications, results, interpretation, new challenges and priorities	Problem solved, scope, model specifications, results, interpretation, new challenges and priorities	Problem solved, scope, model specifications, results, interpretation, new challenges and priorities
		Reducing the judgment gap	
Reducing the judgement gap: Results interpretation	Meaning of classification	Meaning of loss distribution and applications	Identification of states and probability movements
Communication	Presentations to different groups, taking feedback	Presentations to different groups, taking feedback, developing new options	Presentations to different groups, taking feedback, developing new options
		Search of the statistical law	
Search for a statistical law: New generalizations/weak assumptions	Look for panel data, time series indicators	Mixed distribution and special groups for managing claim. Relationships with marketing, pricing	Description with different stochastic processes modifying some assumptions
New applications/input new models	Developing variance metrics, identification new significant variables, benchmarking, development of segmented models (economical sectors, by different clusters)	Loss given default, behavioral models, preventive dashboards, risk indicators management	New structure of portfolio classification, market segmentation

Many steps have common knowledge that need to be aligned and to produce capacity for risk modeling. For instance: describing groups (groups can be defined as the sets of customers according to the due date, delinquency level) clustering, selecting variables from linear approach, classification process profile of payment quality. There is a basis on the loss distribution for other applications such as calculating maximum loss probability. The groups of debt quality can be organized in a different way, producing a sequence of the credit process from selection to control of credit portfolio.

external solutions/answers methodology for problem solving, increasing the sophistication of solutions, managing data/quality, analyzing multi-risk, and selecting solutions development and accessibility.

2.2.2 Risk Knowledge Storage/Retrieval

There are many different components in risk modeling to store and retrieve, such as documents, raw data, data created, taxonomy, metadata, and structured and unstructured data. The action of storing and retrieving implies cleaning data, developing and implementing documentation process, structuring information, and codifying human knowledge with comments of tacit knowledge from individual and groups. There are measures/metrics to develop for identifying the quality data repository, data volume, codified documents/indexed/structured processes to update, metadata structure, comfort with data repositories, documentation incentives, technology used for repositories, process to populate data, document standards and process to access, and use of data repositories.

2.2.3 Risk Knowledge Transfer

Risk modeling knowledge can be transferred through presentations, portals, meetings, discussions, collaboration activities, content management design, distribution, testing reporting, and so on. There are differences to consider when there is a transferring knowledge process between individuals, individuals to groups, between groups, across groups, and groups to organization. All of these differences require actions among the participants to improve the communication processes and willingness to share by fostering the existence and richness of transmission channels, such as unscheduled meetings, informal seminars, coffee breaks, quality of knowledge transfer channels, taxonomies, metadata, forums, bulletins, interdisciplinary solutions search, feedback sessions, discussing forums, and so on.

2.2.4 Risk Knowledge Application and Learning

Application of risk modeling knowledge is represented by decisions, business processes, and models in other organization areas such as impact analysis, evaluation, new developments, and new solutions of strategic and tactical decision. Application is in the process of organizational performance evaluation, testing results, defining and implementing directives, organizational routines, process and technology updating, accessibility, work flow automation, training and experience support, business understanding, results interpretation, speed of the application, and risk cases access.

Companies are competing to optimize their performance on analytical capabilities, which represents getting access to quantitative expertise, capable technology environment, and appropriate data. This analytics capability of risk modeling requires a RAS to support what Pfeffer and Sutton (2006) called the craft of managers that needs to be learned by practice and experience and the use of evidence as a means to constantly update assumptions, knowledge, and skills.

In summary, a RAS has to go further in managing data and information; it goes to support above risk knowledge management processes. As Apte et al. (2002) said, the problem is not just to describe what the organization needs or what its request is. it is to predict, to optimize, and to classify. This means knowledge production, improvement of the attributes, and overcoming the issues of the RAS design. For example, in actuarial science, there is a process of building statistical models describing the claims behavior, creating different policies, and adjusting models according to contract clauses of the products and their potential claim development. Zack (1990) refers in general terms to a RAS as expert systems have contributed to providing competitive capabilities to the organizations, but the bases are in the capacity of acquiring risk management knowledge as it is used in some reinsurers.

As it was introduced in Section 1.4, ERM is above the vision of risk management for individual risks. The holistic view requires support in several dimensions of the risk analytics process. There are three attributes of a holistic view of risk management challenging processes and technology that are the integral, comprehensive, and strategic view (Abrams et al., 2007) of the support system to build. This holistic view complexity is observed when the modeling process is looking for aggregation analysis in light of each organizational section that can have different performance, problems, and resources from the whole organization. Thus, a RAS required is a dynamic bridge between risk knowledge management processes and ERM processes passing through people, business processes, and technology. A RAS design is complete when the performance evaluation subsystem is designed. This step means getting answers to questions such as how to measure, to interpret, and to discover directions of the organization performance connecting risk metrics with risk modeling. There is a search, in this step, for cause-effect indicators related to the risk modeling process and other risk management processes. One of the points of the Basel II, III compliance is to build RAPM (risk adjusted performance management), the adaptation of the principles is worth to have in industries that are not only financial institutions. RAPM comprises risk model development and the construction of risk models requires the understanding of indicators used for enterprise performance evaluation.

The RAS analysis and design of measurement capacity is a core subprocess and it is linked to the search of variables relationships to solve a problem. Risk analytics performance measures are using the relationship between the four types of organizational capital (Fairchild, 2002): intellectual, human, social, and structural. The balanced scorecard (BSC) (Kaplan and Norton, 1999) contributes to using strategy maps to provide a meaning to the intangibles and their influence in the risk modeling process. The inclusion of risk factors and intellectual capital concepts in the balanced scorecard can be a step ahead in the performance evaluation processes in risk analytics. However, more than the metrics for organization performance evaluation, the point is in the process to build the metrics relevant when risk is involved (Wu, 2005). Besides, the KM metrics (Rao, 2005) can be connected to the BSC in different fronts and settings.

The BSC can lead the creation, formation of the strategy of intellectual capital, and its consolidation (Wu, 2005). The integration of the internal perspective, learning and growth and the strategic process of the intellectual capital are a direct consequence of the BSC use. Measures of intellectual capital (Fairchild, 2002) use metrics for financial processes, business processes, learning, client, and human development combining components of intangible assets, growth, renovation efficiency, and stability. Fairchild (2002) explain that KM and BSC can be connected by management of resources with a focus on a combination of resources of intellectual capital with the processes of the organization.

In summary, risk analytics metrics can be included in the BSC and some approaches are developed relating risk factors, intellectual capital, and BSC but not the whole evaluation process of the organization performance under risk. Barquin (2001) identified that managing and leveraging knowledge is crucial for improving organization performance; however, risk was not included as a factor to be evaluated. As a complement, Shaw (2005) presented the risk performance adjusted measures and the process to calculate them. These processes are part of the RAS in the sense of using data, creating models, and interpreting the results and, as Fairchild (2002) said, related to intellectual capital management. However, the integration of the risk measures to the BSC is not evident. There are two ways to develop risk-based performance measures. One is working directly from the definition of the indicators and the inclusion of the risk components in tangible and intangible assets. Another is to build special indicators-metrics (Albretch, 1998) as RAROC (risk adjusted return on capital) and RORAC (return on risk adjusted capital) for example, in order to relate return, expected losses, and exposure (and metrics is in Chapters 3 and 4). In any case, the RAS design requires data architecture and software to support combinations of cause-effect development where the risk modeling processes are involved.

2.3 GENERAL ANALYTICS PROCESS FOR RISK MANAGEMENT

As it was indicated in Section 1.3, risk analytics is fundamental in risk management. Now in general, the analytics process is the basis for developing the solutions in risk analytics. An analytics process (Rodriguez, 2017) compiles the steps and the emphasis on data, data mining, and data management as components associated with the sequence of steps to evolve from data to knowledge. The analytics process in a simplified approach and supplementing the previous section comprises:

- Problem definition, delimitation, and definition of scope through the needs of the business. At this level, it is important to review some possible problem categories of description, visualization, forecasting, classification, optimization, and simulation. This will be part of the connection with the forward steps. It is common that from the beginning the possible models to solve have not been considered and later when data has been gathered and organized some data issues emerge and at the same time opportunities to use more models to tackle the problem. This stage has the following aspects to work on, answering the questions: What is a company trying to accomplish? How is the corporate performance measured? What are the needs of data to support the measurement system? What are the analytics steps and how the analytics projects can support the planning and control of strategy design and implementation?
- Developing understanding and meaning. Review of the context and knowledge domain. This refers to the work of creating meaning that is not only based on the results interpretation side, but also on the initiation of the data selected and the model construction.
- Analytics knowledge sharing and transfer. Analytics work is in most of the cases multidisciplinary and multi-areas of organizations. The analytics process cannot finish when the results are obtained. The results need to create actions. The results need to be embedded in the organization through the adoption of them in business processes. Frame the work of the analytics process under the view of creating an analytics knowledge management system. In principle we should start, if the time allows it, the same as in the systems analysis and design. Prototyping and showing partial/functional results.
- Application, actions and business processes under a permanent plan and act. The analytics process requires a strong and permanent back-and-forth flow of teaching and learning. Contextualization of the results is crucial. The workflow improvement and innovation are part of the objectives in analytics knowledge creation.

The analytics process is supported by the practice of data mining, statistical learning, machine learning, and data analytics techniques in general. A data mining process is to discover significant correlations, patterns, tendencies, by means of the detailed study of great amounts of data stored in repositories, using technologies of recognition of patterns also like mathematical, statistical, and machine learning techniques (see Chapter 7 for more details). There are methodologies to work in data mining, mainly CRISP and SEMMA. The CRISP methodology (Chapman et al., 2000) or cross-industry standard process for data mining starts with the understanding of the business as follows:

- Identification of objectives of the business and criteria of success.
- Evaluation of the present situation.
- To determine goals of mining of data and criteria of success.
- To produce a project plan.
- Develop a conceptual model to describe the ideal solution and the blocks that are required for getting that solution. Identify the blueprint to build the solution by blocks.
- Start from the possible solutions of the problem to solve. That is, assuming a potential solution and identifying the relationships to the organization's strategic and tactical

metrics. Review the measurement process (in case that the metrics are not well defined), identify the metrics that are a priority, and go backward to identify the data that is required for the intermediate steps.
- Build the first model starting with EDA (exploratory data analysis) and visualization.
- Review what is needed in order to have a good model and issues with data and with models.

To develop the models, the fundamental thing is conversion of regular and big data into smart data. The process of this conversion starts with appropriate data management that can use data repositories (see Chapter 6 for describing some technology to use) as it is a data warehouse where ETL (extract, transfer, and load are supplied) is performed and data is usable for modeling. The process of creation of the data warehouse requires considering that the data can be organized in sets, transformed, studied, evaluated, explored, and that has a great implicit value for being useful in the risk analytics process. Fundamentally, the greater advantage of the organized data affluent is that when the tools of data mining are required to be applied, this could be easier to make. Specific repositories of data according to areas or subjects of specialized knowledge are data marts. They can be done with multiple databases that can be accessed by users and can be in several platforms.

The data warehouses have an administrative part that provides the managerial support of the data to produce the expected results. A project of data warehouse will be successful if there is confidence in the source of the data; there exist a clear definition of structure and purpose of problems to solve, exists integration of multiple sources in an only atmosphere, and the levels of risk in each type of risk and the way that they are correlated.

To construct an integrated and centralized data repository of data requires the complete support of top management in the organization, logical model of data, the definition of the specifications, deliverable objectives, and plans of maintenance of the projects. Some problems identified in a process of data warehouse design and implementation are:

- Security of the data sources
- Definition of the required data
- Access of the data and time
- Availability of the historical data
- Possibilities of maintenance
- Possibility of using them throughout the company as suitable information
- Modification of the project management and the managerial levels of the company

For data organization it is required the concept of metadata, that is not another thing that the form to describe the data in a data repository; this is, to observe from above the data, its dimensions, characteristics. Metadata is the data of the data. The metadata requires identification of structure, definition of the fields from the applications, and the rules of transformation from the source. In risk analytics, the process to manage, to clean, and to create usable data is a high consumption consumes a lot of time and resources of the analytics process in general. In that regard everything that is possible to do in advance for populating the data with good data will reduce issues in the analytics steps.

The following (Table 2.3) are aspects that in risk analytics data management will provide a smoother risk analytics use.

Once data is usable, the risk analytics process starts with an exploratory data analysis. The crucial part of this process is to describe data, understand a problem and questions to investigate for answers, connect questions and variables to use in the analytics process, understand the contexts, develop hypotheses, and explain possible relationships to be tested in a formal way. The next section provides basics of an EDA process.

TABLE 2.3

Data Steps for Risk Analytics

Data preparation:
- Data auditing
- Data collection, extraction, and combination from multiple sources/repositories/tables
- Data cleaning: inconsistencies in values, lost data, no correct values, extreme values, outliers
- Data organization:
  - Relational databases/data repositories
  - Raw data quality evaluation
  - Reading data files
  - Definition of population methods

- Data sources and data selection:
  Sampling:
  - Random sample
  - Systematic it uses structure module k for random search
  - Stratified
  - Sampling by segments
  - Sampling with relation to the time
  - Census
  - Big data
  - Stream data

- Data access:
  - Policies of the company
  - Legal barriers
  - Format of the data
  - Limitation of hardware

- Data manipulation:
  - Resources of computers
  - Historical events
  - Precision
  - Representation of the population
  - Number of fields
  - Size of files
  - Training and validation of data sets

New data creation as input for the additional steps in the risk analytics process. The output of models, risk indicators, default rates, key performance indicators, key risk indicators, etc. are input of the chain of step of the risk analytics process.

2.4 EXPLORATORY DATA ANALYSIS (EDA)

In this section, there is a presentation of the techniques to evaluate the quality of data, to create basic metrics and to discover the most relevant variables relationships in a risk analytics process. Exploratory data analysis utilizes different methods to gain a better understanding of a data sets, their structure, relevant variables within the sets, possible relationships among variables, and outliers within each variable. EDA is based mainly on graphical and statistical descriptive techniques. Plotting the data in different ways is one part of visual analytics techniques to reveal the nature of the data. Exploratory analysis is always needed prior to selecting variables or proceeding with the model selection or the modeling itself. For example, creating descriptive metrics, reviewing histograms, creating matrices of scatterplots to understand pairwise relationships among variables, plotting the data (observing data dynamic, changes, proportions, groups, etc.), checking for normality or distribution of probability, linearity, outliers, univariate analysis, etc., is a common practice.

As part of the EDA process, it is required to develop steps and practice in multiple tasks such as:

- Assumption's review. Before the modeling process is started, certain assumptions need to be made on degree of data completeness and integrity, exploratory analysis of data completion, appropriate definition of classes ("bad") of the events, attributes, and the number of observations in the experiment as finite, possible data bias as it is the case in credit risk where sample points in an analytics process could have only the data of the samples that can have a property using data of the customers data that were already part of the exposure and not from accepted and not accepted or those who had access to credit and those who do not.

- Incomplete Data: A common problem encountered when modeling any event is that of missing data. In this circumstance, deleting observations with missing data is not recommended due to the fact that in many instances missing data reflects a pattern in the information that cannot be ignored. Given that incomplete observations yield biased estimators, it is important that they are handled before commencing the data modeling. One possible solution is to use a data imputation method, some of which are presented in the following subsections. These techniques would need to be tried on the data and their validity tested given that certain imputation methods can reduce the inherent variability of data and even distort data distribution.

Another solution is to transform the variables into categorical ones, where missing information would be considered a special category. This is derived from the fact that missing values can be interpreted and can provide clues related to the event of interest. This technique is commonly applied in the credit scoring industry and its use in the modeling process described in this document is recommended as an alternative to imputation.

Data Imputation: There are many methods to deal with the missing data problem. Amongst these methods, the most common ones are mean substitution, multiple regression, last value carried forward and hot deck imputation.

Mean Substitution: This is a very common method where the mean of the total observations for a variable substitutes the missing value. Therefore, the variance of the variable and the correlation with other variables is reduced, thus missing information. Many times, an interpolation between two known values can be made or an extrapolation using the linear trend value.

Regressions: Multiple regression can be used to impute missing values from those observations with no missing values. Because many times this method can unreasonably reduce the noise in data, usually a random noise component is added to the estimates.

Last Value Carried Forward: When dealing with longitudinal data, many times it is possible to replace the missing value with the last know observation for that particular variable.

Hot Deck Imputation: The hot deck method replaces missing data by examining similar units with similar patterns and uses the values of the units known.

2.4.1 Illustration Example of EDA-Data Visualization

This is a strategic risk example applied to the society as a whole. It is considered strategic risk (government state and citizen level of satisfaction with what is developed in the country and where taxes are going to) the change in the perception of happiness in a society. In this example, it is not included the additional data for competitiveness but the illustration of the value of evaluating changes as a way to measure risk is initiated. The data set used is the World Happiness Report 2019 (https://worldhappiness.report/ed/2019). This data set has been selected to illustrate how risk analytics concepts can be used in multiple knowledge domains. In this data set, socio-economic factors are associated with a score that measures perception of outcomes of the society development and the citizens perception of good life. The score is associated with the wellness of living in countries. The negative variation of the score is a risk in the society and risk on implementation of policies. The exploratory data analysis (EDA) shows the aspects related to the data preparation, cleaning, and the relationships among the factors included in the analysis. The concept of risk here is the variation of factors and how they can explain variation of the score of happiness. The data is not perfect, and it is required to clean it. Some variables cannot be used in this example because there are multiple missing values for several countries. From the total of 1949 records of 166 countries with data since 2005, it has been only used the records that have data between 2010–2020 and the variables-factors are fully populated. This is in total data of 59 countries and 649 records were used.

The variables used are life ladder, Log GDP per capita, social support, healthy life expectancy at birth, freedom to make life choices, generosity, perceptions of corruption, positive affect, and negative affect. Table 2.4 shows the summary statistics of all variables and Figure 2.2 indicates at

TABLE 2.4

Basics Statistics of Happiness

Variable	Mean	sd	Se(mean)	IQR	cv	Skewness	Kurtosis	0%	25%	50%	75%	100%
Freedom.to.make.life.choices	0.818	0.096	0.012	0.120	0.117	-0.889	1.024	0.510	0.766	0.830	0.886	0.962
Generosity	-0.007	0.134	0.017	0.214	NA	0.370	-0.644	-0.241	-0.117	-0.015	0.097	0.295
Healthy.life.expectancy.at.birth	67.954	5.150	0.670	7.120	0.076	-0.875	0.150	54.300	65.380	68.900	72.500	75.000
Life.Ladder	5.963	0.974	0.127	1.280	0.163	-0.349	0.140	3.160	5.337	5.964	6.617	7.889
Log.GDP.per.capita	9.864	0.871	0.113	1.139	0.088	-0.758	-0.021	7.684	9.412	9.991	10.550	11.323
Negative.affect	0.294	0.068	0.009	0.088	0.232	0.274	-0.482	0.150	0.245	0.294	0.333	0.440
Perceptions.of.corruption	0.713	0.212	0.028	0.278	0.297	-1.127	0.271	0.164	0.583	0.797	0.861	0.961
Positive.affect	0.719	0.083	0.011	0.120	0.116	-1.176	2.860	0.384	0.665	0.734	0.786	0.849
Social.support	0.861	0.094	0.012	0.137	0.109	-0.924	-0.265	0.617	0.799	0.891	0.936	0.966

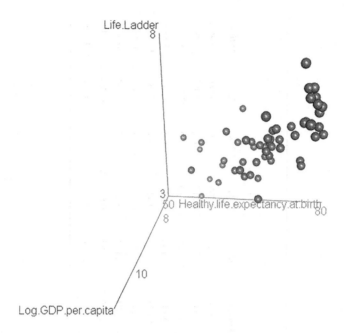

FIGURE 2.2   Scatterplot 3D representing three variables.

least two variables relationship to the life ladder that is used as a target variable. In the graphic, there is an indication of positive correlation among the variables, higher level of health life expectancy at birth and log GDP are pointed in the same direction to a higher life ladder.

The process of visualization requires the creation of means to represent more than three dimensions. Figure 2.2 can be three dimensions and some extra adjustment in data representation can add more dimension view.s For example, colors can represent another variable, size of the points, type of geometric figures used to represent variables triangles, circles, spheres, and so on. In general, in the grammar of graphics there is an understanding of it in the general expression and implementation in R ggplot2.

In ggplot2, the elements to create the graphics are the data source, scales, stats, geoms, coordinates, faceting, and themes. In general, the syntax for correlations and graphics is like this: first it is possible to define the variables to compare, the type of data representation such as regressions, density functions, etc. the same as histograms or not. Figure 2.3 is a representaion of multiple variables observed two by two.

```
scatterplotMatrix(~var1+var2+var3+var4, regLine=TRUE, smooth=FALSE,
diagonal=list(method="histogram"), data=yourdata)

cor(yourdata[,c("var1", "var2","var3", "var4")], use="complete")
```

In the ggplot, the use of variables for graphics can be like:

```
ggplot (data=yourdata, aes(y=var1, x=var2) + geom_point(aes(color=var3),size=3)+
geom_text(aes(label=var4, color=var5),size=3)+ geom_point(aes(color=var2, size=var6))+
coord_trans(y="yourscale"))
+geom_point(aes(color=var3,size=var4))+scale_y_continuous(name="NNNN",trans="log10") +
geom_point(alpha=0.9,aes(size=rvar3))+coord_trans(y="your
scale")+facet_wrap(~var4,nrow=1)+theme(legend.position="top")
```

Scatterplot matrices are powerful to start the identification of relationships and to explain pairwise how a variable can be related to another or how a variable can influence the variation of another. In the experience, the pairwise representation of data is good for stakeholders to understand what is

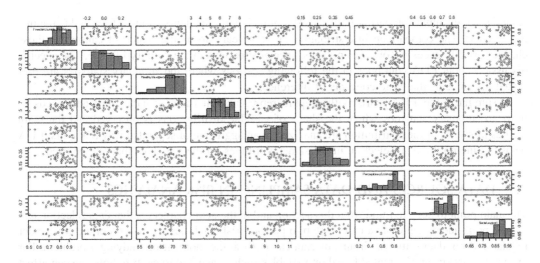

FIGURE 2.3 Scatterplot matrix representing visualization of relationships.

happening in the analyzed problem and showing the data. There is a risk of having people thinking that with identification the understanding of the relationship of variables is complete. That is the reason that description and exploration of data starts with data visualization and the move to modeling where data is possible to review in a multivariate way.

The representation of histograms per variable or per country in Figure 2.4 is appreciated because it is a way to use micro-graphics to easily show comparison of distributions in variables by

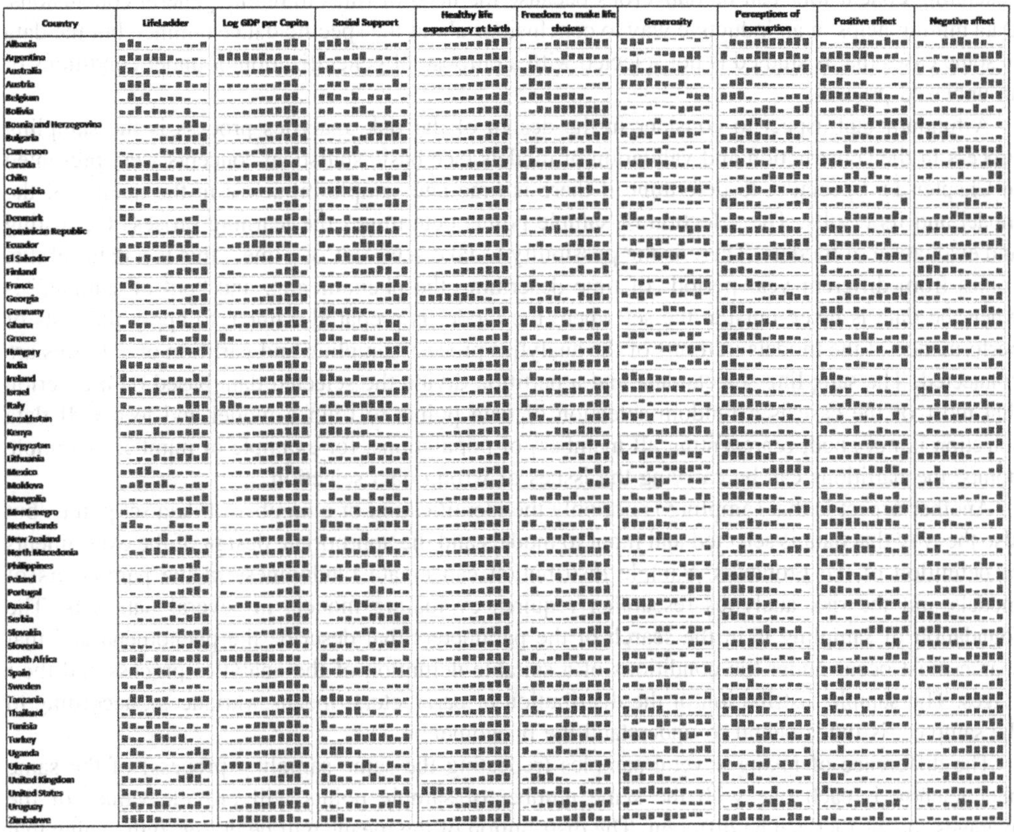

Country	LifeLadder	Log GDP per Capita	Social Support	Healthy life expectancy at birth	Freedom to make life choices	Generosity	Perceptions of corruption	Positive affect	Negative affect

FIGURE 2.4 Histogram per variable per country.

countries for example comparing Italy and Argentina in a life ladder or South Africa and Chile in a log of GDP. The comparison in distribution through years opens the search of causes for those changes or differences in countries policies, special situations in the country life, etc. The specific discussion about EDA continues in the following sections where the summary statistics are presented the same as the basic concepts of inference.

In summary, the EDA starts with graphic representation (data visualization) and needs to move to summary statistics where the shape of variable distributions is observed and the main metrics moments of the distribution are analyzed in an aggregate of separated way risk units. EDA helps to tune up the data selection in the same as it tunes up the variables that can be used.

2.5   DATA SOURCES AND DATA SAMPLING IN RISK ANALYTICS

The main point to keep in mind from this section and in the next chapters is that data selection and sample point identification is a crucial step to perform risk analytics in an appropriate way under regular and big data settings. Groups of data can exist at the moment of studying a problem. For example, a group can be created based on variables such as age and to analyze how age can affect risk in car insurance (important aspect in credibility adjustments of pricing see Chapter 7). Some groups can modify the unbiased analysis, for example taking data only with certain attributes in the data set creates potential bias. The complexity is coming when the groups' differentiation is with unknown definitions of the reasons for group separation or hidden factors that can affect the data quality. In big data analytics, the analytics process can be affected because analysts think that a high volume of data substitutes the good selection of the required data. That is not true. The lack of representativeness needs to be avoided. There are traps to avoid such as bias or reduced capacity to generalize results to the population. The inductive process of observing data points and then generating conclusions can be dangerous because the need of rules to define general conclusions. Data mining helps in an inductive way to conclusions about the specific data examined but the data in some cases that is studied is not selected with a purpose of generalization or under conditions of an unbiased process.

A fundamental aspect to consider in the design of the risk analytics process is the sampling process in the construction and validation of models (see basic statistical concepts were presented in Chapter 1). Specially, to determine if there is time and sample influence in the quality of the model and its results. The selection of sample points determines the learning process the testing and evaluation of models. There is the possibility to take sets "out of Time"; this is a data set that comes from different year periods of time describing the phenomenon, and "out of sample," is when the data is taken outside the set where the model is prepared-trained, to apply the tests of performance of the models in terms of the analytics process sampling and partition of data sets are connected. The sampling selects data and a partition divide the selected data based on a criterion that most of the case is a random selection of data points to train a model and test it. If data selection is not good, representing all members of populations, for example or number of sample points, the partitions can be carrying the issues of wrong data selection.

Another aspect is that sampling is not only the identification of a number of data set points, but also the way that data is selected and input to models and the appropriate design of the experiments or definition of the problems. Sample distribution can create randomness in the parameters of models and the risk analytics researcher requires evaluating models in several data sets. The foundation of sampling is in the search of the parameters that describe the phenomena and that search must occur under the conditions of a suitable definition of the analytics process and their stages. The sample distribution or the distribution of parameters (means, variances), according to the samples, is fundamental to understand the phenomenon.

The difference of taking several samples (repeating the same sampling process) of the same phenomenon is each one with the same number of sample points will provide values of the averages-means that can be different. The distribution of the means will be closer to the value that is the expected value of the population distribution with lower standard deviation when the number of sample points is higher. The distribution of the means is going to be a normal distribution. This is the result that a risk analyst uses very often; the central limit theorem says the higher the sample size the sampling distribution of the mean is closer to the normal distribution despite the distribution of the population and that distribution has a mean equal to the population mean. The central limit theorem supports parameter estimation. Remember that the theorem points that if $\overline{X}$ is the mean of a random sample of size n taken from a population with mean μ and finite variance $\sigma2$, then when n $\rightarrow \infty$ the distribution of $Z = \frac{\overline{X} - \mu}{\sigma / \sqrt{n}}$ is the standard normal distribution N(0, 1).

Sample selection is present in regular or big data. Sampling is for gathering data and for data that already exists, which the risk analyst is going to use in the solution of a problem and in the modeling creation process. In some cases, there is no sense to study big data coming from text, speech, graphics, etc. if the purpose is to obtain certain generalizable results when the data used is only related to certain groups with defined attributes. The error can be to generalize results to the whole population based on the knowledge of only few members of a population. A good example is when there is a study related to tweets, where certain topics or people can be the participants and possible results are valid for the profile of those participants, but not for the whole population as in many cases in politic campaigns people want others to believe the same and use a wrong sample selection.

In sampling, there are valuable terms to keep in mind (See Table 2.5).

The sampling process connects two important subprocesses in risk analytics: selection of data and estimation of parameter. On the one hand, the work with big data does not change the process of selecting the appropriate data for the risk analytics process. On the other hand, when the data is gathered and tested, the results of the modeling process require generalization-control of the risk of overfitting. The issues with samples can be dealt with performing statistical tests and sampling procedures.

The purpose of sampling is to estimate the values of metrics or parameters to use in a measurement process related to the population that is studied. From a population, several samples can be selected and parameters can take values according to the samples. The probability distributions require, after fitting a possible probability distribution, the estimation of the parameters based on the data used to obtain usable models. There are methods to evaluate the variation of results because of calculations using different samples estimators-statistics (random variables that represents the values that a parameter can take from different samples). These methods are in general resampling. It refers to the methods to evaluate the accuracy of the sample statistics for estimating the population parameters. The selection of the points uses subsets from the data points selected randomly with replacement (bootstrapping). Another approach is taking subsets of the data available that is called (jackknifing). Cross validation refers to the methods to evaluate the

---

TABLE 2.5
Terms Used in a Sampling Process

Element: measurement object	Population: collection of elements about as becomes inference
Sample units: collection of disjoint sets of elements in a population	A source of identified data/reference: list of sample units
Sampling error appears because of the use of subsets of the total population	Types of sampling or methods to select the sample points
The standard deviation of the sampling distribution of the mean is called the standard error of the mean $\frac{\sigma}{\sqrt{n}}$	P(estimation error < b) = 1 − a where a is a predetermined value to use for the analysis

possibility to generalize results from the data available. The concept of learning for predictive analytics is based on partitions and the observation of the models results. The partition can select the points in each set for building a model and validate/test the model in a random way or according to the risk analyst method of selection of data.

Once samples are defined, data is selected and organized. A process of parameter estimations will start. In parametric modeling, there is a search of parameters that have properties such as to be unbiased. An unbiased estimator is the one where the expected value of the estimator must be equal to the parameter. In general, the formulas are required to be adapted to maintain the unbiased parameter estimation; for example the S^2 the formula requires $n - 1$ in the

$$s^2 = \frac{\sum_{i=1}^{n} (x_i - \bar{x})^2}{n - 1}$$

denominator and no n in the sample size (one degree of freedom is reduced).

The identification of the parameter distribution of a population in a risk analytics process is critical. The mean of a probability distribution for example is one of the parameters to estimate and different samples can provide different values of the average that is used to estimate the population mean. There is a need to avoid bias and to manage the standard error. Another two concepts that appear in risk analytics are ensembles and Monte Carlo Simulation. In the first one, the purpose is to use several samples to evaluate the models and the algorithms take the samples and form the iterations discover the best model that will be the one used for modeling purposes. In a Monte Carlo Simulation, the sample points are obtained from the probability distribution that describes the variable of analysis using the inverse of the cumulative probability distribution and a random number generation that represents the probability of the sample points.

A summary of sampling methods and some examples of parameter estimation are in the following Figure 2.5.

There are results that are used in estimation of parameters in risk analytics such as the law of large numbers (LLN) that indicates that (under some general conditions such as independence of observations) the sample mean converges to the population mean ($\bar{X}_n \to \mu$) as the sample size n increases (n $\to \infty$). Informally, this means that the difference between the sample mean and the population mean tends to become smaller and smaller as we increase the sample size. The LLN provides a theoretical justification for the use of a sample mean as an estimator for the population mean. Figure 2.5

2.6   DATA PARTITION: TRAINING, TEST, AND VALIDATION DATA

The training set is that on which a model is developed. There are validation and testing data sets to measure fit of models and to find ways generalize results. Different types of methods to test the models and to infer results are used, as mentioned in the previous sections for using multiple samples. Other sets are taken as they are the ones of outside time and outside the training set to prove if the results work suitably. Some of these samples are based on time or selected points in a partition out of sample tests.

In the practice of risk analytics, there are some principles to remember regarding election of data and variables:

- The greater number is not better
- Greater number of variables, more work
- More variables more time of reading
- Avoid redundancies

Simple random sampling the selection of points is assuming the same probability of being selected (uniform distribution). N represent the population and n the sample sizes	Estimation of mean and variance $\hat{\mu} = \bar{x} = \frac{\sum_{i=1}^{n} x_i}{n}$ with $\hat{V}(\bar{x}) = \frac{S^2}{n}\left(\frac{N-n}{N}\right)$ where $S^2 = \frac{\sum_{i=1}^{n}(x_i - \bar{x})^2}{n-1}$ Or proportions $\hat{P} = \bar{x} = \frac{\sum_{i=1}^{n} x_i}{n}$ with $\hat{V}(\hat{P}) = \frac{\hat{p}\hat{q}}{(n-1)}\left(\frac{N-n}{N}\right)$
Systematic sampling – Selecting the elements from a list every certain number k.	$k \le \frac{N}{n}$ $\hat{\mu} = y_{sx} = \frac{\sum_{i=1}^{n} x_i}{n}$ $\hat{V}(\bar{y}_{st}) = \left(\frac{N-n}{N}\right)\frac{S^2}{n}$ where $S^2 = \frac{\sum x_i^2 - \frac{(\sum_{i=1}^{n} x_i)}{n}}{n-1}$
Stratified sampling – data has disjointed subsets or strata and the elements are selected from each subset maintaining proportions. L subsets and N_i sample points for each i.	$\bar{x}_{st} = \frac{1}{N}[N_1 \bar{x}_i + \cdots + N_L \bar{x}_L]$ $\hat{V}(\bar{x}_{st}) = \frac{1}{N^2}\sum_{i=1}^{L} N_i^2\left(\frac{N_i - n_i}{N_i}\right)\frac{S_i^2}{n_i}$ $\hat{P}_{st} = \frac{1}{N}\sum_{i=1}^{L} N_i P_i$ $\hat{V}(\hat{P}_{st}) = \frac{1}{N^2}\sum \frac{N_i^2(N_i - n_i)}{N_i}\frac{\hat{p}_i\hat{q}_i}{n_i - 1}$
Cluster sampling is when the population is divided into clusters and selecting clusters with the use of all data-census in each cluster. N = number of clusters in the population n = number of selected clusters m_i = number of elements of the cluster and x_i total of observations in i-th cluster	$\bar{x} = \frac{\sum_{i=1}^{n} x_i}{\sum_{i=1}^{n} m_i}$ $\hat{V}(\bar{x}) = \left(\frac{N-n}{Nn\bar{M}^2}\right)\frac{\sum_{i=1}^{n}(x_i - \bar{x}_i)^2}{n-1}$ $\bar{m} = \frac{\sum_{i=1}^{n} m_i}{n}$ $M = \sum_{i=1}^{n} m_i$ $\hat{P} = \frac{\sum_{i=1}^{n} a_i}{\sum_{i=1}^{n} m_i}$ $\hat{V}(\hat{P}) = \frac{N-n}{Nn\bar{M}^2}\frac{\sum_{i=1}^{n}(a_i - \hat{p}m_i)^2}{n-1}$

FIGURE 2.5 Sampling methods and parameter estimation.

Definition of aggregation levels

- Records by each person
- Records by cases, by contracts, by products, etc.
- Records by each type of contacts with the organization, services, etc.

Exploration of data and cleaning

- Data of frequencies – variables distribution, histograms
- Visualization different faces, data outside rank, boxplots
- Examining relation between variables by means of crossed tables, OLAP, scatterplots, statistical summary
- Observing patterns of lost data and two potential problems: If the lost data are of a great volume, the number of valid cases can be underneath the amount of data of the file. If it is not at a random loss of data, it reduces the data quality and possibility to use it.

Sampling, partition, and section of variables is an ongoing process according to the problem's definition, availability of data, groups of analysis, and the most important goals of inference. In several cases, the objective of certain processes can be to have more data for prediction but in certain time series like financial ones more years of stock pricing can create bias in the results of return analysis. According to the previous presented point, the next step in risk analytics is to think about inference that start with the presentation in the next section. The main point to keep in mind is that those processes of sampling, partition, and inference are linked.

2.7 INFERENCE AND GENERALIZATION IN RISK ANALYTICS

The process of risk analytics as a scientific process follows a chain of steps: beginning with an experiment design – sampling design – exploratory data analysis – inference – hypotheses testing – modeling – modeling testing – interpretation – review-feedback. Regarding inferences there are metrics such as the arithmetic average can be an estimator of the expected value of a variable distribution. The values to use will depend on many factors one of them is related to the possible selection of a mode, mean or median as representant of the expected variable behavior. The dispersion will be obtained according to the select parameter to use as better descriptor of the variable distribution. There are questions to answer: Which is the best representative of the data to be able to use it in later analyses? The variance with respect to which parameter or metric to use? It is fundamental to understand that the selection will depend on the result of the dispersion of the data. The smaller dispersion identifies a better representing measurement.

Before explaining methods of estimation (next Sections 2.9 and 2.10) there are some estimators that helps in the daily work of the risk analytics process. In the following Exhibit 2.1, there are some average and dispersion metrics used in risk analytics.

In risk analytics, there are several aspects to consider in addition to dispersion or association with variance, there is a lot of work to do on estimating confidence intervals as a way to identify where the expected values of losses or returns can be located, and in the ways that prices of assets/insurance can be adjusted based on the subsets or specific types of risk (credibility).

The first step is to bring to the attention points related to the confidence interval calculations. A confidence interval is the set where the population parameter should belong to according to the probability of estimating with the interval the true population parameter. The probability of estimation is called level of confidence and it is $1 - \alpha$ for α a number between 0 and 1. The level of confidence is usually expressed as a percent; common values are 90%, 95%, or 99%. The normal distribution provides that 90% Z = 1.65, 95% Z = 1.96, and 99% Z = 2.58 values that are used in the calculations. The use of the results formulas depends on the known parameters. The confidence

EXHIBIT 2.1 SUMMARY OF METRICS USED TO DESCRIBE DATA

Moments	Description

Location metrics

Arithmetic mean
Ungrouped data

$\mu = \frac{\sum_{i=1}^{N} x_i}{N}$

Population

$\bar{x} = \frac{\sum_{i=1}^{N} x_i}{n}$

Sample

Arithmetic mean
Grouped data

$\mu = \frac{\sum_{i=1}^{N} f_i x_i}{N}$

$\bar{x} = \frac{\sum_{i=1}^{N} f_i x_i}{n}$

Geometric Mean

$MG = \sqrt[n]{\prod_i X_i}$

$MG = \sqrt[n]{\prod_{f_1} X_1 \dots \prod_{f_n} X_n}$

Harmonic Mean

$MA = \frac{n}{\sum_i \frac{1}{X_i}}$

$MA = \frac{n}{\sum_i f_i \frac{1}{X_i}}$

Median

The middle point/value of the sorted data from min to max
Grouped data with median class X_k

$$med = L + \frac{\frac{n}{2} - CF(X_{k-1})}{FR(X_k)} w$$

n = Number of sample points
$CF(X_{k-1})$ = Cumulative frequency under lower median class boundary
FR = Median class frequency.
w = Length of the median class.
L = Lower median class boundary

Mode

Point/observation that appears with the highest frequency
Grouped data
   Mode for Grouped Data

$Mod = T + \frac{d_1}{d_1 + d_2} j$
T= lower limit of the mode class
d_1= Difference freq. mode class and class before mode class
d_2= Difference freq. mode class and class after model class
j = length of mode class

Midrange

Average of the min and max values of the variable

Dispersion

Range
Interquartile range

After data is sorted it depends on two values that are between the first and
third quartiles

Variance ungrouped data

$\sigma^2 = \frac{\sum_{i=1}^{N}(x_i - \mu)^2}{N}$

$s^2 = \frac{\sum_{i=1}^{N}(x_i - \bar{x})^2}{n-1}$

Variance grouped data

$\mu = \frac{\sum_{i=1}^{N} f_i x_i}{N}$

$s^2 = \frac{\sum_{i=1}^{n} f_i (x_i - \bar{x})^2}{n-1}$

Standard deviation

$\sigma = \sqrt{\frac{\sum_{i=1}^{N}(x_i - \mu)^2}{N}}$

$s = \sqrt{\frac{\sum_{i=1}^{n}(x_i - \bar{x})^2}{n-1}}$

Skewness identifies symmetry
of the distribution

$\frac{\frac{1}{N}\sum_{i=1}^{n}(x_i - \mu)^3}{\sigma^3}$ is the coefficient of skewness (cs)

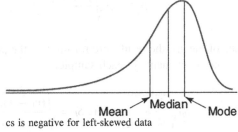

cs is negative for left-skewed data

(Continued)

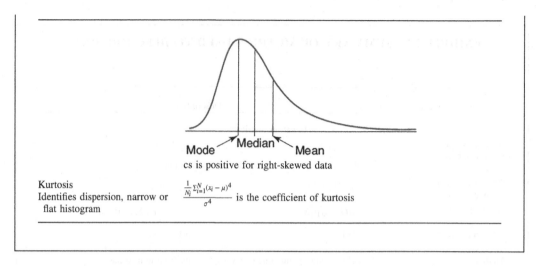

Mode   Median   Mean

cs is positive for right-skewed data

Kurtosis
Identifies dispersion, narrow or $\frac{\frac{1}{N_i}\sum_{i=1}^{N}(x_i - \mu)^4}{\sigma^4}$ is the coefficient of kurtosis
flat histogram

interval is the parameter estimator $+/-Z_{\frac{\alpha}{2}}$ times the standard error $\frac{\sigma}{\sqrt{n}}$. For example, when σ is known, with $\alpha = 0.05$, the value $z = 1.96$.

$$\bar{x} - z_{\alpha \frac{}{2}}\left(\frac{\sigma}{\sqrt{n}}\right) \leq \mu \leq \bar{x} + z_{\alpha \frac{}{2}}\left(\frac{\sigma}{\sqrt{n}}\right)$$

The values are

$$\bar{x} - 1.96\left(\frac{\sigma}{\sqrt{n}}\right) \leq \mu \leq \bar{x} + 1.96\left(\frac{\sigma}{\sqrt{n}}\right)$$

in the case of σ unknown s the sample standard deviation are used:

$$\bar{x} - z_{\alpha \frac{}{2}}\left(\frac{s}{\sqrt{n}}\right) \leq \mu \leq \bar{x} + z_{\alpha \frac{}{2}}\left(\frac{s}{\sqrt{n}}\right)$$

In the case of $n < 30$, the t-distribution is used and it has as parameters α and the number of freedom degrees $v = n - 1$. Then the confidence interval is

$$\bar{x} - t_{\alpha \frac{}{2}, \vartheta}\left(\frac{s}{\sqrt{n}}\right) \leq \mu \leq \bar{x} + t_{\alpha \frac{}{2}, \vartheta}\left(\frac{s}{\sqrt{n}}\right)$$

In the case of proportions, the process is similar,

$$\hat{p} \pm z_{\alpha/2}\sqrt{\frac{\hat{p}(1 - \hat{p})}{n}}$$

In the case of difference of means, the results are for none of the population variances known and assumed equal with n_1 and n_2 elements in each sample:

$$(\bar{x_1} - \bar{x_2}) \pm Z_{\alpha/2}S_P\sqrt{\frac{1}{n_1} + \frac{1}{n_2}} \text{ where } S_P = \sqrt{\frac{(n_1 - 1)S_1^2 + (n_2 - 1)S_2^2}{n_1 + n_2 - 2}}$$

In risk analytics, the fitting process to obtain a loss distribution is a crucial process to develop. The fitting process requires the identification of the distribution and its parameters. To find the best estimators of the parameters and to identify the minimization of the error between the theoretical distribution and the model, there are three approaches included in this book to estimate parameters: method of the moments, maximum likelihood estimation, and optimization.

2.8 METHOD OF THE MOMENTS

The method of the moments is used to consider the parameters of each one of the distributions that study and to be able to choose the best model. Definition: If a parametric family has p parameters, the equations of moments are for x_1, x_2, ..., x_n $i.i.d.$ observations from a distribution:

$$\mu_j' = E(x^j) = \frac{1}{n} \sum_{i=1}^{n} x_i^j \text{ with } j = 1, ..., p$$

The method of the moments for estimation is the solution to these equations, applied to the distributions Lognormal, Gamma, Weibull, and inverse Gaussian.

1. *Method of the Moments* in the estimation of the parameters of the Lognormal distribution:

$$f(x, \mu, \sigma) = \frac{1}{x\sigma\sqrt{2\pi}} e^{-\frac{(\log x - \mu)^2}{2\sigma}}$$

$$E(x^k) = e^{\left(\frac{k\mu + k^2\sigma^2}{2}\right)}$$

$$\hat{\mu} = 2\ln\bar{x} - \frac{1}{2}\ln\frac{1}{n}\sum_{i=1}^{n} x_i^2$$

$$\hat{\sigma}^2 = \ln\frac{1}{n}\sum_{i=1}^{n} x_i^2 - 2\ln\bar{x}$$

2. *Method of the Moments* for the estimation of the parameters of the Gamma distribution:

$$f(x, \alpha, \beta) = \frac{1}{\tau(\alpha)}\beta^\alpha x^{\alpha-1} exp^{-\beta x}$$

$$E(x^k) = \frac{\theta^k \tau(\alpha + \beta)}{\tau(\alpha)}$$

$$\hat{\alpha} = \frac{\sum_{i=1}^{n} x_i^2 - (\sum_{i=1}^{n} x_i)^2}{\sum_{i=1}^{n} x_i}$$

$$\hat{\beta} = \frac{\hat{\alpha}}{\sum_{i=1}^{n} x_i}$$

3. *Method of the Moments* for the estimation of the parameters of the Weibull distribution:

$$f(x, \theta, \tau) = \theta\tau x^{\tau-1} exp^{-\theta x^\tau}$$

p = 25th percentile, q = 75th percentile

$$\hat{\theta} = exp^{\left(\frac{g\ln(p) - \ln(q)}{g-1}\right)}, \quad \hat{g} = \frac{\ln(\ln(4))}{\ln(\ln(4/3))}, \quad \hat{\tau} = \frac{\ln(\ln(4))}{\ln(q) - \ln(\hat{\theta})}$$

4. *Method of the Moments* for the estimation of the parameters of the Gaussian Inverse distribution:

$$E(x) = \lambda, \quad \hat{\mu} = \frac{\bar{x}^3}{\frac{1}{n}\sum_{i=1}^{n} x_i^2 - \bar{x}^2}$$

$$\hat{\lambda} = \bar{x} \qquad Var\ (x) = \lambda^3/\mu$$

$$f(x; \lambda, \mu) = \sqrt{\frac{\lambda}{2\pi x^3}}\ exp^{-\frac{\lambda(x-\mu)^2}{2\mu^{2x}}}$$

2.9   MAXIMUM LIKELIHOOD ESTIMATION

Definition: The function of maximum likelihood for a set of n independent observations is

$$L(\underline{\theta}) = \prod_{j=1}^{n} Lj(\theta)$$

where $L_j(\theta)$ observation to the probability function is the contribution of the j-th observation to the likelihood function. Any proportional function to $L(\theta)$ is any monotonic function of $L(\theta)$ example $l(\underline{\theta}) = \ln L(\theta)$ it will share a common maximum with $L(\theta)$ call $\hat{\underline{\theta}}$. The score function of θ is:

$$S_j(\underline{\theta}) = \frac{\partial}{\partial \theta_j} l(\underline{\theta})$$

And the maximization problem is to solve the equations $S_j(\underline{\theta}) = 0$. For example

1. **The estimator of maximum likelihood** of the parameters of the Lognormal distribution

$$f(x, \mu, \sigma) = \frac{1}{x\sigma\sqrt{2\pi}} exp^{-\frac{(\log x - \mu)^2}{2\sigma^2}}$$

The logarithm of the likelihood function is:

$$L(\mu, \sigma) = \prod_{i=1}^{n} (x_i)^{-1} (2\pi)^{-\frac{n}{2}} (\sigma)^{-n} exp^{-\sum_{i=1}^{n} \frac{(\log x_i - \mu)^2}{2\sigma^2}}$$

$$l(\mu, \sigma) = \sum_{i=1}^{n} \ln x_i - n\ln \sigma - \sum_{i=1}^{n} \frac{(\log x_i - \mu)^2}{2\sigma^2}$$

And the score functions are:

$$S_1(\mu, \sigma) = \frac{\partial l}{\partial \mu} = \frac{\sum_{i=1}^{n}(\log x_i - \mu)}{\sigma^2}$$

$$S_2(\mu, \sigma) = \frac{\partial l}{\partial \sigma} = -\frac{n}{\sigma} + \frac{\sum_{i=1}^{n}(\log x_i - \mu)^2}{\sigma^3}$$

And with $S_1 = S_2 = 0$, the parameters are:

$$\hat{\mu} = \frac{1}{n}\sum_{i=1}^{n} \ln x_i$$

$$\hat{\sigma}^2 = \frac{\sum_{i=1}^{n}(\log x_i - \hat{\mu})^2}{n}$$

2. **Maximum likelihood function** for the parameters of the Gamma distribution:

$$f(x, \alpha, \beta) = \frac{1}{\tau(\alpha)} \beta^{\alpha} x^{\alpha-1} exp^{-\beta x}$$

the likelihood function is:

$$L(\alpha, \beta) = \left(\frac{1}{\tau(\alpha)}\right)^n \beta^{n\alpha} \prod_{i=1}^{n} (x_i)^{\alpha-1} exp^{-\beta \sum_{i=1}^{n} x_i}$$

The logarithm of the likelihood function is:

$$l(\alpha, \beta) = -n \ln(\tau(\alpha)) + n\alpha \ln\beta + (\alpha - 1) \sum_{i=1}^{n} \ln x_i - \beta \sum_{i=1}^{n} x_i$$

The score functions are:

$$S_1(\alpha, \beta) = \frac{\partial l}{\partial \alpha} = \frac{-n\tau(\alpha)'}{\tau(\alpha)} + n \ln\beta + \sum_{i=1}^{n} \ln x_i$$

$$S_2(\alpha, \beta) = \frac{\partial l}{\partial \beta} = \frac{n\alpha}{\beta} - \sum_{i=1}^{n} \ln x_i$$

With S_1 and $S_2 = 0$, the following is obtained:

$$\hat{\beta} = \frac{\alpha}{\sum_{i=1}^{n} x_i} \quad \ln\alpha - \frac{\tau(\hat{\alpha})'}{\tau(\hat{\alpha})} = \ln \sum_{i=1}^{n} x_i - \frac{\sum_{i=1}^{n} \ln x_i}{n}$$

3. **Maximum likelihood function** for the parameters of the Weibull distribution

$$f(x, \theta, \tau) = \theta\tau x^{\tau-1} exp^{-\theta x^{\tau}}$$

The probability function is:

$$L(\theta, \tau) = \theta^n \tau^n \prod_{i=1}^{n} x_i^{\tau-1} exp^{-\theta \sum_{i=1}^{n} x_i^{\tau}}$$

The logarithm of the likelihood function is:

$$l(\theta, \tau) = n \ln\theta + n \ln\tau + (\tau - 1) \sum_{i=1}^{n} x_i - \theta \sum_{i=1}^{n} x_i^{\tau}$$

The score functions are:

$$S_1(\theta, \tau) = \frac{\partial l}{\partial \theta} = \frac{n}{\theta} - \sum_{i=1}^{n} x_i^{\tau}$$

$$S_2(\theta, \tau) = \frac{\partial l}{\partial \tau} = \frac{n}{\tau} + \sum_{i=1}^{n} \ln x_i - \theta \sum_{i=1}^{n} x_i^{\tau} \ln x_i$$

$S_1 = S_2 = 0$, is obtained:

$$\hat{\theta} = \frac{n}{\sum_{i=1}^{n} x_i^{\tau}} \quad \frac{n}{\hat{\tau}} = \frac{\sum_{i=1}^{n} x_j^{\tau} \ln x_i}{\sum_{i=1}^{n} x_j^{\tau}} - \sum_{i=1}^{n} \ln x_i$$

4. **Maximum likelihood function** for the parameters of the Gaussian Inverse distribution

$$f(x; \lambda, \mu) = \sqrt{\frac{\lambda}{2\pi x^3}} \, exp^{-\frac{\lambda(x-\mu)^2}{2\mu^{2x}}}$$

The likelihood function is:

$$L(\lambda, \mu) = \left(\frac{\lambda}{2\pi}\right)^{\frac{n}{2}} \left(\prod_{i=1}^{n} x_i^{-\frac{3}{2}}\right) exp^{-\frac{\lambda}{2\mu^2} \sum_{i=1}^{n} \frac{(x_i-\mu)^2}{x_i}}$$

The logarithm of the likelihood function is:

$$l(\lambda, \mu) = \frac{\mu}{2} \ln\left(\frac{\lambda}{2\pi}\right) - \frac{3}{2} \sum_{i=1}^{n} \ln x_i - \frac{\lambda}{2\mu^2} \sum_{i=1}^{n} \frac{(x_i - \mu)^2}{x_i}$$

The score functions are:

$$S_1(\lambda, \mu) = \frac{\partial}{\partial \lambda} l(\lambda, \mu) = \frac{\mu}{2\lambda} - \frac{1}{2\mu^2} \sum_{i=1}^{n} \frac{(x_i - \mu)^2}{x_i}$$

$$S_2(\lambda, \mu) = \frac{\partial}{\partial \mu} l(\lambda, \mu) = \frac{\lambda}{\mu^3} \sum_{i=1}^{n} \frac{(x_i - \mu)^2}{x_i} + \frac{\lambda}{\mu^2}\left(n - \mu \sum_{i=1}^{n} x_i^{-1}\right)$$

$S_1 = S_2 = 0$, to obtain:

$$\hat{\mu} = \bar{x}$$

$$\hat{\lambda} = \frac{n}{\sum_{i=1}^{n} x_i^{-1} - \frac{n}{\bar{x}}} = \frac{n}{\sum_{i=1}^{n} \left(\frac{1}{x_i} - \frac{1}{\bar{x}}\right)}$$

2.10   ESTIMATORS BY OPTIMIZATION

This process of the estimator is based on the review of the minimum value of the modified χ^2. For a parametric family, let $F(x;\theta)$ the cdf and be $G(x;\theta)$ any function of x that is uniquely related to F. That is, if F and θ are known, then G can be obtained and if G and θ are known, then it is possible to obtain F. Let $G_n(x)$ be obtained from the empirical cdf in the same form. So if there is the value that minimizes θ

$$Q(\theta) = \sum_{j=1}^{k} w_j \left[G(c_j; \theta) - G_n(c_k)\right]^2$$

It is called minimum distance estimator of θ. The values of $c_1 < c_2 < \ldots < c_k$ and $w_1, w_2, \ldots, w_k \geq 0$ are arbitrary selected. This is the minimum χ^2 modified estimator and is given by: $G_j(\theta) = n[F(c_j;\theta) - F(c_{j-1};\theta)], w_j = 1/G_j$.

If $n \rightarrow \infty$, the probability that the likelihood function ($L'(\theta) = 0$) has a solution is going to 1 and the distribution maximum likelihood $\hat{\theta}_n$ converges to a normal distribution with mean θ y variance such that $I(\theta) \ \text{Var}(\hat{\theta}_n) \rightarrow 1$, where

$$I(\theta) = n \int f(x; \theta) \left(\frac{\partial}{\partial \theta} \ln f(x; \theta) \right)^2 dx$$

Thus $[I(\theta)]^{-1}$ is an approximated value for $\text{Var}(\hat{\theta}_n)$. $I(\theta)$ is called the information matrix. The covariance matrix is obtained from the inverse matrix that has as rs_{th} component

$$I(\theta)_{rs} = nE \left[\frac{\partial}{\partial \theta_r} \ln f(x; \theta) \frac{\partial}{\partial \theta_s} \ln f(x; \theta) \right]$$

when the observations are independent and with non-identical distributions.

For the lognormal distribution using the first and second derivatives, the covariance matrix is built as follows

$$I(\theta)_{rs} = - \sum_{j=1}^{n} E \left[\frac{\partial^2}{\partial \theta_s \partial \theta_r} l_j(\theta) \right]$$

Second derivatives:

$$\frac{\partial^2 l}{\partial \mu^2} = -\frac{n}{\sigma^2} \qquad \frac{\partial^2 l}{\partial \sigma \partial \mu} = -2 \sum_{i=1}^{n} \frac{(\ln x_i - \mu)}{\sigma^3} \qquad \frac{\partial^2 l}{\partial \sigma^2} = \frac{n}{\sigma^2} - 3 \sum_{i=1}^{n} \frac{(\ln x_i - \mu)^2}{\sigma^4}$$

The expected values are:

$$E \left[\frac{\partial^2 l}{\partial \mu^2} \right] = -\frac{n}{\sigma^2} \qquad E \left[\frac{\partial^2 l}{\partial \sigma \partial \mu} \right] = 0 \qquad E \left[\frac{\partial^2 l}{\partial \sigma^2} \right] = -\frac{2n}{\sigma^2}$$

And the covariance matrix is

$$\begin{bmatrix} \frac{\sigma^2}{n} & 0 \\ 0 & \frac{\sigma^2}{2n} \end{bmatrix}$$

Another aspect to analyze is the robustness of the parameters and the answer is based on the analysis of *IF* the influence function of a function T in x under a function F_θ

$$IF(x; T, F_\theta) = \lim_{\varepsilon \to 0} \frac{T[(1 - \varepsilon)F_\theta + \varepsilon \Delta_x] - T(F_\theta)}{\varepsilon}$$

when the limit exists. Δx is used in a degenerate *c.d.f.* to give a mass point of 1 in a point x.

If the function IF is zero in a set, those points are not influencing the function. In the lognormal case,

$$\theta_1 \;=\; E\left[\ln x\right] = \int_0^\infty \ln x \, dF_{\underline{\theta}}(x) = T\left(F_{\underline{\theta}}\right)$$

$$\hat{\theta}_1 \;=\; T\left(F_n\right) = \frac{1}{n}\sum_{i=1}^{n}\ln x_i$$

$$\Rightarrow IF\left(x;\,T,\,F_\theta\right) \;=\; \lim_{\varepsilon\to 0}\frac{T\left[(1-\varepsilon)T\left(F_{\underline{\theta}}\right)+\varepsilon\Delta x\right]-T\left(F_{\underline{\theta}}\right)}{\varepsilon}$$

$$=\; \lim_{\varepsilon\to 0}\frac{(1-\varepsilon)\theta_1+\varepsilon\ln x-\theta_1}{\varepsilon} \;=\; \ln x - \theta_1$$

$$=\; \lim_{\varepsilon\to 0}\frac{(1-\varepsilon)\int_0^\infty \ln y \, dF_{\underline{\theta}}(y)+\varepsilon\int_0^\infty \ln y \, d\Delta x(y)-\theta_1}{\varepsilon}$$

$$\Rightarrow \hat{\theta}_1 \;=\; T\left(F_n\right)$$

IF is unbounded in x this means IF $\to \propto$ as $x \to \propto$ it means not robust.

With this review of sampling and estimation processes, the dots are converging to a risk analytics road map as it is presented in the next section.

2.11   RISK ANALYTICS ROAD MAP

Taking the points of the previous sections, risk modeling, risk management processes, risk knowledge management, and components that a RAS has, it is possible to say that the road map is about a mathematical modeling process. A mathematical model (Caldwell and Ram, 1999) starts from a problem and variables definition, introducing observations, data, description of the relationships among variables (generally equations and basic data models), assumptions (experience-knowledge), and with people's knowledge produces solutions-outcomes (required knowledge for solving the model) that can be used for the specific problem solution or with additional knowledge applicable to several problems. Within the process, a loop of formulation and test for different model options is always present and at the same time the question is whether there are mathematical solutions to apply.

Markey R. 2020, presented a view that is summarized in terms of "Smart companies use new models, technologies, and marketing metrics to increase the number of profitable customers, boost retention, and maximize purchases." In this book and concerning risk analytics, is that in the way that organizations are taking care of their users, beneficiaries, clients, or customers a common denominator is the combination of data demographic transactional, project related, etc. the crucial aspects are related to what to evaluate and measure according to a purpose that can be to maximize stakeholders' satisfaction. What is satisfaction, and how are you going to measure it? What are the priority stakeholders? etc. In the next paragraphs, an example is presented showing the steps to deal with engagement of potential customers and possibility to succeed in a project through appropriate use of data analytics. The risk involved is as always to invest money in a project and to have results that possibly are not satisfactory to certain stakeholders such as management or owners.

The risk analytics tools and information structures supporting risk analysis and control areas in organizations that in several cases act as independent organizational areas, with different views, specific objectives, and processes. The independent treatment of risk has effects such as a variety of languages within the organization to talk about risk and the expertise of the analysts is not the same in different areas or applicable to different kinds of problems (Dickinson, 2001, Shaw, 2005). Marshal and Prusak, 1996, Daniell, 2000, Shaw, 2005, presented KM as a discipline that can contribute positively to the ERM implementation regarding data and information management, risk knowledge sharing, and analysis consolidation and reporting. Risk analytics is related to the concept of creating intelligence in organizations (Rodriguez, 2017). The main steps for the analysis are as it has been mentioned before: 1) Business and problem understanding, 2) data preparation and data understanding, 3) modeling, 4) evaluation, and 5) deployment.

In the following paragraphs, there are three illustrations of risk analytics road map components. The first one refers to the problem of defining the target in credit insurance; the second is about combining marketing risk and credit risk. The third refers to the combination of risk and marketing factors to improve effectiveness in a business process.

2.11.1 A View of Combining Marketing Risk and Credit Risk

In the following example, there is a presentation of the aspects to consider in the risk analytics road map. These examples are analyzed in several cases in the book under different perspectives. Every aspect regarding problem definition (target variables definition), data, and models will be completely connected to the practice of risk analytics. No good definition of target means no good definition of required data and model to use. This means the first step in a risk analytics process will be to define the risk. A situation of risk class definition that has several aspects to consider is the credit insurance. A combination of defining the target class that is the contract object to protect the customer who has international trading transactions. Each transaction creates a credit situation if there is a delivery-shipment and payments are not at the same time. In the international transactions, credit insurance uses credit terms such as not more than 360 days of coverage (but generally under 180 days) and pre-shipment periods of not more than 12 months.

An insurance contract is an agreement (policy) between two parties, the insured and the insurer, both having the legal capacity to contract, that specified property (export receivables or work in progress) will be insured against commercial (default, insolvency, repudiation and contract termination) and political risks (war, revolution and insurrection, conversion and transfer risk and cancelation of import or export permits). The customer pays a premium according to the risk levels of the buyers. The amount of the claim paid will be subject to co-insurance or deductible. Credit exposure for the insurer is based on the accounts receivable cycle that commences when an order is placed by the buyer to a seller that produces the good or service to export. An invoice is created, the sale is recorded by the seller, and the account receivable is set up. Afterwards, the delivery of goods or services is made to the buyer. Finally, the payment is made by the buyer based on terms established by the seller.

At each transaction, the risk profile of the buyer is assessed based on current financial and non-financial information. Financial information is obtained from financial statements (both fiscal and interims) as well as from financial statements excerpts. Non-financial information includes demographic and external-credit information.

There is a limit assignment for the credit protection. The risk monitoring process needs to review a risk evolution. The risk assessment and surveillance is a dynamic structure that evolves or *learns* as the conditions of the environment change. A dynamic structure offers the possibility to obtain risk assessment results through time using different performance and observation windows in an automated manner. The continuous process requires the ongoing update of the transactions and the risk assessment according to different times and the required adjustments to the credit system performance measures.

One of the crucial steps in this example is to define the target as it has been mentioned in previous sections. The analytics process requires the definition of the problem in a clear and organized way. This means to define what organization will be consider as a target class to predict or identify it. This is a bivariate problem where there are good and bad risks and the event that generates a loss is a claim paid. The claim paid will have the level of severity of the event according to deductibles and reinsurance. Models to evaluate the severity and to indicate the existence of an event will be part of the definition of a class as bad.

Another example to illustrate marketing and credit risk is based on the data from Moro et al. (2014) from the UCI data repository. This data set can be used to work on classification of customer as good or bad as credit subjects or good or bad to accept a promotion campaign in marketing. This means the target variable can be any of them and the results will be based on demographic, business related and promotion campaign variables (https://archive.ics.uci.edu/ml/data sets/Bank+Marketing).

The first step is to understand the business and to find how risk analytics is connected to the strategic and tactic goals. This means to identify the value that risk analytics will provide to the organization to achieve the goals and desired performance level. For instance:

- Earnings Growth – Earnings per share has grown by 10% in 2018
- Efficiency Ratio (Ratio of Non-interest expenses to Total Revenue) – Improved to 55.6% from 57.2%. 2019 target of 55% and 2022 target of 52%
- Return on Equity – 17.4% achieved vs 15% target
- Shareholder Return – Target of 40%–50%; currently at 43.4%

Banks use as one source of revenue the interest rates that are paid on loans. In this case, personal and small business banking is almost half of the bank's revenue and operations. In order to facilitate the growth of loans, banks require a certain amount of funds from existing clients. This is done through the use of savings accounts where a specific percentage is held for safety/security and another portion is used for the purpose of loans. Loans generate a higher interest rate than the interest that is paid on savings accounts and the difference is the basis of the bank's net income. Since they focus a lot on smaller accounts, the bank would require a good marketing strategy to reach as many potential customers as possible. A bank is looking for optimizing the spread between payment for deposits and rates to charge for loans. This practice increases their margins or profitability. A term deposit is a fixed-term investment that includes the deposit into an account at the bank. If a customer places money in a term deposit, the bank can invest the money in other financial products that pay a higher rate of return than what the bank is paying the customer for the use of their funds.

However, mass marketing is not the most efficient and effective method of marketing. From our data, customers between 18 and 34 years old are the second-largest demographic and are more likely to be engaged by social media ads than mass media.

A second step in the road map is data preparation. Based on the risk identified as GIGO (garbage in garbage out), poor analytics, wrong questions, and insights can be the consequences of not having an appropriate review of data, possible errors, and possible issues in variables definition or methods of gathering the data. In this case, the data structure is (Table 2.6) shown.

In this example, the analysis is presented using variables 5 and 17 as targets and keeping the other variables as explanatory ones. The key is to identify how other variables can affect variable relationships in two different settings because a promotion is about deposits and default is about credit. In this case, only 52 of 45,211 customers accepted the promotion and had a default. The total defaults of the contacted customers is 815 (Table 2.7). Figures 2.6 and 2.7 are examples of variables representation using histograms and bars.

In the descriptive data analysis, univariate and bivariate statistics are calculated (Figures 2.8 to 2.11 and Tables 2.8 to 2.12) where the balance is with a positive coefficient of skewness or right-skewed data that means higher concentration is small balances, the combination of balance an age shows some cases in high balances in young people, or the education levels and aggregated balance concentrated on secondary and tertiary education. These aspects can be a source of segments definition. Using the tables, the concentration of term deposits are higher in tertiary education and singles. What appears is the need to study the intersections of having or not having loans and mortgages and the groups by demographics. And from more relationships, a discovery to move to define how to connect the variables and acceptance of the promotion.

TABLE 2.6
Variables of the Data Bank Promotion

Input variables

Bank client data:

1. age (numeric)
2. job: type of job (categorical: "admin.", "unknown", "unemployed", "management", "housemaid", "entrepreneur", "student", "blue-collar", "self-employed", "retired", "technician", "services")
3. marital: marital status (categorical: "married", "divorced", "single" note: "divorced" means divorced or widowed)
4. education (categorical: "unknown", "secondary", "primary", "tertiary")
5. default: has credit in default? (binary: "yes", "no")
6. balance: average yearly balance, in euros (numeric)
7. housing: has housing loan? (binary: "yes", "no")
8. loan: has personal loan? (binary: "yes", "no")

Data related to the last contact of the current campaign:

9. contact: contact communication type (categorical: "unknown", "telephone", "cellular")
10. day: last contact day of the month (numeric)
11. month: last contact month of year (categorical: "jan", "feb", "mar", ... , "nov", "dec")
12. duration: last contact duration, in seconds (numeric)

Data other attributes:

13. campaign: number of contacts performed during this campaign and for this client (numeric, includes last contact)
14. pdays: number of days that passed by after the client was last contacted from a previous campaign (numeric, −1 means client was not previously contacted)
15. previous: number of contacts performed before this campaign and for this client (numeric)
16. poutcome: outcome of the previous marketing campaign (categorical: "unknown", "other", "failure", "success")
17. y – has the client subscribed a term deposit? (binary: "yes", "no")

TABLE 2.7
Distribution of the Two Possible Target Variables

Frequency	Accepting the Promotion		
Default	no	yes	Grand Total
no	39,159	5,237	44,396
yes	763	52	815
Grand Total	39,922	5,289	45,211

Summary statistics (Table 2.13) indicate the age average of 41 years, and attributes about the marketing campaign. The balance standard deviation is very high, with an indication of having a high dispersion and the values from small amounts to high amounts. Here, the histograms helps to observe the data behavior, fat tails, and new questions appear of the segments with high income, the number of them, and the campaign selection of the potential customers to be interested in the new product. The indication of high balances in a checking account without interest could be a group to consider getting a positive answer to the promotion.

To start analysis, the problem needs to be in the analyst's mind because the first clues to answer research questions are from the objectives. If one objective is to get more potential customers for a product (term deposit), the questions to answer are related to the variables with more influence to make a positive decision and the descriptive part can be with a goal of defining some hypotheses to

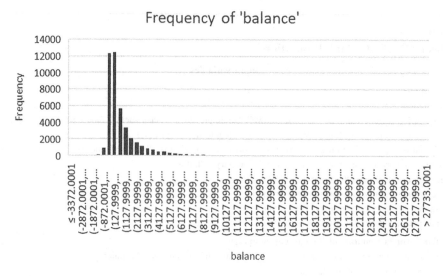

Frequency of 'balance'

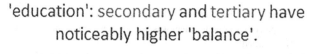

FIGURE 2.6   Histogram balance variable.

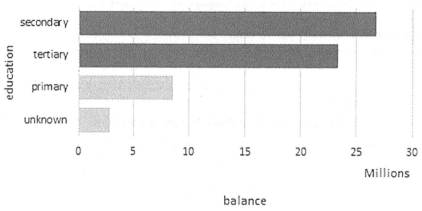

'education': secondary and tertiary have noticeably higher 'balance'.

FIGURE 2.7   Frequency representation of education variable.

statistically test. The use of income is a good way to see prospects and can be a good point to start as well. Table 2.14 indicates that the higher quartile has more acceptance of the promotion of the product and no defaults as part of the risk evaluation and what sounds a good set of prospects in the financial institution. The first bivariate view of data needs to be confirmed or reviewed with a multivariate analysis.

The exploratory data analysis is supported by a matrix that shows relationships variables in scatterplot presentation and histograms of densities as in Table 2.14. The representation of yes or not for acceptance helps to review what the target is, based on the bivariate observation for example where are certain accumulation of points or where there are special cases outside of the mainstream of the sample of customers. For example, with higher age and middle balance, it seems that are more rejections than acceptances. In this way, the modeling process will be a guide and concentrated on reviewing specific questions/hypotheses. EDA guides hypotheses formulation.

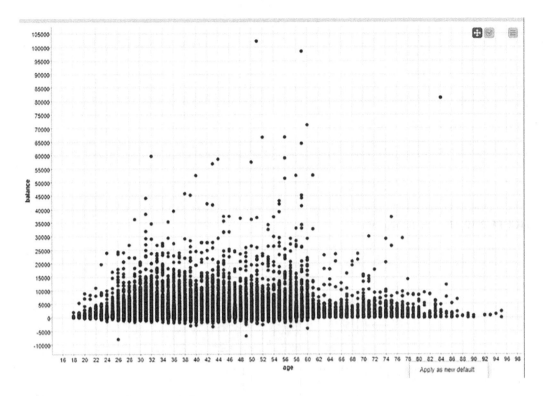

FIGURE 2.8   Scatterplot age vs. balance.

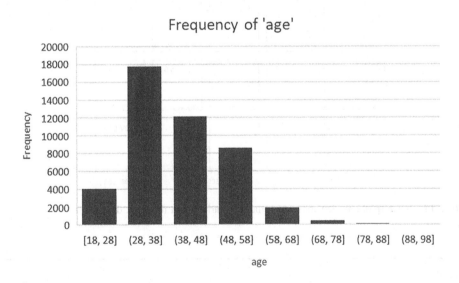

FIGURE 2.9   Histogram age variable.

Table 2.15 shows the categorical variables with each category and the relative frequencies. The additional information from the table can lead to questions such as the balance that can be an indicator of a higher acceptance, but it is the same if the balance is coming from an employee or retired or entrepreneur person. More and more combinations appear to be part of the search of the appropriate treatment of the problems. The next section indicates some ideas of how groups can be created based on multivariate observations and the same as finding how the variables can

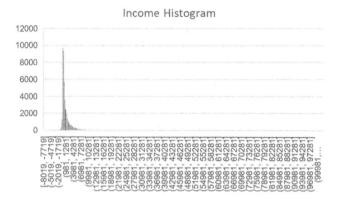

FIGURE 2.10 Income histogram.

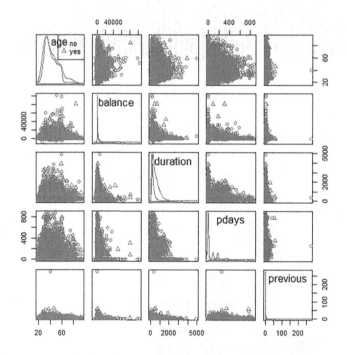

FIGURE 2.11 Scatterplot and densities for numerical variables in the bank data set.

TABLE 2.8
Combined Variables of Marital Status and Type of Clients

Marital Status	# of Clients	# of Clients Split	# of Clients with Term Deposit	Participation Rate
Divorced	5,207	11.52%	622	11.95%
Married	27,214	60.19%	2,755	10.12%
Single	12,790	28.29%	1,912	14.95%

TABLE 2.9
Combined Education Level and Type of Clients

Education	# of Clients	# of Clients split	# of Clients with Term Deposit	Participation Rate
Primary	6,851	15.15%	591	8.63%
Secondary	23,202	51.32%	2,450	10.56%
Tertiary	13,301	29.42%	1,996	15.01%
Unknown	1,857	4.11%	252	13.57%

TABLE 2.10
Combined Balance and Type of Clients

Balance	# of Clients	# of Clients split	# of Clients with Term Deposit	Participation Rate
Negative	3,766	8.33%	210	5.58%
Positive	41,445	91.67%	5,079	12.25%

TABLE 2.11
Combine Mortgage and Type of Clients

Mortgage	# of Clients	# of Clients split	# of Clients with Term Deposit	Participation Rate
No	20,081	44.42%	3,354	16.70%
Yes	25,130	55.58%	1,935	7.70%

TABLE 2.12
Combined Previous Promotion Result and Type of Clients

Outcome of Previous Campaign	# of Clients	# of Clients Split	# of Clients with Term Deposit	Participation Rate
Failure	4,901	10.84%	618	12.61%
Other	1,840	4.07%	307	16.68%
Success	1,511	3.34%	978	64.73%
Unknown	36,959	81.75%	3,386	9.16%

TABLE 2.13
Summary Statistics for Numeric Variables Bank Data

Statistics	Mean	sd	Se(mean)	IQR	cv	Skewness	Kurtosis	0%	25%	50%	75%	100%
age	40.936	10.619	0.050	15	0.259	0.685	0.320	18	33	39	48	95
balance	1362.272	3044.766	14.320	1356	2.235	8.360	140.752	−8019	72	448	1428	102127
campaign	2.764	3.098	0.015	2	1.121	4.899	39.250	1	1	2	3	63
day	15.806	8.322	0.039	13	0.527	0.093	−1.060	1	8	16	21	31
duration	258.163	257.528	1.211	216	0.998	3.144	18.154	0	103	180	319	4918
pdays	40.198	100.129	0.471	0	2.491	2.616	6.935	−1	−1	−1	−1	871
previous	0.580	2.303	0.011	0	3.969	41.846	4506.861	0	0	0	0	275

TABLE 2.14

Summary of Acceptance of Products and Default by Quartiles

Number customer	Balance Quartiles				
Acceptance/Default	Q1	Q2	Q3	Q4	Grand Total
no Acceptance	10,498	10,061	9,891	9,472	39,922
no Default	9,853	9,983	9,858	9,465	39,159
yes Default	645	78	33	7	763
yes Acceptance	819	1,230	1,415	1,825	5,289
no Default	778	1,225	1,409	1,825	5,237
yes Default	41	5	6		52
Grand Total	11,317	11,291	11,306	11,297	45,211

have different influence in the variation or classification of the prospects based on the target variable.

2.11.1.1 Multivariate Analysis

In this part of the example, there are three views of risk analytics that work at modifying the target variable: First, using the binary variable acceptance of the term deposit (variable 17); second, using the binary variable default (variable 5) as target variable; third, creating a new target variable related to the identified clusters (segments).

2.11.1.2 Clustering Using k-Means

After standardizing the numeric-continuous variables it has been used a 5-means clustering process. Results with cluster sizes (number of records) are shown as follows:

Cluster 1. 16,282 risk units
Cluster 2. 17,402 risk units
Cluster 3. 3,592 risk units
Cluster 4. 1,610 risk units
Cluster 5. 6,325 risk units

Table 2.16 shows the center coordinates of the clusters using the standardized variables that have the prefix z_. Figure 2.12 illustrate a 3D scatterplot for variables of age, duration, and balance. As it was indicated before, average balance increases with age and related to duration shows a reduced duration when age increased; however, there are points to review as a potential new group of customer with different behavior regarding the call that is middle ages and having high duration values.

Figure 2.13 shows the ROC curve to identify the models and their performance. The ROC curve closer to the left-top corner of the square is the model with better classification. The diagonal is representing the classification doing nothing for identifying the classes – Naive result. The area under the curve is shown below, *rf* is random forest models, *rpart* is for classification trees, *glm* is generalized linear models, *nnet* neural networks.

- Target Variable – Acceptance of Term Deposit (Variable 17) promotion
  - Area under the ROC curve for the rpart model on bankbook1 [validate] is 0.7725
  - Area under the ROC curve for the rf model on bankbook1 [validate] is 0.9343
  - Area under the ROC curve for the glm model on bankbook1 [validate] is 0.9065
  - Area under the ROC curve for the nnet model on bankbook1 [validate] is 0.4697

TABLE 2.15

Categorical Variables and Relative Frequencies by Category

Total and Relative Frequencies of Categorical Variables

Contact

cellular	telephone	unknown
29,285	2,906	13,020
64.77	6.43	28.8

Default

no	yes
44,396	815
98.2	1.8

Housing

no	yes
20,081	25,130
44.42	55.58

Education

primary	secondary	tertiary	unknown
6,851	23,202	13,301	1,857
15.15	51.32	29.42	4.11

job

admin.	blue-collar	entrepreneur	housemaid	management	retired	self-employed	services	student	technician	unemployed	Unknown
5171	9,732	1,487	1,240	9,458	2,264	1,579	4,154	938	7,597	1,303	288
11.44	21.53	3.29	2.74	20.92	5.01	3.49	9.19	2.07	16.8	2.88	0.64

marital

divorced	married	single
5,207	27,214	12,790
11.52	60.19	28.29

loan

no	yes
37,967	7,244
83.98	16.02

poutcome

failure	other	success	unknown
4,901	1,840	1,511	36,959
10.84	4.07	3.34	81.75

y

no	yes
39,922	5,289
88.3	11.7

month

dec	aug	feb	jan	jun	jul	mar	may	nov	oct	apr	sep
214	6,247	2,649	1,403	5,341	6,895	477	13,766	3,970	738	2,932	579
0.47	13.82	5.86	3.1	11.81	15.25	1.06	30.45	8.78	1.63	6.49	1.28

TABLE 2.16

Transformed (Standardized) Variables and Clusters Identification

Cluster	Z.age	Z.balance	Z.campaign	Z.day	Z.duration	Z.pdays	Z.previous
1	0.0360	−0.0829	−0.1799	−0.8880	−0.2080	−0.3730	−0.2139
2	−0.0255	0.0206	−0.0944	0.8491	−0.2550	−0.3619	−0.2146
3	0.0466	0.2719	−0.1184	−0.0056	2.5378	−0.2465	−0.1470
4	−0.0313	−0.0670	3.9176	0.7512	−0.4327	−0.4019	−0.2425
5	−0.0409	0.0193	−0.2072	−0.2383	−0.0939	2.1981	1.2862

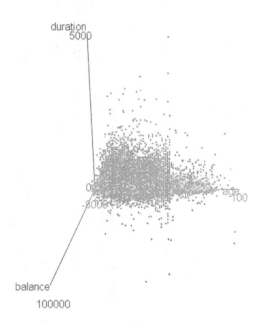

FIGURE 2.12   3D scatterplot for three variables.

- Target Variable – Default (Variable 5)
  - Area under the ROC curve for the rpart model on bankbook1 [validate] is 0.5000
  - Area under the ROC curve for the rf model on bankbook1 [validate] is 0.8506
  - Area under the ROC curve for the glm model on bankbook1 [validate] is 0.8727
  - Area under the ROC curve for the nnet model on bankbook1 [validate] is 0.4997

The variables' importance in the random forest model with two different targets-two different models is reviewed as follows. In the bivariate analysis (Table 2.7), a question appeared around segments related to balance and having or not having default for offering the term deposit. The model 1 uses as target the acceptance of promotion and default as explanatory. The second model uses the default as a target and promotion as explanatory. and using the first target as an explanatory variable in the second model. The most important variables in target 1 are related to the contact of the prospect customer (Table 2.17). Meanwhile, in the default analysis, the most important variables are related to balance and demographics (Table 2.18).

Now, observing with more detail and using the statistical significance in regression model (Tables 2.17 and 2.18), there are points to review. The comparison of the significant variables in each problem illustrates the variables' influence is dependent on the problem to solve. In the case of looking for profiles with different targets, some variables can be simultaneously significant but

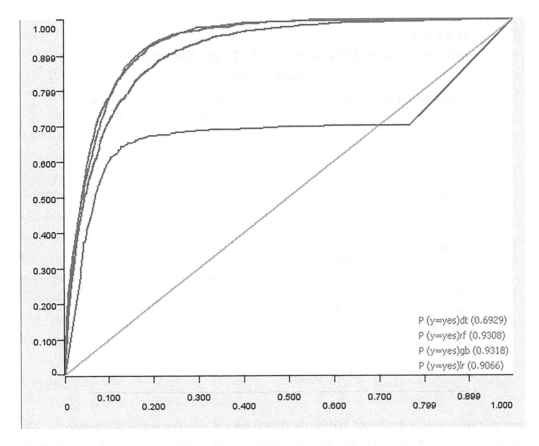

FIGURE 2.13 ROC curves for classification evaluation.

TABLE 2.17
Random Forest Model Outcome for the Target: Acceptance of the Term Deposit Promotion

| Variable Importance | | | | |
Variable Importance	no	yes	Mean Decrease Accuracy	Mean Decrease Gini
duration	149.4	261.14	258.55	1,152.05
month	96.38	27.86	101.54	473.8
contact	56.78	7.15	59.35	70.48
day	57.89	3.04	56.71	323.86
age	47.78	13.69	51.16	366.05
housing	42.13	22.08	48.55	74.54
poutcome	32.01	20.86	44.62	281.89
job	34.45	−7.69	28.24	269.2
pdays	23.84	25.32	27.54	170.21
campaign	17.94	11.17	21.69	145.61
previous	16.88	11.2	17.16	86.97
education	21.11	−3.64	16.81	99.47
marital	6.58	15.8	14.73	79.3
balance	8.64	11.65	13.64	390.4
loan	2.19	12.69	9.07	32.1
default	1.19	8.25	4.98	7.36

TABLE 2.18

Random Forest Model Outcome for the Target: Default or Not

Variable Importance				
Variable Importance	no	yes	Mean Decrease Accuracy	Mean Decrease Gini
balance	29.38	80.01	44.72	174.05
job	26.42	−1.13	25.66	59.26
age	23.35	−3.71	21.56	83.12
housing	20.64	1.53	21.01	12.44
education	22.2	−5.89	20.62	25.44
month	19.17	−1.33	19.42	31.98
day	16.21	−2.26	15.26	73.87
marital	11.87	−0.12	11.42	23.13
y	11.8	−2.42	11.34	4.94
loan	8.69	10.06	10.85	9.12
contact	8.86	0.69	9.01	12.97
duration	9.55	−2.68	8.65	113.81
campaign	9.06	−4.38	7.66	48.63
pdays	3.64	1.17	4.02	7.95
poutcome	3.37	0.11	3.52	2.5
previous	−1.32	2.18	−0.93	5.47

some as it is age that is significant to describe default but not to define potential acceptance of the term deposit in the promotion experiment. However, other variables as balance are significant in each target cases. Another aspect to review is that the variable default is not significant to describe variations in the acceptance of the term deposit promotion. Acceptance in the term deposit promotion is not significant to describe variation in default. This comparison introduces the issues of multiple goals that can be aligned or competing in the definition of action plans. Risk analytics is full of these competitive–conflict targets as it is the case of having less risk investing in the stock market when the companies are more stable while more uncertainty potentially can provide better return or provide higher losses as well in companies less stable (see portfolio model Section 5.8). Tables 2.19 and 2.20 represent the output–results of the models to identiify significant variables.

The combination of clusters and prediction is another step that provides clues of what data is telling to risk analysts. The target variable is multiclass defined using the clusters. The model provides a guide of variables that are related to the clusters segments that are a combination of variables and risk points. The error of the classification (confusion matrix Table 2.21) in each class is less than 10%, which is indicating a possible usable classification. Based on this error observation, the review of the importance of the variables in the model is the next step to perform. The importance of the variables is measured with two indicators: the mean decrease accuracy and the mean decrease Gini. The first one indicates that when the variables are dropped in the different generated trees the accuracy can be reduced. The second one is about the branch split using the Gini impurity index. The importance of the variables in each of the clusters-segments is a guide for selecting the attributes that can influence and belong to a cluster.

The difference with the previous models of classifying the binary variables is that the models were oriented to find variable realtionships to the target variables acceptance of the promotion and the possible default. In the case of the model using clusters is a combination where the used explanatory variables are all original and the clusters are associated with the variables. The values (Table 2.22) open the discussion about the segment that are with very important variables such as

TABLE 2.19

Significant Variables with Target Variable About Acceptance of Promotion in the Same Bank Data Set

Target Variable Acceptance Term Deposit

Target Acceptance of the Term Deposit	Coefficients:				
	Estimate	Std.error	z value	Pr(>|z|)	Significant
(Intercept)	−2.4825	0.220859	−11.24	0	***
job[T.blue-collar]	−0.36231	0.088116	−4.112	3.93E-05	***
job[T.entrepreneur]	−0.44142	0.151578	−2.912	0.003589	**
job[T.housemaid]	−0.50198	0.162349	−3.092	0.001988	**
job[T.management]	−0.18084	0.088621	−2.041	0.041294	*
job[T.self-employed]	−0.27734	0.133825	−2.072	0.038225	*
job[T.services]	−0.24308	0.101334	−2.399	0.016451	*
job[T.student]	0.422209	0.131637	3.207	0.00134	**
job[T.technician]	−0.1862	0.083023	−2.243	0.024916	*
marital[T.married]	−0.17254	0.071021	−2.429	0.015121	*
marital[T.single]	0.167155	0.080728	2.071	0.038396	*
education[T.tertiary]	0.327768	0.090081	3.639	0.000274	***
education[T.unknown]	0.282499	0.123767	2.283	0.022459	*
balance	1.29E-05	6.12E-06	2.101	0.035646	*
housing[T.yes]	−0.67132	0.052921	−12.685	0	***
loan[T.yes]	−0.44904	0.072306	−6.21	5.29E-10	***
contact[T.unknown]	−1.50361	0.086679	−17.347	0	***
day	0.009697	0.002998	3.234	0.00122	**
month[T.aug]	−0.60664	0.09381	−6.467	1.00E-10	***
month[T.dec]	0.773725	0.211531	3.658	0.000254	***
month[T.jan]	−1.29738	0.14792	−8.771	0	***
month[T.jul]	−0.83497	0.093843	−8.898	0	***
month[T.jun]	0.425247	0.1121	3.793	0.000149	***
month[T.mar]	1.648765	0.146573	11.249	0	***
month[T.may]	−0.4669	0.087633	−5.328	9.94E-08	***
month[T.nov]	−0.81007	0.100568	−8.055	7.95E-16	***
month[T.oct]	0.88768	0.131957	6.727	1.73E-11	***
month[T.sep]	0.765301	0.147798	5.178	2.24E-07	***
duration	0.004355	7.90E-05	55.087	0	***
campaign	−0.10002	0.012366	−8.088	6.07E-16	***
poutcome[T.other]	0.195532	0.108247	1.806	0.070863	.
poutcome[T.success]	2.295515	0.098428	23.322	0	***

Signif. codes. 0 (***) 0.001 (**) 0.01 (*) 0.05 (.) 0.1

duration, day, and campaign (clusters 1, 2, 3), while it is not the same in clusters 4 and 5 where campaign and pdays are the most important, respectively.

With this example, it has been illustrated multiple steps in an analytics road map. Classes can be two or many; the same as models to classify. The chapter reviewed the modeling process and the way that modeling is connected to risk management practice, the steps that are common to the ongoing modeling process. This chapter presented the illustration of the modeling process as part

TABLE 2.20

Significant Variables with Target Variable About Acceptance of Promotion in the Same Bank Data Set

Target Having or not Default	Target Variable Default or not Coefficients:				
	Estimate	Std.error	z value	pr(>|z|)	Significant
(Intercept)	−5.2576	0.6957	−7.557	0	***
age	−0.0148	0.0056	−2.624	0.0087	**
job[T.blue-coll	0.4221	0.1758	2.401	0.0164	*
job[T.entrepre	1.2677	0.224	5.659	0	***
job[T.managen	0.7245	0.2	3.622	0.0003	***
job[T.retired]	0.5993	0.2842	2.109	0.035	*
job[T.self-emp	0.7871	0.2644	2.977	0.0029	**
job[T.unemplo	0.875	0.2727	3.209	0.0013	**
marital[T.marri	−0.2982	0.1284	−2.323	0.0202	*
education[T.te	−0.4659	0.177	−2.632	0.0085	**
balance	−0.0023	0.0001	−22.323	0	***
housing[T.yes]	−0.4359	0.105	−4.152	0	***
loan[T.yes]	0.6107	0.0963	6.34	0	***
contact[T.unkn	0.3115	0.1502	2.074	0.0381	*
month[T.aug]	1.1355	0.43	2.641	0.0083	**
month[T.feb]	1.1814	0.4573	2.583	0.0098	**
month[T.jan]	0.9405	0.5247	1.792	0.0731	*
month[T.jul]	1.3734	0.4167	3.296	0.001	***
month[T.jun]	1.224	0.4429	2.764	0.0057	**
month[T.may]	1.0542	0.422	2.498	0.0125	*
month[T.nov]	1.8652	0.4307	4.331	0	***
pdays	0.0026	0.0014	1.908	0.0564	*
poutcome[T.un	1.3126	0.4431	2.963	0.003	**

Signif. codes: 0 (***) 0.001(**) 0.01(*) 0.05 '.' 0.1() 1

TABLE 2.21

Using the Clusters as Target Variables and Misclassification

Clusters	Confusion Matrix					
	1	2	3	4	5	Class.Error
1	11,275	57	24	5	42	0.0112
2	47	12,057	22	1	51	0.0099
3	49	61	2,356	6	40	0.0621
4	3	0	5	1,118	5	0.0115
5	19	26	17	0	4,361	0.0140

TABLE 2.22

Variables Data Set and Their Values Per Cluster

Cluster	Variables and Clusters					Mean Decrease Accuracy	Mean Decrease Gini
	1	2	3	4	5		
duration	281.54	299.35	422.12	29.14	71.98	402.89	2,103.49
day	743.89	707.4	50.77	49.03	43.68	748.05	6,077.24
campaign	141.68	201.98	32.24	377.9	21.48	289.09	1,116.14
balance	43.91	32.38	25.84	2.16	8.74	52.73	178.3
month	14.19	15.87	21.77	12.7	23.31	26.71	380.38
pdays	23.02	23.04	18.3	19.26	189.57	66.76	1,630.98
previous	19.24	21.47	14.08	17.73	23.56	27.02	1,016.82
poutcome	13.31	13.18	11.72	17	16.28	18.13	795.82
contact	11.22	13.09	9.68	7.63	7.17	16.58	52.62
housing	11.48	12.96	7.96	5.54	15.56	20.18	37.9
y	11.22	15.71	7.75	14.45	7.59	20.89	157.74
age	37.06	35.15	6.93	6.14	7.51	46.2	132.77
job	9.22	10.78	6.34	5.25	8.63	16.1	98.29
loan	1.83	6.24	4.66	4.08	6.83	9.86	12.17
education	6.77	7.5	3.22	3.35	5.37	10.51	35.45
default	0.24	−0.95	1.22	−2.07	3.74	0.45	3.19
marital	10.13	6.39	−1.8	2.73	2.24	9.48	26.71

of the risk management subprocesses. The development of the modeling process is not only on the quantitative side, but also requires the conceptualization and qualitative models to understand how to deal with uncertainty to make decisions. The process of creating value from data is in risk analytics the core of the process to produce actionable knowledge. There is a variety of risks, different in the essence of the type of knowledge domains and contexts but all of them with similar steps that are leading the creation of risk analytics systems that help organizations.

Chapters 3 and 4 will present a metrics definition. In general, risk analytics is building metrics and studying their development. Chapter 3 connects the risk analytics process and the decision-making process using benchmarking of the organization. Metrics in an organization are not only on the financial side but some of the quantitative aspects are financial related. The chapter indicates how risk indicators' benchmark can be a powerful tool to identify where the organization vulnerabilities and opportunities are. The main points in the following chapters are about decision making under uncertainty and risk. The chapter indicates how measurement in management is a fundamental process to move in the direction of controlling and mitigating risk. Organizations are looking to achieve goals. Goals are the output of measurement systems and data analytics results is about the variation of expected results (associated with performance and risk) and the losses that can come from adverse events that affect the organization.

TABLE 2.22

Variables Data Set and Initial Values Per Cluster

3 Decision Making Under Risk and Its Analytics Support

In the previous chapter, the main topic was how to connect a risk analytics process and a risk management process with special consideration given to the risk modeling process. At the same time, the concept of measurement and metrics development were fundamental to understand what a RAS could be. This chapter is about the use of general metrics and methods for supporting decisions. Metrics in this chapter are descriptive in nature. Metrics are indicators of risk that can be the first approach to understand and deal with risk in the organization. The examples presented supplement the general review of how the analytics process and the risk management process are connected. Descriptive risk analytics is going beyond data visualization and exploratory data analysis (EDA). Descriptive risk metrics development is more about the rationale to build risk metrics and indicators. There are many possible ratios/rates of change to use or combination of variables to use as risk indicators, but the risk analytics process should define not only rates/rations but also models or a combination (multivariate approach) of those ratios that are the best to use and the ones that are worth having.

Curtis J. (2020) expressed the actuaries (as it was mentioned before risk analytics professionals) and the perspective of actuaries participating more in the business definition, decision-making process. The indication is that actuaries will not just work on prediction, they need to work more on what to do with the outcomes of the risk analytics modeling process. "As more data becomes available and as machines become more adept at identifying trends and performing analyses, actuaries are likely to see their roles change. Employers such as insurance companies will probably look to actuaries less often for the more routine computations needed in common product offerings, pricings, and reserving calculations. Instead, future employers will look to actuaries for more strategic analysis and help answering questions such as:

- How can the data be used to create new, meaningful risk groups?
- What is the business case and financial impact of using the data to deliver products in new ways?
- To what extent can an insurer use the new technology to predict and alter future behaviors?
- What societal and financial impact would such ability to alter future behaviors have on the insurer, the insured and other key parties?"

This view of actuaries and according to the maturity level of data analytics in organizations the trend is applicable to more risk analysts. They are going to be involved in risk analytics for decision making, for providing actionable knowledge, implementation, and deployment of solutions. With that perspective in mind, the first topic in the chapter is to frame the general metrics development about basic methods/tools of decision making; the second topic is about general risk metrics used and its benchmark; the third topic is about comparing results of the metrics, means, and variances in different groups, products, regions; and the fourth topic is dealing with multiple decisions and how to forecast possible results.

3.1 ABOUT GENERAL TOOLS FOR SUPPORTING DECISION MAKING

This review starts with the concepts of controlling projects. Transformation of organizations from functions based on projects oriented where several and diverse resources are part of the reality in management to operate organizations. Risks are present in projects the same as in functional areas.

DOI: 10.1201/9780429342899-4

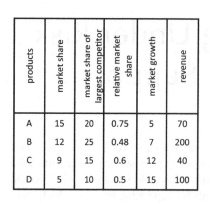

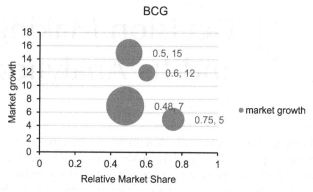

products	market share	market share of largest competitor	relative market share	market growth	revenue
A	15	20	0.75	5	70
B	12	25	0.48	7	200
C	9	15	0.6	12	40
D	5	10	0.5	15	100

FIGURE 3.1   Representation of three KPIs.

Risk in projects will connect directly results in multiple functional areas involved in the project. The qualitative tools are in general guidelines to the use of quantitative results. These qualitative tools are linked to the risk analytics subprocess of developing a benchmarking approach that indicates what are appropriate levels of indicators according to industries. The main idea is to clarify what a metric is and how to build it. Furthermore, multiple decisions will use a variety of metrics and the complexity to overcome will be in how the develop the methods to combine decisions that in some cases can have contradictory outcomes or they are not possible to achieve simultaneously. The BCG (Boston Consulting Group) model helps to compare specific key performance indicators (KPIs); for example, relative market share versus market growth and revenue (Figure 3.1) where the size of the circle is the revenue amount. In terms of risk analytics, the use of historical data is a way of obtaining more knowledge, comparing changes in each of the variables per each of the products (A,B,C,D) or companies (tables below are based on the contributions to strategy analysis of Boston Consulting Group, General Electric, Dupont, McKinsey, Arthur D. Little).

The changes of location and using an absolute value of the change in the review as a measure of magnitude gives a different view of the products or companies. A change in a competitive position is strategic risk (Figure 3.2). The capacity for organizations to adapt them to a new business environment is a matter of controlling variation of expected results. The metrics used can be many in terms of defining the best for specific problems: growth, losses, turnover, churn, etc. but the surrounding analytics work is similar. Data care and its organization, modeling risk care-control, and creation of indicators time series are common to all metrics and their implementation for supporting decision-making processes.

Several qualitative models are developed to understand how to make decisions based on a combination of factors. The mainstream of these models has been to connect competitiveness and

Change relative market share	Change market growth	Change revenue
0.013	-0.667	0.0769
0.036	0.125	0.0526
-0.200	-0.091	0.1429
0.167	-0.500	0.0526

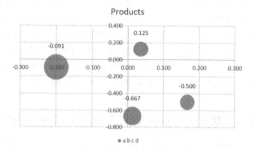

FIGURE 3.2   Changes in the KPIs.

TABLE 3.1

Building the Matrix of Market Attractiveness and Competitiveness Used for Business Units or for Programs or Groups of Products (Arthur D. Little, McKinsey, BCG, GE)

Attractiveness	Weight	Score	Weighted score
size	15	4	0.6
growth	12	3	0.36
pricing policy	5	3	0.15
market diversification	5	2	0.1
competitive structure	5	3	0.15
return of the industry	20	3	0.6
technical role	5	4	0.2
inflation threat	5	2	0.1
cycles	5	2	0.1
strength finances	10	5	0.5
energy impact	8	4	0.32
human resources	5	4	0.2
	100		3.38
Competitiveness	**Weight**	**Score**	**Weighted Score**
market share	10	5	0.5
growth rate	5	3	0.15
line products depth	5	4	0.2
distribution	10	4	0.4
Innovation	5	3	0.15
prices	5	5	0.25
communication	15	3	0.45
location	10	2	0.2
capacity/productivity	10	4	0.4
experience	15	4	0.6
cost control	5	2	0.1
quality	5	3	0.15
	100		3.55

market attractiveness. The issues related to risk analytics are connected to the evaluation of the variation of the performance indicators, the metrics used, the identification of the importance of the factors to use, and so on. Risk analytics aims to identify how certain factors affect performance, the targets, and goals variations according to risk indicators or factors that can describe risks. Table 3.1 shows some items/variables that are found in management literature as qualitative models. The risk analytics view recommends testing if this type of factors on others are creating value in what attractiveness and competitiveness will be for the organization.

The identification of qualitative and quantitative models has in common the identification of classes or categories to link them and actions/decisions to make. As it was explained in the previous chapter, the classes definition of the target variables will be an important decision to make because it is the problem definition in a specific, concrete, and precise way. Associated with the identification of these classes or categories is the concept of a strategy to develop. Depending on the goals, a strategy will be defined. In general, in risk analytics the use of KPIs (key performance indicators) and KRIs (key risk indicators) has several facets: first, the identification of groups, classes, and categories in the factors used to define the strategy matrices. A strategy matrix is a combination of factors such as attractiveness and capabilities-competitiveness. A second aspect is related to the definition of factors to evaluate and compare the way to obtain the scores. These factors should be associated with a type of event: bankruptcy, business failure, high performance, and so on. The use of regressions or tools for variable relationships identification could help to clarify the factors that influence the events. Tables 3.2, 3.3, and 3.4 are examples of categories used and the cut-offs of the categories an analytics works to perform, the same as the identification of the components of the items that are included on Table 3.1.

The variation and combination of variables is indicating actions to take/decisions to make. The spectrum of the scales needs clear definition and evaluation to identify where the organization's efforts can provide value added to the stakeholders. The issue of identifying cause-effect in

TABLE 3.2

Matrix Market Attractiveness and Business Position (McKinsey, GE Matrix)

Market Attractiveness/ Business Position	High	Medium	Low
High	Invest/grow	Invest/grow	Selective investment
Medium	Invest/grow	Selective investment	Harvest/divest
Low	Selective investment	Harvest/divest	Harvest/divest

TABLE 3.3

Strategic Actions Related to Combine Markets and Products (Ansoff Matrix)

		Products	
		current	new
markets	current	penetration	product development
	new	market development	diversification

TABLE 3.4

Factors Affecting Attractiveness of Industries

- Growth
- Efficiency/productivity
- Resources use
- Return to shareholders
- Customer's return
- Employee's return
- Society's return
- Sales dollars and units
- Profits to sales
- ROI, ROA, EPS, Market Cap ...
- Levels of quality
- Salaries/stability
- Taxes paid
- Control

- Geographical extension
- Markets and segments
- Product lines
- Distribution channels
- Service
- Prices
- Credit
- Promotion/advertisement
- Brands
- Production/operation
- R&D
- Product design
- HR and talent
- Organizational structure

categorical models can be approached, indicating the effects of the factors and actions presented in the matrices. Table 3.2 leads to connecting for example high market attractiveness and high business position with the action of investing and pushing the company to grow. Table 3.3 indicates the combination of new products and new markets is a diversification strategy. Possibly there is a correlation, or there are ways to expect certain results, but in risk analytics the cause-effect requires at least to start with the influence diagrams and to evaluate correlations with results, variability measures, etc.

In the creation of a decision-making process, the identification of goals is crucial and they are the targets for evaluation of models in general and reference to measure the variation of results (risk) in organizations. Objectives as metrics require the attribute identification to be clear and specific in their formulation. Attributes like dimension, scales, ranges, periodicity, etc. define where the objective and its metrics are determined and identified. The objectives and metrics are based on what previous knowledge is showing about results; this means a goal can be with a connection of time series analysis, results in industry benchmark, with the addition or reduction of the values based on the organization's experience. These goals have to be real-achievable in a time window forecast. This means with a definition of confidence intervals where the values of the goal can be or in practice to be achievable in a time frame. The end the purpose, in terms of risk analytics of measurement, is to guide the path to increase the probability of achieve results closer to where the expected values of the goals are.

Decision making is related to the balanced scorecard (BSC) definition where the four factors considered need to be aligned to a strategy and its implementation: benefits or financial results, operations or processes, people or talent development, and customers or users or stakeholders. All four factor categories require definitions of metrics and indicators and the evaluation of aspects such as presented in Table 3.4.

These items in Table 3.4 are examples of variables that in risk analytics data will be sources to assess and mitigate changes in the final performance evaluation of the organizations. Similar lists are the input to understand how to implement the process of a SWOT analysis: strengths, weaknesses, opportunities, and threats. These four categories of potential events and attributes are defined as the way that differentiate the organization and to adapt the organization to new competitive and risk conditions. For example, to have a network of ATMs in a bank in the 80s could be a strength; it was only for a limited time, after some years the ATM network was part of the business model and definition of banking, a generic attribute across the industry. If the entity did not have ATMs, it was a possible threat because an opportunity is for a time frame or in market for limited circumstances. Nowadays, organizations' digital transformation is a priority; efficiency is on the one hand a goal but on the other hand it can be a limitation to maintain the organization in a good performance level because products and services can be substituted by blockchain, data products, automation in several areas, and a combination of human and machine interaction. Organizations have at the same time SWOT factors; however, it is in the hands of the organization the capabilities development to obtain adaptive competitive advantages. The risk analytics process, monitoring risk and finding where the highest losses/effects can be, is a way to guide the decision maker to define where to allocate resources and push and pull actions.

A good example is the analysis of portfolios applied to multiple areas of organizations (see the optimization model in Chapter 9). There are portfolios, such as:

- Product portfolio
- Business units portfolio
- Market portfolio
- Promotion portfolio
- People portfolio
- Investment portfolio

TABLE 3.5
Portfolio of Products (BCG Matrix)

Relative Market Share vs. Market Growth Rate	High	Low
High	Star Products	Question products
Low	Cash Cows	Dogs

These portfolios are looking for gaining the best return on the investments or the best revenue structure knowing that the reduction of variability of results (risk) has to be minimized. In a product portfolio (BCG Table 3.5), the concept is that products with different market growth and different market share require different resources of the organization and at the same time generate different benefits to the organization. This means qualitative models support the search of cause and effect as it could be that oriented actions are according to situations as a portfolio of products that are having low market share and low growth can be important to keep because of branding.

Again, classification is a matter of risk analytics because the criteria to classify and to define classes will be the first step to start to clarify where actions should be. After classification, the evaluation and time series analysis will show where the expected results will be for the organization adaptation. In the same way, simulations will provide the possible results in metrics that an organization wants to control.

Another aspect to keep in mind related to decision making is the definition of indicators of risk that are possible to find in projects. Furthermore, in terms of tools and strategy implementation and decision making in risk analytics, the projects are under uncertainty and it is required to evaluate risks in the execution of a project. Projects are ways to organize work and risks are related to time of completion, costs related to the project development, resources used, etc. The variation of the expected results in achieving the goals of projects is what is required to study in risk analytics. This is an example (Table 3.6) to review project risks.

The approach reviewing the activities time required to estimate the expected time of completing of the activities and then to use the calculation of the sequence of actions in the network to define the best path to complete the project. The expected time calculation uses the beta distribution presentation as PERT distribution and triangular distribution. For these two distributions, the parameters to define are:

- Optimistic time – time that assume that the project will not have development issues
- Pessimistic time – time that includes a stress test of complex circumstances to complete the project
- Most likely time – according to the experiences. the experts estimate the time of completion

The beta function is the basis of the beta distribution that is providing the foundation of risk evaluation in project development:

$$B(\alpha, \beta) = \int_0^1 x^{\alpha-1}(1-x)^{\beta-1}dx = \frac{\Gamma(\alpha)\Gamma(\beta)}{\Gamma(\alpha+\beta)}, \quad \text{for } \alpha, \beta > 0.$$

TABLE 3.6

Summary of Data and Basic Calculations of Times of the Project in a Deterministic Approach

Project in Risk Analytics Weeks Time

Activity	Time	Activity description	Sequence
ip	2	Identify the problem	—
id	3	Identify data available	—
q	2	Review questions to answer	A
v	4	Identify variables to use	A, B
d	4	Select the required data	C
o	3	Organize/clean data	C
m	5	Test models to use	D, E
r	2	Review results	F, G

ACTIVITY	EARLIEST START ES	EARLIEST FINISH EF	LATEST START LS	LATEST FINISH LF	SLACK LS – ES	ON CRITICAL PATH
ip	0	2	0	2	0	Yes
id	0	3	1	4	1	No
q	2	4	2	4	0	Yes
v	3	7	4	8	1	No
d	4	8	4	8	0	Yes
o	4	7	10	13	6	No
m	8	13	8	13	0	Yes
r	13	15	13	15	0	Yes

The distribution has the mathematical formulation with parameters α and β with a random variable between 0 and 1 identifying mean and variance, as below:

$$f(x) = \begin{cases} \frac{1}{B(\alpha,\beta)} x^{\alpha-1} (1-x)^{\beta-1}, & 0 < x < 1, \\ 0, & \text{elsewhere.} \end{cases}$$

$$\mu = \frac{\alpha}{\alpha+\beta}$$

$$\sigma^2 = \frac{\alpha\beta}{(\alpha+\beta)^2(\alpha+\beta+1)}$$

The PERT distribution is a specific case of the beta distribution used for the project evaluation. In risk analytics, it is very important mainly when there is not enough data available and very good input for a Monte Carlo sSimulation. The mean and variance (Table 3.7) are given by

$$t = (a + 4m + b)/6$$

Variance of activity completion times:

$$v = [(b - a)/6]2$$

TABLE 3.7

Calculation of Expected Times and Variances in Each Activity

Time Estimates (in Weeks) for Milwaukee Paper's Project

ACTIVITY	OPTIMISTIC a	MOST LIKELY m	PESSIMISTIC b	EXPECTED TIME $t = (a + 4m + b)/6$	VARIANCE $[(b - a)/6]^2$
Ip	1	2	3	2	.11
Id	2	3	4	3	.11
Q	1	2	3	2	.11
V	2	4	6	4	.44
D	1	4	7	4	1.00
O	1	2	9	3	1.78
M	3	4	11	5	1.78
R	1	2	3	2	.11

and in the project case, they are the calculation of the project risk. See the details for PERT distribution in Vose (2000). A triangular distribution is similar to the PERT given the parameters definition. The PERT distribution is a way to smooth the triangular distribution. See Johnson (1997) for details about triangular and beta distribution relationship.

With this in mind, the calculation of the expected activity time and variance is:

$$\sigma_p^2 = \text{Project variance}$$

=Σ (variances of activities on critical path) the assumption is that each activity is independent from another, this means activities behave as independent random variables. If there is no independence, the covariance correction has to be included. The concept of a project is that a project takes the maximum time that an activity uses to perform as input to calculate the critical path or the slack time equal zero activities. However, once the beta (PERT) distribution is used, the assumption is that the parameters μ and σ are used as parameters for calculations under the assumption of time of completion normally distributed. This means the variance is calculated on the critical activities addition, the same as the expected time values. The expected time is for the critical activities ip, q, d, m, and r and summing the expected times the result is the expected time of the project.

What is the probability this project can be completed on or before any number of weeks deadline?

Z = (weeks deadline − expected time of completion)

/σₚ for example in the 16 weeks deadline the result is:

= (16 weeks − 15 weeks)/1.76

= 0.57

Once projects and general strategy are under a risk monitoring framework, a step to perform is benchmarking scoring. In that regard, in the following section, there is a presentation of creating scores of risk indicators or metrics based on what is observed in the industry indicators; this means a benchmark process with score definition for risk analysis.

3.2 BENCHMARK APPROACH FOR DEFINING METRICS

The purpose is to illustrate how with metrics and benchmark a risk analytics process will provide valuable components to build a risk analytics system (RAS). Descriptive risk analytics is the set of steps to build diagnostic metrics and basic risk assessment metrics. The main methods are based on identification of no-model based risk indicators and the way that these risk indicators can be compared to industries and behavioral metrics of organizations.

Risk indicators need to be aligned with the key performance indicators (KPI) and some of risk indicators will be converted into key risk indicators (KRI) (please review Chapter 8). A risk indicator should not be only financial but also it should be based on business processes. The main value of risk indicators is to provide guidelines to monitor risk behavior of the business factors.

The use of benchmarking for financial analysis is a controversial one; on the one hand there is an important value added to compare a company with its industry, and on the other hand it is difficult to avoid confusion for the company's classification as a bad or good performer or good or bad risk. In this section, there is an exploration of opportunities to use financial benchmarking as a risk quality indicator. It is possible to create scores and to define structural variables to review in risk management assessment. The use of the outcomes of a descriptive analysis will be related to the definition of risk levels and definition of classes in risk classification. A benchmarking system assigns a place for a company in its industry and then it is required to structure a system to create, validate, and use the score. In particular, benchmarking of risk indicators finds application in the development of strategic risk descriptive models.

In general, a method is based on the data source but it can be created using tables from sources such as Yahoo Finance, Market-watch, and Google finance, using the indicators reported in each case comparing values in each of the categories. It is possible to take the variables and to find relationships among risk indicators violations, variables used for benchmark scores, and variables in absolute values (ratios).

The first point to review in this type of descriptive analytics project is as mentioned in previous sections, data requirements, variables definition, issues in distribution (for example benchmark based on quartile comparison), structure definition, data integrity, and variable relationship to a claim/target event. In this specific system, there are points to consider for a correct treatment of negative ratios, quartile definitions, missing values treatment, age of financial statements, variable correlation, and scores calculation.

To illustrate some of the steps to develop a benchmark-descriptive analytics process, there are aspects that are important to review in detail (see Section 3.3 ahead). On the one hand, the definition of variables and ways to compare organizations is crucial. There is a need to define how the classes (as it was indicated in Chapter 2) will be organized the same as to identify the variables to describe the risk profiles. On the other hand, the presentation of how variables can be related to the target or event of interest. For instance, the analysis of the variable's contribution is provided with different approaches, such as logistic regression and decision trees methodologies. It has been identified that some of the principal attributes correlated with the claim event, using the logistic regression for scores, ratios, and using or not dummy variables to identify violation of thresholds.

As it has been stablished in the introduction and Chapter 2, the analytics process has meaning if the outcomes of the analysis are associated with the performance improvement of the organization. The association is based on the effect of the outcomes/classification/probabilities of events on approval rates, revenue strategy, and on the bottom line of the company's results. The analysis and report were classified by questions and in each one identified the issues and a possible answer for improvement. In summary, benchmarking provides evidence to be confirmed in posterior studies, present the methodological points to discover some of the variable relationships, issues to confirm, and impact to measure.

The creation of indicators has many steps to clarify the metric. The metrics need to be consistently well defined. The indicators are going to be time series and the wrong definition, changes, and lack of comparability can create issues in analysis. The first point to review is about assumptions and definitions used. The meaning of the variables, metrics definition, cleansing data by asking questions such as if negative values for variables are with meaning, if data is related to financial statements, if the age of the statements can affect the metrics, use or not ise weights of certain factors or the possible correlation of variables or redundancy in the use. For example, to use variables that are functions of others such as benefits can be a result of revenue and costs.

3.3   STEPS TO START THE DEFINITION OF METRICS

The first step is to review what is currently measured and how the current metrics were created. In this presentation, metrics are defined as scores. This means the metrics can be a combination of other factors to provide an output. After the identification of current metrics, a comparison of results is needed with and without changes introduced to the definition and assignation of scores or metrics. This means to review or recalculate scores under different conditions. Then, connect the metrics and the main events of a phenomenon that is expected to be measured. For example, to clarify the contribution of metrics on a realization of events that affect organization's performance (claims, default, loss of customers, etc.). In evaluation or target event that is based on claims, it could be appropriated to know about a variable combination of financial indicators of performance quality, such as negative loss, negative equity, rations, and general market related variables (e.g., market share).

A second step is about data selection and metrics:

The review of current metrics leads to build new ones based on using samples through time and using complete and clean data. For example, to answer if metrics use financial statements that are updated/audited at the measurement time. The time frame is a selected window for the observations and a clear point of reference in time to compare results. In the definition of metrics, it can be possible to have a reference variable (such as a score or a specific market) that can be part of the decision support system, goals, targets or optima identified/expected/desired. In the following steps, a financial indicator >0 is used. A financial indicator in this example is the input that can come from experts or from a model that gives a score of financial health in the organization. At the same time, one market can be predefined, knowing that the replication of the process can be performed for other cases. The numbers ahead are based on 31,068 risk units from one country market with 634 claims; under the condition of a financial indicator >0, the subset is counting 7,983 risk units and 149 claims. In the case of using all markets in this data set, there are 17,123 risk units with financial statements and financial indicator >0.

A third step is to review metrics and using benchmarking through the comparison with the industry using quantiles/quartiles of a metric common to the industry and then to review several metrics in integrated ways. The first step is to review the metrics individually in the market and then to review these metrics as a combination in a multivariate way. The following aspects are important to consider in the evaluation of benchmark using quartiles:

- Definition of how sectors are selected according to the SIC/NAICS industry classification. It is important to determine the level of desired granularity in the classification. In practical terms, it can be based on the data available. For example, a general two-digit aggregation of the industries to compare with the economic sector can be appropriate.
- In terms of building risk indicators, it is possible to use a score defined as a ratio of quartile values and an accepted minimum of the value of a financial ratio according to the risk policies. The changes in the minimum accepted will modify the number of customer/ transactions that can go through the next steps in a business process. The expressions below show the quartiles ratios (Q_i represents the quartile i) and the minimum LL accepted. The LL value is a calculation as the average of the distance between the third and second weighted quartile. The general expression will take values that are calculated and presented as follows, where ratios are pre-calculated values used as risk indicators and a number-score assigned using the position in the benchmark (relative position) of the risk unit and its industry (Table 3.8).

TABLE 3.8

Definition of Scores Based on Quartiles Position for Risk Indicators

Quartiles and scale	Assigned Score	Financial Ratio Value Bound That Defines the Score and are Thresholds Provided by the Organization and Its Experience and Policies		
		Quartile Value and Scale	**Quick and Current Ratio**	**Other Financial Ratios**
Above Upper Quartile	1	Upper quartile ($Q1$)	2	2
Between Upper quartile and Median	2	Median($Q2$)	1.5	1.5
Between the Median and the Mid-Lower = Average of the Median and the lower quartile	3	Mid-Lower Level	1.25	1.25
Between Mid-Lower and the Lower Quartile	4	Lower Quartile ($Q3$)	1	1
Between Lower quartile and Lower-Lower Level (LL) = average of b times lower quartile and median	5	Lower- Lower Level	0.375	0.75
Below Lower-Lower level	6			

The procedure to assign the scores based on the benchmark is sensitivite to the way that the scales are defined. For example, the scale can be only based on quartiles/quantiles or as it is in this presentation, using the estimation of new scale points based on a rule defined by a risk analyst.

$$\frac{|Q_3(low) - LL|}{|Median - LL|} = 0.33$$

$$\frac{|Q_3 - 0.1|}{|Q_2 - 0.1|} = 0.375$$

$$\frac{\left|Q_3(low) - \frac{bQ_3 - Q_2}{2}\right|}{\left|Q_2 - \frac{bQ_3 - Q_2}{2}\right|} = 0.375$$

This means the selection of the transactions/customers/risk units according to the risk indicators, for example the level of current or quick ratios will depend on the value b that the organizations decide to use (a level of risk tolerance). In this illustration, the number b is 2.8. This number shows us the possible new definition of LL. The sensitivity to the changes of the indicators calculation and use is a step of continuous evaluation for example the data set used to modify the metric produced important changes in the risk units that were accepted in the portfolio through a univariate filter of the benchmarks. The total number of risk units that can be accepted is modified as in Table 3.9 is indicated.

Thresholds are numbers defining the rules for controlling risk conditions (Table 3.10). The system starts with initial values and the experience will indicate the way to calibrate the cut-offs based on the risk appetite and markets condition. A threshold is a variable in time and the number of risk units that are accepted out of a range of possible risk results. This modification of the calculation increases the number of risk units in different risk class and at the same time the new risk units can possibly increase the overall risk level of the portfolio. Additionally, it is possible to provide the scale changes can be using the values of the quartiles through time and managing the average as the threshold for defining the scales.

A fourth step is working with calibration of thresholds using a predefined probability of the events that are expected to have in certain limits. For example, the risk units will not be accepted if

TABLE 3.9
Lower Levels Definition Per Risk Indicators

Financial Ratio	Changes using the new Lower- Lower level (LL) definition Using financial statements less than a year		
	Original risk units with score 6	Percentage of risk units with score 6	New additions to 5 score (from the ones classified in score 6) because of changes in the metric and LL definition
Sales to total assets (S/TA)	732	57	148
Profits to total assets (P/TA)	401	71	185
Total liabilities to total net-worth (TL/TNW)	539	71	259
Quick ratio (QR)	102	70	3
Current ration (CR)	23	87	0

TABLE 3.10
Different Thresholds and Specific Scores at Violation

Type	Name of the Risk Indicator/Threshold	Score at Violation
Risk Indicators directly from financial statements	Net Loss (pre or after tax)	
	Negative equity	
	Quick ratio	6
	Current ratio	6
	Operating loss	
	Fin indicator that is calculated	>5
Risk indicators that can be predefined and precalculated	Credit rating	6
	Bank rating	5, 6
	Exporter payment experience	5, 6
	Legal/labor	5, 6
	Payment rating	5, 6
	Trade experience	6
	Supplier payment history	5, 6
	Management experience clear	6
	Record clear (business reputation clear)	6

there is not a score within the specification 1.50 ± d, d as tolerance or accepted deviation. For answering a question like this, it is required to have more information about the distribution of the scores. If the assumption is normality and a value 1.5 is the mean and there is standard deviation of 0.2, to find a d that is providing acceptance of the risk units 95% of the case the solution could be: that in $N(01)$, $P(-1.96 < Z < 1.96) = 0.95$. The equation of the transformation is $1.96 = (1.50 + d) - 1.50/0.2$ and $d = (0.2)(1.96) = 0.392$. The values where the filter will be are 1.108 and 1.892.

A fifth step, is to consider in the definition of metrics and evaluation based on benchmark is the possibility of taking negative values by the metric. This is the case of the relationship between a negative operation profit-loss and the way that it affects a financial ratio as profit/total assets. One decision from the risk analyst is to consider some indicators with negative values with minimum scores or not acceptable. This is the case when TNW and working capital are negative and then the scores assigned for the ratios net profit/TNW, sales/working capital and TL/TNW can be directly assigned as the lowest in the scale. The other approach is that for a negative profit (operating loss), negative ratio, or financial data very old it is better to use a historical data to assign a score. Historical data for each ratio is available and it is available for previous years, in each quartile. A five-year average for each quartile can be used and to re-calculate the medium-lower and lower-lower values, using the average results and to compare the actual data with this new scale. After this step, a score is determined with the same methodology.

Furthermore, to consider in the creation of risk metrics is that possibly a benchmark in a market cannot take into consideration the good companies that can be in a highly competitive industry with high-performance players. The risk for the company could be not to be alarmed, but the company can get a bad score because the company does not have a high-performance level in the industry. This means it is necessary to obtain a new scale to assign a fair score. In the same way, there are cases with a very bad industry and the company looks good in that industry, but this company itself has a poor result and a risk level that is critical. The process of a benchmark rating can identify companies as good in a bad industry; however, these risk units could continue being a bad risk and it creates a potential riskier environment and anti-selection.

The way to manage the benchmark issue because of relative position of a company in a good or bad industry: first, to consider the historical data of the industry, second to introduce an evaluation of the company itself independently of the industry, and third consider the benchmark with the industry using other variables and creating clusters of companies (Section 3.4). A regression of the values in the variables of interest can help to guide comparisons of companies. Another approach for evaluating the metric is including new variables such as growth rate of the industry compared with the growth of the company to identify a company trend. More strategic variables can be included, growth is appropriate to consider, because it is related to market share and economies of scale and scope. The company will be a-priori good when its general growth is bigger than the industry growth and the ratio is positive, and bad when the company has a lower growth than the industry and a negative ratio.

Figure 3.3 shows how the adjustments of the quartiles method can be improved if the companies are in good and bad markets just using the average of historical quartile data points by categories/classes of good and bad performance industries.

The final step to review is about possible issues in defining a risk indicator metric based on financial statements or financial data that can be related to missing values and age of the data available. Methods of statistical imputation can be used for solving missing data, in general historical average can be an option of the variance is not very high. Regarding the age of the financial statements or data sources for evaluating the risk units, there is a need of having the scores based on current financial statements and to avoid providing scores if they are not compared to the benchmark quartile at the time when the financial statements of the risk units are.

3.4 CREATING CLUSTERS OF COMPANIES BASED ON THEIR RETURNS

Benchmarking using quartiles for risk indicators is a powerful method; however, it is a univariate method of comparison. A suggested method that supplements the univariate vision of benchmarking can be clustering based on certain selected variables. For example, it could be the return of the stocks or return on investment or on assets or using any other risk indicator. In risk analytics, a priority action is the understanding of strategies, the qualitative data that is available to understand what is happening in the market, and how the companies are reaching goals of return. Strategy results are expressed with prices and returns in the stock market behavior. The concept of strategic groups is crucial to define where to go and with whom to compete in a market. However, when the risk is the attribute to observe to define/study a behavior of portfolios can be or how companies are expected to get certain results, a clustering process of companies based on return can help to define investment portfolios. This example shows 58 companies in a period of time with 296 data points in the time window and shows a hierarchical clustering process indicating the final set of clusters that in the companies can exist. The

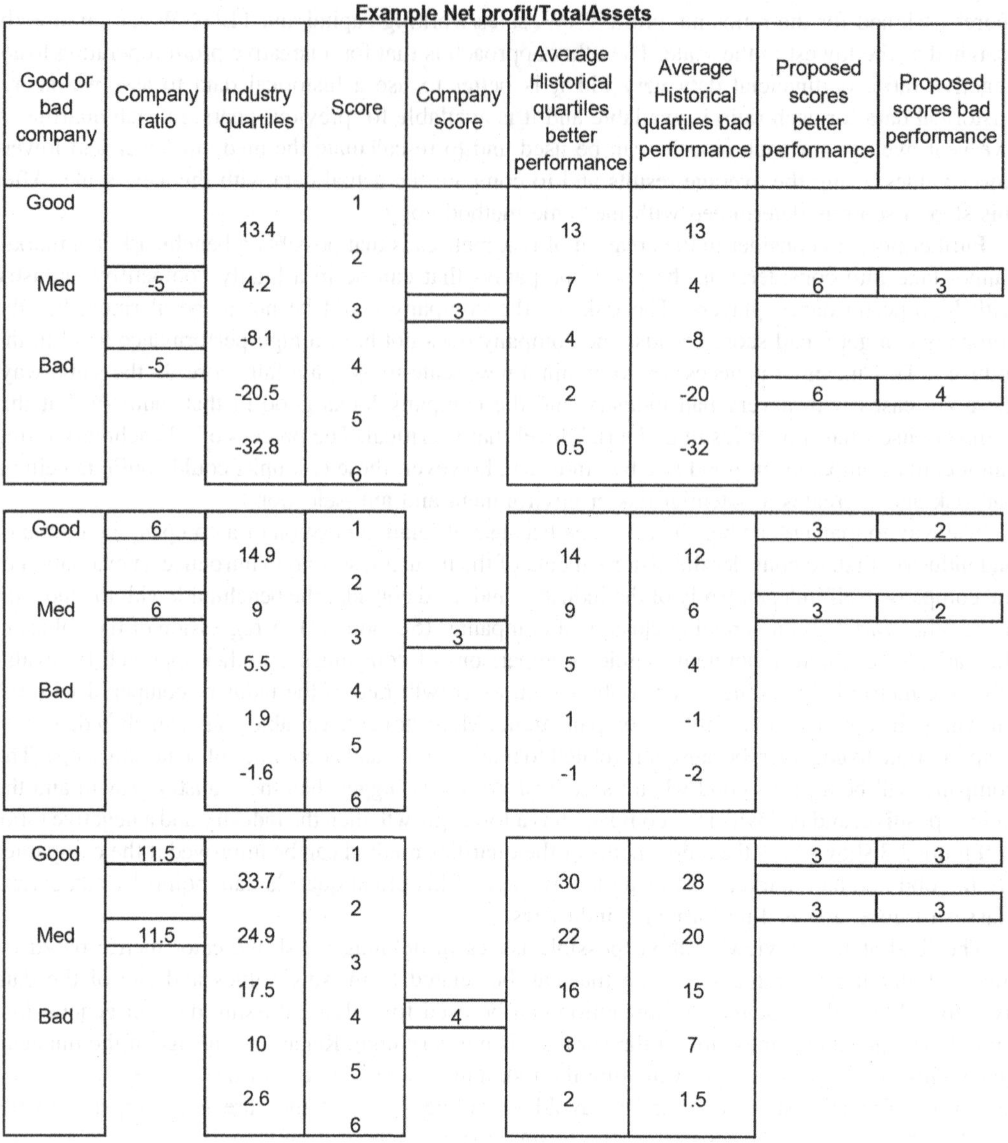

Example Net profit/TotalAssets

Good or bad company	Company ratio	Industry quartiles	Score	Company score	Average Historical quartiles better performance	Average Historical quartiles bad performance	Proposed scores better performance	Proposed scores bad performance
Good		13.4	1		13	13		
			2					
Med	-5	4.2			7	4	6	3
			3	3				
		-8.1			4	-8		
Bad	-5		4					
		-20.5			2	-20	6	4
			5					
		-32.8			0.5	-32		
			6					
Good	6	14.9	1		14	12	3	2
			2					
Med	6	9			9	6	3	2
			3	3				
		5.5			5	4		
Bad			4					
		1.9			1	-1		
			5					
		-1.6			-1	-2		
			6					
Good	11.5	33.7	1		30	28	3	3
			2				3	3
Med	11.5	24.9			22	20		
			3					
		17.5			16	15		
Bad			4	4				
		10			8	7		
			5					
		2.6			2	1.5		
			6					

FIGURE 3.3 Risk indicators and scores based on historical quartiles of company and industry.

clustering procedure here is on the variables (companies) and the data points are return values in the period of observation (in Chapters 5 and 7 there are details about return analysis and the foundations of clustering). The results help to identify for an investor what companies can have similar behaviors in return even though they are not in the same industry.

Clustering algorithm converged.

As Table 3.11 indicates, seven clusters have a maximum of 13 sample points-companies and a minimum of 4. None is showing a possible outlier behavior. Clusters 3, 4, and 5 are with the same number of members. One example to review is cluster 5, where members are retail companies. Clusters 3 and 6 are composed of companies in the pharmaceutical and food industries, respectively. Other clusters are a mix of companies in different sectors. Cluster 4 is special because it includes technology companies and a company in the energy business (oil). Table 3.12 represents the clusters members by companies as variables and defining the groups of comparables organizations.

TABLE 3.11

All Clusters for Variables = Companies for Historical Return –
Stock Market data

Cluster Summary for 7 Clusters

Cluster	Members	Cluster Variation	Variation Explained	Proportion Explained	Second Eigenvalue
1	10	10	5.33974	0.5340	0.7834
2	13	13	6.340436	0.4877	0.8544
3	7	7	3.558656	0.5084	0.7702
4	7	7	3.811006	0.5444	0.8065
5	7	7	4.354941	0.6221	0.7792
6	10	10	4.736225	0.4736	0.9680
7	4	4	2.498407	0.6246	0.6982

TABLE 3.12

Cluster by Variables – Companies Show Similarities Among
the Groups

7 Clusters		R-squared with		1-R**2 Ratio
Cluster	Variable	Own Cluster	Next Closest	
Cluster 1	3m	0.5089	0.3335	0.7369
	avon	0.3499	0.1876	0.8003
	goodrich	0.6194	0.3581	0.5928
	goodyear	0.4075	0.3095	0.8581
	honeywell	0.5950	0.3548	0.6277
	itt	0.6880	0.3913	0.5126
	lockheed	0.3923	0.2268	0.7860
	nike	0.4749	0.3297	0.7834
	rockwell	0.6275	0.3747	0.5958
	unitedtech	0.6765	0.4260	0.5636
Cluster 2	Generalmotors	0.4188	0.2729	0.7994
	harley	0.4966	0.2962	0.7153
	jpmorgan	0.6945	0.4535	0.5590
	marriot	0.4890	0.3624	0.8016
	mattel	0.3851	0.3040	0.8835
	officedep	0.4907	0.3029	0.7306
	officemax	0.5479	0.3897	0.7408
	sherwin	0.4762	0.3583	0.8162
	southwest	0.4146	0.2347	0.7649
	staples	0.5914	0.4886	0.7990
	supervalu	0.2185	0.1433	0.9122
	tjx	0.5460	0.4370	0.8064
	unitedparcel	0.5712	0.4047	0.7203
Cluster 3	abbot	0.5434	0.3157	0.6673
	baxter	0.4709	0.2272	0.6847

(Continued)

TABLE 3.12 *(Continued)*
Cluster by Variables – Companies Show Similarities Among the Groups

7 Clusters		R-squared with		1-R**2 Ratio
Cluster	Variable	Own Cluster	Next Closest	
	hershey	0.4680	0.2829	0.7419
	j&J	0.5763	0.3776	0.6806
	mckesson	0.4061	0.2570	0.7993
	pfizer	0.6621	0.4354	0.5984
	schering	0.4319	0.2181	0.7266
Cluster 4	halliburton	0.5492	0.2775	0.6240
	motorola	0.3242	0.1558	0.8006
	nucor	0.6358	0.4095	0.6167
	occidental	0.6627	0.3241	0.4989
	smurfith	0.4159	0.2885	0.8210
	sunoco	0.5881	0.2823	0.5739
	unitedsteel	0.6351	0.4383	0.6496
Cluster 5	barnes	0.3516	0.2086	0.8193
	jcpenney	0.7053	0.4381	0.5244
	kohl	0.7575	0.4217	0.4194
	lowe	0.6400	0.5184	0.7475
	nordstrom	0.6574	0.4496	0.6225
	ross	0.6034	0.4959	0.7868
	target	0.6397	0.4112	0.6119
Cluster 6	generalmills	0.5131	0.3590	0.7595
	kellogs	0.5408	0.2997	0.6558
	kimberly	0.4701	0.3466	0.8111
	kroger	0.4848	0.3550	0.7988
	pepsico	0.5270	0.3389	0.7154
	procter	0.5551	0.2943	0.6305
	reynolds	0.4126	0.2658	0.8001
	safeway	0.4495	0.2856	0.7705
	sprint	0.2758	0.1384	0.8406
	verizon	0.5074	0.3317	0.7370
Cluster 7	hewlett	0.6658	0.3602	0.5224
	ibm	0.7083	0.3450	0.4454
	intel	0.6869	0.3312	0.4681
	liberty	0.4374	0.2951	0.7981

Figure 3.4 shows the dendrogram that is the tree representation of the clusters and each of the branches shows the selection of the companies belonging to the cluster.

The R code in Exhibit 3.1 illustrates the use of the package quantmod and it is possible to get the time series of the stock prices and to obtain the summary statistics and main charts showing the price changes over time along with the same as volume (Figures 3.5, 3.6, and 3.9) and the graphics of the returns (Figures 3.7, 3.8, and 3.10). These three companies in the same industry sector experienced different levels of volatility. The prices in INTC where growth and during

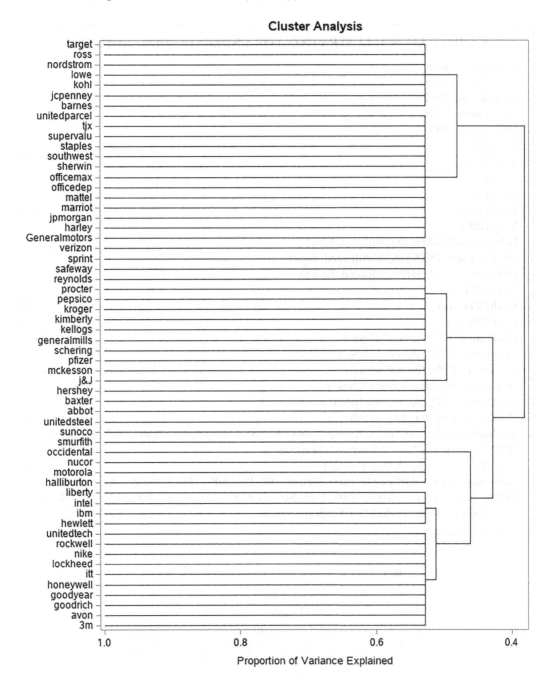

FIGURE 3.4   Dendrogram showing the companies grouping for returns.

the last months volatility was higher, IBM the prices move up and down with high volatility during the whole observation period, and HPE the price behavior were similar to IBM and volatility with high variations in the observation period as well; however, the transaction volume in IBM and HPE were not having similar results. IBM had higher picks during the last periods and HPE had steadier transaction results.

EXHIBIT 3.1   R ILLUSTRATION FOR UNDERSTANDING RETURNS

```
library(quantmod)
library(fBasics)
getSymbols('IBM')
getSymbols('INTC')
getSymbols('HPE')
dim(IBM)
dim(INTC)
dim(HPE)
head(IBM)
head(INTC)
head(HPE)
IBM.rtn=diff(IBM$IBM.Adjusted, lag=1)
INTC.rtn=diff(INTC$INTC.Adjusted, lag=1)
HPE.rtn=diff(HPE$HPE.Adjusted, lag=1)
head(IBM.rtn)
head(INTC.rtn)
head(HPE.rtn)
chartSeries(IBM, theme='white')
chartSeries(INTC, theme='white')
chartSeries(HPE, theme='white')
chartSeries(IBM.rtn, theme='white')
chartSeries(INTC.rtn, theme='white')
chartSeries(HPE.rtn, theme='white')
numSummary(ibmintc[,"IBM.Adjusted", drop=FALSE], statistics=c("mean", "sd", "se(mean)",
"IQR", "quantiles", "cv", "skewness", "kurtosis"),
quantiles=c(0,.25,.5,.75,1), type="2")
mean sd se(mean) IQR cv skewness kurtosis 0% 25% 50% 75% 100% n NA
0.01969505 1.527857 0.02480798 1.451546 77.5757 −0.8319563 9.661331 −13.24834
−0.685669 0.045105 0.765877 10.15506 3793 1
```

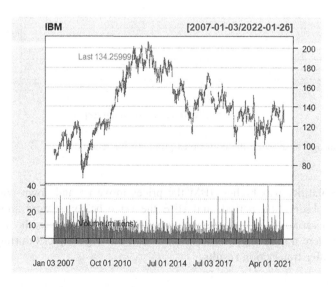

FIGURE 3.5   Stock prices IBM and volume 14 years.

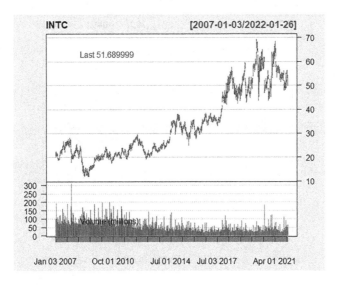

FIGURE 3.6 Stock prices INTC and volume 14 years.

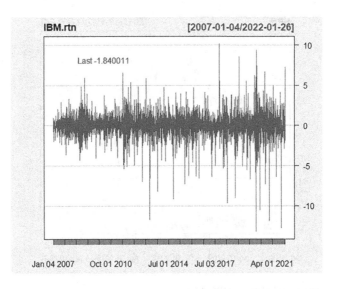

FIGURE 3.7 Return IBM 14 years.

The representation of the prices-returns and volume brings a lot of questions about a probability distribution of returns, the same as the identification of factors that can affect the results that explain differences in companies in the same sector with different stock results. What are the strategies behind the results? What are the perceptions of the company's stockholders, and so on? A scatterplot (Figure 3.11) contributes to identifying how companies are related. The cluster analysis is applied and the explanation of how the behavior of volatility in the cluster, volume, and possible prices forecast helps to understand dynamic portfolios and can supplement the use of the connection between risk-variance of prices and expected returns of the companies.

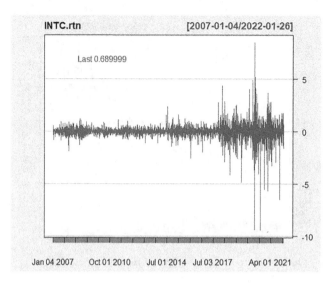

FIGURE 3.8   Return INTC 14 years.

FIGURE 3.9   Stock prices and volume HPE 14 years.

EXHIBIT 3.2   CREATION OF A SCATTERPLOT FOR RETURN OF MULTIPLE COMPANIES

Using the data of returns
scatterplot(INTC.Adjusted~IBM.Adjusted, regLine=TRUE, smooth=list(span=0.5,
spread=TRUE), boxplots=FALSE, ellipse=list(levels=c(.5, .9)),
    data=ibmintc)

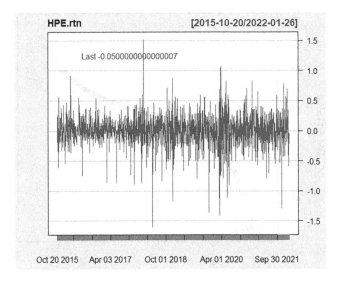

FIGURE 3.10 Return HPE 14 years.

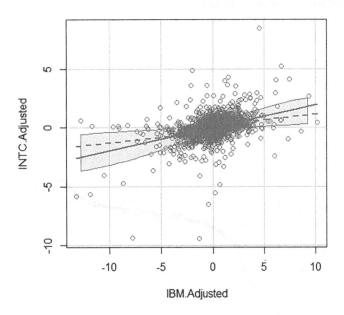

FIGURE 3.11 Scatterplot and approach with linear models and band representation.

The analysis of the distribution of returns is in Figures 3.12 to 3.15 and tests are funda-mental and show how normal distribution can describe the return data, the symmetry is clear, the tails are heavy, and kurtosis shows narrow distribution. Possibly, normal distribution can be substituted by Laplace distribution or something similar. The hypotheses of normality cannot be rejected.

Pairwise correlations indicate as well it was mentioned before that IBM and INTC are not having similar results. Correlations are significant but the values are less than 0.5 and it could indicate weak correlation. This a step that will be discussed in the next chapters.

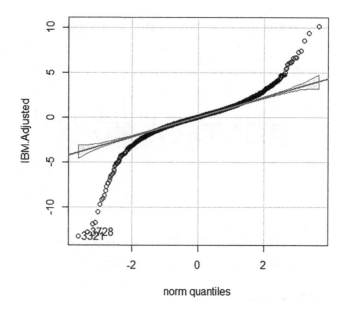

FIGURE 3.12   IBM returns normality QQ-plot.

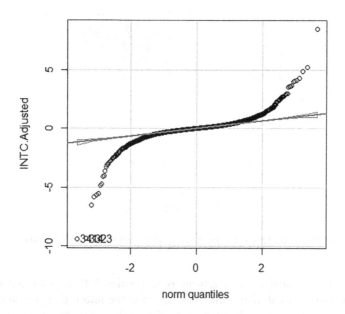

FIGURE 3.13   INTC returns normality QQ-plot.

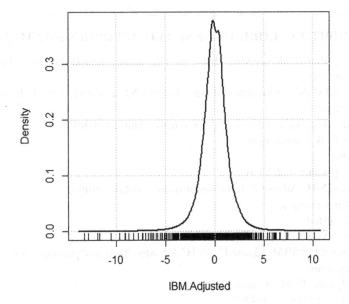

FIGURE 3.14 IBM density of returns.

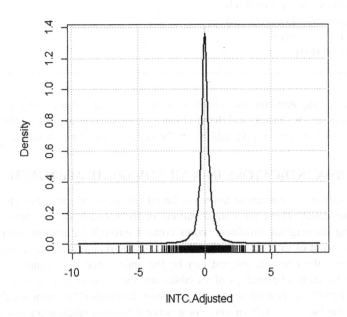

FIGURE 3.15 INTC density of returns.

EXHIBIT 3.3   CODE TO GENERATE GRAPHICS 3–12 TO 3–15

with(ibmintc, qqPlot(IBM.Adjusted, dist="norm", id=list(method="y", n=2, labels=
rownames(ibmintc))))
densityPlot(~ IBM.Adjusted, data=ibmintc, bw=bw.SJ, adjust=1, kernel=dnorm,
method="adaptive")
normalityTest(~IBM.Adjusted, test="shapiro.test", data=ibmintc)
    Shapiro-Wilk normality test
data: IBM.Adjusted
W = 0.90512, p-value < 2.2e–16
normalityTest(~INTC.Adjusted, test="shapiro.test", data=ibmintc)
Shapiro-Wilk normality test
data: INTC.Adjusted
W = 0.74196, p-value < 2.2e–16
rcorr.adjust(ibmintc[,c("IBM.Adjusted","INTC.Adjusted")], type="pearson", use="complete")
Pearson correlations:
    IBM.Adjusted INTC.Adjusted
IBM.Adjusted   1.0000   0.4365
INTC.Adjusted   0.4365   1.0000
Number of observations: 3793
Pairwise two-sided p-values:
    IBM.Adjusted INTC.Adjusted
IBM.Adjusted   <.0001
INTC.Adjusted <.0001
Adjusted p-values (Holm's method)
    IBM.Adjusted INTC.Adjusted
IBM.Adjusted   <.0001
INTC.Adjusted <.0001

The next section supplements the vision of comparing companies using clusters based on returns using as classes the clusters and then to identify the variables explaining the classes in order to control factors that are creating variability in the organization's performance.

3.5   ABOUT RISK INDICATORS IN A MULTIVARIATE APPROACH

In the previous sections, a univariate approach based on quartiles and using clusters for benchmarking were presented. There are considerations in the creation of the metrics related to relationships among the original variables, scores created through the market comparison, and the description of an event of interest or in the direction of the relationship identification to define a score. For instance, the event of interest can be the appearance of a claim or default and the approach to identify their relationships of variables and the event of having or not a claim can be tackled through logistic regression or any classification technique. In a non-multivariate analysis sales/total asset can have a weight of zero for a score definition-calculation, but the multivariate analysis can show its influence in a claim event. This means it is possible to recalculate the weights based on the claim event, using a statistical/machine learning tool and the financial and non-financial data for identifying how the risk units can be classified.

The use of a group of explanatory variables to describe the claim event and the search of relationships could be original raw financial and non-financial variables, indicator of violation variable thresholds, and ratio variables. In Chapter 7, the models used for multivariate analysis are explained. Logistic regression was used in a sample data set and some aspects were observed: first, the use of scores based on the benchmark and the use of the raw data – ratio can bring different results of relationships that require a cautious review. For example, a low score associated with the quick ratio appears to point to a higher probability of claim or default. However, a good quick ratio in general has an inverse direction to the probability of claim or default. In summary, it has to be very clear if the variable used is the raw-original one or it is a function of the original variable such as a calculated score. The value of the multivariate analysis is that the introduction of variables can indicate that variables not considered can be good to describe the event of interest. The contrary is to review, too, some variables originally considered important at the end can be insignificant to describe the variation of the event of interest. The variables can be, for example, financial and non-financials such as the behavior of the risk units in commercial transactions, or the composition of the management groups or legal aspects or relationships to the society. Another point to consider is the use of non-correlated variables to avoid issues in the modeling process (collinearity). The data set used for this chapter indicates that there is a weak correlation between cost of sales with sales over total assets, cost of sales with profit to total assets or strong correlations between, current and quick ratio (as expected), current ratio and cost of sales over payable accounts, and quick ratio with cost of sales over payable accounts.

In general, the results of a logistic regression model create risk knowledge about the relevance of the variables and the explanatory power of the claim-default event and for the claim-default probability calculation. A multivariate approach not only shows the relationships of variables with the claim-default event of interest, but also shows the importance of the requirement of good definition and interpretation of the variables at the moment of using a risk analytics process because it is not the same as using raw financial ratios or to use scores or violation to certain conditions as variables to describe an event of interest.

The explanation of steps to create risk indicators based on benchmarking or using models bring reflections to keep in mind for the good risk analytics process implementation:

1. It is part of the analytics process to differentiate between a mathematical model that discriminates risk and a procedure which includes some arithmetic manipulations and rules of decision regarding risk. In risk analytics, the desire is to combine rules of decision and mathematical models this means an expert model/system has to be built as a combination of decision rules and model outcomes. Something to think about is that risk indicators, thresholds, and any other rule have to be consistent with the mathematical model approach to supplement and not to substitute the interaction for a univariate rule that a business process or organization created.

2. As a task the clarification of differences among risk types (e.g., risk of insolvency and default or overdue and financially distressed companies) is critical. This means to clarify in a complete way what the target variable or variables are. The concept of evolution of the models is a component of building risk indicators, that when there are time series it is required to examine temporal statistical dependences/correlations in the data set. Specially, for financial data. It is necessary to include time series for risk units with experience as customers or already evaluated. The variables to evaluate the risk event can be diverse according to the experience/relations of the risk unit and an organization.

3. The variables to include in a risk indicator creation is an ongoing process. For example, there are models that use ratios of cash flow to total debt that are predicting bankruptcy; other models use additional predictors such as network capital/total assets, retained earnings/total assets, earnings before interest and taxes/total assets, market value of equity/book value of total debt, and sales/total assets.

4. Machine learning models include very valuable methodologies like decision/classification/regression trees/random forest that help to identify and evaluate risk in a process of risk analytics. The reason is that analysts can organize the search of risk units and their relation

to risk events following the way that tree is opening the tree branches. The same can be used to proceed in a surveillance and follow-up of the evolution of the risk units.

5. Using methods to connect the risk indicators and default rates provide new perspectives to monitor and control risks. Default rates can be individually or in combination calculated by the use of risk indicators. Risk indicators are metrics that define, according to the experience, the possible good or bad risk event outcome. Default rates (see Section 4.2) by risk indicator, individual and in combination, can guide the decision-making process and support the design of operations. Variables that are identified and influencers in final results can be the priority to control and evaluate, mainly in the process of surveillance and follow-up of the risk units after acceptance in risk processes (credit, fraud, investment).

The structure of analysis of risk indicators and default rates (see Section 4.2) requires the following components:

- First, to define the denominator of the default rate as a measure of the exposure to the risk event under analysis in a time window.
- Second, count the number of events occurrences in the window of time using a cohort methodology, or an occurrence of the event in the time window. The metric has to be consistent.
- Third calculate the ratios and identify the confidence intervals. If data is enough, the distribution of each of the default rates will be valuable to keep.
- Fourth, proceed with same steps by groups or classes according to the needs of business process definition. For instance, to separate groups based on predefined rules, steps of the business process to perform, markets, products, etc. In particular, it is a good practice to find clusters of risk units to compare default rates in the groups and the communalities.
- Fifth, using different perspectives and comparing the variables that are significant to describe the event of interest in multiple samples/classes.

Different methods can be used and each one is necessary to define which variables can be or not used as the main risk indicators. In the multivariate case, if regression types models are used, the stepwise process can help to identify the variables to keep or to release. In the random forest process, the importance of the variables can give a guide to define variables to use as well. The main point is to maintain the connection about the analytics process and how the outcomes will be translated to the actions/decisions to make to improve/enhance the business process.

3.6 COMPARING RISK METRICS IN GROUPS

Once a benchmark has been performed and metrics are related to risk events, a new step in the analysis is required. This section illustrates the use of one method to compare metrics in groups. ANOVA tests the equality of means and proportions. Assume that the events are evaluated regarding car claims. The groups are showing different results in the average of claims (Tables 3.13, 3.14, and 3.15). The question is if the segmentation is showing differences using education as the

---

TABLE 3.13
Value of Claims Estimators

Segment by Education	Average of Claims Number
College graduate	3.444444444
Graduate degree	4.5
Some college	3.142857143
Grand Total	**3.708333333**

TABLE 3.14
Frequencies of Claims

College Graduate	Graduate Degree	Some College
2	5	4
4	5	1
3	3	4
3	4	4
3	4	4
3	5	3
5	5	2
3	5	
5		

TABLE 3.15
ANOVA Summary

	Output ANOVA			
Groups	Count	Sum	Average	Variance
College graduate	9	31	3.444444	1.027778
Graduate degree	8	36	4.5	0.571429
Some college	7	22	3.142857	1.47619
		ANOVA			
Source of Variation	SS	df	MS	F	P-value	F crit
Between groups	7.878968	2	3.939484	3.924652	0.035635	3.4668
Within groups	21.07937	21	1.003779			
Total	28.95833	23				

main factor. The answer to that a question is based on ANOVA comparing the means equality. The null hypothesis is that all means are equal and the alternative is that at least one is different.

H_o: $\mu_1 = \mu_2 = \mu_3 = \ldots = \mu_n$ and H_a is at least there is one different from the others

Using a tool such as Excel with the data.

The solution is based on: one factor, the hypotheses of equality of the means is rejected, the p-value is small at alpha=5%, and the F value is greater than the F critical value.

The interpretation of the result is that there is a difference in segments in terms of claims, and this could influence changes in premiums if the combination with severity will affect the final losses. The next step is to study the meaning of severity and frequency combination. The model to work on is a compound Poisson process model, as it was indicated in Chapter 1, Section 1.8.

3.7 DECISION MAKING ON INVESTMENTS IN A RISK PRESCRIPTIVE ANALYTICS APPROACH

In the previous sections, the presentation of metrics as a means to support decisions is supplemented by prescriptive analytics. The predictive part produces outcomes that can be used to define rules, guidelines to operate, and it is where optimization for example can help. In this section, there are illustrations of using return on investments as metrics that guide risk analysis with the use of a deterministic prescriptive analytics. Assuming that investments in assets are decisions of yes or no, a problem to consider is if the asset is selected or not in an investment process. For example, if there are four projects and there is a known budget to invest in dollars, the amount that each investment return is a problem that could be with the following structure.

Decision Variables: X_i with $i=1,2,3,4$ projects and representing 1 if there is an investment in the project X_i and 0 if there is no investment. First project returns 20,000, second 28,000, third one 15,000, and fourth one 10,000 economic units. The problem is to maximize the return of the investment, this is: Using (000) thousands, the equation of total return can be written as $20X_1 + 28X_2 + 15X_3 + 10X_4$. There are, for example, preferences to select the projects and they are included in the budget selection assigning weights to each project and there is a maximum investment budget of 14,000. For instance, $6X_1 + 5X_2 + 4X_3 + 5X_4 \leq 14$. The variables are representing the real values and they should be greater or equal than zero. The Solver in Excel input and output is shown in Exhibits 3.4 and 3.5.

The solution using Excel Solver follows.

Maximum value of objective function z is 53; the values of the decision variables are:

x1	0
x2	1
x3	1
x4	1

and the value of the constraint is 14; that means that all of the budget was consumed.

Examples of arbitrage, financial control, and several others can be studied using prescriptive analytics; for example, the possible transactions in currency or with markets and goods with prices

EXHIBIT 3.4   FORMULATION OF THE LINEAR MODEL IN EXCEL SOLVER

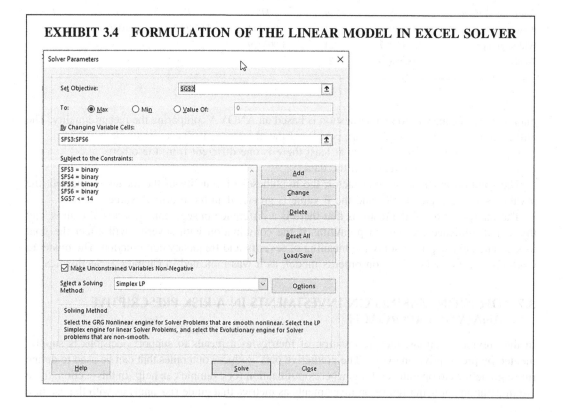

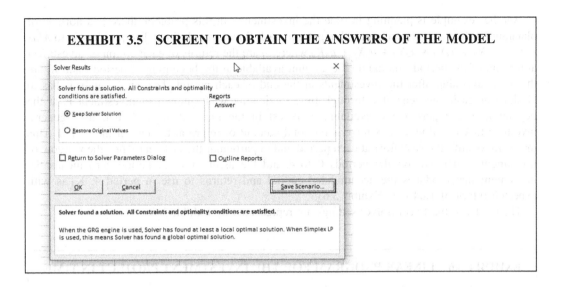

EXHIBIT 3.5   SCREEN TO OBTAIN THE ANSWERS OF THE MODEL

TABLE 3.16
Conversion Table of Currencies

| Excel Reference | M | N | O | P | Q | R |
Row/Column	cu1	cu2	cu3	cu4	cu5	cu6
3 cu1	1	10	15	0.5	2	0.8
4 cu2	0.1	1	0.4	2	3	0.9
5 cu3	0.066667	2.5	1	3	2	4
6 cu4	2	0.5	0.333333	1	0.3	0.2
7 cu5	0.5	0.333333	0.5	3.333333	1	3
8 cu6	1.25	1.111111	0.25	5	0.333333	1

in currencies from different countries. Assume that there are six currencies, and there is a variable X_{ij} that represents the transaction amount that is converted using an exchange rate among i and j currencies-countries.

Constraints that are in the syntax of Excel are expressed in Table 3.17, such as the variable in Excel Solver is in the \$M\$13:\$M\$17 and constraints are in M19 to M24.

TABLE 3.17
Syntax in Excel for Formulation

=SUMPRODUCT(M4:M8,M13:M17)-SUM(N12:R12)

=N3*N12+N5*N14+N6*N15+N7*N16+N8*N17-(M13+O13+P13+Q13+R13)

=O3*O12+O4*O13+O6*O15+O7*O16+O8*O17-(M14+N14+P14+Q14+R14)

=P3*P12+P4*P13+P5*P14+P7*P16+P8*P17-(M15+N15+O15+Q15+R15)

=Q3*Q12+Q4*Q13+Q5*Q14+Q6*Q15+Q8*Q17-(M16+N16+O16+P16+R16)

=SUMPRODUCT(R3:R7,R12:R16)-SUM(M17:Q17)

Another example is planning in time the investments. In this problem, there is a horizon of planning for financial investment, a budget and cash flow through time. The problem is to *Max* $a_1X_1 + a_2X_2 + a_3X_3 + a_4X_4 + a_5X_5 + a_5K_4$ where a_i are the returns of each option of investment at the end of the period i including the amount available at the beginning of period i and K_i are the funds available after the investments at the end of each period. The whole analysis has to be done as cashflow generated through time, reviewing what amount of investment is at the beginning of the period and available to invest in the main assets and then in a general investment. A function to maximize is the total amount of return at the end of the period. This means to identify the cash flow at each period and in particular the last year when the window of investment is defined. Be the periods 0 to 4 and the assets 1 to 5. Period zero means the investment that produces the accumulated capital and returns to use in period 4. K_4 is with expected return of 1.04 (see Exhibit 3.6).

The model in the Excel Solver settings are represented by Exhibit 3.7.

EXHIBIT 3.6   LINEAR PROGRAM FOR THE INVESTMENT PROJECT IN TIME

	0	1	2	3	4	Excel formulas
asset1	−1	1.15	1.05	0	1.02	$z=1.02Asset_1+1.02Asset_3+1.02Asset_4+1.01Asset_5-Asset_2+1.04K_4$
asset2	0	−1	1.15	1.05	−1	$z=1.02*C11+1.02*C13+1.02*C14+1.01*C15+1.04*C19$
asset3	−1	1.25	0	0	1.02	a1 100000
asset4	−1	0	0	1.2	1.02	a2 100000
asset5	0	0	−1	1.25	1.01	a3 49999.9999999999
						a4 0
						a5 100000
						k0 0
						k1 77499.9999999999
						k2 200600
						k3 438624
						k4 610168.96
						Constraint's formulas
						c1 =C11+C13+C14+C16
						c2 =1.15*C11+1.25*C13+1.04*C16-C12-C17
						c3 =1.05*C11+1.15*C12+1.04*C17-C15-C18
						c4 =1.05*C12+1.2*C14+1.25*C15+1.04*C18-C19
						c5 =1.02*C11+1.02*C13+1.02*C14+1.01*C15+1.04*-C19- C12-C20
z						710169
a1						100000
a2						100000
a3						50000
a4						0
a5						100000
k0						0
k1						77500
k2						200600

k3	438624
k4	610169
c1	150000
c2	0
c3	0
c4	0
c5	0

EXHIBIT 3.7   USE THE SOLVER IN EXCEL

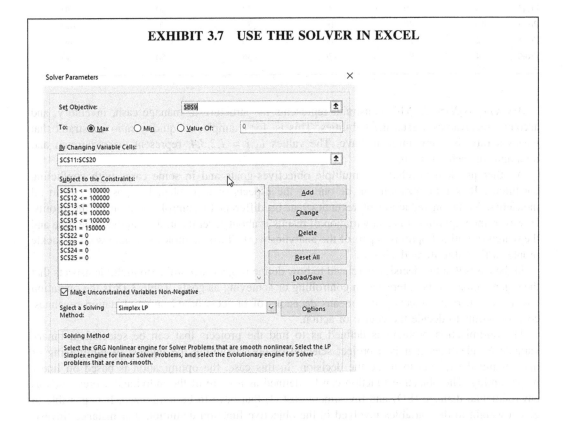

Another situation is a planning process of a company's financial project according to the product's portfolio, cash generation, and resources use. The challenges are to find the conditions of the operation that can be or would like to be prioritized to control and to distribute (data available, revenues, costs, and expenses by products):

Max $C_1X_1+C_2X_2$
S.T.
$X_1 <= L_1$ This is for example the capacity or demand for a product in the portfolio
$X_2 <= L_2$ This is the capacity or demand for a product in the portfolio

$Cf_1X_1+Cf_2X_2 <= L_3$ In this case, this is the cash flow value required that is a result of what was in cash at the beginning of the period plus account receivables, less expenses, and costs related to each product.

TABLE 3.18

Operation Costs

	min	max	min	min	min	max
	1	2	3	4	5	6
	Cost Hours People (P)	Production output (PO)	Investment (I)	Operation Cost (OC)	Environment damage/cost (ED)	Work conditions (WC)
Proj1	80	90	60	54	80	50
Proj2	65	58	20	97	10	10
Proj3	83	60	40	72	40	70
Proj4	40	80	100	75	70	100
Proj5	52	72	60	20	30	80
Proj6	94	96	70	36	50	60

$Ass_1X_1+Ass_2X_2>=L_4$ This constraint represents the structure to manage cash, inventory, and accounts receivables versus the liabilities. This is, for example, a liquidity ratio constraint that means a ratio is a minimum to have. The values L_i $i = 1,2,3,4$, represent the maximum and minimum in each constraint.

Another problem is related to multiple objectives-goals and in some cases with conflicting conditions. Risk minimization can be one of the aspects of a problem but possibly not to all indicators. Variation reduction of revenues can be different to control variation of the profits. However, the requirement is that variation of results is about several variables at the same time and the search of optimal options is part of the analytics work. Two examples illustrate ways to tackle problems in multicriteria decisions:

In the cases that the decision is related to how define projects according to multiple aspects that the organization can be interested in controlling or achieving as goals. Table 3.18 is the operation cost for comparing projects – this means decisions of projects based on combination revenues, costs or profits to decide the course of action.

The optimization problem is defined as to find the projects that can be selected (a binary variable X_i identifies if it is a project selected or not) assuming the interest of minimizing or maximizing the factors to make the decision. In this case, the optimization is based on linear programming. The objective function can be defined as a score of the individual scores, such as environmental damage (ED) and investment cost (I) that have to be minimized. It is possible to give a weight to the variables involved in the objective function definition. For instance, investment can be 2 of 5 and environment cost can be 3 of 5 points. This means:

$$Z = 2^*I + 3^*ED$$

Subject to:

People cost/hours $80^*x_1+65^*x_2+83^*x_3+40^*x_4+52^*x_5+94^*x_6$ lower or equal the total hours available.

Production output $90^*x_1+58^*x_2+60^*x_3+80^*x_4+72^*x_5+96^*x_6$ greater or equal the minimum expected or required

Operation costs $54^*x_1+97^*x_2+72^*x_3+75^*x_4+20^*x_5+36^*x_6$ lower or equal the available budget

Work conditions $50^*x_1+10^*x_2+70^*x_3+100^*x_4+80^*x_5+60^*x_6$ to have a result of conditions greater or equal a minimum standard for workers

---

**EXHIBIT 3.8   DEFINING A PROGRAM WITH DIFFERENT CONDITIONS/
CONSTRAINTS**

original	two more constraints
Max $Z=400x_1+300x_2$	max $z=400x_1+300x_2$
s.t.	s.t.
$10x_1+15x_2<=150$	$10x_1+15x_2<=150$
$x_1>=3$	$x_1>=3$ minimum demand
$x_2>=4$	$x_2>=4$ minimum demand
$x_1,x_2>=0$	$x_1<=5$ maximum demand
	$x_2<=6$ maximum demand
	$x_1,x_2>=0$

Goal programming as a tool for decision making is a powerful tool. The same as linear programming, the identification of what is adding value to have an improved goal is what in general in risk analytics and in management is in search of. On the one hand, to have several criteria to decide what to do is supplemented to define how to obtain the goals that have been defined (Exhibit 3.8). On the other hand, the definition of the goals before the optimization can come from forecasting, classification, prediction methods, etc. For example, the expected value of a random metric can be the goal and to define how to achieve the goal can be a combination of operation conditions in the organization.

Using the variables x_1 x_2 s_{1-} s_{2-} s_{3-} s_{4-} s_{5-} s_{6-} s_{1+} s_{2+} s_{3+} s_{4+} s_{5+} s_{6+} the full model is as follows.

Maximize $Z=300s_{4+}+300s_{5+}+300s_{2-}+300s_{3-}+20s_{1+}+10s_{6-}$

s.t.

$10x_1+15x_2+s_{1-} - s_{1+}=150$	machine	priority 3
$x_1+s_{2-} -s_{2+}=3$	demand	priority 2
$x_2+s_{3-}-s_{3+}=4$	demand	priority 2
$x_1+s_{4-}-s_{4+}=5$	demand	priority 1
$x_2+s_{5-}-s_{5+}=6$	demand	priority 1
$400x_1+300x_2+s_{6-}-s_{6+}=4800$	net profit	priority 4

All variables $>=0$

And the solution is as follows.

Z	1050
variables	
x_1	7.5
x_2	6
s_{1-}	0
s_{2-}	0
s_{3-}	0
s_{4-}	0
s_{5-}	0
s_{6-}	0
s_{1+}	15
s_{2+}	4.5
s_{3+}	2
s_{4+}	2.5
$s5+$	0
$s6+$	0

Another aspect in metric definition is the use of time series for obtaining new insights from the metrics realization in different periods. The next section introduces some ideas about the process of using time series metrics analysis.

3.8   FORECASTING AND TIME SERIES AS A MEANS TO SUPPORT DECISION MAKING

In risk analytics forecasting, there are:

1. Qualitative techniques
2. Stochastic processes/time-series models
3. Explanatory/inferential causal models

To develop a forecasting process, the first step is to identify where to use the forecast and how many factors can be used or are required. Data gathering is going to define the capacity to develop the model. Define the possible models and then to evaluate these models, create the models, and evaluate the best model's performance. In risk analytics, the use of raw data and created data as input of the forecast is a way to connect the metric creation and the metric control.

- "A time series model accounts for patterns in the past movement of a variable and uses that information to predict its future movements."Pindyck and Rubinfeld (1998)
- There are deterministic and stochastic models
- Deterministic models:
  - ◦ Linear trend model: the series growths with constants absolute increases
  - ◦ Log linear regression equation or exponential growth curve: in this case the changes are with constant percentage increases
  - ◦ Autoregressive trend model $y_t = c_1 + c_2 y_{t-1}$
- There are many others quadratic, logistic etc.
- Another type is moving averages where a forecast term ahead is given by

$$\hat{y}_{T+1} = \frac{1}{12}(y_T + y_{T+1} + \dots + y_{T-11})$$

The number of periods depends on the time series to study. MA (moving average) is a series of arithmetic means that is: Used if little or no trend exists, and used often for smoothing the time series and to provide overall impression of data over time. MA are for obtaining – estimiating trends and cycles. Trend and seasonality are part of non-stationary time series. A stationary time series have only a random behavior and in general a time series representation is as a product of four factors: trend, seasonality, cyclicity and randomness. This means moving averages provide an estimation of trend times cyclicity because the moving averages are reducing the seasonality and random behavior. A trend is a movement upward or downward with a direction of a time series.

- This means to have (L*C). Or it is better to say each moving average reduces the seasonal and random.
- Using the notation L*S*C*I that appears in the literature. L is a long-term trend.
- This means the ratio of the original and the moving average result provides an estimate of seasonal and random components.
- And new moving average on the z_t will reduce the random component.
- For instance, it can be a moving average by 12 periods-months or by quarters.

$$\tilde{y} = \frac{1}{12}(y_{t+6} + \dots + y_t + y_{t+1} + \dots + y_{t-5})$$

TABLE 3.19

Data by Quarters Year and Calculation of Moving Averages and Pieces of the Time Series Decomposition

Date	Number Date	Time	Value LSCI	moving average (4 periods)	Moving Av. Centered is estimation of trend and cycle= reducing the seasonality and random = LC	Adjustment original value LSCI/LC=SI
1999-09-30	36433	1	398			
1999-12-29	36523	2	352			
2000-03-28	36613	3	283	371.75	371.00	0.7628
2000-06-26	36703	4	454	370.25	369.38	1.2291
2000-09-24	36793	5	392	368.50	367.38	1.0670
2000-12-23	36883	6	345	366.25	358.50	0.9623
2001-03-23	36973	7	274	350.75	338.00	0.8107
2001-06-21	37063	8	392	325.25	308.38	1.2712
2001-09-19	37153	9	290	291.50	284.50	1.0193
2001-12-18	37243	10	210	277.50	276.25	0.7602
2002-03-18	37333	11	218	275.00	286.50	0.7609
2002-06-16	37423	12	382	298.00	314.25	1.2156
2002-09-14	37513	13	382	330.50	340.50	1.1219
2002-12-13	37603	14	340	350.50	359.25	0.9464
2003-03-13	37693	15	298	368.00	373.13	0.7987
2003-06-11	37783	16	452	378.25	382.25	1.1825
2003-09-09	37873	17	423	386.25	391.00	1.0818
2003-12-08	37963	18	372	395.75	397.75	0.9353
2004-03-07	38053	19	336	399.75	395.25	0.8501
2004-06-05	38143	20	468	390.75	382.88	1.2223
2004-09-03	38233	21	387	375.00	366.00	1.0574
2004-12-02	38323	22	309	357.00	348.38	0.8870
2005-03-02	38413	23	264	339.75	342.38	0.7711
2005-05-31	38503	24	399	345.00	355.88	1.1212
2005-08-29	38593	25	408	366.75	382.38	1.0670
2005-11-27	38683	26	396	398.00	423.63	0.9348
2006-02-25	38773	27	389	449.25	470.63	0.8266
2006-05-26	38863	28	604	492.00	506.63	1.1922
2006-08-24	38953	29	579	521.25	536.38	1.0795
2006-11-22	39043	30	513	551.50	558.63	0.9183
2007-02-20	39133	31	510	565.75		
2007-05-21	39223	32	661			

In the example (Table 3.19), the averages are calculated by quarters. In general, time series are decomposed in four components: seasonality, trends, cyclicity, and randomness LxSxCxI. The models will deal with these components to provide the best expected results. An example of finding the components of a time series in a manual way, assuming the LxSxCxI multiplicative decomposition model of the series, is given by the discovery of trend (L), seasonality indexes (S), cyclicity index (C), and random component (I).

Cycle identification factors (Table 3.20).

TABLE 3.20
Cycle Identification

Quarters year	Original data LSCI	Trend value L	seasonal index S	LxS	LSCI/ LS=CI*100	getting cycle moving average	C	CI/C=I
3	398	291.73	107.59	313.87	126.80			
4	352	298.07	91.11	271.57	129.62	372.37	124.12	104.43
1	283	304.41	80.18	244.08	115.95	366.19	122.06	94.99
2	454	310.75	121.12	376.38	120.62	351.47	117.16	102.96
3	392	317.09	107.59	341.16	114.90	352.60	117.53	97.76
4	345	323.43	91.11	294.68	117.08	335.61	111.87	104.66
1	274	329.77	80.18	264.41	103.63	317.00	105.67	98.07
2	392	336.11	121.12	407.10	96.29	278.63	92.88	103.68
3	290	342.45	107.59	368.44	78.71	241.08		
4	210	348.79	91.11	317.78	66.08			

TABLE 3.21
Seasonal Index Calculation

Year	Quarter				
	1	2	3	4	Total
	76.30	123.00	106.80	96.10	
	81.10	126.90	101.80	76.10	
	76.00	121.30	112.00	94.70	
	79.90	118.30	108.20	93.50	
	85.10	122.20	105.70	88.50	
	77.00	112.10	106.50	93.40	
	82.60	119.10	107.80	91.80	
Total	558.00	842.90	748.80	634.10	
Average	79.71	120.41	106.97	90.59	397.69
Adjusted Seasonality Index	80.18	121.12	107.59	91.11	400

And calculation of the seasonality factor by quarters calculation (Table 3.21) includes the trend as illustrated in Figure 3.16 and Table 3.22.

Table 3.16 represents the time series and the trend line is included; the error generated by factors affecting the time series is part of the required adjustments.

In particular, each factor to correct the approach of the trends is based on the calculation in Table 3.22.

Models of the forecasting can be evaluated using the rule searching for the minimum error of the forecast and the reality, using the following criteria:

- Mean absolute deviation (MAD)

$$MAD = \frac{\sum_{t=1}^{n} |A_t - F_t|}{n}$$

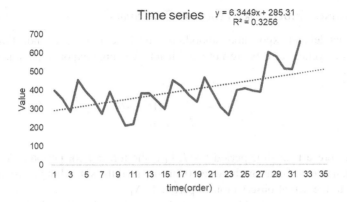

FIGURE 3.16 Positive trend of the data set and fit to review small R-squared.

TABLE 3.22

Manual Calculation for the Time Series Components Including the Trend Calculation

Quarter	X	Y	Trend	Year quarter	Original data Y	Total four quarters	Moving average 4 quarters	Centered moving average	Value of S*I
			Yt= 285.39+6.34X	col1	col2	col3	col4	col5	col 2 divided by col 5
3	1	398	291.73	3	398				
4	2	352	298.07	4	3 52				
1	3	283	304.41	1	283	1,487	372	371	76.3
2	4	454	310.75	2	454	1,481	370	369	123
3	5	392	317.09	3	392	1,474	368	367	106.8
4	6	345	323.43	4	345	1.465	366	359	96.1

- Mean square error (MSE)

$$MSE = \frac{\sum_{t=1}^{n} (A_t - F_t)^2}{n}$$

- Root mean square error (RMSE)

$$RMSE = \sqrt{\frac{\sum_{t=1}^{n} (A_t - F_t)^2}{n}}$$

- Mean absolute percentage error (MAPE)

$$MAPE = \frac{\sum_{t=1}^{n} \left| \frac{A_t - F_t}{A_t} \right|}{n} \times 100$$

3.8.1   Forecasting Models for Stationary Time Series

Moving average model and exponential smoothing model are useful over short time periods when trend, seasonal, or cyclical effects are not significant. A simple exponential smoothing model is given by:

$$
\begin{aligned}
F_{t+1} &= (1 - \alpha)F_t + \alpha A_t \\
&= F_t + \alpha(A_t - F_t)
\end{aligned}
$$

where F_{t+1} is the forecast for time period $t + 1$, F_t is the forecast for period t, A_t is the observed value in period t, and α is a constant between 0 and 1 called the smoothing constant. To begin, set F_1 and F_2 equal to the actual observation in period 1, A_1.

Double moving average and double exponential smoothing is based on the linear trend equation. The forecast for k periods into the future is a function of the level a_t and the trend b_t. The models differ in their computations of a_t and b_t.

$$
F_{t+k} = a_t + b_t k
$$

Double exponential smoothing:

$$
\begin{aligned}
a_t &= \alpha F_t + (1 - \alpha)(a_{t-1} + b_{t-1}) \\
b_t &= \beta(a_t - a_{t-1}) + (1 - \beta)b_{t-1}
\end{aligned}
$$

When autocorrelation is present, successive observations are correlated with one another; for example, large observations tend to follow other large observations, and small observations also tend to follow one another. A graphic of the time series is recommended first to identify the appropriate type of model to use. When time series exhibits seasonality, different techniques can provide different forecasts, for instance multiple regression models with categorical variables for the seasonal components or Holt-Winters models, similar to exponential smoothing models in that smoothing constants are used to smooth out variations in the level and seasonal patterns over time. The Holt-Winters additive model applies to time series with relatively stable seasonality and is based on the equation

$$
F_{t+1} = a_t + b_t + S_{t-s+1}
$$

The Holt-Winters multiplicative model applies to time series whose amplitude increases or decreases over time and is given by

$$
F_{t+1} = (a_t + b_t)S_{t-s+1}
$$

Figures 3.17 to 3.22 and Tables 3.23 to 3.36 show the results of multiple models and their errors. The evaluation of errors provides a guide to select the most appropriate model to use. The graphics used on the x-axis are the numeric value of the date as it is in Table 3.19. For the Holt-Winter (H-W) model, there are examples of different parameter values of α, β, γ, season length, and number of seasons. The corresponding confidence intervals are indicated. Model 1H-W fits better with a forecast value of 607. 7; the error indicators show lower values.

Using double exponential and exponential models, the results are as follows: (See Figures 3.21 and 3.22 and Tables 3.33 to 3.36):

Models as before use the results of the past in linear combination with weights or coefficients that are static in time. However, another aspect to keep in mind is that a time series generator

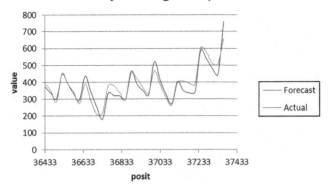

FIGURE 3.17   Model 1 Holt-Winter.

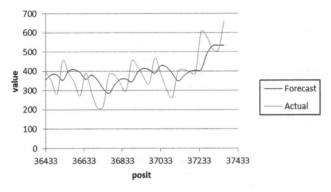

FIGURE 3.18   Model 2 Holt-Winter.

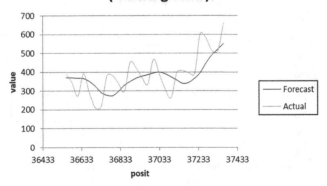

FIGURE 3.19   Model 3 MA 4 periods.

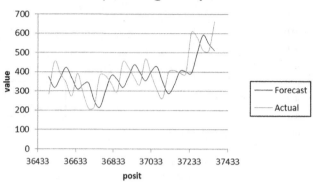

FIGURE 3.20　Model4 MA 2 periods.

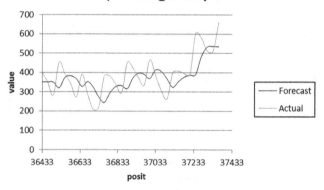

FIGURE 3.21　Double exponential smoothing.

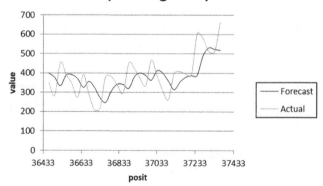

FIGURE 3.22　Exponential smoothing.

TABLE 3.23

Error Evaluation Model 1 Holt-Winter

Mean Absolute Percentage Error (MAPE)	8.322632
Mean Absolute Deviation (MAD)	31.83303
Mean Square Error (MSE)	1511.35
Tracking Signal Error (TSE)	6.756872
Cumulative Forecast Error (CFE)	215.0917
Mean Forecast Error (MFE)	6.721617

TABLE 3.24

Error Evaluation Model 2 Holt-Winter

Mean Absolute Percentage Error (MAPE)	19.68519
Mean Absolute Deviation (MAD)	69.0784
Mean Square Error (MSE)	6831.493
Tracking Signal Error (TSE)	−2.0371
Cumulative Forecast Error (CFE)	−140.72
Mean Forecast Error (MFE)	−4.39749

TABLE 3.25

Forecasted Value and Confidence Interval Model 1 Holt -Winter

posit	Forecast	LCI	UCI
1	607.6883	483.7979	731.5787

TABLE 3.26

Forecasted value and confidence interval Model 2 Holt-Winter

posit	Forecast	LCI	UCI
1	590.6343	339.894	841.3747

TABLE 3.27

Parameter Estimation Model 1 Hold-Winter

Parameters/Options	
Optimize Weights	Yes
Alpha (Level)	0.858485672
Beta (Trend)	0.003509629
Gamma (Seasonality)	0.917050691
Season length	4
Number of seasons	8
Forecast	Yes
#Forecasts	1

TABLE 3.28

Parameter Estimation Model 2 Holt-Winter

Parameters/Options	
Optimize Weights	Yes
Alpha (Level)	0.350566118
Beta (Trend)	0.007721183
Gamma (Seasonality)	0.034272286
Season length	1
Number of seasons	32
Forecast	Yes
#Forecasts	1

TABLE 3.29

Error Evaluation Model 3 MA 4 Periods

Mean Absolute Percentage Error (MAPE)	18.08122
Mean Absolute Deviation (MAD)	66.17857
Mean Square Error (MSE)	6422.531
Tracking Signal Error (TSE)	7.600648
Cumulative Forecast Error (CFE)	503
Mean Forecast Error (MFE)	17.96429

TABLE 3.30

Error Evaluation Model 4 MA 2 Periods

Mean Absolute Percentage Error (MAPE)	21.96836
Mean Absolute Deviation (MAD)	82.5
Mean Square Error (MSE)	9088.317
Tracking Signal Error (TSE)	4.424242
Cumulative Forecast Error (CFE)	365
Mean Forecast Error (MFE)	12.16667

TABLE 3.31

Forecasted Value, Parameters, and Confidence Intervals Model 3 MA 4 Periods

posit	Forecast	LCI	UCI
1	565.75	412.5341	718.9659
Parameters/Options			
Interval	4		
Forecast	Yes		
#Forecasts	1		

TABLE 3.32

Forecasted Value, Parameters, and Confidence Intervals Model 4 MA 2 Periods

posit	Forecast	LCI	UCI
1	585.5	404.234	766.766
Parameters/Options			
Interval	2		
Forecast	Yes		
#Forecasts	1		

TABLE 3.33

Error Evaluation Model Double Exponential Smoothing

Mean Absolute Percentage Error (MAPE)	18.34874
Mean Absolute Deviation (MAD)	68.33695
Mean Square Error (MSE)	6975.547
Tracking Signal Error (TSE)	8.063227
Cumulative Forecast Error (CFE)	551.0163
Mean Forecast Error (MFE)	17.21926

TABLE 3.34

Error Evaluation Model Exponential Smoothing

Mean Absolute Percentage Error (MAPE)	18.87438
Mean Absolute Deviation (MAD)	69.87572
Mean Square Error (MSE)	7252.168
Tracking Signal Error (TSE)	5.752874
Cumulative Forecast Error (CFE)	401.9862
Mean Forecast Error (MFE)	12.9673

TABLE 3.35

Forecasted Value, Parameters, and Confidence Intervals Model Double Exponential Smoothing

posit	Forecast	LCI	UCI
1	599.1188	435.4231	762.8145
Parameters/Options			
Optimization Selected		Yes	
Alpha (Level)		0.398754845	
Beta (Trend)		0.074617756	
Forecast		Yes	
#Forecasts		1	

TABLE 3.36

Forecasted Value, Parameters, and Confidence Intervals

Model Exponential Smoothing

posit	Forecast	LCI	UCI
1	582.9281	418.6469	747.2093
Parameters/Options			
Optimization Selected		Yes	
Alpha (Level)		0.460036012	
Forecast		Yes	
#Forecasts		1	

(stochastic process) can change with respect to time. If there is no change, the time series is stationary (similar to regression); in other case, the time series is non-stationary. The concept of time correlation of the data is led by the autocorrelation function: this function will tell us how much correlation there is between neighboring data points in the series. Autocorrelation with lag k is $\rho_k = \frac{cov(y_t, y_{t+k})}{\sigma_{y_t}\sigma_{y_{t+k}}}$; in stationary processes, the covariances are equal: "The probability distribution of the random variable y_t is the same for all t and its shape can be inferred by looking at a histogram of the observations y_1, y_2, ..., y_T that make up the observed series," Pindyck and Rubinfeld (1998).

A white noise is the stochastic process $y_t = e_t$, where e_t is an independent random variable with zero mean, where the autocorrelation is zero when k > 0 and 1 when k = 0. When the autocorrelation is close to zero, there is small value of using a model to forecast a time series. In most cases, it is needed to convert the original time series into a non-stationary one for that a differentiation process is used. A new series is created using a stationary series transformation $w_t = y_t - y_{t-1} = \Delta y_t$; if it is not stationary, then the second order is calculated $W_t = \Delta y_t - \Delta y_{t-1}$ or $W_t = \Delta^2 y_t$.

A moving average process of order q, MA(q) is a process where each observation is generated by a weighted average of random disturbances going back q periods; the random disturbances are assumed to be independently distributed across time and this is generated by a white noise process $Y_t = \mu + e_t - \theta_1 e_{t-1} - \theta_2 e_{t-1} - ... -\theta_q e_{t-q}$ where $\theta_1, ..., \theta_q$ can be positive and negative. In this case, each e_t is a random variable normally distributed with mean 0, variance σ_e^2, and covariance equal zero for k≠0.

An autoregressive model of order p is where y_t is obtained by a weighted average of past observations using p periods back, together with a random changes in the current period AR(p) $Y_t = \varphi_1 y_{t-1} + \varphi_2 y_{t-2} + ... +\varphi_p y_{t-p} + \delta + e_t$ δ is a constant term that relates to the mean of the stochastic process, for example AR(1):

$$\mu = \frac{\delta}{1 - \varphi_1}$$

If the autoregressive process is stationary, the mean μ will be invariant with respect to time; this is $E(y_t) = E(y_{t-1}) = ... = \mu$. A mix of MA(q) and AR(p) models is through an ARMA(p,q) model with parameters p and q, with $Y_t = \varphi_1 y_{t-1} + \varphi_2 y_{t-2} + ... +\varphi_p y_{t-p} + \delta + e_t -\theta_1 e_{t-1} - \theta_2 e_{t-1} - ... -\theta_q e_{t-q}$.

The assumption is that the process is stationary and the mean $\mu = \varphi_1 \mu + ... +\varphi_p \mu + \delta$ is constant through time. When the series is not stationary, it is required to perform differentiation and a model including differentiation appears with three parameters in number of differentiation and parameters of the AR(p) and MA(q) models involved ARIMA(p,d,q) $\varphi(B)\Delta^d y_t = \delta + \theta(B)e_t$ with $\varphi(B) = 1 - \varphi_1 B - \varphi_2 B^2 - ... -\varphi_p B^p$ autoregressive operator and $\theta(B) = 1 - \theta_1 B - \theta_2 B^2 - ... -\theta_q B^q$ the moving average operator.

Using the ARIMA model for the data in Table 3.19 for forecast and comparing three models (Figures 3.23 to 3–31) and different parameters first with p=1; second with p=q=1; third p=q=2 indicate that the smallest and model to use is Model 3. A criterion to identify the best model is the AIC Akaike Information Criterion. A lower value is better. The process of selecting candidates of models is based on ACF and PACF; the number of spikes outside the band of UCI and LCI and then to use the AIC information criteria (Tables 3.37 to 3.41) (Figures 3.23 to 3.31).

TABLE 3.37

Forecasted Values and Confidence Intervals ARIMA Model 2, 95% Confidence

posit	Forecast	Lower	Upper
Forecast 1	551.4717	387.5991	715.3443
Forecast 2	529.6759	350.4512	708.9006
Forecast 3	510.8221	320.9201	700.7241
Forecast 4	494.5133	296.9991	692.0275
Forecast 5	480.4058	277.3824	683.4293
Forecast 6	468.2026	261.1527	675.2526
Forecast 7	457.6467	247.6344	667.6589
Forecast 8	448.5156	236.3138	660.7174
Forecast 9	440.617	226.7915	654.4425

TABLE 3.38

Parameters Estimation and Model Fitting ARIMA Model 1, 95% Confidence

ARIMA	Coeff	StErr	p-value
Const. term	149.929	6.976654	1.9E-102
AR1	0.615567	0.341457	0.071425
Mean	390		
−2LogL	375.2003		
Res. StdDev	85.63917		
#Iterations	200		

TABLE 3.39

Forecasted Values and Confidence Intervals ARIMA Model 2, 95% Confidence

ARIMA	Coeff	StErr	p-value
Const. term	52.64308	2.449643	1.9E-102
AR1	0.865018	0	0
MA1	−0.42214	0	0
Mean	390		
−2LogL	374.7533		
Res. StdDev	84.53472		
#Iterations	200		

TABLE 3.40
Parameters Estimation and Model Fitting ARIMA Model 3, 95% Confidence

posit	Forecast	Lower	Upper
Forecast 1	572.3284	411.9065	732.7503
Forecast 2	520.9139	335.7486	706.0792
Forecast 3	508.671	316.0602	701.2818
Forecast 4	495.6645	296.8918	694.4373
Forecast 5	484.2005	280.6887	687.7124
Forecast 6	473.973	266.7711	681.1749
Forecast 7	464.8564	254.7685	674.9443
Forecast 8	456.7295	244.3762	669.0828
Forecast 9	449.4849	235.3485	663.6213

TABLE 3.41
Forecasted Values and Confidence Intervals ARIMA Model 3, 95% Confidence

ARIMA	Coeff	StErr	p-value
Const. term	44.97886	2.093003	1.9E-102
AR1	0.829133	1.430487	0.562174
AR2	0.055537	0.785609	0.943642
MA1	−0.2527	0.911083	0.781498
MA2	−0.20287	1.178948	0.863375
Mean	390		
−2LogL	373.4459		
Res. StdDev	82.6939		
#Iterations	200		

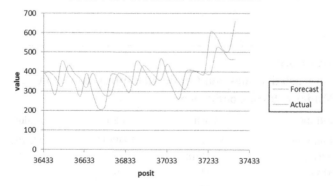

FIGURE 3.23 ARIMA Model 1 95% confidence.

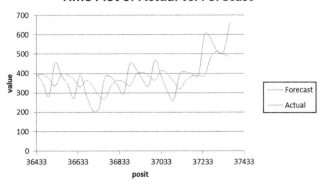

FIGURE 3.24 ARIMA Model 2 95% confidence.

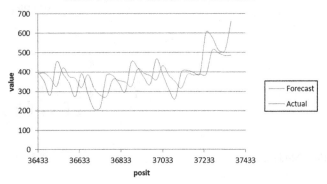

FIGURE 3.25 ARIMA Model 3 95% confidence.

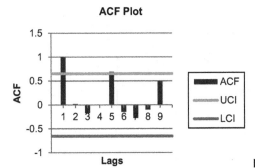

FIGURE 3.26 ARIMA Model 1.

This chapter introduced general concepts of decision making and how to measure through risk indicators using several techniques. The principles of consistency and maintenance of the meaning of the risk indicators are the bases of comparisons to generate time series and to generate data that can be used as input for predictive models. Metrics are new data to the risk analytics process generated by a RAS. Creation of metrics is the process of defining functions outcomes to continue with multiple layers of a RAS. As the examples illustrate, measurement can be directly from

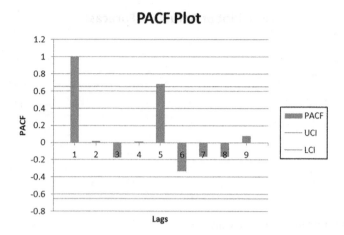

FIGURE 3.27   ARIMA Model 1.

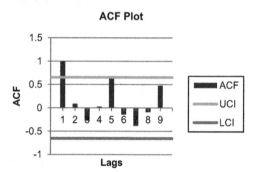

FIGURE 3.28   ARIMA Model 2.

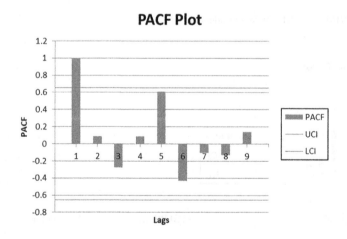

FIGURE 3.29   ARIMA Model 2.

internal results or in comparison with the market. Benchmarking is a means to know competitive positions and at the same time to understanding how the organization is performing according to the market conditions, to know where to be for developing the business, and to position the organization to evaluate strategic risks. Measurement results are used for inputting problems in optimization and at the same time to forecast.

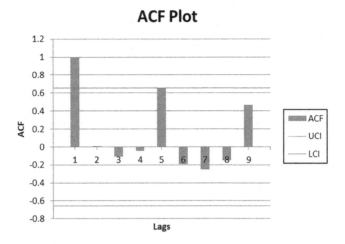

FIGURE 3.30 ARIMA Model 3.

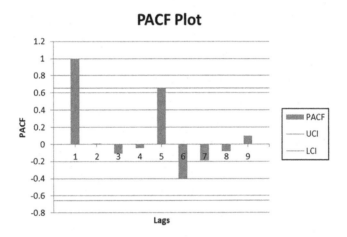

FIGURE 3.31 ARIMA Model 3.

In the following chapter, a discussion of measurement continues but is concentrated on concepts of measuring exposure, losses, and multiple concepts related to control and orientation of resources allocation in organizations to better performance. Chapter 4 will indicate how an exposure analysis is the basis to obtain meaningful risk understanding because the risk exposure that organizations have will influence losses and expected results. It is not the same risk exposure for all organizations; it depends on the business definition and the market. Risk exposure is coming from multiple dimensions-factors from products, operations, financial activity, socio-economic conditions, etc. and losses will potentially exist with frequency and severity based on the exposure and loss treatment before, during, and after realization of risk events.

4 Risk Management and Analytics in Organizations

The previous chapter indicated techniques to support metrics that are descriptive in nature and how they can be organized in a multivariate analysis. Benchmark metrics are fundamental to understand the conditions in a market-society to improve a risk assessment process. It was an introduction to a means to develop estimators/parameters and to compare parameters using ANOVA. Similarly, it was indicated how issues of measurement appear from the treatment of multiple decisions and metrics connected to those decisions. Simultaneously, Chapter 3 presented a possible start to a more non-deterministic approach of monitoring risk. This chapter comprises a review of the risk measurement process as a component of a risk analytics system creation supplementing what was exposed in Section 1.5 and previous chapter concentrated on default rates and probabilities of default.

This chapter prepares the land to use techniques on ML as Mashrur A. et al. (2020) pointed out: "Financial risk management avoids losses and maximizes profits, and hence is vital to most businesses. As the task relies heavily on information-driven decision making, machine learning is a promising source for new methods and technologies. In recent years, we have seen increasing adoption of machine learning methods for various risk management tasks. Machine-learning researchers, however, often struggle to navigate the vast and complex domain knowledge and the fast-evolving literature." This chapter starts with the fundamental question of what to measure and then how to measure. In general, risk indicators are metrics to use but the level of sophistication can vary depending on the definition of the problem and metric to use. In that regards, a loss ration can be just a beginning of measuring but the default rate can be a better view in the case of more factors to observe and how they affect the metrics. ML will be introduced in Chapter 5 to deal with multivariate data and to combine the pure mathematical approach to measuring with the AI-ML approach.

In addition, this chapter is supplemented with the understanding of LGD that is presented in Chapter 9. A measurement can be based on deterministic and stochastic approaches and in this chapter, there is a combination of metrics that are deterministic and stochastic that add value to describe the event of interest and its possible realization. The metrics development such as probabilities of default, default rates analysis, or metrics scales definition are part of the risk exposure understanding and the guide to risk analytics for risk monitoring and control of the risk management processes. As part of the principles of the RAS design, one of these principles is keeping the orientation of controlling identified factors that are related – have incidence to targets variability in strategy and its risk management.

4.1 HOW TO START A RISK MEASUREMENT SYSTEM

The first steps of creating a risk measurement system are based on the understanding of the difference of having static, dynamic, deterministic, and stochastic metrics. On the one hand, the creation of metrics starts with the definition of ratios, rates, or indicators relating multiple variables internally and externally from the business the same as raw or created variables that describe risk sub-processes. For example, as it was presented in the previous chapters, using risk indicators and their benchmark, a loss ratio is a ratio of losses versus premium in insurance, but it might be used in the same way substituting the denominator by revenues, exposure measurement values, or others. The numerator can be a value or calculation of expected values of losses. In general, metrics are random variables, and their calculation will modify the results used by organizations.

DOI: 10.1201/9780429342899-5

The definition and consistency of use of the metrics will provide the value of comparison power and possibility to control. A metric is a vehicle to help management to control events and operation. Another aspect to keep in mind is the clear sources of a metric. Depending on the maturity level of the organization and the sophistication and complexity of the measurement of risk, the components of the metric will require diverse sources of data and data processing. This is the case when an organization requires the outcome of forecast coming from a GARCH model, possibly higher level of sophistication and analytics process development or from just an average of historical results that can be enough to start a forecasting process. (See forecasting Section 3.8)

Data analytics focuses on the creation of the metrics and the possibility to use those metrics to support decisions and actions. The metric is possible to use when data is available to feed the components of the metric. Data provides the possibility to create the metric and then the metric itself will require the definition adjustments based on model outcomes. The question is if the organization has the capacity to use the model to create knowledge from data. A good example is in the default rates calculations that are static and continuous, using data that is from financial statements or from stock prices. But default rates can be stochastic based as well as they are when loss models-distributions are used and the moments of the loss distributions are the indicators. The main issue for a better modeling process of losses by segments (granularity by groups of factors) can be the number of sample points or better said the capacity to slice and dice to get from data the views that are desired; for example, loss distributions by product, by customer types, by regions, by industries, etc. Depending on the organization or the availability of data, specific steps will be performed to create the components of the metrics. In a first step, it can be to create ratios of static values coming from financial statements in another can be the expected result of simulated variables; for example, if it is required to use the expected net present value that can be the input for another metric. A metric requires several steps before using it; it is the case of RAROC metrics to evaluate needs of economic capital. It is a ratio, but the ratio needs a denominator that requires several steps from a risk assessment process.

On the other hand, the definition of metrics requires connecting the metric to organizations' goals. This means, for instance, to have the balanced scorecard alignment and an enterprise risk management plan and execution, when it is possible. The desire is to achieve the integral view of risk perspectives, but in several cases, data and mathematics are not providing the possibilities to move as far as organizations would like. However, alignment with goals is crucial for metrics definitions and interpretation. The other three aspects to mention are, first, adjustments of the metrics. Definition of what is required to the metric. For example, the loss ratio can be initially using in a numerator the reported claims, but it can be in another more specific case the use of the claims not reported. The same regarding the currency conversion or the inflation levels. Second, metrics are related to dimensions which are in analytics words the application of general metrics to subsets; for example, if the metric is by period of time, or region, or distribution channel or product. The issue with slicing and dicing has to be solved through data management, describing the subsets of data, visualization, and then on the modeling part by the possibility to use enough sample points to create appropriate models (review the concept of the power of the measurement in sampling to obtaining statistical significant results). Third, metrics are potentially the same in structure, but the interpretation is according to the specific problem that needs to be clearly determined. An example is the loss ratio meaning for decisions is different at the level of underwriting or at the level of prices calculation or in terms of predictive analytics.

A risk measurement system is integrated to the planning process in all levels of the organization, and it includes the metrics definition, data sources selection, validation of models, stress testing, and several testing evaluation interactions depending on the risk types. Some risks, such as credit, market, liquidity, and insurance risks, are with more data, tools, and conceptual support while other risks are more data limited for risk assessment, such as operational, reputation, strategic, legal, and regulatory and compliance risks. For the risks that are more difficult to quantify, the emphasis is on qualitative risk factors definition-identification. Quantification will be related to the direct measurement of a factor or to consequences, impact or to the complementary concepts as it is in the case of expected loss evaluation. In the case that is possible, quantifying expected losses or losses that are statistically expected to occur as a result of conducting business in a given time period a measurement – quantification of unexpected loss or the estimation of the deviation of actual earnings from expected earnings, in a time window of observation is crucial for risk management.

Stress testing helps to evaluate the potential effects of a set of specified changes in risk factors, corresponding to possible high-impact adverse economic and financial market/operational events. Additionally, back-testing maintains the validity of the metrics over time according to regulation and economic capital and viability in medium/long term of the organization. In addition, simulation/scenario analyses by different risk types, several settings, and portfolios support a measurement system.

The next section indicates metrics that a risk measurement system needs to create. The evaluation of the metrics can be as mentioned above, deterministic and stochastic. In the first approach, the emphasis is on deterministic metrics and a brief view of stochastic analysis. Additionally, as it has been indicated, it is fundamental to understand how organizations goals and strategies to deal with risk have to be aligned and clearly oriented for measurement processes implementation.

4.2   DEFAULT RATES, PROBABILITIES OF DEFAULT, AND RISK SCALES

The concepts of default rates and probabilities of default are similar, but they are not the same and in this section is presented how they are distinguished. Default rates are metrics calculated based on a ratio of risk events appearances to exposure in an observation window of time. The probabilities of default are calculations based on fitted probability distribution models to data, that combine several factors to determine the possible risk event realization. Risk scales refer to the importance of the dimension of the metrics and the comparable structure that metrics have (consistency through time).

The creation and use of risk metrics incorporate the calculation of the metrics themselves and their use. Additional analytics will be included after the metrics creation, such as the time series study of those metrics. The analytics component of the created metrics provides the possibility to develop more sophisticated and accurate risk metrics and confidence of intervals for appropriate use of the metric. Risk metrics development is a joint work among technical and business areas in order to define how they are going to answer risk management problems. The variety of metrics goes from default rates (loss ratios) to the outcomes of models in volatility analysis, time series analysis and risk or prescriptive analytics based on risk allocation. The first step is to go through the default rate and to deal with exposure and losses. A purpose of the time series generation of default rates is to identify its variability and to introduce the possibility to have access to the reasons of this variability through time. Time series of default rates will provide predictive analytics opportunities as a powerful instrument to control the portfolio and to construct better forecasting tools, using the best-fitted models. Variance measures include among many a range of the default rate, geometric variation, and variance related to the expected value of the default rate. The variance measures have to be studied to identify the random effects and the variance components of the metric. Some of the most important concepts associated with the possibility of building time series is the computation of covariance structures and correlation functions.

The probabilities of default are the source to define scores that in turn will be rescaled to classify risk according to risk cut-offs defined by the organization's risk appetite definition (risk groups/classes). The classes are determined based on the probability of default and the granularity (number of classes to use) level that is used. The number of levels depends on differentiation of classes. Higher the number is not necessary the better. The determinant of number of classes is the power of differentiation among risk levels. At the same time, it could be possible to have different classes for example by groups/industries. It is crucial to have a method of transformation or equivalence of one class to another. It is the case of having Moody's, S&P, Fitch, etc. scales for risk levels but with identifiable probability cut-offs for equivalency purpose. The assignment of cut-offs requires continuous adjustments based on the level of risk that is acceptable, the exposure that has to be in control according to policies or other managerial considerations. The separation between risk scales is part of the way to structure the risk exposure portfolio. The problem of exposure management is at the end an exposure allocation problem, a portfolio problem where the total exposure amount that should be in each class will be according to the organization's acceptable risk levels.

Probabilities of default can be related to the heads of credit (risk units) and to their transactions. The first set would be a probability of default for each customer (and the score associated to that probability) and a risk rating derived from that particular probability of default. The second set of results would be a probability of default for each transaction in the customer relationship and the organization, the score associated to that probability and a risk rating for that particular transaction. Moreover, there is at the strategic level a probability of default referred to the organization default as a whole or bankruptcy, which is the aggregation of factors affecting the organization's performance.

Another important aspect to consider in risk analytics is the identification of risk scales and the consideration of the time window for the application of the scales. It can be related to the probability of having default in hours, days, months, and years. Risk analysis needs to take into consideration the outlook and factors affecting results/outcomes in time. The presentation and interpretation of results in this chapter are based on a year of observation. The cumulative probabilities of default and the respective ratings are a mean to review the improvement, deterioration, or tactics of surveillance and follow-up of risk exposure. The probabilities of default in the practice can be benchmarked with the Moody's/S&P's letter scale. At the same time, the organization keeps the classification that is based on in-house calculations and what is from external, and market related. A point to keep in mind is in the use of the comparable risk scales. This means the type of organization, instrument, or product to use and to create means to compare results.

In a nutshell, the risk analytics methods are associated with the estimation of loss distributions (see Chapter 9 for a review of loss given default and loss distribution analysis) or the identification of the probability distribution of the indicator that is used in the risk management process. Once the loss distribution is defined, the mean, variance, and standard deviation will be converted into the structure of risk control. The procedure that needs to be followed is to identify the probability density function of losses for the general credit portfolio. The definition of loss will be considered including recoveries. The process of evaluation of the general estimators of parameters will include the possibility of using different methodologies and choosing the best according with the test run for this purpose. The procedure has to include the analysis of the losses in different years and the construction of the probability distribution that best fits to the data available. A loss distribution will need to be tested for different theoretical probability distributions (Figures 4.1–4.4).

4.2.1 Graphical Review of Loss Distribution Fitting

The lower the values, the better the fit. Laplace distribution provides a better fit for the data. The Laplace distribution is acute and the merge of two exponentials. The idea of having other probability distributions with a good fit is worth it because the description of the phenomenon can be appropriate and the implementation of the systems can be developed according to experiments and how fat the tails are. Fat tails mean the combination skewness and kurtosis. High acute histogram and narrow is an indicator of fat tails. Different methodologies to identify the fit approach will be used, particularly chi-square and Kolmogorov-Smirnov tests. Some methods of estimation and fitting, Q-Q and probability plots, the empirical comparison, will have to be included in the analysis. A set of descriptive characteristics, including different probability distribution moments,

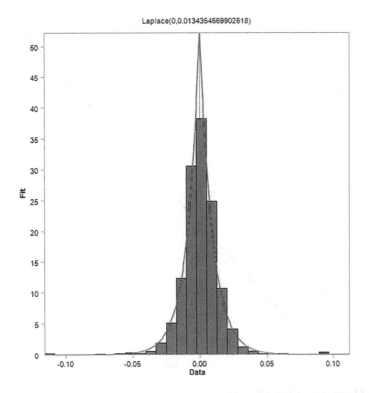

FIGURE 4.1   First step is a histogram of the data and test possible probability distributions.

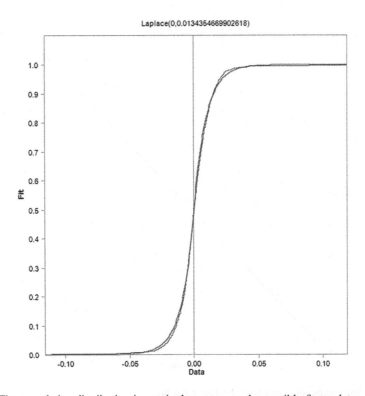

FIGURE 4.2   The cumulative distribution is required to compare the possible fits to data.

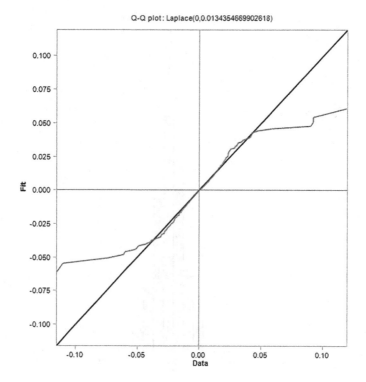

FIGURE 4.3 QQ plots shows best fits.

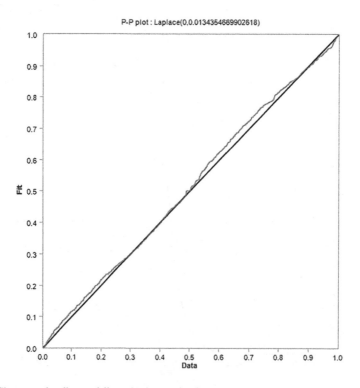

FIGURE 4.4 Closer to the diagonal line, the better the fit.

TABLE 4.1

Information Criteria Helps to Define the Best Fit. Three Fit Measurements -SIC, -AIC and -HQIC

Results of the fitting process

Name	-SIC	-AIC	-HQIC
Laplace	7417.647	7428	7424.056
Logistic	7387.844	7398	7394.253
NormalMix	7316.369	7332	7325.982
Normal	7083.608	7094	7090.017

Input	Data		
Total points	1254		
Used points	1254		
Location		Laplace	
Mean	0.00040635	0	
Spread			
St. dev.	0.014284	0.013435	
Variance	0.00020403	0.00018051	
CofV	35.151	N/A	
Shape			
Skewness	0.0035073	0	
Kurtosis	17.706	6	
Percentiles			
1%	−0.035771	−0.037165	
3%	−0.024029	−0.026728	
5%	−0.019474	−0.021875	
8%	−0.015748	−0.01741	
10%	−0.013844	−0.01529	
15%	−0.010459	−0.011438	
20%	−0.0079104	−0.008705	
25%	−0.0062483	−0.0065851	

have to be identified and created in the fitting process to evaluate estimators and means to test hypotheses. Furthermore, a table has to be built, including specifications for the use of default probabilities forecast in the general problem of portfolio assessment (Table 4.1).

4.3 EXPOSURE AND DEFAULT RATE CONSTRUCTION

The risk analytics process incorporates the creation of metrics that describe risks and risk units (objects, events, people, artifacts, etc. where the risk event appears). The following section illustrates the default rate creation process using the credit risk event with classes according to risk levels and steps of the risk management process, such as risks under surveillance and non-surveillance, and according to periods of time. Surveillance and non-surveillance are components of the risk monitoring process that in this book is a RAS main objectives to achieve: to be area of risks units lives-evolution. Moreover, the periods of exposure can be different according to the risk units. This means not all risk units will be exposed at the same time in a portfolio. The default rates allow to quantitatively assess the effectiveness of the risk rating classes, i.e., scales such as: low, moderate, medium, priority watch, critical, and unacceptable. To select the most appropriate default rate framework, different options need to be evaluated. In particular, the type of risk is the basic to build metrics. Risks such as credit are similar to car or health risks in terms of assessment approaches because of the possibility of having not only one claim event but several in a period of time or the number of risks in car and health exposure are associated with partial and total losses, the same as in credit can be default and insolvency. Default rates require the definition of two components: the claims/default/event realization and exposure calculation. Steps to determine exposure are illustrated using a credit case.

There are two main factors to consider in losses at an exposure situation: frequency of loss events (counting), severity of loss events (amounts of potential damages). These factors are associated with the calculation of default rates according to exposure and loss event definitions. At the same time, exposure management can be affected by the definition of the risk events. For example, in credit risk, it is required to define what the rules will be to define a good or bad event/ prospect. Additionally, the analysis of losses and exposure are associated with the definition of the window of events and data observations that can affect risk events. Exposure can be equally split into classes such as direct exposure or extended exposure in terms of considering the scope of the analysis. For instance, in credit risk analysis, direct exposure can be related to a transaction and extended exposure can be related to the associated business parents' risks.

A calculation of exposure by risk units or frequency is the number of risk units that can be in risk management processes, such as in the surveillance and non-surveillance portfolio. The definition of a time window for an analysis is essential to identify the risk units that were at the beginning of the period, the new ones that remain in the portfolio during the period of observation and the risk units that were out (canceled, left the organization) of exposure during the observation time period. This is an adjustment for exposure made based on the weight by time of each risk unit exposure duration in the portfolio (e.g., 1/10 of risk units had three months of exposure, 2/10 of the risk units had the whole year exposure, and so on). Risk units are associated with dollar exposure and the aggregation analysis is based on the time of exposure currency (dollar) to use.

The identification of dates is crucial because depending on them the losses will be taken into consideration for the analysis and relationship among prices, exposure, events costs, etc. The alignment of periods of declaration of losses and exposure has to be precise and consistent for the whole default rate calculation process. For example, a year when a loss/claim/default is paid is the period of time and the reference to compare the aggregated loss values by risk units and then compare them to the exposure of total of risk units.

Moreover, there are decisions to make for organizing data in exposure; for example, using a sample cohort where the default rate is calculated as fractions in which the numerator represents the number of risk units in the portfolio at the beginning of a n-month period that had a loss/claim during that period. The denominator represents the number of risk units that could have had a loss/ claim during the period (i.e., the total number of risk units evaluated at the beginning of the period). However, it is better for calculating a better approach of risk unit-year as an actuarial exposure approach where a default rate is calculated as fractions in which the numerator represents the number of risk units under observation in the portfolio during the one-year period that had a loss/claim. The denominator represents the number of risk units that remained at the end of the period minus the time-weighted number of risk units withdrawals plus the time-weighted number of new entries. Important factors in choosing the most adequate methodology should be the availability of up-to-date data that is usable and comparable through time and the best approximation to the riskiness of the risk units.

In a default rate, the numerator of the ratio the number or value of the risk events (claims, defaults, losses, etc.) that occurred in the period of time can be segmented and performed using groups, classes that are business and decision related such as customer segments, regions, industries, teams, risk classes, exposure levels, etc. Another way to approach the default rate in operational risk is as a failure rate or the hazard rate, also known as the force of mortality and the failure rate and usually denoted $h_X(x)$ or $h(x)$ is the ratio of the density and survival functions when the density function is defined. That is, $h_X(x) = f_X(x)/S_X(x)$.

4.4 AN ILLUSTRATION OF DEFAULT RATE CALCULATION

The definition of data to use has to be consistent with the risk analytics process of modeling and definition of metrics to be consistent for the future use. The metrics are initially pictures of the actual situation of the risks, but the aggregation of the metrics in time series will provide the opportunity of predictive analytics for the organization. The losses/claims cannot all be claims, only paid and an indicator could be built with incurred claims reported and not reported (IBNR). As an illustration, the following calculations can guide to create the default rates starting by the identification of all risk units month by month, marking the exposure time, and counting the number of time periods (months) that the risk unit was in the portfolio. At the end of the observation period, the weighted result will use the number of exposure months; for example (Table 4.2), 100 risk units were in the portfolio 12 months, 90 were exposed by 11 months; 80 were exposed by 10 months, etc.

One element of control in this calculation is to observe the portfolio stability in number of exposure units, how the withdraws and newcomers to the portfolio are during the year. In the credit setting, it is, for example, to have 100.000 loans at the end of the year n, new loans will be accepted every month during the following year, some will finish the term $n+1$ (this is like the inventory calculation in operations). The number of exposed risk units weighted by time of exposure will be used in the aggregation of the number of risk units exposed during the period of the default rate calculation. The underwriting control by periods of time is crucial to identify if policies of acceptance can affect the level of acceptable risk in the organization. This type of analysis is related to predictive and prescriptive analytics to figure out what the best level of return, revenues, or expected losses the organization can have.

Regarding the numerator, for example, in a portfolio of a year 1,000 claims (defaults) were paid in period n+1, 900 were the claims corresponding to the risk units exposed using the selected method of calculation (it could be for example 700 using another calculation method). Once the numerator and denominator are with the required definitions for numerators and denominators and the data gathered, the next step is to define how to slice and dice all ratios. This means to calculate default rates by risk classes, by regions, by products, or combinations for products and regions of risk levels. This process of slicing and dicing helps to define the cut-offs of the probabilities of default, for example, required by a control according to a class (e.g., the default classification that credit rating agencies use according to probabilities of default). The classes in risk classification will have a level of granularity that is determined by management and the value of differentiation in risk levels. The control will be supported by descriptive analytics as well by creating the representation of the default rate behavior and the possibility to have a forecast based on the risk classes.

TABLE 4.2
Example of Exposure (Denominator) Calculation Considering the Months of Exposure

Number of months	12	11	10	9	8	7	6	5	4	3	2	1
Number of risk units exposed during the number of months	100	90	80	70	60	50	40	30	20	10	10	10
Product risk units * periods of exposure in a year	1200	990	800	630	480	350	240	150	80	30	20	10
Number of risk units that were with exposure during a year period without considering number of months exposed												570
Number of risk units weighted by the number of months that in the year period were exposed. This is the denominator to use												415

The default rates can provide knowledge about the behavior if new risk acceptance and withdraws are in the outlook. For instance, in some cases, the surveillance process advises to change conditions of risk units or to close transactions or even to finish the commercial (risk unit) contract. As any ratio, if the number of the risk events is controllable the control is on the numerator but if the control is on the number of risk units exposed the control will be on the churn and maintenance of acceptable risk units. Furthermore, a time series of default rates can be generated by rolling the cohorts forward on a monthly/quarterly basis. This would allow tracking the rate behavior over time and to sweep more claims during the year. In any case, the purpose is to have a clearer approach to get numerator and denominators closer to the reality of risk exposure and potential events.

Depending on the risk unit aggregation, the calculation of the inputs of the default rate can change. For example, the previous calculations have been on the head of a risk unit represented by a credit contract, or a company or a person. However, the default rates can be related to transactions, converting the transaction as the risk unit to study. To measure transaction risk, transaction-based default rates will be generated, where the units under observation are the denominators and the transactions with claims will be the numerators of the default rates. The numerator will be defined as the total number of claims in the time window associated to transactions of the observation window. The denominator will be defined as all transactions during the observation window. Dollar transaction-based default rates would be calculated by dividing the total claims paid in the performance window by the total transaction exposure for a particular observation window.

In summary, to build default rates, the same as any metric development, needs multiple steps to keep the metric relevant and possible to use for building a robust measurement system. Table 4.3 summarizes aspects in the risk measurement process and data use. Each of the figures in Table 4.3 suggests steps for maintaining a clean data, updated, organized data sets that are not only because of having relational data bases or any NoSQL repository but also to have the discipline and organization to produce and keep data as the organization requires in a risk analytics process (Figures 4.5–4.9).

Moreover, as mentioned in Section 1.11, there are several other risk metrics in risk analytics. Sections 5.20 and 9.1 are the calculation and interpretation of VaR and CVaR. Conditional value-at-risk (CVaR) in a portfolio is the biggest loss that is generated by default of credit customers at certain confidence levels and time observation window.

TABLE 4.3

Summary of Maintenance of Data Quality for Risk Measurement

- Data is not just another resource. Data is the fuel for information and knowledge creation. Everything that organizations can do on improving data will have big returns in the future. Alignment, standard, and coordination of sources and use of data is required.
- Data steps for quality improvement and source use requires a general plan with defined blocks and specific goals (e.g., use AI for data gathering in underwriting).
- Controlling data quality is a management duty to support operations and strategy. In general, the whole risk analytics process.
- Data complexity starts with "numbers-figures" but the complexity will increase with unstructured data used in risk assessment, e.g., comment screen or unstructured data used for risk assessment.
- It is required to answer the question of what is the consistency among data, business and assessed risk: Risk of cash flow default in a short-term scenario?
- Data and models, measurement systems are in an ongoing interaction, that is a loop data support metric creation/models and them creates data clarity to use and to develop (new variables).

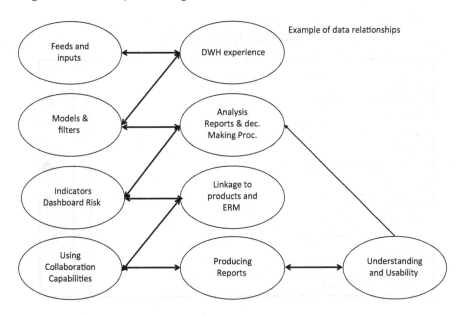

FIGURE 4.5   Possible steps to create usable data.

Data structure basis

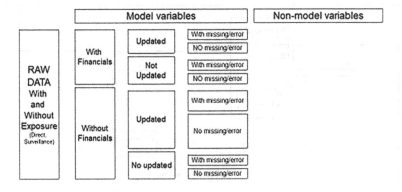

FIGURE 4.6   Data for risk measurement and variables.

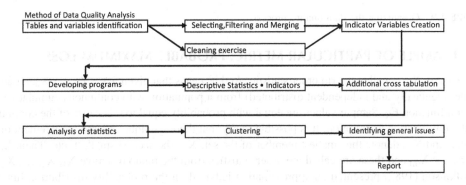

FIGURE 4.7   Following steps to maintain data quality.

Data Quality Dashboard			
Negative data	●	○	○
Outliers	○	◐	○
Zero values categories	○	○	●
Age of data	○	◐	○
Variable identification	◐	○	○
Population	○	◐	○
Related cash flow variables	○	○	●
Variable use	●	○	○
Data by sectors	○	○	●
Data by country	○	◐	○
Agreement (working capital)	●	○	○
Repetition	○	◐	○
Certified source-statement	●	○	○
Exposure with issues	○	◐	○

FIGURE 4.8   Creating evaluation dashboards of data quality.

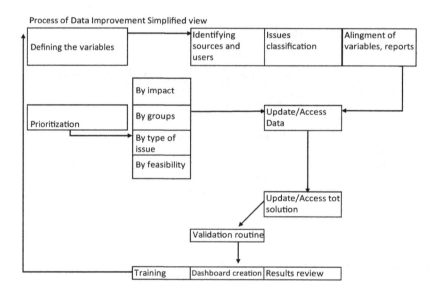

FIGURE 4.9   Organizing the data quality process.

4.5   EXAMPLE OF PARTICULAR METRIC: PROBABLE MAXIMUM LOSS

For $1 \leq r \leq n$, $X_{(r)}$ is called the rth order statistic. And it means that given a $X_1, X_2, ..., X_n$, a random sample (identically and independent distributed) from a population with continuous cumulative distribution function F_X. Sample values are equal with probability equal to 0 because of the continuous distribution function assumption. It is possible to say that there a unique ordered arrangement of the sample. And $X_{(1)}$ denote the smallest member of the set, $X_{(2)}$ the second smallest, etc. Then, $X_{(1)} < X_{(2)} < ... < X_{(n)}$ and these are called the order statistics from the random sample $X_1, X_2, ..., X_n$.

Wilkinson (1982) presented an approximation is based on the probability distribution function of $X_{(n)}$, which is the maximum value of the loss sample. It is defined as a good estimator for the PML, the expected value of the n-order statistics. Specifically,

$$F_{X_{(n)}}(x) = \Pr(X_{(n)} \leq x)$$

This means all the values of the random variables should be lower than a given value x, where $X_{(1)} < X_{(2)} \ldots < X_{(n)}$ for any n. $E(X_{(n)})$ represents the expected value under the assumption of the *i.i.d* random variables with distribution F_x. The sub-index shows the position of interest. In the case that our loss distribution is a Lognormal (hypothesis to be validated), it is possible to estimate the values in the following way:

$$E(X_{(n)}) \cong \Lambda_x^{-1}\left(\frac{n}{n+1}\right)$$

where Λ_x represents the lognormal distribution. Now

$$\Lambda_x^{-1}\left(\frac{n}{n+1}\right) = e^{\left[\sigma Z^{-1}\left(\frac{n}{n+1}\right)+\mu\right]}$$

where Z represents the standard normal distribution. The PML is given by the value and the interval around it.

$E(X_{(n)}) + k(Var(X_{(n)}))^{1/2}$ k is possible to select according to the risk appetite and which needs a variance approximation:

$$Var(X_{(n)}) \cong \left(\frac{n}{(n+1)^2}\right)\frac{1}{n+2}\left[\lambda_x(E(X_{(n)}))^{-2}\right]$$

where λ_x represents the lognormal density function of Λ_x.

Now that a PML is under a possible approximation, the following section introduces how expected losses for individual risk units and a portfolio could be.

4.6 ADAPTING METRICS TO RISK CONDITIONS: BANKS ILLUSTRATION

In general, risk analytics requires multiple steps that are interconnected; risk classification and expected losses evaluation is an example of the connection in risk analytics. Risk conditions affected the risk metrics and their interpretation. In this section, there is review and illustration of external and internal circumstances are influencing the steps to design the risk measurement system. Risk classification has related costs and benefits that require the review during the definition of the risk classes. A proper cost-benefit analysis needs to be carried out to determine the risk analytics model's best risk classification so that organization value is maximized. In particular, a confusion matrix of risk classification will have an impact on the way that classification is processed and contextualized. For example, cost can be related to human intervention or analytics technology use and data requirements.

Furthermore, metrics and classification impact in risk analytics are connected through the definition of limits of exposure. A well-defined, robust mechanism to calculate the ideal cut-offs to assign risk levels and allocate limits is needed. The process of defining limits is inherently based on the weighted-loss ratio and the utilized exposure in business operation. Such a process has direct implications, for example, when there is a need of analysis of transition matrices for risk migration. Transition matrices are the calculation of probabilities of how risk units can be in a risk class and how they can move to other classes. For example, in credit risk, to pass from a group of credits at zero days overdue to a class of more than 30 days. In other words, when analyzing migration is not only important to know how many risk units are going to migrate to worse risk scales but also to know what the amount at risk is being downgraded and possibly defaulted. An optimization analysis is required to assign and allocate limits. This optimization analysis relies on mathematical programming that is associated with goal achievement. The purpose of this analysis is to identify the best combination of variables that will yield an optimal allocation of limits. The limit allocation problem is seen as the minimization of the weighted-loss ratio or as the maximization of the credit-granting capacity.

If the problem of metrics and exposure starts with the minimization of the weighted-loss ratio, it is appropriate to identify constraints such as:

- Credit-granting capacity
- Total amount of exposure is allocated by risk tool or model
- Loss ratios defined by segments
- Segment and tool allocation accepted
- Margins in operations
- Human intervention – underwriting process definition
- Relationship premium to loss ratio
- Net loss ratio combination
- Limits used structure
- Segments mixed
- Increments accepted by tools
- Cost of data

A tool that helps to guide the risk measurement by guiding the selection of dimensions of control is the balanced scorecard as it was introduced in Sections 3.1 and above. It connects risk analytics development in the organization under uncertainty as Figure 4.10 illustrates.

Table 4.3 translates into the reality some aspects of what is in Figure 4.10.

Risk and a BSC

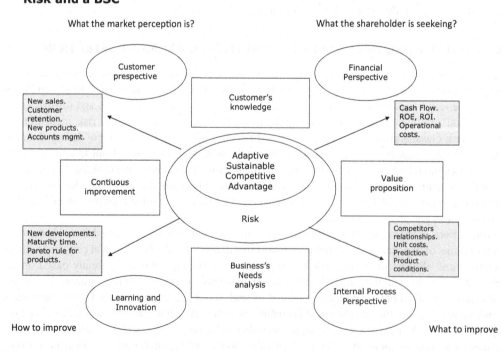

FIGURE 4.10 Risk and balanced scorecard a guide in the RAS development.

TABLE 4.4

Example of Balanced Scorecard Aspects Related to the Risk Analytics Process

Concept	Targets and Action orientation/lead in the BSC and related to support risk control
Clients/customer evaluation	• Clients with benefit of a relief programs • Digitalization and mobile bank use • Investment excellence • Customer service
Employees/learning and innovation	• Diversity and policies for people promotion • Support in case of crisis as COVID • People satisfaction – meaningful work • Satisfaction of knowledge transfer for operation
Society	• Support segments in need and development • Support to mitigate COVID effects • Taxpaying • Renewable energy power purchase agreement

Financial perspective
Shareholders financial
performance metrics
	• Defining earnings per share (EPS)
	• Estimating ROE
	• Metrics related to:
	  • EPS growth
	  • Capital ratio
	  • Payout ratio
	  • Shareholder return
	  • Benchmark

External factors – Disruptive e.g., COVID risk	• Evaluation, control, and follow-up to implement measures of recovery, increased market volatility, unemployment rates, impact financial results in business segments to several degrees. Programs in support of liquidity and funding programs, and so on.

An illustration about the real risk measurement process is given through the banks approach. The review of the risk management structure provides support on how to use analytics and risk management development, providing the framework of how risk analytics will add value to an organization. To keep in mind, a business is about managing the risks that are part of organization, industry, and society. Dealing with risk requires development of skills and management in the organization to deal with the targets (Table 4.5) and their potential risk changes and new risks through all subprocesses of the risk management process.

At the same time, goals indicate how risk measurement and actions in risk management are related to the factors associated with risk governance, risk appetite, risk management tools, risk identification and assessment, creation risk awareness and capacities to deal with it across the organization, and strategic priorities, for example (Table 4.6).

Risk monitoring and development of risk capacity depend on risk areas and risk-related sources as in Table 4.7.

Risk monitoring and risk measurement are linked in any risk analytics process given the requirement of identifying strategies to deal with the identified risks the examples in Table 4.8 provide a presentation of what certain commercial banks are looking for implementing in periods of crisis.

Furthermore, any complete process for developing a risk analytics system requires risk management principles that provides an effectively balance risk and reward to enable sustainable growth; clear responsibility for risk management; clear combination of purpose and vision, and appropriate values and code of conduct to keep reputation and public trust of all stakeholder, decisions are based on future healthy and robust control environment that protect stakeholders.

TABLE 4.5

Example of Goals in a Real Bank Operation that are the Basics and Target in Metrics Measurement

Key Performance Data All data ended October 31, 2020	1-year	5-year	10-year
Average annual total shareholdelder return	−14.6	5.1	7.3
Average growth in annual EPS	−12.8	3.2	5.2
Average growth in annual adjusted EPS	−18.2	2.6	5.2
Average annual ROE	10.1	12.2	13.4
Average annual adjusted ROE	10.3	13.1	13.9
Compound growth in annual dividends declared per share	4.4	5.5	4.2
Dividend yield	5.3	4.2	4.3
Price to earnings multiple	10.5	11.7	11.7
Market value/book value ratio	1.02	1.39	1.46
Common equity tier 1 ratio	11.9	na	na

Source: 1-year measure at Oct. 31, 2020, 5 and 10 years are averages
Source Bank of Montreatl Annual Report 2020.

TABLE 4.6

Example of Objectives and Actions According to Risk Conditions

Objectives Associated With	Course of Action
Transformation of customer service and providing more digital solutions	Several approaches • Identification of customers, verification methods • Free, real-time streaming quotes and enables clients to trade • Chatbots
Increasing the speed of growth	• Segmentation • Association with organizations to distribute services

The implementation of principles thorough policies and operational management actions has risk drivers defined in general enterprise risk management framework. Starting with a risk governance, the crucial aspect is to define a business strategy as the core of defining the risk appetite; this means to identify and maintain a business portfolio based on risk profile changes. Strategic risk control and management is the mandate of the organization's management using the strategic planning process, policies definition to align resources financial, operational, marketing, and technological to achieve the goals.

Risk appetite is part of an effective risk management to protect the organization from unacceptable losses or undesirable outcomes with respect to earnings volatility, capital adequacy or liquidity, reputation risk, or other risks while supporting and enabling our overall business strategy. Risk appetite is the amount and type of risk that the organizations are able and willing to accept to achieve business objectives. The risk appetite determines levels internal regulatory limits and constraints, and influences the risk management philosophy, code of conduct, business practices, and resource allocation. Figure 4.11 illustrates a statement of risk appetite.

TABLE 4.7

Identification of Risks and Sources of Risk in a Process of Risk Monitoring

Risk Areas	Risk-related Sources
Business environment	• Capacity and attitude to savings • Consumption, spending, payment, purchasing • Changes in inflation, unemployment • External adverse events such as pandemic • Decisions about interest rates
Knowledge, Information technology and network risks	• Cyber attacks, data breaches, cyber extortion, and use of Internet-based operations/transactions • Data sharing and use of data form external suppliers, sharing data, use of devices, etc. • Business disruption, losses in transactions, in intellectual property • Use of external services for storage and services in the cloud • Privacy, data gathering, management, and governance of data, that are connected to wrong or abusive/misuse of data, and confidentiality
International trading and geopolitical adverse conditions	There are issues to solve in agreements and threats because of trade concentration, factors affecting good countries relationships, etc., volatility in currency exchange and international capital markets
Traditional products such as mortgage	Consequences of unemployment, credit defaults, house affordability, rent, vacancy rates
Regulatory changes	Anti-money laundering regulations, the Interest rate benchmark reform, as well as data, privacy, consumer protection regulations Canadian benchmark rate for qualifying insured mortgages and client-focused reforms, continue to provide challenges and impact our operations and strategies. Money laundering, terrorist financing, and sanctions compliance continue to receive significant attention as nations attempt to deal with the harmful legal, economic, and social consequences of criminal activities. Governments, law enforcement agencies, and regulators around the world employ a variety of means, including establishing regulatory requirements on financial institutions, to curtail the ability of criminal and terrorist elements to profit from, or finance, their activities
Environmental and social risk (including climate change)	Recent events have put organizations, including us, under increasing scrutiny to address social and racial inequality and human rights issues, and failure to do so may result in strategic, reputational and regulatory risks. Additional risks are emerging associated with climate change as it relates to extreme weather events and the global transition to a low carbon economy, which could result in a broad range of impacts including potential strategic, reputational, regulatory, compliance, operational, and credit-related risks for us and our clients.
Digital disruption and innovation	Demand for digital banking services has increased, and while this represents an opportunity for us to leverage our technological advantage, the need to meet the rapidly evolving needs of clients and compete with non-traditional competitors has increased our strategic and reputational risks. Additional risks also continue to emerge as demographic trends, evolving client expectations, the increased power to analyze data and the emergence of disruptors are creating competitive pressures across a number of sectors. Moreover, established technology companies, newer competitors, and regulatory changes continue to foster new business models that could challenge traditional banks and financial products. Finally, while the adoption of new technologies, such as AI and machine learning, presents opportunities for us, it could result in new and complex strategic, reputational, operational, regulatory, and compliance risks that would need to be managed effectively.
Culture and conduct risks	the behaviors, judgments, decisions, and actions of the organization and our employees. Culture and conduct risks are considered top risks for the financial services industry due to the impact our choices, behaviors, and overall risk governance can have on outcomes for our stakeholders.

TABLE 4.8

Risks and Possible Strategies to Deal With Them

Risks	Strategies to Deal With Risk (The Bank)
Money laundering, terrorist financing, and sanctions compliance	Prevention, detection, deterrence, and the exchange/reporting of information Bank's AML Risk program includes policies, procedures, and control standards relating to client identification and due diligence, transaction monitoring, payment and name screening, investigating, and reporting of suspicious activity, and evaluation of new products and services to prevent and/or detect activities that may pose risk to the Bank. The AML Risk program also facilitates an annual enterprise-wide AML/ATF and sanctions risk assessment process and ensures that all employees, including executive management, and the board of directors undergo initial and ongoing AML/ATF and sanctions training. Information Technology and cybersecurity risk technology, information and cyber security risks continue to impact financial institutions and other businesses in Canada and around the globe.
Threat actors are adapting to the changing environment and continue to increase in sophistication, severity, and prevalence as adversaries use ever evolving technologies and attack methodologies	Proactively monitors and manages the risks and constantly updates and refines programs as threats emerge to minimize disruptions and keep systems and information protected. In addition, the bank has purchased insurance coverage to help mitigate against certain potential losses associated with cyber incidents.
Speed of digital transformation	To support this strategy the Bank is in process of opening digital factories and its key international focus markets, in Mexico, Peru, Chile, and Colombia to contribute to financial innovation, while continuing to monitor for evolving risks in new technology tools. Investments in agile, analytics and digital technology have supported the banks' response to the pandemic, its shifting portfolio, and addressing customer needs faster and with greater insight.
Supplier management – third-party use development	There is a growing dependency on the effectiveness of the control environment in place at vendors to limit the impacts of vendor availability and security incidents on the bank's operations, intellectual property, and reputation. Additionally, third-party service providers to those third parties (i.e., fourth-party vendors) can also fall victim to systems, data, and privacy breaches if their control environments fail to operate effectively.
Legal and compliance risk	Regulatory environment experienced a shift away from regulatory forbearance to increased regulatory reporting obligations and information requests with respect to certain subjects, such as customer assistance programs, liquidity, trade reporting, and market conduct. The bank proactively adjusts lending strategies across all markets and portfolios to reflect any change in risk profile, while considering government support programs available for temporary relief and customers enrolled in the bank's customer relief programs. Additional steps have been taken to expand collections capabilities to enable the bank to support customers that are experiencing prolonged or acute financial distress. The bank also performs stress tests considering these sensitivities and continues to enhance risk management capabilities through investments in technology and analytics.
External risk socio- and environmental liabilities	Emerging policy/regulatory actions on climate can elevate the bank's reputational, legal, and regulatory compliance risks. There are also emerging climate change and sustainable finance opportunities to invest in.
Model Risk	Regulatory guidelines for model risk set out expectations for the establishment of an enterprise-wide risk management framework, including policies and procedures to identify, assess, and manage the risks inherent in any model. The Bank proactively monitors and manages the risks associated with the development and use of models. It has an enterprise-wide model risk management policy in place, supported by appropriate processes and procedures, that support the identification and management of material risks associated with models.

Risk Appetite statements

Quantitative Statements	Qualitative Statements
• Manage earning volatility and exposure to future losses under normal and stressed conditions • Avoid excessive concentrations of risk • Ensure Capital adequacy and sound management of liquidity and funding risk • Maintain strong credit ratings and a risk profile that is in the top half of our peer group	• Undertake only risk we understand. Make thoughtful and future-focused risk decision taking environmental and social considerations into account • Effective balance risk and reward to enable sustainable growth • Maintain a health and robust control environment to protect our stakeholders • Always be operationally prepared and financially resilient for a potential crisis • Always uphold our Purpose and Vision and consistency abide by our Values and Code of Conduct to maintain our reputation and the trust of our clients, colleagues and communities

FIGURE 4.11 Example of risk appetite statement (Royal Bank Annual Report 2020).

Risk control is based on the definition of a framework for enterprise risk management. In the practice, delegated authorities and limits for credit, market, liquidity and insurance risks are established by the board of directors and delegated to senior management at levels below risk appetite and regulatory requirements. Senior management can then delegate some or all of their authorities onwards to others in the organization. The delegated authorities enable the approval of single name, geographic and industry sectors, and product and portfolio exposures within defined parameters and limits. They are also used to manage concentration risk, establish underwriting and inventory limits for trading and investment banking activities and set market risk tolerances. Transactions that exceed senior management's delegated authorities require the approval of the risk committee of the board of directors.

Risk review and approval processes are part of risk control mechanism and are established by the organization authority according to the nature, size, and complexity of the risk involved. The control process is associated with risk monitoring, reporting, and a culture of risk about taking risk, deal with current and future risks. Risk culture is developed through a learning process where the decisions and development of tactics is associated with the best understanding of factors influencing variation of expected results.

4.6.1 METRICS IN A BANK SETTING

As a supplement of the previous paragraphs presentation in this subsection, there is an illustration of the practice in banking to use metrics to organize risk in the management process. According to the type of risk, metrics can be defined aligned to the type of events to analyze and mitigate risks. For instance, the following risk types can use the risk mitigation strategies as indicated (Table 4.9).

Examples of developing metrics to benchmark and to control risk in financial markets can be defined by alignment of rates values or indicators of compliance with regulation. In general, ratings are created by external agencies, organizations, and internal in each organization, the translation of the risk levels according to the probabilities of events is a key process to clarify where the cut-offs of risk are, how a comparison can be performed, and what the meaning of the risk level is represented by sectors, product, corporations, etc. Exhibit 4.1 shows a sample of table equivalence for bond and scales from different credit risk agencies.

In a similar way, regulation requires having an evaluation that is the most uniform possible across markets, products, and activities. An example related to capital requirements is presented as an example in the OSFI control body of financial institutions in Canada. See Exhibit 4.2.

In addition to mitigation strategies, the capital structure through the risk-weighted assets and exposure can be summarized as in Table 4.4.

TABLE 4.9
Risks and Mitigation Strategies in Banking

Type of Risk	Risk Mitigation Strategy
Credit risk: default of issuer, debtor, counterparty, borrower or policyholder, guarantor, reinsurer), transactions where risk exposed such accounts receivables trading and non-trading activities.	Including guarantees, collateral, seniority, loan-to-value requirements, limits by segments, thresholds (tolerance levels), collaterals and their appropriate valuation, using portfolio approach (goals) for products, markets, transactions, and under constraints of risk appetite and levels of concentration.
Retail credit risk about a particular credit risk transactions and the selection of customers/clients in business with and without experience in the organization.	Individual and portfolio analysis of expected and unexpected losses the same a s the variance of possible results (volatility). Use of the metrics related to the time period observation of economic capital, probability of default (PD), exposure at default (EAD), and loss given default (LGD), Exposure assessment and its relationship to ratings. See the examples in Exhibit 4.1, 4.2, and 4.3.
Counterparty credit risk is about compliance in the obligations/agreements in transactions with futures, forwards, swaps, and options or repos.	Close-out netting or calculation/agreement of a net value between accounts payable or in case of default or risk event emerges. A way to mitigate is using predefined agreements. The mitigation policies are related to the ISDA - International Swaps and Derivatives Association Master Agreement. At the same time, the exploration of collaterals through liquid assets agreement in margin definitions.
Wrong-way risk is about positive correlation to the PD of the counterparty, credit quality, underlying assets quality, or economic-market factors.	Monitoring systems that simulate and stress test conditions related to factors such as concentration, cash flows, and liquidity.
Market risk is about effects changes in market prices because of factors such as interest rates, credit spreads, foreign exchange rates, commodity prices, equity prices, and so on.	Measurement in market risk is related to the fair value through profit or loss, aggregated income, economic value, hedge effectiveness, capital sufficiency, and so on.
Liquidity and funding risks or not capacity to generate payment means to pay obligations.	Alignment of limits, marketability of assets, conditions of markets evaluation of simulations of the assets and liabilities, and other cash flow factors under multiple appropriate assumptions. The review of the risk methodologies and underlying assumptions needs to be an ongoing process with validation and calibration of the models and information systems. The process of monitoring can be for a medium term, short term, and contingency planning.
Operational risk is associated with the effects of resources issues, measurement systems, operation flows, human skills use, capacity and capabilities development, etc.	Monitoring and systems of control for internal operation and external operations, quality of suppliers, possible threats form sources such as cybersecurity, data management, activities that are because of socio-economic conditions, corruption, bribery, supply chain, agreements, and events that affect the continuity of the operation in the organization during and/or after an adverse event.
Strategic risk is the risk that the organization that modify the adaptive competitive advantages according to formulation and implementation of strategies. For instance, image changes, reputation, social intervention, employment conditions, market competitive positions, answers to attractiveness of markets and sectors, disputes and quality of services and products, mismatch of organization's offer and customers, and society expectations.	This is basically DOFA monitoring and to work on strengthening and maintaining adaptive intelligence for competing. Deal with concentration of clients and suppliers, external-business environment information, simulation of markets, and portfolio diversification.

EXHIBIT 4.1   INTERNAL PROBABILITIES OF DEFAULT AND EQUIVALENT SCALES OF CREDIT RATING ORGANIZATIONS (SOURCE ROYAL BANK ANNUAL REPORT 2020)

| Ratings | PD Bands | | BRR | S&P | Moody's | Description |
	Business and Bank	Sovereign				
1	0.0000% – 0.0300%	0.0000% – 0.0150%	1+	AAA	Aaa	
2	0.0000% – 0.0300%	0.0151% – 0.0250%	1H	AA+	Aa1	
3	0.0000% – 0.0350%	0.0251% – 0.0350%	1M	AA	Aa2	
4		0.0351% – 0.0475%	1L	AA-	Aa3	
5		0.0476% – 0.0650%	2+H	A+	A1	Investment Grade
6		0.0651% – 0.0875%	2+M	A	A2	
7		0.0876% – 0.1150%	2+L	A-	A3	
8		0.1151% – 0.1475%	2H	BBB+	Baa1	
9		0.1476% – 0.1925%	2M	BBB	Baa2	
10		0.1926% – 0.3170%	2L	BBB-	Baa3	
11		0.3171% – 0.5645%	2-H	BB+	Ba1	
12		0.5646% – 0.9360%	2-M	BB	Ba2	
13		0.9361% – 1.5380%	2-L	BB-	Ba3	
14		1.5381% – 2.3030%	3+H	B+	B1	
15		2.3031% – 3.3460%	3+M	B	B2	Non-investment Grade
16		3.3461% – 6.7890%	3+L	B-	B3	
17		6.7891% – 10.2880%	3H	CCC+	Caa1	
18		10.2881% – 13.0635%	3M	CCC	Caa2	
19		13.0636% – 22.1820%	3L	CCC-	Caa3	
20		22.1821% – 99.9990%	4	CC	Ca	
21		100%	5	D	C	Impaired
22		100%	6	D	C	

*   This table represents an integral part of our 2020 Annual Consolidated Financial Statements.

EXHIBIT 4.2   TARGETS OF THE OSFI (CANADIAN REGULATOR) AND A BANK COMPLIANCE (SOURCE ROYAL BANK ANNUAL REPORT 2020)

| Basel III capital and leverage ratios | OSFI regulatory target requirements for large banks under Basel III | | | | | RBC capital and leverage ratios as at October 31, 2020 | Domestic Stability Buffer (3) | Minimum including Capital Buffers, D-SIB/G-SIB surcharge and Domestic Stability Buffer |
	Minimum	Capital Buffers ( )	Minimum including Capital Buffers	D-SIB/G-SIB Surcharge (2)	Minimum including Capital Buffers and D-SIB/G-SIB surcharge (2)			
Common Equity Tier 1	4.5%	2.5%	7.0%	1.0%	8.0%	12.5%	1.0%	9.0%
Tier 1 capital	6.0%	2.5%	8.5%	1.0%	9.5%	13.5%	1.0%	10.5%
Total capital	8.0%	2.5%	10.5%	1.0%	11.5%	15.5%	1.0%	12.5%
Leverage ratio	3.0%	n.a.	3.0%	n.a.	3.0%	4.8%	n.a.	3.0%

(1)   The capital buffers include the capital conservation buffer and the countercyclical capital buffer as prescribed by OSFI.
(2)   A capital surcharge, equal to the higher of our D-SIB surcharge and the BCBS's G-SIB surcharge, is applicable to risk-weighted capital.
(3)   Effective March 13, 2020, in accordance with the revised guidance noted above, OSFI lowered the level for the DSB to 1.0% of RWA from 2.25%. On June 23, 2020, OSFI reaffirmed the DSB at 1.0% of total RWA.
n.a.   not applicable.

Figures 4.12 and 4.13 summarize the sequence of metrics development related to weighted assets and capital.

And Table 4.10 illustrates the comparison of banks according to economic capital discriminated by type of risk in a personal banking operation.

All of these examples of how risk management and data analytics are related lead to giving more emphasis to the appropriate analysis of the risk exposure. An example is indicated in the next section, according to supply-chain risk.

EXHIBIT 4.3   SAMPLE OF A STRUCTURE OF CAPITAL IN A BANK (SOURCE ROYAL BANK ANNUAL REPORT 2020)

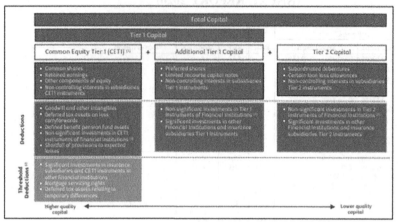

(1)   Effective March 27, 2020, in accordance with OSFI's regulatory adjustments, modifications for increases in expected credit loss provisions for CET1 capital are subject to applying a 70% after-tax exclusion rate for growth in Stage 1 and Stage 2 allowances, relative to January 31, 2020 balances.

(2)   First level: The amount by which each of the items exceeds a 10% threshold of CET1 capital (after all deductions but before threshold deductions) will be deducted from CET1 capital. Second level: The aggregate amount of the three items not deducted from the first level above and in excess of 15% of CET1 capital after regulatory adjustments will be deducted from capital, and the remaining balance not deducted will be risk-weighted at 250%.

(3)   Non-significant investments are subject to certain CAR criteria that drive the amount eligible for deduction.

EXHIBIT 4.4   EXPOSURE AND RISK WEIGHTED ASSETS (SOURCE ROYAL BANK ANNUAL REPORT 2020)

As at October 31 (Millions of Canadian dollars, except percentage amounts)	Exposure (1)	Average of risk-weights (2)	2020 Risk-weighted assets Standardized approach	Advanced approach	Other	Tota	2019 Total
Credit risk							
Lending-related and other							
Residential mortgages	$ 302,980	8%	$ 9,294	$ 15,310	$ –	$ 24,604	$ 23,629
Other retail	299,180	20%	6,848	53,696	–	60,544	59,443
Business	378,188	58%	51,175	167,628	–	218,803	215,342
Sovereign	281,426	5%	2,385	12,986	–	15,371	9,400
Bank	29,911	17%	1,720	3,508	–	5,228	7,648
Total lending-related and other	$1,291,685	25%	$ 71,422	$253,128	$ –	$324,550	$315,462
Trading-related							
Repo-style transactions	$ 857,349	1%	$ 88	$ 9,352	$ 56	$ 9,496	$ 10,469
Derivatives – including CVA – CET1 phase-in adjustment	93,930	46%	2,073	22,347	18,497	42,917	33,617
Total trading-related	$ 951,279	6%	$ 2,161	$ 31,699	$18,553	$ 52,413	$ 44,086
Total lending-related and other and trading-related	$2,242,964	17%	$ 73,583	$284,827	$18,553	$376,963	$359,548
Bank book equities	3,456	143%	–	4,931	–	4,931	4,583
Securitization exposures	64,421	18%	5,270	6,219	–	11,489	7,794
Regulatory scaling factor	n.a.	n.a.	n.a.	17,385	–	17,385	17,089
Other assets	29,459	129%	n.a.	n.a.	38,053	38,053	28,821
Total credit risk	$2,340,300	19%	$ 78,853	$313,362	$56,606	$448,821	$417,835
Market risk							
Interest rate			$ 2,309	$ 5,532	$ –	$ 7,841	$ 7,264
Equity			2,066	1,562	–	3,628	3,381
Foreign exchange			2,544	373	–	2,917	1,756
Commodities			238	49	–	287	296
Specific risk			4,932	1,053	–	5,985	8,885
Incremental risk charge			–	6,716	–	6,716	7,335
Total market risk			$ 12,089	$ 15,285	$ –	$ 27,374	$ 28,917
Operational risk			$ 70,047	n.a.	n.a.	$ 70,047	$ 66,104
Total risk-weighted assets	$2,340,300		$ 160,989	$328,647	$56,606	$546,242	$512,856

(1)   Total exposure represents EAD which is the expected gross exposure upon the default of an obligor. This amount is before any allowance against impaired loans or partial write-offs and does not reflect the impact of credit risk mitigation and collateral held.

(2)   Represents the average of counterparty risk weights within a particular category.

n.a.   not applicable.

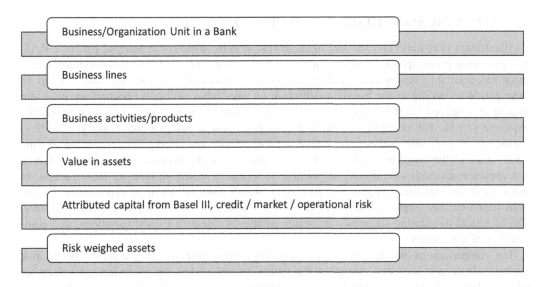

FIGURE 4.12   Business structure and risk weighted assets.

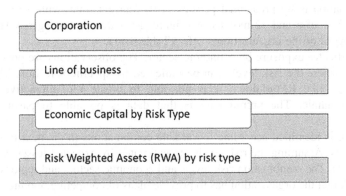

FIGURE 4.13   Economic capital and RWA.

TABLE 4.10

Comparison of Economic Capital by Risk in Personal Banking

Bank	Line of Business	Economic Capital			
		Credit Risk	Market Risk	Op. Risk	Other
Bank 1	PersonalBanking	65	0	9	26
Bank 2	PersonalBanking	78	7	15	0
Bank 3	PersonalBanking	60	1	18	12
Bank 4	PersonalBanking	75	0	18	7

Source Banks Annual Reports.

4.7 EXPOSURE MANAGEMENT IN SUPPLY-CHAIN RISK

As illustration is to build an exposure management system, which is an integral part of a RAS. The following paragraphs indicates variables and steps to create what a system requires to have using risk related to supply chain and credit risk associated with it. First, exposure is based on aggregation according to the business definition of who, what, and how. Second, an exposure system in a second layer is based on how at the customers or risk units and their levels the exposure can be, for example, buyers in the supply chain of international trading. The illustration of the exposure analysis shows the need of slicing and dicing data according to time observation of the variables such as risk levels, markets, and economic sectors. This means a risk measurement/indicator should be possible to calculate based on three or more factors. In that regard, the exposure analysis uses frequency of risk units and value of exposure of the risk units based on risk levels, markets, and economic sectors for premiums, losses, and exposure. The historical monitoring requires time series creation to identify trends, variations, and combination of the factors.

The comparison of the changes in each indicator though time is part of control, and the risk appetite/tolerance is indicated through a thresholds definition showing when metrics values are taking values that are out of policies or expectations. In this example, the expected losses are compared to the premiums and the differences in risk levels, sectors, and regions/markets appear as important matter to control risk.

First, at an aggregated level comparing frequencies (number of risk units) and values of exposure, the evaluation is by predefined periods in the current time, with a review of previous months in a window of 6 and 12 months. All figures are calculated using risk levels, economic sectors, and by types of the organization's offer (Table 4.11).

Table 4.12 indicates exposure by economic sector. The observations are possible to develop in data products where the risk levels can be indicated by specific selection. This means with the use of means like RMarkdown it is possible to create the interactive report that is shareable and dynamic. The prerequisite is that data is possible to partition in multiple dimensions.

Once exposure is identified according to variable combinations in the next level is to identify the expected losses. Assuming the risk levels are calibrated by expected losses can be calculated (Tables 4.13, 4.14). The combination risk levels and economic sectors and regions will define the conditions of risk that the organization has to provide plans of competing, monitoring, and control of risk.

Premium and expected values need to be compared to identify variation of results and potential adjustments to perform and obtain positive results. Table 4.15 summarizes by economic sector and region the values of premium. Again, the main point is to have the capacity to separate premium by the required dimensions of economic sectors, geographic regions, markets, products, etc.

Tables 4.16 to 4.17 are indicating what changes of risk can be in a portfolio. Several aspects can be derived of these tables, but one that is crucial is the comparison with thresholds (expected results or levels of risk appetite). The comparison provides the guideline to adjust what performance goals can be, the estimation of approaching the goals, and as it mentioned in Chapter 1 the possible indication of confidence intervals according to ongoing circumstances in the business environment. Each threshold can be identified as percentage variation that is acceptable in the risk appetite of the organization (Table 4.18).

In addition, creation of historical dashboards including figures that are interactive with structure as Figures 4.14, 4.15, 4.16 where the summary of the main results exposure, claims/losses, premiums, and any other risk indicator metrics that can be functions of basic factors such as the case of taking risk levels and expected losses by exposure (Figure 4.16). All of them will provide clues of what the behavior of the organization can be in a fluctuating market.

TABLE 4.11

Frequencies and Values of Exposure by Types of Risk and Business Offer

		Number of risk units					Exposure ($ mlns)				
		March 2019	Share	Quarter	6 Months	15 months	March 2019	Share	Quarter	6 Months	15 months
Exposure	Total										
	LOW	31,064	49.03%	7.37%	4.25%	1.87%	11,377	31.34%	1.28%	-1.37%	6.56%
	MOD	18,376	26.01%	1.61%	1.63%	6.27%	11,562	31.85%	-1.27%	-1.02%	7.72%
	MED	13,882	17.29%	-13.39%	-9.56%	-3.56%	7,731	21.30%	-0.06%	2.62%	-4.62%
	HI	5,628	6.72%	-16.58%	-11.63%	-24.89%	4,125	11.36%	-7.43%	-5.23%	-27.26%
	PRI	261	0.31%	-2.42%	-7.82%	-3.79%	564	1.55%	17.34%	-35.61%	-42.06%
	CRI	265	0.42%	55.41%	107.67%	274.40%	871	2.40%	39.40%	235.01%	605.44%
	UNX	160	0.24%	63.30%	79.41%	133.81%	70	0.19%	18.37%	13.10%	313.09%
	Total	69,691	100.00%	0.00%	0.00%	0.00%	36,300	100.00%	0%	0.00%	0.00%
	Main										
	LOW	31,040	50.02%	7.96%	4.81%	2.80%	10,688.13	29.44%	0.59%	-1.87%	4.97%
	MOD	16,142	26.01%	1.53%	1.66%	6.43%	10,475	28.86%	-1.06%	-0.66%	3.21%
	MED	10,393	16.75%	-14.60%	-10.68%	-5.13%	6,168	16.99%	-1.23%	2.11%	-14.38%
	HI	3,929	6.33%	-18.31%	-13.41%	-27.48%	3,307	9.11%	-9.62%	-6.73%	-33.87%
	PRI	192	0.31%	-3.38%	-5.67%	-4.03%	430	1.19%	8.68%	-10.43%	-11.90%
	CRI	215	0.35%	52.24%	100.19%	259.52%	243	0.67%	61.41%	136.95%	261.45%
	UNX	139	0.22%	70.12%	94.14%	145.85%	37	0.10%	38.60%	49.28%	176.52%
	Total	62,050	100.00%	0.00%	0.00%	0.00%	31,349	86.36%	-1%	-0.89%	-5%
	Additional										
	LOW	1,974	37.31%	-0.84%	-3.24%	-7.55%	689	1.90%	13.24%	7.02%	39.41%
	MOD	1,373	25.95%	2.53%	1.24%	4.04%	1,087	3.00%	-3.18%	-4.33%	86.07%
	MED	1,248	23.59%	-2.16%	0.53%	7.95%	1,562	4.30%	4.89%	4.69%	73.45%
	HI	595	11.25%	-3.52%	1.35%	-6.41%	818	2.25%	2.60%	1.32%	22.07%
	PRI	14	0.26%	13.69%	-29.96%	4.38%	134	0.37%	57.59%	-66.14%	-72.38%
	CRI	66	1.25%	64.91%	132.34%	278.54%	628	1.73%	32.41%	298.91%	1016.88%
	UNX	21	0.40%	27.90%	17.41%	56.58%	32	0.09%	1.31%	-11.62%	860.52%
	Total	5,291	100.00%	0.00%	0.00%	0.00%	4,951	13.64%	7%	6.02%	55%

TABLE 4.12
Exposure by Economic Sector

Economic Sectors		March 2019	Share	Quarter	6 Months	15 months	March 2019	Share	Quarter	6 Months	15 months
				Exposure of risk units					Exposure dollars		
	Mining	1,599	2.37%	0.45%	2.56%	4.91%	3,725	10%	-6.84%	-2.96%	35.49%
	Oil & Gas	638	0.95%	-0.06%	1.53%	7.44%	4,206	12%	0.45%	-3.66%	9.84%
	Knowledge Base	7,692	11.42%	-1.26%	-1.69%	0.46%	2,644	7%	3.62%	4.19%	-7.18%
	Media & Telecom	2,812	4.18%	-2.93%	-3.03%	-5.22%	3,092	9%	12.48%	11.79%	5.04%
	Engineering	12,620	18.74%	0.67%	-0.30%	0.10%	3,087	9%	0.57%	-0.78%	-10.85%
	Environment	309	0.46%	-10.55%	-0.19%	4.46%	147	0%	-35.48%	-31.91%	-27.39%
	Financial Services	747	1.11%	-3.08%	-0.99%	-0.03%	639	2%	-22.23%	-37.49%	-36.13%

TABLE 4.13

Expected Losses by Risk Level

			Expected Loss				
			March 2019	Share	Quarter	6 Months	15 months
Exposure	Total	LOW	10,934,111	13.60%	−16.07%	−4.19%	6.26%
		MOD	19,976,626	24.84%	−7.54%	−4.91%	5.66%
		MED	21,913,686	27.25%	−5.35%	−6.77%	−11.85%
		HI	12,380,758	15.40%	2.99%	−9.52%	−28.74%
		PRI	4,305,334	5.35%	10.68%	−37.65%	−41.06%
		CRI	10,024,560	12.47%	37.75%	221.26%	596.08%
		UNX	883,145	1.10%	−20.21%	12.86%	260.28%
		Total	80,418,220	100.00%	0.00%	0.00%	0.00%
	Main	LOW	10,317,978	13%	−14.99%	−4.52%	4.43%
		MOD	18,059,967	22%	−6.06%	−4.86%	1.54%
		MED	17,702,215	22%	3.51%	−10.42%	−20.55%
		HI	10,048,375	12%	8.03%	−11.11%	−35.01%
		PRI	3,287,057	4%	18.59%	−13.41%	−10.81%
		CRI	2,881,098	4%	18.03%	126.98%	258.29%
		UNX	510,358	1%	16.13%	46.16%	153.50%
		Total	62,807,048	78%	−3.69%	−5.22%	−10%
	Additional	LOW	616,132.62	1%	−42.54%	1.67%	50.15%
		MOD	1,916,659	2%	−34.49%	−5.41%	71.15%
		MED	4,211,471	5%	−48.95%	12.47%	63.30%
		HI	2,332,383	3%	−28.47%	−1.98%	22.01%
		PRI	1,018,277	1%	15.90%	−67.25%	−71.86%
		CRI	7,143,462	9%	33.02%	285.90%	1023.14%
		UNX	372,788	0%	2.03%	−13.97%	751.07%
		Total	17,611,173	22%	15.83%	24.46%	71%

TABLE 4.14

Economic Sectors Exposure, Premium, and Expected Losses

Economic Sectors	Mining	5,705,577	7%	−8.20%	−4.55%	28.91%
	Oil & Gas	5,057,238	6%	−3.65%	−11.06%	−7.16%
	Knowledge Base	5,411,754	7%	−1.37%	−3.02%	−10.81%
	Media & Telecom	6,862,136	9%	18.17%	9.68%	6.21%
	Engineering	6,694,404	8%	−0.74%	−5.04%	−12.07%
	Environment	200,963	0%	−43.66%	−35.03%	−28.12%
	Financial Services	979,391	1%	−32.21%	−36.58%	−43.92%
	Government Services	91,886	0%	21.63%	−10.54%	−24.02%
	Total	80,392,207	100%	0.00%	0.00%	0.00%
Geographic Regions	AFRICA & THE MIDDLE EAST	2,634,268	3%	−15.32%	−13.08%	2.92%
	ASIA & FAR EAST	6,684,668	8%	−0.91%	−2.57%	19.38%
	CANADA	5,373,090	7%	−5.63%	−6.71%	−23.39%
	CENTRAL AMERICA & CARIBBEAN	4,996,870	6%	0.55%	−1.69%	14.13%

TABLE 4.15

Premium by Sectors and Regions, Current Supply-Chain Share and Changes

Economic Sectors					
	Mining	11,750,208	0.92%	−5.14%	39.14%
	Oil & Gas	1,198,445	4.04%	7.08%	−14.98%
	Knowledge Base	4,591,516	3.61%	−2.14%	−5.02%
	Media & Telecom	5,595,584	13.19%	6.34%	39.08%
	Engineering	5,744,431	−1.35%	−3.34%	−10.12%
	Environment	702,605	−10.54%	−12.31%	−18.73%
	Financial Services	1,108,093	18.81%	9.52%	58.22%
	Government Services	1,092,153	−6.18%	−15.86%	3.08%
	Total	76,874,761	1.91%	−1.27%	6.95%
Geographic Regions	AFRICA & THE MIDDLE EAST	3,557,585	0.49%	6.65%	70.05%
	ASIA & FAR EAST	6,683,626	3.91%	−5.50%	20.37%
	CANADA	4,996,824	1.24%	1.40%	−12.74%
	CENTRAL AMERICA & CARIBBEAN	5,190,662	1.69%	−0.30%	18.13%
	EASTERN EUROPE	882,132	6.60%	4.06%	32.37%
	FORMER SOVIET UNION	975,366	−8.15%	−8.75%	65.48%
	JAPAN, AUSTRALIA, NEW ZEALAND	3,913,862	5.94%	5.07%	31.44%
	SOUTH AMERICA	6,056,671	−6.25%	−10.71%	58.41%
	USA	47,295,956	2.34%	0.55%	1.31%
	WESTERN EUROPE	9,757,775	0.90%	−3.41%	1.83%
	Total	89,353,212	1.60%	−0.84%	8.85%

TABLE 4.16

Premium Calculation Aggregated by Risk Levels and Its Changes

Premium Risk Units

March 2019	Quarter	6 Months	15 months
		Premium by risk levels	
89,353,212	1.60%	−1%	8.85%
	Premium economic sector risk units		

TABLE 4.17

Ratio Loss/Exposure by Risk Level and Economic Sector

	Change in Risk (Expected Loss/Exposure) By Risk Level and Economic Sectors			
	March 2019	Quarter	6 Months	15 months
Risk level	0.096%	−1.48%	0.39%	−2.09%
	0.173%	−1.99%	−0.72%	−3.69%
	0.283%	−8.60%	−6.11%	−9.25%
	0.300%	−1.77%	−1.33%	−3.80%
	0.763%	−0.16%	0.07%	−0.11%
	1.151%	0.13%	−0.90%	−3.12%
	1.270%	2.11%	3.12%	−14.36%
	0.222%	−0.47%	3.35%	−1.81%
Economic sector	0.097%	−1.19%	0.55%	−2.31%
	0.172%	−2.37%	−1.02%	−3.40%
	0.287%	−10.07%	−9.33%	−8.88%

TABLE 4.18

Use of Percentage of Changes vs. Threshold as a Warning to Surveillance, Policy Changes, or Price Adjustments

Thresholds	Exposure Risk Units Change	Exposure Dollars Change	Expected Losses Change	Premium Change	Expected loss/ Exposure Change	Premium /Expected Loss Change
By risk level	%	%	%	%	%	%
By Industry	%	%	%	%	%	%
By Country	%	%	%	%	%	%

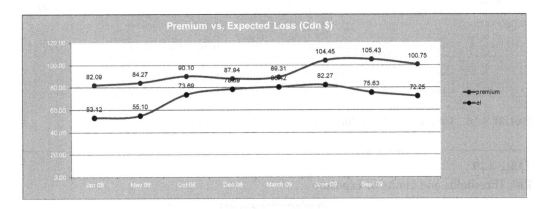

FIGURE 4.14   Review of expected losses and premium dollar amount.

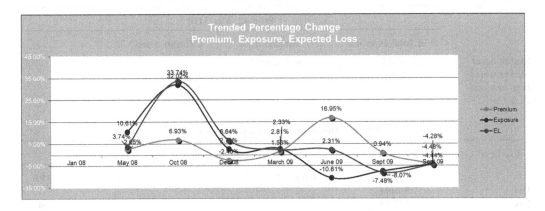

FIGURE 4.15   Comparison of exposure and expected losses and premium.

Second, at the level of customer, the systems for monitoring risk can contain these elements (Tables 4.19 to 4.21 and Figures 4.17 to 4.20 ahead):

1. According to risk-level distribution of exposure and amounts compared to thresholds
2. Risk levels, exposure, and risk units in the allowed levels (thresholds compliance)
3. Risk levels by risk units and economic sectors/industries – concentration and conditions of markets

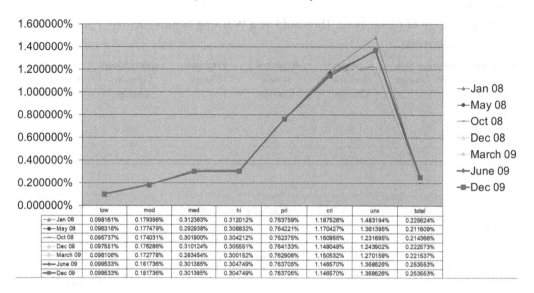

FIGURE 4.16 Time and risk levels for expected losses and exposure comparison.

TABLE 4.19
Risk Thresholds and Limits of Exposure

Threshold Measurement			
Risk Thresholds – Risk Ratings			
Risk Rating	**Exposure Guideline/Threshold**		
	Product (Mar 31st)		
	% of Total Exposure	Threshold	% Thresh. Used
Mod or better	67.32	No threshold	
Med or worse	32.64	45	72.50%
High or worse	17.11	17	100.70%
Ri & Cri•	3.16	4	79.10%

Obligor Thresholds (Risk weighting factor 33%)					
Risk Level	Obligor_ Thr.	Risk Units that are over limits as at March. 31st			
		100%*	75%	50%	25%
Low	S650M				
Mod	$450M				e4
Med	$250M				e5
Hi	Sl 25M		el	e2	e6
pri	Sl 25M			e3	e7
Cri	Sl 25M				

4. Limits by markets – countries, limits thresholds, and compliance
5. Risk concentration by variables such as region, risk level, economic sector, etc. by risk units and exposure.

TABLE 4.20

Thresholds and Industries

Industry Thresholds

| Sector | Total Exposure | | $ 31,07,75,81,041 | | Compliant | |
	Exposure	Risk Weighted	Limit	Difference	25% Oftotal Exposure	10% Oftotal Exposure
Consumer Goods	7,99,32,47,330	2,63,77,71,619	7,76,93,95,260	5,13,16,23,641	yes	yes
Media & Telecom	3,56,11,42,254	1,17,51,76,944	7,76,93,95,260	6,59,42,18,316	yes	yes
Knowledge Base	3,54,36,59,402	1,16,94,07,603	7,76,93,95,260	6,59,99,87,658	yes	yes
Mining	2,80,10,72,279	92,43,53,852	7,76,93,95,260	6,84,50,41,408	yes	yes
Engineering	2,30,83,51,390	76,17,55,959	7,76,93,95,260	7,00,76,39,302	yes	yes
Autos/trucks	1,91,34,99,263	63,14,54,757	7,76,93,95,260	7,13,79,40,503	yes	yes
FOW er	1,33,04,31,598	43,90,42,427	7,76,93,95,260	7,33,03,52,833	yes	yes
Bulk Agriculture	1,32,04,28,741	43,57,41,485	7,76,93,95,260	7,33,36,53,776	Yes	yes
Oil & Gas	1,27,85,89,979	42,19,34,693	7,76,93,95,260	7,34,74,60,567	Yes	yes
Lumber	92,65,78,530	30,57,70,915	7,76,93,95,260	7,46,36,24,345	yes	yes
Pulp & Paper	87,27,02,471	28,79,91,815	7,76,93,95,260	7,48,14,03,445	yes	yes
Fisheries	61,33,04,772	20,23,90,575	7,76,93,95,260	7,56,70,04,685	yes	yes
Aerospace	56,23,83,759	18,55,86,640	7,76,93,95,260	7,58,38,08,620	yes	yes
Transportation ser	52,99,02,949	17,48,67,973	7,76,93,95,260	7,59,45,27,287	yes	yes
Financial Services	47,82,93,567	15,78,36,877	7,76,93,95,260	7,61,15,58,383	yes	yes
Life Science	38,61,46,154	12,74,28,231	7,76,93,95,260	7,64,19,67,029	yes	yes
Meat	27,32,93,163	9,01,86,744	7,76,93,95,260	7,67,92,08,516	yes	yes
Environment	15,47,52,360	5,10,68,279	7,76,93,95,260	7,71,83,26,981	yes	Yes
Buses & Specialty	8,68,73,166	2,86,68,145	7,76,93,95,260	7,74,07,27,115	yes	yes
Govenment Service	5,39,24,897	1,77,95,216	7,76,93,95,260	7,75,16,00,044	yes	yes
Shipbuilding	3,19,82,257	1,05,54,145	7,76,93,95,260	7,75,88,41,115	yes	yes
Rail	3,07,21,669	1,01,38,151	7,76,93,95,260	7,75,92,57,109	yes	yes
Tourism	2,36,50,338	78,04,612	7,76,93,95,260	7,76,15,90,649	yes	yes

Visualization of how risk units concentrate exposure is helpful to identify risk levels, economic sectors, distribution of the portfolio, and entities-organizations-individuals that require surveillance and assessment under new risk conditions.

For instance, Figure 4.20 summarizes the customers-risk units or organizations that have the highest volume of exposure and with the risk monitoring process will be oriented and defined for improving efficiency and effectiveness.

With this review of exposure and the value in supply-chain risk analysis, this chapter guided the analysis of exposure and the way to create basic measurement systems to maintain updated knowledge to develop risk management. Risk analytics is mainly structured by the means to deal with the data, reports, metrics, and means to put risk analytics knowledge in the middle of the management practice. Data science is supporting the rational part when data and knowledge from

TABLE 4.21

Example of country as variable for thresholds definition

Country Thresholds

Figures in Thousands

Country Name	Exposure	Risk Weighted Exposure	Limit	Availability of Limit	Compliant
UNITED STATES OF AMERICA	1,44,09,820	47,55,241	n/a	n/a	yes
CANADA	14,53,651	3,67,841	n/a	n/a	yes
UNITED KINGDOM	11,23,573	3,43,909	n/a	n/a	yes
JAPAN	10,43,075	3,40,666	n/a	n/a	yes
MEXICO	9,05,930	3,08,196	74,88,800	71,80,604	yes
BRAZIL	8,54,093	2,80,393	74,88,800	72,08,407	yes
FRANCE	7,27,860	2,34,126	n/a	n/a	yes
GERMANY	7,19,734	2,22,523	n/a	n/a	yes
ITALY	7,04,574	2,20,525	n/a	n/a	yes
INDIA	6,51,242	1,95,738	74,88,800	72,93,062	yes

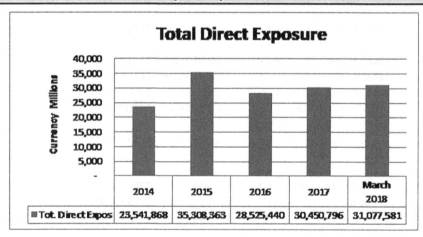

FIGURE 4.17   Historical total direct exposure.

data is possible to create and to use. Methods are multiple and the selection of the appropriate ones is part of the complexity in organizations because options are several and the experience with the methods is what will improve expertise in risk management. The work in risk analytics is not only with more and a variety of models but to use the appropriate methods/techniques to use data to support management practice.

The following chapter is about tools. Tools are in this book associated with algorithms, software, and means to deal with data to create risk analytics knowledge, understanding capacity to share, and the possibility to interact and produce dynamic in the risk analytics process. In this book, the understanding of tools starts with return analysis, data types, and statistical and machine

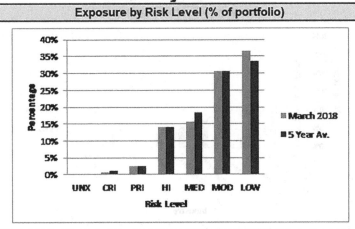

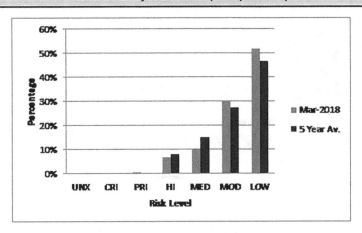

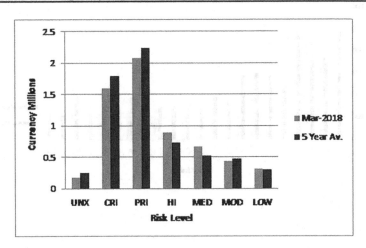

FIGURE 4.18 Risk level and portfolio exposure.

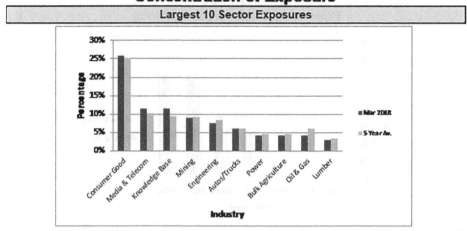

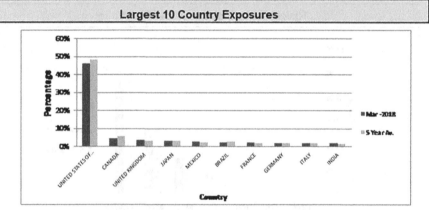

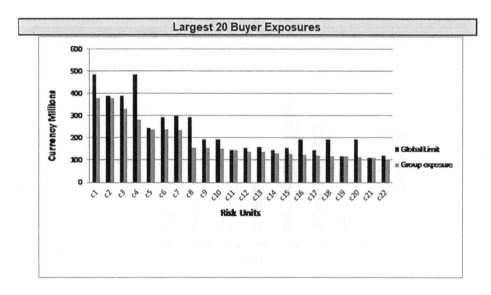

FIGURE 4.19   Concentration by risk units, segments, regions, etc.

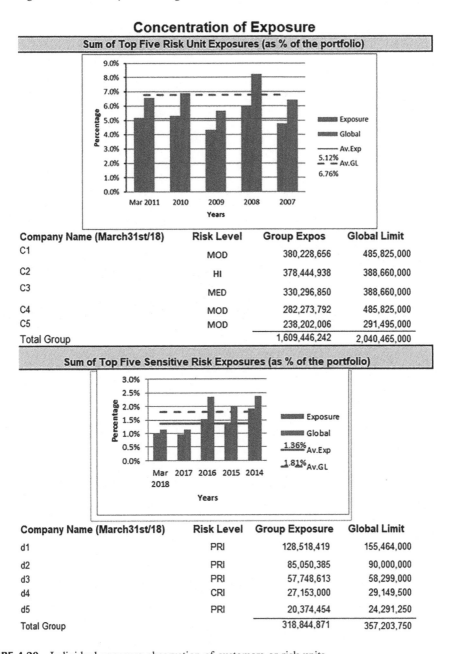

FIGURE 4.20 Individual exposure observation of customers or risk units.

learning methods/techniques used in data analytics. Tools depend on the type of data that is used and the problem to solve. The problem can be about calculations using mathematical tools such as return models or prediction as it is risk classification or optimization in portfolios. Tools are not necessarily quantitative and computational machine based; the tools can be qualitative that supplement the quantitative views providing more value according to quantitative approaches. In particular, the next chapter introduces the interest rate analysis in financial products that helps to review deterministic and stochastic approaches to measure factors that can affect risk exposure and losses.

5 Tools for Risk Management

In this chapter, there is a presentation of the risk analytics process to be implemented in a RAS design following two approaches: first, qualitative models and improvement of knowledge to deal with uncertainty and manage risk and second, to connect the approaches of dealing with risk through financial concepts of risk management based on return-interest theory, portfolios, and products for risk management (derivatives). The combination of qualitative and quantitative approaches is crucial in the development of more robust solutions in risk analytics. In general, in this book, there is a presentation of the risk analytics process for keeping the balance between understanding what qualitative models require to add value to the organization and what quantitative models use from actuarial science, finance, and statistical and machine learning techniques. The possibility of using multiple types of data in risk management is a key part of the required balance of discovering techniques to obtain better knowledge to deal with uncertainty.

To start with a more specific study, if the analytics arsenal that risk management has the first step is understanding interest (more general return of assets analysis) behavior and related traditional products in the financial practice. In 2021, Longbing Cao (2021) expressed that AIDS (artificial intelligence and data science) has changed multiple conditions of the current financial world: "AIDS consist of (1) classic techniques including logic, planning, knowledge representation, statistical modeling, mathematical modeling, optimization, … natural language processing (NLP); and (2) modern techniques such as recent advances in representation learning, machine learning, optimization, data analytics, data mining and knowledge discovery, computational intelligence, event analysis, …, AIDS largely defines the objectives, products and services of the new era of EcoFin and FinTech and nurtures waves of EcoFin transformations toward increasingly proactive, personalized, intelligent, interconnected, secure and trustful products and services, forming smart FinTech …)."

In that order of ideas, the evolution of finance risk is about creating a Fintech set of smarter solutions and that include the interaction of humans and machines. This general topic will be divided into three chapters in this book, the current one, Chapter 6 for understanding more about data and Chapter 7 where machine learning basics will be reviewed. The first step in that direction is understanding what is presented in the following sections, where there is a description of managing risk knowledge as an instrument of strategic development in organizations and how return analysis in the traditional way has been used for dealing with risk. The presentation of the topics includes, on the one hand, a view of how the risk analytics process is performed in risk management implementation that is supplementary to what is in Chapter 1, Section 1.3. And, on the other hand, how multiple variables can affect risk management subprocesses such as risk classification. The assumption in this view of risk analytics is that better knowledge through analytics can help to mitigate risk. Risk analytics uses tools of financial mathematics and tools from data science. There are limitations in the use according to regulation, but multiple problems have been solved and can be tackled with statistical and machine learning tools. In that regard, what is fundamental is to understand how human capital is created and developed in the analytics capacity of the organization to improve the capabilities for strengthening adaptive competitive advantages. This chapter discusses the need of the search of models where it is not only to find the best model but also to find the best variables describing the risk classes. In risk classification, there are variables that can be related to demographic data, transactions, experience with products, marketing, etc. In risk analytics, the ongoing improvement is in the calibration of models in order to detect better variables, models, and data sources to use for better understanding of risk factors/causes and their control.

DOI: 10.1201/9780429342899-6

TABLE 5.1

Combination of Types of Analytics and Applications

Type of Application/Type of Analytics	Descriptive Analytics	Predictive Analytics	Prescriptive Analytics
Strategic			
Managerial			
Operational			
Customer – facing			
Scientific			

Moreover, there is a gap in the identification of the relationship between risk and the expertise of the company. The gap appears between the know-how of what the company does for creating value and what it does with data analytics using data, models, techniques, and methods for dealing with risk. For instance, variables defining the expertise of the company and its management are used to identify relationships with risk evaluation and possible investment in the company's shares. To pave the gap, it is possible to use risk analytics as a human development and machines interaction for supporting decisions and problem-solving processes in an organization's risk control. Risk analytics will be a competitive advantage according to the degree that organizations grow in the adoption and adaptation of the risk analytics process. There are different tasks that need to be connected, as is illustrated in Table 5.1, which indicates in one dimension the types of analytics and the other the level of applications.

In general, the questions to answer in risk analytics implementation are related to the value of data, models, and systems, plus other factors in organizations to strengthen adaptive competitive advantages. Networks and data-enabled learning are a good mix to improve and maintain strategic positions in the market. What is difficult is to develop learning and networks based on data (Hagiu and Wright 2020). The concept of using data enabled learning to compete and deal with risk is about three main points. First, access to data and capacity to maintain it in good standing and protected. Second, answer to the questions of how data is developing differentiation in the offer of the organization, in the dimensions of how the organizations make things, in the way that analytics and AI means will provide value added to operation and (product, services, social participation, etc.) to the organization. Who in the sense of identifying and maintaining customers and transactions in the desired direction of strategies (revenue balanced and appropriate customer experience) and what in the sense of data product creation for supporting the business operation. Third, answer the question of what data, strategies, and products are designed and oriented according to a better risk knowledge of the market, competitors, and socio-economic environment.

A business can change faster than people think. For instance, financial services are under the pressure of adaptation to new FinTech-Blockchain, healthcare operation and HealthTech, government and supervision and RegTech, insurance market development and InsurTech, educational models and EdTech, and more AI use and applications. Intermediation business is changing and the business model needs to change. The questions that emerge regarding risk management are about risks of data, software, analytics models, and in general the objects and actions in the risk analytics process. The analysis of operational risks and their implications in other additional risks is growing and requires new risk management approaches. For instance, new digital banks are growing and AI and Fintech are used in underwriting and controlling risk events. These are cases:

1. Ant Financial Services: No cash society, what is the value of financial intermediaries, P2P loans.

2. Zebra Medical Vision: Image diagnosis in what is required, enhancing the radiologists capabilities using AI.
3. Wayfair: All about automated logistic clusters in anywhere to be closer to the final user/costumer.
4. Indigo AG: Digitalization at the service of farmers improving environmental sustainability and profitability.
5. Ocado: The online grocery looking from effortless of the customers of getting their food.
6. Microsoft AI Factory: The means to understand AI through experiences of start-ups to support digital transformation.
7. Waymo: Driving for changing the transportation business, automotive industry using AI.

These above examples illustrate changes in business models for organizations. Business models bring new risks, and it is required conceptual models to connect data, creation of basic metrics, and the way that business need to adapt the risk analytics process balancing intuition and reason. A qualitative conceptual model approach leads to knowing where the models and their outcomes will add value to the organization. In a simplified way, the strategy of the organizations is connecting problems, data methods, techniques, and solutions for the business to achieve goals. Organizations will embed the solutions in their offer of products and services and will search for keeping adaptive competitive advantages in their markets (Figure 5.1).

In general, organizations compete and perform well, create models, financial engineering processes, products based on models and technology, etc. The creation and implementation of strategies and tactics move the whole organization in all levels to define data and analytics capabilities to be part of people's capabilities/skills. These skills are crucial to operate and to incorporate new knowledge to manage risks and guide business processes to achieve goals. People in organizations converted into creation and integration units of the digitalization-automation process in organizations (Figure 5.2).

Technology is a means to support what humans are developing in descriptive, predictive, prescriptive analytics, AI, and the support of multiple technologies that are emerging from assisted intelligence, augmented intelligence, and autonomous intelligence to the process of data analytics. New capacity is added to risk analytics with technology improvement, for example: parallel

FIGURE 5.1 Connecting risk analytics and the strategy in business.

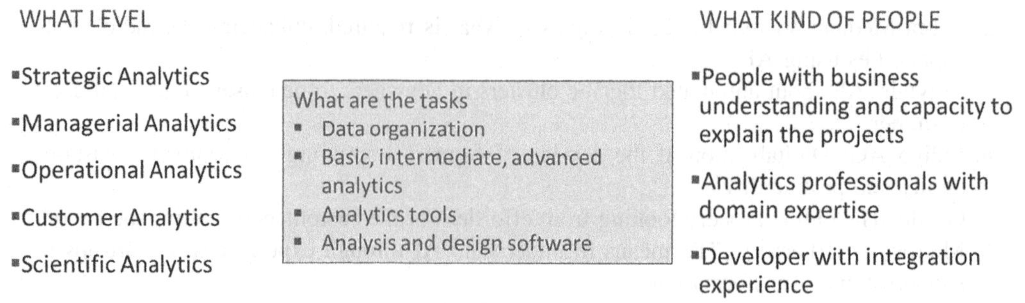

WHAT LEVEL   WHAT KIND OF PEOPLE

▪Strategic Analytics

▪Managerial Analytics

▪Operational Analytics

▪Customer Analytics

▪Scientific Analytics

What are the tasks
▪ Data organization
▪ Basic, intermediate, advanced
   analytics
▪ Analytics tools
▪ Analysis and design software

▪People with business
understanding and capacity to
explain the projects

▪Analytics professionals with
domain expertise

▪Developer with integration
experience

FIGURE 5.2 Analytics levels and people's skill requirements.

computing: divide tasks in small units to perform them in parallel; multithread computing, distributed computing, freestanding analytics, etc. all of them require the integration of analytics process, the capacity to identify new risks in organizations, and then to prepare the arsenal of risk analytics tools to deal with old and new risks that affect strategies and tactics.

The chapter is divided into 11 sections. The first four sections indicate how risk knowledge evolves, and assets tangibles and intangibles are included in RAS design and their influence in the development of return in organizations. Sections 5 to 11 show principles for defining products in risk management and finance with the purpose of showing the analytics part based on a basic mathematical development of return.

5.1 PREVENTION, RESILIENCE, AND PREDICTION

In the first four chapters, the presentation has been centered around the risk analytics process, the way to create the bases of measurement systems, all with the principle of the search to control risk, to minimize losses, variation of expected results, etc. The concept of prevention is associated with predictive analytics. The risk events can occur, but the losses could be manageable if prediction about risk events and their effects are in place. For example, in terms of pricing, the accumulation of customers payment covers the claims in insurance and in the case of natural disasters the event can occur, and the society can act according to a plan to mitigate additional adverse events avoiding increasing the losses. Vaccines are not immunizing people to infections at 100%, but they are acting as a means to build barriers to the infections and in the case of the infections to have a body with better answers to the adverse event (infection) effects. In car accidents, the numbers show the way that casualties are reduced because of the use of the seat belts, but it does not mean that accidents will not occur. In this case, risk analytics can guide organizations to find variables, factors, and means where the effect of the adverse risk events can be reduced, the losses minimized, and the risk units keeping the operation.

In the case of the airline business, the big impact of September 11, 2001, created huge losses, bankruptcies, and several related industries suffered economical damage. However, the understanding of the business operation knowledge, forecasting techniques, evaluation of cost structures, simulation of passenger's movement, transportation networks evaluation, etc. created a high number of operational protection methods/systems. In the times of COVID-19, the organizations could manage the effects of the adverse event, reducing the negative impact, developing systems to deal with the pandemic, and structuring platforms for the operation of human life. The stand-alone solutions or research results are not adding enough value if there is no a way to integrate it, a way to create the system that will help to operate hospital, enterprises, prevention, education, etc. Airlines learn to share resources to have a better organization to manage costs that add means to control operational and financial risks.

Predictive Methodology and Techniques

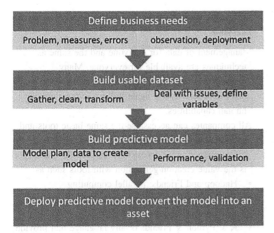

- Statistical and machine learning techniques smaller differences
- Using big data and BDA
- Supervised, unsupervised and reinforcement learning
- Data visualization: Tableau, PowerBI, R ggplot2, Python
- Bayesian networks
- Clustering
- Dimension reduction – principal components
- Relationships regressions – generalized linear models

FIGURE 5.3   Sequence of analytics and techniques.

Predictive Methodology and Techniques

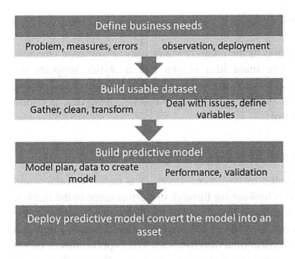

- Survival analysis time is the interest
- Trees decision, classification
- Ensembles: Random forest, ADAboost, gradientboost, Bagging
- Naïve Bayes Classifier
- Neural networks
- Deep Learning

FIGURE 5.4   Sequence of analytics and techniques.

Figures 5.3 and 5.4 indicate the same steps of predictive methodology with multiple techniques to use. All of these techniques are appropriate in risk analytics. The learning process for the modeling process is as it was illustrated in the bank example in the previous chapter. An important aspect in risk analytics is that predictive methodologies have to be connected to prescriptive analytics methodologies. This means after we have ideas of what kinds of events or effects the events can have the problem will be to develop structures of rules, decisions, automation, and operation in organizations.

In general, the creation of competitive advantages is sustainable based on risk management development. A risk analytics process provides answers to what organizations are looking for, as is

TABLE 5.2

Differentiation and Use of Analytics

Examples of What Organizations Want to do	Differentiation can Exist But Many Resources are for Everyone
• Not only to deal with the issue with model selection but also with the capacity to automate processes. • Manage the mix of the blended models of people's minds and machines. • Maintain the analytics process with a complete view every time. Do not see any project of analytics in silo way. It can be very costly. • Try to think without the noise of vendors! This helps for decisions. • Use the best of each tool and be clear with the scope of the need/problem to solve. There is no need of overcapacity all the time! Learn to do/use something very well and then move to work with other models. • Differentiate using multiple areas of organizations, for example the capacity for testing, to create workflows, to develop the last mile-deployment process of solutions in a smooth way, etc.	Management of data for everyone and the same as techniques are available for everyone. Many organizations will use the same data in the same sector, and the differentiation again will come from people: human capabilities. All companies can access/use the same basic tools and computational capacity, the open source created no differentiation in the access to resources. The crucial part is the value creation/generation with tools such as: • Hadoop and Friends: parallel computing • Spark: large-scale data processing very fast • Karma: data integration tool • R & Python & Friends or any language that provide support to modeling and automation • Technology for processing is cheaper and closer to final users.

indicated in Table 5.2, and the point is that risk analytics is part of human capabilities that can lead to differentiation in organizations.

The following sections present an introduction of the chain risk analytics, knowledge creation, and development of return-profit analysis. The main idea is that risk analytics supports the knowledge creation that will support organizations to deal with return and profits development. The perspective in this chapter is that return theory is based on predictive analytics, portfolio analysis, risk modeling, monitoring, and control.

5.2   RISK ANALYTICS KNOWLEDGE OF RETURN

This section includes a review of the knowledge management theory as a means to understand what a company as investment and return goal is looking for through its performance in the market. The organization's knowledge and risk relationship is based on the company risk evaluation, the value of its shares, years in business of the company, the experience of its management, financial statement quality, and variables identifying organizational development. The expectations of future returns are considered as part of the understanding of the risk level and the quality of the knowledge that the company currently possesses. Potential relationships are indicated using descriptive and predictive analytics. The human and financial relationships are explained first, identification of the significant variables and description of the relationship(s); and second, as a step towards opening a methodological path to evaluate risk and knowledge perception from the investor point of view.

Human attributes in management and the modeling process development are part of the risk analytics capacity. According to Figure 1.5, the main point to keep in mind is that data analytics is a means to create knowledge and knowledge is a way to deal with uncertainty/risk through risk analytics knowledge consolidation. Knowledge requires appropriate use, orientation, and development. The review of the concepts in the chapter is based on the observation of how risk analytics is connected to an analytics process and how human intervention is crucial for increasing the value of risk analytics. One goal in the search of the value of analytics knowledge or risk analytics in risk control is to seek potential relationships between investor's knowledge about an organization and the volatility of the stock return and the credit rating evaluation from credit agencies. Reputation of the firm is represented by innovation, quality of products and services, years in business, and identification of the firm as a leader in some fields or as being possessed of attributes such as being a good employer.

In risk analytics, a purpose is to protect the value of the organization. The value proposition of an organization is related to alignment of the elements of support to the business, securing of the information risks, speed in the delivery of service, reduction in the cost of service, and improvement of the service quality and management of risks. Management of an organization is looking for creating value for the internal and external client. Organizations use it to create value not only for the accumulation of knowledge, experience to improve IT and business processes, and alignment of business strategies and technology, but also establishing a series of relations between the administration of the organization and the different groups of interest, organizing structures that comply with the strategic development of the organization, and providing transparency in the information in terms of conditions, decisions, and actions.

As is indicated in Figure 1.5, knowledge can be considered a factor to reduce risk (Dickinson, 2001). Knowledge transfer can be influenced adversely by the existence of knowledge silos, and business units can require education in how to transfer experiences (Horton-Bentley, 2006), taking into consideration that the pace of change can reduce the value of experience in some specific fields (Hayward, 2002). Thus, the relationships sought between risk and knowledge to create competitive advantages are based on the identification of associations between factors related to firm reputation, competitiveness, and structural capacity for achieving positive results for its stakeholders. Bowman (1980) describes the paradox of having a negative association between corporate return and risk when there is a positive relationship, from the portfolio point of view, between return and risk. The meaning is that companies with lower risk and higher return have a higher share price, reducing the return for the owner or buyer of the stocks. This result has inspired many different articles and in particular this one in order to understand whether the better the organization knowledge, the better the risk, which will have consequences for the investor's decision depending on the return appetite.

The search of relationships includes factors divided into three groups:

- Value of the firm, credit decisions, and intangibles in organizations
- Consumer and customers' risk perception, and investment behavior
- Value of the brand and reputation in investment decisions

5.3 VALUE OF THE FIRM, CREDIT DECISIONS, AND INTANGIBLES IN ORGANIZATIONS

Risk analytics is a means to contribute to identifying the relationship between intangible and tangible assets in risk management processes, to build measurement systems, and to use risk knowledge creation as a means to mitigate and control risk before, during, and after the risk event. Miller and Bromiley (1990) examined the risk factors used for different measures affecting strategic risk management. The factors are related to the risk of income stream, stock returns, and strategic risk. The measures of risk and the association with performance are not clear and, in some cases, contradictory results have been presented in different studies because of the measures used for risk and its attributes. This means that a first step in the analysis is to define what risk measure(s) will be used (as it was indicated in Chapter 3). In this chapter, the description of risk is in the variance of return and the credit agency evaluation of the firm. Miller's and Bromiley's (1990) results show a negative association in performance of the income stream risk.

Johnson et al. (2002) studied the relationship between knowledge, innovation, and share price. They found that the knowledge-based enterprise obtains firm value based on human capital, research and development, patents, and technological assets. The evaluation of companies is based on intangible assets when the financial statement of the organization is more based on intellectual capital than on the valuation models of traditional accounting practice. Johnson et al. (2002) indicate that it is difficult to find how research and development influences the share price because of the different ways in which R&D affects organization performance. Similarly, goodwill is considered significant in the share value for non-manufacturing companies but not for manufacturing organizations.

Catasus and Grojer (2003) demonstrated that credit decisions take into consideration the value of the intangibles and that it is possible to get access to capital markets if a company is intensive in intangible assets. Guimon (2005) observed the value of the intellectual capital report in the credit decision process and presented a wide set of references where investment decisions and cost of capital are based on intangibles disclosure. Patton (2007) studied metrics for knowledge in organizations where traditional project management may not be most effective. The concept of intangible assets as skills and their strategic value imputes an important role to intellectual capital and intellectual property in creating competitive advantage. Patton's study is complemented by that of Hillestad (2007), who examined ratios on the Oslo Stock Exchange and found that intangible assets add value to increase equity and to produce better equity ratios.

Fiegenbaum and Thomas (1988) examined a broad list of studies of risk-return association. They found that individuals mix risk averse and risk-seeking behavior when there is a search for a target return. Their main result was therefore to validate the paradox of the risk-return association based on the target of the organization; This means there is a negative correlation between risk and return. The conclusion is that firms with losses and companies under the target return level are risk seekers, according to McNamara and Bromley (1997), who studied the influence of cognitive and organizational factors on risky decisions. The setting selected was risk assessment in commercial lending, where human judgment is important for credit decisions. The study examined behavioral factors that can modify the risk assessment based on willingness to take risk and suggested examination of the risk assessment presented by managers in order to identify the patterns of decisions related to cognitive and organizational factors.

Thus, the credit assessment process as an indicator of risk relationship with behavior leads on to the value of additional information in investment decisions. Lim and Dallimore (2002) analyzed the information that is needed and valuable for the investors. They presented a difference between the relationship with the disclosure of the intellectual capital in manufacturing and services, showing that better disclosure of intellectual capital is related to better understanding of the health of the company. This means a better understanding of the organization's intangible assets.

Brammer et al. (2004) studied U.K. companies in the "list of the best" in *Management Today* and found that in the short term, reputation led to a higher return. This important result has as its complement Mulligan's and Hastie's (2005) work on the impact of information on investment decisions. They found that when information is used for the risk judgment, negative (i.e., adverse) information has a high impact. In addition, Wong et al. (2006) studied the behavior of individuals regarding selling securities. Investors, whether winners or losers, decide to keep or to sell according to attributes of the people involved in the trading process. Orerler and Taspinar (2006) did research into utility and risk and the decision-making process. Their conclusion is that the psychological component of the investment decision, in terms of how much risk to take, is important in the process and there is more risk tolerance for the decision when there is more knowledge or control.

Moreover, Baker and Wurgler (2007) used two main assumptions. First, investors follow their beliefs about future cash flows and investment risk that are not supported by information or facts and, second, that making decisions against people's feelings can be risky and costly. They conclude that it is possible to measure the sentiment of the investors and that it is possible that the results affect the stock market. Additionally, Desai et al. (2008) presented a relationship between the consumer's perception of risk when they manage business and the years in business for the organization. Operational and strategic risk are associated with years in business in the way of sustainability of the competitive level of the organization in the market.

Thus, there are several examples of relationships between the investor's psychology and the perception of risk. Perception of risk can affect decisions, and in turn can be affected by knowledge and information about reputation, business longevity, and perception of organization competitiveness. Brand equity or brand value play an important role in the investment decision. Brand equity includes the human factors associated with the brand evaluation. Motameni and Shahrokhi (1998) identified several perspectives on brand equity valuation and their associated measures. Factors such as style, culture, and attitude are those that people need to keep the value of the brand. Jucaityte and Virvilaite (2007) went on to introduce the influence of the consumer into the traditional view of the economical value of the brand. The influence of the consumers is represented by psychographic and behaviorally-oriented metrics for the brand evaluation. Finally, Mizik and Jacobson (2008) presented the pillars of the brand evaluator model developed by Young and Rubicam (a leading marketing communication agency). They showed that the most important for brand valuation was to identify the financial impact of the perceptual brand attributes. They concluded that the stock return is associated with three elements: energy, perceived brand relevance, and financial performance measures.

Therefore, risk analytics has a lot of room to grow and to connect the risk knowledge creation and application to create value and to improve risk management processes and systems. The above presentation identifies three components in an investment decision related to intangibles, psychological factors, and brand value. Risk and knowledge are clearly intertwined in this discussion. Applying risk analytics in the search of relationships, three questions were studied: Is there a difference in risk level between companies with different levels of knowledge? Are intangible assets directly associated with investment risk level? What are the variables that can identify groups of companies based on risk, knowledge, and structural capacity?

The search of how to align risk analytics and organizations value requires the study of organizations' use of data analytics/risk analytics. Organizations use data/risk analytics with the hope of improving knowledge to deal with uncertainty and it requires effort in studying different scenarios. Preliminary results show a differentiation of the groups of companies based on a combination of risk and knowledge management variables which suggest a differentiation among organizations. A risk analytics process includes the creation of indices describing levels of risk, knowledge, and structural capacity, clusters to define classes, and identification of variables describing clusters. In the next section, an approach to find the contribution of knowledge to performance guides a search for understanding how to improve risk analytics to be more productive/efficient. The variables independently analyzed suggest that not all clusters of organizations include risk variables as differentiators and when the cluster includes risk variables, they appear with score variables such as years in business of the company, number of years on the 500 list, people management quality, and innovation. The score level of the indexes shows relationships, especially with the low and high scores, because of clusters' attributes and a relationship between low- and high-risk index levels with a high and low index of KM and nonstructural index levels.

5.4 ASSETS AND RETURNS

The following is an illustration of a data/variables definition and organization in a risk analytics process for the identification of intangibles and tangible assets factors in performance and risk management:

1. Construction of a database of selected companies and appropriate variables from several data sources.
2. Conversion of data into a consistent format to enable manipulation of the variables. The raw data included continuous variables, ratios and amounts; ordinal variables in the form of scores, and binary variables – indicators of belonging to a list or not. As far as possible, all variables were converted into an ordinal scale based on quartile rankings, with a score

of 4 being the best. Variables such as volatility therefore had the scale reversed in this
process, because smaller volatility is better.

3. Creation of three new variables called indices of risk, knowledge, and structural capacity.
   These indices are based on the sum of the values in each group of variables related to risk,
   knowledge management, and structural capacity: financial variables and number of
   employees.
4. Search for relationships, firstly by exploratory analysis such as cross tabulation and
   correlations, and then using multivariate techniques, specifically cluster analysis and
   decision trees, using the algorithms from the SAS 9.4 tool.

Part of the steps to follow implies the selection of tests and methods to validate metrics and results.
For instance, Spearman's Rho was the main criterion used because of rank correlation search
among variables. The probability level of rejection of the null hypothesis was put at $\alpha = 0.05$. The
null hypotheses are in general that the variables are not associated with the score of the risk index.
To identify variable relationships techniques, clustering and decision trees are used.

A clustering process allocates companies into groups according to the data. The purpose is that
in each group the components are considered similar according to the rule of the pattern similarity
defined. The purpose is to differentiate the most among the groups-clusters and the maximum
internal cluster pattern similarity. The clustering method uses different algorithms such as SAS
fastclus proc for the application of the k-means algorithm. Additionally, classification trees can
offer results based on a tree representation, the percentage, and variables that split the company
sets. The split is based on the classes of the dependent variables. The variables with the higher
percentage of members in each category at the end of the tree (leaves) allow the identification of
the attributes of the companies in each level of the risk index. Figure 5.5 illustrates the possibility
of using clusters and trees to define groups of organizations according to risk metrics.

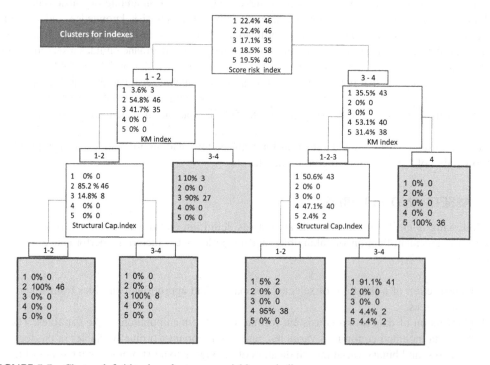

FIGURE 5.5 Cluster definition based on new variables as indices.

There were four main steps in the analysis:

1. Construction of a data base of selected companies and appropriate variables (shown in Table 1). Data sources included *Fortune* 500, 500 most admired, Make list, ASTD list, Yahoo finance, Orbis, Moody's, Standard & Poor's, and Dun & Bradstreet. The database includes 205 companies in a range of sectors.
2. Conversion of data into a consistent format to enable manipulation of the variables. The raw data included continuous variables, ratios, and amounts; ordinal variables in the form of scores, and binary variables-indicators of belonging to a list or not. As far as possible, all variables were converted into an ordinal scale based on quartile rankings, with a score of 4 being the best. Variables such as volatility, therefore, had the scale reversed in this process, because smaller volatility is better. This conversion would also serve to reduce the effect of an unusual value for one variable for a specific company in the particular year.
3. Creation of three new variables called indices of risk, knowledge, and structural capacity. These indices are based on the sum of the values in each group of variables, as shown in Table 5.3.
   • Risk
   • Knowledge management/intangibles
   • Structural capacity: financial variables and number of employees
4. Search for relationships, firstly by exploratory analysis such as cross tabulation and correlations, and then using multivariate techniques, specifically cluster analysis and decision trees, using the SAS Enterprise Miner algorithms.

Exploratory analysis is concentrated on the defined scores instead of the original data variables. The reason is to obtain comparable scales using ordinal variables. The variables associated with the risk index following $\alpha = 0.5$ are the scores of belong to Make list (Make is a survey for benchmark regarding use of KM and intangibles), number of years of 500 list, percentage of intangibles, working capital, number of employees, operating result, total asset amount, revenues, and profits. This means most of them are from the structural capacity variables group except belonging to the Make list, number of years on the 500 list, and percentage of intangibles.

However, taking independently the variable scores of S&P, Moody's, and volatility, it is found that for the first two the correlation exists with the scores of belong to the Make list, most admired, number of years on 500 list, years in control, innovation, social responsibility, long-term investment, quality of management, and financial soundness. Volatility is associated with the scores of belong to the Make list, number of years on 500 list, years in business, percentage of intangible assets, and structural capacity variables. According to the multivariate techniques and the scenarios used, the summary of results is the following per each scenario and per each technique:

Scenario 1 Using Only Indices:

Using clusters

Five clusters are used (see Figure 5.5). The results show that the three variables define the attributes of the clusters according to the SAS importance indicator, thus:

Cluster1: Conformed by 46 companies with 41 companies with structural capacity index and risk index high and very high (3 and 4) and with KM index not very high

Cluster2: Conformed by 46 companies with low–medium levels (1 and 2) in all three indexes

Cluster3: Conformed by 35 companies with 27 companies with KM index high and very high (3 and 4) and Risk index low and medium (1 and 2)

TABLE 5.3

Variables Used to Define the Indexes

Variable Used	Variables Structural Capacity	KM Variables	Risk Variables
Belong to the list of the best 100 companies to work for		x	
Score number of employees	x		
Score volatility			x
Score fixed assets	x		
Score working capital amount	x		
Score for intangibles assets	x		
Score operating revenue turnover	x		
Score for profit margin	x		
Score return on shareholder's funds	x		
Score return on capital employed	x		
Score total assets amount	x		
Score years in control		x	
Score years in business		x	
Score years of management experience		x	
Belong to the ASTD list			
The company is considered global		x	
Number of years in the 500 list		x	
Knowledge management index		x	
Belong to the Make list		x	
Moody's credit rating as a score			x
Belong to the *Fortune* 500 most admired companies list		x	
Percentage of intangible assets		x	
Amount of profits last year	x		
Revenues amount	x		
Score of the asset use		x	
Score for current ratio			
Score of financial soundness	x		
Score for innovation		x	
Score KM index		x	
Score of the long investment	x		
Score of people management		x	
Score for profit amount	x		
Score for quality of products		x	
Score for quality management		x	
Score for revenues amount	x		
Score for risk index with S&P component			x
Score for social responsibility		x	
Score for structural capacity index	x		
S&P credit rating as a score			x
Index of structural capacity	x		
Volatility score			x

Cluster4: Conformed by 40 companies with 38 companies with low and medium (1 and 2) structural capacity index, with low, medium, and high KM index (1,2,3), and very high and high Risk index (3 and 4)

Cluster5: Conformed by 38 companies with 36 companies characterized mainly by a KM index very high (4) and the Risk index high and very high (3 and 4)

In summary, cluster 5, composed of the highest index scored companies, shows an association among the indexes, and cluster 2 the lowest score in all indexes suggests an index association among low score companies as well.

Using decision trees, the purpose is to classify the companies according to the risk index that has four levels:

Risk Level 1: 49 companies in total. This level is mainly defined by companies that have a low level of structural capacity index and KM index low; these are 11 companies the highest number among all the leaves and 31% of the companies that have this combination.

Risk Level 2: This distribution is similar for all the terminal nodes of the tree, only 8 companies represent the highest percentage in a branch when KM index is low and structural capacity index is low as well.

Risk Level 3: This is a risk level that is present mainly with 16 companies that have the highest structural capacity index and KM index not very high.

Risk Level 4: This is the best risk level and the largest number of companies is when the highest KM index and the highest structural capacity index are combined. This combination represents 80% of the companies in high and very high risk index.

In summary, companies having a good KM index and structural capacity index are better in terms of risk and on the other extreme, low KM index and low structural capacity can describe companies with no good risk index. The models have been presented using multiple variables (See Figures 5.6–5.10).

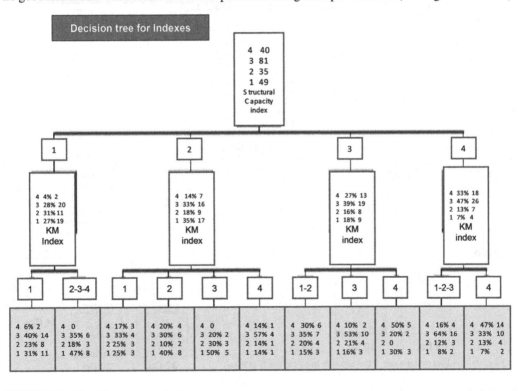

FIGURE 5.6   Decision trees for indexes.

Scenario 2 Using the Non-structural Capacity Variables and Risk Index Components:

Using clusters

This scenario uses ten clusters. The variables that define the clusters are the scores of innovation, years in business, number of years on 500 list, years in control, volatility, and people management. There are 110 companies that are related to volatility score in the clusters 3, 4, 5, 6, and 7. The cluster 7 has 31 companies and shows the largest differentiated group with 23 companies that have low and medium volatility, years in control low, medium and high, people management high and very high, innovation not low, and number of years on 500 list equal to 4 and 5. In the other clusters 3, 4, 5, and 6, the number of companies per volatility score level is not, as a percent, well discriminated (Figure 5.7).

Using decision trees

Risk Level 1: This low-risk index is concentrated on companies with 1, 2, or 3 times on the 500 list.

Risk Level 2 and 3: The differentiation is not totally clear; the distribution is similar in all levels. In the risk level 3, there is a group of companies (12 in total) with people management in low level, medium level in years of expertise, and 5 on the 500 list.

Risk Level 4: This level is present mainly in companies that are part of the most admired list that have years of expertise high and very high (level 3 and 4) and with 5 on the 500 list (44% of the leaf the highest percentage in all leaves).

This scenario shows only the variable scores: years in business, years in control, people management, number of years on 500 list, and innovation appear with the risk variable volatility in the

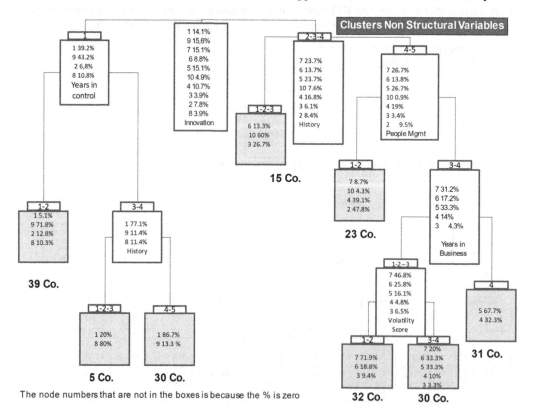

FIGURE 5.7   Clusters for non-structural variables.

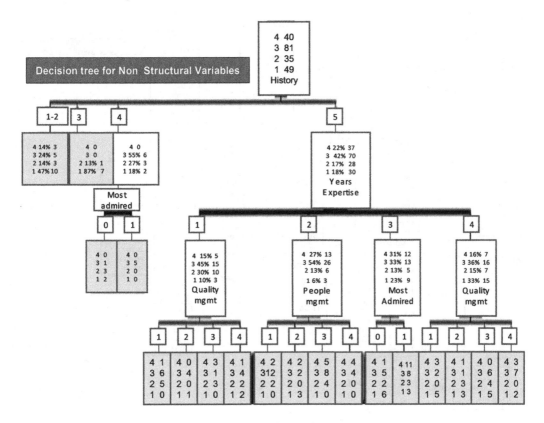

FIGURE 5.8 Decision trees for non-structural variables.

definition of 5 of 10 company clusters. The best risk level is characterized by the high and very high level of years of management expertise, belong to the list of the most admired companies, having high-quality management, and to number of years on 500 list for five years (Figure 5.8).

Scenario 3 Using All Variables: Non-structural and Structural Variables:

Using clusters

The score variables that describe the clusters are innovation, asset use, volatility, working capital, profits, and long-term investments. The total of companies classified using volatility is 92 represented by 2, 4, 6, and 10. For instance, cluster 6 has 38 of 42 companies with no low volatility, low and medium innovation, working capital is not very high, and not low in profits. Only clusters 2 and 10 show most of the companies (13 of 21 and 12 of 20, respectively) with a low volatility score and with low and medium asset use, and low and medium innovation levels (Figure 5.9).

Using decision trees: The results show a clearer classification for risk levels 1, 3, and 4 than for level 2.

Risk Level 1: The characteristics of this level are mainly low and medium total assets score, low and medium profits score, and 5 on the 500 list. However, the case of very high score year of expertise and low people management and high profits belong to this risk level.

Risk Levels 2 and 3: This is a combination similar to the risk level 1 with additional companies when the people management score is medium and moderate in the highest score of revenues and profits. Risk level 3 can be reached with moderate profits, and low people management and years of expertise scores.

Risk Level 4: The combinations at this risk level are mainly in companies with a very high score in people management, very high score in revenues, and very high score in profits. Additionally,

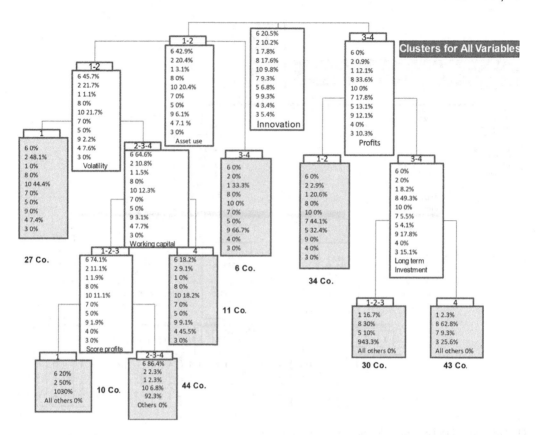

FIGURE 5.9 Clusters for all variables.

this risk level is present when the scores are very high for percentage of intangibles and high for profit and people management.

In summary, in this scenario, innovation, use of corporate assets, working capital, profits, and volatility define 4 of 10 clusters. The clusters 2 and 4 suggest that low volatility score, low innovation score, low asset use, and low profit can be associated within the clusters. Furthermore, the best risk level is found when the variables people management, percentage of intangibles, revenues, and profits are located in the best scores. However, the low-risk scores do not include the KM-associated variables years of expertise, people management, and percentage of intangibles (Figure 5.10).

With the above points of observations, several hypotheses can lead to further investigation to supplement this first approach of analyzing variables that describe risk, structural capacity, and knowledge management. Three different scenarios of analysis were presented and analyzed with statistical techniques. The differentiation of the groups of companies based on the combination of risk and knowledge management variables suggest a differentiation among organizations. The score level of the indexes shows relationships, especially with the low and high scores, because of clusters' attributes and a relationship between low- and high-risk index levels with high and low index of KM and non-structural index levels.

The variables independently analyzed suggest that not all the clusters include risk variables as differentiators and when the cluster includes risk variables, they appear with score variables such as years in business of the company, number years on the 500 list, people management quality, and innovation. Regarding risk levels, it is possible to say that levels 2 and 3 are not well differentiated but levels 1 and 4 are. The best scores in people management, revenues, profits, and years of expertise suggest a high-risk index level. On the other extreme, the low levels include low number of years on the 500 list, low profit scores, and low assets. Variables like people management, percentage of

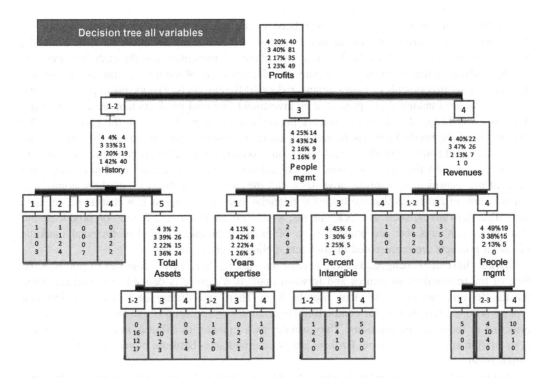

FIGURE 5.10 Decision tree for all variables.

intangibles, years of expertise, and quality management appear in the splits describing risk levels, which means the variables are important, however the variable categories are not clear indicators of risk classification.

This section opens a research area for discovering the relationships among risk, knowledge management-data analytics use, financial, and operational capacity. The sample can be increased and the analysis can be searched with more emphasis in specific sectors. Finally, understanding the relationships among intangible assets value, reputation, share value, and decision-making process can help the organization to develop KM strategies. These KM strategies could support the mitigation process of strategic risk of the organization and develop analyses based on the investor point of view.

5.5 RISK ANALYTICS AND THE ANALYTICS OF RETURN

The previous section has been concentrated on how to connect various qualitative models, business variables, risk index, and performance. In this section, there is presentation of the several topics that are part of risk analytics related to return and financial products valuation that will be developed in the following sections. A risk analytics process applied in the return understanding is based on processes for creating pricing models of financial products, understanding transaction costs or returns depending on the contract conditions, creating metrics to evaluate products and investments, and variation according to changes in inputs such as interest rates.

Risk analytics in the return analysis requires the discrete and continuous treatment of the variables for understanding what is happening in the present and in the future of financial operations. In the first part, there is a description of the general model of return and valuation of products. After that description, the sections are presenting the concepts of traditional interest treatment for products and financial transactions and then a review of several financial instruments and concepts related to financial portfolios. In particular, the concepts associated with the main characteristics of the return concept are related to the pricing process of financial assets and transaction costs. There is an introduction to the interest treatment and products such as bonds, loans, deposits, and derivatives. At the same time, there is a presentation to the cash flow analysis.

The analysis of return and risk management indicates some of the most common tools on the market to cover investments or assets against risks of different kinds. The means to protect against several risks are fundamentally presented as investment financial products that are nothing more than insurance/hedge structures for which a premium must be paid to obtain the protection. The description of the products/means behavior is using models that can be seen in discrete or continuous time that combine mathematical results and computational calculations such as simulation.

The discounted values of cash flows that are delivered to the owners are used to calculate the value of the securities. In addition, nowadays with the dynamics of the stock markets, bonds, and mutual funds of portfolios that are traded in financial markets, appear as new market participants the called derivatives, such as stock options, swaps on interest rates, futures of products, and reinsurance contracts that are another form of financial products traded in financial markets. Financial products are represented in contracts, policies, certificates, etc.

Markets have also changed, as there may or may not be delivery of securities or goods at the time of the transaction; in futures and forward markets the price is defined in the current time but the delivery can be made many months later. There is a difference between dealers and brokers who are responsible for conducting negotiations and promoting products. Dealers act as principal in securities transactions. They usually own inventories offered on the basis of a sell price margin and purchase price. Brokers act as intermediaries between buyers and sellers, for a commission.

Option contracts are similar to futures where the purpose is to cover the possible change of a price of an item, generating a contract that has value by fulfilling a promise to recognize a preset price. Swaps allow parties to exchange cash flows. They are traded over the OTC market; the exchange markets are more liquid than the OTC markets. OTC means a market for dealer titles that may not be members of a recognized stock exchange. These products act as protection from interest rate, price, and other risks, implying that their role is not only an investment but also is to become a way to manage risk. According to the above, the next sections will be concentrated on describing the analytics process to deal with return and its influences in product design, portfolio, and support to financial transactions.

5.6 GENERAL MODEL FOR FINANCIAL ASSETS VALUATION

This introductory presentation of the models of pricing theory is based on Panjer et al. (1998). Assume N assets/securities S_1, S_2, ..., S_N with two observations at times 0 and 1. At 0, the investor knows the values and at 1 the results are random variables. Therefore, the information structure that a market has is analyzed through time. It is defined $\Omega = \{\varpi_1, \varpi_2, ..., \varpi_M\}$ such as the sample space of a finite M number of possible outcomes. It is known that the probability of each result is greater than zero. The value of the asset j at state ϖ at time k is represented by $S_j(k, \varpi)$, assuming non-negative values. $S_j(0, \varpi) = S_j(0)$ is the same for all ϖ of Ω.

At the time 1, the value is given by the matrix $S(1, \varpi)$ as:

$$\begin{bmatrix} S_1(1, \varpi_1) & S_2(1, \varpi_1) & . & . & S_N(1, \varpi_1) \\ \vdots & & & & \vdots \\ S_1(1, \varpi_M) & & . & . & S_N(1, \varpi_M) \end{bmatrix}$$

The selection of the portfolio is at time 0. There are j assets maintained between 0 to 1 with θ_j items per asset, $j = 1 ... N$. This is known as the strategy component of the trading strategy. If $\theta_j > 0$, then θ_j units of the asset j are purchased. If $\theta_j < 0$, then $|\theta_j|$ units of asset j are sold in short

$$\theta = \begin{bmatrix} \theta_1 \\ \vdots \\ \theta_N \end{bmatrix} \text{ is a negotiation/trading strategy.}$$

The value of the portfolio at 0 is the product of asset prices at time 0 (Vector $S(0)$ all asset prices at time 0) and the number of assets at the time of analysis

$$S(0)\theta = \theta_1 S_1(0) + \theta_2 S_2(0) + \ldots + \theta_N S_N(0)$$

The portfolio value at time 1 will depend on possible Ω values that are realized. If ϖ_j occurs, the portfolio value is $\theta_1 S_1(1, \varpi_j) + \theta_2 S_2(1, \varpi_j) + \ldots + \theta_N S_N(1, \varpi_j)$, which is the j-th component of the column vector:

$$S(1, \Omega)\theta = \begin{bmatrix} \theta_1 S_1(1, \varpi_1) + \theta_2 S_2(1, \varpi_1) + \cdots + \theta_N S_N(1, \varpi_1) \\ \vdots \\ \theta_1 S_1(1, \varpi_M) + \theta_2 S_2(1, \varpi_M) + \cdots + \theta_N S_N(1, \varpi_M) \end{bmatrix}$$

The results at time 1 of the portfolio depend on the trading strategy and the components of $S(1,\Omega)\theta$ are random variables indicating the portfolio value.

The portfolio concept uses the arbitrage term representing the simultaneous purchase and sale of the same securities, goods, and foreign currency in different markets to generate profit given the prices difference in each market. These models are applicable under the case of non-arbitrage. An arbitrage opportunity is such a trading strategy that:

$S(0)\theta \leq 0$ and $S(1,\Omega)\theta > 0$. The securities market model is said to be free of arbitration if there are no arbitrage opportunities. The multi-period model is constructed by defining the stochastic S_j process with the $S_j(k)$ variables with k ranging from 1 to T this is with T+1 time points, the S_j family or vector of values of stochastic processes is the one studied in the model. All of this is based on what is known as the fundamental asset pricing theorem. The theorem indicates that in the single period model there is free arbitrage is equivalent to have no a vector of prices of all traded assets.

The stochastic process that is associated with these models is that of geometric Brownian movement, which is defined as: If $\{Y(t), t \geq 0\}$. This is a Brownian movement process with mean μt and variance $t\sigma^2$, then the process $\{X(t), t \geq 0\}$ defined by $X(t) = e^{Y(t)}$ is called a geometric Brownian process. To be a Brownian process requires $X(0) = 0$, the set $\{X(t), t \geq 0\}$ has independent and stationary increments, and it is normally distributed with mean μt and variance $t\sigma^2$.

The relationship starts from the force of interest and all the handling of the present value of the securities values are associated with a function like the previous one, where each of the variables generated by the logarithm of the quotient of two consecutive prices is related to a Brownian process and therefore the prices will follow a geometric Brownian process. From these strong model structures, it is possible to obtain pricing formulas as is the case of the Black & Scholes.

With this fast view of the fundamental model for financial data analysis, it is possible to move to the specific cases of return analysis and products-securities review that will be vehicles for risk management. The presentation illustrates the analytics process based on mathematical development to obtain values that can be used for evaluating investments, costs or risk related to transactions, investments and financial products use to deal with risk. Be $S_t > 0$ is the price of an asset at time t and $S_t - S_a$ is the price change that the owner finds when buying at the time a and selling at the time t. The asset may have dividends, coupons, or expenses. Be $D(a,t)$ the accumulated cash distributed to the owner in (a,t). The return obtained is the solution to:

$$e^{(t-a)R(a,t)} = \frac{S_t + D(a,\, t)}{S_a}$$

Assuming the reinvestment of dividends and considering the continuous capitalization, at time a, the price S_t is a random variable. The period $(a,\, t)$ is a month, a week, or a day; then consider $R = R$ $(t-1,\, t)$. The simplest model of pricing is the one period model where an asset is traded in t and $T > t$, without dividends or costs. $S = S_t$ the actual price and $\tau = T - t$. Then $R = R(t,\, T)$ is a Bernoulli *variable*, where R is equal to u with probability P or d with probability $1-P$. The S_T prices that are at time T are equal to a Se^{ut} with a probability P or to Se^{dt} with probability $1-P$. Generalizations of multiple periods allows changes of prices per trading period that follow a Bernoulli law:

$$R(t,\, T) = \frac{u}{N}K + \frac{d}{N}(N - K)$$

where K is the random number of prices going up and N the number of trading periods. The first specific step in understanding return is to keep in mind the general models and to go through the review of interest dynamic in transactions as it is presented in the following section.

5.7　THE EQUIVALENCE CONCEPT

Once the return concept is defined, the next step is to work with it in the form of interest rate. The first part of the review is considering the deterministic behavior of the interest. The following concepts of interest rate understanding are part of financial assets that are short-term loans for companies or government with maturity of less than one year: certificates of deposit, treasury securities, repurchase agreements known as repos, are made by negotiators with the titles used as collateral. LIBOR (London interbank offered rate) is used for interbank lending in London and is a reference for short-term interest rates in European markets.

Simple interest: In this case, the interest caused and not withdrawn, does not earn interest.

If $i = 5\%$ paid at he end of each month, $P = \$10,000$. At the end of the year period, the accumulated $[\$500 \times 12] + \$10,000 = \$16,000$.

Compound interest: interest caused and not withdrawn earns interests. If $i = 21\%$ year paid at the end of each quarter, $i_t = 5.25\%$ $\$P = \$100$ the flow is:

Balance	Interests
1st Q 100	5.25
2st Q 105.25	105.25 × 0.0525 = 5.5256
3rd Q 110.7757	110.77 × 0.0525 = 5.8157
4th Q 116.5913	116.59 × 0.0525 = 6.1210

At the end of the year, $122.7123.

If an individual is indifferent between receiving $P today or receiving $(P+C) within a period (one month, one semester, one year), it is said that for that person $P today are equivalent to $(P+C) within a period with an opportunity interest rate of, C/P × 100% (the amount that needs to be paid (C), which reflects the ability of money to generate wealth in n time periods to the person). The equivalence between a present sum and a future sum depends on the calculation of interest:

S = P * (1 + equivalent interest rate at the end of the period)
S = Future value
P = Present value

If the calculation is compounded (interest are gaining interests), then:

$S = P (1 + i)^n$ i = interest rate per period of liquidation or payment. Therefore, S is the amount of money an individual agrees to receive within n periods if the person gives $\$P$ to another (opportunity $i\%$) person.

The interest can be paid at the end of the periods; that means that interest payments are made for each $\$P$ invested or calculated once "past" the posting period. Or interest paid at the beginning when interest is paid on every $\$P - i\% * P$ of investment. Nominal Interest: It is the advertised rate, rates are not comparable for example two projects that offer the 22% nominal per year and 21% because it will depend on how the interest will be paid. Effective interest is that rate that involves the periodicity of payments of the nominal rate and according to the conditions of at end of the period or at the beginning.

How to calculate effective interest when the interest is paid at the beginning: $\$P = 100$, the original investment will be $P - i\% * P$ and if the interest is $i = 21\%$ paid by quarters the calculation is

$$\frac{100\left(\frac{0.21}{4}\right)}{\text{investment}} = \frac{0.0525 \times 100}{100 - 5.2.5}$$
$$= \frac{5.25}{94.75}$$
$$= 5.5409$$

Thus, $S = P (1.055409)^4$ to calculate S at the end of the year.

5.7.1 EQUIVALENCE BETWEEN A FUTURE SUM AND A SERIES OF UNIFORM SUMS

R is a uniform sum with i = the rate of opportunity for the period. S = Future amount and n = number of periods. Procedure: Calculate the sum of the future values of R. In this first approach, the R is paid at the end of the period. Then

$$S = R + R(1 + i) + \dots + R(1 + i)^{n-1} \tag{A}$$

Multiplying both sides of the equality by $(1 + i)$, it is obtained

$$(1 + i)S = R(1 + i) + R(1 + i)^2 + \dots + R(1 + i)^n \tag{B}$$

And

$$(B) - (A) = iS$$
$$= R(1 + i)^n - R$$

Thus $iS = R ((1 + i)^n - 1)$:

$$S = \frac{R((1 + i))^n - 1}{i}$$

If instead it is required to see the relationship with P of R, it is only required to "bring" S to the present value.

$$P = S\left(\frac{1}{1+i}\right)^n$$
$$= \frac{R((1 + i)^n - 1)}{i(1 + i)^n}$$

This is "a methodology" of work to reduce your problem to present value and future value in each calculation. There is a situation where there are payments growing at a G rate, this means first payment at the second period is G, third 2G, fourth 3G, and so on up to the last payment at n that is $(n - 1)$G:

$$P = \text{sum of the present values of kG with k} = 1 \ldots (n - 1)$$

$$= G\left(\frac{1}{(1+i)^2} + \frac{2}{(1+i)^3} + \cdots + \frac{n-2}{(1+i)^{n-1}} + \frac{n-1}{(1+i)^n}\right) \text{ (A) beginning with } n = 2$$

$$P(1 + i) = G\left(\frac{1}{(1+i)^1} + \frac{2}{(1+i)^2} + \cdots + \frac{n-1}{(n+i)^{n-1}}\right) \text{ (B) then}$$

$$(B) - (A) = P(1 + i) - P$$

$$= G\left[\frac{1}{(1+i)} + \frac{2}{(1+i)^2} + \cdots + \frac{n-2}{(1+i)^{n-1}}\right] - \frac{[n-1]G}{(1+i)^n}$$

$$Pi = G\left[\frac{1}{(1+i)} + \frac{2}{(1+i)^2} + \cdots + \frac{1}{(n+i)^{n-1}} + \frac{1}{(n+i)^n}\right] - \frac{Gn}{(1+i)^n}$$

$$P = \frac{G}{i}\left[\frac{(1+i)^n - 1}{i(1+i)^n}\right] - \frac{Gn}{i(1+i)^n}$$

$$= \frac{G}{i}\left[\frac{(1+i)^n - 1}{i(1+i)^n} - \frac{n}{(1+i)^n}\right]$$

For example:
The following joint financing system has been submitted for the purchase of machinery:

1. Ten annual installments of $2,500, delivering the first at the time of the transaction.
2. $1,500 at the end of the 3rd year, $2,000 at the end of the 4th year, $2,500 at the end of the 5th, and so on until the tenth.
3. $20,000 in year 7.

To solve this problem, the best is to use all operations in present value equivalence of all transactions. $P_1 = P'_1 + P''_1$ where

$$P'_1 = \textit{Present value of } \$\, 2,500 \textit{ for } 9 \text{ periods. And}$$
$$P''_1 = 2,500 \textit{ at the beginning}$$

$P'_2 =$ is the uniform sum with gradient (500, 12%, 8 periods) + uniform sum of (1500), everything at present value.

$P_2 =$ Present value of P'_2 and $P_3 =$ Present value of $20,000. This means the solution is:

$$P = P_1 + P_2 + P_3$$

5.7.2 SPECIAL TREATMENT OF ANNUITIES

Annuities: They are a succession of installments made at equal time intervals. Future and present value of a series (any) number of finite terms. The future value of the p-th in an annuity $a_1, \ldots a_p, \ldots, a_n$ is $a_p(1 + i)^{n-p}$ then

$$VF_n = a_1(1 + i)^{n-1} + \ldots\ldots\ldots + a_p(1 + i)^{n-p} + \ldots\ldots a_n$$

The present value of the *p-th* term is $\frac{a_p}{(1+i)^p}$

$$VP_0 = \frac{a_1}{(1+i)} + \ldots + \frac{a_p}{(1+i)^p} + \ldots + \frac{a_n}{(1+i)^n}$$

The annuities $a_1, \ldots, a_p, \ldots, a_n$ are not uniform; this means it is not required that $a_{p+1} = a_p$ $p = 1 \ldots, n$; however, the concept is in place. Moreover,

$$VF_n = VP_0(1+i)^n$$

If there is an annuity that is deferred in time – *d–periods*, then its present value is:

$$VP_d = \frac{a_1}{(1+i)^{1+d}} + \ldots \ldots + \frac{a_p}{(1+i)^{p+d}} + \ldots \ldots + \frac{a_n}{(1+i)^{n+d}}$$

$$VP_d = \frac{VP_0}{(1+i)^d} \Leftrightarrow (1+i)^d \, VP_d = VP_0$$

Payment of annuities due in a specific period.

If a_1 is the first installment and $V = VP_0(1+i)$ is the amount at the beginning of the analysis – transaction, the loan is $V - a_1$ that is equal to:

$$(V - a_1) = \frac{a_2}{1+i} + \frac{a_3}{(1+i)^2} + \ldots + \frac{a_n}{(1+i)^{n-1}}$$

Similarly, if there is an interest rate paid at the beginning of the period, the analysis should be as follows. It is known that the equivalence between a future sum and a present sum is:

$$S = P(1+i)^n \quad i = \text{opportunity interest in the period}$$
$$n = \text{Number of times interests are paid}$$

If the i is paid at the end it is not required the transformation. In the case of interest paid at beginning of the period to use in the annuity calculation:

$i^0 = \frac{i}{1-i}$ and $1 + i^0$ is $1 + \frac{i}{1-i}$ that is equal to $\frac{1}{1-i}$

Therefore, if capitalized interest paid at the beginning is the equivalence between present and future value, it should look like this:

$$S = P\left(\frac{1}{1-i}\right)^n \Leftrightarrow (1-i)^n \, S = P$$

Therefore, a series or annuity with interest paid at the beginning of the period is equivalent in present value to the following:

VP_0^A = Present value of the annuity with interest paid at the beginning of the period

$$VP_0^A = a_1(1-i) + a_2(1-i)^2 + \ldots + a_p(1-i)^p + \ldots + a_n(1-i)^n$$

if $a_i = a_j$ with $i \neq j$ then $VP_0^A = \frac{a\left[(1-i) - (1-i)^{n+1}\right]}{i}$

If the desire is to calculate the early annuity with early interest rate it is:

$$V^A = (1 + i) VP_0^A$$

5.7.3 FINITE ANNUITIES WITH ARITHMETIC PROGRESSION CHANGE

a_1 is the first term and $- R -$ the arithmetic progression rate

$$VF_n = a_1 (1 + i)^{n-1} + a_2 (1 + i)^{n-2} + \ldots \ldots + a_{n-1} (1 + i) + a_n$$

The arithmetic rate of change $a_{p+1} - a_p = R$. Using the same method to solve the finite sum:

$$VF_n (1 + i) - VF_n \text{ for } p = 1 \ldots (n - 1) \text{ with } a_n - a_1 = (n - 1)R.$$
$$VF_n (n + i) = a_1 (1 + i)^n + a_2 (1 + i)^{n-1} + \ldots \ldots + a_{n-1} (1 + i)^2 + a_n (1 + i)$$
$$VF_n = a_1 (1 + i)^{n-1} + \ldots \ldots + a_{n-2} (1 + i)^2 + a_{n-1} (1 + i) + a_n$$

Operating
$$VF_n. i = a_1 (1 + i)^n + R[(1 + i)^{n-1} + \ldots \ldots + (1 + i)] - [a_i + (n - 1)R$$
$$VF_n. i = a_1 [(1 + i)^n - 1] + R\frac{(1 + i)^n - 1}{i} - nR$$
$$VF_n = \frac{\left(a_1 + \frac{R}{i}\right)[(1 + i)^n - 1] - nR}{i}$$

In the case that annuity is changing geometrically, a is the first term q, the geometric rate of change such as the *p-th* term is aq^{p-1}

$$\rightarrow VF_n = a(1 + i)^{n-1} + aq(1 + i)^{n-2} + \ldots + aq^{n-1}$$
$$VF_n = a(1 + i)^{n-1} \left[1 + \frac{q}{1+i} + \left(\frac{q}{1+i}\right)^2 + \ldots + \left(\frac{q}{1+i}\right)^{n-1} \right]$$

To solve, it is needed to review two cases:

$$q \neq 1 + i$$

Subtracting $\frac{q}{1+i} VF_n$ of VF_n

$$\frac{q}{1 + i} VF_n = a(1 + i)^{n-1} \left[\frac{q}{1 + i} + \left(\frac{q}{1 + i}\right)^2 + \ldots + \left(\frac{q}{1 + i}\right)^n \right]$$

$$\rightarrow \left(1 - \frac{q}{1+i}\right) VF_n = a(1 + i)^{n-1} \left[1 - \left(\frac{q}{1+i}\right)^n \right]$$

$$\rightarrow VF_n = \frac{a[q^n - (1 + i)^n]}{q - (1 + i)} \longleftarrow \text{ This is the reason to study the cases.}$$

If $q = 1 + i \rightarrow VF_n = na(1 + i)^{n-1} \rightarrow$ using the above equation.

Using actuarial notation to obtain extra equivalences, it is possible to simplify formulas $v = \frac{1}{1+i}$ the annuity with payments at the end of the period will be:

$$a_{n]} = v + v^2 + \cdots + v^n$$

That is, $a_{n\rceil} = \frac{1-(1+i)^{-n}}{i}$ and when the payments are at the beginning

$$\ddot{a}_{n\rceil} = 1 + \upsilon + \cdots + \upsilon^{n-1}$$

$\ddot{a}_{n\rceil} = \frac{1-\upsilon^n}{d}$ where $d = 1 - \upsilon$ known as a discount rate.

In that regard, if there is a situation of payments that is with arithmetic progression starting with P payment and growing with Q every period ahead.

$$VPannuity = Pa_{n\rceil} + Q\frac{a_{n\rceil} - n\upsilon^n}{i}$$

The previous equations of annuities can be represented using the simplified actuarial notation. Now the continuity concept in interest calculations can be treated as follows, using the concept of the force of interest: Using the notation of $a(t)$ as the accumulation function for $t \geq 0$ for 1 dollar invested at $t = 0$. Thus, $a(t) = (1 + i)^t$. In the case of expressing the effective interest in a period n of time as $i_{eff} = \frac{a(n) - a(n-1)}{a(n-1)}$ for a small interval $(t, t + \Delta t)$, it is possible to measure the interest rate as $\lim_{\Delta t \to 0} \frac{i(t, t+\Delta t)}{\Delta t} = \frac{a'(t)}{a(t)}$ that represents the force of interest and it is represented as $\delta(t)$ and where $a(t)$ represents the accumulation function at time t of one initial investment of 1 dollar.

From this definition, $\delta(t) = \frac{\partial \ln(a(t))}{\partial t}$ and $a(t) = \exp\left(\int_0^t \delta(s)ds\right)$.

And in compound interest rate, the approach is $e^\delta = 1 + i$.

If the annuities continue forever, this means $n \to \infty$, they are called perpetuities; the example can be dividends in preferred stocks or in England they had the consols or perpetual bonds paying interest forever. Consols were all redeemed in 2015.

There are cases where installments are with different periods of compounding interest; it can be observed in a case where installments are more frequent than the interest compounding period and on the contrary with installments less frequent.

5.7.4 Principles of Loan Amortization

There is a question about the decomposition of installments in what part of the amount is repaid and what the interest/cost of the loan is. Depending on the conditions of the loans, if they have different methods of interest calculations or if the loans are indexed, etc. The formulas will change, but the principles will be the same as follows:

$$\begin{aligned} a_p &= iK_{p-1} + M_p \\ M_p &= K_{p-1} - K_p \end{aligned}$$

where a_p is the annuity-instalment and time p.

$i\,K_{p-1}$ = It is the interest of the balance of the capital (main of the loan at time $p - 1$) = K_{p-1}
M_p = This is the amount of a_p that is going to pay the loan-capital
The total amount of the loan is the sum of the M_p $p = 1, ..., n$.
If the annuity is constant, this is a

$$\begin{aligned} VP_0 &= \frac{a[(1+i)^n - 1]}{i(1+i)^n} \\ M_1 &= a - Ki = K\frac{i}{(1+i)^n - 1} \end{aligned}$$

amortization varies in geometric reason progression $(1 + i)$

Equating the annuities $\rightarrow i\,K_{p-1} + M_p = K_p i + M_{p+1}$

$$= (K_{p-1} - M_p)i = +M_{p+1}$$

$$M_{p+1} = M_p(1 + i) \text{ and } M_p = M_1(1 + i)^{p-1}.$$

To check the amortized part in the last annuity. In this situation, $K_{n-1} = M_n$ payment and $M_n\,i$ interest

$$a = M_n\,i + M_n = M_n(1 + i)$$

$$M_n = \frac{a}{(1+i)}$$

$\uparrow$
fix

The capital included in the p-th annuity is

$$M_p = \frac{a}{(1 + i)^{n-p+1}}.$$

The amortized capital before the p-th annuity

$$B_p = M_{1+\ldots+}M_p = M_1\frac{(1+i)^p - 1}{i}$$

$$= K\frac{(1+i)^p - 1}{(1+i)^n - 1}$$

The balance to pay after the p-th annuity is

$$K_p = K - B_p$$

$$= K\frac{(1+i)^n - (1+i)^p}{(1+i)^n - 1}$$

And the total interest paid is

$$S = na - k$$

5.7.5 Basics of Investments, Cash Flows, and Transactions Analysis

In investment analysis, there are several factors to consider. This means to review alternatives before and after taxes or the effects of inflation and devaluation, at the same time the concept of opportunity value that is part of the decision-maker conditions of analysis. Opportunity value is a basic concept to obtain results to compare values in the future and present, to identify the contribution of cash flows in any investment and its return. The net present value is a metric-indicator of the behavior of cash flows in the future and under their equivalent evaluation in the present. It is not a profitability metric but it is a support to decisions as goodness or the attractiveness of transactions, products results, operations, etc. It can be said that the net present value of an investment is the value of this measured in dollars today of all the future income and expenses that constitute a project. The NPV is calculated based on the opportunity interest (i_{op}) of the analyst (investor); therefore, the analysis depends on who does it. NPV decision criterion:

- It is advisable if the NPV > 0
- It's indifferent if NPV is 0
- It is not convenient if NPV < 0

When the NPV is 0, the invested money earns an interest equal to the one used to calculate the NPV. The NPV is the value of opportunity in dollars at the time of the analysis of the alternative in question, if the result is positive it represents the extraordinary benefits of the project. The roots of polynomial equations are known as internal VPN(i) return rates = 0. This is known as yield. The internal rate of return – yield (IRR) is based on the money that remains invested in the project. An important aspect as a metric is that it is independent of the opportunity interest rate. The polynomial is

$$VPN(i*) = \sum_{j=0}^{n} \frac{a_j}{(1 + i)^j} = 0$$

where the cash flows are a_j discounted an interest rate i.

If $i* > i_{op}$ a project/investment is advisable
$i* < i_{op}$ Rejection
$i_{op} - i* = 0$ Indifference

A concept to remember is that the assumption for IRR to represent the return is that the money remains in the project. If this is not the case, the new flows have to be evaluated under the new investment conditions or to discover the true return; for example, a person buys a tractor for $10 million that generates net revenue of $4.5 million and at the end of the fifth year sells it for $4.5 million. Find out what the true return is for an investor who has an i_{op} = 32% and another who has an i_{op} of 24%. The IRR is 39.97% (Table 5.4).

Calculating the return of the withdrawals using the rates 32% and 24% the IRR has different with future values of S (32%) = 46'79 and S (24%) = 40'72.

The projects are equivalent to these simplified flows

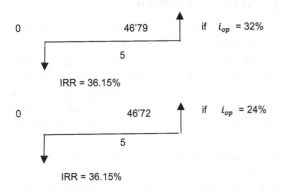

TABLE 5.4

Basic Cash Flow Generated with Interest Accumulation and Withdrawals

Period	Beginning Invest.	Accumulated	Interest	Balance	Withdrawals
0–1	10^1	10^1	3.997	13.997	4.5
1–2		9.497	3.796	13.293	4.5
2–3		8.793	3.515	12.308	4.5
3–4		7.808	3.121	10.929	4.5
4–5		6.429	2.570	8.999	9.0

Returns are affected because of taxes. For example, a term deposit at 32% is equivalent to 39.588% at the end of a year after taxes is $K = effective\ rate\,(1 - t)$.

If the tax rate is $t = 30\%$, then $K = 0.39588(1 - 0.30) = 27.71\%$.

On the other hand, inflation can affect the return as well.

$$\frac{\$P(1+i)}{(1+inf)}$$

$\$P$

Generating a real return of $(1 + t_R) = \frac{1+i}{1+inf}$

$$t_R = \frac{1 + i}{1 + inf} - 1$$

The same will happens with a devaluation rate at DEV rate $\frac{1+i}{1+DEV} - 1$.

Now, in the case that the cash flows are continuous, it is possible to use a function (t) that indicates the rate per unit of time of payments at time t. In an interval $[t_1, t_2]$, the present value of the payments is given by PV is equal to $\int_{t_1}^{t_2} v^t p(t)\,dt$ where v is the discount factor.

Flows can theoretically be continuous (non-discrete) and in that case, the expression to use is

$$\text{P.V of discrete cash flow} = c_1 v^{t_1} + c_2 v^{t_2} + \ldots + c_n v^{t_n} = \sum_{j=1}^{n} c_j v^{t_j}.$$

5.8 RETURN ANALYSIS IN STOCK MARKETS AND BONDS

Companies issue property titles in the form of shares. Shareholders have a right to profits that will be distributed based on dividend policies. The shareholders are not responsible in the case of bankruptcy, but they are at risk of their investment. At the beginning of the company, there is a private issuance of shares and after there are negotiations that are regulated to prevent fraud. An investment bank is required to coordinate lawyers, accountants, and marketing experts for the initial public offering, known as an IPO. It can be presented for entirely new companies or for cases where there is privatization of companies or the demutualization of insurance companies, which were owned by the policymakers.

New shares from an existing company can be offered or partition of the current ones. The process of partition does not dilute the property. The new issuance can lower the share price. Each case is given according to the financial conditions of the company. In the current economic system, there are concepts related to the acquisition such as IBO, MBO, and IPO. IBO (institutional buyout) refers to the acquisition of the organization by an institutional investor, the MBO (management buyout) is when management of the organization is acquiring the organization, and IPO (initial public offer) when a company that traded on the market becomes a private owner of the shares. Likewise, a company can change to a mutual.

The shares are negotiable; there is an active secondary transaction market (OTC), which is owned by distributors authorized to negotiate and earn commissions. The Nasdaq (National Association of Securities Dealers Automated) quotation has performed a very large volume of operations, as it is a network of distributors that pay their costs through a purchase and sale price margin. Some transactions are direct; for example, pension plans exchange insurance companies for annuities. There are some ways to perform these transactions, such as:

- Market orders: They are made by buyers and sellers with brokers or distributors, they negotiate at the price that arrive and end at the end of the trading day.
- Limit Orders: Sales limit orders are executed only when purchase offer prices exceed the limits. Similarly, purchase limits can never be executed but reduce price uncertainty.
- Stop orders: Stop-loss orders are market orders subject to a specific X price and T expiration time. If prices fall below X before T, they become sales orders. If they increase above X, they become purchase orders. Stop-loss is known as sell orders and the opposite is the stop-buy order.
- Short sales: Traders usually do not have the shares; they are held by brokers and registered as owners by issuers. Brokers lose dividends from stocks in their inventory. Brokers can lend shares to short sell. These shares are eventually replaced, and dividends paid in the meantime.

A concept that emerges in stock transactions is the margin one. Buying on margin is when brokers pay short-term interest on cash held in traders' accounts and extend credit lines for stock purchases. If a person has borrowed b to buy n shares at an s price, ns − b is the investor's equity and is used as *collateral-guarantee*. A minimum collateral pns ≤ s − b is required (p as percentage). If the share price falls below ns − b/(1 − p) it leads to a margin call or margin request. This concept is used when the investor buys a margin account with the expectation that the share price will grow or in a short sale with the expectation that the price will decline and the prices of the shares go against the investor, the brokerage firm will send a margin requirement requesting that the investor add funds or title them to the account to protect the broker price. margin is the amount paid by a client when he uses credit to buy a title, and the balance is borrowed by the broker against an acceptable collateral.

Short seller margins: The broker lends shares of an investor to short sell to others. It must place the benefits in the investor's account plus a margin taken as a guarantee. There are two risks between two investors: breaking the deal and withdrawing, and may not have enough resources to comply with the agreement. The margin concept is used to deal with risks. In a margin account, the broker will require the investor to deposit funds into the account. An initial margin is the amount that must be deposited at the time the contract is entered. A maintenance margin is the amount to ensure that the balance in the margin account never becomes negative. And a margin call is when the balance in the margin account falls below the margin maintenance and it will be requested for money, or margin call.

5.8.1 RETURN ANALYSIS FOR STOCKS

This example corresponds to the analysis of the price of shares and dividends of a set of shares. The example uses the sample mean and the covariance matrix of the returns. There is also a search of minimum value of the variance by taking three companies and using an expected return of 1.5% per month. There is a graphic showing returns between 1% and 3%, changing by 0.5%. The calculation for the return uses the following:

$$\frac{S_t - S_a + D(a, t)}{Sa}$$

where S_t is the price at the end of the period and S_a the price at the beginning of the period. $D(a, t)$ represents the dividend paid in period (a, t). Three companies with prices and dividends with monthly data are shown in Table 5.5.

For the return calculation (see Table 5.6).

In the case of having different periods of interest aggregation and maturity, the calculations for annualized/comparable rates can be performed as is indicated in the following tables (5.7, 5.8, 5.9). For the return analysis for the selected week period (see Table 5.7).

TABLE 5.5
Figures of Prices and Dividends for Three Organizations. Columns Date, Stock Price Company, And Dividends

Date	Comp 1		Comp 2		Comp 3	
1987 dec	42	0	17.625	0	28.625	0
1988 Jan	41.5	0	14	0.05	31.875	0
1988 feb	43	0.08	18	0	30.875	0.53
1988 mar	40	0	14.625	0	29	0
1988 apr	41	0	14.625	0	28.75	0
1988 may	41.5	0.08	15.25	0.05	30.625	0.55
1988 jun	46.25	0	15.125	0	30.5	0
1988 Jul	44.375	0	15	0.05	30.375	0
1988 aug	39.875	0.08	14.25	0	29.875	0.55
1988 sep	43.25	0	14.5	0	31.25	0
1988 oct	38.625	0	13.5	0.05	31.5	0
1988 nov	37.625	0.1	13	0	30.5	0.55
1988 dec	40.25	0	12.625	0	31.125	0
1989 Jan	37.75	0	13	0	31.5	0
1989 feb	36.25	0.1	14.5	0.05	29.875	0.55
1989 mar	35.625	0	13.875	0	29.75	0
1989 apr	39	0	13	0	30.625	0
1989 may	47.75	0.1	12.75	0.05	31.25	0.57
1989 Jun	41.25	0	13.25	0	30.875	0

TABLE 5.6
Return Calculation for the Three Organizations in Table 5.5

1987 dec			
1988 jan	−0.01190	−0.20284	0.11354
1988 feb	0.03807	0.28571	−0.01475
1988 mar	−0.06977	−0.18750	−0.06073
1988 apr	0.02500	0.00000	−0.00862
1988 may	0.01415	0.04615	0.08435
1988 jun	0.11446	−0.00820	−0.00408
1988 jul	−0.04054	−0.00496	−0.00410
1988 aug	−0.09961	−0.05000	0.00165
1988 sep	0.08464	0.01754	0.04603
1988 oct	−0.10694	−0.06552	0.00800
1988 nov	−0.02330	−0.03704	−0.01429
1988 dec	0.06977	−0.02885	0.02049
1989 jan	−0.06211	0.02970	0.01205
1989 feb	−0.03709	0.11923	−0.03413
1989 mar	−0.01724	−0.04310	−0.00418
1989 apr	0.09474	−0.06306	0.02941
1989 may	0.22692	−0.01538	0.03902
1989 jun	−0.13613	0.03922	−0.01200
1989 jul	−0.03636	−0.04717	0.06478

TABLE 5.7

Calculation of Returns by Weeks

	Prices and Returns for 10 weeks for the whole Portfolio											Dividends
prices	1 week	2 weeks	3 weeks	4 weeks	5 weeks	6 weeks	7 weeks	8 weeks	9 weeks	10 weeks	11 weeks	
agrainc	10.85	10.75	10.5	10.5	10.6	11	10.95	11	11	10.6	10.75	4
clarica	22.35	21.65	21.85	22.3	21.25	21.3	22.9	23.8	24.3	26.6	26.6	0.15
searscan	33.65	34.05	34.35	34.8	34	31.05	34.3	32.5	35	37.1	37	0.06
research	52.75	49.2	39	44.3	45.25	44.45	48.4	45.85	56.5	61.1	80.4	0
corel	8.8	9.25	10.75	10.4	10	8.7	7.7	9.75	9.95	12.95	16.15	0
shellcan	31.8	32.7	32.65	33.3	30	29.3	32	31	31.3	30	31.5	0.18

To see the annual equivalent returns (see Table 5.8).

Return annual calculations of the portfolio value considering the six companies during the selected period can be performed as follows (Table 5.9):

$$5.4383 = 52 \ln\left(\frac{1.229, 60}{1.107, 50}\right)$$

$$4.3641 = 26 \ln\left(\frac{1.229, 60}{1.039, 60}\right)$$

$$4.1513577 = 52/2 \ln\left(\frac{1.229, 60}{960, 72}\right)$$

$$\vdots$$

$$1.126413 = 52/10 \ln\left(\frac{1.229, 60}{990, 12}\right)$$

As a first example of portfolio, the following paragraphs indicate the steps to analyze a portfolio. Two examples are presented with different level of details in the calculations. To analyze a portfolio it is used the Markowitz model (Section 9.5 has more details about calculations). The three companies' stocks used in Table 5.5 and the analysis requires the Covariance Matrix of the returns (Table 5.10).

The purpose of the Markowitz model is to minimize the variance with the constraint of a level of expected return. The variance is represented by $X' \Sigma X$ and the constraints are $\sum_{i=1}^{n} X_i \mu_i = \mu_p$ and $\sum_{i?1}^{n} X_i = 1$. The X_i are the percentages of investment in each stock. μ_p represents the expected return of each stock and in this example, taking values of 0.01, 0.015, 0.02, −0.025, and 0.03.

Using the Excel Solver calculation for non-linear models (see Table 5.11).

Figure 5.11 shows how the relationship is between return and standard deviation (risk). The values of the optimization based on several expected returns are in Table 5.12.

In the case of two assets, the expression of expected return and variance based on X% selection are represented by:

$$E(XR_1 + (1 - X)R_2) = XE(R_1) + (1 - X)E(R_2) = X\mu_1 + (1 - X)\mu_2$$

$$V(XR_1 + (1 - X)R_2) = X^2 V(R_1) + (1 - X)^2 V(R_2) + 2X(1 - X)Cov(R_1, R_2)$$

Through calculations of the optimal values of variance, there is a graphic of standard deviation and expected return after iterations with different expected returns that provides what is called the efficient frontier (Figure 5.12).

The following example provides more details using a portfolio of six companies. There is a review of results in even weeks calculating the returns in each case. The amount for investing

TABLE 5.8
Annualized Returns

Date	Security	Price	1 week	Returns on Prices 2 weeks	3 weeks	4 weeks	5 weeks	6 weeks	7 weeks	8 weeks	9 weeks	10weeks
19-11-1999		$10.75	73.07%	-59.77%	-39.85%	-23.96%	-23.91%	12.18%	17.48%	15.29%	0.00%	-4.81%
12-11-1999		$10.60	-192.61%	-96.31%	-56.31%	-48.15%	0%	8.21%	7.04%	-9.13%	-13.47%	
05-11-1999	Agrainc	$11.00	0.00%	11.85%	0.00%	48.15%	48.38%	40.32%	17.08%	8.92%		
29-10-1999		$11.00	23.69%	0.00%	64.20%	60.48%	48.38%	19.92%	10.20%			
22-10-1999		$10.95	-23.69%	84.46%	72.74%	55%	19.17%	7.95%				
15-10-1999		$11.00	192.61%	120.95%	80.63%	29.89%	14.28%					
08-10-1999		$10.60	49.29%	24.64%	-24.36%	-30.30%						
01-10-1999		$10.50	0.00%	-61.18%	-56.84%							
25-09-1999		$10.50	-122.36%	-85.25%								
17-09-1999		$10.75	-48.15%									
10-09-1999	Purchase	$10.85										

TABLE 5.9
Annual Equivalent of Returns

Date	Portfolio Value	1 week	2 weeks	3 weeks	4 weeks	5 weeks	6 weeks	7 weeks	8 weeks	9 weeks	10weeks
				Annual Yields	Using Continuous Compounding						
19-11-1999	1229.6	5.438	4.36418	4.151358	3.0726	3.058984	2.169323	1.6223	1.600228	1.281702	1.126414
12-11-1999	1107.5	3.29	3.50786	2.284029	2.4641	1.515517	0.986296	1.05192	0.762121	0.64731	
05-11-1999	1039.6	3.726	1.78105	2.188857	1.0719	0.525555	0.678912	0.401	0.316974		
29-10-1999	967.72	-0.16363	1.42042	0.187288	-0.27449	0.06955	-0.15313	-0.17			
22-10-1999	970.77	3.004	0.36275	-0.31144	0.1278	-0.15102	-0.17105				
15-10-1999	916.27	-2.279	-1.9694	-0.83103	-0.9399	-0.80616					
08-10-1999	957.32	-1.66	-0.10706	-0.49354	-0.438						
01-10-1999	988.37	1.446	0.08959	-0.03066							
25-09-1999	961.27	-1.267	-0.76884								
17-09-1999	984.97	-0.271									
10-09-1999	990.12										
08-09-1999	1000										

TABLE 5.10
Covariance Matrix of the Three Organizations' Return

Covariance Matrix

Company 1	Company 2	Company 3
0.012423	−0.00137	0.000439
−0.00137	0.009529	0.000361
0.000439	0.000361	0.001791

TABLE 5.11
Expected Return by Stocks in the Portfolio

μ_p	X_1	X_2	X_3
0.01	0.095	0.097	0.81
0.015	−0.0345	−0.3876	1.422
0.02	−0.16398	−0.8718	2.036
0.025	−0.29	−1.356	2.65
0.03	−0.423	−1.84	3.263

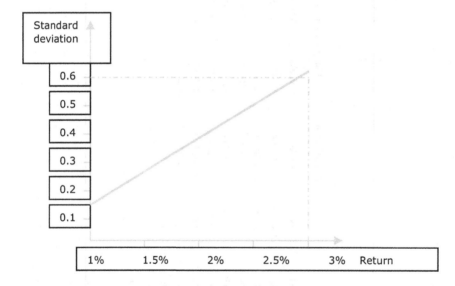

FIGURE 5.11   Relationship of higher a return potentially higher risk.

TABLE 5.12
Standard Deviation of Returns – Risk

μ_p	Standard Deviation
1.0%	0.148
1.5%	0.260
2.0%	0.378
2.5%	0.497
3.0%	0.616

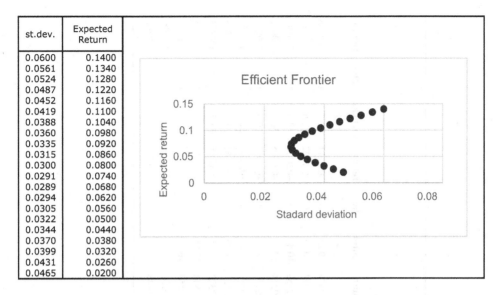

st.dev.	Expected Return
0.0600	0.1400
0.0561	0.1340
0.0524	0.1280
0.0487	0.1220
0.0452	0.1160
0.0419	0.1100
0.0388	0.1040
0.0360	0.0980
0.0335	0.0920
0.0315	0.0860
0.0300	0.0800
0.0291	0.0740
0.0289	0.0680
0.0294	0.0620
0.0305	0.0560
0.0322	0.0500
0.0344	0.0440
0.0370	0.0380
0.0399	0.0320
0.0431	0.0260
0.0465	0.0200

FIGURE 5.12 Representation of risk and expected return according to the portfolio selection.

is $1,000 and the six stocks were in the portfolio for during the whole period of analysis (Table 5.13).

Th calculation of the variance-covariance matrix provides the evaluation of changes in the random variables used (returns of stocks) (Table 5.14).

A result of the program is presented in Table 5.15.

That means only three of six companies are considered appropriate to reduce the variance and to get the expected results. The main company option appears to be under these assumptions; the company 1 with using almost 80% of the total investment budget.

5.8.2 RETURN ANALYTICS IN BONDS

In this section, the review is about pricing different types of bonds and building metrics to understand the behavior of the bonds through years. A way for a company or a government agency to gather cash is issuing and selling bonds in the market. A bond is an interest-based security where the issuer is committed to pay a defined amount (or amounts) of money at some future date (or dates). The company or government agencies or dependencies that are issuing bonds identify the total financial needs and define the amount borrowed for a period of time at certain interest rate that is offering to pay. The lenders to the organization in this case are the bond buyers/holders who will receive the interest and payment according to the issue agreement. Bonds as long-term loans for organizations are issued through investment banks or the central banking system. Bonds have coupons to be paid periodically and redemption values to maturity. Coupons are negotiated on secondary markets. In the case of corporate bonds, stockholders promise to pay the coupons before taking the dividends. The coupon is the agreement of payment for the investment during the life of the bonds.

The term of the bond is the number of units of time between the issue and the maturity time or time when final payment is done/agreed/defined. Bonds with an infinite term are called perpetuals and at the same time there are bonds that allow the payment before the maturity time. Those bonds are the callable bonds. Any date prior to, or including, the maturity date on which a bond may be redeemed is the redemption date. The par value or face value is the amount that is agreed to pay to bondholders when the maturity date due. When a callable bond is paid, possibly there is a penalty for the transaction, $C > F$.

TABLE 5.13

Example of Calculation of Returns in a Portfolio

RETURNS FOR THE STOCKS

prices	agrainc	div	return	clarica	div	return	searscan	div	return	resea rch	div	return	corel	div	return	shellcan	div	return
1 week	10.85			22.35			33.65			52.75			8.8			31.8		
2 weeks	10.75	0	−0.0092	21.65	0	−0.031	34.05	0	0.0119	49.2	0	−0.0673	9.25	0	0.0511	32.7	0	0.0283
3 weeks	10.5	0	−0.0233	21.85	0	0.0092	34.35	0	0.0088	39	0	−0.2073	10.75	0	0.1622	32.65	0	−0.0015
4 weeks	10.5	0	0	22.3	0	0.0206	34.8	0	0.0131	44.3	0	0.1359	10.4	0	−0.0326	33.3	0	0.0199
5 weeks	10.6	0	0.0095	21.25	0	−0.047	34	0	−0.023	45.25	0	0.0214	10	0	−0.0385	30	0	−0.0991
6 weeks	11	0	0.0377	21.3	0	0.0024	31.05	0	−0.0868	44.45	0	−0.0177	8.7	0	−0.13	29.3	0	−0.0233
7 weeks	10.95	0	−0.0045	22.9	0	0.0751	34.3	0	0.1047	48.4	0	0.0889	7.7	0	−0.1149	32	0	0.0922
8 weeks	11	0	0.0046	23.8	0	0.0393	32.5	0	−0.0525	45.85	0	−0.0527	9.75	0	0.2662	31	0	−0.0313
9 weeks	11	0.04	0.0036	24.3	0.15	0.0273	35	0.06	0.0788	56.5	0	0.2323	9.95	0	0.0205	31.3	0.18	0.0155
10 weeks	10.6	0	−0.0364	26.6	0	0.0947	37.1	0	0.06	61.1	0	0.0814	12.95	0	0.3015	30	0	−0.0415
11 weeks	10.75	0	0.0142	26.6	0	0	37	0	−0.0027	80.4	0	0.3159	16.15	0	0.2471	31.5	0	0.05
mean			−0.0004			0.019			0.0112			0.0531			0.0733			0.0009
s.deviation			0.0193			0.0412			0.0554			0.1448			0.152			0.0505

TABLE 5.14

Portfolio Variance-Covariance Matrix for Returns

Covariance Matrix

	Agrainc	Clarica	Searscom	Research	Coral	Shellcam
Agrainc	0.0003716	−0.00037	−0.00064	0.000689	−0.00149	−3.3E−05
Clarica	−0.000372	0.001699	0.001235	0.00105	0.001773	0.000613
Searscom	−0.000641	0.001235	0.003071	0.002863	−0.00014	0.001466
Research	0.0006888	0.00105	0.002863	0.020961	0.000422	0.002477
Coral	−0.001489	0.001773	−0.00014	0.000422	0.023115	−0.0012
Shullcam	−3.3E−0.5	0.000613	0.001466	0.002477	−0.0012	0.002549

TABLE 5.15

Solution of the Model for Portfolio Optimization

Variance Minimization

			Variables	
minimal value	1E-04	**x1**	0.79934	
of variance		**x2**	0	
		x3	0.175714	
		x4	0	
		x5	0.024946	
		x6	0	

A C redemption value that is paid to maturity at time T is defined as part of the bonus structure. The rate of coupon c as a value relative to the original (face) value of the title F. Usually C is F. There are zero coupons with recognition of interest when they are mature at the end of the term. The price of the bond is the PV of the payments that the bondholder will receive. A risk analytics person keeps in mind the rule of taking and understanding the transaction with the PV transformation. The transaction price at the time t of a bond for a maturity return y is given by:

$$P = \frac{1 - (1 + y)^{-N}}{y} cF + (1 + y)^{-N} C$$

where $N = T - t$ is the number of coupons. In some countries, coupons are semestral and some bonds are issued indexed with inflation-adjusted coupons.

In a simple way, there are several classifications of bonds:

- Accumulation bond is one in which the redemption price includes the original loan plus accumulated interest. Examples of such bonds are the Series E savings bonds.
- Bonds with coupons are periodic payments of interest made by the issuer of the bond prior to redemption.
- Registered and unregistered bonds. There are bond where the name of the owner is registered and any transaction require the corresponding changes in the registration. One bond in which the lender is not listed in the records of the borrower is the unregistered

bond. In this case, the bond belongs to whomever has legal possession of it. Again, these bonds are occasionally called coupon bonds, due to the physically attached coupons.

- Fixed-rate and floated-rate bonds. A fixed-rate bond keeps the same rate the whole term, while the second has a rate that is changing during the term.
- Mortgage and debenture bonds. The first is a secured bond that has a collateral a mortgage/real estate. The second is unsecured and based on the creditworthiness of the issuer.
- Income or adjustment bonds. High-risk bonds pay coupons if the bond issuer has funds/income to pay the coupons.
- Junk bonds. This is a high probability of default bond that pays higher yield.
- Convertible bond. The bond can be paid by the issuer through common stocks of the company at a price that has discount related to the market value.
- Serial bonds. A set of bonds issued at the same time with various maturity dates. These are used when a borrower is in need of a large amount of money.
- Treasury bonds. Issued by the U.S. Treasury. Terms of seven or more years.
- Treasury bills. Short-term debt with maturities of 13, 26, or 52 weeks. T-bill yields are computed as rates of discount. These yields are computed on a simple discount basis. The basis for counting time periods for T-bills is actual/360.
- Municipal bonds. These are bonds issued by state and local governments to finance large, long-term capital projects (e.g., hospitals, highways, schools).

In bond return analytics, a main question is about determining the purchase price that will produce a given yield rate to an investor. This question is in the previous section. When considering the price of a bond, we make the following assumptions:

- All obligations will be paid by the bond issuer on the specified dates of payments. Any possibility of default will be ignored.
- The bond has a fixed maturity date.
- The price of the bond is decided immediately after a coupon payment date, or alternatively, at issue date if the bond is brand new. The following symbols and notations will be used in connection with bond valuation:

P = The price paid for a bond.

F = The par value or face value or face amount. This amount is usually printed on the front of the bond and is often the amount payable at the maturity date.

C = the redemption value of a bond, i.e. the amount of money paid at a redemption date to the holder of the bond.

r = The coupon rate is the effective rate per coupon payment period used in determining the amount of the coupon. The default payment period is a half-year. For example, r = 0.035 for a 7% nominal coupon paid semiannually.

Fr = The amount of a coupon payment.

g = The modified coupon rate. It is defined by $g = Fr/C$. Thus, g is the coupon rate per unit of redemption value, rather than per unit of par value.

i = The yield rate of a bond, or the yield to maturity. The interest rate actually earned by the investor, assuming the bond is held until redemption or maturity.

n = The number of coupon payment periods from the date of calculation until maturity date or redemption date.

K = The present value, computed at the yield rate, of the redemption value at the maturity date, or a redemption date, i.e. $K = Cv^n$ at the yield rate i.

G = The base amount of a bond. It is defined by $G_i = Fr$ or $G = Fr/i$. Thus, G is the amount which, if invested at the yield rate i, would produce periodic interest payments equal to the coupons on the bond.

The quantities F, C, r, g, and n are given by the terms of a bond and remain fixed throughout the bonds life. On the other hand, P and i will vary throughout the life of the bond. Price and yield rate have a precise inverse relationship to each other; i.e., as the price increases the yield rate is going down and on the contrary.

There are three different quoted yields associated with a bond:

1. Nominal yield is the ratio of annualized coupon payment to par value. For example, two coupons per year of $3.50 on a $100 par value bond result in a 7.00% nominal yield.
2. Current yield is the ratio of the annualized coupon payment to the original price of the bond. For example, if you paid $90 per $100 of par value of the bond described above, the current yield would be $7.00/$90 = 7.78%.
3. Yield to maturity is the actual annualized yield rate, or internal rate of return.

Four formulas for price are reviewed, similar to loans, the price of a bond is defined to be the present value of all future payments. The formulas are derivable one from the other: there are situations where one may be more useful than another for specific applications. The first of these is called the basic formula. It is found by writing the equation of value at time t = 0 of the time diagram and is given by

$$P = Fra_{\overline{n}|i} + Cv_i^n = Fra_{\overline{n}|i} + K.$$

This formula has a verbal interpretation: the price of a bond is equal to the present value of future coupons plus the present value of the redemption value.

It is possible derive expressions for the premium and discount using and recalling that $Fr = Cg$.

Premium/Discount Valuation Formula
$$P = Fra_{\overline{a}|,i} + Cv^n$$
$$= Fra_{\overline{n}|,i} + C\left(1 - ia_{\overline{n}|,i}\right)$$
$$= C + (Fr - Ci)a_{\overline{n}|,i} = C\left(1 + (g - i)a_{\overline{n}|,i}\right)$$
Price = Redemption Value ± The Premium/Discount.]

There are questions on bond pricing such as to find the price of a ten-year bond with a par value of $1,000 with coupons at 8.4% convertible semiannually and redeemable at $1,050. Or to find a bond price to produce a yield rate of a nominal rate of annual interest of 10% convertible semiannually. Or to find the price of a ten-year bond with a par value of $5,000 with coupons at 6.2% convertible semiannually and redeemable at $6,000. The bond is priced to produce a yield rate of a nominal rate of annual interest of 10% convertible semiannually.

$$F = 5000 \quad C = 6000 \quad i = \frac{0.10}{2} = 0.05 \quad r = \frac{0.062}{2} = 0.031 \text{ and}$$
$$g = \frac{5000}{6000}0.031$$
$$n- = 20$$
$$K = 6000\left(\frac{1}{1.05}\right)^{20}$$
$$G = \frac{0.031}{0.05}5000$$

$12.46 is annuity that is in Excel functions = PV(0.05,20,–1)

$$a_{n]i} = v + v^2 + \cdots + v^n = \frac{1-v^n}{i}$$

$$v = \frac{1}{1+i}$$

Where

And $4,192.98 is the price. In Excel, using the previous result in position J13, the calculation is = 5000 * 0.031 * J13 * (6000 * ((1/1.05)^20)).

In that case

Premium

$$P - C = (Fr - Ci)a_{n],i} = C(g - i)a_{n],i}$$

Discount

$$C - P = C(i - g)a_{n],i}$$

The bond return analysis has many questions to answer; for example, a 20-year bond matures for its par value of 50,000. The price of the bond is 40,000 at a 10% yield convertible semiannually. Calculate the coupon rate convertible semiannually. Coupon payment is defined to be the product of the face value and the coupon periodic rate. Also, the price of a bond is the present value of all future payments.

The first step is the conversion to the right interest rate to use. Let k be the semiannual effective coupon rate. Then

$$40000 = 50000/1.05^{40} + 50000k(1 - 1.05^{-40})/0.05$$

or

$$50000k(1 - 1.05^{-20})/0.05 = 32.897.72$$

Get k and multiply it by 2 because is a semiannual rate. The same type of questions are with direct application of the price expression, It is important to review if the interest is with the equivalent effective rate in the calculation of the annuity, or with different frequencies. This means if it is asked the price to yield to the investor a r% effective the conversion is required.

In the case of different frequencies, the price is calculated using the actuarial notation as:

$$P = Fr\frac{a_{n]}}{s_{n]}} + Cv^n$$

5.8.3 Price of a Bond Between Coupon Payments

There are many transactions between coupon payments because the bonds are traded every day. A method to calculate the price of a bond at any time prior to maturity date is assuming that the interest period is the same as the coupon payment period, and the search is to find the price of a bond at time $n + t$, where $0 < t < 1$. The computation would be P_n (the price at time n) with $P_{n+1} = P_n(1 + i)^n$ then if a bond is ten years term with coupons of 1,000 and looking for a yield of 10 % semiannually with the same C and F values of 100,000, it is required to know the price after three and half years. The price after three years is $P = 1000a_{n]0.05} + 100000v_{0.05}^n$, where n is

14 periods to get coupons. The price for the transaction is approximated by $p(1 + 0.05)^{6/6}$, where 6/6 is six months of the semiannual liquidation; in the case of having two months, after three years the exponent will be 2/6.

5.8.3.1 Callable Bonds

In a callable bond, the issuer includes in the agreement that can pay the bond in different dates different from the original term. The call dates lead to defined redemption prices, and the main calculation to identify if the bond is hedging against the changes in interest rates is if the interest rates dates. To evaluate the risk to the investor, it is useful to be able to complete the yield rate for each of the call dates. Of a bond with F, P, and the same C for all dates, the price P is calculated as

$$P = Fra_{m]i_m} + Cv^m$$

where i_m is the equivalent of the yield rate at m periods.

The regular price calculation is when m and n are the same. In particular, if the desired yield is 5% payable semiannually, i_m is 2.5%.

5.9 RETURN AND TERM STRUCTURE OF INTEREST: SPOT AND FORWARD

This section shows how the analytics process of interest rates is about dependency of time, the term of the rate, and equivalences in calculations based on how the interest rates are negotiated or related to products.

5.9.1 SPOT AND FORWARD RATES

The calculation of the yield of a bond that is zero-coupon calculated at time 0 and with a term of n periods of time is the spot rate, different maturity times give different spot rates. The graphic of the spot rates versus the time to maturity is called the yield curve. The forward is the rate that is agreed to use in the calculation of a loan of a one-year term, but the loan will be in n years from now. The year 0 and n years later will be the rate to pay during the period n to $n+1$. If s_k is the spot rate, the payment is a unique payment of a currency unit at the time k is $P = (1 + s_k)^{-k}$ and the spot rate is a geometric average of the forward rate f_k.

$$(1 + s_k)^k = \prod_{i=1}^{k-1} \left(1 + f_i\right)$$

That at k is

$$f_k = \frac{(1 + s_{k+1})^{k+1}}{(1 + s_k)^k} - 1$$

That is

$$(1 + s_{k+1})^{k+1} = \left(1 + f_k\right)(1 + s_k)^k$$
$$= \left(1 + f_k\right)\left(1 + f_{k-1}\right)(1 + s_{k-1})^{k-1}$$

Then it is possible obtain the spot rate

$$(1 + s_{k+1})^{k+1} = \left(1 + f_0\right)\left(1 + f_1\right) + \cdots \left(1 + f_k\right)$$
$$s_{k+1} = \left(\left(1 + f_0\right)\left(1 + f_1\right) + \cdots \left(1 + f_k\right)\right)^{\frac{1}{k+1}} - 1$$

The Vasicek model uses the recursive relationship $r_{k+1} = r_k + a(b - r_k) + \sigma Z_k$.

EXHIBIT 5.1   USE OF R FOR BONDS CALCULATION JRVFINANCE PACKAGE

Bonds R in jrvFinance (jrvFinance Usage, Jayanth R. Varma,2021-11-05)

```
library(jrvFinance)
#cashflows
duration(cf=c(1500,2500,3500),rate=0.055)
duration(cg=c(1500,2500,3500),rate=0.055, modified=TRUE)
# Annuities
annuity.pv(rate=0.09, n.periods=20)
annuity.pv(rate=0.09, n.periods=20, immediate.start=TRUE)
annuity.fv(rate=0.09, n.periods=20)
annuity.fv(rate=0.09, n.periods=20, immediate.start=TRUE)
#bond price
bond.price(settle="2021-12-31", mature="2025-01-01", coupon=0.05, yield=0.06)
#In case that timing for frequency of coupons and yield are not the same
bond.price(settle="2012-04-15", mature="2022-01-01", coupon=8e-2,
yield=8.8843e-2, freq=1, comp.freq=2)
#In case of callable bonds
bond.yield(settle='2018-01-01', mature='2023-01-01', coupon=5e-2,
price=101,redemption_value = 102)
```

See the presentation in the option examples ahead in this chapter in Section 5.11.4, where b is the rate of long term, a is the intensity of r rate movement, and Z_k are independent and identically distributed random variables. The performance at maturity and a bonus zero coupons is equal to the spot rates. Or in a continuous case, $\partial r_t = a(b - r_t)\partial t + \sigma\delta W_t$ where W_t is the Wiener stochastic process describing the market risk, σ is the volatility, a is the speed of the interest rate to go back to the estimated long term rate, b is the estimated long term rate as forecast from historical experience, and r_t is the short-term rate.

The computation of many of the concepts that are in these sections are performed using R packages such as jrvFinance, Quantmod, Quantlib, and some others available in the CRAN repository.

Additionally, Excel is equipped with several functions that help with the calculations:

- PV(rate, nper, pmt, fv, type)
- FV(rate, nper, pmt, fv, type)
- COUPDAYSBS(settlement, maturity, frequency, basis)
- YEARFRAC(Strat_date, end_date, basis)
- PRICE(settlement, maturity, rate, yld, redemption, frequency, basis)
- YIELD(settlement, maturity, rate, pr, redemption, frequency, basis)
- DURATION(settlement, maturity, coupon, yld, frequency, basis)
- MDURATION(settlement, maturity, coupon, yld, frequency, basis)

5.9.2 SENSITIVITY ANALYSIS OF INTEREST RATES

This section is about changes in interest rates through time. A unit risk is having an obligation for a certain amount and the payment is based on bond selection with different terms. The bonds are zero coupon; this means the yield i produces a value of $F(1+i)^n$ at redemption where n is the term period of the bond. This means that if there are different terms, there are different amounts at the end of the periods that have to be reinvested to pay the loan. In general, what is possible is to find a combination of rates that are known now and rates that are estimated or expected to have in the future to get the amount to pay the loan. Finally, it is possible to buy bonds with different terms that can be more than five years and to achieve the goal of paying the loan in five years. The terms of the bonds can be eight years and the benefit of having it will depend on the expectation of the future rates and to reduce potential losses.

It is possible to define the price function as the accumulated of the discounted cash flows generated by transactions. The function is created with the assumption of positive values for transactions, with finite number of transactions. With the expression that is the price function such as

$p(i) = \sum_{t \geq 0} c_t (1 + i)^{-t}$ that in a small variation of the I can be written as

$$P(i + \Delta i) \approx P(i) + \Delta i P' + \frac{\Delta i^2}{2} P''(i)$$

where the C_t are cash flows at time $t \geq 0$. This function is with attributes such as concave up, first derivative is negative, and second derivative is positive.

$$\frac{d}{di} P(i) = P'(i)$$
$$\frac{d^2}{di^2} P(i) = P''(i)$$

The meaning of the first derivative is speed/rate of change in pricing because changes in the interest rates and evaluation of the acceleration of the change is possible to describe with the second derivative.

5.9.2.1 Duration

There are in risk analytics multiple metrics to guide the risk understanding of one set of metrics is associated with the sensitivity to changes in interest rate and how they can influence prices of assets or financial planning estimations. Duration and convexity are examples of these metrics. From their way to build, it is possible to learn how to build other metrics when they are required. Duration will provide an indication of how the bond price can change given changes in interest rates. Duration is not the term of the bond.

Duration is the first derivative of the function $P(i)$, $P'(i)$ and a volatility metric is given by the measure of the relative rate of change. The i used in this context of the indicators is the yield to maturity. The modified duration per unit period of conversion is expressed as

$$\frac{d}{di} P(i) = - \sum_{t \geq 0} \frac{t C_t}{(1 + i)^{t+1}}$$

When the interest is compounded in each period, with the equivalence of the nominal rate $i^{(m)}$ and m times per year the calculation incorporates the interests transformation. The negative sign is used to maintain the ratio positive. The conversions follow the interest rate previous rule calculations including the ratio $- \frac{\frac{dP(i)}{di^{(m)}}}{P(i)} = \left(- \frac{P'(i)}{P(i)} \right) \left(\frac{1 + i}{1 + \frac{i^{(m)}}{m}} \right)$.

In the continuous case, $r = ln(1 + i)$ with $A = \sum_{t \geq 0} e^{-rt} C_t$ duration is $Duration = \frac{1}{A} \sum_{t \geq 0} te^{-rt} C_t = -\frac{d}{dr} \ln A$.

Another metric is **Macaulay duration**, which is expressed as:

$$D_{Mac} = \frac{1}{P(i)} \sum_{t \geq 0} \frac{t C_t}{(1 + i)^t}$$

5.9.2.2 Convexity

Convexity is a metric that is based on the Taylor polynomial for the price curve and is closely related to the concavity of the graph. Recall that the second-degree Taylor polynomial

$$Convexity = \frac{P''(i)}{P'(i)}$$

In the continuous case, using the force of interest, that with A defined above gives $Convexity = \frac{1}{A}\frac{d^2}{dr^2}A$ or

$$Convexity = \frac{1}{A}\sum_{t\geq0} t^2 e^{-rt}C_t$$

where $r = ln(1 + i)$, which is the continuously compounded rate of interest and called the force of interest.

5.9.2.3 About Immunization

Immunization is a term used to express the use of the combination of assets according to the rates of interest to cover potential losses because of interest rates changes. The procedure is in the bond market to identify the C value of the alternative bond investment according to the time it is expected to buy in the future. The first bond is bought for a two-year term and the second bond with term of six years. If the loan is required to pay in five years, there is information to have: the C redemption values of the first and second bond, the yield in each bond, at the sum of the C value of the first bond plus the equivalent of the C value of the second bond at the end of the second year/ beginning of the third year will be invested a $i\%$ for the rest of the loan term to get the amount that is required.

As an illustration of the analytics process, it is assumed that there are available assets (A_t) at time t, the same as due liabilities (L_t) at the same time. The difference between assets and a liabilities in present value is the surplus function $S(i)$.

$$S(i) = \sum_t (A_t - L_t)(1 + i)^{-t} = \sum_t A_t(1 + i)^{-t} - \sum_t L_t(1 + i)^{-t}$$

This function will be positive, negative, or equal to zero depending on the assets and liabilities amounts, periods of time, etc.; one objective is to have positive surplus and optimize based on constraints defined by organizations. The problem to solve is a minimization problem searching the interest rate that minimizes the function.

Redington immunization matches the cash flows at the present value, the same as the duration at present value and convexity of liabilities lower or equal to the convexity of liabilities; this means assets and liabilities match $\frac{L}{(1+i)^t} = \sum_k \frac{A_i}{(1+i)^{t_k}}$, where assets are available at different times t_i.

The duration is weighted by the present values, with liability and asset of equivalent duration and d_i for asset duration:

$$\frac{d}{di}\frac{L}{(1 + i)^t} = \frac{d}{di}\sum_k \frac{A_i}{(1 + i)^{t_k}}$$

And the convexity is given by

$$\frac{d^2}{di^2}\frac{L}{(1 + i)^t} \leq \frac{d^2}{di^2}\sum_k \frac{A_i}{(1 + i)^{t_k}}$$

M-Squared

Another metric that is used evaluates the duration metric change regarding r rate. This means $\frac{d}{dr} Duration = -M^2$ representing the continuous case as $A = \Sigma_{t \geq 0}\ e^{-rt}A_t$ or in the discrete situation as $P(i)$.

That is in a general expression $M^2 = \frac{1}{A} \Sigma_{t \geq 0}\ (t - Duration)^2 e^{-rt}A_t$.

5.10 METRICS IN A PORTFOLIO

The metrics used in the previous section can be used in portfolios with multiple assets/securities/financial instruments. The calculation of duration and convexity add knowledge to the set of analysis done using percentiles of the loss distribution (VaR, CvaR, SVaR). The aggregated metrics of the portfolio are the weighted duration and convexity of the individual assets. This means there is a linear property to use.

A portfolio is $Port = \Sigma_{k=1}^{m} P(i)_k$, the sum of the individual $P(i)_k$ of the k assets. Thus

$$Duration_{port} = -\frac{\frac{d}{di}Port}{Port} = \sum_{k=1}^{m} \frac{P(i)_k}{Port}(Duration\ of\ Asset\ k)$$

The same applies to convexity

$$Convexity = \sum_{k=1}^{m} \frac{P(i)_k}{Port}(Convexity\ of\ Asset\ k)$$

There are concepts to review such as VaR, SVaR, and CVaR as part of a risk management process and methodology (see Section 9.4 for the numeric example of VaR simulation). VaR measures the value of potential losses in a portfolio that will not exceed more than a fraction of possible events. The second measures the potential losses of the entire portfolio of the organization. The loss distribution concept and the understanding of percentiles of the distribution are the bases of the VaR concept, as a range is established at the level of losses, in which above the expected losses there is a scale of unexpected losses and exceptional losses. The VaR concept is linked to unexpected losses where the probability of loss is less than VaR. Basic models of VaR variance assume normality, meaning that the percentages of change in prices in financial markets are normally distributed.

Value-at-risk (VaR) is a statistical measure of potential loss for a financial portfolio computed at a given level of confidence and over a defined holding period. In the practice organizations measure VaR at the 99th percentile confidence level for price movements over a one-day holding period using historic simulation of the last two years of equally weighted historic market data. These calculations are updated daily with current risk positions, with the exception of certain less material positions that are not actively traded and are updated on at least a monthly basis.

Stressed value-at-risk (SVaR) is calculated in an identical manner as VaR with the exception that it is computed using a fixed historical one-year period of extreme volatility and its inverse rather than the most recent two-year history. The stress period used needs to be updated covering the global financial crisis to a one-year period and high market volatility through time. CVaR represents the calculation beyond the VaR point through a weighted average of losses or expected value of losses.

VaR and SVaR are statistical estimates based on historical market data and should be interpreted with knowledge of their limitations, which include the following:

- VaR and SVaR will not be predictive of future losses if the realized market movements differ significantly from the historical periods used to compute them.

- VaR and SVaR project potential losses over a one-day holding period and do not project potential losses for risk positions held over longer time periods.
- VaR and SVaR are measured using positions at close of business and do not include the impact of trading activity over the course of a day. VaR and SVaR are measured through multiple means validating the VaR against daily marked-to-market revenue. The search is to find possible events where trading results/revenue are above VaR estimation.

The VaR number, in a portfolio for a one-day time horizon, is the product between the one-day volatility by the present position value of that day. Remembering that volatility is described as the standard deviation of the loss distribution, a definition can be given to VaR by saying that it measures the amount of money that can be lost in a period of time, within a predefined level of trust. There are mainly two ways to obtain the VaR value: the first is using the correlation and variance values of each asset or as it is known using the covariance method, and the second is by introducing simulation using the Monte Carlo method.

The first method: $VaR = \sqrt{VCV^T}$. V is the matrix of the invested quantities in each asset times the volatility and C represents the correlations. This means that the matrix entries are the invested amounts of each asset in the portfolio multiplied by its volatility. C represents the matrix of correlations. In the case where the interest is the VaR approximation for options two problems must be solved: the first presents that in options there are several factors involved and second to options have a high kurtosis distribution with respect to the underlying asset of the option.

The VaR value can be calculated using a simulation by knowledge of historical price data, taking a series of many days. The variance of the portfolio is calculated based on the variances of individual assets. Simulation uses the covariance in a series of historical values. Price changes are obtained for all assets or risk factors needed to analyze the portfolio. Portfolio change data is organized into percentiles. The VaR value will be the value of the change corresponding to the confidence level. Correlations and variances or volatility are then calculated for each of the portfolio's components or risk factors. The Monte Carlo Simulation is then random numbers that are generated applying the inverse of the cumulative normal distribution function to each random number generated. These numbers represent the change in prices. The inverse is searched with data from a normal zero, one distribution. For the calculation the experiment is performed multiple times both for the number of events and repetitions of the simulation. Then, with those repeated values, the mean, standard deviation, and range data, in particular for the VaR value, are taken. The VaR value of each asset represented is the product of the change by the value of the position in each of the events.

Now for the case where multiple assets are made, the eigenvalues and eigenvectors are calculated and correlated price changes are generated for all assets. This is done because the values and vectors themselves indicate how price changes in one group of risk factors behavior relative to the others. When calculating for a multi-asset portfolio the prices are correlated the analysis of principal components of the correlation matrix is required. The eigenvalues and eigenvectors are calculated solving the characteristic equation $det(X - \lambda I) = 0$. Once these eigenvalues and eigenvectors have been calculated, it is defined as the sum of the changes of all individual assets of the product of the square root of the eigenvalue of the i-th asset, multiplied by the random price change calculated by applying the inverse of the normal distribution by the k-th element of the i-th eigenvector of the volatility of the k-th asset.

After the correlated price changes are generated, they are applied to the portfolio assets and a historical series of portfolio changes will be generated. That is, each change of the asset multiplied by the position of the asset and then added all the results. Portfolio changes are sorted by percentiles and according to the defined confidence level it is set which is the VaR value. In the case of options, the change in the option value is obtained using Taylor's polynomial approximation. Risk factors measured by portfolio changes are considered to be denoted in Greek letters.

Δoption value

$$= \partial \Delta value \ underlying \ asset_i + \frac{1}{2}\gamma \Delta value \ underlying \ asset_i$$
$$+ \ \nu \Delta volatility \ of \ underlying \ asset_i + \rho \Delta free \ risk \ rate$$
$$+ \ \theta \Delta \ period \ of \ time$$

In the case of non-normality, the skewness and kurtosis structure of the distribution should be observed, as should the study of the behavior of the tails. In practice, it should try to approximate the condition of the normativity study. Of course, with the knowledge of the distribution, the same procedure can be performed, only that the values will be calculated by the inverse of the function that best describes the phenomenon. Volatility calculation can be performed by calculating the standard deviation, simple moving averages or by simulation. It may be presented that volatility is assumed to be constant in time or not constant, in which case an exponentially weighted moving average is used.

Stress tests are used to identify and control risk that is related to considerable changes in market prices and rates. Organizations perform stress testing daily on positions that are marked-to-market. The stress tests are using simulation based on historical and hypothetical events that can have important impact in the duration/term periods up to 90 days. Regulation changes can appear or catastrophes as well. In 2013, an important change came with the policy of reducing the speed of buying the Treasury bonds or what happened with the CDOs (collateralized debt obligations) and subprime mortgages in a financial crisis. The stress testing is an ongoing process that includes the review of the current positions and under the assumption of revaluation in the moment of the calculation and with no other external factors intervention.

In Exhibit 5.2, the average VaR is showing an increment that is required to investigate the cause, in this particular case can be explained because of market volatility. When the comparison is on SVaR, the difference is smaller and it is possibly because the impact of the periods of time where the calculations are performed and the volatility in those periods is different, or conditions of credits spreads require more analysis. Exhibit 5.3 indicates organizations in the same period and the comparison of the trading revenue and VaR calculation where patterns show similarities in the same period of time of trading revenue losses. Only one of the four organizations did not have trading losses higher that the VaR calculation.

Additional details of the metrics will be presented in Chapter 9. Now with the previous concept, it is possible to connect the creation of financial products that help to manage risk and to identify specific metrics by products and portfolios.

EXHIBIT 5.2   EXAMPLE OF A BANK SUMMARY OF TWO YEARS COMPARISON AT THE SAME DAY VAR AND SVAR CALCULATIONS (ROYAL BANK ANNUAL REPORT 2020)

| | October 31, 2020 | | | | October 31, 2019 | | | |
| | | For the year ended | | | | For the year ended | | |
(Millions of Canadian dollars)	As at	Average	High	Low	As at	Average	High	Low
Equity	$ 23	$ 33	$ 64	$ 13	$ 22	$ 19	$ 32	$ 11
Foreign exchange	3	3	6	1	3	4	13	2
Commodities	3	3	7	1	2	2	4	1
Interest rate (1)	47	54	178	11	13	14	19	11
Credit specific (2)	7	6	7	4	5	5	6	4
Diversification (3)	(18)	(25)	n.m.	n.m.	(17)	(17)	n.m.	n.m.
Market risk VaR	$ 65	$ 74	$ 232	$ 18	$ 28	$ 27	$ 45	$ 15
Market risk Stressed VaR	$ 86	$ 109	$ 228	$ 49	$ 85	$ 106	$ 161	$ 76

*   This table represents an integral part of our 2020 Annual Consolidated Financial Statements.
(1)   General credit spread risk and funding spread risk associated with uncollateralized derivatives are included under interest rate VaR.
(2)   Credit specific risk captures issuer-specific credit spread volatility.
(3)   Market risk VaR is less than the sum of the individual risk factor VaR results due to portfolio diversification.
n.m. not meaningful

**EXHIBIT 5.3   COMPARING THE TRADING REVENUE AND MARKET RISK
VAR DIFFERENT ORGANIZATIONS (SOURCE: BANKS YEAR REPORTS 2020)**

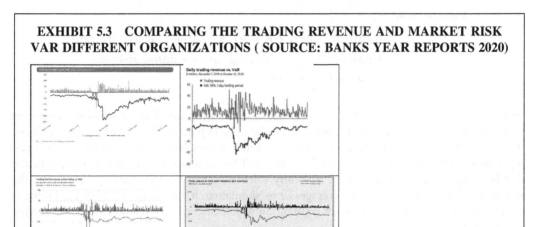

5.11   ANALYTICS OF PRODUCTS TO DEAL WITH RISK

Part of risk analytics in dealing with investments is the use of products/financial contracts to hedge organizations, transactions, and generate opportunities for investors. This section presents examples of products based on the interest rate treatment for supporting transactions and dealing with risk. A derivative is a title that pays its owner an amount that is a function of the value of another main title (underlying asset). A derivative product is obtained from the main title of options, forwards, futures, swaps, etc. For example, if insurance is a title, then reinsurance is a derivative title. Derivative valuation is based on derivative trading, the underlying asset and risk-free bonds. This means that the information of the three elements is taken to identify how to value it. For example, risk-free bonds identify the risk-free investment rate that is a parameter of these models. If the prices of a bond and a main title are known and their combination can replicate derivative payments, the market price of the derivative must be equal to the price of the bond combination and the main title. This is the price policy of non-arbitration. Remember that arbitrage consists of the simultaneous purchase and sale of a title for a risk-free benefit.

In an arbitration-free market, two assets with identical future cash flows must have the same current price. The opportunity for arbitration is the possibility to make a trading profit without the possibility of loss. In the insurance business there are multiple interesting situations of risk control, from cash flows to the definition of product prices. An insurer invests premiums, pays expenses, and handles customer claims when they take place. An insurance risk portfolio is financially more stable, risks are uncorrelated, but analogous to an asset portfolio.

In risk theory, a person buys a policy that commits the insurer to pay claims in (0, T), P is paid at time zero in exchange for a future cash flow of claims. These are uncertain for bonds and divisions. The insurance market does not have a secondary market for policyholders for the reserved subscription right. Some life insurance products give rise to the secondary market. Another form of secondary market is transactions that are made with reinsurers. Reinsurance contracts are insurance contract derivatives.

5.11.1   INTEREST RATE SWAPS

This is a contract between two entities or counterparties that indicates payment of interest according to the contract. There is a fix-rate payment form of a part of the contract and the

---

TABLE 5.16
Swap Price Calculation

Terms	Spot Prices	Spot Rate	Swap Rate
1	100	5%	$P(0, 1) = \frac{1}{1.05}$
2	200	5.5%	$P(0, 2) = \frac{1}{1.005^2}$
3	300	6%	$P(0, 3) = \frac{1}{1.06^3}$

---

counterpart has a variable rate. This is a way to convert variable rates into fixed rates. LIBOR is used for defining forward rates based on the spot LIBOR rate. The payments are interest rates times the contract amount/loan/principal. Assuming loans amount equal in all periods and the calculation of the interest swap rate is $P(0,k) = P_k$ at time k or zero coupon bond price.

This means $P_k = \frac{1}{(1 + s_k)}$ in terms of the yield rate of a zero-coupon k year bond and the swap rate is at N time $swaprate = \frac{1 - P_N}{\sum_{k=1}^{N} P_k}$ that is when in bond face amount or par value = price of the bond = C redemption value or par coupon bond. This P_k is the bond price.

And in terms of the forward rates, f_t the swap price is $\frac{\sum_{k=1}^{n} P_k f_{k-1}}{\sum_{k=1}^{n} P_k}$ and changing to swap with m periods ahead $\frac{\sum_{k=m}^{n} P_k f_{k-1}}{\sum_{k=m}^{n} P_k}$. That is equivalent to the formula above. As an example, if there are three terms, the calculations will be (Table 5.16).

The price is the weighted calculation:

$$r = \frac{100P(0, 1) + 200P(0, 2) + 300P(0, 3)}{\sum_1^3 P(0, k)}$$

5.11.2 Forward Contracts

A forward contract specifies, at the time it is written, t, the terms under which a transaction may take place at some point T in the future. The terms that are specified are the quantity and quality of goods, plus other details. The forward contract is usually a personal contract that is not easily transferred to a third party. It is made to the measure of the people involved in the transaction. It is assumed that the underlying asset is traded at a price S_t at time t. Forward negotiators agree to trade the asset at a $F(t,T)$ price at the time T, $t < T$. Both parties must respond to the contract, regardless of what the market changes have been like.

If the time goes to T, the price goes to S_T. The forward buyer pays $F(t,T)$ for the asset even though $S_T < F(t,T)$ and the seller must deliver the asset at $F(t,T)$ price even though $S_T > F(t,T)$.

An example of a forward contract can be given for the currency transaction. The market dynamic appears with the concept of bid (offer purchase), ask (offer to sell) and spread, that is, offer to buy for b monetary units, offer to sell for $b+1$ monetary units and the difference that will be that spread, respectively. Forward contract distributors make their profit as the difference-margin between offered price and demanded price, negotiators pay a fee to the distributor for providing the transaction. The cost of non-payment and transaction costs are ignored here. For example, a company wants to make an investment of ninety thousand monetary units in a pension fund in country A, maturing in a year in a hundred thousand monetary units. The organization to protect itself from the exchange rate, opens a forward contract with a bank with $S_0 = F(0,1) = 1.25$.

The forward markets change daily. For instance, if today is $t = 0$ in January, it will be a price at delivery in a year of $F(0,1) = 1.25$, and July $F(0.5,1) = 1.2$, converging to a spot price of $F(T,T) = S_T$. The forward interest rates are related to forward contracts. For example, a forward contract can be written at $t = 0$ asking for delivery at $t = k$ of a zero coupon bond with n years to maturation at a value of 1. In that if a forward contract with price $F = F(0,k)$ at time $t = 0$ and with investment window of $(0, k + n)$ with possibilities of acquiring a bond with price $P(n + k) = (1 + S_{n+k})^{-(n+k)}$ that has $n + k$ years maturing at 1 and S_{n+k} the spot rate ay time 0 for a bond $n+k$ discount bond. Or open a forward contract agreeing to buy aa n-year bond when $t = k$ at the same time that buying a zero coupon bond with maturity at $t = k$ with initial value F. Then to buy the bond of n years under the forward contract at $t = k,$ the initial the cost of the forward is $FP(k) = P(n + k)$ or

$$FP(k) = F(1 + S_k)^{-k}$$

Because of no-arbitrage, where S_k is the spot rate at $t = 0$ for a bond of k years to discount. And it is possible to obtain that $F = F(0,k)$ is given by

$$F(0, k) = \frac{P(n + k)}{P(k)} = \frac{(1 + S_{n+k})^{-(n+k)}}{(1 + S_k)^{-k}} = \frac{1}{(1 + f_k)\ldots(1 + f_{k+\mu-1})}$$

where f_k are forward rates for the period.

The relationship between spot and forward markets is given by connecting a trade strategy. On the one hand, if there is a purchasing strategy of an asset at time t in the spot market at S_t prices and an known accumulated cash at $T > t$ of $D(t, T)$ that is with end value of $S_T + D(t, T)$. On the other hand, a forward contract open at time t will pay $F(t, T)$ at time T and the transaction includes to deposit in a saving account the present value of F and $D(t,T)$ at a rate between t and T of $r = R(t, T)$ per year. The cash flow at time t will be $(F + D(t, T))e^{-(T-t)r}$ and at time T the saving account has accumulated $F + D(t, T)$ and the buyer pays F for the asset that is with market value equal S_T. The two ways to trade in general $F(t, T) = S_t e^{(T-t)r} - D(t, T)$ have the same payoff.

5.11.3 FUTURES CONTRACTS

When it is required to have several forward contracts, it is necessary to create a standardized contract, which is known as a futures contract. The nature of forward contracts makes it difficult to change a position. The futures contracts are offered through exchanges and are standardized with maturity, size, and major assets or indices. Futures markets do not require immediate transfer of the principal asset or title. The contract is given today, at today's market prices, but the item may be delivered in the future. They can exist from multiple types of assets such as consumer goods, securities, and currencies.

The futures market involves hedgers (the ones that are protected) who are corporations or individuals who trade in the stock or goods market and buy or sell future contracts to protect their possessions, or expected possessions in the money market, i.e., use contracts as insurance. There are also speculators who are those who use the sale and purchase of futures contracts for profit. Currency markets are the most developed of the forward markets. By standardization, coin futures do not always provide optimal protection. While a futures position is open, traders earn and pay losses on a daily basis.

An example is like when a trader opens a future position on day 1. The contract requests the delivery of 100 units of the asset to 100 monetary units each on the 60th. So, $F(1,60) \times 100$. Assume that the trader has a balance sheet account of 1,000 on day 1. Price changes are as follows with newspaper sources (Table 5.17).

An example is related to futures on Treasury bonds. Assume that there is a transaction in which a three-month bond future contract is purchased in May for delivery in July of 1,000,000 monetary units. It is known that for an October maturity the spot price is 5% annual discount yield; that is, there are 150 days to do the calculation until maturity:

TABLE 5.17

Example of Prices and Contract Values

Day	Value of Account	Price	Contract Value
1	1.000	100.00	10.000
2	1.500	105.00	10.500
3	2.500	110.00	11.000
4	2.500	110.00	11.000
5	1.000	100.00	10.000
6	900	99.00	9.900

$$S_t = 1.000.000[1 - 150/360 * 0.05] = 979.166 \text{ May price}$$

If the return of the Treasury bonds is 4.5% at the beginning of May and ending in July the price for the bonds would be

$$1.000.000[1 - 60/360 * 0.045] = 992.500$$

Then the price of the future is $F = S_t e^{r(T-t)}$ where r is the risk free interest rate and $1.000.000 = 992.500e^{r\ (T-t)}$ is the solution value of the future $1.001.447 = 979.166e^{r(T-t)}$.

5.11.4 OPTIONS

The following presentation is not a complete review of options and their operations and details of how the options work and how to obtain the prices in many types of products, but this is an illustration of how risk analytics works in a valuation of a contract. The option price requires to understand at least three aspects: exercise or not the right, the market condition of arbitrage or not, and the payment of dividends. Models identification is based on the combination of theses aspects and main idea of the risk analytics modeling is to consider the two outcomes (Bernoulli process) and repeat several periods the same possible outcome generation to work based on a binomial distribution analysis and then through a continuous assumption of interest capitalization to use a normal approach.

In options analysis there is a good application of probability distributions knowledge such as normal, binomial, and lognormal distributions plus other analytics concepts in the evaluation of option contracts. An option is a contract that allows buying or selling a security/asset at a certain defined price. Options generate obligations and rights as follows: The call options for whom the holder or buyer pay a premium and has the right to buy the interest asset at a fixed price; for the seller or subscriber receives a premium and is obliged to sell if required, within a period of time. The put options for the holder or buyer pay a premium and have the right to sell, while for the seller or subscriber they receive a premium and are required to buy if requested (Figures 5.13 to 5.16 illustrate the way that options work).

The contract has a term, but it does not mean obligation to buy or sell. The price for buying or selling the stock is the exercise price. One option offers protection against unfavorable price movements but does not reduce the benefit by increasing prices. A premium is paid when the contract is opened.

- S is the price of the asset and S_t the price at t of the underlying asset of the option.
- k is the exercise price at $T > t$.

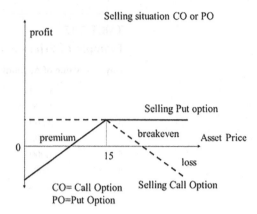

FIGURE 5.13 Payment of the seller.

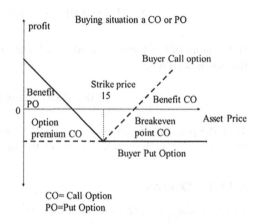

FIGURE 5.14 Payment for the buyer.

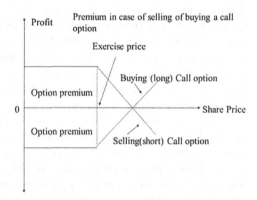

FIGURE 5.15 Benefits for sellers and buyers Call.

The right to buy is a decision of the option owner at time T who can obtain $S_T - k$, dado $S_T > k$, because of using the option and sale immediately the asset in the market. If $S_T < k$, the option is not used. The value of using the option is a function of the closed price $(S_T - k)^+$, where in general the function is:

$(Z)^+ = \max (Z,0)$, this is equal to Z if $Z > 0$ or 0 if $Z < 0$. The rights of the options can be negotiated in the stock exchange market.

A call option or purchase option for a stock gives to the owner the right to buy the stocks at fixed exercised price. The option expires at T with $\Delta t = T - t$ as the option term. A put option gives the

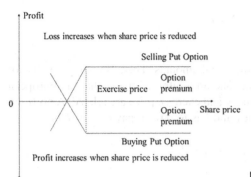

FIGURE 5.16 Benefits for sellers and buyers Put.

right to sell stocks at a specified price during the term of the option. The value of the exercise of a sell option is $(k - S)^+$, where S is the market price of the asset. The value of the sell option on the expiration date should be the less market price of the stock.

In the case of the put option, the buyer receives a positive payment only if the value of the main asset is or falls below the strike price. The call option gives a positive pay value to the buyer only if the value of the principal asset exceeds the strike price. The call option protects whether the price of the stock or the main asset goes up, because for the producer the profit would be reduced. The put option protects if the share or asset price falls, because the profit of the supplier would be reduced.

There are three concepts associated with option transactions: *In the money* that in the case of the call option, is when the strike price is lower than the price of the underlying asset at the time T. For the case of the put option, it is the opposite situation. *Out of the money* means that in the call option, the strike price is higher than the price of the main asset at the time T. In the case of the put option is the opposite. *At the money* is understood when the equality of the price of the exercise and that of the main asset at the time T is presented for both call and put options.

Types of options

European style: They can only be exercised at the expiration date of the contract. American style: They can be exercised at any time before expiration. Exotic options: They include different modalities, among them are the Asian and transaction mechanisms that are modified.

Options have also been classified according to the underlying assets stock options, currency options, bonus options, stock index options, and OTC options that are custom-made contracts that have been defined. Some factors influence the value of option premiums, such as the relationship between the price of the underlying asset and the exercise price of the option, the expiration time, interest rate, price volatility of the underlying assets and *dividends*.

Now, in the following paragraphs is presented, some of the characteristics of the options and the way that there are relationships based on the assumptions as any risk analytics work. c and p are the prices of a European option, buy and sell; C and P prices of the equivalent American options.

$$C > c \text{ and } P > p.$$

Then, $C \geq (S - k)^+$ because the American option can be used immediately to have S at a k price. In case of the price is lower than k the owner is not obligated to buy. The condition is that C is non-negative and $P \geq (k - S)^+$ in the case of a put option.

5.11.4.1 Parity Between Put and Call Options

In the case of a European option with no-arbitrage, no dividends, a risk-free rate is possible to get from traders, no transaction fees, no taxes, and possible short selling and access to credit, the European put and call options are related through

$$c + ke^{-r(T-t)} = S + p$$

where p, c, S, and e^{-rt} are known.

The securities are traded in any amount, even in fractional amounts. There is no opportunity for arbitration in or around the asset and options market. The no arbitrage implies that the European options that are on the same asset with the same maturity and exercise price are related. A portfolio with a long purchase and short selling cost $c - p$ at t and has to have a payment at T of

$$(S_T - k)^+ - (k - S_T)^+ = S_T - k$$

The payment $S_t - k$ at T can be obtained without using options buying an asset S at t and a loan of

$$ke^{-r(T-r)}$$

Obtaining

$$c - p = S - ke^{-r(T-t)}$$

Black and Scholes Model

The assumption is that the spot prices of the securities are changing according to a geometric Brownian motion. The return in a period (t, T) is normal with mean $\mu(T - t)$ and variance $\sigma^2 (T - t)$, with μ and σ constant and independent in disjoint time intervals.

$S = S_t$ the price of the security at time t, the term of the option is $\Delta t = T - t$, r the interest rate of risk free bond with the assumption of compounded continuously. $R = R(t, T)$ is a random variable Bernoulli distributed with possible values u and d with $d < u$ and probability parameter π with probability π, $S_T = Se^{ut}$ and probability $1 - \pi$, $S_T = Se^{dt}$.

f is a function that pays at T $f(S_T)$ that applied to s the spot price is defined as:

$$f(s) = (s - k)^+ \text{call option}$$
$$f(s) = (k - s)^+ \text{put option}$$

The evaluation is based on the portfolio of the spot asset and one investment risk free with n units of the asset and B dollars loan at free risk rate. If $n > 0$, there is a long position on the asset and if $n < 0$, there is a short position, then $nS - B$ ($S = S_t$ is the current price per unit) is the price of the portfolio at time t and $nS_T - Be^{r\Delta t}$ is at maturity time. The purpose is to identify n and B.

Define $f_u = f(Se^{u\Delta t})$ and $f_d = f(Se^{d\Delta t})$ that at maturity produces the payoffs $nSe^{u\Delta t} - Be^{r\Delta t} = f_u$ and $nSe^{d\Delta t} - Be^{r\Delta t} = f_d$ that is providing the solutions

$$nS = \frac{f_u - f_d}{e^{u\Delta t} - e^{d\Delta t}} \text{ and } B = e^{-r\Delta t}\left(\frac{f_u e^{d\Delta t} - f_d e^{u\Delta t}}{e^{u\Delta t} - e^{d\Delta t}}\right)$$

This portfolio duplicates the derivative payments and it is the hedge portfolio. The price $nS - B$ is equal to the derivative price $nS - B = e^{-r\Delta t}(pf_u - qf_d)$ for $p = \frac{e^{r\Delta t} - e^{d\Delta t}}{e^{u\Delta t} - e^{d\Delta t}}$ and $q = 1 - p$.

Then $c = e^{-r\Delta t}E(f(S_T))$ with expectation based on the used distribution where

$$E(S_T) = pSe^{u\Delta t} + (1 - p)Se^{d\Delta t} = Se^{r\Delta t}$$

For a call option, $c = e^{-r\Delta t}(pf_u - qf_d)$ is equal 0 if $k \geq Se^{u\Delta t}$ or $e^{-r\Delta t}p(Se^{u\Delta t} - k)$ if $Se^{d\Delta t} \leq k \leq Se^{d\Delta t}$ or $e^{-rt}(pSe^{u\Delta t} + qSe^{d\Delta t} - k)$ if $k \leq Se^{d\Delta t}$.

For the analysis of multiple periods, it is assumed using the binomial model with two *i.i.d.* variables in [t, T], the return $R(t, t_m) = R(t_m, T)$ is equal to $\frac{u\Delta t}{2}$ with probability π and $\frac{d\Delta t}{2}$ with probability $1 - \pi$ and a time in the middle $t_m = \frac{(t+T)}{2}$ with an annual return of

$$R(t, T) = \frac{Nu}{2} + \frac{(2 - N)}{2}d$$

where N is binomial $(2,\pi)$ and in general the price is conditioned to the price at the time t_2 and given by $gp(s) = e^{-\frac{r\Delta t}{2}}E(f(S_T)|S_{t_m} = s)$.

Applying at t_m the previous results is $e^{-\frac{r\Delta t}{2}}E(gp(S_{t_m})) = e^{-r\Delta t}E(f(S_T))$ or price.

Obtaining the option price when the process is extended to N using a random variable binomial (N, p_n) and

$$R(t, T) = N\frac{u}{n} + (n - N)\frac{d}{n}$$

a price result of

$$p = \frac{e^{\frac{r\Delta t}{n}} - e^{\frac{d\Delta t}{n}}}{e^{\frac{u\Delta t}{n}} - e^{\frac{d\Delta t}{n}}}$$

The exercise price is k, the current stock price is S, and the option is exercised in Δt years from now. R is the instant return rate for $S_T = Se^{\Delta tR}$, a European call option with no dividends. Assuming the parity put and call, the Black and Scholes model and R a random variable is assumed normally distributed with variance $\sigma^2\Delta t$. The prices of the put and call options are given by

$$c = sN(d_1) - ke^{-r\Delta t}N(d_2) \text{ and } P = ke^{-r\Delta t}N(-d_2) - SN(-d_1)$$

where

$$d_1 = \frac{\ln\left(\frac{S}{k}\right) + \left(\frac{r+\sigma^2}{2}\right)\Delta t}{\sigma\sqrt{\Delta t}}$$

And $d_2 = d_1 - \sigma\sqrt{\Delta t}$

In case of dividends at a continuous rate $\phi \geq 0$, the result can be modified changing S by $e^{-\Delta t\phi}S$ considering that the dividends are reinvested in stocks as well.

5.11.4.2 American Options

American options are exercised before the maturity date. In the case of call options, there are options including the payment or not of dividend. Under arbitrage assumption with dividends, the soft bounds are:

$$S_t \geq C_t \geq [S_t - k]^+$$

For the lower bound, in order to prevent risk-free arbitrage, C must be non-negative. If $C_t < [S_t - k]^+$, the investor could buy this option and exercise it immediately, and earn a risk-free profit so arbitrage exists. For the upper bound, if $C_t > S_t$, then the investor would make an immediate profit by buying the stock or selling the call option, this because the investor can exercise his right at any time. If the option expires without positive cash flow, then the investor has no liabilities under the option but still owns the asset. This strategy increases the profit without risk, and then arbitrage would exist.

The strong bounds with C > 0 and it is true that $C > [S_t - k]^+$ if $S_t < k$. Assume $S_t < k$ at time t_1 the American call value is $S_{t_1} - k$ at time t_1 that is between dividend dates. An investor can make an arbitrage profit by purchasing a call option, shorting the underlying asset, and investing the strike price k in discount bond that matures and time t_1. A rational investor will not exercise an American call option between the underlying asset dividend payment days. The early exercise of the option is optimal in an American call option just before the payment date if the price of the asset exceeds the critical value. If the price of the asset falls below the critical value, then it is not optimal to exercise even immediately before the payment date.

From the second result of the American call options without dividends, the price of the call option will be the same as the European call option and it is never optimal to exercise the option early. For American put without dividends, it is optimum to exercise the option early while the option call without dividends should not be exercised early, because it is not optimal.

Using the parity of the call and put European options with $P > p$, $P > C + ke^{-rT} - S$ and the parity $c + Ke^{-rT} = p + s$ that in the case of not dividends provides $c = C \rightarrow P > C + Ke^{-rT} - S$ or $C - P < S - Ke^{-rT}$.

5.11.4.3   Valuation

1. *Binomial method of valuation by periods in the case of a put option.* Two possibilities either go up with probability p or goes down with probability $1 - p$.

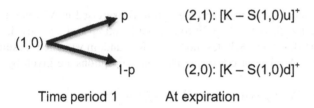

$$\text{(2,1): } [K - S(1,0)u]^+$$

$$(1,0)$$

$$\text{(2,0): } [K - S(1,0)d]^+$$

Time period 1   At expiration

Explicitly, if it is assumed that the option has not been exercised on the node $(1, 0)$, from the risk-neutral valuation, the value of the European put option on the node $(1, 0)$ is:

$$P(1, 0) = e^{-r\Delta t}\{q[k - S(1, 0)u]^+ + (1 - q)[k - S(1, 0)d]^+\}$$

And the American put option at zero is

$$
\begin{aligned}
P(1, 0) &= max\{[k - S(1, 0)]^+, p(1, 0)\} \\
&= max\{k - S(1, 0), e^{(-r\Delta t)}(q[k - S(1, 0)u]^+ + (1 - q)[k - S(1, 0)d]^+)\}
\end{aligned}
$$

Three cases for the exercise price k:
   First:

$$k > S(1, 0)u$$

If the option is exercised immediately in the node $(1,0)$:

$$P(1, 0) = k - S(1, 0) > ke^{-r\Delta t} - S(1, 0) = p(1, 0)$$

Second:

$$k < S(1, 0)d$$

The option has no difference gain in the two nodes, if it is exercised.

Third:

$$S(1, 0)u < k < S(1, 0)d$$

Assuming that the S^*_1 is the critical share price at time 1:

$k - S^*_1 = e^{-r\Delta t}(1 - q)$ [k $-$ S(1, 0)d] where the critical price of the share is a cut-off price between the decision to exercise or maintain the option. For an American put option, it is always optimal to exercise the option immediately when the share price is less than some critical share price.

In the case of n periods in general, when it comes to evaluating the American type option for multiple periods, a binomial approximation can be made allowing multiple states. There is also a way to approximate by partial differential equations, and in particular there is no formula like that of Black and Scholes for the case of European options. Taking in general the value to be approximated for the value of an option of many periods, it would be as in this example, in addition to being multiplied by the value of the binomial coefficients (N, p) by each of the states j and then added on the value i:

In the case of no dividends, the life of the option is divided in N subintervals of length Δt

f_{ij} = Option value at time when the price of that stock is $Su^j d^{i-j}$ $0 \le i \le N, 0 \le j \le i$

at expiration time $f_{Nj} = \max [K - Su^j d^{N-j}, 0]$ j = 0, 1, ... , N

with early exercise a period before expiration

$f_{ij} = \max\{k - Su^j d^{N-1-j}, e^{-r\Delta t} [pf_{Nj + 1} + (1-p)f_{Nj}]\}, 0 \le i \le N - 1, 0 \le j \le i$

with early exercise i periods before expiration

$f_{ij} = \max \{k - Su^j d^{i-j}, e^{-r\Delta t}[pf_{i-1,j+1} + (1- p)f_{i-1,j}]\}$ and $0 \le j \le n-i$

Finally, the risk analytics work includes the review of the concepts for pricing, transactions, operations, and interest rates analysis based on stochastic approaches. The Brownian motion model has the stochastic differential equation

$$dS_t = \mu S_t dt + \sigma S_t dW_t$$

where S_t is the stock price at time t and S_0 is today's price, σ is the volatility, and the solution is

$$S_t = S_0 e^{\left(\mu - \left(\frac{1}{2}\right)\sigma^2\right)t + \sigma\sqrt{t}Z_t}$$

when the W_t the Wiener process or Brownian motion has zero mean and variance t, and Z_t is the N (0,1). The Wiener process has the properties

1. $W_0 = 0$
2. The application t $\rightarrow$ W_t is continuous in t with probability 1
3. W_t for t $\ge$ 0 has increments that are stationary and independent
4. $W_{t+s} - W_t$ is N(0,t)

This solution allows simulations assuming the mean, sigma, period of time, and original price. Z_t is the sample point in the simulation that is coming from inverse of the normal distribution applied to the generated random number.

The Vasicek model for interest rates is a model for analyzing instant interest rates, following the stochastic differential equation:

$$dr_t = k(\mu - r_t)dt + \sigma dW_t$$

where t is the time period, μ is mean of interest rate, the difference $k(\mu - r_t)$ is the expected change of the interest rate, k is the speed to the reversion to the mean, and σ is the volatility.

The solution for s ≤ t is

$$r_t = r_s e^{-k(t-s)} + \mu(1 - e^{-k(t-s)}) + \sigma e^{-kt} \int_s^t e^{ku} dW_u$$

as Brigo and Mercurio (2006) indicated.

The conditional to σ-algebra F_s of expected and variance values are given by

$$E(r_t|F_s) = r_s e^{-k(t-s)} + \mu(1 - e^{-k(t-s)})$$

And

$$var(r_t|F_s) = \frac{\sigma^2}{2k}(1 - e^{2k(t-s)})$$

Illustrating the calculations:

An illustration of the calculations using R (there are many R packages for options and financial mathematics calculations) can be using "derivmkts" Package of Robert McDonald (2022), FinancialMath at includes additional functions in products valuation, and Rmetrics that include Black and Scholes calculations. With the first one, the approach is mainly on the options. This package has two functions to use binomopt and binomplot to calculatae put and call European and American options. What it is required is to provide the parameters and obtaining the values and graphics (see the derivmkts package documentation https://cran.r-project.org/web/packages/derivmkts/derivmkts.pdf for the meaning of parameter/arguments of the functions).

With the parameters/arguments, it is possible to get the Greeks using the *greeks* and *greeks2* functions, or additional values required with the boolean selection of the parameter values. At the same time it is possible to obtain the results of the European option prices using the function *bscall* and *bsput* (see Exhibit 5.4).

EXHIBIT 5.4   BASIC STRUCTURE OF FUNCTION SYNTAX FOR DERIVMKTS R PACKAGE

```
# European and American Options, calls and puts
binomopt(s, k, v, r, tt, d, nstep = 10, american = TRUE, putopt=FALSE,
specifyupdn=FALSE, crr=FALSE,
jarrowrudd=FALSE, up=1.5, dn=0.5, returntrees=FALSE, returnparams=FALSE,
returngreeks=FALSE)
binomplot(s, k, v, r, tt, d, nstep, putopt=FALSE, american=TRUE, plotvalues=FALSE,
plotarrows=FALSE,
drawstrike=TRUE, pointsize=4, ylimval=c(0,0), saveplot = FALSE,
saveplotfn='binomialplot.pdf', crr=FALSE,
jarrowrudd=FALSE, titles=TRUE, specifyupdn=FALSE, up=1.5, dn=0.5,
returnprice=FALSE, logy=FALSE)
greeks(f, complete=FALSE, long=FALSE, initcaps=TRUE) # must used named list entries:
greeks2(fn, …) bsopt(s, k, v, r, tt, d)
# European Options, puts and calls
bscall(s, k, v, r, tt, d)
bsput(s, k, v, r, tt, d)
assetcall(s, k, v, r, tt, d)
cashcall(s, k, v, r, tt, d)
assetput(s, k, v, r, tt, d)
cashput(s, k, v, r, tt, d)
```

Calculation using derivmkts American option, see Exhibit 5.5 that has stock and strike prices equal to $50, a risk-free interest rate of 10%, standard deviation (volatility) of 40% with non-dividend stock and T = 0.4167, Δt = 0.0833, with $u = e^{\frac{\sigma\Delta t}{2}}$ = 1.1224 and $d = e^{-\frac{\sigma\Delta t}{2}}$ = 0.8909.

In addition to derivmkts in R, it is possible to find several packages for calculations. The syntax, for example, using Financial Mathematics package https://rdrr.io/cran/FinancialMath/ is as follows (Figure 5.17).

EXHIBIT 5.5   OUTCOME OF CALCULATIONS WITH MULTIPLE PARAMETERS USING DERIVMKTS FOR AN AMERICAN PUT OPTION

Basic Code

```
library(derivmkts)
s <- 50; k <- 50; r <- 0.10; v <- 0.40; tt <- 0.4167; d <- 0;nstep=7
binomopt(s, k, v, r, tt, d, nstep = 7, american = TRUE, putopt=TRUE, specifyupdn=TRUE, crr=FALSE,
jarrowrudd=FALSE, up=1.1224, dn=0.8909, returntrees=TRUE, returnparams=TRUE,
returngreeks=TRUE)
binomplot(s, k, v, r, tt, d, nstep, putopt=TRUE, american=TRUE, plotvalues=TRUE,
plotarrows=TRUE,
drawstrike=TRUE, pointsize=4, ylimval=c(0,0), saveplot = FALSE,
saveplotfn='binomialplot.pdf', crr=FALSE,
jarrowrudd=FALSE, titles=TRUE, specifyupdn=TRUE, up=1.1224, dn=0.8909,
returnprice=FALSE, logy=FALSE)
```

$price price	$params	$oppricetree [,1] [,2] [,3]	$stree [,1] [,2] [,3] [,4]	$probtree [,1] [,2] [,3] [,4]
5.385193	s k v r	[,4] [,5]	[,5] [,6]	[,5]
$greeks	50.00000000 50.00000000	[1,] 5.385193 3.02239	[1,] 50 56.120 62.98909	[1,] 1 0.4970653
delta gamma theta	0.40000000 0.10000000	1.319153 0.3412499	70.69895 79.35250	0.2470739 0.1228118
−0.41140044 0.02870032	tt d nstep p	0.0000000	89.06525	0.06104550
−0.01483505	0.41670000 0.00000000	[2,] 0.000000 7.78435	[2,] 0 44.545 49.99731	[2,] 0 0.5029347
	7.00000000 0.49706527	4.741631 2.3013045	56.11698 62.98570	0.4999828 0.3727861
	up dn h	0.6825684	70.69515	0.24706537
	1.12240000 0.89090000	[3,] 0.000000 0.00000	[3,] 0 0.000 39.68514	[3,] 0 0.0000000
	0.05952857	10.883973 7.2097675	44.54260 49.99462	0.2529433 0.3771881
		3.9284694	56.11396	0.37497416
		[4,] 0.000000 0.00000	[4,] 0 0.000 0.00000	[4,] 0 0.0000000
		0.000000 14.6445083	35.35549 39.68300	0.0000000 0.1272140
		10.5383625	44.54020	0.25293463
		[5,] 0.000000 0.00000	[5,] 0 0.000 0.00000	[5,] 0 0.0000000
		0.000000 0.0000000	0.00000 31.49821	0.0000000 0.0000000
		18.5017925	35.35359	0.06398033
		[6,] 0.000000 0.00000	[6,] 0 0.000 0.00000	[6,] 0 0.0000000
		0.000000 0.0000000	0.00000 0.00000	0.0000000 0.0000000
		0.0000000	28.06175	0.00000000
		[7,] 0.000000 0.00000	[7,] 0 0.000 0.00000	[7,] 0 0.0000000
		0.000000 0.0000000	0.00000 0.00000	0.0000000 0.0000000
		0.0000000	0.00000	0.00000000
		[8,] 0.000000 0.00000	[8,] 0 0.000 0.00000	[8,] 0 0.0000000
		0.000000 0.0000000	0.00000 0.00000	0.0000000 0.0000000
		0.0000000	0.00000	0.00000000
		[,6] [,7] [,8]	[,7] [,8]	[,6] [,7] [,8]
		[1,] 0.000000 0.000000	[1,] 99.96684 112.20278	[1,] 0.03034360
		0.000000	[2,] 79.34823 89.06046	0.01508275 0.007497111
		[2,] 0.000000 0.000000	[3,] 62.98231 70.69134	[2,] 0.15350952

0.000000	[4,] 49.99192 56.11094	0.09156510 0.053099471
[3,] 1.365274 0.000000	[5,] 39.68087 44.53781	[3,] 0.31064439
0.000000	[6,] 31.49651 35.35168	0.23161581 0.161179445
[4,] 6.508388 2.730823	[7,] 25.00022 28.06024	[4,] 0.31431255
0.000000	[8,] 0.00000 22.27269	0.31246770 0.271804478
[5,] 14.646412 10.319133		[5,] 0.15901201
5.462195		0.23711804 0.275014004
[6,] 21.938247 18.503488		[6,] 0.03217793
14.648315		0.09596719 0.166956857
[7,] 0.000000 24.999784		[7,] 0.00000000
21.939758		0.01618340 0.056309440
[8,] 0.000000 0.000000		[8,] 0.00000000
27.727308		0.00000000 0.008139193

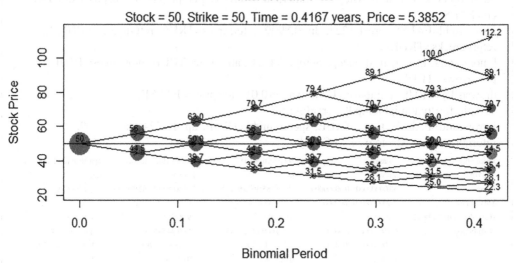

FIGURE 5.17   Output for a put American option suing derivmkts package in R.

Bonds

bond(f,r,c,n,i,ic=1,cf=1,t=NA,plot=FALSE)
f face value
r coupon rate convertible cf times per year
c redemption value
n the number of coupons/periods for the bond
i nominal interest rate convertible ic times per year
ic interest conversion frequency per year
cf coupon frequency- number of coupons per year
t specified period for which the price and write up/down amount is solved for, if not NA
plot tells whether or not to plot the convexity

Forwards

forward(S,t,r,position,div.structure="none",dividend=NA,df=1,D=NA,k=NA,plot=FALSE)
S spot price at time 0

t time of expiration (in years)
r continuously compounded yearly risk free rate
position either buyer or seller of the contract ("long" or "short")
div.structure the structure of the dividends for the underlying ("none", "continuous", or "discrete")
dividend amount of each dividend, or amount of first dividend if k is not NA
df dividend frequency- number of dividends per year
D continuous dividend yield
k dividend growth rate per df
plot tells whether or not to plot the payoff

Options
Call

option.call(S,K,r,t,sd,price=NA,position,plot=FALSE)
S spot price at time 0
K strike price
r continuously compounded yearly risk free rate
t time of expiration (in years)
sd standard deviation of the stock (volatility)
price specified call price if the Black Scholes pricing is not desired (leave as NA to use the Black Scholes pricing)
position either buyer or seller of option ("long" or "short")
plottells whether or not to plot the payoff and profit

Put

option.put(S,K,r,t,sd,price=NA,position,plot=FALSE)
S spot price at time 0
K strike price
r continuously compounded yearly risk free rate
t time of expiration (in years)
sd standard deviation of the stock (volatility)
price specified put price if the Black Scholes pricing is not desired (leave as NA to use the Black Scholes pricing)
position either buyer or seller of option ("long" or "short")
plot tells whether or not to plot the payoff and profit

In case of using Rmetrics packages (Wurtz et al., 2015) for the Black Scholes option prices, there are many functions that are possible to use for computation in finance. Some of them are for return analysis, fMultivar; for trading/technical analysis, fTrading; for other problems analysis such as regression, time series, correalations, portfolios, options: fRegression, fCopulae, fOptions, fExoticOptions, fAsianOptions, fPortfolio, fAssets, and so on.

This chapter has illustrated the use of concepts associated with return in financial products. The tools indicated are mathematical based, with the understanding of mathematical definitions of possible operations that return required, time changes, prices of assets, etc. Return is measured as variation in financial products, their prices, and in values of the money involved in investments, but in general the main aspects are connected to the need of evaluating activities that can be performed in the future and there is uncertainty on the outcomes and it is required means to evaluate possible results. The closer the results are to the reality, the better. Keeping in mind that the outcomes of models are going to be that estimators, they are not going to be the reality, the results will fall in confidence intervals, and the results will have probability of appearance. The key points are that a risk analytics approach helps to clarify where the expected results could be, and it can help to organize the resources in the direction that looks the bets for the organization. And again the risk analytics is a means to support what the orientation can be for strategy and tactics, thinking that everything requires adjustments and calibration according to new data arrival.

The following chapter is about types of data and how to proceed with risk analytics tools to create knowledge using statistical and machine learning. Models are means to obtain knowledge that will be adapted and adopted according to the variety of data, structured, semi-structured, unstructured, the process to change unstructured data to structured data, etc. text data, speech data, and other similar required transformations to move in the direction of structured data where mathematics and algorithms are used. The creation of special matrices with frequencies in text analytics, or the definition of matrices for videos or speech recognition are the bases for data analytics. It is important to maintain the orientation that big data or unstructured data are types of data and they need data analytics for getting the valuable knowledge to obtain results in the organization and actions to perform.

6 Data Analytics in Risk Management

In this chapter, the main message and learning is about the type of data that is required to use in risk analytics according to the variety of data. In the current big data time, the concepts of data analytics are not only around volume, but also in many cases the issue of good risk analytics is about the good use of the variety of the data. Volume can be important for understanding and solving problems, but it is not the most important attribute of data to consider in risk analytics. In several cases, variance affects the data to use; it is possible to have many years of time series data for return analysis for example, but it does not mean that the analysis can avoid a fall in the trap of potential bias.

In the editorial of IMDS (2020): "Data intelligence and risk analytics develop dramatically in recent years. However, the relevant research work is still lack of attention. The purpose of this special issue is to innovative research methodologies from the perspective of data intelligence and risk analytics." And continued: "However, such massive and invaluable data from risk analytics may bring new challenges such as data processing, data visualization, data-driven decision models, risk decision support systems, etc., in the era of big data." This is the reason of having this book and the orientation to design a RAS. Starting with all varieties of risks and possible work with the risk management processes, data is the center of supply to the system. In particular, in this chapter, the aim is to reflect on the data challenges for working with risk analytics. Data is coming from many sources, but the creation of data to sue is limited, the understanding of what data to use, what frequency, how to deal with issues of continuity of the processes in financial markets, institutions, smart fintech, etc. make risk analytics regarding data a very special field to do more research and to pay more attention to deal with it.

The type of data is a factor affecting all that is in the analytics process. Models will be accommodated based on the type of data and interpretation will be subject to the type of data as well. In several cases, data needs transformation and the final results have to be translated to the original variables/values of the raw data set. Data in analytics is possible to divide into raw data and usable data. Raw data is the data that populate the repositories directly from sources. This is the source to create the usable data. Usable data is after all steps of organizing the data, cleaning, and preparing data from different tables or sources that will be used. In the development of the steps to prepare data there is a huge consumption of the analytics process time. It is interesting that the entry-level jobs of people working in analytics is about cleaning and preparing data; however, with the experience it is clear that in the process of organizing the data for analytics posterior step is really the critical step and do it requires a lot of experience of the data scientist/analytics professional. This means that in some cases the work can be tedious and not very grateful; it is in the creation of making the data usable that is the determinant of the next steps to have a good analysis and then offer results with meaning in the problem-solving and decision-making process.

It is crucial to understand that data is the realization of the variables' value. This means the process to keep in mind is that data is not valuable it is not clear what variables for solving the problem will be used. As mentioned in risk analytics, the size of the data is not the priority. The priority is to identify the variables and the sources of data that can be used for a good solution of the problem. This means that a data analytics process will start with the scientific process to determine the data selection and the way that data will be available. The way to get the data is the same as it is in a problem-solving process. Data scientists need to design the process starting with the end in mind and go back to the root of the data to see if it is possible to get the required data (Figure 6.1).

DOI: 10.1201/9780429342899-7

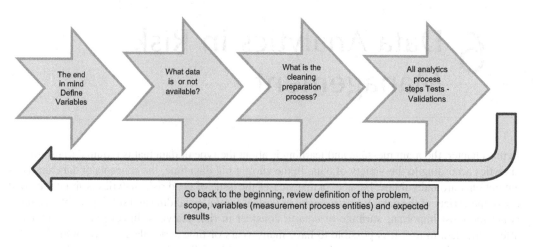

FIGURE 6.1   Data organization/preparation process is a continuous process.

The risk analytics purpose is the creation of knowledge that helps to mitigate and control risk. Risk knowledge creation is a step to find protection, hedging, insurance, or means to mitigate and manage risks. Data is the result of the measurement process (discussed in Chapters 3 and 4) that variables have and that are represented by text, numbers, pictures, videos, etc. In Chapter 1, a matrix representation was indicated and it is the way that data will be used after the required transformations; text will be transformed in matrices and videos as well, etc. Risk knowledge creation starts with obtaining information from data to continue in the analytics process for giving sense and meaning to what the original data says to solve the problem. Information will flow through information systems to move all pieces of the organization. The sources of data are extensive in number and variety as a list as the following shows: annual reports, accounting audits, financial profitability analysis, economic trends, marketing research, operations management performance reports, human resource measurements, web behavior, page views, visitor's country, time of view, length of time, origin and destination paths, products they searched for and viewed, products purchased, what reviews they read, and many others.

Terms related to data organization and use are many; for example, data sets as a collection of data: marketing survey responses, a table of historical stock prices, and a collection of measurements of dimensions of a manufactured item. Database as a collection of related files containing records on people, places, or things. A database file is usually organized in a two-dimensional table, where the columns correspond to each individual element of data (called fields, or attributes), and the rows represent records of related data elements. Big data refers to massive amounts of business data from a wide variety of sources, much of which is available in real time, and much of which is uncertain or unpredictable. IBM calls these characteristics volume, variety, velocity, and veracity. Big data is treated as another type of data that requires certain additional steps for developing computational capacity, but, for example, the application of analytics capabilities will be with the analytics techniques that are used in regular data. Some people confuse big data with big data analytics and this confusion can create a misunderstanding that more data will be the solution for good knowledge creation. Biased data can be huge, and the knowledge will be wrong as it can be the case with social network.

Ladley (2016) pointed out the concept meaning of data attributes that is key for the analytics process. For example, it is crucial to define the level of detail not only in the scales and number of categories that are required in the analysis and that is called granularity, but also aspects related to the changes in the data such as data updating, dimensions of the metrics, and the way that the measures are used in terms of dimensions such as regions, products, time-periodicity, etc. An important data clarity aspect is the consistency in the measurement process. This means seeing if there is consistency in the metric calculation/methods and components used at different times of experiments to be possible to compare or to identify changes through time. For example, GDP needs to be consistently measured to be comparable; no changes in the GDP metric definition can be expected to keep consistency of economic country comparisons. If changes are required, they will point to another new variable/metric creation. Thus, there is a need to change the name or to identify the methods of conversion from old to new versions of metrics. It is a very common error of having measurement through time that has been changed and the results are not comparable, and the time series has been used as comparable. In circumstances of inflation, constant prices/currency conversion of the variables in time series is part of the key points to time data analytics.

Moreover, methods and techniques in risk analytics that deal with data implies several challenges, such as the time among the measurements, the sequence, appropriate measurement times, and speed of measurement (for instance, cases where the IoT is used to generate data). Data collection for creating time series analysis has to be planned from the beginning. For example, in certain cases, organizations create metrics for performance measurement or risk-related evaluation and they are used once or few times in a period of time, but nobody collects and organizes the metrics to a posterior study. This is the case of financial ratios or operation metrics or measurement of goals and variations to goals. The purpose again is to learn through data how a potential future could be and how solutions can be under certain patterns of observed data. Other important aspects to consider in data organization and preparation are distribution of data across internally and externally conditions of an organization, connection and retrieval of data from multiple sources that deal with data variety and need data integration (for example, using web data), data management factors such as who and how to take care of the data maintenance, quality, availability, cost, means of extracting, and transforming data to get the usable data (Hair et al., 2010).

In Chapter 2, the review of data indicates several steps and methods to improve the risk analytics data understanding process; however, depending on the problem, a unique relationship among data, technique, or method is not enough in several problems; there are a wide variety of techniques that can be used from mathematics-statistic based on ML/AI based. In certain problems, data issues are different and require various roads to deal with them. For instance, in stock price data-return analysis, the sensitivity can be affected because of data missing in periods of time, while in clustering, the issue can be because of the mix of quantitative and qualitative variables or discrete of continues data. One of the aspects to consider most of the time is to deal with missing data. Missing data is the value referred to a variable, value that should be registered, and it is not in the source. Missing data is different in the case of structured and unstructured data. To deal with missing data in structured data, an approach can be first to determine the type of missing data, how big the missing data is, identification of possible patterns (for example, the missing data is coming from a type of risk unit or from a region), to identify possible imputation methods, etc.

Several decisions appear in the process of correcting a data set; for example, to delete variables, delete records, to use only records with full data, deal with outliers, manage correlations, consistency of variables/data definition, etc. All these decisions need to be well referenced and thought in the way that potential bias can be identified, errors estimated, and ways to improve in the following data collection process. As mentioned in Chapter 2, there are rules of thumb that 10% of the data can be ignored (not good) or better to find imputation methods if there is a random occurrence of the missing data. Of course, the percentage is just a potential guide because in several problems the number of sample points is not of good size and any lost point can jeopardize the analytics process. Imputation methods using regression or model-based methods can be used. Missing at random (MAR) model methods are preferred. Missing completely at random (MCAR), for example, regression is preferred. The imputation in a simple approach can be with the mean or mode of the variables' values; assign a value determined by the analyst or with value of a variable in similar records Larose and Larose (2014).

In the data organization process, there are potential outliers, and there are methods of identifying outliers; however, the outlier candidates need to be studied independently to clarify if the sample points are really outliers or they are members of a different sample/group. In general, what is important is not to delete the potential outlier immediately if they have been identified; those sample points can be, for example, members of a type of risk attribute that has been observed in few cases. Only after a clear identification of the possible outlier as an outlier is when it cannot be used. Models can be affected by the outliers and metrics as well, as it is case of the mean, but in any case, the best practice is to go back to the original experiment, the source of data, and the event review to be sure that the sample point is for sure an outlier.

Some guides to detect potential outliers (Hair et al., 2010):

- Standardize data and then identify outliers in terms of number of standard deviations.
- Examine data using box plots, stem and leaf, and scatterplots.
- Multivariate detection (D2) using clustering.
- Univariate methods – examine all metric variables to identify unique or extreme observations.
- For small samples (80 or fewer observations), outliers typically are defined as cases with standard scores of 2.5 or greater.
- For larger sample sizes, increase the threshold value of standard scores up to 4.
- If standard scores are not used, identify cases falling outside the ranges of 2.5 versus 4 standard deviations, depending on the sample size.
- Bivariate methods – focus their use on specific variable relationships, such as the independent versus dependent variables.
- Use scatterplots with confidence intervals at a specified alpha level.
- Multivariate methods – best suited for examining a complete variate, such as the independent variables in regression or the variables in factor analysis.

In the data review and organization, there are additional aspects to consider:

- Identifying data as deterministic vs. randomness, facts vs. probability distributions outcomes
- Development of the metrics and their follow-up. Such as Mean and variance and their follow-up. In some cases, the median or mode is used to identify central measurement.
- Visualization, visualization … exploration, description
- Unbiasedness avoidance
- Consistency search in definitions and source standards
- Sufficiency of the records required for a study

Other possible data issues that are common in risk analytics data include (Cady, 2017):

1. Formatting
2. Content of data
3. Issues of generating data that is not related to the research questions
4. Duplicate in data entries
5. Multiple entries for a single entity
6. Missing entries (we already saw how to deal with missing data)
7. Nulls and what is a zero
8. Inconsistencies in data definitions
9. Outliers we already talked about them
10. Time related issues – out-of-date
11. Wrong definition of variables – inconsistent definition of variables when you merge data from different sources
12. Aggregated data issues
13. Spacing or delimitation of data

14. Type of characters used – invalid and inconsistent
15. Dates and their formats
16. Versions of tools used
17. Structure of the syntax in some languages
18. Issues in the definition of the variables or the new created data
19. Irregular capitalization
20. Inconsistent delimiters
21. Irregular NULL format
22. Invalid characters
23. Weird or incompatible datetimes
24. Operating system incompatibilities
25. Wrong software versions
26. If the data is text, look directly at the raw file rather than just reading it into a script.

Data changes that can be promoted to proceed in the creation of the final data table to use include (Larose and Larose, 2014) one approach to normalize/standardize data. In algorithms related to similarity, evaluation-clustering the range intervals of the data and its scales can affect the results. Min-max normalization works by seeing how much greater the field value is than the minimum value min(X), and scaling this difference by the range. That is:

- $X*mm = X - min (X)/range(X)$
  $= X - min (X)/max(X) - min(X)$
- Z-score standardization, which is one of the most common transformations used and works by taking the difference between the field value and the field mean value, and scaling this difference by the standard deviation of the field values.
  That is Z-score $= X - mean(X)/SD(X)$
- Decimal scaling ensures that every normalized value lies between −1 and 1.
  $X*decimal = X /10^d$ where d is selected by the number of digits of the numerator.

Once data is for testing, it is crucial to go back and to ask the following questions (Table 6.1).

Risk analytics requires a systematic and methodic data gathering and organization process. The idea is that risk-related data will be a combination of several data types and the repositories will be SQL and NoSQL. The process for finding patterns will be represented by three main concepts: supervised learning when a partition of data is used to create a model through one subset of the original data set (this data set is the training data set) and the supplement subset that will be used to validate the model; the whole process is looking for describing a target or dependent variable. This

TABLE 6.1

Guide of Aspects to Review in Quality of Usable Data

Possibility of updating	How is the update process? Structure to repeat and to have secure outcomes
Creation of new variables	Use original data to create new variables, new data
Data quality collection, formatting	The variables took correct values
Data population	How the variables are populated
Keep trough time	Validity of data timewise
Cleaning records	Are events and data well connected? Events represented by data?
Time attributes	Is the data current with respect to business requirements? What about changes and new definition through time-consistency

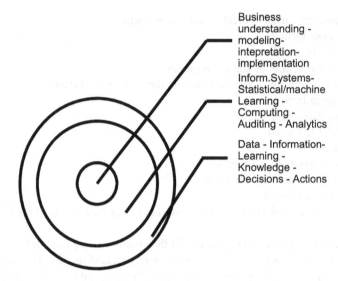

Business understanding - modeling- intepretation- implementation

Inform.Systems- Statistical/machine Learning - Computing - Auditing - Analytics

Data - Information- Learning - Knowledge - Decisions - Actions

FIGURE 6.2 Suppeort of finding knowledge in data and to produce understanding.

process is used for risk classification. A second pattern identification method is using the unsupervised learning in which the search of pattern is with the whole data set and there is no target to describe and the algorithms are based on the similarity definitions. The third process is what is called reinforcement learning, where the purpose is to build a system (agent) that takes the feedback from the environment (reward of performance of the system) to improve and to learn a series of actions to develop the reward results. This means, for example, in risk analytics depending on the conditions of an economic sector, changes in a company performance can appear and decisions are developed based on the business environment. Other types of learning, such as federated learning and transfer learning, are above the scope of this book.

In summary, in risk analytics data understanding includes comprehension of different types of problems to solve, techniques to use, representation of results, evaluation of models, and implementation steps. A large amount of data, with different dimensions and heterogeneity have given the possibility of finding patterns and to identify information that is not explicit from the basic observation of data. The data that are in the data repositories, data warehouses, or data lakes that have no schema (NoSQL) for the storage includes structured and unstructured data. In Figure 6.2, the description of the layers of risk analytics include the center of understanding the business and then go out to find the analysis and design of methods and systems, and data transformation into actions.

6.1 HOW TO USE TECHNOLOGY, AND STORE AND MANAGE STRUCTURED AND UNSTRUCTURED DATA

In the process of designing a risk analytics systems, not only data itself can bring points to study with the case but how to manage it, store it, and process it. Several answers are coming according to the use that the data analytics process will give to the data or according to the data analytics steps in the solution of a problem. Structured data such as transactional can be stored in relational databases, including, for example (sales, payroll), people (employees), and places (warehouses, stores). The most common business databases today are relational database management systems (DBMS). And the database models include:

- Hierarchical database model – information is organized into a tree-like structure (using parent/child relationships) in such a way that it cannot have too many relationships.

- Network database model – a flexible way of representing objects and their relationships.
- Relational database model – stores information in the form of logically related two-dimensional tables.
- Entity class – a category of person, place, thing, or event about which information is stored.
- Entity – an individual person, place, thing, or an individual occurrence of an event about which information is stored.

In a relational database, each table collects the data for an entity class; for example, one table is for Customers, another for Orders, and another for Products. In each table (entity class), each row, or record contains the data for each entity belonging to that class. The characteristics or properties of an entity class are the attributes for which we collect data. In a DBMS, these are columns in the table called fields. For example, in a risk unit, it could be:

- Risk unit ID
- Risk unit ID-label-name
- Contact name
- Location or risk – address, phone, latitude, longitude

The way to connect tables will be based on the identification of primary keys or fields or attributes (or group of fields) that contain values that uniquely identify a given record in a table. It is possible to use what is called a foreign key, a primary key of one table that appears in a field in another table. A value in the foreign key of one table corresponds to the value in the primary key of another table. The idea in the creation of data management means to generate relationships and keep tables linked to other ones through the matching between the values in a primary key to the values in the foreign key of another table. Database advantages from a business perspective include:

- Increased flexibility.
- Increased scalability and performance.
- Reduced redundancy.
- Increased integrity (quality).
- Increased security.

The design of the database requires handling changes quickly and easily, providing users with different views, slicing and dicing, to be the source for creating data warehouses and data marts, having only one physical storage with several logical views, possibility to update and to grow, providing good performance results, and avoiding redundancy (same data in different locations or duplications in the same data repository).

Databases and in general data repositories have potential problems to solve in their design and the risk analytics system (RAS) has to deal with:

- Inconsistency of data describing the same thing.
- Waste of space, waste of time to enter and update data.
- Difficulty securing data in many places.
- Information integrity – measures the quality of information.
- Integrity constraint – rules that help ensure the quality of information.
- Relational integrity constraint – rule that enforces basic and fundamental information-based constraints.
- Business-critical integrity constraint – rule that enforces business rules vital to an organization's success and often requires more insight and knowledge than relational integrity constraints.

Nowadays, the use of cloud-based database server architecture uses cloud computing service providers to supply some or all database services. Deloitte Insights (2019) indicates that the cloud is one of the nine macro forces moving business: analytics, cloud, digital experience, core systems, risk, business of technology, cognitive systems, blockchain, digital reality. All of these forces with common risk such as ethics in the creation and use. There are aspects to consider in the development and use of cloud services and in particular operational risks to evaluate depending on the service levels. Cloud computing includes the capacity for processing data, a central repository of software, access to use the software itself, and means to collaborate and develop projects that integrate many different resources. There are some acronyms, such as IAAS (infrastructure as a service), PASS (platform as a service), and SAAS (software as a service), that are included in the cloud computing conceptualization.

Cloud computing can be associated with the service science concept, which has as one of its objectives keeping the study of mutual value creation (co-creation) between service systems (in our case organizations). Co-creation and cloud computing are concepts to leverage the risk knowledge management. Cloud computing will possibly allow a better collaborative use of system tools, process capabilities, and knowledge in the organization; however, the proper use requires the understanding of the benefits that it generates and the possible risk factors/areas that demand more attention. Therefore, the first reflection is about the identification of answering the question: What are the benefits of cloud computing for risk management? There are many ways to describe the value that cloud computing brings to the organization of risk management. Some of these benefits are:

- Potential reduction of technology costs. Possibly computing time, computing resources and modeling can gain synergies because of the use of the cloud.
- Faster access to technology and with the possibility to use a more connected and collaborative risk management.
- Management of resources based on pay-as-you-go for applications that are only required for some projects.
- Access to new services for the customers and options in product-service development.
- Reduction of activities related to infrastructure management.
- Potential acceleration of compliance and development of the organization's capacities.
- Improved access to risk management data that support the decision-making process and the studies/research consolidation.
- Extended use of services, such as open source and collaborative developments around the world.
- Awareness and early warning systems based on the experiences in different regions of the world, economic sectors, products, natural phenomena, etc.
- Data mining possibilities for credit risk management, or any other kind of risk.

All of these benefits are possible to obtain based on the proper use of cloud computing, co-creation, and its risk control. These benefits introduce the need to analyze the potential risks that organizations might deal with when they are using cloud computing. Thus, a second reflection is about the need of analyzing risks of cloud computing. These risks are related to many factors, which can be observed from different perspectives: user, provider, or creator of the cloud. In this section, the focus is on factors related to the adaptation and evolution of the organizations and the associated strategic and operational risks:

- Lack of understanding of the technology trends by the executives and other stakeholders.
- Potential threats on the security of data and protection of the digital capital.
- Lack of capacity to organize the enterprises to use in a different way the information resources or the need to answer properly how to manage the digital capital of the organization.

- Blindness as to the value of cloud computing as a solution for the organization and no appreciation to cloud computing inside the organization using more resources than are probably needed.
- Control, reliability, regulation, and support are issues to be estimated, analyzed, and evaluated in any decision-making process; in particular in any cloud computing decision, given the strategic value of the digital and human capital that will manage the cloud resources. Intellectual capital is always growing in importance for financial services and for the economy in general demanding more attention from the decision makers.

Cloud computing is a way to manage the services of the organization, to reorganize technology management and to redefine the use of digital capital in the organization (possibly in the human and AI capital as well). The analysis related to collaboration, risk knowledge transfer, and risk knowledge creation require time and clarity from the organizations to leverage the benefits of cloud computing. Every step in the understanding improvement of cloud computing will be very valuable to develop capabilities to operate more efficiently and effectively under controlled risks (Table 6.2).

From a database, the data repositories evolve to data warehouses that are a logical collection of data coming from several databases of specific purpose – production, customers, sales, accounting, transactions etc., supporting the actions that the organization performs. The data warehouse is a physical repository that organizes data from relational databases after a process of data preparation to be closer and accessible by to the user. The primary purpose of a data warehouse is to aggregate information throughout an organization into a single repository for decision-making purposes. There are some subprocesses to organize and populate the data warehouse: extraction, transformation, and loading (ETL). A DataMart contains a subset of data warehouse data obtained with the purpose of satisfying specific business units or objectives.

Cloud computing allows the use of structure and unstructured data. Risk analytics is associated with the use of unstructured data in multiple ways as a supplement to the knowledge that can be created from structured data or data source can be unstructured to perform a specific analysis, e.g., sentiment of buyers in markets according to changes of interest rates, inflation, new regulation, etc. In the past, most of the models and ways to classify, assess, and evaluate risk were related to structured data. Nowadays, organizations are incorporating data that is coming from sources such as the web, tweets, speech, documents, e-mails, pictures, videos, etc. The use of data of unstructured data is extremely interesting because it is supplementing the structured data analysis, it is providing new insights, and the techniques are challenged to be possible to use in a transition unstructured data to structure that data.

TABLE 6.2
Cloud Computing Basic Aspects to Consider in the RAS

Structure/Architecture	Control	Services
• Interaction with current databases	• I/O use/access	• Procession/computation
• Networks relationships	• Tests for quality, data population,validation	• Dealing with users' demand
• Access, connectivity, support to data sourcing	• Fraud, cybersecurity, encryption, decryption, access, face, finger, ... recognition	• Data analytics
• Types of data, volume, interaction, transformation capacity, streaming ...	• Several users from internal and external organizations	• Creation of AI solutions
	• Data recovery, access protection to APIs ...	• Connection to other solutions, IoT, digitalization
		• Operational support-service e.g. chatbot, ...

A good example of using structured and unstructured data is related to having methods of underwriting, that use quantitative data and the models use data in producing for example classifications. Underwriters help organizations interpreting the outcomes of the quantitative models, generating a report that includes additional observations about the risk events or risk units and identification of qualitative aspects of the risk subject to analysis. After the report is written, it is read and used in the decision-making process. However, the identification of patterns in reports is another risk analytics area of risk management improvement. There are interesting questions to answer such as the possible bias of the analysis, outlook of the economic sector, use of techniques for risk assessment, etc. In similar cases, a claims evaluation and control that can be related to pictures or data that is not only structure data but also images that can help to review patterns or cause of accidents and risk occurrence. For instance, it can be related to identify pieces of damage in car accidents, signalization in transit accidents, and conditions of the risk event. Said in the most precise way in improving city administration: "Smart cities need to focus on improving outcomes for residents and enlisting their active participation in shaping the places they call home" (McKinsey Global Institute, 2018).

Evolution of risk analytics is associated with what Iansiti and Lakkhane (2020) showed regarding the connection of financial services/advantages and risk analytics-data analytics: "… Ant Financial uses artificial intelligence and data from Alipay—its core mobile-payments platform—to run an extraordinary variety of businesses, including consumer lending, money market funds, wealth management, health insurance, credit-rating services, and even an online game that encourages people to reduce their carbon footprint."

In risk analytics, the interaction of multiple types of data is at the same time as the interaction of intelligences, to have in the human talent the time to dedicate to problems that are not automatable and that require more attention, the tails of distribution of events, the innovation process, capacity to create better evolving competitive advantages, better early warning systems and resilience capacity, etc. The intelligences such as assisted intelligence, augmented intelligence, autonomous intelligence, and digitalization capabilities will grow in use and the data combination will require more support and organization of data (Figure 6.3).

Platforms integrating open source and proprietary solutions such as SAS Viya, Azure, Amazon, and others are going in the direction of flexible systems that use open source core of Hadoop, MapReduce, and Spark to create the means to obtain data analytics solutions. Moreover, on the one hand, solutions are going in the direction of integrating multiple tools and platforms and to have the visual programming is the KNIME platform. In KNIME, there are integration opportunities of MATLAB, Weka, H2O, R, Python, etc. The new computing left aside the proprietary and re-invention of the wheel to move in the direction of doing more with what is available and working more with scope economies in mind. On the other hand, the software solutions are supported by

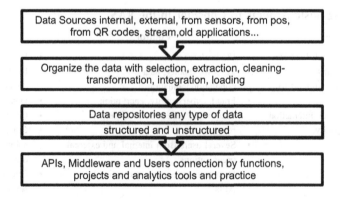

FIGURE 6.3 Data in a RAS.

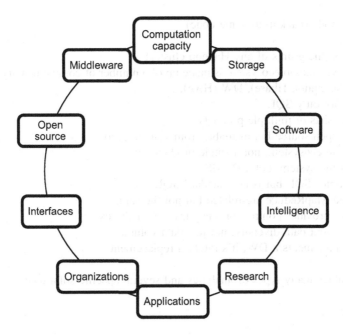

FIGURE 6.4 RAS connection of its components in multiple levels of development.

computational capacity in the form of parallel computing, which divides tasks in small units to perform in parallel, multithread computing, distributed computing, freestanding analytics, partially integrated analytics, in database analytics, and in Hadoop analytics. The RAS connects multiple points, as is shown in Figure 6.4 that are in different levels of development and with possibilities to increase capabilities for organizations. Organizations use the talent of data science to compete and evolve but keeping the basic computational capacity common for members of markets.

The following paragraphs describe the core of platforms and tools that are used in risk analytics. Hadoop ecosystem is an open-source framework for storing and analyzing massive amounts of distributed, unstructured data. Originally created by Doug Cutting at Yahoo!, Hadoop clusters run on inexpensive commodity hardware in the way that projects can scale out inexpensively. Hadoop is now part of Apache Software Foundation. Hadoop is open source; hundreds of contributors continuously improve the core technology. The combination is MapReduce + Hadoop that is a core technology and a means for working with big data. Hadoop works in a simplified presentation, as follows:

- Access unstructured and semi-structured data (e.g., log files, social media feeds, other data sources).
- Break the data up into "parts," which are then loaded into a file system made up of multiple nodes running on commodity hardware using HDFS (Hadoop distributed file system).
- Each "part" is replicated multiple times and loaded into the file system for replication and failsafe processing.
- A node acts as the facilitator and another as job tracker.
- Jobs are distributed to the clients, and once completed the results are collected and aggregated using MapReduce.

Hadoop has attributes such as the following:

- Hadoop distributed file system (HDFS)
- Name node (primary facilitator)

- Secondary node (backup to name node)
- Job tracker
- Slave nodes (the grunts of any Hadoop cluster)
- Additionally, Hadoop ecosystem is made up of a number of complementary sub-projects: NoSQL (Cassandra, Hbase), DW (Hive), …
- NoSQL = not only SQL
- Hadoop consists of multiple products
- Hadoop is open source but available from vendors, too
- Hadoop is an ecosystem, not a single product
- HDFS is a file system, not a DBMS
- Hive resembles SQL but is not standard SQL
- Hadoop and MapReduce are related but not the same
- MapReduce provides control for analytics, not analytics
- Hadoop is about data diversity, not just data volume
- Hadoop complements a DW; it's rarely a replacement

And Hadoop enables many types of analytics and several specific solutions:

- MapReduce …
- Hadoop …
- Hive
- Pig
- Hbase
- Flume
- Oozie
- Ambari
- Avro
- Mahout, Sqoop, Hcatalog, ….

MapReduce distributes the processing of very large multi-structured data files across a large cluster of ordinary machines/processors. The goal is achieving high performance with "simple" computers. Developed and popularized by Google, MapReduce is good at processing and analyzing large volumes of multi-structured data in a timely manner; example tasks: indexing the web for search, graph analysis, text analysis, machine learning, and so on. MapReduce takes the raw data that is used and it is separated and organized through the MAP functions in the way that data requires to be sorted and reduce function separate the data in different servers. The first steps are to input data files (load to HDFS), then to split data/jobs in tasks according to attributes; second, the map steps assign a pair with a key identifier per data element coming from different sources, each data component start with 1 as key (key value pairs the assignments are stored as records). The shuffling step is to sort data based on the data and keys. Then the reduce step sorts the data and puts all repeated together with a data piece with a key of the accumulated number of repetitions of the piece of data. The process is repeated in all nodes of the cluster (Figure 6.5).

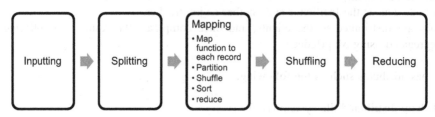

FIGURE 6.5   MapReduce sequence of steps.

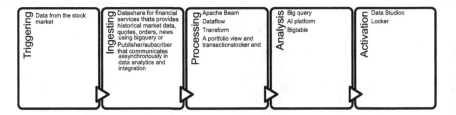

FIGURE 6.6   Data flow in a financial application.

To the transfer from structured relational databases/data warehouse, use Sqoop. Hadoop acts as the organization of the data in a data warehouse; first, copy files from sensor data, pictures, blogs, emails, web data, documents, speech, etc. and then ETL actions to use Hadoop to provide developers the input for data analysis or basic analysis to move ahead with other tools. Hadoop is not a database but in its ecosystem the database can be Hive, HBase, or external as MongoDB.

A cloud data flow is defined as a data process that is fast, does not use servers, and is cost effective for stream and batch data. The steps in general are to get the data from the source and then transform it, and the data is put in what is called a sink. The process can use Apache Beam libraries. The promise is that it is possible to use an AI problem resolution through predictive analytics, fraud detection, transactions with outliers, pattern recognition, changes in patterns, in real time (Figure 6.6).

Additional tools are the combination of Eclipse for development of MapReduce Java programming and Spark instead of Hadoop. Spark is faster and it is possible to not use it in batch processing. Spark has the interfaces to RStudio and Python. In sparklyr, the use of dplyr is a tool for dealing with data, changes, cleaning, transformation, etc. and extensions packages such as H2O. The capabilities of Spark and R are possible to use, keeping the operation local or in clusters/cloud. Streaming is possible with a R/Python and Spark combination, creating a folder for the data stream and it will create an output folder that will be the stream and Spark will use automatically its capabilities for parallel process of data.

The following are names to use to move to where technology is leading in the use of structure and unstructured data, big data, integration of open source and proprietary, and connecting data warehouses and NSQL databases. The short descriptions are from the tools' websites.

A concept to review for a RAS analysis and design is schema and non-schema: In the previous paragraphs, there was a description of tools for storing structured data. The relational databases require a schema for writing-loading data. Once data is in the repository, tools to retrieve data such as SQL are used. The issue with unstructured data includes the use of non-schema to store data. This means the repository can have unstructured data and there is flexibility with the type of data to store. The schema is applied when data is retrieved through a query process. In risk analytics, the structured and unstructured repositories coexist. A modeling process will use techniques on the created usable data that is the input for a solution development.

In the paragraphs above, the definition of repository of data was indicated as a task to perform; however, there are some extra points to consider in using unstructured data. This is the case of using the concept of data lakes: the data is stored as is. The volume stored is massive and with the format as the data was created. The components of the data lake are using identifiers and metadata tags. Another concept is data vault, used for historical data that can be used maintaining chronological keys, links, and it is possible to maintain the historical data entities using the satellites concept.

Examples of tools to work with different types of data in addition to the Hadoop ecosystem are: Openstack as a cloud infrastructure to use virtual machines, the cloud services coming from AWS, Azure, and several others that provide the capacity to work with stream data and data with a big volume in what is cloud parallel computing. From Exhibit 6.1, there is a special attention to MongoDB: "A NoSQL database is used to store large quantities of complex and diverse data, such as product catalogs, logs, user interactions, analytics, and more." MongoDB is one of the most

EXHIBIT 6.1 SHORT DESCRIPTION OF TOOLS TO DEAL WITH STRUCTURED, UNSTRUCTURED, BIG DATA, AND ANALYTICS CAPACITY

MONGO

https://www.mongodb.com/nosql-explained

NoSQL databases (aka "not only SQL") are non tabular, and store data differently than relational tables. NoSQL databases come in a variety of types based on their data model. The main types are document, key-value, wide-column, and graph. They provide flexible schemas and scale easily with large amounts of data and high user loads.

RStudio

Take control of your R code

RStudio is an integrated development environment (IDE) for R. It includes a console, syntax-highlighting editor that supports direct code execution, as well as tools for plotting, history, debugging and workspace management. Click here to see more RStudio features.

RStudio is available in **open source** and **commercial** editions and runs on the desktop (Windows, Mac, and Linux) or in a browser connected to RStudio Server or RStudio Server Pro (Debian/Ubuntu, Red Hat/CentOS, and SUSE Linux).

Generality

Combine SQL, streaming, and complex analytics.

Spark powers a stack of libraries including SQL and DataFrames, MLlib for machine learning, GraphX, and Spark Streaming. You can combine these libraries seamlessly in the same application

Spark SQL	Spark Streaming	MLlib (machine learning)	GraphX (graph)
		Apache Spark	

Welcome to Spark Python API Docs!

scikit-learn
Machine Learning in Python

- Simple and efficient tools for predictive data analysis
- Accessible to everybody, and reusable in various contexts
- Built on NumPy, SciPy, and matplotlib
- Open source, commercially usable – BSD license

Classification
Identifying which category an object belongs to.
Applications: Spam detection, image recognition.
Algorithms: SVM, nearest neighbors, random forest, and more...

Regression
Predicting a continuous-valued attribute associated with an object.
Applications: Drug response, Stock prices.
Algorithms: SVR, nearest neighbors, random forest, and more...

Clustering
Automatic grouping of similar objects into sets.
Applications: Customer segmentation, Grouping experiment outcomes
Algorithms: k-Means, spectral clustering, mean-shift, and more...

sparklyr: R interface for Apache Spark

- Connect to Spark from R. The sparklyr package provides a complete dplyr backend.
- Filter and aggregate Spark datasets then bring them into R for analysis and visualization.
- Use Spark's distributed machine learning library from R.
- Create extensions that call the full Spark API and provide interfaces to Spark packages.

established NoSQL databases, with features such as data aggregation, MongoDB allows that the records are not having the same number of attributes, it is flexible and provide the possibility to deal with data that is evolving-changing. The queries can filter and group data and to search text, it has intuitive and a rich query language. The concept of ACID transactions: atomicity, consistency, integrity, and durability. Atomicity is a property indicating that if any operations fail the full set operations will go back to the state before the failure. Consistency is about rules in the database that have to be maintain in all operations. Isolation for operations only with the required data separating the data that is in the transactions. Durability protect the changes in the transactions. High performance and high availability means it is appropriate to manage the use of multiple nodes of data processing and storage, Finally, scalability is the possibility to scale to have databases in horizontal growth through many nodes.

The NoSQL databases are different from the traditional databases that are defined with schema to store data; these are relational databases. In MongoDB or in general NoSQL databases, data is stored as documents, which allows multiple types of data or multiple attributes related to same record. This means there is a flexible structure to deal with data. As it was mentioned before, in risk analytics, for example, a company's data for analysis can come from several sources and it can be data from tweets or form the stock market or from the financial statements; all of the attributes are different and refer to the same company of analysis.

In Table 6.3, there is a presentation of examples of using risk analytics for unstructured data, illustrating the examples mainly with text analytics through supervised and unsupervised learning techniques.

The review of unstructured data in risk management has two faces. On the one hand, the possibility to use it for monitor, identify, and control risk. On the other hand, unstructured data

TABLE 6.3
Examples of Using Unstructured Data in Risk-Related Field

Unstructured Data Use	Reference
Twitter moods were used to predict the stock market. Expert investors in microblogs were identified and sentiment analysis of stocks was performed.	Bar-Haim et al., 2011; Feldman et al., 2011
Blog and news sentiment analysis was used to study trading strategies.	(Zhang and Skiena, 2010)
The desire to enhance their analytical capabilities and automate across business lines, including risk management, by managing and mining these increased volumes and a variety of data has led financial institutions to explore powerful and analytical solutions, a consequence of which is the rise in interest and the popularity of machine learning and artificial intelligence within the FI community.	VanLiebergen, 2017
Use of text analysis in finance to examine the sentiment of numerous news items, articles, financial reports, and tweets about public companies.	Loughran and McDonald, 2011; Garcia, 2013
Unsupervised can be related to classification based on the words and parts of the speech, texts/documents.	Taboada et al., 2011
"The lexicon-based analysis showed that sentiment scores reflect major economic events between 2002 and 2014 very well. In addition, there is a strong correlation between uncertainty, negativity, and the Tier 1 capital ratio evolution over time."	Nopp and Hanbury, 2015
"Sentiment analysis has been widely applied in financial applications since Robert Engle (Engle and Ng, 1993) suggested the asymmetric and affective impact of news on volatility. In recent years, researchers exploited various text resources e.g. news, microblogs, reviews, disclosures of companies to analyze the effects on markets in multifarious manners: impacting on price trends (Kazemian et al., 2016), volume of trade (Engelberg and Parsons, 2011), volatilities (Rekabsaz et al.,2017) and even potential risks (Nopp and Hanbury, 2015)."	Luo et al., 2018

creates risk to the owner of the data. Corporations and institutions need to pay a lot of effort in dealing with unstructured data and the way that it is used in the markets. In the first perspective, the use of the shared systems, emails, social media, etc. is storing and sharing a lot of data that can be wrongly used. Moreover, the filtering capacity about what data is circulating can create a high level of confusion. This confusion is coming in cases when people, for example, believe that higher numbers-frequencies of occurrence of events/things can demonstrate the true of events/things. As mentioned before, a higher number of records can come from sources like tweets with a huge bias and it can produce a very complex issue to solve about the value of data and knowledge in data analytics (data risk). Fake news, wrong data/concepts/information, etc. can create underestimated damage as it is panic or alteration of massive behavior.

In this book, it has been indicated that qualitative variables/studies supplement quantitative variables analysis; the same happens with unstructured data that can supplement what is discovered using structured risk data and with both to support risk control in organizations and its general management. There are several ways to use unstructured data in risk analytics, from using pictures in car insurance when events happen to describing how people are thinking and behaving according to what happens in the stock market, for example. There are applications of clustering, classification, and other possible techniques to discover what is inside/behind recommendations, reputation/image possible variations, use of social media, potential fraud, comments about topics, etc. that can support several risk monitoring systems or to create basic early warning systems.

The general practices of sentiment analysis bring the attention of how to identify sentiment in an automatic way. Taboada et al. (2011) describe the lexicon base approach and indicate that an approach based on statistical and machine learning techniques to develop supervised learning models. There is another approach that is a semi-supervised approach that is based on a dictionary approach combining labeling examples in the training process. Taboada et al. (2011) indicate that sentiment analysis is associated with the use of polarity and subjectivity in the texts or speeches. Moreover, these authors commented that support vector machines as classifiers are good in the prediction of polarity when the classifier is in the same type of topic-domain but not good when the topic-domain is changed. Pang et al. (2002) indicated that: "… k-Nearest Neighbors (simple, powerful), Naive Bayes (simple, very efficient as it is linearly proportional to the time needed to read in all the data); Support-Vector Machines (relatively new, more powerful); K-Nearest Neighbor classification (simple, expensive at test time, high variance, non-linear); Vector space classification using centroids and hyperplanes that split them (simple, linear discriminant classifier); and AdaBoost (based on creating a highly accurate prediction rule using a weighted linear combination of other classifiers)."

Taboada et al. (2011) expressed that the lexicon-based analysis can be manual of automated created, and the scores that are created. In the case of risk analytics, Nopp and Hanbury (2015) pointed out: "The lexicon-based analysis showed that sentiment scores reflect major economic events between 2002 and 2014 very well. In addition, there is a strong correlation between uncertainty, negativity, and the Tier 1 capital ratio evolution over time. Hence, the sentiment scores could be used in regression models for predicting the T1 evolution. However, the results are only meaningful if the figures are aggregated by year. Applying the model on data of individual banks leads to inaccurate results. It should also be noted that this method is not meant to be used as a stand-alone estimator for the T1 evolution. Instead, it should be combined with other estimation methods." Tier 1 label capital ratio is used in banks and it is the ratio of equity and reserves to risk-weighted assets.

According to the experiments in using unstructured data from the text, there are several aspects to develop capabilities to provide better and accurate results. Sarkis and Kolm, (2017) commented that growth of the content from multiple sources is generating barriers to accomplish what risk analysts are doing: "(such Twitter, Reddit, Facebook, Bloomberg Finance, Google Finance, Yahoo Finance, etc.) it is becoming increasingly difficult to analyze this large media content." This is not a problem only on the algorithms or approaches, the volume and the diversity create complexity for answering questions of investors.

Sarkis and Kolm (2017) say the literature is indicating several examples where sentiment analysis is used. In the stock market, the use of weblogs can be identified text related to sentiments of fear, anxiety, worry, even mentioned studies where the queries about issues can be correlated to the volumes of Nasdaq-100, but at the end the good use of models and clarity of data will allow to put filters and organize the appropriate data analytics process. The application of opinion mining or sentiment analysis can be in areas such as fraud analytics through the expressions and exchange of communications that can lead to doing something that is not part of a contract or under conditions of operation. In the case of credit risk, there is a good set of structured data for evaluating organizations and people; however, to complement and to improve the accuracy of risk identification and assessment, the use the text analytics of evaluation notes, the presentation of results in organizations, the new projects reports, or data that is describing what is happening to organizations and people in the current operation.

6.2 TECHNOLOGY IN THE RAS DESIGN

This section is about what is expected and the directions of using technology for risk analytics, product development, and support organization and society in areas related to the risk management process. The OECD (2021) brings reflections/principles about the use of AI, machine learning and big data in finance:

- AI is for people's benefit, to improve conditions of quality of life and production.
- AI is under the rules, regulations, and compliance of what societies are looking for to improve the citizens.
- Transparency and disclosure to ensure that citizens are benefit of the AI development.
- Evaluate and control risks of AI. For example, issues in SPOOFING in trading that is to manipulate information in the markets that affects operations and actions. It can be in e-business and in financial trading.
- Accountability review of operators and developers of the AI in societies.

The applications and risks are as follows (Table 6.4).

In particular, blockchain is having momentum. Deloitte Insights Blockchain A technical Primer 2018 indicates that "a blockchain is a digital and distributed ledger of transactions recorded and replicated in real time across a network of computers or nodes." Part of the value of this process is that the transaction is peer to peer, with encryption and validation with a possibility of seeing the transaction record but it is not possible to modify. The concept of P2P means that there is no need of central or intermediaries in the transaction. The blockchain is a means to store digital records based on the created digital entities at the same time it is possible to deal with digital contracts defined as codes. Blockchains are open with and without permission to read, write, or commit, or closed that can be in a consortium/group or totally private.

In the document of distributed ledger technology (DLT) and blockchain World Bank Group (Krause et al., 2017), advantages and disadvantages are indicated:

Advantages

- Decentralization and disintermediation
- Greater Transparency and easier auditability
- Automation and programmability
- Immutability and verifiability
- Speed and efficiency
- Cost reductions
- Enhanced cybersecurity resilience

TABLE 6.4

Areas of Development Connected to RAS

Area of Operation	Applications and Solutions
Asset Management	Portfolio monitoring, allocation, reconciliation, use of unstructured data and use of multiple sources of data simultaneously, trade execution. Develop and improvement of hedge funds.
Algorithmic Trading	Analysis and execution of trading strategies, selection of strategies, prediction of results, prediction of events, brokers and traders connectivity, evaluation of several markets, adjust parameters.
Credit Management	From risk assessment, control-surveillance, including factors, streaming data conditions of markets and operations, liquidity, conditions of markets, matching operations, risk, adjust parameters of models. Not only quality of prospects with certain data in banking but using several variables, or based on transactions, payments, fraud detection, consumer habits, etc. Definition of policies for credit resources allocation against bias, concentration.
Contracts - Blockchain	Development of transaction capacity, trading, exchange and based on secure systems. Cryptocurrencies, data repositories exchange.
Insurance (Insurtech)	Support to all steps in insurance from underwriting to investments. Development of means to deal with contracts, pricing, fraud, regulators, suppliers, and so on.
Health (Healthtech)	To use data access, connectivity between patients and medical service providers, control of the illness, prediction, continuity of care, dealing with administration of health contracts, and access to services. Support clinical trials and connect stakeholders of the healthcare system.
Regulators (RegTech)	Deal with people identity, relationships with the state, property records, criminal records, elections, transparency, support to access citizens services.
Supervision (SupTech)	Control and development of the areas of supervision in governments, societies, and their services suppliers to citizens.

Disadvantages

* Maturity level
* Scalability – transaction speed
* Interoperability and integration
* Cybersecurity
* Governance
* Regulatory – legal clarity – industry standards
* Privacy
* Environmental costs

In general, blockchain technology is transforming trading, transactions, and operations in several organizations. There are many applications of blockchain that are coming and require observation/ follow-up of its development. There are multiple unknowns: legal standards and controls. The impact in the society is in modifying not only business models and operations but also accounting, products and services development, smart communities, etc. The energy consumption of the network is a point to consider in the cost of using blockchains that require consensus methods and the way that ledgers are updated and storage of data. In terms of the application, cryptocurrencies have been operating and growing; however, the market value of the cryptocurrencies has been volatile. Finally, blockchain is a great opportunity to develop business and at the same time a time for a strategic review of the business models of intermediaries and traditional players in transactions.

This chapter showed that risk analytics data can be structured, the traditional data coming from data warehouses/relational databases; data from other types of human actions, speech, pictures, videos, text, with batches and continues actualization such streaming. The multiple types of data put conditions to use techniques of analysis. Exploration of more techniques for unstructured data is valuable to supplement the work done on structured data. This is the case of analyzing companies where data can come from financial statements, stock markets, or conversations about what people feel regarding a company growth or investments or plans. In general, a risk analytics system has to deal with the combination of data and combination of techniques.

The next chapter has a discussion of the types of problems that are or coming in risk analytics, such as grouping companies according to certain attributes, identifying risk classes, finding the way to predict results based on performance, finding ways to allocate resources, and guide decisions based on the best possible solution. Of course, the growth of tools, problems, and packages is according to the identification of risks and the specialties of them. The approach to tackle the problems can be similar as to what was presented in previous chapters but the specialties of risk can be treated with appropriate techniques. For example, the analysis of the risks of AI is not developed as it is in credit risk classification.

7 Machine and Statistical Learning in Risk Analytics

In this chapter, there is an introduction to a variety of analytics techniques used in risk analytics that are essential for the RAS analysis and design. The statistical and machine learning techniques exposed in this chapter are used in combination to the previous models that are leading to solve problems in pricing, valuation, transactions, etc. The use of the techniques presented in this chapter support knowledge discovery through description, classification, optimization, simulation, etc. These techniques supplement the direct creation of metrics by products or stages in a risk management process. The techniques presented in this chapter are part of the arsenal of statistical and machine learning tools and are selected to guide the reader to the relationship type of problem to solve and possible technique to use; however, there is not an extensive review of many algorithms because the number of packages/algorithms is growing very fast and expanding immensely, but the basic group of models is exposed. The examples are mainly related to risk classification and the impact in pricing and business decisions. The purpose is to identify certain aspects that in risk management are crucial for the appropriate use of the techniques for solutions of problems in risk analytics.

In general, there are more processes and societies with multiple levels of advances in areas of using statistical and machine learning for risk management especially in enterprise risk management (ERM). A good example of understanding gaps is what is happening in China where the advance of new fintech is moving very fast through P2P lending-banking, using special apps such as Alipay, and a flourish of digital banks, the practice of risk management requires a lot of work to do to deal with the high speed of the exposure growth that needs more control. This chapter provides a set of explanations about models that can be used to develop the ERM practice. Jia and Wu (2022) indicated "… innovation of this paper is as follows. (1) challenge of applying machine learning in the risk management industry is not how to use machine learning, but how to obtain data and how to obtain data in the correct format. Companies often have more data available than they think they have. How to obtain the required and available data with innovative ideas and structure the data is a big challenge. (2) Although the research on risk management in China started relatively late, more researchers and institutions have begun to devote themselves to the research and exploration of the theoretical aspects of risk management. Compared with countries and regions, China still has many aspects that need to be improved in theory and practice."

Following the need of connecting statistical and machine learning with risk management process, the first aspect shown in Figure 7.1 refers to the development of a brief of what an organization is in terms of the relationship among strategy, data, and operational capabilities and then to move to the risk analytics looking for possibilities to develop capabilities to solve problems from data to results and decisions using technology: modeling and computational capacity.

A crucial point to understand is what modeling implies in risk analytics support (review the topic in Chapter 2). There are two aspects to review one is in general modeling in risk analytics and the other is model risk. In this book model risk is the core concept under the assumption that wrong or misuse of modeling techniques lead to bad solutions and the connected implementations (wrong decisions). In general, model risk is related to the potential of adverse consequences of decisions that are based on incorrect or misused of model results. These adverse consequences can include financial loss, poor business decision making or damage to reputation. Model risk arises from the use of quantitative analytical tools (including the models in previous chapters and the

DOI: 10.1201/9780429342899-8

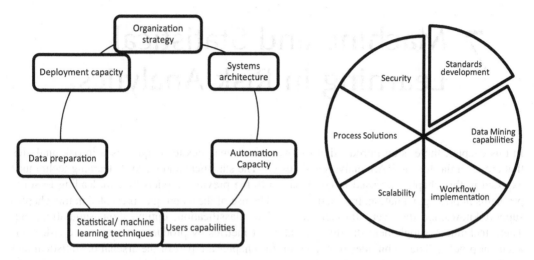

FIGURE 7.1 General representation of technique aspects for using and implementing in risk analytics solutions.

models in this chapter) that apply to statistical, mathematical, economic, algorithmic, or other advanced techniques such as artificial intelligence (AI) and machine learning (ML) to process input data and generate quantitative estimates.

Examples in the practice is in the banks' use of analytics tools include:

- From simple models to sophisticated models for transactions, risk assessment, prediction, etc.
- Techniques are related to guide business decisions in risk and capital management and to support the continuous operation in lending, trading, underwriting, funding, investment, and operational development.
- Quantitative tools support the definition of assumptions and limitations of models, and it is required controls though the stages of solutions development, validation, implementation, and different types of models.
- Models from the techniques require the combination with qualitative review, judgment and follow-up, calibration, and awareness of operational changes that can modify the model definitions.
- The key aspect is to consider the models as models and not as the reality. This means models guide and help to disclose possible states of the nature, their probabilities, multivariate relationships, possible results, and estimation of required parameters, but models are not the reality.
- A model can be good and model risk also arises from the potential for misuse of models or model output. This framework sets out an end-to-end approach for model risk governance across the model life cycle and helps to ensure that model risk remains within the limits of the bank's risk appetite.
- Organization to deal with model risk includes identification of model risk management principles that requires detailed risk management processes with roles and responsibilities of the multiple areas/groups involved in modeling. Three main levels to deal with model development and its risk: first model is owners, developers, and users; second is modelers; and third is auditing groups. The modelers team develops, compliant with internal and external directives of frameworks, and keeps the complete organization/control/support of the variety of models that are available, conditions to use them and connection to risk knowledge sharing.

- Modelers team requires permanent monitoring, meetings, review of results related to model development, calibration, simulation, outcomes analysis, back-testing, variation analysis, error/loss analysis, time series and metrics evaluation, identification of confidence intervals of metrics, validation, parameter estimation methods and improvement, models selection, etc. performance.

The search of solutions starts with the good problem definition, for example, in the classification problem the classes definition is crucial step. As it was mentioned in previous chapters a crucial step is to shape, give scope and clarify the target. Fundamental to understand the metrics keeping in mind what was presented in Chapter 4 that is not the same to have a default rate defined as number of accidents per year with a denominator given by number of cars in a year and to have number of accidents per year with denominator number of miles on the road of cars per year. In credit risk, the definition of what a bad credit could be different from time, institutions, policies, strategies, etc., this means the classes' definition will be part of the problem definition and on the contrary the problem definition will be about classes definition. The problem definition is related to the scope of work, the shape of the problem itself, and the expected results. A way to define the problem is to define the questions to answer, define the variables related to those questions, and start reviewing what it is known, what is unknown, and the project would like to know. The level of knowledge is key; there are different steps regarding, for example, the definition of a classification problem with binary classes or a level of granularity (more than two risk levels) such as the risk categories in a credit agency.

Models in risk analytics that combine statistical and machine learning are of many types. From descriptive models (Visual Analytics and EDA Exploratory Data Analysis) in the sense to identify measures of tendency, variability analysis, test of hypothesis search of variable relationships, up to mathematical models, prediction, and definition of rules and simulations through prescriptive analytics. In a risk analytics process, the identification of groups of risk units or type of risk is an important task. A sampling plan (see Section 2.5) even though there is big data access or full work with population data the filters to clarify the experiment data to use is crucial. In the process of data selection, special attention is required in the search of structures of similarity to identify groups. Once the groups-classes are identified, a problem to solve is to define how certain profiles can be classified. The classification process will have an impact in operation and strategy, in decisions and final models, and implementation evaluation. There are several models for classification and in this chapter, there is a brief description of models used in classification, relationships definition, and variable distribution analysis.

7.1   MANAGING MODELS

Through the book, there has been a presentation of concepts used in the risk analytics process. The data mining process is based on thinking how to solve problems (inductive process) and with deterministic or stochastic approaches to solve those problems diving into data that has been accumulated, and to use models of multiple structures, algebraic, statistical, machine learning based, etc. to find patterns or possible clues that help to solve a problem. Data mining is an inductive process. For generalizing the result, it is required to test hypotheses, cross tabulation, resampling, etc. methods that support the findings and possibility to use in a population where the data has been obtained. The steps presented ahead are covering not only the model creation but also the testing of the models, calibration, comparison, assessment/evaluation, and their assumptions. Assumption validation is crucial. The analytics process has to be connected to the context and the assumptions of the modeling process need to be systematic and with orientation to evaluate a variety of cases, not only the one that is considered at the time and people in the experiment design and execution.

The risk analytics professional has to keep in mind that the creation of models is under the principle of simplicity (parsimony) and understanding better than creating solutions extremely complex and not easy to digest procedures. Testing assumptions opens the gate for modeling testing, revising the risk model, prototyping, delivery of partial and final results in each step, validation, and feedback of results. Permanent feedback from each step is needed. This is a back-and-forth process to get appropriate models for the problem solution, the data available and constraints related not only to the operation but also to understanding of outcomes and possibilities of implementation/deployment. The agile approach is highly recommended in the risk analytics process. Keep in mind the process of modeling the creation of time series of developed metrics (not only one-time NPV calculation, but simulation of the distribution of the NPVs) in order to perform further analysis when the same experiment/business problem solution is repeated.

Some terms used in this chapter are:

- Classification: it consists of examining attributes of new objects and assigning them to a set of classes predefined.
- Estimation: it works with results and continuous evaluation. Example: neuronal networks. Given a data set to estimate means to find a possible value(s) to describe the behavior of variables and their relationships.
- Prediction: the records are classified according to a predicted or possible future behavior or future value.
- Affinity groups: activity to establish the groups of similar attributes.
- Group-clusters: segmentation, organization in homogenous groups.
- Description: identification of patterns.

Evaluation and reporting are part of the risk analytics process. The evaluation depends on which the organization wants to develop in a project and how the approach to solve the problem has been. Evaluation means to define criteria of success of the business and alignment of results to determine possible recommendations, to generate actions, and decisions. In the reporting process, the key concept is that reports are expected to be alive (ongoing updating process), dynamic, interactive, and accessible from many users in different locations. This means that more than reports the purpose is to create data products that are using the capabilities of markdown in R, Python, the Jupyter notebook, etc.

The variety of models are based on the problems to solve, forecasting, classification, grouping-clustering, optimization, visualization, etc. As mentioned before, clustering is for identifying possible groups of observations in a population. In other words, cluster analysis identifies a set of groups that will minimize within-group variation and maximize between-group variation. Cluster analysis is very useful when trying to reduce the number of variables in a data set and to discover similarities in the information available. Factor analysis reduces the dimensionality of a data set and illustrates the structure of a set of variables. Factor analysis converts a large number of variables into a smaller number of factors. The original variables have the highest correlations with the factors. These factors are orthogonal and uncorrelated and thus solve a multicollinearity problem in the data. Principal components analysis (PCA) is a form of factor analysis that analyzes total variance that is commonly used. PCA finds a linear combination of variables such that the maximum variance is extracted from the variables. This variance is removed, and a second linear combination is calculated, this second combination explains a large fraction of the remaining variance and so forth. All principal components are orthogonal.

The possibility of working with data to approach the reality involves the creation of methods that support their suitable use and give sense to the models. For example, the expected value of a phenomenon, described from the general model that is known, but it is unknown the probability distribution to describe this type of phenomenon, or the relationships among variables that are associated with the phenomenon. In the conceptual design of the model, variables that have already been established as predictive of failure/default in relevant literature would be tested and included, if they are or not significant for the study and its explanation capacity of variation. In the practice, there are several models already used with multiple variables and significant according to the combination and target definitions such as Altman's models, RMA, Moody's, etc., have already tested and used sets of variables that have a greater power in predicting financial distress/default. A model would use the most available information to select the appropriate variables that reduce issues of multicollinearity, data population of the variable, cost of obtaining the data, and so on, such as bond ratings, financial information, credit information, and possibly macro variables (GDP, inflation, etc.) that prove to be significant in the exploratory analysis.

7.2 BASICS OF MEASUREMENT TO CREATE GROUPS

Measurement has been one of the most important activities in science and technology to support the development of problem-solving processes in societies (see Chapters 1, 3, and 4 for creation of measurement systems and metrics without an emphasis on data mining). In risk analytics, organizations are in a continuous process of creating solutions that are related to the measurement process, definition of metrics, and the way that in the reality the concepts associated with risk management can be described as measured among numbers and non-numeric variables. Probability and statistics are measurement means for risk analytics. Metrics and indicators start as deterministic and move to stochastic. For example, ratios in financial analysis are deterministic at the beginning and they move to be considered random variables and analyzed through several models (as presented in Sections 4.4 and 4.5). In risk analytics, measurement of probability can be an indicator of similarity in risk classes or possible events. Different types of variables are comparable using a similarity measure. The measure of the distance between two objects with the Euclidean definition using the location of the objects is one common way to work with numerical variables. The situation to represent the distance between categories of variables requires a specific definition of the similarity. Probability distribution of default is a way to define the levels of risk/categories in credit risk. There is a need to define the scale, units, and way to interpret the results. In risk analytics, for example, the measurement of positive-negatives or negative-positives in a classification problem can be a similarity measure among classification techniques.

As it was indicated in Chapter 1, the distance measure used is part of the analytics steps in risk management. The general concept to use is the measurement of similarity based on distance measurements definition for quantitative and qualitative variables. In similarity, the higher the value of the metric is representing more similar sets, events, objects, variables, etc. The selection of the similarity measure is crucial in the goodness of the algorithm or technique to risk analytics. In quantitative data, there is a definition of distance as part of L_p – norm definition that will be for example with $p = 2$ the Euclidean distance or with $p = 1$ the Manhattan distance metrics. A distance function has the following attributes: distance from A to B, d[A,B] has four properties:

1. $d[A,B] \geq 0$
2. $d(A,A) = 0$
3. $d(A,B) = d(B,A)$
4. $d(A,B) \leq d(A,C) + d(C,B)$ when C is between A and B

Similarity measures give a statistical distance between two p-dimensional vectors of observations, for instance $d(x, y) = \sqrt{[(x - y)'A(x - y)]}$ where $A = S^{-1}$ and S is the sample variance-covariance matrix (see Chapter 1). Other possible norms are the Euclidean, Minkowski, Camberra, and Czekonowski distances [see Johnson (1998)].

For instance, the two points $A = (x_1, \dots x_k)$ and $B = (y_1, \dots, y_k)$ and the L_p-norm are given by $(\sum_{i=1}^{k} |x_i - y_i|^p)^{\frac{1}{p}}$.

There are factors affecting the use of L_p-norm because of the data distribution, the type of attribute that is used to describe the phenomenon, how the values are separated, etc. In certain cases, there are other measures of similarity to use, such as the Minkowski distance ($\sum_{i=1}^{k} w_i |x_i - y_i|^p)^{\frac{1}{p}}$ that can give a weight (w_i of the attribute i) to a parameter that could be more relevant in a problem to solve.

Another example of improving the definition similarities can be related to the variation of the data around points which will determine how correlations can affect the metric. The Mahalanobis distance defined between two points $A = (x_1, \ldots x_k)$ and $B = (y_1, \ldots, y_k)$ as $\sqrt{(A - B)\Sigma^{-1}(A - B)^T}$ where Σ^{-1} represents the inverse of kxk covariance matrix (See Chapter 1).

Now categorical data is common in risk analytics. The questions emerge around the definition of similarity if attributes of risk units are not numeric but categorical or a mix. How could a measurement of similarity be built? Examples of the process are found in the following: Develop similarity functions that are based on defining that two individual attributes are similar when $x_i = y_i$ and this is represented as $S(x_i, y_i) = 1$ or $x_i \neq y_i S(x_i, y_i)$ is represented as zero. Once all individual comparisons are done, the aggregation can provide a measure of similarity using $\sum_{i=1}^{k} S(x_i, y_i)$. Of course, the issue with similarity measure is that is not possible to differentiate attribute weights. When there is a mix of quantitative and qualitative data an approach is to create a similarity measure as a combination of quantitative similarity and qualitative similarity measures, this means that each data record will be a combination of quantitative and qualitative variables. If a record is with n numerical variables and m categorical, the similarity can be similarity of R_1 and R_2 (two records) equal to ρ·quantsimilarity of the n numerical variables plus (1-ρ)·qualsimilarity of the m categorical variables. The correction of the metric will be done dividing all components of similarity measures by the standard deviation as a normalization process to compare.

Additional aspects of the similarity measurement include not only the evaluation of the distance between points but also the evaluation of the angles between vectors, or frequencies of aspects, or attributes in common in sets (category frequencies). Categories can be treated in different ways if they are ordinal and nominal. When the categories are ordinal, it is possible to assume a continuous scale and use distance metrics as numeric variables. At the same time, when there are ranks, the adjustments of transformation of the variables are used to compare the values: to divide all variables by the mean, normalize, reduce the minimum value of the variable, and after to divide by the range. Similarity measurement can be through a cosine similarity measurement that is based on representing text data vectors of the document features and to compare based on the angle between the two vectors describing the documents and they will be similar if the cosine is close to 1. Another similarity measurement used for general sets where the comparison is based on the ratio of the number elements in the intersection over the number of elements of the union of the sets. The closer the ratio to 1, the more similar the sets will be (Figure 7.2, 7.3).

Strengths and weaknesses of the method of using distances in similarity measurement: Similarities evaluation/measurement is fundamental, but everything starts with descriptions (Figure 7.5) and a potential modeling plan. A process of data mining, similarities testing, and steps on data organization modeling is having multiple steps. A good road map in analytics helps a lot, as it was mentioned before, but in the modeling process can be very valuable to have a diagram that connects the thinking of risk analytics and the creation of solutions. Here is where a tool like KNIME plays a very important role. Figure 7.4 is an example of the steps that the modeling process will follow using the representation of the workflow using KNIME: read data (I/O process), clarify if there is a need of data manipulation; for example, similarities will be appropriate if the scale intervals are comparable, selection of records and variables for defining the models. In the workflow a next step is selection of models. The models can be for supervised and unsupervised learning and then the models to tests are several according to the purpose of the modeling and the technique will be compared. Scoring and clarifying the assessment process for defining models to use is not only based on indicators or accuracy, but it will also be, as mentioned before, a part of practical and aligned view of implementation, understanding, and capacity to control factors. Models not necessarily are the answer for the prediction, only the answer that in several cases is crucial is what factors can be potentially controlled to keep the variation of results inside a target set.

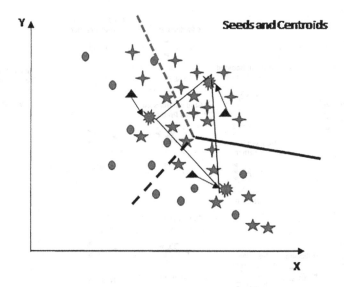

FIGURE 7.2 Separation of groups based on similarities to centroids.

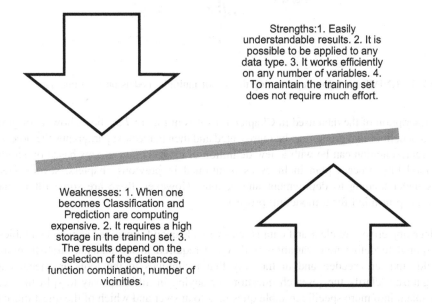

Strengths:1. Easily understandable results. 2. It is possible to be applied to any data type. 3. It works efficiently on any number of variables. 4. To maintain the training set does not require much effort.

Weaknesses: 1. When one becomes Classification and Prediction are computing expensive. 2. It requires a high storage in the training set. 3. The results depend on the selection of the distances, function combination, number of vicinities.

FIGURE 7.3 Balance use of similarity measurement, variables, and models according to targets.

One process in risk analytics is to determine groups of risk units, and after to find the way to classify new data records from new transactions, events, risk units, individuals, companies, etc. in classes. For example, the risk related to segmentation can be measured regarding a good target selection for investing in marketing capacity to be more efficient and effective in achieving goals such as profitability, revenue, market share, etc. The search for groups is based on the similarity measurement; it is a process to find the groups containing the most similar risk units and to find the way to separate the maximum or differentiate the maximum of the groups. The process is converted into an optimization process where the similarities within groups should be the maximum and the separation (no similarity) in the groups the maximum too. The normalization of data is a good practice to use the data in the scale of difference of data to the mean to standard deviation.

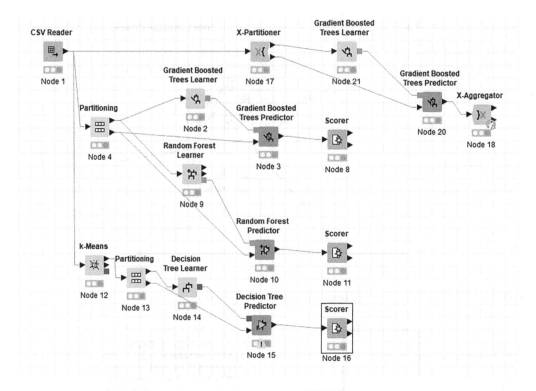

FIGURE 7.4 KNIME workflow representing the use of multiple models on the same data.

The description of the data used in Chapter 1, as it is in Figure 7.5, shows how an original target variable that defines two groups can be represented and then in the next paragraphs the process shows how the representation can be with a new definition of categories or groups based on similarities.

The modeling process plan includes as mentioned in previous chapters, several steps from business understanding to deployment and actions. However, there are some filters and guide points to keep in mind for a modeling process:

1. Once objectives are clear and data is relatively clean and organized as raw data tables it is required to define new variables if they are required in the analysis, transforming the fields that are needed and in the way that techniques in the tools are needed to be organized, clarify the research questions or saying in different way to split the general problem into more specific testable questions to answer and which of the questions can be converted into hypotheses to test. Answers to questions will need the planning to level of aggregation and groups where the answers can be used. Models for subsets of data is a good practice if that adjustment supports decisions in those groups. In marketing for example, it can be segmentation and in credit risk the types of loans, groups of customers, or policies because of combination of product, etc.
2. Build several models that are compatible with data and objectives. At this level, it is important to recognize that a model can be the structural model type and the other the model to calculate results. The first concept of structural model in this book refers to the models such as regression with the multiple forms of regressions according to the variables used. The second concept of model to use is when the structural model as regression has a parameter estimated from data and the estimators in the model will be the source to calculate the values of interest. This means the final model to implement is a structural model (one or many) with specific estimated parameters.

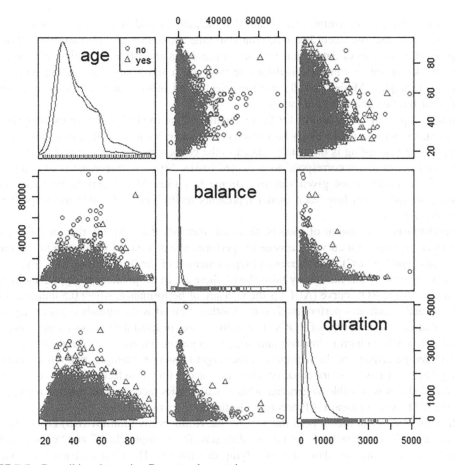

FIGURE 7.5   Describing data using R scatterplot matrix.

3. In general, a modeling process is successful not only because of accuracy indicators, it is about the possibility to assess the model, limitations/constraints to operate, and develop the models. Availability of data, the same as measurement of outcomes, possible ways for automation and data feeding, are requirements to support the modeling process.

With these three points in mind, it is possible to dig deeper in the machine and statistical learning modeling process as it is followed in next sections.

7.3   MODELS, VALIDATION, TESTING, AND PERFORMANCE

Models in risk analytics can be mainly under the supervised and unsupervised learning modeling processes and introducing other ways of learning as it is reinforcement learning. The unsupervised learning models require the evaluation and test based on the selection of the algorithms, similarity measures, data use, and data organization. For example, on the one hand, in the case of having a model for clustering-creating groups of risk units, the variables values should be in similar scale, most of the cases creating a normalized data to work. On the other hand, the test and evaluation of models in supervised learning requires the partition of data. Partition in a minimum of two sets, one for training the model and another to testing it. Model validation and testing are crucial parts of developing risk analytics systems. If the model is not validated and tested, there is no certainty that the results of the model do agree with reality and that it can be generalized. One of the complex aspects can come with overfitting; this means that the model could fit very well to the original data but not to a new data set. Records can be related to time and in that case the partition will be based on the selection of a set of data points in time for training and another for testing. For the purpose of this book, an out of sample/out-of-time testing and a sensitivity analysis are performed in Chapter 9 examples. Models usually use the selection of records in a random way to create a partition of training and testing a model.

Another aspect in risk analytics for the evaluation of the models is sensitivity analysis. In the evaluation, the purpose is to identify how results can change because of changes in parameters and assumptions. Back testing is intimately related to the concept of credit value-at-risk. Back testing assures that actual losses correspond to projected losses. Stress testing consists of analyzing the results of the model output given various extreme scenarios. Model performance measures are necessary to understand how each model represents reality and to be able to compare models among themselves.

In performance evaluation of models, there are methods that help the risk analytics process. ROCs (receiving operator curves) measure the performance of a model with a categorical outcome (e.g., "bads" and "goods"). It is a graphical representation of the fitting process quality, e.g., how many real "goods" versus how many false "bads" there are in the predictions (type I and II errors). The area under the ROC curve (AUC) is the measure of performance, where 0.5 indicates random prediction and 1 indicates perfect prediction. Another method is the cumulative accuracy profiles (CAPs) that are a special type of ROCs. This method uses ordered data points by the scores in the scales of classes from high to low risk and selecting a percentage of the total number of risk units as calculated percentage of the members of the target class (for example, risk units that are performing low) that have a score equal or lower than score for the selected fraction of companies. With the CAPs, it is possible to generate what is called ARs (accuracy ratios) that represent how close the CAP is to an ideal CAP according to the data set in analysis.

Other two metrics of model performance are: the Kolmogorov Smirnov (KS) D statistic that is an indication of the separation between two data sets, for example "bads" and "goods." KS does not make any assumptions about the underlying distribution. The Gini criterion for model performance measures identify the quality of the separation in models, especially in some algorithmic (machine learning) approaches like classification trees, to identify the quality of splitting. It compares the frequency of cases in the branch with the total associated with a parent node. The purpose is to minimize the value of the index. Gini is appropriate when the contribution of the variables to explain the event of interest needs to be identified.

$$Gini\,(t) = 1 - \sum_{j=1}^{n} p\,(j|t)^2$$

where the p represents the relative frequency of class j at node t. The Gini coefficient takes a cumulative distribution curve to compare the distribution of a specific variable with the uniform distribution. The greater the deviation of the cumulative distribution from the uniform one is, the greater the divergence or separation.

A simplified guide to models according to different questions to answer are indicated as follows in Table 7.1.

Grouping is done based on similarities or distances. Common algorithms for sorting objects in groups are: similarity measures, hierarchical clustering methods, multidimensional scaling, and correspondence analysis. In clustering, the intention is to find a partition of the data in which the differences among members of a group is diminished. All the measures are taken with respect to a centroid and points near the centroids are assigned (see Figure 7.6), the centroids are modified in different iterations and the allocation of points is repeated until the centroids do not modify the minimum differences in group members. The algorithm should converge, and the process is affected by the initial selection of the points. The first selection of points is based on the

TABLE 7.1

A Brief of Problems and Techniques Relationships

Need/Action	Technique/Method/Tool	General Aspects to Review
Exploration and visualization	EDA, statistical summaries, distribution variable analysis, scatterplots, correspondence analysis	The appropriate research questions lead to data and model selection. In another level, the type of learning that is required: supervised, unsupervised, reinforcement. Additionally, the concept behind techniques selection is about selecting inferential and not inferential techniques. Identify type of variables and appropriateness of the models or transformations required.
Data dimension reduction	Factor analysis, principal components analysis	
Optimization	Calculus-based optimization, numerical methods, and specific algorithmic optimization – mathematical programming models – DEA	
Prediction Classification	Discriminant analysis, logistic regression, classification trees, ensemble algorithms, ANN, CNN, deep learning	Predictors continuous, discrete, categorical, dummies, targets continuous, categorical. There are many algorithms for solving problems as mentioned in the left columns.
Prediction Regression	Multiple-linear and multivariate regression -stepwise - ANOVA Generalized linear models Adjusted Regression – Lasso-Ridge Poisson, Tobit, Burr, Weibull regression	
Prediction Forecasting	Time series models with or without stationarity data, with and without variance weights: ARMA, ARIMA, GARCH family	
Association	Link Analysis Network Analysis Sequence Analysis	
Clustering	K-means, k-medoids, k-modes, hierarchical, single-complete link, minimum spanning tree, PAM portioning around medoids, or using genetic and NN algorithms for clustering, BIRCH, CURE	
Simulation	Monte Carlo, discrete events simulation	
Cause and effect identification	Econometric approach – structural equations- causal inference	

observation of the points where there is high density, and they are separated widely. The centroids are updated depending on the minimization of the squared error or distances among points. Averages or middle points are taken as centroids for groups (see Figures 7.7, 7.8, and 7.9 and Exhibits 7.1 and 7.2). The points are allocated by proximity to the centroid. There is a difference in finding the centroid inside the group or outside. The k-mode, k-medoid, k-medians, or k-prototypes (the algorithms use the higher frequency or center of distribution of a mix) used with categorical variables inside the group as center of it. Distance methods for identifying similarities include a concept of vicinity that is a circle around the centroid, it can be an issue to solve in certain data where there are irregular, not convex, sets or that outliers affect the vicinity definition.

One of the methods to find groups of risk units is the k-means algorithm. With the k-means, the number of groups is predefined by the researcher and the k number is tested with different k values up to the point the clusters are not improving. There is a method known as the elbow graphic that helps to identify the best k to select; elbow method, silhouette method, and gap static method. The idea is to test several k's, looking for the total within-cluster variation minimization.

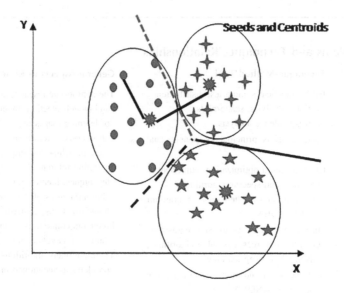

FIGURE 7.6 Illustration clustering process.

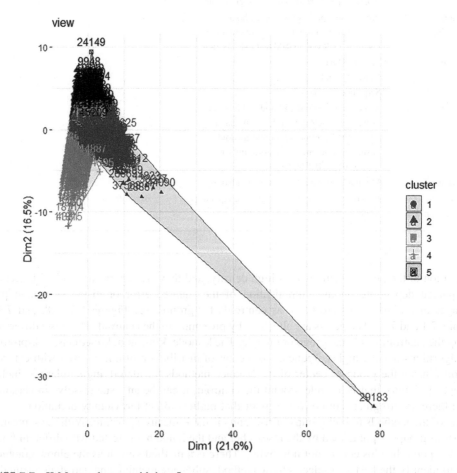

FIGURE 7.7 K-Means clusters with k = 5.

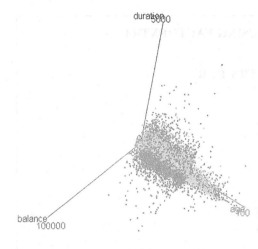

FIGURE 7.8 Cluster three dimensions view 1, not standardized data.

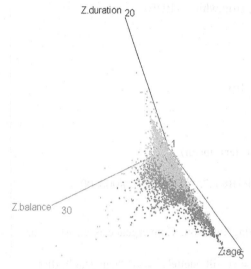

FIGURE 7.9 Cluster three dimension view 2, standardized data.

Algorithm k-means:

1. To choose the number of groups (measured it uniforms for example) that are desired to form.
2. K is the number of seeds to determine the centroids. Each seed is a combination of values by each measurement.
3. To each record in the database , the allocation of group is based on the closer points to the seed.
4. The centroids of the new groups are calculated, and the complete process initiates with new centroids taking the role from the seeds. The points can be moved from a group to another one.
5. Iterate several times.

In summary, is the search of separate groups of a certain number of members with the search of k minimizing the within-groups sum of squares for all variables.

EXHIBIT 7.1   CODE FOR USING FACTOEXTRA

GENERAL APPROACH USING FACTOEXTRA IN R

```
# Install
install.packages("FactoMineR")
# Load
library("FactoMineR")
install.packages("factoextra")
library("factoextra")
library("Rcmdr")
library("dplyr")
library("ggplot2")
library("NbClust")
bankat1 <- read.table("yourfile", header=TRUE, stringsAsFactors=TRUE,
          sep=",", na.strings="NA", dec=".", strip.white=TRUE)
bankat11<-select(bankat1,-KMeans)
dim(bankat11)
banka <- scale(bankat11)
set.seed(123)
kmeansres <- kmeans(banka, centers=5, nstart = 10)
kmeansres$size
kmeansres$centers
#find means of each cluster
aggregate(bankat1, by=list(cluster=kmeansres$cluster), mean)
fviz_cluster(kmeansres, data = banka,
          palette = c("#00AFBB","#2E9FDF", "#E7B800", "#FC4E07","#000000"),
          ggtheme = theme_minimal(),
          main = "view")
#In general the optimization is using the following function. Convergence is an issue for
a large file
fviz_nbclust(banka,FUNCluster=NULL, method = c("silhouette", "wss","gap_stat"), diss =
NULL, k.max = 10, nboot = 100, verbose = interactive(), barfill = "steelblue",barcolor =
"steelblue", linecolor = "steelblue",print.summary = TRUE)
```

**EXHIBIT 7.2   R CODE FOR K-MEANS ALGORITHMS USING THE
STANDARDIZED DATA**

R CODE AND OUTPUT FOR K=MEANS CLUSTERING

```
bank <- local({
 .Z <- scale(bank[,c("age","balance","campaign","day","duration","pdays","previous")])
 within(bank, {
   Z.previous <- .Z[,7]
   Z.pdays <- .Z[,6]
   Z.duration <- .Z[,5]
   Z.day <- .Z[,4]
   Z.campaign <- .Z[,3]
```

```
      Z.balance <- .Z[,2]
      Z.age <- .Z[,1]
   })
})
.cluster <- KMeans(model.matrix(~-1 + Z.age + Z.balance + Z.campaign + Z.day + Z.duration +
Z.pdays + Z.previous, bank), centers = 5, iter.max = 10,
   num.seeds = 10)
.cluster$size # Cluster Sizes
.cluster$centers # Cluster Centroids
.cluster$withinss # Within Cluster Sum of Squares
.cluster$tot.withinss # Total Within Sum of Squares
.cluster$betweenss # Between Cluster Sum of Squares
biplot(princomp(model.matrix(~-1 + Z.age + Z.balance + Z.campaign + Z.day + Z.duration
+ Z.pdays + Z.previous, bank)), xlabs =
   as.character(.cluster$cluster))
bank$KMeans <- assignCluster(model.matrix(~-1 + Z.age + Z.balance + Z.campaign + Z.day +
Z.duration + Z.pdays + Z.previous, bank), bank,
   .cluster$cluster)
remove(.cluster)
#The output
> .cluster$size # Cluster Sizes
[1] 3592 6325 16282 17402 1610
> .cluster$centers # Cluster Centroids
```

	new.x.Z.age	new.x.Z.balance	new.x.Z.campaign	new.x.Z.day	new.x.Z.duration	new.x.Z.pdays	new.x.Z.previous
1	0.04664426	0.27186125	−0.11841345	−0.005574846	2.53783887	−0.2464828	−0.1470301
2	−0.04089308	0.01928427	−0.20721081	−0.238291783	−0.09389153	2.1980835	1.2861634
3	0.03598506	−0.08286049	−0.17990678	−0.888009508	−0.20803796	−0.3730144	−0.2138889
4	−0.02554245	0.02060556	−0.09436448	0.849117087	−0.25503630	−0.3618612	−0.2145665
5	−0.03125246	−0.06704470	3.91759156	0.751214685	−0.43269416	−0.4018522	−0.2424999

```
> .cluster$withinss # Within Cluster Sum of Squares
[1] 30407.46 58751.43 39077.42 50076.57 12251.21
> .cluster$tot.withinss # Total Within Sum of Squares
[1] 190564.1
> .cluster$betweenss # Between Cluster Sum of Squares
[1] 125905.9
> biplot(princomp(model.matrix(~-1 + Z.age + Z.balance + Z.campaign + Z.day +
Z.duration + Z.pdays + Z.previous, bank)), xlabs =
+ as.character(.cluster$cluster))
> bank$KMeans <- assignCluster(model.matrix(~-1 + Z.age + Z.balance + Z.campaign +
Z.day + Z.duration + Z.pdays + Z.previous, bank), bank,
+ .cluster$cluster)
> remove(.cluster)
```

In k-means, the selection of k is a problem of identifying the number of clusters that can be using the elbow (Figure 7.11) approach that is based on the graphic of the average distance of the points to the clusters centroid and observing when the value of the average changes in a speed of reducing the value. Another way to obtain k is using silhouette (see Figure 7.12 and Exhibit 7.3) score, that provides a way to decide the k based on, higher the value the clusters are better defined.

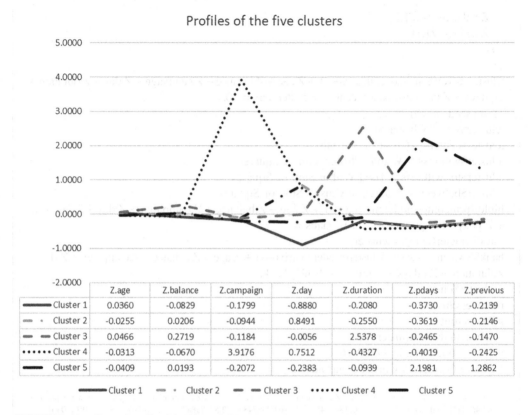

Profiles of the five clusters

	Z.age	Z.balance	Z.campaign	Z.day	Z.duration	Z.pdays	Z.previous
Cluster 1	0.0360	-0.0829	-0.1799	-0.8880	-0.2080	-0.3730	-0.2139
Cluster 2	-0.0255	0.0206	-0.0944	0.8491	-0.2550	-0.3619	-0.2146
Cluster 3	0.0466	0.2719	-0.1184	-0.0056	2.5378	-0.2465	-0.1470
Cluster 4	-0.0313	-0.0670	3.9176	0.7512	-0.4327	-0.4019	-0.2425
Cluster 5	-0.0409	0.0193	-0.2072	-0.2383	-0.0939	2.1981	1.2862

Cluster 1   Cluster 2   Cluster 3   Cluster 4   Cluster 5

FIGURE 7.10 Cluster profiles identify variable means that separate the groups.

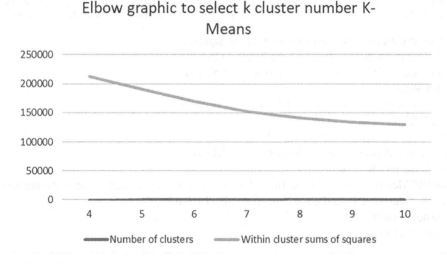

Elbow graphic to select k cluster number K-Means

Number of clusters   Within cluster sums of squares

FIGURE 7.11 Elbow representation to select K.

A tool to use is the R package *factoextra* that helps in multivariate analysis for optimizing the k selection; however, it is highly computationally demanding to get elbow (known as WSS total within groups sum of squares), silhouette, and Gap_stat charts. The algorithms for the k-means are mainly Hartigan-Wong (1979) is used in the package that has improvements to Lloyd, MacQuee, and Forgy previous years' algorithms.

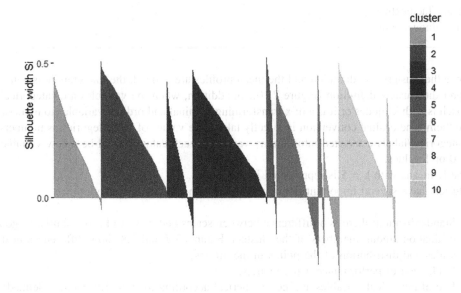

Clusters silhouette plot
Average silhouette width: 0.2

FIGURE 7.12 Silhouette outcome.

EXHIBIT 7.3 OBTAINING SILHOUETTE RESULTS

```
# load the data
# Install
install.packages("FactoMineR")
# Load
library("FactoMineR")
install.packages("factoextra")
library("factoextra")
library("Rcmdr")
library("dplyr")
library("ggplot2")
library("NbClust")
bankat1 <- read.table("C:/Users/eduar/OneDrive/IQAnalytics2019t/bookriskanalytics/book-
july2021/bankat.csv", header=TRUE, stringsAsFactors=TRUE,
          sep=",", na.strings="NA", dec=".", strip.white=TRUE)
# 1. Loading and preparing data
bankat11<-select(bankat1,-KMeans)
dim(bankat11)
banka <- scale(bankat11)
# 2. Compute k-means
```

```
set.seed(123)
kmeansres <- kmeans(banka, 10, iter.max = 1000, algorithm="MacQueen")
kmeansres$size
kmeansres$centers
# calculate silhouette
library(cluster)
sil <- silhouette(kmeansres$cluster, dist(banka))
# plot silhouette
library(factoextra)
fviz_silhouette(sil)
```

Once the clusters are identified and the mean profiles are defined, the line graphic is helping to interpret the clusters definition (Figure 7.10). In addition, when the variables are categorical, the approach is with k-modes or it is a mix transforming nominal and ordinal variables to numeric and to use them. The ordinal conversion is directly taking the values of the categories as numbers and the categorical/labels converted into dummy variables; each category will be a new variable that takes 0 or 1 values.

The K-means with k = 5 is represented in Figure 7.7.

Clusters have several important points to keep in mind for implementation:

1. Standardization: there is a difference between scales and ways to keep a similarity good evaluation among members of the clusters. Figures 7.7 and 7.8 show differences in the scales and distribution of the points in the groups.
2. Evaluation of performance using metrics.
3. Use of numerical variables and non-numerical according to similarity metrics defined in each case.

Silhouette calculation is based on $S_i = (b_i - a_i) / \max \{(a_i, b_i)\}$ for each of the points a_i, b_i $i = 1 \dots n$. The comparison of the level of dot line (Figure 7.12) when a number of different clusters is tested will indicate the best number of clusters to use, the higher the value better the separation of the clusters. For the example, it can be taken the value of seven as the elbow rule suggests Table 7.2.

The correlations are calculated with the quantitative non-normalized and normalized values (the same correlation value) of the variables and shown using Table 7.3. This is to illustrate that the clustering process is different when the clusters is for data points or for variables. Table 7.3 combined indicate how correlated are the profile variables of the clusters.

Another clustering method is the hierarchical clustering method, which is a linkage method where the smallest distance in a matrix $D = (d_{ik})$, of all the distances between points is found. Merging the corresponding objects, say U and V, produces cluster UV. The distance between (UV) and any other cluster W are computed by $d_{(UV)W} = \min[d_{UW}, d_{VW}]$, where the distances are between the nearest neighbors of clusters U and W and clusters V and W, respectively. The procedure of group by hierarchic use of dendograms or clustering. In summary, there are clustering methods to select according to problem and data. For example, in agglomerative clustering, starting with a cluster defined by each observation, the algorithm combines clusters according to similarity (distance), obtaining bigger clusters and the process is repeated up to have a root cluster that is with observations. The graphic of the process is the dendogram. This uses a proximity matrix and it can be of down to top or top to down. Each element is based on similarity measures, or variables belong to an individual group, is combined in the most similar groups, become divisions until it is left a group of a single element that stays.

TABLE 7.2

Summary of centers with k=7 that seems the best according to elbow observation

K = 7 for k-means elbow shows a good selection for this dataset

> .cluster$size # Cluster Sizes

[1] 2986 9965 929 5744 11670 12504 1413

Cluster	Z.age	Z.balance	Z.campaign	Z.day	Z.duration	Z.pdays	Z.previous
1	−0.042	−0.020	−0.102	0.005	2.770	−0.241	−0.144
2	1.289	−0.013	−0.116	−0.074	−0.210	−0.307	−0.172
3	0.290	4.896	−0.084	0.030	−0.054	−0.090	−0.022
4	−0.147	−0.075	−0.202	−0.259	−0.094	2.294	1.326
5	−0.536	−0.178	−0.193	−0.912	−0.178	−0.366	−0.210
6	−0.468	−0.133	−0.074	0.940	−0.229	−0.358	−0.213
7	−0.028	−0.137	4.159	0.753	−0.455	−0.401	−0.241

> .cluster$centers # Cluster Centroids

> .cluster$withinss # Within Cluster Sum of Squares

[1] 15123.24 24071.97 13601.73 51762.01 16707.33 20967.97 10014.75

> .cluster$tot.withinss # Total Within Sum of Squares

[1] 152249

> .cluster$betweenss # Between Cluster Sum of Squares

[1] 164221

The corresponding dendogram is presented in Figure 7.13. The number of clusters units in the hierarchical algorithm is

Cluster number	1	2	3	4	5
Total Units	9980	5606	8513	13724	7388

That compared to the k-means results where total units are 3592 6325 16282 17402 1610 showing a higher concentration on two clusters.

The opposite view of the agglomerative method is the divisive hierarchical clustering that begins with the root, in which all observations are included in a single cluster and the algorithm looks for a set with the highest dissimilarity. The branches definition can be maximum or complete linkage clustering that looks for the maximum value of the dissimilarities among clusters. Another is minimum or single linkage clustering where the groups are created based on the minimum dissimilarities. The mean or average linkage clustering does not take maximum or minimum but averages to group observations and centroid linkage clustering that is based on the definition of centroid (for example the mean) of the groups and measuring the dissimilarities using the centroids. Finally, the Ward's minimum variance method is reducing to the minimum the variance in the cluster/group and having the maximum separation of the groups.

7.4   RISK CLASSIFICATION: RELATIONSHIPS AND PREDICTIONS

The development and use of statistical and machine learning require probability and statistics theory. Statistical learning is oriented to inference and discovering the variables relationships, the validation of the models is not on testing data sets as it is in machine learning; they are based on mathematical optimization or mathematical definitions of the model structure. In a classification problem, let X the set of variables $(X_1, X_2, ..., X_p)$; each one takes a value per risk unit and it produces a vector $x = (x_1, x_2, ..., x_p)$ with all the attributes. Let A the set of all possible answers and

TABLE 7.3
Variable Correlations

	Z.pdays	pdays	day	Z.day	duration	Z.duration	Z.previous	previous	campaign	Z.campaign	balance	Z.balance	Z.age	age
Z.pdays	1.000	1.000	-0.092	-0.092	-0.004	-0.004	0.430	0.430	-0.090	-0.090	0.009	0.009	-0.022	-0.022
pdays	1.000	1.000	-0.092	-0.092	-0.004	-0.004	0.430	0.430	-0.090	-0.090	0.009	0.009	-0.022	-0.022
day	-0.092	-0.092	1.000	1.000	-0.033	-0.033	-0.050	-0.050	0.164	0.164	0.008	0.008	-0.009	-0.009
Z.day	-0.092	-0.092	1.000	1.000	-0.033	-0.033	-0.050	-0.050	0.164	0.164	0.008	0.008	-0.009	-0.009
duration	-0.004	-0.004	-0.033	-0.033	1.000	1.000	0.000	0.000	-0.090	-0.090	0.020	0.020	-0.004	-0.004
Z.duration	-0.004	-0.004	-0.033	-0.033	1.000	1.000	0.000	0.000	-0.090	-0.090	0.020	0.020	-0.004	-0.004
Z.previous	0.430	0.430	-0.050	-0.050	0.000	0.000	1.000	1.000	-0.032	-0.032	0.013	0.013	-0.002	-0.002
previous	0.430	0.430	-0.050	-0.050	0.000	0.000	1.000	1.000	-0.032	-0.032	0.013	0.013	-0.002	-0.002
campaign	-0.090	-0.090	0.164	0.164	-0.090	-0.090	-0.032	-0.032	1.000	1.000	-0.018	-0.018	0.008	0.008
Z.campaign	-0.090	-0.090	0.164	0.164	-0.090	-0.090	-0.032	-0.032	1.000	1.000	-0.018	-0.018	0.008	0.008
balance	0.009	0.009	0.008	0.008	0.020	0.020	0.013	0.013	-0.018	-0.018	1.000	1.000	0.098	0.098
Z.balance	0.009	0.009	0.008	0.008	0.020	0.020	0.013	0.013	-0.018	-0.018	1.000	1.000	0.098	0.098
Z.age	-0.022	-0.022	-0.009	-0.009	-0.004	-0.004	-0.002	-0.002	0.008	0.008	0.098	0.098	1.000	1.000
age	-0.022	-0.022	-0.009	-0.009	-0.004	-0.004	-0.002	-0.002	0.008	0.008	0.098	0.098	1.000	1.000

EXHIBIT 7.4   HIERARCHICAL CLUSTERING SHOWING FIRST 5 LEVELS

Using RCmdr HClust.1 <- hclust(dist(model.matrix(~–1 +
Z.age+Z.balance+Z.campaign+Z.day+Z.duration+Z.pdays+Z.previous, hierbank)) ,
method= "ward")
plot(HClust.1, main= "Cluster Dendrogram for Solution HClust.1", xlab=
"Observation Number in Data Set hierbank",
sub="Method=ward; Distance=euclidian")
summary(as.factor(cutree(HClust.1, k = 5))) # Cluster Sizes
by(model.matrix(~–1 + Z.age + Z.balance + Z.campaign + Z.day + Z.duration +
Z.pdays + Z.previous, hierbank), as.factor(cutree(HClust.1, k = 5)),
colMeans) # Cluster Centroids
biplot(princomp(model.matrix(~–1 + Z.age + Z.balance + Z.campaign + Z.day +
Z.duration + Z.pdays + Z.previous, hierbank)), xlabs =
as.character(cutree(HClust.1, k = 5)))

> summary(as.factor(cutree(HClust.1, k = 5))) # Cluster Sizes

1	2	3	4	5
9980	5606	8513	13724	7388

> by(model.matrix(~–1 + Z.age + Z.balance + Z.campaign + Z.day + Z.duration +
+ Z.pdays + Z.previous, hierbank), as.factor(cutree(HClust.1, k = 5)),
+ colMeans) # Cluster Centroids
INDICES: 1

Z.age	Z.balance	Z.campaign	Z.day	Z.duration	Z.pdays	Z.previous
–0.1354786	–0.2130704	–0.1825825	–1.1401635	–0.1647099	–0.4109482	–0.2495451

INDICES: 2

Z.age	Z.balance	Z.campaign	Z.day	Z.duration	Z.pdays	Z.previous
0.16712262	0.85446215	–0.14003685	0.09658426	1.59414582	–0.21963165	–0.11819733

INDICES: 3

Z.age	Z.balance	Z.campaign	Z.day	Z.duration	Z.pdays	Z.previous
1.00078012	–0.06252073	0.69643612	0.62552481	–0.29610097	–0.38337006	–0.23607768

INDICES: 4

Z.age	Z.balance	Z.campaign	Z.day	Z.duration	Z.pdays	Z.previous
–0.5445929	–0.1499400	–0.1210321	0.5065741	–0.2672447	–0.4108431	–0.2506090

INDICES: 5

Z.age	Z.balance	Z.campaign	Z.day	Z.duration	Z.pdays	Z.previous
–0.08533589	–0.00996980	–0.22475597	–0.19490182	–0.14951304	1.92671333	1.16434232

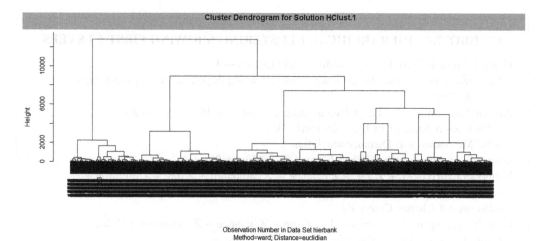

FIGURE 7.13 Hierarchical clustering observations using Euclidean distance and ward.

this is assumed finite. This set represents the sample space or the set of all possible answers. This means, for example, to use two classes. The general problem to solve is to get **x** set G and B where $G \cup B = A$. G can represent the set of good risk profile and B the set of bad risk profile. The definition of bad risk profile for the classification is defined according to the business and it can be modified through time. The change will modify the classification results. In general, there are two general cost associated with the classification C_1 if a good risk is wrong classified and not accepted and C_2 if a bad risk prospect is accepted. Calling P_G and P_B, the proportion of applicants good risk profile and bad risk profile, respectively. For this set of expressions, the random variable is considered discrete and **x** is a vector.

The error is the classification of wrong profiles. There are expressions in terms of conditional probability that provide the structure of all the conceptualization. The first step is to define $p(x|G) = \frac{p(x \cap G)}{p(Good)}$ as the probability of a good risk applicant with attributes **x** divided by probability of a good risk profile. And we call $q(G|x)$ the probability that a risk unit is good given the attributes **x**. $p(x)$ is the probability to have attributes **x**. Then $q(G|x)p(x) = P(x|G)P_G$ or $q(G|x) = \frac{P(x \mid G)P_G}{p(x)}$; thus, the cost of misclassification will be $C_1 \cdot \sum_{x \in B} q(G|x)p(x) + C_2 \cdot \sum_{x \in G} q(B|x)p(x)$.

If the level of acceptance is r, the G has to satisfy $\sum_{x \in G} P(x|G)P_G + \sum_{x \in G} P(x|B)P_B = r$. The problem is converted into minimize $\sum_{x \in G} P(x|B)P_B$ the default rate,

subject to

$$\sum_{x \in G} p(x) = r$$

because

$$\sum_G p(x) = \sum_G P(G|x)p(x) + \sum_G P(B|x)p(x)$$

$$\sum_G p(x) = \sum_G (1 - P(B|x))p(x) + \sum_G P(B|x)p(x)$$

The general condition to belong to the good risk profile set has to be addressed by the following set definition where c defines the condition to be considered a good risk profile:

$$G = \left\{ x \left| \frac{P(x|B)P_B}{P(x)} \leq c \right. \right\} = \left\{ x \left| \frac{1 - c}{c} \leq \frac{q(G|x)}{q(B|x)} \right. \right\}$$

In the continuous case of the random variable, all the previous approaches have to be changed for a probability density and the sums transformed by integrals, but the relationships to be defined are the same. For example, what is used in the logistic case:

$$\ln\left(\frac{p_i}{1 - p_i}\right) = \ln\left(\frac{P_G f\left(x|G\right)}{P_B f\left(x|B\right)}\right)$$

Risk classification involves different steps with several approaches available at each step:

1. Collecting the data, in this case, numerical or categorical data can be used. The sampling should be defined, wherever possible to reflect the characteristics of the data. For example, values of claims or profiles of clients can be used or a mix of both.
2. Classification of the groups of insureds/risk units. Here we have two different problems; one is the definition of groups and selection variables, the other is to classify a new client into one of these groups. Discriminant analysis, correspondence analysis, or cluster analysis techniques are used to define the profiles of the groups with numerical data. Logistic regression is also used, especially with categorical data.
3. Cross validation of the classification with the current data.
4. For new data, assign each new insured/risk unit to the classification group with closest characteristics.
5. Review the results and perform a misclassification analysis.

In general, the solution of a classification problem requires the identification target with two-variable model with different categories, or for a n-variable models with multiple categories. This means to use explanatory variables that are numerical or categorical and classification to two or to multiple groups. Clustering and classification models have relationships to risk selection of prospect insureds, credit users, customer in organizations, etc. In the following paragraphs, models with qualitative and quantitative variables are considered. Some of the most important characteristics in risk analysis and a few applications are given. An automobile insurance illustration is given. The main problem can be defined as a set of steps from grouping, sampling, and classification up to the price-premium-revenue calculation.

The risk classification problem is one of the most important subjects in financial services, in marketing, and in particular in insurance and reinsurance companies. Classification is the bases for underwriting, for actuarial calculation of premiums, reserves, and ruin problems evaluation. For example, classification methods based on scoring are used in bank loans analysis. The process requires identifying good or bad prospects, the probabilities of monetary losses on a portfolio and the survival of loans to maturity. Risk classification and credit analysis have a probability of misclassification, which must be minimized. However, in risk classification, there is a prior problem, which is to define the classes or groups used to separate risks. The definition for example of what is the target, what is bad or good, what is a success or not represents the crucial part as it has been mentioned before. From the definition, using the business and theoretical knowledge the data and models will be organized. Moreover, in industries such as insurance classification requires to have into account some important issues:

- Risk can be classified relative to frequency; for example, bad or good drivers, winter season or not. Besides the intensity of the risk can change and it is possible to have a small number of large claims. The strategy of the company can be given for a mix between number-frequency and intensity/severity. This, in terms of the model, means a different set of the variables for making decisions about the risk in each group.

- Classification methods require complete data. For example, in insurance, sometimes data is missing, as variables important to the claim process may be difficult to find in a file. For example, car parts that are expensive can impact on the claim costs in automobile insurance, but this amount of detail is usually not kept on record.
- Loss distributions are usually heavy tailed; that is, they depart from the normal distribution and in many cases are mixed distributions.
- The effect of time is very important; the risk is good today, but it can change in the future.
- Some of the variables in insurance are categorical and it is necessary to create dummy variables to include them in models.
- Contracts in insurance have different simultaneous risk coverages. It means some groups could be good for one risk but bad for others.
- There is a difference between collective and individual contracts. The analysis of collective contracts is similar to that of a company.
- These are some differences with the analysis done using scoring methods in the banking industry.

With this initial view of risk classification, in the next section models used in risk classification are described in detail. The concept is to connect the predictive analytics techniques and risk classification following the context such as insurance business and banking; however, the techniques and concepts are possible to use in multiple knowledge domains.

7.5 SEARCH OF RELATIONSHIPS AMONG VARIABLES USING GENERALIZED LINEAR MODELS

The generalized linear models are the bases of many risk modeling processes. In this section, it is included in the possibility to use more options to identify the good relationship between explanatory variables and the dependent variable (target). There is a generalization relative to the assumption of the probability distribution of the events in the population. It is possible to consider different distributions for the errors, random effects (because of risk units), and for the dependent variable, not only normal, for instance: Poisson, binomial, normal, gamma, inverse Gaussian (exponential family members). At the same time, different link functions can be used to obtain the linear structure required in the analysis.

The link function gives us the relationship between the mean of the i_{th} observation and its linear predictors. $y_i = g_i(\mu_i) = x_i^T \beta$. The link function is a means to transform the dependent variable to use least squares method. A specific case used in a study is the logistic regression where the assumption of the probability distribution is binomial and the link function is the natural log of the odds. In the same way, the generalized linear models give the possibility to include Anova, Ancova, and Manova analysis, very important in transactional models, because it is introduced the risk level as a factor affecting the transaction risk. The approach using generalized linear models has been used in similar problems for instance, survival modeling and graduation, multiple stage models, risk classification, premium rating, and claim reserving in non-life insurance.

At this level of the search of relationships among variables, it is important to distinguish what is multiple linear regression and multivariate linear regression. In both cases, there are several variables that are influencing the behavior of one output variable (multiple linear regression) or several output variables (multivariate linear regression). An example of multiple linear regression in risk analytics there can be the interest of describing the severity of a risk event based on the variables related to the risk unit, market environment, or any other set of possible attributes. In the case of multivariate linear regression, an example is when there are demographic variables, product use in an organization, and a marketing campaign with output variables of revenue and volume generated by marketing strategy. In a multiple linear regression, where:

1. The dependent variable is continuous
2. A set of continuous independent variables is used
3. The points of deviation of the line follow a distribution normal
4. The residuals are independent of the values that are predicted
5. The objective is to construct a linear function of the independent variables that allows to explain or to predict the value of the dependent variable

The assumptions in multiple linear regression are:

1. All the predicting variables must have a linear relationship
2. Error distribution is normal. The expected value of the error of the model must be zero
3. It must not have autocorrelation of the remainders of the models
4. It must not have correlation between the independent error and variables
5. It must have absence of multicollinearity between the predicting variables

In the following paragraphs, it is presented in the case of finding the classification models using various regression related models. The models will classify risk units as organizations and risk units as transactions. In the first stage, all risk unit-specific variables are considered to predict the risk unit-risk. In the second stage, the risk unit model output is used as an input for the transactions model. Subsequently, all other transaction-related variables are used simultaneously with the risk unit model to determine the transaction risk. This two-stage approach was chosen to assure that no risk unit-specific information is lost in modeling the transaction risk. This way, the level of significance associated with multiple variables will be distributed among the risk unit and transaction-specific variables and not only on transactional variables.

7.6 MODELING RISK UNIT

This subsection explores different alternatives to model risk units and to improve risk differentiation. Risk differentiation refers to the ability to classify risk units in groups that are homogeneous within each class and heterogeneous among classes. A good data structure is considered necessary to improve a model's robustness. Particularly, a data structure that includes changes over time is preferred (panel/longitudinal data). Many alternative methodologies have been reviewed, but there are two that are worth focusing on. The first one is a traditional logit model using cross-sectional data for a cohort of risk units that includes several years of data. The second one is based on longitudinal data analysis for unbalanced panels. An unbalanced panel is that in which each individual (risk unit) has a different number of observations through time; in other words, the entry and exit points of each buyer are different. Unbalanced panel handles entries due to new exposure added to a portfolio on a risk unit and exits due to withdrawal, exclusion, expired cases, or events of interest submission. Based on this technique, a logit model with fixed- or/and random-effects would be employed. The second modeling structure is preferred, given that the advantages between the explanatory variables and time are combined under a logistic structure. The selection of this model is a fundamental step in the perspective of a modeling dynamic structure. A panel data model allows to control for heterogeneity and variability caused by the explanatory variables and time for each particular risk unit.

The data used in risk analytics requires the combination of data sources and profile attributes. For example, in this illustrative case, two approaches are tried. The first one consists of building two sub-models, one will rate risk units with available non-financial and financial information, and the other will rate risk units with only non-financial information available. Each sub-model would be calibrated based on each of the subpopulations. The structure of each sub-model would be, in principle, similar and the criteria used to define which variables remain in each sub-model will be given by the significance level or the variables and the sub-models themselves. The outputs of the sub-models would then be amalgamated into a unique score, the model's score. Each particular score level would represent a certain probability of default (or a range of probabilities of default). The second approach is to transform certain variables into categorical variables, where missing information would be considered one special category. One such variable could be the existence or non-existence of financial information, another variable could be age of financial statement if available. This is derived from the fact that missing value can be interpreted and can provide clues related to the event of interest.

There is in a modeling process a special consideration about specific variables, for example, industry and country, which are potential factors affecting the risk unit and transaction models. Three approaches are common ground in the real applications. The first approach or the ideal one is to have one model per combination of country and industry. In this case, several models would be fitted to the data for a specific combination of country and industry and the results of each model would then be harmonized in an equivalent scale through the probabilities of default. The second is to fit several models per industry sector or per geographic area. The results would then be combined in a score according to their particular probabilities of default. The third is to introduce categorical variables to account for industry- and country-specific variations. These variables would be included in the general model.

In the analysis of having separated models, a point to consider is the number of events of interest that are related to the input data. The number of events of interest can be an issue of unbalanced data for performing an appropriate model. The number should have a number of events that provides capacity to create a model with an appropriate level of robustness (power of the model-sampling process). In most of the cases having different models per combination of industry and country cannot be feasible, given the amount of events information that would be needed per sector. Information would be unavailable in many of the combinations or in some cases results would not be robust and thus lack any meaning. The design of models per industry sectors or geographical areas is possible to explore. This alternative would be perhaps the most efficient, but availability of the event of interest observations is still a factor that can limit the modeling capacity. Introducing a categorical variable is an alternative that will provide knowledge about the significance or not of the sector and region variables in explaining the events of interest to implement in practice.

In the search of variables to include in a risk model, there is one to consider, in particular for default or bankruptcy, that is the relationship to parents in financial or industrial conglomerates. The organizations that are related because of ownership will be affected by risk events in each risk unit. The impact of the effect will be associated with the level of equity ties in the organization ownership. There is a higher chance that the parent will take its subsidiary to bankruptcy if the parent itself goes bankrupt.

As mentioned at the beginning of the section, two possible models are cross-sectional and longitudinal logistic regressions. First, the data selection and modeling process is a cohort of risk units and their attributes (cross-sectional data) at a specific point in time is selected and the events of interests are observed at the end of the chosen period. Once data is prepared, a logistic regression is run on the data to model the probability of the event of interest and to identify those attributes that contribute to explaining the events of interest. This procedure would be repeated by changing the cohorts and performance windows to obtain cumulative probabilities of default for different time periods (Table 7.4).

Second, longitudinal (panel) data refers to a cross-sectional observation that are followed over time. An independent variable and a set of explanatory variables are observed at each time, permitting the study of the dynamics of an event; for instance, the claims event. Tracking each risk unit over time has advantages compared to cross-sectional analysis. When using cross-sectional data, individual variation cannot be separately identified. However, by taking repeated observations per risk unit, risk unit-specific variations are identifiable, thus accounting for heterogeneity of the risk units is possible.

TABLE 7.4

Working with Cross-Sectional Data Advantages and Disadvantages

Advantages	Disadvantages
• Predicts the probability of failure per risk unit for the period under observation.	• Does not account for time variations among individual risk units.
• Easy to replicate.	• Available data is reduced.
• Straightforward.	• Resulting probability is related to the chosen period.

7.7 MIXED MODELS

There are possible variations in linear regression model because of the records-risk units evaluated. In a linear regression, the coefficients are considered fixed, but it is possible to think that the coefficient can have random behavior according to the risk units. Evaluation of variables risk units can be correlated. The simplest case could be to have through time observations of attributes of one risk unit, e.g., a patient, a driver, etc. The **general mixed model** is defined as $y_{it} = z_{it}'\alpha_i + x_{it}'\beta + \varepsilon_{it}$, each risk unit i is observed at each time t_i. y_{it} is the response variable that can be, for example, taking values 0 or 1, if there is an event of interest or not. The explanatory variables are $x_{it} = (x_{it1}, \ldots x_{itK})'$ and its parameters are $\beta_{it} = (\beta_1, \ldots \beta_K)'$. The model uses an additional set of explanatory variables $z_{it} = (z_{it1}, \ldots z_{itq})'$ whose parameters $\alpha_{it} = (\alpha_{it1}, \ldots \alpha_{itq})'$ represent the randomness of the variable's coefficients because of the risk units. The α_I are assumed *i.i.d.* N(0, σ_α^2) and ε_{it}' are *i.i.d.* In addition, α_i and ε_{it} are independent and not observable.

The fixed-effects logit model is given by: $\text{prob}(Y_{it} = 1(bad)) = \frac{exp^{\alpha_i + x_{it}'\beta}}{1 + exp^{\alpha_i + x_{it}'\beta}}$ where $\alpha_{it} = (\alpha_{it1}, \ldots \alpha_{itq})'$ are individual effects that are constant over time and risk unit-specific, and $x_{it} = (x_{it1}, \ldots x_{itK})'$ are the explanatory variables and its parameters are $\beta_{it} = (\beta_1, \ldots \beta_K)'$.

The **mixed** (fixed- and random-effects) **logit model** is given by: $Prob(Y_{it} = 1(bad)) = \frac{exp^{z_{it}'\alpha_i + x_{it}'\beta}}{1 + exp^{z_{it}'\alpha_i + x_{it}'\beta}}$ where $\alpha_{it} = (\alpha_{it1}, \ldots \alpha_{itq})'$ are risk unit-specific and are *i.i.d.* N(0, σ_α^2), $x_{it} = (x_{it1}, \ldots x_{itK})'$ are exploratory variables with parameters are $\beta_{it} = (\beta_1, \ldots \beta_K)'$, and $z_{it} = (z_{it1}, \ldots z_{itq})'$ are an additional set of explanatory variables related to the α_i's.

The pros and cons of using a mixed model are the following Table 7.5.

TABLE 7.5

Advantages and Disadvantages of Mixed Models

Advantages	Disadvantages
• Allows us to study a change in the response over time in reference to each risk unit.	• Difficult interpretation of fixed- and/or random effects.
• Allows us to separate dynamic relations from static comparisons.	• Predictions are not straightforward.
• Provides a larger set of observations.	• Difficult to program.
• Provides more robust estimates and conclusions.	• Difficult to estimate.
• Allows us to identify factors that are not observable in cross-sectional analysis.	
• Allows us to identify changes in performance through an economic cycle.	
• Allows us to account for individual variation.	

The mixed model methodology is recommended to account for heterogeneity of the risk units and to analyze the dynamics of a portfolio as well as the attributes that explain the probability of the event interest. Fixed-effects are adequate when risk units in a portfolio are unique, e.g., large quoted companies, i.e., where the sample is not random. The fixed-effects model applies to cross-sectional observations and all inferences are made with respect to the specific variations within the sample. A random-effects approach is appropriate if the cross-sectional observations are drawn randomly from a population. The random-effects approach makes inferences with respect to the population characteristics. As an example, an unbalanced panel (some observations can have for certain years missing values, this means the time dimension is specific to each individual) of m years of data is used with $t = 1, \ldots m$ and $i = 1, \ldots n$, where n = total risk units at each time t. As the dependent variable, the event of interest would be modeled. As independent variables, all relevant variables defining profiles (financial, demographic, macroeconomic, etc.) would be used. This model would be used to measure the probability event of interest at each time t, and would allow to identify the variables that are related to the event of interest. The model's output would be the probability of a risk unit of indicating the appearance of an event of interest in $1, \ldots, m$ years. The probability output would then be converted into a score to define risk levels. In the actuarial practice for pricing, the general mixed model is the balanced Bühlmann Model that is used in the context of the credibility theory to calibrate the pricing of different risk units and risk types. As Frees (2004) pointed out: "Data used for insurance pricing in the credibility rate-making context often fit into this panel data design. For insurance pricing, 'subjects' may be individual or group policyholders, rating territories or industries. Explanatory variables, or covariates, help to explain claims differences among subjects and thus provide useful information for pricing different risks. For the panel data design, the critical component is that the claims (the response) and the explanatory variables are tracked over time, for each subject."

Prediction of the risk unit-specific probabilities of default has the following connotations:

- Prediction of a probability of an event for a period of time,
- Prediction with the variables of the expected loss and the portfolio structure,
- Prediction under variance components of the most important effects affecting a portfolio,
- Prediction of changes in the default rates though time and their impact in the risk level distribution.

In general (Frees, 2004), the effects of the risk unit-specific explanatory variables through time are part of the questions to answer in risk analytics. Particularly, in the panel, the data model based on the prediction power is given by a linear mixed effects model:

$$y_{i,T_i+L} = Z'_{i,T_i+L}\, \alpha_i + x'_{i,T_i+L}\, \beta + \varepsilon_{i,T_i+L}$$

where L is a time in the future, and the random variables α_i effects of the i-th specific subject included in the data set, the vectors x of explanatory variables, and Z as the risk unit specific are assumed to be known. Then, the forecasts will be given by the use of the covariance matrices and the BLUP (best linear unbiased estimator) estimation (vector of coefficients estimators for Z) for a_{BLUP}.

For example, the forecast for a one-year period would be represented by,

$$\hat{y}_{i,T_i+1} = x'_{i,T_i+1}\, b_{GLS} + z'_{i,T_i+1}\, a_{BLUP} + r'^{V_i^{-1}}(y_i - X_i b_{GLS}), \quad \text{where}$$

r represents the correlation vector and V is the variance-covariance matrix for the model.

GLS represents the estimation method in this case generalized least squares to estimate the $\beta's$. And BLUPs represent the best linear unbiased predictors for the random effects. The concept behind is that given two random variables, for example, following a joint bivariate normal distribution, the estimate mean of one corresponding to a specified value of the other is unknown as a predictor of the particular realization of the random variables.

It is common that a model includes fixed and random effects for the description of the relationship between dependent variables and predictors (independent variables). The estimators and interpretation have to be produced in order to generate the predictions. Prediction power of the models can be identified with a set of assumptions and constraints. The general improvement process for prediction will consider a simulation framework for the portfolio. The results of the distribution modeling and a general set of empirical results are included in the Monte-Carlo Simulation process, following the next steps:

- Identify a rule for acceptance of buyers based on the probability of default. The rule has to identify a cut-off, at the beginning the cut-off is only for the classification purposes (acceptable or not).
- Generate observations with the attributes used in the default event analysis.
- Determine which applicants will be granted a credit limit; this step is necessary to calculate the expected default probabilities. Then the rules for all these that have an approval are applied and the total credit losses on the portfolio are calculated.
- The process has to be repeated in order to calculate an approximation of the loss distribution, based on the number of cases generated.
- Finally, the process is tested many times to validate results.

There is a problem to solve in risk analytics related to transactions. A risk unit can be good prospect or belong to a class that is desired, but some factors can affect a transaction of a risk unit generating changes in the risk levels. A transaction can be a new contract, new exposure, changes of conditions of contracts, etc. This risk considers not only the unit-specific risk but also a set of variables that are defined in a contract or in any business/operational interaction with the risk unit. The statistical model to use is a cross-sectional logit for cohort data. The general structure of the risk unit transaction model assumes that the risk unit risk level is an input. The balance of the explanatory variables is the transaction-specific variables such as terms of contracts, participation in promotion campaigns/tactic specific, business groups/teams/areas/methods/conditions, amount requested, past transactions' history (frequency and quality), first covered, highest exposure, deductible, max credit period, etc. The dependent variable represents whether or not at least one event of interest was registered during the observation period. The explanatory variables to be used in the model will be the ones that prove to be significant and yield a robust model.

7.8 LOGISTIC REGRESSION

In general, in regression, in ordinary least squares what is solved is to find coefficients that produce this equality $y_i = \beta_0 + \beta_1 x_i + \varepsilon_i$ where the residuals (difference estimation and actual values) are minimized. The y_i are response-dependent variables or targets that depend on x_i that are explanatory variable-independent variables. A maximum likelihood estimation in regression is applicable from the definition of logit/probit model where $p(y_i = 1) = F(X_1, ..., X_k) = \beta_1 X_1 + ... + \beta_k X_k$ looking for the probability of an event such as $y_i = 1$ through a function F, that is the probability of a category for the response variable. The purpose is to maximize the function that is called likelihood of the events probability calculation that is the product of having the value $y_i = 1$ in each observation. The formalization is presented in the next paragraphs. A scoring system that can be expressed as a decision rule is based on a linear function F where X_i are the relevant variables and β_i are the weights or scores corresponding to variables X_i.

Discriminant analysis is the most frequently used to determine the coefficients β_i. However, it imposes the assumption of normally distributed variables X_i, which is violated for categorical variables. Each variable can have different categories. The assumption in the two-response model is that the risk units can be classified as good or bad, depending on the variables X_i. In the binary case, the dependent variable is Bernoulli distributed and in that case the linear regression (linear combination of the independent variables) or mean response is the probability of one of the two values in y and the variance as it is in Bernoulli distribution. The logistic regression model is used under the assumption that the probability of a risk unit (for instance, insured individual risks) being good is dependent on the level of the variable X_i. To formalize the logistic regression model, the function (P) that indicates the relationship of expectation of a response variable and explanatory variables will be given by P_k, indicated below, and the parameters are estimated using maximum likelihood. This means the response variable is binary with p explanatory variables. For n cases, the data will then consist of n vectors

$$(y_k, x_{1k}, \cdots, x_{pk})$$

of jointly observed values of the response variable and the explanatory variables. Y_k is equal to 1 with probability P_k and 0 with probability $1 - P_k$, $k = 1, \cdots, n$ and denoted like

$$P_k = P(Y_k = 1 | x_{1k}, \cdots, x_{pk})$$

$$P_k = \frac{\exp\left(\beta_0 + \Sigma\beta_j x_{jk}^p\right)}{1 + \exp\left(\beta_0 + \Sigma\beta_j x_{jk}^p\right)}$$

$$\ln(P_k/1 - P_k) = \beta_0 + \sum_{j=1}^{p} \beta_j x_{jk}$$

This means the natural logarithm of the ratio of the posterior probability of a good risk unit and the posterior probability of a bad risk unit is equal to a linear function of the variables (profile) X_i. The likelihood function for a set of n observations $y_1, \cdots, y_n$, where Y_i are independent, is given by:

$$L = P(Y_1 = y_1, \cdots, Y_n = y_n) = \prod_{k=1}^{n} P_k^{y_k}(1 - P_k)^{1-y_k}$$

The transformation using the natural logarithm is used and it offers benefits to the maximization of the function. The likelihood function represents probabilities, the values are between 0 and 1, and the log will be negative. Another aspect to remind us is that the hypotheses testing in regression is the null hypothesis of having coefficients equal zero; the difference with OLS (ordinary least squares) and maximum likelihood estimation test is that OLS is used in the hypotheses testing the F-test, while in the case of ML the test is based on the likelihood ratio test ($-2(\ln L - \ln L_0)$) where L_0 represents full (all variables) model likelihood, and L the reduced (less variables) model likelihood. The log-likelihood becomes:

$$\ln(L(\beta_0, \cdots, \beta_p)) = \sum_{k=1}^{n} y_k [\beta_0 + \sum_{j=1}^{p} \beta_j x_{jk}]$$
$$- \sum_{k=1}^{n} \ln[1 + \exp(\beta_0 + \sum_{j=1}^{p} \beta_j x_{jk})]$$

Equivalently

$$\ln(L(\beta_0, \cdots, \beta_p)) = y \cdot \beta_0 + \sum_{j=1}^{p} \beta_j \sum_{k=1}^{n} y_k x_{jk} - ng(\beta_0, \cdots, \beta_p)$$

where $g(\beta_0, \cdots, \beta_p)$ is independent of $y_1, \ldots, y_n$. With the assumption of this it has dimension $p + 1$. The estimates of $\beta_0, \cdots, \beta_p$ are found solving the equations:

$$y. = E(Y.) = \sum_{k=1}^{n} P_k$$

and

$$\sum_{k=1}^{n} y_k x_{jk} = \sum_{k=1}^{n} x_{jk} P_k = \sum_{k=1}^{n} x_{jk} E(Y_k)$$

The new prospect is classified with the good risk units (e.g., insureds) if its predicted probability P_k is higher than a cut-off level c, determined finding a good or bad classification with a trial cut-off, in order to obtain the percentage of good classifications. The variable selection requires a stepwise logistic regression procedure. The stepwise begins with a model with one variable and adds, one by one, the variables that give the best improvement in goodness of fit of the model, until no further single addition achieves a specified significance level. When several models need to be compared, the likelihood ratio test and a R-statistic with a correction for the number of estimated parameters, can be used. The likelihood ratio test χ^2 distribution is used to test the hypothesis of coefficients equal zero except for the constant, with q degrees of freedom with q as deleted variables or variables that are not used in the model (difference between degree of freedom of restricted model and unrestricted model). L_0 is the likelihood function for the full model and L is the likelihood function for the reduced-restricted model. The hypothesis of independence is rejected if LR (likelihood ratio) is too large. The p-values that are smaller give the most important variables, and the hypothesis of coefficients equal zero is rejected.

$$LR = -2(\ln L - \ln L_0)$$
$$R^2 = \frac{-2\ln L_0 + 2\ln L}{-2\ln L_0}$$

Now R^2 is the measure of goodness of fit. It measures the proportion of uncertainty in the data that is explained by the model. If the full model is with $L = 1$, $lnL = 0$, and $R^2 = 1$. If the reduced model yields the same likelihood as the full model, then $LnL = LnL_0$ and $R^2 = 0$. The small p-values give the most important variables such that the hypothesis of values not zero for the coefficients of the variables is rejected. H_0: $\beta_i = 0$; H_1: $\beta_i \neq 0$

In addition, to test hypotheses and select variables, it is required to define the classification criteria to differentiate groups; for example, the profit over one time period. With this criteria, the percentages of good or bad risk units can be calculated. A sample is then taken and the criteria applied. If the classification is not good with this cut-off level, it is changed and the above procedure repeated.

The response variables are indicator variables explaining whether the risk units had, for example, claims or nor in the current and previous year. The variables in an insurance situation can be family dependents between 18 and 22 years old, younger dependents, car value, level of education, age, and profession (see Exhibit 7.5).

This example uses P like the probability of not a claim. Two periods of time are reviewed. In the first group for E_1, E_2 show that when they increase, P increases. These variables E_1 and E_2 have the smallest p-value. In the second model – group inverse relationships for variables appeared such as A, ED, and EDUC a professional is more likely to have claim. This type of results open the eyes to segmentation and policies related to groups of risk units.

The model can be used to obtain the value of $\widehat{P}_i$ for each observation by determining the value of $\ln\left(\frac{\widehat{P}_i}{1-\widehat{P}_i}\right) = \tilde{\beta}_0 + \sum_{j=1}^{r} \tilde{\beta}_j x_{ij}$ and then solving for $\widehat{P}_i$ where $\tilde{\beta}_j$ is the estimator for β_j. This is $\widehat{P}_i = \frac{e^{x_i \tilde{\beta}}}{1+e^{x_i \tilde{\beta}}}$.

The assumption is that the observation is placed in the category $Y = 0$ if $\widehat{P}_i < 0.5$; otherwise, the observation is placed in the category $Y = 1$. The proportion of correctly classified observations is given by $\frac{n_{00}+n_{11}}{n}$ with $n = n_{00} + n_{01} + n_{10} + n_{11}$ where n_{00} is the relation $Y = 0$ with $\widehat{P}_i < 0.5$ and $Y = 0$ with $\widehat{P}_i \geq 0.5$, $Y = 1$ with $\widehat{P}_i < 0.5$, $Y = 1$ with $\widehat{P}_i \geq 0.5$.

EXHIBIT 7.5 CLASSIFICATION USING LOGISTIC REGRESSION AND DIFFERENT TARGET DEFINITION

```
data claims;
  input claim1 claim0 e1 e2 a c ed age;
  cards;
0 0 0 0 0 4340 12 42        1 1 0 0 0 27938 12 46
0 0 0 1 0 13648 12 31       1 1 0 1 0 6704 12 27
1 1 0 1 1 4973 10 38        1 1 0 0 0 7711 12 32
0 1 0 0 0 8427 12 46        0 1 0 1 0 8576 16 38
0 1 0 0 0 18320 18 46       0 0 1 0 0 7223 16 26
0 1 0 1 1 7680 10 29        0 0 1 0 0 11259 16 31
1 1 0 1 0 5612 12 25        0 0 0 1 0 26063 12 30
0 0 0 1 0 13554 12 32       1 1 0 0 0 11776 12 42
1 0 0 0 0 5329 12 26        0 1 0 1 1 12793 18 46
1 1 0 0 0 10511 12 29       1 1 0 0 0 11080 12 44
0 1 0 0 0 10486 12 34       1 1 0 0 0 7074 12 31
0 1 0 0 0 14071 16 38       1 1 0 1 0 6679 12 36
1 1 0 0 0 9024 12 32        0 1 0 0 0 15868 12 45
1 1 0 1 0 14329 12 36       1 1 0 0 0 7972 16 42
1 1 0 0 1 5118 18 28        0 0 1 0 1 0 12 29
0 1 0 0 0 3044 12 37        1 1 0 0 0 3030 10 43
1 0 0 1 2640 7 38           1 1 0 0 0 2970 16 27
1 1 0 0 1 2050 7 43         1 1 0 0 0 9305 12 40
0 0 0 1 1 6750 12 23        1 1 0 0 0 8125 12 30
0 0 0 0 0 3383 12 24        0 0 1 1 13033 10 29
1 1 0 0 0 6630 12 40        1 1 0 1 0 12 39
1 1 0 0 0 7000 12 46        1 1 0 1 1 2781 12 30
0 1 0 0 0 8815 12 42        1 1 0 0 1 3010 12 35
1 1 0 0 0 3450 12 46        0 0 0 0 0 26056 12 40
0 0 0 0 0 12031 12 42       0 0 0 0 0 5795 12 46
1 1 0 0 1 6144 12 31        1 1 0 1 0 12 36
0 0 1 0 11513 12 39         1 1 0 1 0 2639 12 28
0 1 0 1 0 12167 12 46       1 1 0 0 0 9087 12 24
0 0 1 0 0 9968 16 28        0 0 0 0 0 12312 12 34
0 1 0 0 0 5888 12 23        0 0 0 0 0 7325 12 33
1 1 0 0 0 10232 12 32       1 1 0 0 0 3517 10 26
1 1 0 0 0 8017 12 40        1 1 0 0 0 17140 12 35
1 1 0 0 0 11686 12 45       1 1 0 0 0 24054 12 40
1 1 0 0 0 28363 12 31       0 1 0 0 1 13211 12 34
1 1 0 0 1 4343 7 46         0 1 0 0 0 9309 12 45
1 1 0 0 0 10554 12 38       1 1 0 0 0 3135 10 40
1 1 0 1 0 2484 10 29        1 1 0 0 0 2935 10 45
0 0 0 0 0 5672 12 44        1 1 0 0 0 9607 12 41
                            0 1 0 0 0 10629 12 44
                            1 1 0 0 0 8207 12 24
```

```
1 1 0 0 1 13319 18 31
1 1 0 0 1 7678 18 35
1 1 0 0 0 7162 12 24
0 0 0 0 0 7804 12 34
0 1 0 1 0 13648 16 28
0 0 0 1 0 9311 12 27
```

```
1 1 0 0 0 9772 12 42
1 1 0 0 0 8955 12 46
1 1 0 0 0 6204 10 46
0 1 0 0 1 9378 12 32
0 0 0 0 0 54281 12 45
1 1 0 1 0 7525 12 31
0 0 1 0 0 11504 12 32
0 1 0 0 0 5763 12 42
0 0 0 1 0 5683 12 32
0 1 0 0 0 10937 12 40
1 1 0 0 0 9361 12 45
0 0 1 0 0 6342 12 35
1 0 0 0 0 7160 10 31
1 0 0 1 0 7788 12 31
1 1 0 0 1 2402 10 25
;
run;
proc logistic data = claims;
model claim1= e1 e2 a c ed age;run;
proc logistic data = claims;
model claim0= e1 e2 a c ed age;
run;
;
```

Multiple Response Insured

The LOGISTIC Procedure

Data Set: WORK.CLAIMS
Response Variable: CLAIM1
Response Levels: 2
Number of Observations: 100
Link Function: Logit

Response Profile

Ordered Value	CLAIM1	Count
1	0	35
2	1	65

Model Fitting Information and Testing Global Null Hypothesis BETA=0

Criterion	Intercept Only	Intercept and Covariates	Chi-Square for Covariates
AIC	131.489	120.653	.
SC	134.094	138.890	.
-2 LOG L	129.489	106.653	22.836 with 6 DF (p=0.0009)

Multiple Response Insured

The LOGISTIC Procedure

Data Set: WORK.CLAIMS
Response Variable: CLAIM0
Response Levels: 2
Number of Observations: 100
Link Function: Logit

Response Profile

Ordered Value	CLAIM0	Count
1	0	28
2	1	72

Model Fitting Information and Testing Global Null Hypothesis BETA=0

Criterion	Intercept Only	Intercept and Covariates	Chi-Square for Covariates
AIC	120.591	102.104	.
SC	123.196	120.341	.
-2 LOG L	118.591	88.104	30.486 with 6 DF (p=0.0001)

Score .   21.243 with 6 DF
                                               (p=0.0017)

Analysis of Maximum Likelihood Estimates

Variable	DF	Parameter Estimate	Standard Error	Wald Chi-Square	Pr > Chi-Square	Standardized Estimate	Odds Ratio
INTERCPT	1	-6.3654	2.5600	6.1828	0.0129	.	.
E1	1	3.6944	1.2905	8.1962	0.0042	0.486163	40.223
E2	1	1.6935	0.6461	6.8714	0.0088	0.406336	5.439
A	1	0.0877	0.6556	0.0179	0.8936	0.019061	1.092
C	1	0.00008	0.000001	3.7723	0.0521	0.315003	1.000
ED	1	0.0913	0.1241	0.5420	0.4616	0.103821	1.096
AGE	1	0.0870	0.0456	3.6349	0.0566	0.341118	1.091

Association of Predicted Probabilities and Observed Responses

Concordant = 78.1%   Somers' D = 0.564
Discordant = 21.7%   Gamma = 0.566
Tied = 0.2%   Tau-a = 0.259
(2275 pairs)   c = 0.782

Score .   27.768 with 6 DF
                                               (p=0.0001)

Analysis of Maximum Likelihood Estimates

Variable	DF	Parameter Estimate	Standard Error	Wald Chi-Square	Pr > Chi-Square	Standardized Estimate	Odds Ratio
INTERCPT1	1	6.0633	3.2988	3.3783	0.0661	.	.
E1	1	4.5179	1.5736	8.2426	0.0041	0.594527	91.645
E2	1	1.1244	0.6051	3.4527	0.0631	0.269774	3.078
A	1	-1.5451	0.9427	2.6865	0.1012	-0.335866	0.213
C	1	0.000108	0.000045	5.7842	0.0162	0.426445	1.000
ED	1	-0.4777	0.2293	4.3409	0.0372	-0.542916	0.620
AGE	1	-0.0774	0.0441	3.0077	0.0794	-0.303331	0.926

Association of Predicted Probabilities and Observed Responses

Concordant = 80.7%   Somers' D = 0.615
Discordant = 19.2%   Gamma = 0.616
Tied = 0.1%   Tau-a = 0.251
(2016 pairs)   c = 0.808

For categorical variables, the groups of responses may not only be bad or good risk units. In general, there will be several groups: bad, moderate, good, excellent. For that reason, it is very important to study the classification problem using logistic regression for multiple groups. Various generalizations have been proposed; one is to take the response variables categories two by two. Another is the solution proposed by McCulloch with additive parameters for the levels introduced in the following way:

Let Y_k be a politomous response variable, with response categories $t = 1, \cdots, T$ and explanatory variables with values $x_{1k}, \cdots, x_{pk}$. Then denote by

$$P_{kt} = P(Y_k = t | x_{1k}, \cdots, x_{pk}),$$

which satisfies

$$\sum_{t=1}^{T} P_{kt} = 1.$$

There are $T - 1$ different logistic regression models, $t = 1, \cdots, T - 1$:

$$\ln\left[\frac{P_{kt}}{1 - P_{kt}}\right] = \beta_0^{(t)} + \sum_{j=1}^{p} \beta_j^{(t)} x_{jk},$$

$$\ln\left[\frac{P_{kt}}{P_{kT}}\right] = \beta_0^{(t)} + \sum_{j=1}^{p} \beta_j^{(t)} x_{jk}$$

$$\ln\left[\frac{P_{kt}}{P_{kt+1}}\right] = \beta_0^{(t)} + \sum_{j=1}^{p} \beta_j^{(t)} x_{jk}$$

$$\ln\left[\frac{P_{kt}}{\sum_{l \geq t+1} P_{kl}}\right] = \beta_0^{(t)} + \sum_{j=1}^{p} \beta_j^{(t)} x_{jk}.$$

One model introducing the response levels with additive parameters is called MLR1:

$$\ln\left[\frac{\sum_{l=1}^{t} P_{kl}}{\sum_{l=t+1}^{T} P_{kl}}\right] = \alpha_j + \sum_{j=1}^{p} \beta_j x_{jk}$$

Another model describing the data as a weighted sum of the logarithms of the P_{kt}, with preassigned weights $(w_1, \cdots, w_T)$ is given the following. This model is loglinear and it is possible to derive the likelihood function with different sets of explanatory variables for each value of the response variable (called MLR2):

$$P_{kt} = \frac{\exp[(\beta_0 + \sum_j x_{jk}) w_t]}{\sum_{t=1}^{T} \exp[(\beta_0 + \sum_j \beta_j x_{jk}) w_t]}.$$

This is when is assumed that there is one Y-value for each combination of X's. The case considered is when there are several observed Y-values for each combination of the explanatory variables. The likelihood function for this last model is obtained by denoting the binomial counts n_i for the number of cases with values $x_{1i}, \cdots, x_{pi}$, of which z_{it}, say, have an observed response $Y_k = t$. Then

$$L = \prod_{i=1}^{I} \binom{n_i}{z_{i1}, \cdots, z_{iT}} \prod_{t=1}^{T} P_{it}^{z_{it}}$$

where

$$P_{it} = \frac{\exp[(\beta_0 + \Sigma_j \beta_j x_{ji})w_t]}{\Sigma_{t=1}^{T} \exp[(\beta_0 + \Sigma_j \beta_j x_{ji})w_t]}$$

and $n = \Sigma_{i=1}^{I} n_i$ is the number of observations. From these equations, are derived as

$$\sum_{t=1}^{T} z_{.t} w_t = \sum_{t=1}^{T} w_t \sum_{i=1}^{I} n_i P_{it}$$

$$\sum_{t=1}^{T} w_t \sum_{i=1}^{I} z_{it} x_{ji} = \sum_{t=1}^{T} w_t \sum_{i=1}^{I} x_{ji} n_j P_{it},$$

$$E[Z_{it}] = n_i P_{it}.$$

With these equations, it is possible to compute the estimators $\widehat{\beta_0}, \cdots, \widehat{\beta_p}$ using iterative procedures. This model can be seen as a regression model for the weighted averages of the logarithmically transformed expected numbers:

$$\sum_t w_t \ln P_{it} = (\beta_0 + \sum_j \beta j x_{ji}) \sum_t w_t^2$$

$$- \sum_t w_t \ln \sum_{s=1}^{T} \exp[(\beta_0 + \sum_j \beta_j x_{ji})w_s]$$

Hence, if location and scale for the weights $w_1, \dots, w_I$ are chosen such that

$$\sum_t w_t = 0$$

$$\sum_t w_t^2 = 1,$$

$$\sum_t w_t \ln P_{it} = \beta_0 + \sum_j \beta_j x_{ji}.$$

The goodness of fit test statistic for the models MLR1 and MLR2 is:

$$Z = 2 \sum_{i=1}^{I} \sum_{t=1}^{T} Z_{it} \left[\ln Z_{it} - \ln(n_i)\widehat{P}_{it} \right]$$

where for MLR1

$$\widehat{P}_{it} = \hat{Q}_{it} - \hat{Q}_{it-1}$$

with

$$\hat{Q}_{it} = \frac{\exp(\hat{\alpha}_0 + \Sigma_j \hat{\beta}_j z_{ji})}{1 + \exp(\hat{\alpha}_j + \Sigma_j \hat{\beta}_j z_{ji})}$$

and in the second model MLR2

$$\widehat{P}_{it} = \frac{\exp[(\hat{\beta}_0 + \Sigma_j \hat{\beta}_j z_{ji})w_t]}{\Sigma_{t=1}^{T} \exp[(\hat{\beta}_0 + \Sigma_j \hat{\beta}_j z_{ji})w_t]}$$

The degrees of freedom for the approximating χ^2 are $I(T-1) - p - (T-1)$ for the first model MLR1 and for the second model MLR2 $I(T-1) - p - 1$.

After obtaining the estimated coefficients for the logistic regression models for $\ln(P_r/P_g)$ with $r = 1, \cdots, g - 1$, it is possible to solve the estimated equations for P_r and $P_g = 1 - \sum_{r=1}^{q-1} P_r$. The resulting equations, one for each P_r, $r = 1, \cdots, g$, can then be used to determine the values of P_r for each unknown. The unknown is then placed in the category corresponding to the largest value of P_r obtained.

This example represents the use of multiple response for logistic regression. There are different deductibles to choose. The options of deductibles are four, represented by three indicator variables: X_1, X_2, X_3. The response variable has nine levels to choose from in terms of the benefits for the customer.

The results are given by the coefficient of the model. The score chi-square for testing the proportional odds is 17.287, which is nonsignificant with respect to a χ^2 distribution with 21 degrees of freedom. This indicates that a proportional odds model is appropriate for the data. The positive value for the parameter estimate of X_1 indicates a tendency towards the lower numbered categories of the first deductible option relative to the fourth. In other words, the four deductible option is better than the first. Each of the second and the third options is less favorable than the fourth. The relative magnitudes of these slope estimates imply this preference ordering: fourth, first, third, second.

The representation of the logit model for transactions including the input of the probability of default is:

$$\ln \frac{P_i}{1 - P_i} = a_0 + a_1 RiskUnit_{riskLevel} + a_2 T_1 + \cdots + a_{n+1} T_n + \varepsilon_i$$

where T_i represents transactional variables and p_i represents the probability of the occurrence of the event of interest. The models can be created using different windows of the transactions and how long the transactions last. The purpose is to obtain the probability of default associated with a particular transaction. The prediction ability is related to the performance window. In other words, the model will yield the probability of default in the next n years, where n equals the performance window. In general, the effects of the transaction-specific exploratory variables are sought. In this case, the prediction power will be given by:

$$\ln \frac{P_i}{1 - P_i} = a_0 + a_1 RiskUnit_{risklevel} + a_2 T_1 + \cdots + a_{n+1} T_n$$

The example presented in Section 2.10 is now revisited, reviewing the logistic regression model Exhibit 7.7, where the multiple categories for the explanatory variables have been identified.

To explain the model, the example used in the paragraphs presents the case of two predictor variables and introduces the issue of missing values. Suppose there are missing values in the second covariate. Let X_1 have categories $1, \cdots, J$ and X_2 have categories $1, \cdots, K$. The $P(Y = 1|X_1 = j, X_2 = k)$ is given by $\dfrac{\exp\left(\beta_0 + \beta_{1j} X_{1j} + \beta_{2k} X_{2k}\right)}{1 + \exp\left(\beta_0 + \beta_{1j} X_{1j} + \beta_{2k} X_{2k}\right)}$ [Vach (1994)].

The observability of x_2 is indicated by an indicator random variable O_2 with two values 0 when X_2 is not observable and 1 when X_2 is observable. Instead of X_2, the random variable $Z_2 = X_2$ is used when O_2 is equal to 1 and $Z_2 = K + 1$ when $O_2 = 0$, where K is the number of categories; that is, Z_2 has an additional category for missing values. The joint distribution of (Y, X, Z_2) can be written in terms of the conditional distribution of O_2 given (Y, X_1, X_2).

This conditional distribution is called the "missing value mechanism" described by the observation probabilities:

$$q_{ijk} = P(O_2 = 1|Y = i, X_1 = j, X_2 = k)$$

EXHIBIT 7.6　LOGISTIC REGRESSIONS INCLUDING MULTIPLE CATEGORIES

Multiple Response Insured

```
data insured;
  drop z1-z9;
  x1 = 0; x2 = 0; x3 = 0;
  if n = 1 then x1 = 1;
  if n = 2 then x2 = 1;
  if n = 3 then x3 = 1;
  array z z1-z9;
  input z1-z9;
  do over z;
    y = _i_ ;
    freq = z;
    output;
  end;
cards;
0 0 1 7  8 8 19 8 1
6 9 12 11 76 1 0 0
1 1 6 8 23 7 5 1 0
0 0 0 1  3 7 14 16 11
;
run;
proc logistic
  data=insured;
  freq freq;
  model y = x1-x3;
  title1 'Multiple
    Response
    Deductibles';
run;
```

The LOGISTIC Procedure

Data Set: WORK.INSURED
Response Variable: Y
Response Levels: 9
Number of Observations: 28
Frequency Variable: FREQ
Link Function: Logit

Response Profile

Ordered Value	Y	Count
1	1	7
2	2	10
3	3	19
4	4	27
5	5	41
6	6	28
7	7	39
8	8	25
9	9	12

NOTE: 8 observation(s) having zero frequencies or weights were excluded since they do not contribute to the analysis.

Score Test for the Proportional Odds Assumption

Chi-Square = 17.2868 with 21 DF (p=0.6936)

Model Fitting Information and Testing Global Null Hypothesis BETA=0

Criterion	Intercept Only	Intercept and Covariates	Chi-Square for Covariates
AIC	875.802	733.348	.
SC	902.502	770.061	.
-2 LOG L	859.802	711.348	148.454 with 3 DF (p=0.0001)
Score	.	.	111.267 with 3 DF (p=0.0001)

Analysis of Maximum Likelihood Estimates

Variable	DF	Parameter Estimate	Standard Error	Wald Chi-Square	Pr > Chi-Square	Standardized Estimate	Odds Ratio
INTERCP1	1	-7.0802	0.5624	158.4865	0.0001	.	.
INTERCP2	1	-6.0250	0.4755	160.5507	0.0001	.	.
INTERCP3	1	-4.9254	0.4272	132.9477	0.0001	.	.
INTERCP4	1	-3.8568	0.3902	97.7086	0.0001	.	.
INTERCP5	1	-2.5206	0.3431	53.9713	0.0001	.	.
INTERCP6	1	-1.5685	0.3086	25.8379	0.0001	.	.
INTERCP7	1	-0.0669	0.2658	0.0633	0.8013	.	.
INTERCP8	1	1.4930	0.3310	20.3443	0.0001	.	.
X1	1	1.6128	0.3778	18.2258	0.0001	0.385954	5.017
X2	1	4.9646	0.4741	109.6453	0.0001	1.188080	143.257
X3	1	3.3227	0.4251	61.0936	0.0001	0.795146	27.735

Association of Predicted Probabilities and Observed Responses

Concordant = 67.6%	Somers' D = 0.578
Discordant = 9.8%	Gamma = 0.746
Tied = 22.6%	Tau-a = 0.500
(18635 pairs)	c = 0.789

EXHIBIT 7.7   MULTIPLE CATEGORIES IN EXPLANATORY VARIABLES

EXAMPLE MULTIPLE CATEGORIES IN EXPLANATORY VARIABLES LOGISTIC REGRESSION

Using Rattle, the code indicates some of the main aspects to provide a training and test data for a logistics model. At the same time, the output is about a mix of quantitative and qualitative variables. The test for coefficients and for ANOVA and the variables indicate the significant variables testing the null hypotheses of coefficients equal zero. The concept of deviance is about the minus two times the difference of the two models restricted and unrestricted:

nobs=45211 train=31648 validate=6782 test=6781

```
set.seed(crv$seed)
crs$nobs <- nrow(crs$dataset)
crs$train <- sample(crs$nobs, 0.7*crs$nobs)
crs$nobs %>%
  seq_len() %>%
  setdiff(crs$train) %>%
  sample(0.15*crs$nobs) ->
crs$validate

crs$nobs %>%
  seq_len() %>%
  setdiff(crs$train) %>%
  setdiff(crs$validate) ->
crs$test
```

```
# selection of variables for the model
crs$input <- c("age", "job", "marital", "education", "default", "balance", "housing", "loan",
"contact", "day", "month", "duration", "campaign", "pdays", "previous", "poutcome")

crs$numeric <- c("age", "balance", "day", "duration", "campaign", "pdays", "previous")

crs$categoric <- c("job", "marital", "education", "default", "housing", "loan", "contact",
"month", "poutcome")

crs$target <- "y"
crs$risk <- NULL
crs$ident <- NULL
crs$ignore <- NULL
crs$weights <- NULL

crs$glm <- glm(y ~ .,data=crs$dataset[crs$train, c(crs$input, crs$target)], family=binomial
(link="logit"))
```

```
# review of model summary

print(summary(crs$glm))

cat(sprintf("Log likelihood: %.3f (%d df)\n",
    logLik(crs$glm)[1],
    attr(logLik(crs$glm), "df")))
```

```
cat(sprintf("Null/Residual deviance difference: %.3f (%d df)\n",
    crs$glm$null.deviance-crs$glm$deviance,
    crs$glm$df.null-crs$glm$df.residual))
```

```
cat(sprintf("Chi-square p-value: %.8f\n",
    dchisq(crs$glm$null.deviance-crs$glm$deviance,
        crs$glm$df.null-crs$glm$df.residual)))
```

```
cat(sprintf("Pseudo R-Square (optimistic): %.8f\n",
    cor(crs$glm$y, crs$glm$fitted.values)))
```

```
cat('\n==== ANOVA ====\n\n')
print(anova(crs$glm, test="Chisq"))
cat("\n")
```

Time taken: 5.76 secs
Summary of the Logistic Regression model (built using glm):

Call:
glm(formula = y ~ ., family = binomial(link = "logit"), data = crs$dataset[crs$train,
    c(crs$input, crs$target)])
Deviance Residuals:

Min	1Q	Median	3Q	Max
−4.7621	−0.3746	−0.2525	−0.1508	3.2765

	Estimate	Std. Error	z value	Pr(>|z|)	
(Intercept)	−2.422770218	0.221485800	−10.94	< 2e-16	***
age	−0.001756971	0.002637083	−0.666	0.505248	
job[T.blue-collar]	−0.33249268	0.085932420	−3.869	0.000109	***
job[T.entrepreneur]	−0.622825426	0.158802737	−3.922	0.0000878	***
job[T.housemaid]	−0.432269194	0.158769629	−2.723	0.006477	**
job[T.management]	−0.181899551	0.087139118	−2.087	0.036846	*
job[T.retired]	0.291897024	0.116639497	2.503	0.01233	*
job[T.self-employed]	−0.255843397	0.132512067	−1.931	0.053518	.
job[T.services]	−0.313048133	0.101308150	−3.090	0.002001	**
job[T.student]	0.331616759	0.130922262	2.533	0.011311	*
job[T.technician]	−0.248330641	0.082211531	−3.021	0.002522	**
job[T.unemployed]	−0.209808790	0.131626334	−1.594	0.110942	
job[T.unknown]	−0.198952098	0.272221003	−0.731	0.464872	
marital[T.married]	−0.236802448	0.069741602	−3.395	0.000685	***
marital[T.single]	0.012225921	0.079697409	0.153	0.878079	
education[T.secondary]	0.231447330	0.077224659	2.997	0.002726	**
education[T.tertiary]	0.396557684	0.089529288	4.429	9.45E-06	***
education[T.unknown]	0.324928317	0.124060327	2.619	0.008816	**
default[T.yes]	0.025900792	0.195994884	0.132	0.894865	
balance	0.000013862	0.000006433	2.155	0.031176	*
housing[T.yes]	−0.644829814	0.052488480	−12.29	< 2e-16	***
loan[T.yes]	−0.498960994	0.072489624	−6.883	5.85E-12	***
contact[T.telephone]	−0.044940638	0.088610524	−0.507	0.612035	
contact[T.unknown]	−1.510556491	0.087337702	−17.3	< 2e-16	***
day	0.00961882	0.002987838	3.219	0.001285	**

month[T.aug]	−0.691453072	0.093441118	−7.400	1.36E-13	***
month[T.dec]	0.566244918	0.205438477	2.756	0.005846	**
month[T.feb]	−0.13427387	0.106071411	−1.266	0.205555	
month[T.jan]	−1.370863616	0.148639924	−9.223	< 2e-16	***
month[T.jul]	−0.816619158	0.091861941	−8.890	< 2e-16	***
month[T.jun]	0.358126853	0.113025342	3.169	0.001532	**
month[T.mar]	1.573434695	0.143999301	10.927	< 2e-16	***
month[T.may]	−0.502399829	0.086596654	−5.802	6.57E-09	***
month[T.nov]	−0.894687737	0.100322304	−8.918	< 2e-16	***
month[T.oct]	0.793457950	0.128141079	6.192	5.94E-10	***
month[T.sep]	0.813140983	0.145317271	5.596	2.2E-08	***
duration	0.004224001	0.000077584	54.444	< 2e-16	***
campaign	−0.099563098	0.012412418	−8.021	1.05E-15	***
pdays	0.000054804	0.000365540	0.150	0.880823	
previous	0.019404622	0.012673020	1.531	0.125726	
poutcome[T.other]	0.107062593	0.108966413	0.983	0.32584	
poutcome[T.success]	2.313798331	0.099089840	23.351	< 2e-16	***
poutcome[T.unknown]	−0.049398169	0.118053322	−0.418	0.675626	

Signif. codes: 0 '***' 0.001 '**' 0.01 '*' 0.05 '.' 0.1 ' ' 1

(Dispersion parameter for binomial family taken to be 1)

Null deviance: 22824 on 31646 degrees of freedom
Residual deviance: 15078 on 31604 degrees of freedom
AIC: 15164

Number of Fisher Scoring iterations: 6

Log likelihood: −7539.099 (43 df)
Null/Residual deviance difference: 7745.907 (42 df)
Chi-square p-value: 0.00000000
Pseudo R-Square (optimistic): 0.55885466

==== ANOVA ====
Analysis of Deviance Table

Model: binomial, link: logit

Response: y

Terms added sequentially (first to last)

	Df	Deviance	Resid. Df	Resid. Dev	Pr(>Chi)	
NULL			31646	22824		
age	1	18.0	31645	22806	2.17E-05	***
job	11	486.2	31634	22320	< 2.2e-16	***
marital	2	93.8	31632	22226	< 2.2e-16	***
education	3	80.8	31629	22145	< 2.2e-16	***
default	1	14.9	31628	22130	0.000112	***
balance	1	40.0	31627	22090	2.58E-10	***
housing	1	353.8	31626	21737	< 2.2e-16	***
loan	1	113.4	31625	21623	< 2.2e-16	***

contact	2	533.2	31623	21090	< 2.2e-16	***
day	1	33.0	31622	21057	9.26E-09	***
month	11	938.0	31611	20119	< 2.2e-16	***
duration	1	3961.1	31610	16158	< 2.2e-16	***
campaign	1	109.4	31609	16048	< 2.2e-16	***
pdays	1	95.4	31608	15953	< 2.2e-16	***
previous	1	50.6	31607	15902	1.16E-12	***
poutcome	3	824.3	31604	15078	< 2.2e-16	***

Signif. codes: 0 '***' 0.001 '**' 0.01 '*' 0.05 '.' 0.1 ' ' 1

Time taken: 5.76 secs

Observing n independent realizations $Y_r, X_{1r}, Z_{2r},\ r = 1, \cdots, n$ it is found a table of $2 \times J \times (K + 1)$ with entries and n_{ijk} is the number of r such that $Y_r = i,\ X_{1r} = j,\ Z_{2r} = k$.

and with the cell probabilities given by:

$$p_{ijk} = q_{ijk} p_{ijk}^*, \quad if\ K \neq K + 1$$

and

$$p_{ij(k+1)} = \sum_{k=1}^{K} (1 - q_{ijk}) p_{ijk}^*,$$

where $p_{ijk}^* = P(Y = i, X_1 = j, X_2 = k)$ or, equivalently,

$$p_{ijk}^* = P(Y = 1 | X_1 = j, X_2 = k)^i (1 - P(Y = 1 | X_1 = j, X_2 = k))^{1-i}$$

$$P(X_2 = k | X_1 = j) P(X_1 = j)$$

Using factors as explanatory variables is possible to perform regression. The following example of car insurance rating and variable selection is found in Stroinsky and Currie (1989); that is, using a factor model with the factors as explanatory variables and used with a small few values and the data can be presented in two ways: individual or cumulative form with a generalized linear model (GLM) for each of these forms. To describe the automobile insurance portfolio, the independent observations y_i of the number of claims produced by each individual policy is given by $y_i = \lambda_i + \epsilon_i, i = 1, \cdots, n$; that is, the sum of the systematic and random components. Where there is an invertible link function $g(\lambda) = X\beta$, the link function linearizes λ_i with respect to p unknown parameters β_j. The matrix X consists of the values x_{ij}, for $i = 1, \cdots, n$ and $j = 1, \cdots, p$, of the explanatory variables and is full rank p. βX is called the linear predictor and is denoted by η.

In the cumulative model, the matrix X gives the total number of claims from the policies having equal combination of factor levels. The matrix X^{cum} consists of only the explanatory matrix in the original matrix X with different policy profiles. It is a way to reduce the computational problems. Y_i denote the number of claims produced by policy i in a certain rating unit period.

Theorem:

Let $\hat{\beta}$ be the vector of estimates obtained by fitting the GLM to the data y_i using the formulas

$$\hat{\beta}^* = \hat{\beta} + (X\hat{V}^{-1}X)^{-1}X^T\hat{Z}^*,$$

where

$$\hat{\mathbf{V}} = diag a_i(\phi) b''[k(\hat{\eta}_i)][g'(\hat{\lambda}_i)]^2$$

$$\hat{z}_i = \hat{\eta}_i + (y_i - \hat{\lambda}_i) g'(\hat{\lambda}_i)$$

$$\hat{\eta}_i = x_i^T \hat{\beta}, \hat{\lambda}_i = g^{-1}(\hat{\eta}_i)$$

and a chosen vector of initial estimates $\widehat{\beta_0}$. Then, if $\tilde{\beta}$ is the vector of estimates obtained by fitting the corresponding cumulation model y_j^{cum}, using the formulas for the cumulation model and starting from the same initial estimates $\widehat{\beta_0}$ the identity $\hat{\beta} = \tilde{\beta}$ follows.

The set of factors could be large, and it is possible to have a large number of potential cross classifications. Then, with the classical additive regression model (normal errors and identity link) and the standard multiplicative model (Poisson errors with logarithmic link), the main effects models are selected using forward and backward selection.

The set of ten factors splits into three subsets in a hierarchy of importance. Age, rating group, and class are the most important. Voluntary excess, experience, voluntary restriction, and year of manufacture are the second. District and sex are not statistically significant. There are methods for clustering or segmentation of portfolio risks. For example, Beirlant et al. (1998) use the Burr regression. The Burr regression model is given with the density function:

$$f(y) = \frac{\lambda \tau \beta^\lambda y^{\tau-1}}{(\beta + y^\tau)^{\lambda+1}}, \quad y > 0, \beta, \tau, \lambda > 0$$

and the regression model:

$$Y|\mathbf{x} \sim Burr(\beta(\mathbf{x}), \lambda, \tau), \quad \beta(\mathbf{x}) = \exp(\tau \Theta' \mathbf{x})$$

where Θ is the p-dimensional vector of regression coefficients. The variables for the model are related to claim ratios and the groups of automobiles. The model uses dummy variables $d_{ij} = 1$ if observation belongs to automobile category j, $d_{\{ij\}} = -1$ if observation i belongs to the automobile category $k+1$ and $d_{ij} = 0$; otherwise $j = 1, \cdots, k$.

7.9   CORRESPONDENCE ANALYSIS

A model with two response variables could be, for example, bad and good risks. The choice depends on the expected forecasting power. To evaluate the number of insureds in each group, the tests χ^2 and Student-T values are used. Examples of variables and categories are marital status, sex, age, class of tariff, car trademark, driving experience, profession, bonus-malus class, geographic zone, selected coverage, or type of driving [for more details see Greenacre (1984), Andersen (1990)].

With this information, the following steps are carried out:

1. Correspondence analysis.
2. Choice of axis.
3. Factorial discriminant analysis, analysis of the results, two-way classification. Definition of the good and bad characteristics.
4. Validation sample test.
5. Analysis of a new sample and relation with the results.
6. Analysis of the cross-classification variables and interaction effects. Here, a reduction of the correlation effect is sought to improve the predictive power of the model.

Loss ratios of claims over premiums in a given period, for example three years, can be used, to identify good and bad risks. The definition of bad is part of the complexity of the process. The researcher/analyst will decide the criteria. For example, values greater than two claims or at least one claim with corporal damages in one period would be classified as bad. Variables and categories are obtained from the sample. Correspondence analysis is built through a contingency table (see Exhibit 7.8) with the following attributes (see Johnson, 1998).

X is a $I \times J$ two-way table of unscaled frequencies or counts. $I > J$ and X is of full column rank J. I is the number of individuals and J is the total number of response categories to the questionnaire. P is called the correspondence matrix. $\tilde{P}$ is centered by subtracting the product of the row total and the column total from each entry. That is

$$\mathbf{P} = (P_{ij}) = \frac{(X_{ij})}{n} = \frac{1}{n}\mathbf{X},$$

for i = 1, $\cdots$, I and j = 1, $\cdots$, J. Now

$$r = \mathbf{P}1$$
$$c = \mathbf{P}'1$$

and hence

$$\tilde{p}_{ij} = p_{ij} - r_i c_j,$$

which gives

$$\tilde{\mathbf{P}} = \mathbf{P} - rc'.$$

For diagonal matrices $D_r = \text{diag}(r_1, r_2, ..., r_I)$ and $D_c = \text{diag}(c_1, c_2, ..., c_J)$ define the scaled matrix

$$\mathbf{P}^* = \mathbf{D}_r^{-1/2}(\tilde{\mathbf{P}})\mathbf{D}_c^{-1/2}$$

The following steps are required to find the coordinates of the points in the graph:

Step 1. Find the singular value decomposition of P*

$$\mathbf{P}^* = \mathbf{U\Lambda V'},$$

with $\text{rank}(\mathbf{P}^*) = \text{rank}(\tilde{\mathbf{P}}) \leq J - 1$ and $\Lambda = \text{diag}(\lambda_1, \cdots, \lambda_{J-1})$, contains the singular values ordered from largest to smallest.

$$\mathbf{U'U} = \mathbf{V'V} = \mathbf{I}.$$

Step 2. Set

$$\tilde{\mathbf{U}} = \mathbf{D}_r^{1/2}\mathbf{U},$$

And

$$\tilde{\mathbf{V}} = \mathbf{D}_c^{1/2}\mathbf{V}.$$

The singular value decomposition of $\tilde{P}$ is given by

$$\tilde{P} = P - rc' = \tilde{U}\Lambda\tilde{V}'$$
$$= \sum_{j=1}^{J-1} \lambda_j \tilde{u}_j \tilde{v}_j',$$

where $\tilde{u}_j$, $\tilde{v}_j'$ are the j-th column vector of $\tilde{U}$ and $\tilde{V}$, respectively.

$$\tilde{U}'D_r^{-1}\tilde{U} = \tilde{V}'D_c^{-1}\tilde{V} = I$$

The columns of $\tilde{U}$ define the coordinate axes for the points (see Exhibit 7.10) representing the column profiles of P and the columns of $\tilde{V}$ define the coordinate axes for the points representing the row profiles of P.

$$Y = D_r^{-1}\tilde{U}\Lambda$$

Step 3. Calculate the coordinates of the row profiles and the coordinates of the column profiles

$$Z = D_c^{-1}\tilde{V}\Lambda.$$

The two first columns of Y and Z contain the points and column points in the best two-dimensional representations of data.

Step 4. The total inertia (see Exhibit 7.9) is the sum of squares of the non-zero singular values

$$\text{Total inertia} = \sum_{i=1}^{K} \lambda_i^2,$$

where $\lambda_1 \geq \lambda_2 \cdots \geq \lambda_k \geq 0$, K = rank($\tilde{P}$) and rank($\tilde{P}$) = min($I - 1, J - 1$) usually.

The χ^2 statistic measures the degree of association between the row and column variables in a two-way contingency table with I rows and J columns. $O_{ij} = x_{ij}$ is the observed frequency and the E_{ij} is the expected frequency in the $(i, j)th$ cell if the row variable is independent of the column variable. Then

$$\chi^2 = \sum_{i,j} \frac{(O_{ij} - E_{ij})^2}{E_{ij}}.$$

With $E_{ij} = nr_i c_j$ the latter can be re-written as

$$\chi^2 = n\sum_{i,j} \frac{(p_{ij} - r_i c_j)^2}{r_i c_j},$$

which is seen as a discrepancy between P and rc'. Equivalently the matrix notation

$$\text{Inertia} = \frac{\chi^2}{n} = \text{trace}(D_r^{-1}(P - rc')D_c^{-1}(P - rc')') = \sum_{k=1}^{J-1} \lambda_k^2$$

where the inertia is the weighted sum of the square distances of the row profiles (or column profiles) to the centroid. The inertia associated with the row points is the same as the inertia associated with the column points

$$\mathbf{Y'D}_r\mathbf{Y} = \Lambda^2 = \mathbf{Z'D}_c\mathbf{Z}.$$

The following illustrates the process using SAS. Consider a contingency table and the procedure PROC CORRESP in SAS. The data gives the variable, claim, and driver gender and age. The categories are: Yes or No Claim, Male or Female, and Age 60+, 18–25, 25–35, 35–45, 45–60 denoted in the output by E1, E2, E3, E4, E5 the age levels; no1, no2 represent no claims for males and females; Yes1, Yes2 represent claims for males and females, respectively.

The following Exhibit 7.8 of frequencies gives the relation among the three variables.

It is shown that the males with claims of age 60+ and the females with claims of ages 18–25 make the largest individual contribution to the χ^2. For the row profiles, the males with claims and the females with claims yield the largest χ^2 contribution, whereas for column profiles the largest contributions to the χ^2 come from age 60+ and ages 18–25.

The following exhibits show the vectors of row and column conditional densities.

The Pearson χ^2 statistic is 70.917, which has a p-value of 0.000. The total inertia represents the magnitude of the departure from independence that needs to be explained. The term departure from independence is the departure of the observed cell frequencies from the cell frequencies expected under independence. The total inertia in this example is 0.17597. This can be allocated to the three dimensions, four rows, and four columns.

With these values, it is possible to build a chart. It uses two dimensions with 0.14191 and 0.03286 inertias. The first dimension reflects a contrast between females of different ages and males with claims. The second-row dimension is a measure of males with different ages but not claims. The column profile represents a contrast between ages 18–25, ages 35–45, and age 60+. The second dimension for column profile deviations seems to reflect a contrast among the three ages 25–25, 35–45, 45–60 with age 60+. These points mean males tend to have higher rates of claims at age 60+ and lower rates of claim for other ages.

Now the multiway correspondence analysis is indicated for multiple responses when there are different groups of insureds. The method used $Z = [Z_1, \cdots, Z_Q]$, is a Q-variate indicator matrix. Each Z_Q is a matrix representing the variable and the categories of this variable [see Greenacre (1984) and Andersen (1994)]. The problem in multiway tables is to find n appropriate two-way matrices to perform the decomposition. The Burt-matrix B is used; $Z^T Z$ is defined as:

EXHIBIT 7.8   CREATION OF CONTINGENCY TABLE FOR CORRESPONDENCE ANALYSIS

Contingency Table

	E1	E2	E3	E4	E5	Sum
no1	8	11	5	7	12	43
no2	5	15	3	1	6	30
yes1	105	32	11	23	37	208
yes2	32	57	6	2	25	122
Sum	150	115	25	33	80	403

Contributions to the Total Chi-Square Statistic

	E1	E2	E3	E4	E5	Sum
no1	4.0037	0.1315	2.0396	3.4372	1.4057	11.0178
no2	3.4051	4.8434	0.6970	0.8636	0.0003	9.8096
yes1	9.8256	12.6070	0.2807	2.0910	0.4458	25.2501
yes2	3.9598	14.1387	0.3250	6.3905	0.0252	24.8392
Sum	21.1943	31.7207	3.3423	12.7823	1.8771	70.9167

EXHIBIT 7.9　DEFINITION OF THE PROFILES IN CORRESPONDENCE ANALYSIS

Row Profiles

	E1	E2	E3	E4	E5
no1	0.186047	0.255814	0.116279	0.162791	0.279070
no2	0.166667	0.500000	0.100000	0.033333	0.200000
yes1	0.504808	0.153846	0.052885	0.110577	0.177885
yes2	0.262295	0.467213	0.049180	0.016393	0.204918

Column Profiles

	E1	E2	E3	E4	E5
no1	0.053333	0.095652	0.200000	0.212121	0.150000
no2	0.033333	0.130435	0.120000	0.030303	0.075000
yes1	0.700000	0.278261	0.440000	0.696970	0.462500
yes2	0.213333	0.495652	0.240000	0.060606	0.312500

Inertia and Chi-Square Decomposition

Singular Values	Principal Inertias	Chi-Squares	Percents	16　32　48　64　80
				----+----+----+----+----+---
0.37672	0.14191	57.1917	80.65%	*************************
0.18127	0.03286	13.2414	18.67%	******
0.03464	0.00120	0.4835	0.68%	
	-------	-------		
	0.17597	70.9167	(Degrees of Freedom = 12)	

EXHIBIT 7.10　IDENTIFICATION OF COORDINATES OF THE POINTS IN CORRESPONDENCE ANALYSIS

Row Coordinates

	Dim1	Dim2
no1	0.044308	0.503481
no2	0.554074	0.089193
yes1	-.344733	-.050263
yes2	0.435876	-.113695

Column Coordinates

	Dim1	Dim2
E1	-.338434	-.163372
E2	0.521948	-.058182
E3	0.075066	0.342023
E4	-.498154	0.372821
E5	0.066295	0.129288

$$Z^TZ = \begin{bmatrix} \mathbf{Z}_1^T\mathbf{Z}_1 & \mathbf{Z}_1^T\mathbf{Z}_2 & \cdots & \mathbf{Z}_1^T\mathbf{Z}_Q \\ \mathbf{Z}_2^T\mathbf{Z}_1 & \mathbf{Z}_2^T\mathbf{Z}_2 & \cdots & \mathbf{Z}_2^T\mathbf{Z}_Q \\ \vdots & \vdots & \ddots & \vdots \\ \mathbf{Z}_Q^T\mathbf{Z}_1 & \mathbf{Z}_Q^T\mathbf{Z}_2 & \cdots & \mathbf{Z}_Q^T\mathbf{Z}_Q \end{bmatrix}$$

where $Z_q^TZ_{q'}$ for $q \neq q'$, is a two way contingency table. It condenses the association between variables q and q' across the I individuals (I rows). $Z_q^TZ_q$ is the diagonal matrix of column sums of Z_q or QIc^Z. Z^TZ is positive, semidefinite and symmetric. It has $J = J_1 + \cdots + J_Q$ columns where the q-th matrix Z_q, corresponding to the q-th discrete variable, has J_q columns for each of the J_q categories.

There are QI ones in Z, I in each submatrix Z_q; the other entries are zero. The vector c^Z of column masses of Z is given by $c^Z = (1/QI)Z^T1$, while the subset of masses for the columns of Z_q are denoted by the vector $c_q^Z = (1/QI)Z_q^T1$. The following results suppose that there are responses in all the categories of response.

1. The sum of the masses of the columns of Z_q is $1/Q$ for all $q = 1, \cdots, Q$.
2. The centroid of the column profiles of Z_q is at the origin of the display; that is at the centroid of all the column profiles.
3. The column profile total inertia is $inertia(J) = J/Q - 1$ (similarly for the row profiles).
4. The inertia of the column profiles of Z_q is $inertia(J_q) = (J_q - 1)/Q$.
5. The inertia of a particular category j is $inertia(j) = 1/Q - c_j^Z$.
6. The number of non-trivial dimensions with positive inertia is at most $J - Q$.
7. The standard coordinates in the analysis of Z^TZ are identical to the standard coordinates of the columns in the analysis of Z. And $\lambda^B = (\lambda^Z)^{1/2}$ the principal inertias λ^B in the analysis of the Burt matrix have the squares of those of the indicator matrix.

The correspondence analysis of Z or Z^TZ does not take into account associations among more than two discrete variables but rather looks at all the two-way associations jointly.

The standard coordinates are given by $\Gamma^B = R^B\Gamma^B(D_\lambda^B)^{-1/2}$, where R^B is defined as

$$\begin{bmatrix} \mathbf{I} & \mathbf{R}_{12} & \cdots & \mathbf{R}_{1Q} \\ \mathbf{R}_{21} & \mathbf{I} & \cdots & \mathbf{R}_{2Q} \\ \vdots & \vdots & \ddots & \vdots \\ \mathbf{R}_{Q1} & \mathbf{R}_{Q2} & \cdots & \mathbf{I} \end{bmatrix}$$

Here, R_{qq} is the matrix of row profiles of the two-way contingency tables $Z_q^TZ_q$ and Γ^B can be partitioned into Q sets of rows Γ_q^B with $q = 1, \cdots, Q$, in which case

$$\Gamma_q^B = \left(\frac{1}{Q}\right)(\Gamma_q^B + \sum_{q'\neq q} \mathbf{R}_{qq'}\Gamma_{q'}^B)(\mathbf{D}_\lambda^B)^{-1/2},$$

for $q = 1, \cdots, Q$.

Collecting terms in Γ_q^B and remembering that $\Gamma^Z = \Gamma^B$ and $D_\lambda^Z = (D_\lambda^Z) = (D_\lambda^B)^{-1/2}$, the expression for the coordinates of the categories of variable q in terms of those of the other variables in the correspondence analysis of Z are

$$\Gamma_q^Z(Q\mathbf{D}_\lambda^Z - I) = \sum_{q'\neq q} \mathbf{R}_{qq'}\Gamma_{q'}^z.$$

One remark about correspondence analysis is that the coordinates of the points are re-parametrizations of the x_{ik}, y_{jk} scores in the general canonical correlation model. Correspondence analysis uses adjusted scores

$$x_{ik}^* = \lambda_k x_{ik} \text{ and } y_{jk}^* = \lambda_k y_{jk}$$

As an illustration, consider the relations among number of drivers, claim size, drink or no alcohol (Exhibit 7.11):

The Burt matrix is obtained from the contingency table (Exhibit 7.12). The variable I represents the level of claim, with four categories. The variable D represents the number of drivers with two categories. Finally, S means if the driver consumes alcohol or not.

The correspondence analysis procedure illustration:

The multiple correspondence analysis of the Burt matrix yields five dimensions. Two dimensions yield principal inertias of 0.444 and 0.3587. Here, distances between points do not have a direct interpretation. Higher claim levels are associated with the categories drink alcohol and more than one driver.

EXHIBIT 7.11   MULTIFACTOR CORRESPONDENCE ANALYSIS SAS CODE

```
data cars;
input i1 i2 i3 i4 d1 d2 s1 s2;
cards;
78776 0 0 0 74471 4305 12813 65963
0 4647 0 0 4123 524 647 4000
0 0 3001 0 2616 385 2642 359
0 0 0 345 275 70 42 303
74471 4123 2616 275 81485 0 13486 67999
4305 524 385 70 0 5284 375 4909
12813 647 2642 42 13486 375 13861 0
65963 4000 359 303 67999 4909 0 72908
;
proc corresp mca data=cars outc=results all nvars=3;
var i1 i2 i3 i4 d1 d2 s1 s2;
run;
data results;
set results;
y=dim1;
x=dim2;
xsys='2';
ysys='2';
text=_name_;
size=1.5;
label y='dimension1'
      x='dimension2';
keep x y text xsys ysys size;
run;
proc gplot data=results;
symbol1 v=none;
axis1 length=3.6 in order=-2 to 8 by 1;
plot y*x=1 / annotate=results frame haxis=axis1 vaxis=axis1
      href=0 vref=0;
run;
```

EXHIBIT 7.12 MULTIPLE CORRESPONDENCE PROCESS

The Correspondence Analysis Procedure

Contingency Table

	I1	I2	I3	I4	D1	D2	S1	S2	Sum
I1	78776	0	0	0	74471	4305	12813	65963	236328
I2	0	4647	0	0	4123	524	647	4000	13941
I3	0	0	3001	0	2616	385	2642	359	9003
I4	0	0	0	345	275	70	42	303	1035
D1	74471	4123	2616	275	81485	0	13486	67999	244455
D2	4305	524	385	70	0	5284	375	4909	15852
S1	12813	647	2642	42	13486	375	13861	0	43866
S2	65963	4000	359	303	67999	4909	0	72908	216441
Sum	236328	13941	9003	1035	244455	15852	43866	216441	780921

Column Profiles

	I1	I2	I3	I4	D1	D2	S1	S2
I1	0.333333	0.000000	0.000000	0.000000	0.304641	0.271575	0.292094	0.304762
I2	0.000000	0.333333	0.000000	0.000000	0.016866	0.033056	0.014749	0.018481
I3	0.000000	0.000000	0.333333	0.000000	0.010701	0.024287	0.060229	0.001659
I4	0.000000	0.000000	0.000000	0.333333	0.001125	0.004416	0.000957	0.001400
D1	0.315117	0.295746	0.290570	0.265700	0.333333	0.000000	0.307436	0.314169
D2	0.018216	0.037587	0.042764	0.067633	0.000000	0.333333	0.008549	0.022681
S1	0.054217	0.046410	0.293458	0.040580	0.055168	0.023656	0.315985	0.000000
S2	0.279116	0.286923	0.039876	0.292754	0.278166	0.309677	0.000000	0.336849

Contributions to the Total Chi-Square Statistic

	I1	I2	I3	I4	D1	D2	S1	S2	Sum
I1	736	4219	2725	313	3	51	16	3	8066
I2	4219	77724	161	18	13	205	24	5	82369
I3	2725	161	80871	12	15	224	9024	1829	94859
I4	313	18	12	86080	7	114	4	1	86551
D1	3	13	15	7	322	4962	4	1	5328
D2	51	205	224	114	4962	76523	298	60	82438
S1	16	24	9024	4	4	298	52714	12158	74243
S2	3	5	1829	1	1	60	12158	2782	16839
Sum	8066	82369	94859	86551	5328	82438	74243	16839	450694

The Correspondence Analysis Procedure

Inertia and Chi-Square Decomposition

	Singular Values	Principal Inertias	Chi-Squares	Percents	5 10 15 20 25
I1	0.66647	0.44418	121021	26.85%	*************************************
I2	0.59891	0.35870	97731.9	21.68%	*****************************
I3	0.57735	0.33333	90820.7	20.15%	***************************
I4	0.55984	0.31342	85393.9	18.95%	*************************
D1	0.45225	0.20453	55726.1	12.36%	*****************
		1.65415	450694		(Degrees of Freedom = 49)

Column Coordinates

	Dim1	Dim2
I1	-0.12000	-0.19403
I2	-0.28283	2.31210
I3	4.44321	0.69746
I4	-0.41519	6.14177
D1	-0.00931	-0.19224
D2	-0.08582	2.99573
S1	1.75047	-0.19149
S2	-0.37156	0.04109

Summary Statistics for the Column Points

	Quality	Mass	Inertia
I1	0.500188	0.302627	0.019037
I2	0.306983	0.017852	0.190749
I3	0.724599	0.011529	0.194568
I4	0.151268	0.001325	0.200714
D1	0.565586	0.313034	0.012395
D2	0.582408	0.020299	0.189250
S1	0.670225	0.056172	0.157109
S2	0.647241	0.277161	0.036178

Partial Contributions to Inertia for the Column Points

	Dim1	Dim2
I1	0.009810	0.031764
I2	0.003215	0.266054
I3	0.512411	0.015635
I4	0.000514	0.139377
D1	0.000061	0.032253
D2	0.000337	0.507871
S1	0.387504	0.005742
S2	0.086148	0.001305

Indices of the Coordinates that Contribute Most to Inertia for the Column Points

	Dim1	Dim2	Best
I1	0	0	2
I2	0	2	2
I3	1	0	1
I4	0	2	2
D1	0	0	2
D2	0	2	2
S1	1	0	1
S2	0	0	1

Squared Cosines for the Column Points

	Dim1	Dim2
I1	0.138374	0.361814
I2	0.004526	0.302457
I3	0.707175	0.017425
I4	0.000688	0.150580
D1	0.001323	0.564263
D2	0.000478	0.581930
S1	0.662300	0.007926
S2	0.639421	0.007820

7.10 MORE ABOUT MULTIVARIATE TOOLS

Once groups and variables have been defined, it is possible to assign observations to these groups. This is the following step in the classification process where the problem no longer requires a cluster analysis but a classification analysis. For numerical continuous variables, a discriminant analysis is used, while for categorical variables it is logistic regression presented before or any of the machine learning tools that are appropriate for the problems, data, and implementation needs.

In the case of numerical data, the value of claims and the coverage taken by the risk unit are used. These depend on the automobile value, the coverage, the premiums paid, and the value of deductibles or franchises. In a case like this, it is possible to use discriminant analysis. The populations are assumed normally distributed. There are cases in the analysis where it is required to reduce the dimensionality of the data and principal components and factor analysis can help to identify the best combination of variables to use.

The essential concepts and results of an analysis of principal components looks for explaining the variance-covariance structure of a set of variables by means of the linear combination of these variables. The search is now about a p variable k principal component with n measurements. The principal components are the linear combinations of not correlated variables with the highest variances as possible (see examples Table 7.6). Take p random variables $X_1, X_2 \ldots X_p$, the random vector $X' = [\, X_1, X_2 \ldots X_p]$ with covariance matrix Σ and with eigenvalues $\lambda_1 \geq \lambda_2 \ldots \geq \lambda_p \geq 0$. The linear combinations:

$$Y_1 = a'_1 X$$
$$Y_2 = a'_2 X \ldots$$
$$Y_p = a'_p X$$

the i-th principal component is the linear combination $a'_i X$ that maximizes $Var(a'_i X)$ subject to $a'_i a_i = 1$ and $Cov(a'_i X, a'_k X) = 0$ for $k < i$. The coefficients are the components of the eigenvectors; this means $Yi = e'_i X$ where e_i are the eigenvectors associated with the eigenvalues λ_i of Σ. Where

TABLE 7.6
Principal Components Example

Loadings	Review of the principal components						
	Comp.1	Comp.2	Comp.3	Comp.4	Comp.5	Comp.6	Comp.7
age	0.022	0.118	0.692	0.242	0.658	0.117	0.036
balance	−0.029	0.144	0.693	−0.150	−0.679	−0.115	0.013
campaign	0.255	−0.612	0.126	−0.124	0.136	−0.710	0.077
day	0.271	−0.512	0.128	−0.475	0.006	0.649	0.041
duration	−0.059	0.450	−0.028	−0.815	0.286	−0.215	0.021
pdays	−0.668	−0.207	0.014	−0.050	0.018	0.031	0.712
previous	−0.641	−0.288	0.084	−0.108	0.064	−0.011	−0.695
Variances	Comp.1	Comp.2	Comp.3	Comp.4	Comp.5	Comp.6	Comp.7
	1.5093	1.1550	1.0970	0.9750	0.8974	0.8262	0.5401
	Importance of components						
	Comp.1	Comp.2	Comp.3	Comp.4	Comp.5	Comp.6	Comp.7
Standard deviation	1.229	1.075	1.047	0.987	0.947	0.909	0.735
Proportion of variance	0.216	0.165	0.157	0.139	0.128	0.118	0.077
Cumulative proportion	0.216	0.381	0.537	0.677	0.805	0.923	1.000

$$var(Y_i) = a_i' \Sigma a_i = \lambda_i$$
$$Cov(Y_i, Y_k) = a_i' \Sigma a_k = 0$$

Where i and k are from 1 to p.

It is possible to define the proportion of the variance generated by the k-th principal component as $\lambda_k/\lambda_1+\lambda_2+ \ldots +\lambda_p$. This is a consequence of having the variances of the principal components as the eigenvalues. The correlation coefficients between Y_i and the variables X_k is given by: $\rho_{Y_iX_k} = e_{ik}\lambda^{0.5}/\sigma_{kk}^{0.5}$ with $i, k = 1,2, \ldots, p$.

Now a factor analysis is looking for the relations of covariance among many variables in terms of a small group of underlying variables called factors. This is an extension of the analysis of principal components. Factor analysis can be used in segmentation and classification identifying the underlying variables in groups of clients. The same as in product investigation, determining the product attributes that influence in the selection of products. Also, sensitivity to price of the consumers can be identified. Variables can be grouped by their correlations and that the variables in a group are highly correlated, but that have low correlation with other variables in a different group. The principal components analysis and factorial analysis are looking for to approximate the covariance matrix Σ. The random vector Xs with p components, mean μ, and covariance matrix Σ. The model is $X - \mu = LF + \varepsilon$ where L is the matrix of the weights of the factors with μ_i = mean of variable i:

ε_i = i-th specific factor

F_j = j-th common factor

l_{ij} = weight of i-th variable of the j-th factor satisfying the following conditions:

$$E(F) = 0, \ Cov(F) = I, \ E(\varepsilon) = 0, \ Cov(\varepsilon) = \Psi$$

where Ψ is the diagonal matrix, F and ε are independent.

There is a difference with regression analysis, in regression the independent variables are observable whereas F and ε they are not observable. Now the variance of i-th variable that is determined by the m common factors is called i-th commune. The specific variance is the part of the variance of X_i due to a specific factor. The relations are the following ones:

$$\vec{\Sigma} = \lambda_i \vec{e_1}\vec{e_1}' + \cdots + \lambda_p \vec{e_p}\vec{e_p}' + \vec{\Psi}$$

$$\Psi_i = \sigma_{ii} - \sum_{j=1}^{m} l_{ij}^2$$

$$\vec{L} = \left[\sqrt{\lambda_1}\vec{e_1}, \ldots, \sqrt{\lambda_m}\vec{e_m} \right]$$

$$\vec{\Sigma} = \vec{LL}' + \vec{\Psi}$$

where the eigenvalues are ordered and the weights are the correlations.

Using the bank data, the principal components and factors are indicated in the following results (Table 7.6).

Each of the components has a variance definition and it is represented in Figure 7.13.

And Table 7.7 shows the results for the factor analysis. It shows that three factors describe the dependent variables. The method used was Varimax Figure 7.14.

factanal(x = ~age + balance + campaign + day + duration + pdays + previous, factors = 3, data = bankbook, scores = "none", rotation = "varimax")

Uniqueness:

age	balance	campaign	day	duration	pdays	previous
0.990	0.005	0.538	0.938	0.984	0.165	0.752

TABLE 7.7
Factor Analysis Output

		Factor1	Factor2	Factor3
age				
balance			0.994	
campaign				0.679
day				0.235
duration				−0.126
pdays		0.908		
previous		0.497		
		Factor1	Factor2	Factor3
SS Loadings		1.083	1.004	0.543
Proportion Var.	Var	0.155	0.143	0.078
Cumulative Var		0.155	0.298	0.376

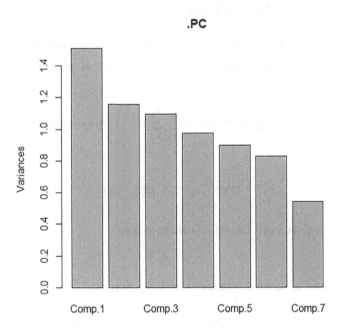

.PC

FIGURE 7.14 Representation of the variance and principal components relationship.

Test of the hypothesis that three factors are sufficient. The chi-square statistic is 22.86 on three degrees of freedom. The p-value is 0.0000431.

The next section presents some facets of a classification process that are possible to use for continuous dependent variables through discriminant analysis and using the concept of principal components.

7.10.1 Discriminant Analysis

Fisher's discriminant analysis can be used as a first step to separate groups-discrimination- classification. It is assumed that the $p \times p$ population covariance matrices are equal and of full rank

(Johnson 1998). Consider the linear combination $Y = a'X$, which has expected value $a'\mu_i$ for population π_i and variance $a'\Sigma a$.

The ratio $\frac{a'B_\mu a}{a'\Sigma a}$ measures the variability between the groups of Y-values relative to the common variability within groups. Objective: Select a to maximize the above ratio. Estimation of the values for μ *and* Σ (the variance-covariance matrix) are required, taking a sample from the populations. Let B be the sample between groups and $\bar{x}$ the estimator for μ. For Σ is used, the sample within groups matrix $W/(n_1 + \cdots + n_g - g) = S_{pooled}$. The sample size n_i from population π_i, $i = 1, \ldots, g$. The x_i are the data set from population π_i and g is the number of groups.

$$\bar{x} = \frac{\sum_{i=1}^{g} n_i \bar{x}_i}{\sum_{i=1}^{n} n_i} = \frac{\sum_{i=1}^{g} \sum_{j=1}^{n_i} x_{ij}}{\sum_{i=1}^{g} n_i}$$

Let $\widehat{\lambda}_1, \cdots, \widehat{\lambda}_s > 0$ denote the $s \leq min(g - 1, p)$ nonzero eigenvalues of $W^{-1}B$ and $\widehat{e}_1, \cdots, \widehat{e}_s$ be the corresponding eigenvectors (scaled so that $\widehat{e}' S_{pooled} \widehat{e} = 1$). Then the vector of coefficients $\hat{a}$ that maximizes the ratio

$$\frac{\hat{a}'\mathbf{B}\hat{a}}{\hat{a}'\mathbf{W}\hat{a}} = \frac{\hat{a}'[\sum_{i=1}^{g} n_i (\bar{x}_i - \bar{x})(\bar{x}_i - \bar{x})']\hat{a}}{\hat{a}'[\sum_{i=1}^{g} \sum_{j=1}^{n_i} (x_{ij} - \bar{x}_i)(x_{ij} - \bar{x})']\hat{a}}$$

is given by $\widehat{a}_1 = \hat{e}_1$. The linear combination $\widehat{a_1'}x$ is called the sample first discriminant. The choice $\widehat{a}_2 = \widehat{e}_2$ produces the sample second discriminant $\widehat{a_2'}x$ and in general the discriminant k is $\widehat{a_k'}x = \widehat{e_k'}x$ for $k \leq s$, where

$$\mathbf{W} = \sum_{i=1}^{g} (n_i - 1)\mathbf{S}_i = \sum_{i=1}^{g} \sum_{j=1}^{n_i} (\bar{x}_{ij} - \bar{x}_i)(\bar{x}_{ij} - \bar{x}_i)'.$$

and

$$\mathbf{B} = \sum_{i=1}^{g} n_i (\bar{x}_i - \bar{x})(\bar{x}_i - \bar{x})'$$

The discriminants give the basis for the classification rule.

$$Y_k = a_k'\mathbf{X}$$

for $k \leq s$. The measure of squared distance from $Y = y$ to μ_{iY} is

$$(y - \mu_{iY})'(y - \mu_{iY}) = \sum_{j=1}^{s} (y_j - \mu_{iY_j})^2$$

A reasonable classification rule is one that assigns y to population π_k if the square of the distance from y to μ_{ky} is smaller than the square of the distance from y to μ_{iY} for $i \neq k$.

If only r discriminants are used the rule is allocate x to π_k. If

$$\sum_{j=1}^{r} (y_j - \mu_{kY_j})^2 = \sum_{j=1}^{r} [a_j'(x - \mu_k)]^2$$

$$\sum_{j=1}^{r} (y_j - \mu_{kY_j})^2 \leq \sum_{j=1}^{r} [a_j'(x - \mu_k)]^2,$$

for all $i \neq k$.

Let $y_j = a_j' x$ where $a_j = \Sigma^{-1/2} e_j$ and e_j is an eigenvector of $\Sigma^{-1/2} B \Sigma^{-1/2}$. Then

$$\sum_{j=1}^{p} \left(y_j - \mu_{iY_j} \right)^2 = \sum_{j=1}^{p} [a_j'(x - \mu_i)]^2,$$

$$\sum_{j=1}^{p} \left(y_j - \mu_{iY_j} \right)^2 = (x - \mu_i)' \Sigma^{-1}(x - \mu_i) = -2d_i(x) + x'\Sigma^{-1}x + 2\ln p_i$$

If $\lambda_1 \geq \cdots \geq \lambda_S > 0 = \lambda_{S+1} = \cdots = \lambda_p$, $\sum_{j=S+1}^{p} \left(y_j - \mu_{iY_j} \right)^2$, is constant for all populations $i = 1, 2, \cdots, g$, so only the first s discriminants y_j, or $\sum_{j=1}^{s} \left(y_j - \mu_{iY_j} \right)^2$ contribute to the classification. Also, if the prior probabilities are such that $p_1 = p_2 = \cdots = p_g = 1/g$. This rule with $r = s$ is equivalent to the population version of the minimum TPM rule (total probability of misclassification). This is, allocate x to π_k if the linear discriminant score $\widehat{d_k}(x)$ is the largest of $\widehat{d_g}(x)$ for all g.

Where

$$d_i(x) = \mu_i' \Sigma^{-1} x - \frac{1}{2}\mu_i' \Sigma^{-1}\mu_i + \ln p_i$$

$$\hat{d}_i(x) = x_i^{-1} S_{pooled}^{-1} x - \frac{1}{2}\bar{x}_i' S_{pooled}^{-1} x_i + \ln p_i$$

for $i = 1, 2, \cdots, g$ and

$$S_{pooled} = \frac{1}{n_1 + \cdots + n_g - g} \left(\sum_{j=1}^{g} (n_j - 1)s_j \right)$$

are the discriminant scores.

Now for the first $r \leq s$ sample discriminants, the allocation rule is:

$$\sum_{j=1}^{r} \left(\hat{y}_j - \bar{y}_{kY_j} \right)^2 = \sum_{j=1}^{r} [\hat{a}_j'(x - \bar{x}_k)]^2$$

$$\sum_{j=1}^{r} \left(\hat{y}_j - \bar{y}_{kY_j} \right)^2 \leq \sum_{j=1}^{r} [\hat{a}_j'(x - \bar{x}_i)]^2.$$

For all $i \neq k$ and $\overline{y_{kj}} = \widehat{a_j' \bar{x}_k}$ and $r \leq s$.

In this example, (Exhibit 7.13 indicates the points reached by the risk units in insurance when given a value to the different variables. The scores are previous experience and second the joint profile between automobile and driver characteristics. The first variable is *driv*1 and the second *driv*2. There are three possibilities for grouping the prospects. The groups are accepted, not accepted, and to study by the underwriter. The results are shown as insured 1, 2, 3, respectively.

Each group has these frequencies, with the covariance matrix given by the following Exhibit 7.14:

For this example, the point to classify has the values 3.21 and 497. The distances are calculated using the pooled within-class covariance matrix with DF = 82. The formula used is: $D_i^2 = (x_0 - x_i)' S_{pooled}^{-1}(x_0 - x_i)$. The values were 2.58, 17.10, and 2.47. That means the smallest distance is to the group mean is three. Then the point is applied to the group three or to study of underwriter. The multivariate statistics are with the likelihood ratio criterion Wilks-Lambda and not based on this as Lawley-Hotelling, Pillai, and Roy. The test is for $H_{0k}: \lambda_{k+1} = \cdots \lambda_r = 0$; the first k eigenvalues are zero.

The Wilk's Lambda is the ratio $\|W\|/\|T\|$. The Lawley Hotelling is given by $trace[W(T - E)^{-1}]$; the Pillai is $trace(WT)^{-1}$. Where T is the sum of the square's matrices, for groups, for blocks, for interactions, and for error. The statics is given by $n_{2k}(1 - \Lambda_k^{1/\nu_k}/n_{1k}\Lambda_k^{1/\nu_k})$, which has an F distribution with n_{1k} and n_{2k} degrees of freedom and

EXHIBIT 7.13   DISCRIMINANT ANALYSIS

Discriminant Analysis

85	Observations	84	DF	Total
2	Variables	82	DF	Within Classes
3	Classes	2	DF	Between Classes

Class Level Information

INSURED	Frequency	Weight	Proportion	Prior Probability
1	31	31.0000	0.364706	0.333133
2	28	28.0000	0.329412	0.333433
3	26	26.0000	0.305882	0.333433

EXHIBIT 7.14   COVARIANCE MATRIX

```
Within-Class Covariance Matrices

              INSURED = 1     DF = 30

     Variable         DRIV1           DRIV2

       DRIV1        0.043558        0.058097
       DRIV2        0.058097     4618.247312


-----------------------------------------------
           INSURED = 2     DF = 27

     Variable         DRIV1           DRIV2

       DRIV1        0.033649       -1.192037
       DRIV2       -1.192037     3891.253968


-----------------------------------------------
           INSURED = 3     DF = 25

     Variable         DRIV1           DRIV2

       DRIV1        0.029692       -5.403846
       DRIV2       -5.403846     2246.904615


Pooled Within-Class Covariance Matrix     DF = 82

     Variable         DRIV1           DRIV2

       DRIV1        0.036068       -2.018759
       DRIV2       -2.018759     3655.901121

Pooled Covariance Matrix Information

          Covariance       Natural Log of the Determinant
          Matrix Rank      of the Covariance Matrix

               2               4.85035289
```

$$v = \sqrt{\frac{(p-k)^2(g-k-1)^2 - 4}{(p-k)^2 + (q-k)^2 - 5}}, \quad n_1 = (p-k)(g-k-1)$$

and

$$n_{2k} = v_k\left[(n-1) - \frac{1}{2}(p+g)\right] - \frac{(p-k)(g-k-1)}{2} + 1$$

and $\Lambda_k = \sum_{j=k+1}^{r} \ln(1 + \lambda_j)$

Then the eigenvalues are different of zero, and the p-value is small.

EXHIBIT 7.15 COMPLETE OUTPUT OF DISCRIMINANT ANALYSIS

Pairwise Generalized Squared Distances Between Groups

Generalized Squared Distance to INSURED

From INSURED	1	2	3
1	2.19843	33.48542	12.26006
2	33.48722	2.19662	9.63026
3	12.26186	9.63026	2.19662

Multivariate Statistics and F Approximations

Statistic	S=2 Value	M=−0.5 F	N=39.5 Num DF	Den DF	Pr > F
Wilks' Lambda	0.12637661	73.4257	4	162	0.0001
Pillai's Trace	1.00963002	41.7973	4	164	0.0001
Hotelling-Lawley Trace	5.83665601	116.7331	4	160	0.0001
Roy's Greatest Root	5.64604452	231.4878	2	82	0.0001

Linear Discriminant Function

INSURED

	1	2	3
CONSTANT	−241.47090	−134.99723	−178.41407
DRIV1	106.24991	78.08637	92.66953
DRIV2	0.21218	0.16541	0.17323

Classification Results for Calibration Data: WORK.INSURED

Resubstitution Results using Linear Discriminant Function

Generalized Squared Distance Function:

Posterior Probability of Membership in each INSURED:

Posterior Probability of Membership in INSURED:

Obs	From INSURED	Classified into INSURED	1	2	3
2	1	3 *	0.1201	0.0020	0.8779
3	1	3 *	0.3652	0.0004	0.6344
24	1	3 *	0.4764	0.0000	0.5236
31	1	3 *	0.2962	0.0004	0.7034
58	2	3 *	0.0001	0.2450	0.7550
59	2	3 *	0.0001	0.1326	0.8673
66	3	1 *	0.5334	0.0000	0.4666

* Misclassified observation

Posterior Probability of Membership in each INSURED:

	1	2	3	Total
1	27	0	4	31
	87.10	0.00	12.90	100.00
2	0	26	2	28
	0.00	92.86	7.14	100.00
3	1	0	25	26
	3.85	0.00	96.15	100.00
Total	28	26	31	85
Percent	32.94	30.59	36.47	100.00
Priors	0.3331	0.3334	0.3334	

Error Count Estimates for INSURED:

	1	2	3	Total
Rate	0.1290	0.0714	0.0385	0.0796
Priors	0.3331	0.3334	0.3334	

Posterior Probability of Membership in INSURED:

Obs	From INSURED	Classified into INSURED	1	2	3
1	1	3 *	0.4870	0.0054	0.5076
2	1	3 *	0.0933	0.0017	0.9050
3	1	3 *	0.3346	0.0004	0.6650
24	1	3 *	0.3973	0.0000	0.6027
31	1	3 *	0.2592	0.0004	0.7404
58	2	3 *	0.0001	0.1971	0.8029
59	2	3 *	0.0002	0.0952	0.9047
66	3	1 *	0.6859	0.0000	0.3141
75	3	2 *	0.0002	0.5089	0.4909

* Misclassified observation

Number of Observations and Percent Classified into INSURED:

	1	2	3	Total
1	26	0	5	31
	83.87	0.00	16.13	100.00
2	0	26	2	28
	0.00	92.86	7.14	100.00
3	1	1	24	26
	3.85	3.85	92.31	100.00
Total	27	27	31	85
Percent	31.76	31.76	36.47	100.00
Priors	0.3331	0.3334	0.3334	

Error Count Estimates for INSURED:

	1	2	3	Total
Rate	0.1613	0.0714	0.0769	0.1032
Priors	0.3331	0.3334	0.3334	

The results in Exhibit 7.15 show that the number of observations and percent classified into insured shows the distribution of the data in the three groups. The 84% of the accepted are located as accepted and the 16% of the accepted are located as to study by the underwriter.

7.10.2 Artificial Neural Networks (ANNs), Deep Learning, and Tensorflow

This model is emulating the brain and the way that communication and results appear in the connected neurons, from an input layer (attributes that can be demographic, transactional, promotion, etc.), the creation of hidden layers and output layers (classification or prediction result) in a model definition. It is modeled as basic units on biological neurons with each unit that has many inputs that combines in a specific value of result. The units are connected in such a way that the output of one is the input of another one. The connections create a network with flow in a direction that can be given (feed-forward, recurrent, probabilistic, etc.). The model architecture feed-forward combines a multi-layer perceptron with a backpropagation learning algorithm. Artificial neural networks (ANNs) are possible to use not only for prediction but also for clustering. There are different algorithms according to the learning algorithms and the type input: discrete or continuous in a supervised or unsupervised learning process. Moreover, the architecture for supervised learning is recurrent and feedforward, while for unsupervised learning the groups of algorithms are estimator and extractor Figures 7.15, 7.16.

A single neuron is represented by $S = \sum_{i-1}^{n} X_i W_i$ (*Combination function*) that has a transfer function $f(S)$ to obtain the outcomes $Y = (Y_1, Y_2, ..., Y_n)$. The main concept is activation function that is defined by two parts: a combination/summation function and a transfer function. For several neurons, the combination function can take a form such as in the case of two inputs and three outcomes with different inputs each one:

$$Y_1 = X_1 W_{11} + X_2 W_{12}$$
$$Y_2 = X_1 W_{12} + X_2 W_{22}$$
$$Y_3 = X_2 W_{23}$$

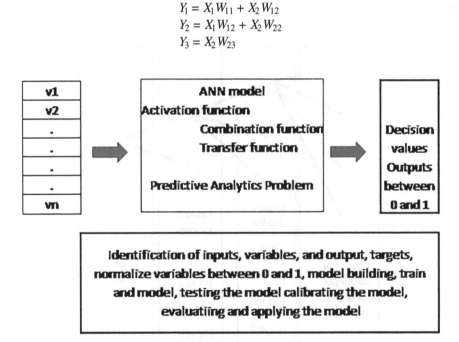

FIGURE 7.15 Descrition of ANN model.

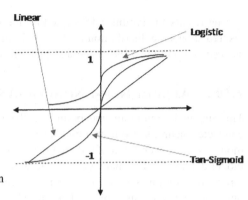

FIGURE 7.16 Activation functions that can be used in
the ANN network model definition.

7.10.2.1   Structure of the ANN

In the case of having only one layer of calculations $f(w_1x_1 + w_2x_2 + b) = y_1$ where f is the activation
function and the linear combination of the inputs x_i has weights w_i, b is called the bias and y_1 is the
target. In the case of having several layers of calculations, the functions are composed. Assuming two
hidden layers with four variables, the first layer is three neurons and the second layer is two neurons,
two different activation functions by the two layers. The composition could be as follows:

Using the notation based on the layers and the connection among neurons, the composition will
be like Figure 7.17 using the notation:

$w_{i,j}^k$ where k is arriving layer, i is origin node, and j is arriving node in the arriving layer
z_p^r activation function output where r is the layer and p is the node in the activated layer

This means that if the variables are x_i, the first summation and outcome of the activation
function is:

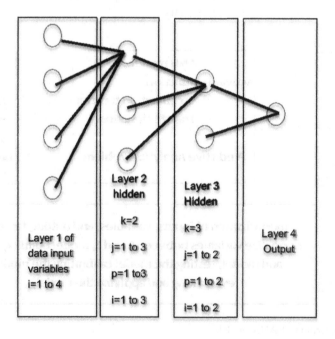

FIGURE 7.17 ANN layers structure.

$$f_1\left(\sum_{i=1}^{4} w_{i,1}^2 x_i\right) = z_1^2$$

$$f_1\left(\sum_{i=1}^{4} w_{i,2}^2 x_i\right) = z_2^2$$

$$f_1\left(\sum_{i=1}^{4} w_{i,3}^2 x_i\right) = z_3^2$$

And then

$$f_2\left(\sum_{i,p=1}^{3} w_{i,1}^3 z_p^2\right) = z_1^3$$

$$f_2\left(\sum_{i,p=1}^{3} w_{i,2}^3 z_p^2\right) = z_2^3$$

$$f_2\left(\sum_{i,p=1}^{3} w_{i,3}^3 z_p^2\right) = z_3^3$$

The last node will be the output – target of the models. The activation functions can be the same in the hidden layers. The activation functions can be:

1. Linear or ReLu that is $f(x) = max(0,x)$ zero up to zero and then the identity
2. Tanh is a function between -1 and 1 and the form is

$$f(x) = \frac{2}{1 + e^{-2x}} - 1$$

3. Sigmoid that is between 0 and 1 with the form $f(x) = \frac{1}{1+e^{-x}}$ this is the logistic function

The *Tanh* function performs better in several cases (Goodfellow et al., 2016) than logistic or linear.

In the analysis of ANN, Softmax is used to identify the target as classes and a vector of outcomes; each class will have a defined probability. The form of the function is coming from multinomial distribution and used for multinomial logistic classification:

$$softmax(x_i) = \frac{exp(x_i)}{\sum_{j=1}^{n} exp(x_j)}$$

This is the normalization of values of the $exp(x_i)$ by the sum of all those calculated exponentials of the data set. The optimization method can be given by the gradient descent algorithm that is an optimization algorithm to find local optimum (minimum/maximum) of a loss function and requires the review of two concepts.

First, the differentiable function, that is when there is a derivative in the whole domain of the function. The derivative will not exist when the limits from the right and from left of differentiation quotient are not equal this happens in very acute functions, functions with jumps or infinite discontinuity. Second, the concept of a convex set, that is when all the points of the segment line connecting two elements of set are inside the set, this means that

$$f(\lambda x_1 + (1 - \lambda)x_2) \le \lambda f(x_1) + (1 - \lambda)f(x_2)$$

In the case of n variables, the search of optimum is using the gradient in a point a

$$\nabla f(a) = \begin{bmatrix} \frac{\partial f(a)}{\partial x_1} \\ \vdots \\ \frac{\partial f(a)}{\partial x_n} \end{bmatrix}$$

And the algorithm is using the iterative definition

$$a_{n+1} = a_n - \eta \nabla f(a_n)$$

The algorithm is finishing if the number of iterations is ended or if the movement to the next position is smaller than a defined value; for example, 0.001, is called tolerance. Another optimization algorithm can be used. For example, in the case of saddle points, the use Newton Raphson can be appropriate or there are algorithms that help the optimization process as extensions of the gradient descendent method such as stochastic gradient descent method or ADAM, AdaGrad, or RMSProp.

For instance, the stochastic gradient descent is in this case with the calculation of the gradient as a function i that is a loss function for the x vector parameter and where the assumption is that the loss function is an average of loss functions by the data vector of the data set (for more details, Zhang et al. (2022) optimization algorithms Chapter 12 at https://d2l.ai/d2l-en.pdf Dive into Deep Learning).

$$f(x) = \frac{1}{n} \sum_{i=1}^{n} f_i(x)$$

And

$$\nabla f(x) = \frac{1}{n} \sum_{i=1}^{n} \nabla f_i(x)$$

is using this approach to calculate the gradient descent algorithm.

Training of the network in back propagation (Figure 7.18):

1. The network takes an example from training data set using existing steps in the network, calculates the results.
2. The error makes a revision of the difference between the actual results and the expected one, residuals.
3. Searching for reducing the error.
4. Each unit receives a specific identification of the error. The weights are adjusted.
5. The adjustment of weights is called generalized delta rule in feed-forward ANN. This is based on two parameters: Momentum is related to the trend of the weights in each unit of change of the direction in which the algorithms are guiding.

Learning rate that is controlling the speed of change of weights. The recursive formula provides the means to calculations:

$$W_{ji}(t + 1) = W_{ji}(t) + nd_j O_i - \alpha [W_{ji}(t) - W_{ji}(t - 1)]$$

W_{ji} is the weight connecting i to neuron j, t is the test number, n is the rate of learning and d_j is the gradient error j, O_i is the activation level of a node (nonlinear function applied is the result of the combination of weights and inputs), and α is the momentum term.

A review of backpropagation algorithm to train and learn is in Figure 7.18.

To choose the training set, follow the principles of sampling that are applied in the partition of training and evaluation – testing for the models. The set consists of the records whose prediction or classification is already known, and it is the source for the model to identify the variables relationships to support the classification modeling process. The training set includes the values for

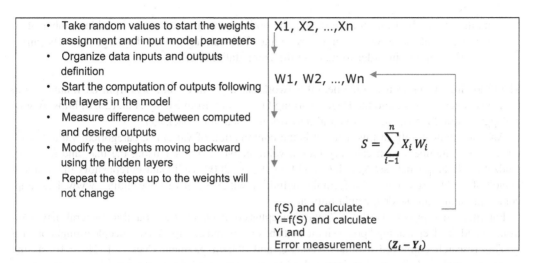

FIGURE 7.18 Simplified view of the back propagation algorithm.

all the attributes and the number of attributes, including an identification. Decide the network architecture and its organization, indicating a learning algorithm to use. Start the parametrization with initial values and to review the weights of a first iteration and validation, and continue to create feedback to tune the inputs, weights, parameters. When the tests are showing appropriate results, use the ANN to predict.

A step that is crucial to start the understanding of the ANN black-box process is the sensitivity analysis. It uses the test data set to determine sensitivity to the inputs generating and observing changes in the outputs.

1. Use averages and measure the results when averages are the inputs.
2. Measure the result of the network when each entrance is modified simultaneously with the maximums and minimums.

Neuronal networks have strengths and weaknesses as models to use. Understanding of the model for implementation is several cases is a priority for analytics deployment and ANN can be reconsider as model to support certain solutions but underatnding keep questions on the black box of the model. As strengths are possible to mention:

1. Applicable in a wide number of problems. It is possible to use with nonlinear relation-ships of the variables. It can be used with numerical and categorical variables through a transformation.
2. The model still produces good results in complex types of problems
3. The model can work with categorical variables continuous and in general no normality or independence assumptions
4. The results in comparison with other models produce better classifications

To keep in mind, there are certain weaknesses:

1. Inputs of ranks 0,1 required.
2. The explanation of results are not straightforward. They do not present/display explicit rules. To find what inputs is more important than others is not clear.
3. The model can converge prematurely to an inferior solution (one does not know if the

module is the best one for the data). The optimal solution for a considerable number of parameters of the network is not easy to find. The training process for large data sets can require sampling in order to manage the computational effort.

The following examples use some neural network packages in R, data sets from UCI, data sets in the R packages as Mass, and the Deep Learning Open Book from Zhang et al. (2022) https://www.r-bloggers.com/2015/09/fitting-a-neural-network-in-r-neuralnet-package/

An issue to deal with in this data set is the combination of variables; categorical variables are codified with numbers each category took a value between 0 and 1 using the max and min normalization. Example data set Yeh, I. C. and Lien, C. H. (2009) UCI Dataset repository that is about default of credit cards clients. for formulas definition with several variables https://www.datacamp.com/community/tutorials/r-formula-tutorial

For timeseries prices, use https://datascienceplus.com/neuralnet-train-and-test-neural-networks-using-r/ and the deep leaning book as indicated above is found at https://www.deeplearningbook.org/

This research employed a binary variable, and default payment (Yes = 1, No = 0), as the response variable. This study reviewed the literature and used the following 23 variables as explanatory variables (see model and results for Exhibits 7.16 to 7.20):

X1: Amount of the given credit (NT dollar): it includes both the individual consumer credit and his/her family (supplementary) credit.
X2: Gender (1 = male; 2 = female).
X3: Education (1 = graduate school; 2 = university; 3 = high school; 4 = others).
X4: Marital status (1 = married; 2 = single; 3 = others).
X5: Age (year).
X6-X11: History of past payment. We tracked the past monthly payment records (from April to September, 2005) as follows: X6 = the repayment status in September, 2005; X7 = the repayment status in August, 2005; … ; X11 = the repayment status in April, 2005. The measurement scale for the repayment status is: −1 = pay duly; 1 = payment delay for one month; 2 = payment delay for two months; … ; 8 = payment delay for eight months; 9 = payment delay for nine months and above.
X12-X17: Amount of bill statement (NT dollar). X12 = amount of bill statement in September, 2005; X13 = amount of bill statement in August, 2005; … ; X17 = amount of bill statement in April, 2005.
X18-X23: Amount of previous payment (NT dollar). X18 = amount paid in September, 2005; X19 = amount paid in August, 2005; … ; X23 = amount paid in April, 2005.

EXHIBIT 7.16   ANN MODEL PRESENTATION IN R USING NEURALNET LIBRARY

```
library(neuralnet)
set.seed(1234)
default<-read.table("c:folder/default of credit card clients1.csv",header=TRUE,
stringsAsFactors=TRUE, sep=",", na.strings="NA", dec=".",strip.white=TRUE)
head(default)
str(default)
hist(default$default)
maxval<-apply(default,2,max)
minval<-apply(default,2,min)
default1<-as.data.frame(scale(default,center=minval, scale=maxval-minval))
head(default)
```

```
head(default1)
dim(default1)
samdef<-sample(1:nrow(default1),21000)
traindef<-default1[samdef,]
testdef<-default1[-samdef,]
dim(traindef)
dim(testdef)
default2 = subset(default1, select = -c(ID) )
head(default2)
fullvar<-colnames(default2)
predvar<-fullvar[!fullvar%in%default]
predvar<-paste(predvar,sep="+")
predvar
equat<-as.formula(paste("default~",predvar,sep="+"))
NNmod<-neuralnet(formula = equat,hidden=c(4,2), linear.output = T,data=traindef)
equat
plot(NNmod)
```

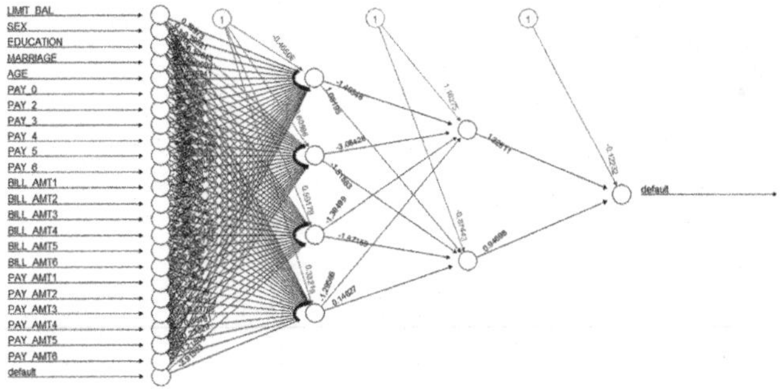

The section of the number of layers is part of the modeler decision. Each one can have the same or different activation function. The model to start using is sequential and recurrent for the time series. The units value is the number of outputs of the dense layer. The activation function is any of the ones introduced before (relu, sigmoid, softmax, tanh, selu, etc.). A dense layer is the layer where all nodes before and after of the layer are connected. The process of creating the linear combinations for the layers is the same as the representation of mxn matrix A multiply by the variables vector $nx1$ to obtain the matrix $mx1$ of the linear combinations (Ax). In that regard, the units number will be n variables. This is not the complete code but gives the structure indication.

EXHIBIT 7.17   ANN WITH DIFFERENT LAYERS, FIVE HIDDEN LAYERS INSTEAD OF FOUR

```
NNmod1<-neuralnet(formula = equat,hidden=c(5,2), linear.output = T,data=traindef)
plot(NNmod1)

#prediction
predictval<-compute(NNmod,testdef[,1:24])
dim(predictval)
resultsdef<-data.frame(actual=testdef$default,prediction=predictval$net.result)
resultsdef
```

```
#Test the resulting output
roundedresultsdef<-sapply(resultsdef,round,digits=0)
roundedresultsdef=data.frame(roundedresultsdef)
attach(roundedresultsdef)
table(actual,prediction)
```

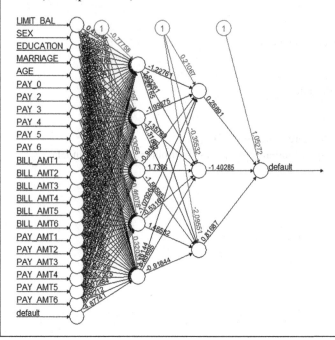

EXHIBIT 7.18   RESULT USING LOGISTIC REGRESSION

Using logistic regression

glm(formula = default ~ ., family = binomial(link = "logit"),
data = crs$dataset[crs$train, c(crs$input, crs$target)])

Deviance Residuals:

Min	1Q	Median	3Q	Max
−3.1543	−0.7007	−0.5458	−0.2810	3.4099

Coefficients:

	Estimate	Std. Error	z value	Pr(>|z|)
(Intercept)	−0.5299038522	0.1425898378	−3.716	0.000202 ***
LIMIT_BAL	−0.0000007011	0.0000001869	−3.752	0.000176 ***
SEX	−0.1285160846	0.0366849039	−3.503	0.000460 ***
EDUCATION	−0.1152783086	0.0254178706	−4.535	0.00000575148 ***
MARRIAGE	−0.1942948049	0.0381769084	−5.089	0.00000035933 ***
AGE	0.0067759674	0.0021396321	3.167	0.001541 **
PAY_0	0.5640624228	0.0212135660	26.590	< 2e-16 ***

PAY_2	0.0916063036	0.0241529943	3.793	0.000149 ***
PAY_3	0.0645600206	0.0272372350	2.370	0.017774 *
PAY_4	0.0264463413	0.0298369908	0.886	0.375423
PAY_5	0.0433500315	0.0320445382	1.353	0.176118
PAY_6	0.0111967540	0.0265948661	0.421	0.673746
BILL_AMT1	−0.0000063655	0.0000014272	−4.460	0.00000819059 ***
BILL_AMT2	0.0000041519	0.0000018111	2.292	0.021879 *
BILL_AMT3	−0.0000003000	0.0000015982	−0.188	0.851096
BILL_AMT4	−0.0000002996	0.0000016583	−0.181	0.856629
BILL_AMT5	−0.0000003150	0.0000018947	−0.166	0.867973
BILL_AMT6	0.0000024350	0.0000014593	1.669	0.095196 .
PAY_AMT1	−0.0000189699	0.0000031707	−5.983	0.00000000219 ***
PAY_AMT2	−0.0000093284	0.0000026752	−3.487	0.000488 ***
PAY_AMT3	−0.0000028349	0.0000019967	−1.420	0.155679
PAY_AMT4	−0.0000065912	0.0000023468	−2.809	0.004976 **
PAY_AMT5	−0.0000036633	0.0000020569	−1.781	0.074920 .
PAY_AMT6	−0.0000003384	0.0000014448	−0.234	0.814786

Signif. codes: 0 '***' 0.001 '**' 0.01 '*' 0.05 '.' 0.1 ' ' 1

(Dispersion parameter for binomial family taken to be 1)

   Null deviance: 22176 on 20999 degrees of freedom
Residual deviance: 19454 on 20976 degrees of freedom
AIC: 19502

Number of Fisher Scoring iterations: 6
Log likelihood: −9727.070 (24 df)
Null/Residual deviance difference: 2721.468 (23 df)
Chi-square p-value: 0.00000000
Pseudo R-Square (optimistic): 0.40212006

==== ANOVA ====
Analysis of Deviance Table
Model: binomial, link: logit
Response: default
Terms added sequentially (first to last)

	Df	Deviance	Resid. Df	Resid. Dev	Pr(>Chi)
NULL			20999	22176	
LIMIT_BAL	1	519.65	20998	21656	< 2.2e-16 ***
SEX	1	30.94	20997	21625	2.658e-08 ***
EDUCATION	1	1.86	20996	21623	0.173060
MARRIAGE	1	59.56	20995	21564	1.187e-14 ***
AGE	1	8.06	20994	21556	0.004528 **
PAY_0	1	1805.66	20993	19750	< 2.2e-16 ***
PAY_2	1	67.68	20992	19682	< 2.2e-16 ***
PAY_3	1	17.51	20991	19665	2.865e-05 ***
PAY_4	1	3.53	20990	19661	0.060316 .
PAY_5	1	2.91	20989	19658	0.087915 .

PAY_6	1	0.01	20988	19658	0.907614
BILL_AMT1	1	73.17	20987	19585	< 2.2e-16 ***
BILL_AMT2	1	0.09	20986	19585	0.766463
BILL_AMT3	1	1.24	20985	19584	0.264752
BILL_AMT4	1	0.37	20984	19583	0.542516
BILL_AMT5	1	0.12	20983	19583	0.729888
BILL_AMT6	1	1.84	20982	19581	0.175527
PAY_AMT1	1	86.30	20981	19495	< 2.2e-16 ***
PAY_AMT2	1	22.50	20980	19473	2.100e-06 ***
PAY_AMT3	1	3.98	20979	19469	0.046168 *
PAY_AMT4	1	10.85	20978	19458	0.000986 ***
PAY_AMT5	1	3.58	20977	19454	0.058649 .
PAY_AMT6	1	0.06	20976	19454	0.813900

Signif. codes: 0 '***' 0.001 '**' 0.01 '*' 0.05 '.' 0.1 ' ' 1

Using the logistic regression for multicategory explanatory variables requires the same rule of k-1 number of variables that appear in the outcome because the k variable will be the complement. Some categories will be significant. The aggregation by variable can summarize if the variable itself will be significant or not.

A brief intro of using the connection to Spark in the case of using big data is as follows, which includes what modeling processes in the local machine, but it is notable the use of the R commands to deal with the modeling process.

EXHIBIT 7.19   CODE USING SPARKLYR

```
Using Sparklyr
library(sparklyr)
spark_install()
spark_install("2.3")
system("java -version")
#start the connection
sc <- spark_connect(master = "local", version = "2.3")
cars <- copy_to(sc, mtcars)
cars
#check spark functioning
spark_web(sc)
#using the SQL capability
library(DBI)
dbGetQuery(sc, "SELECT count(*) FROM mtcars")
#You can use dplyr less code
library(dplyr)
#example using spark Plot
select(cars, hp, mpg) %>%
  sample_n(100) %>%
  collect() %>%
```

```
 plot()
#example using spark modelling
model <- ml_linear_regression(cars, mpg ~ hp)
model
#add entries and predict
model %>%
 ml_predict(copy_to(sc, data.frame(hp = 250 + 10 * 1:10))) %>%
 transmute(hp = hp, mpg = prediction) %>%
 full_join(select(cars, hp, mpg)) %>%
 collect() %>%
 plot()
#read data
spark_write_csv(cars, "cars.csv")
cars <- spark_read_csv(sc, "cars.csv")
#extensions
install.packages("sparklyr.nested")
sparklyr.nested::sdf_nest(cars, hp) %>%
 group_by(cyl) %>%
 summarise(data = collect_list(data))
#streaming
dir.create("input")
write.csv(mtcars, "input/cars_1.csv", row.names = F)
#defining the stream
stream <- stream_read_csv(sc, "input/") %>%
 select(mpg, cyl, disp) %>%
 stream_write_csv("output/")
dir("output", pattern = ".csv")
# Write more data into the stream source
write.csv(mtcars, "input/cars_2.csv", row.names = F)
# Check the contents of the stream destination
dir("output", pattern = ".csv")
stream_stop(stream)
#disconnecting
spark_disconnect(sc)
spark_disconnect_all()
#connect again
sc <- spark_connect(master = "local", version = "2.3")
library(dplyr)
#importing to spark
cars <- copy_to(sc, mtcars)
#start understanding the data
summarize_all(cars, mean)
summarize_all(cars, mean) %>%
 show_query()
cars %>%
 mutate(transmission = ifelse(am == 0, "automatic", "manual")) %>%
 group_by(transmission) %>%
 summarise_all(mean)
#using built functions in Spark SQL
summarise(cars, mpg_percentile = percentile(mpg, 0.25))
summarise(cars, mpg_percentile = percentile(mpg, 0.25)) %>%
```

```
  show_query()
summarise(cars, mpg_percentile = percentile(mpg, array(0.25, 0.5, 0.75)))
summarise(cars, mpg_percentile = percentile(mpg, array(0.25, 0.5, 0.75))) %>%
 mutate(mpg_percentile = explode(mpg_percentile))
#correlations
ml_corr(cars)
library(corrr)
correlate(cars, use = "pairwise.complete.obs", method = "pearson")
correlate(cars, use = "pairwise.complete.obs", method = "pearson") %>%
 shave() %>%
 rplot()
library(ggplot2)
ggplot(aes(as.factor(cyl), mpg), data = mtcars) + geom_col()
#group and summarize are in spark and collected into R
car_group <- cars %>%
 group_by(cyl) %>%
 summarise(mpg = sum(mpg, na.rm = TRUE)) %>%
 collect() %>%
 print()
#only 3 records passed to the plotting
ggplot(aes(as.factor(cyl), mpg), data = car_group) +
 geom_col(fill = "#999999") + coord_flip()
#facilitating the translation to spark
library(dbplot)
cars %>%
 dbplot_histogram(mpg, binwidth = 3) +
 labs(title = "MPG Distribution",
 subtitle = "Histogram over miles per gallon")
ggplot(aes(mpg, wt), data = mtcars) +
 geom_point()
# a different scatterplot
dbplot_raster(cars, mpg, wt, resolution = 16)
#iterating in spark
cars %>%
 ml_linear_regression(mpg ~ .) %>%
 summary()
cars %>%
 ml_linear_regression(mpg ~ hp + cyl) %>%
 summary()
cars %>%
 ml_generalized_linear_regression(mpg ~ hp + cyl) %>%
 summary()
#compute() command can take the end of a dplyr command
#and save the results to Spark memory
cached_cars <- cars %>%
 mutate(cyl = paste0("cyl_", cyl)) %>%
 compute("cached_cars")
cached_cars %>%
 ml_linear_regression(mpg ~ .) %>%
 summary()
spark_disconnect(sc)
```

Deep learning-Tensorflow and time series

1. What is deep learning? It is a process from data observations to outcomes/results through multiple layers. Layers are transformations of data. The transformation are functions that are differentiable for stochastic gradient descent. There is a calculation of weights for data.
2. What are tensors? They are multidimensional arrays this means scalars, vectors, matrices, matrices of matrices and matrices of matrices of matrices, this means for dimensions. This is possible to review in terms of data that is pictures and then attributes
3. The tensorflow computing library that support machines learning and deep learning
   Can use CPU, GPU, TPU (tensor processing unit), automatic differentiations
4. What is a tensorflow? it is a graph of units of computation in nodes that is defined in R and the data tensors are computed in the nodes, this means executing functions-models, flowing the defined graph

The use of KERAS and Tensorflow through RStudio requires only the installation of the two packages directly from the CRAN repository. KERAS in in Tensorflow. You can use convolutional and recurrent networks as it is time series. The idea is to work in the modeling process using layers from sequential or functional API to layers to organize the data and then to mode to functions such as the loss function to create and evaluate the metrics.

Good sources of examples are https://tensorflow.rstudio.com/tutorials/beginners/ and https://tensorflow.rstudio.com/guide/

The main structure for using tensorflow is as follows:

EXHIBIT 7.20   USING KERAS-TENSORFLOW

```
#using KERAS-Tensorflow
#usinf Rcmdr
library(Rcmdr)
library(keras)
library(tidyr)
library(dplyr)
default <-read.table("C:/yourfilelocation/default of credit card clients1.csv",
    header=TRUE, stringsAsFactors=TRUE, sep=",", na.strings="NA", dec=".",
    strip.white=TRUE)
normaliz.Z <- scale(default[,c("AGE","BILL_AMT1","BILL_AMT2","BILL_AMT3",
    "BILL_AMT4","BILL_AMT5","BILL_AMT6","default","EDUCATION","ID",
    "LIMIT_BAL",
    "MARRIAGE","PAY_0","PAY_2","PAY_3","PAY_4","PAY_5","PAY_6",
    "PAY_AMT1",
    "PAY_AMT2","PAY_AMT3","PAY_AMT4","PAY_AMT5","PAY_AMT6",
    "SEX")])
within(default, {
Z.SEX <- .Z[,25]
Z.PAY_AMT6 <- .Z[,24]
Z.PAY_AMT5 <- .Z[,23]
Z.PAY_AMT4 <- .Z[,22]
Z.PAY_AMT3 <- .Z[,21]
Z.PAY_AMT2 <- .Z[,20]
Z.PAY_AMT1 <- .Z[,19]
Z.PAY_6 <- .Z[,18]
```

```
Z.PAY_5 <- .Z[,17]
Z.PAY_4 <- .Z[,16]
Z.PAY_3 <- .Z[,15]
Z.PAY_2 <- .Z[,14]
Z.PAY_0 <- .Z[,13]
Z.MARRIAGE <- .Z[,12]
Z.LIMIT_BAL <- .Z[,11]
Z.ID <- .Z[,10]
Z.EDUCATION <- .Z[,9]
Z.default <- .Z[,8]
Z.BILL_AMT6 <- .Z[,7]
Z.BILL_AMT5 <- .Z[,6]
Z.BILL_AMT4 <- .Z[,5]
Z.BILL_AMT3 <- .Z[,4]
Z.BILL_AMT2 <- .Z[,3]
Z.BILL_AMT1 <- .Z[,2]
Z.AGE <- .Z[,1]
})
head(normaliz.Z,10)
head(normaliz.Z)
```

After normalization, the training and test files are generated and the KERAS model will be defined identifying the parameters of layers, the activation function to use and finally to compile the model according to a loss function definition and optimizer method. In KERAS, the components are layers and models. The general syntax is as follows:

Another option of using R and deep learning is through Torch. Torch in R was launched in 2020. Torch is originally the pyTorch now with R native.

EXHIBIT 7.21   SYNTAX USING KERAS

```
# create the model
model <- keras_model_sequential()
model %>%
  layer_dense(units = XXXX, activation = 'relu', input_shape = c(XXXXXX)) %>%
  layer_dense(units = XXXX, activation = 'relu', input_shape = c(XXXXXX)) %>%
# the last layer is the output
  layer_dense(units = 1)
# the next step is to compile the model
model %>% compile(
  loss = "mse",
  optimizer = "adam"
)
```

Furthermore, the integration with tools like KNIME is powerful and it is indicated the main nodes to use. In KNIME, the integration with KERAS and Tensorflow is found in the nodes repository as integration after deep learning and then selecting keras or tensorflow. Once the node is selected, the definition the layers of the network will be available.

EXHIBIT 7.22   KNIME WORKFLOW TO USE TENSORFLOW

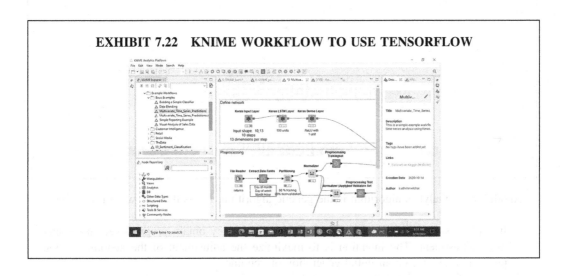

EXHIBIT 7.23   KNIME MODULES TO USE FOR TENSORFLOW

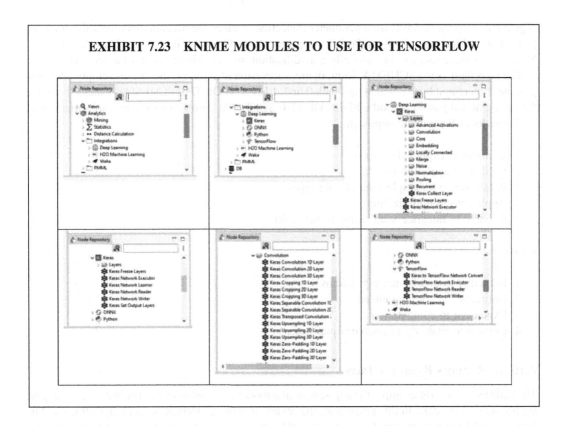

EXHIBIT 7.24   TENSORFLOW IN KNIME INDICATING THE USE OF METANODES

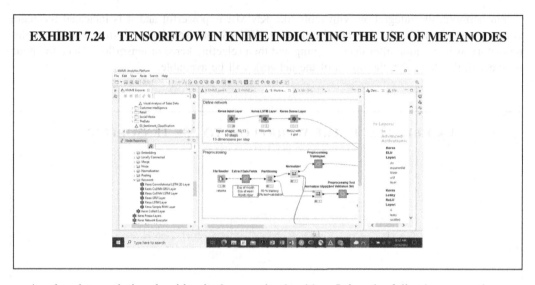

Another data analytics algorithm is the genetic algorithm. It has the following properties:

1. It evolves successive generations of genomes that they obtain progressively more and more adjustment. The intention is to maximize the adjustment of the genomes in the population. To create an initial generation of genomes.
2. To modify the initial values when applying selection, crossings, and mutations.
3. To repeat step 2 until they do not obtain more improvements.

A genome is a gene of 5 bits for a parameter. Selection: it takes the measurement from the constant population and increases the fit of the following generation. Crossing: it forms to change 2 genomes. Mutation: to make random, occasionally a modification, in a position random of a genome.

The algorithm uses a SCHEMA: form, figure, succession of symbols, the first and empty ones of a genome is increased by (*), that agrees with 0 or 1. LENGTH OF THE SCHEMA: distance between the most external positions. And ORDER OF THE SCHEMA: number of fixed positions that it has.

Strengths of the genetic approach

1. It produces explicable results
2. Facility to apply the results
3. It can handle an ample rank of data types
4. Applicable to optimization
5. Possible to integrate with neuronal networks

Weaknesses

1. Difficulty to codify many problems
2. Optimality is not guaranteed
3. Expensive in computation
4. Limited availability in analytics platforms

7.10.3   ANALYSIS BASED ON TREES

The traditional procedures imply the adjustment of a model (regression or discriminant) according to the behavior of the data. In this subsection, the review is about classification trees algorithms and in Section 7.10.4 there is an introduction to ensembles that includes the random forest approach. The decision trees divide the data, successively, based on a criterion that implies relationships between the predicting variables and the objective-target variable. Breiman et al. (1984) developed C&RT (classification and regression trees). It does successive binary separations in the data guiding themselves by a criterion, not a statistical test as it is in the CHAID algorithm. In each node, the predicting variable that improves plus the criterion, is used to make the following partition. The trees created with this criterion let themselves grow widely and later they are pruned: to prune diminishing the complex cost. The terminal nodes show the groups that can have a greater concentration of cases with the wished characteristic. There are advantages in using decision trees in classification. The trees are designed to work with an elevated number of variables; as nonparametric methods capture relations that the linear models cannot capture (relations nonlinear and complex interactions); different methods can handle different types of variables; use or not of statistical criteria now for choosing and for dividing variables in branches. See examples Exhibit 7.25 and Figure 7.19.

There are concepts associated with the tree algorithms. One of those is impurity; that is the name of the criterion to grow the tree with a nominal objective variable. Impurity captures the degree in which the cases, within a node, are concentrated in a single category. A pure node is that in which all the cases are in a single category. The greater degree of impurity occurs when all the categories of a predicting variable contain the same amount of cases. The impurity is possible to measure.

The impurity criterion stays but it is moderate according to the variance to the interior of the node. It captures the degree in which the answers within a node are concentrated around a single value. The impurity of a branch is the weighed average of the variances of the terminal nodes. The Gini metric-index guides the evaluation of impurity. The index of Gini is described: If the set T_o has elements of n classes and f_j is the relative frequency of class j in A, then $gin(A) = 1 - \sum_{j=1}^{n} f_j^2$. If T_o in two sets of sizes $|A_1|$ and $|A_2|$ defines the index of Gini like a weighed average. The Gini minor is the used one in the partition of the branch.

$$Gini(A) = \frac{|A_1|}{|A|} gini(A_1) + \frac{|A_2|}{|A|} gini(A_2)$$

To grow a tree indefinitely reduces the impurity almost always. The measurement of complex cost increases in the measurement in which the tree is greater. It is equal to $R(T) + a*|T|$ where $R(T)$ is the measurement of substitution of risk of the tree or branch, a is the penalty coefficient, and $|T|$ is the number of terminal nodes of the tree or branch. In order to improve the measurement of cost complex, the component of substitution of risk must diminish more than the penalty. The measurement of complex cost works well if the tree grows and then it is pruned using this criterion. The method consists of pruning branches of successive way with base in the Maxima reduction of the measurement of complex cost. Trees are selected; the smallest tree whose risk (probability of classifying erroneously) is within a rank of one standard error of the smaller risk is found during the growth of the tree.

The tree partitions for predicting continuous or ordinal following these steps: Sort data within the nodes by the values of the categories of the predicting variable. Calculate the reduction in impurity for all the possible cut points. The best partition is determined. For nominal predictors (explanatory variables/attributes), all the possible combinations of their categories are evaluated, and the partition becomes when it is found the greater reduction in impurity. This causes a same predicting variable that can often appear within a branch. The costs of erroneous classification can be included in C&RT, but not of a totally satisfactory way, because symmetrical costs are created. If these costs are taken up the growth of the tree, the allocation of cases and the summaries of risk will be influenced. Another way to incorporate the costs is using the probabilities a priori. The nodes show the frequency results in front of a dependent variable and are part of the results of a statistical test.

The CHAID algorithm is used for analysis of categorical variables. The idea is always from the root to be developing a chain of implications if A then B, where A and B they are the attributes. The algorithms can stop and become leaves of the tree when a node no longer has other element samples. In the case of having the elements belong to the group or defined class the algorithm stop. Each algorithm defines the shutdown rules.

1. The predicting variables are categorical like the target variable
2. The objective is to find the relationship or association between the set of the predicting variables and the target
3. The report is made in a diagram of arbol representing but the significant difference in the percentages of the dependent variable.
4. CHAID = chi-square automatic interaction detection which is a method of heuristic search that consist of examining relations between several predicting variables and an objective or dependent variable. The algorithm is:
   1. For each predicting variable x looks for the pair of categories of x whose difference presents/displays the smaller significance with respect to the variable criterion y. The method to calculate the critical level depends on the level of the y measure.
      - If y is continuous it is used the F test
      - If y is nominal it is formed a contingency table with the categories of x like rows and the categories of y like columns. To use the test chi-square for evaluation
      - If y is ordinal it is adjusted the model of association of y. To use the test of the likelihood ratio.
   2. For the pair of categories of x with the greater critic level compare the value of the critical level with the pre-specified level alpha.
      If the critical value is greater than alpha join the pair in a single compound category. As result forms a new set of categories of x and the process becomes to initiate from the step 1 if the value of the critical level is smaller than alpha move to step 3.
   3. To calculate the critical level for the set of the categories of x and the categories of y, by means of the correction of Bonferroni test
   4. To select to the predicting variable x whose corrected critical level is the minimum. To compare its critical level with the pre-established level alpha
      - If the critical level is smaller or equal to alpha to divide the node according to the set of categories of x
      - if the critical level is greater than alpha not to divide the node, it is a terminal node
   5. To continue until the shutdown rule is fulfilled

Another algorithm that is found in analytics platforms is the QUEST algorithm that means: quick unbiased efficient statistical. This algorithm deals with the problems classification, making in separated from the segmentation of the selection of the variables. The methods are parametric and the data must fulfill assumptions. QUEST has the quality to make the calculations of more efficient way from the computational point of view than C&RT and CHAID. The dependent variable can be nominal and predicting variables continuous.

The QUEST algorithms is:

1. For each variable x, if x is categorical nominal, to calculate the critical level of a chi-square test between x and the categorical dependent variable. If x is continuous to use F test.
2. To compare the smaller critical level with the pre-established level of alpha, corrected using Bonferroni test (multiple comparisons test).
   - If the critical level is smaller than the elected alpha to select the corresponding predicting variable to divide the node. Go to step 3
   - If the critical level is greater than alpha for each x that is ordinal or continuous use the Levene test on unequal variances, to calculate its critical level
   - To compare the smaller critical level of the Levene test with a new corrected level of alpha by using Bonferroni

- If the critical level is smaller than alpha, to select to divide the node the corresponding predicting variable with the smaller critical level in the Levene test to go to step 3
- If the critical level is greater than alpha to select the predicting variable of step 1 whose critical level is smaller to divide the node. Go to step 3

3. Suppose that x is the predicting variable of step 2. If x is continuous or ordinal to go to step 4. If x is nominal, to transform x is a ghost variable z and to calculate. The greater discriminant coordinate of z. becomes x to maximize differences between categories of the criterion variable.

4. If y has two categories, go to step 5. On the contrary, to calculate the average of x. For each category of y apply an algorithm of conglomerate of two averages to average happiness to obtain two super-classes of y.

5. To apply to the quadratic discriminant analysis to determine the division point. The cut points are two and the one is chosen that is closer to the average sample of each class.

6. A node will not be divided if some of the following conditions is fulfilled:
   - All the cases of a node have identical values in all the predicting ones
   - The node becomes pure, all the cases have the same value in the variable criterion
   - The depth of the tree has reached the pre-established maximum value
   - The number of cases that constitute the node is minor who the pre-established minimum size for a parental node. The division of the node has as result a filial node whose I number of cases is minor who the pre-established size minimum for a filial node

For continuous predicting variables, it makes an analysis of variance, and according to the value of the F it decides with what variable making the partition. Additionally, in the case of using the explanatory nominal variables a chi-square test and adjustments of Bonferroni are the selected test to apply.

Once chosen, the variable with which it is going away to make the partition, that partition is done by means of a discriminant analysis using the predicting variable in groups created by the objective categories. For more than two categories in the objective variable, QUEST makes an analysis of conglomerates of 2 K-means based on the predictive variable. This way, a binary partition is appropriate. The nominal predicting variables become dummy variables. Finally, the algorithm replaces lost values, using other predicting variables.

The function of information gain exists to deal with entropy in classification. Having two classes A and B and there is a C can be in A or B and it can be defined as information (a,b)

$$ information\,(a,\,b) = -\frac{a}{a+b}log_2\frac{a}{a+b} - \frac{b}{a+b}log_2\frac{b}{a+b} $$

In general, the entropy is defined for k classes as $E = -\sum_{i=1}^{n} p_i log_2 p_i$.

If an attribute O is taken, a set C can be divided in sets $\{C_1, C_2 \dots , C_k\}$ each one having to a_i elements of A and b_i elements of B. The entropy is the expected value of information O

$$ E(O) = \sum_{i=1}^{k} \frac{a_i + b_i}{a+b} I(a_i, b_i) $$

where a and b are the totals and the gain by branch is $I(a, b)-E(O)$.

EXHIBIT 7.25 EXAMPLE USING CLASSIFICATION TREES AND THE RULES OUTPUT OF A TREE MODEL

n= 31647

(node), split, n, loss, yval, (yprob)

   * denotes terminal node

1) root 31647 3706 no (0.88289569 0.11710431)
  2) duration< 448.5 27084 1911 no (0.92944174 0.07055826)
    4) poutcome=failure,other,unknown 26251 1404 no (0.94651632 0.05348368) *
    5) poutcome=success 833 326 yes (0.39135654 0.60864346)
     10) duration< 132 157 32 no (0.79617834 0.20382166) *
     11) duration>=132 676 201 yes (0.29733728 0.70266272) *
  3) duration>=448.5 4563 1795 no (0.60661845 0.39338155)
    6) duration< 827.5 3330 1059 no (0.68198198 0.31801802)
     12) poutcome=failure,other,unknown 3164 922 no (0.70859671 0.29140329) *
     13) poutcome=success 166 29 yes (0.17469880 0.82530120) *
    7) duration>=827.5 1233 497 yes (0.40308191 0.59691809) *

Classification tree:
rpart(formula = y ~ ., data = crs$dataset[crs$train, c(crs$input,
    crs$target)], method = "class", model = TRUE, parms = list(split = "information"),
    control = rpart.control(usesurrogate = 0, maxsurrogate = 0))

Variables actually used in tree construction:
[1] duration poutcome

Root node error: 3706/31647 = 0.1171

n= 31647

	CP	nsplit	rel error	xerror	xstd
1	0.037777	0	1.00000	1.00000	0.015435
2	0.029142	3	0.88667	0.92364	0.014909
3	0.025094	4	0.85753	0.87345	0.014546
4	0.010000	5	0.83243	0.83864	0.014285

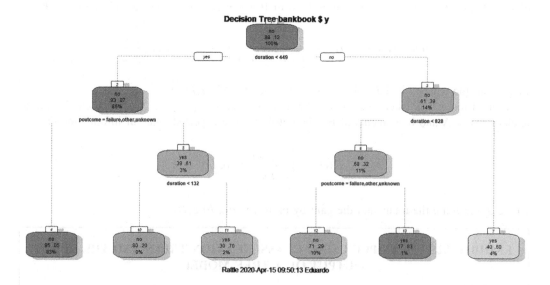

FIGURE 7.19   Display of the output for a tree model.

7.10.3.1   Additional Non-Parametric Analysis

Models for risk classification can be parametric and non-parametric. Some authors indicate that a classification problem cannot be distribution-free in the good sense [see Anderson (1994)]. However, there are ML algorithms doing good work through a non-parametric structure. Some models belong to these main categories.

- Consider a good rule assuming that the distributions are known. The cdf and pdf are replaced by their respective sample estimates.
- Use a well-known tests for the non-parametric samples.
- Some ad-hoc methods which are typical, like minimum distance.

As an additional non-parametric models as option to classification trees is the nearest neighbor (K-NN) that proposes a classification rule for the two-population problem based on non-parametric estimates of the pdf. The method of estimating a density f can be described as follows: Let $X_1, \cdots, X_n$ be i.i.d r.v's with common pdf. f which is continuous at x. Let S_n be a sequence of sets in the sample space with corresponding volumes V_n such that: $\lim_{n \to \infty} sup_{y \in S_n} \|x - y\| = 0$ and $\lim_{n \to \infty} nV_n =$. And let K_n be the number of observations that lie in S_n. Then $\hat{f}(x) = \frac{k_n}{nV_n} \to f(x)$ in probability when k_n and n go to infinity. From here it is possible to use the K-NN rule.

Let X be the observation to be classified. Consider the distance function d and order all the values $d(X_{ij}, X)$, where X_{ij} are the random sample from the i-th population. $j = 1, \cdots, n_{i\$}$ and $\$i = 1, \cdots, m$. The rule assigns X to the population π_i

if $\frac{k_i}{n_i} = max_j \left(\frac{k_j}{n_j}\right)$ *where* k_i is the number of observations from π_i in the k observations "nearest" to x.

7.10.4   Ensembles – Bagging – Boosting and Stacking

Random forest description belongs to this section about ensembles. The ensemble models provide the support to reduce overfitting and to obtain more generalizable models for risk classification. The ensembles take a set of estimators that is better than the individual components. The ensembles are identified as meta-classifiers because of using the set of individual classifiers. Classifiers are the techniques to classify. This can have the analogy of a combination of solutions to get through the ensemble process a better solution using the individual solution.

The creation of ensembles can be using the same data set and different algorithms or using different samples with the algorithm-classifier. The voting system is used for different samples and different algorithms in the ensemble process. Classifiers used in the ensemble with algorithms are decision tress, support vector machines, logistic regression, and so on. For the different samples generation, the bootstrap method is used.

7.10.4.1   Bagging – Bootstrap Aggregating

The purpose is to reduce the variance of estimators. One example is **random forest:** this technique creates decision trees using bootstrap samples as training data sets and random feature selection for fitting the individual tree models that use a majority voting system to select the best prediction of the target. Voting systems mean that the class for a solution is selected based on the higher number of individual solutions (the mode of the solutions) that show a selected class.

In the case of using a GUI as Rattle, the results and the possible comparison are given through the area under the curve, indicating the variables used in the splits, checking the error rate, different number of observations, and different number of variables considered to random sample in each split.

EXHIBIT 7.26   RANDOM FOREST OUTCOME AND ROC CURVE

Summary of the Random Forest Model

======================================

Number of observations used to build the model: 31647

Missing value imputation is active.

Call:

randomForest(formula = y ~ .,

        data = crs$dataset[crs$train, c(crs$input, crs$target)],

        ntree = 500, mtry = 4, importance = TRUE, replace = FALSE, na.action = randomForest::na.roughfix)

        Type of random forest: classification

          Number of trees: 500

No. of variables tried at each split: 4

      OOB estimate of error rate: 9.14%

Confusion matrix:

	no	yes	class.error
no	26940	1001	0.03582549
yes	1893	1813	0.51079331

	no	yes	Mean Decrease Accuracy	Mean Decrease Gini
duration	149.4	261.14	258.55	1152.05
month	96.38	27.86	101.54	473.8
contact	56.78	7.15	59.35	70.48
day	57.89	3.04	56.71	323.86
age	47.78	13.69	51.16	366.05
housing	42.13	22.08	48.55	74.54
poutcome	32.01	20.86	44.62	281.89
job	34.45	-7.69	28.24	269.2
pdays	23.84	25.32	27.54	170.21
campaign	17.94	11.17	21.69	145.61
previous	16.88	11.2	17.16	86.97
education	21.11	-3.64	16.81	99.47
marital	6.58	15.8	14.73	79.3
balance	8.64	11.65	13.64	390.4
loan	2.19	12.69	9.07	32.1
default	1.19	8.25	4.98	7.36

95% CI: 0.7186–0.7348 (DeLong)

Area under the curve: 0.7267

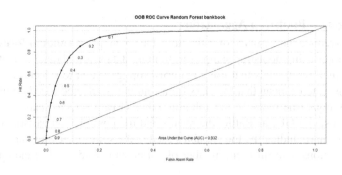

EXHIBIT 7.27 CODE AND ROC USING RANDOM FOREST

Code presented by RATTLE package, and it guides to the main components of modeling process.
Random forest
Number of observations used to build the model: 21000
Missing value imputation is active.
Call:
randomForest(formula = as.factor(default) ~ .,

data = crs$dataset[crs$train, c(crs$input, crs$target)],
ntree = 500, mtry = 24, importance = TRUE, replace = FALSE, na.action = randomForest::na.roughfix)

Type of random forest: classification
Number of trees: 500
No. of variables tried at each split: 23

OOB estimate of error rate: 18.79%
Confusion matrix:

	0	1	class.error
0	15317	1045	0.0638675
1	2901	1737	0.6254851

Analysis of the Area Under the Curve (AUC)
==

Call:
roc.default(response = crsrfy, predictor = as.numeric(crsrfpredicted))

Data: as.numeric(crsrfpredicted) in 16362 controls (crsrfy 0) < 4638 cases (crsrfy 1).
Area under the curve: 0.6553

95% CI: 0.6481–0.6625 (DeLong)

Variable Importance
=====================

	0	1	Mean Decrease Accuracy	Mean Decrease Gini
PAY_0	118.10	106.05	181.57	724.98
PAY_2	61.09	1.39	66.69	165.22
BILL_AMT3	48.76	−15.26	52.85	200.94
BILL_AMT4	46.83	−11.84	52.00	193.88
BILL_AMT2	47.83	−11.21	51.73	209.21
PAY_6	42.74	8.55	50.32	51.49
BILL_AMT5	44.05	−8.04	48.95	186.32
BILL_AMT6	32.28	9.44	43.43	217.20
PAY_4	40.57	−4.75	42.93	46.76
PAY_AMT5	32.71	3.57	41.03	201.76
BILL_AMT1	25.89	25.72	39.01	303.79
PAY_AMT1	35.53	−3.49	38.45	218.89
PAY_AMT6	31.26	10.56	38.22	237.74

PAY_AMT3	26.83	13.19	37.92	225.13
PAY_5	23.65	22.87	37.27	50.03
LIMIT_BAL	30.12	12.02	35.39	273.63
PAY_3	31.00	1.78	34.48	42.71
PAY_AMT2	29.91	0.94	33.66	262.94
PAY_AMT4	14.13	27.56	30.50	206.76
AGE	30.21	6.04	30.05	341.49
MARRIAGE	18.61	2.55	18.14	58.99
SEX	4.06	4.19	5.69	54.21
EDUCATION	3.63	0.23	3.31	89.08

Rules examples
Tree 1 Rule 1 Node 1160 Decision 1

```
 1: PAY_0 <= 1.5
 2: PAY_2 <= 1.5
 3: PAY_AMT2 <= 1500.5
 4: PAY_AMT4 <= 585.5
 5: PAY_3 <= 1
 6: PAY_AMT1 <= 1022
 7: AGE <= 53.5
 8: LIMIT_BAL <= 25000
 9: PAY_AMT1 <= 383
10: PAY_AMT6 <= 890
11: AGE <= 33.5
12: PAY_AMT2 <= 238
13: BILL_AMT1 <= -174
```

Tree 1 Rule 2 Node 1392 Decision 0

```
 1: PAY_0 <= 1.5
 2: PAY_2 <= 1.5
 3: PAY_AMT2 <= 1500.5
 4: PAY_AMT4 <= 585.5
 5: PAY_3 <= 1
 6: PAY_AMT1 <= 1022
 7: AGE <= 53.5
 8: LIMIT_BAL <= 25000
 9: PAY_AMT1 <= 383
10: PAY_AMT6 <= 890
11: AGE <= 33.5
12: PAY_AMT2 <= 238
13: BILL_AMT1 > -174
14: PAY_2 <= -0.5
```

Tree 1 Rule 3 Node 1604 Decision 1

```
 1: PAY_0 <= 1.5
 2: PAY_2 <= 1.5
```

```
 3: PAY_AMT2 <= 1500.5
 4: PAY_AMT4 <= 585.5
 5: PAY_3 <= 1
 6: PAY_AMT1 <= 1022
 7: AGE <= 53.5
 8: LIMIT_BAL <= 25000
 9: PAY_AMT1 <= 383
10: PAY_AMT6 <= 890
11: AGE <= 33.5
12: PAY_AMT2 <= 238
13: BILL_AMT1 > -174
14: PAY_2 > -0.5
15: BILL_AMT1 <= 8698.5
```

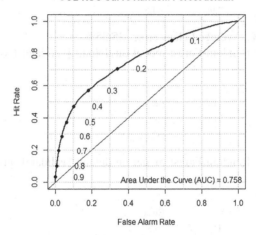

OOB ROC Curve Random Forest default

7.10.4.2 Boosting

An example is **AdaBoost,** which is adaptive boosting. In general, the boosting method selects without replacement random sub-data-sets (samples) for training the models. The first selection trains a model, a percentage (50%) of the wrong classified examples (points) is added to a second subset random selected without replacement, and with this new data set train a new model. Then, with the examples that were misclassified by the first and second iteration, join the new random selection to train a new model. In particular, in the AdaBoost method the technique uses the whole training data set to train the models. The training points are with new weights in each iteration for getting classifiers that learn from the errors of previous iterations with low performance models. The misclassified points take a higher weight and use them for training models. Every iteration will modify the weights of them and train another classifier. After several models with a low performance, the technique uses the majority voting to select the model to use.

Exhibits 7.28 and 7.29 indicate the use of Extreme Boost in R presenting the error levels and variables to select for obtaining the classification levels. The risk analyst is going to calibrate those models through review of variables definition, variables to start with, data volume to use, etc. The identification of where the error will be acceptable and with variables identification to

EXHIBIT 7.28   BOOSTING MODEL

Boosting

Error matrix for the Extreme Boost model on default [validate] (counts):Boosting

Predicted

Actual	0	1	Error
0	3278	216	6.2
1	649	357	64.5

Error matrix for the Extreme Boost model on default [validate] (proportions):

Predicted

Actual	0	1	Error
0	72.8	4.8	6.2
1	14.4	7.9	64.5

Overall error: 19.3%, Averaged class error: 35.35%

Error matrix for the Random Forest model on default [validate] (counts):

Predicted

Actual	0	1	Error
0	3275	219	6.3
1	629	377	62.5

Error matrix for the Random Forest model on default [validate] (proportions):

Predicted

Actual	0	1	Error
0	72.8	4.9	6.3
1	14.0	8.4	62.5

Overall error: 18.8%, Averaged class error: 34.4%

Error matrix for the Linear model on default [validate] (counts):

Predicted

Actual	0	1	Error
0	3391	103	2.9
1	778	228	77.3

Error matrix for the Linear model on default [validate] (proportions):

Predicted

Actual	0	1	Error
0	75.4	2.3	2.9
1	17.3	5.1	77.3

Overall error: 19.5%, Averaged class error: 40.1%

Error matrix for the Neural Net model on default [validate] (counts):

Predicted

Actual	0	Error
0	3494	0
1	1006	100

Error matrix for the Neural Net model on default [validate] (proportions):

Predicted

Actual	0	Error
0	77.6	0
1	22.4	100

Overall error: −77.6%, Averaged class error: 50%

Comparing models using ROC
Area under the ROC curve for the xgb model on default [validate] is 0.7620

Area under the ROC curve for the rf model on default [validate] is 0.7506
Area under the ROC curve for the glm model on default [validate] is 0.7150
Area under the ROC curve for the nnet model on default [validate] is 0.5000

EXHIBIT 7.29 ITERATIONS IN EXTREME BOOST R

Summary of the Extreme Boost model:
    ada(y ~ ., data = crs$dataset[crs$train, c(crs$input, crs$target)],
        control = rpart::rpart.control(maxdepth = 6, cp = 0.01, minsplit = 20,
           xval = 10), iter = 50)
Loss: exponential Method: discrete Iteration: 50
Final Confusion Matrix for Data:
        Final Prediction

True value	no	yes
no	27224	717
yes	2178	1528

Train Error: 0.091

Out-Of-Bag Error: 0.092 iteration= 50

Additional Estimates of number of iterations:

train.err1 train.kap1

42	48

Variables actually used in tree construction:

[1]	"age"	"balance"	"campaign"	"contact"	"day"	"duration"
[7]	"education"	"housing"	"job"	"loan"	"marital"	"month"
[13]	"pdays"	"poutcome"	"previous"			

Frequency of variables actually used:

duration	month	contact	poutcome	pdays	age	housing	day
48	44	42	16	15	14	13	11
campaign	job	balance	loan	education	previous	marital	
10	10	8	5	3	3	2	

take the next step will be to define the action of reviewing the process where these variables are going to be controlled. Many variables can be involved in risk analytics – management processes. This means not only to have the suggested variables to control will be enough or a reason to stop the risk analysis but also to clarify the feasibility of controlling the suggested variables and the possibility to test new variables that can be controllable in reality to achieve better results. For example, if age is affecting the results in a clear way, to improve results possibly age is controllable but another variable as it could be the length of the call can be more difficult to control because of the contact conditions and ways that the communication is going be developed.

Another example of boosting is **gradient boosting**. The difference from AdaBoost is basically in the application of the weights in points to include in the iterations and how the classifiers are used together to select the best model. In analytics platforms as it is R and Python the XGBoost is implemented. The technique uses the regression techniques to train the models. The models produce errors and with several iterations the purpose of achieving the best points predict the target Figure 7.20.

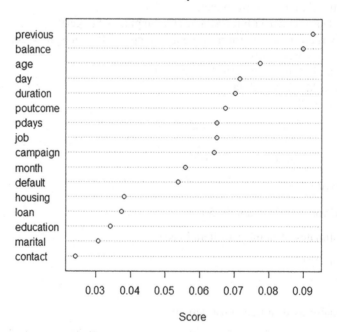

FIGURE 7.20 The identification importance of variables in a model outcome is a guide to actions of control, mitigation, and strategy.

In general, in risk analytics, there is the concept of model risk that is related to the issue of a model not performing as it should, the issues with assumptions, the lack of proper testing, etc. There is another risk to consider associated with model risk and that is the operational risk of implementation. This means the cost of implementations against the cost of new knowledge-solution that is gained. In ensembles, there are improvements, but the computational complexity will be increased in the implementation and in some solutions it could be more expensive to get a better solution with not gaining that justify the costs of using it. In the Netflix competition, the situation was like the ensemble model and was the best solution for classifying but the implementation-deployment was so expensive that the company decided not to use it.

7.10.4.3 Stacking

In this method, there is a combination of classifiers and ensembles; for example, a random forest can be combined with a logistic regression.

7.11 BEYOND CLASSIFICATION RELATED PROBLEMS

This section includes aspects related to classification to enhance final actions in risk management, pricing, reserves, forecasting, calibration, etc. A few aspects are indicated ahead: analysis of variance components, misclassification, credibility, Markov chains, and ruin problems.

7.11.1 ANALYSIS OF VARIANCE AND ITS COMPONENTS

To illustrate, in pricing, after the classes are identified and the risk classified, the model is used to calculate the premiums. This requires identifying the risk level for each class and defining credibility premiums. One of the problems is to find the effects of distributions of related variables defined in a model for the profiles of the risk units-insureds, for example:

A/B	B_1	B_2	$\cdots$	B_b	Total
A_1	r_{11}	r_{12}	$\cdots$	r_{1b}	$r_{1.}$
A_2	r_{21}	r_{22}	$\cdots$	r_{2b}	$r_{2.}$
$\vdots$	$\vdots$	$\vdots$	$\vdots$	$\vdots$	$\vdots$
A_a	r_{a1}	r_{a2}	$\cdots$	r_{ab}	$r_{a.}$
Total	$r_{.1}$	$r_{.2}$	$\cdots$	$r_{.b}$	1

A divides the population in classes $A_1, \cdots, A_a$ and B divides the population in classes $B_1, \cdots, B_b$. The proportion of the population that is classified as both A_a and B_b is r_{ab}, while $r_{a.}$ = the proportion of the population classified as A_a and $r_{.b}$ = the proportion of the population classified as B_b.

The components of variance are useful to analyze. Models used to assign premiums to risk are based on components of variance. Here it is illustrated in the use of one- and two-way ANOVA. For example, fixed effects ANOVA can be used to detect the effect of cellular phones on driving ability. Consider five groups of people with various cellular phone use habits and 200 observations within each group. The mean and standards deviation are given as follows:

Group	Mean	S.D.
Non-users	3.78	0.79
Passive users	3.30	0.77
Light users	3.23	0.78
Medium users	2.73	0.81
Heavy users	2.59	0.82

The variances are similar, but the means are different. There are relationships among the various population. The model response is $y_{ij} = \mu_i + e_{ij}$ for member j of group i, where the uncorrelated errors e_{ij} have the same distribution with average zero and variance σ_i^2.

An example for random effects is when it is considered a population of 200 auto-insurance policies who had claims. Randomly select seven policies. Then for each policy choose a sample of 50 automobiles. An inference conclusion is sought for the whole population. This means μ_i, the individual policy, means score were drawn randomly from a population. Mean scores with overall mean μ and variance σ_A^2 made up of the N eligible policies of the company. σ_i^2 represents the within variance for policy i and σ_A^2 represents the between variance for a population of true means.

The model is $y_{ij} = \mu + a_i + e_{ij}$ where $\mu_i = \mu + a_i$. The two-way model is $y_{ijk} = \mu + a_i + b_j + e_{ijk}$ where a_i describe the effect on y due to i-th level of first factor and b_j is the effect of j-th of second factor. There are two models; one is nested $Y_{ijk} = a_i + b_{ij} + \mu_{ijk}$ and classification with interaction $Y_{ijk} = \mu + a_i + b_j + c_{ij} + e_{ijk}$. c_{ij} is the interaction effect of i-th level of first factor and j-th of the second factor. In the case of random effects, a_i, b_j, c_{ij} are random with variances σ_a^2, σ_b^2, σ_c^2, σ_e^2; these are the variance components.

The insured claim ratio is decomposed in a sum of uncorrelated random variables. Each of these new random variables represents the contribution of a risk factor or the contribution of an interaction between risk factors to the total variance of the insured's claim ratio random variable. This total variance is broken up into variance components. A hierarchical approach is not adequate if there is an interaction between the various risk factors. For example, an automobile insurance portfolio would be given a hierarchical classification first by gender of the driver and then by age, where gender and age represent the two qualitative risk factors. However, some young women share risk with young men who themselves share driving characteristics with older men. The parameters give $\Theta_i^{(1)}$, $\Theta_j^{(2)}$, $\Theta_k^{(3)}$, $X_{ijk1} \ldots .. X_{ijkT_{ijk}}$ the description of the risk. t goes from 1 to T_{ijk}.

Classification, variance components, and related concepts are looking for clarifying the changes that can be different in certain groups. One concept in risk analytics is to find the metrics of risk adjusted to group conditions. This is approached by credibility theory. Define P as the number of risk factors, and let J_p be the number of categories available within the p-th risk factor $p = 1, \cdots, P$. Category $j_p (=1, \cdots, J_P)$ of the p-th risk factor is characterized by $\Theta_{j_p}^{(p)}$.

The available set of data consists of a P-dimensional array with realizations of risks $X_{j_1 j_2, \cdots, j_p t}$ in cells $(j_1, j_2, \cdots, j_{P-1}, j_P)$ for $t = 1, \cdots, T_{j_1, \cdots, j_p}$. The multiway crossed classification model consists of the following assumptions [see Dannenburg (1995)]:

1. For fixed p, the $\Theta_{j_p}^{(p)}$ are i.i.d; all ocurring $\Theta's$ are independent.
2. For certain functions. For $q, i_1, \ldots, i_q \in 1, \ldots, P$; $j_{i_1} = 1, \ldots, J_{i_1}$; and so on.

$$E\left[X_{j_1, \cdots, j_P t} | \Theta_{j_{i_1}}^{(i_1)}, \cdots, \theta_{j_{i_q}}^{i_q}\right] = \mu_{i_1, \cdots, i_q}\left(\theta_{j_{i_1}}^{(i_1)}, \cdots, \theta_{j_{i_q}}^{i_q}\right)$$

3.
$$E\left[cov\left[X_{j_1, \cdots, j_P, t}, X_{k_1, \cdots, k_P, u} \Big| \Theta^{(1)}, \cdots, \Theta^{(P)}\right]\right] = \delta_{j_1, \cdots, j_P, k_1, \cdots, k_P, u} \frac{s^2}{w_{j_1, \cdots, j_P, t}}$$

Here, $\Theta^{(q)} = \left(\theta_1^{(q)}, \cdots, \theta_{J_q}^{(q)}\right)'$

In terms of credibility, the variance components models play an important role. In the Buhlmann-Straub model, the loss ratio of an insured is the random variation around the collective mean m

$$X_{it} = m + \Xi_i^1 + \Xi_{it}^{(12)}$$

where Ξ_i represents the variability between the insureds and $\Xi_{it}^{(12)}$ is the variability in the insureds claim over time. In the hierarchical model, the variable sector is component 1. Class is component 2. Insured is component 3. Time is component 4.

It means that time t, the claim ratio of insured i in class k of sector p, can be written as:

$$X_{it}^{kp} = m + \Xi_p^{(1)} + \Xi_{pk}^{(12)} + \Xi_{pki}^{(123)} + \Xi_{pkit}^{(1234)},$$

where there are the interactions between time and components i, (i, j), (i, j, k).

In the cross-classification credibility model with q, l_1, l_2, $\cdots$, $l_q = 1, 2, 3$ then

$$X_{ijtk} = m + \Xi_i^{(1)} + \Xi_j^{(2)} + \Xi_k^{(3)} + \Xi_{ij}^{(12)} + \Xi_{ik}^{(13)} + \Xi_{jk}^{(23)} + \Xi_{ijk}^{(123)} + \Xi_{ijkt}^{(1234)}$$

The random variables $\Xi^{(l_1, \cdots, l_q)}$ have mean zero and variance $b^{(l_1, \cdots, l_q)}$.

7.11.2 Misclassification Problem

Misclassification in the insurance model produces an erroneously greater or lower premium for the insured (Johnson, 1998). The total probability of misclassification is given by the probability of the observation and comes from group 1 and is misclassified plus the probability of the observation comes from group 2 and is misclassified. The objective is to find the smallest value of the total probability of misclassification. The minimum expected cost rule with equal misclassification costs is given by:

Allocate x to group k if

$$p_k f_k(x) > p_i f_i(x) \, for \, all \, i \neq k$$

The minimum total probability of misclassification rule for normal populations, with unequal Σ_i is: Allocate x to the group k if the k-th quadratic score is the largest of other quadratic scores. The quadratic scores is:

$$d_i^Q(x) = -\frac{1}{2}\ln\Sigma - \frac{1}{2}(x - \mu_i'\Sigma_i^{-1}(x - \mu_i) + \ln p_i$$

The same rule is accepted if there are several normal populations, and the quadratic score is

$$d_i^Q(x) = -\frac{1}{2}\ln\mathbf{S} - \frac{1}{2}(x - \bar{x}_i)'\mathbf{S}_i^{-1}(x - \bar{x}_i) + \ln p_i$$

The problem of misclassification can be solved by an analysis of the portfolio indicating allocation optimization based on the classes used for risk evaluation. Not all risks have to be perfect; the portfolio will have risks units in all categories as it was expressed in previous chapter.

7.11.3 Migration of risk levels with Markov's model

This model is possible to apply with the redefinition of the risk levels based on the scoring model design. The consistency of the risk evaluation for different periods of the portfolio has to be reached. The possibility of having current conditions of the risk level definition and the administrative rules involved in the process produce distortion in the transition matrices and the comparison is not allowed. The score function S has to be applied to the portfolios in different time periods; this is $S(P_1)$, $S(P_2)$ and so on, to redefine for all these portfolios the risk levels and then to start the process of the matrices building.

N_{jk} is the number of buyers in the risk category j in the time i, which move to the category k in the time $i+1$. With this values, we create the matrix N.

P_{ik} is the quotient $\frac{N_{jk}}{\sum_{k=0}^{n} N_{jk}}$ where the n categories include the credits paid and defaulted.

With these values, it is created the from transition matrix P with i and j entries. The categories corresponding to credits paid and defaulted are considered absorbent categories. The matrix P is partitioned in the following way with n transient states and r absorbing states:

$$ P = \begin{bmatrix} I & O \\ R & Q \end{bmatrix} $$

The matrix I is the identity matrix of rxr, the matrix O is matrix of zeros with dimension rxn, R is a matrix of nxr created with the absorbent states, and Q is a matrix of nxn with the transient states. The process has to define the fundamental matrix N in the following way:

$$ N = (I - Q)^{-1} = I + Q + Q^2 + Q^3 + \cdots + Q^k + \cdots $$

where this is an expansion based on a matrix polynomial. The movement through time is based on the transition matrix multiplication this means to calculate P^n for a period n. The vector $B_i = (B_{i0}, B_{i1}, \ldots, B_{in-1})$ represents the number of risk units in the moment i for each risk level. The matrix product BNR give us the number of expected of credit paid and defaulted from a risk level vector B. A variance can be calculated and a π value can be calculated as

$$ A = b\,[\pi NR - (\pi NR)_{sq}] $$

The b value is the total number of buyers of the portfolio. The vector $\pi = (1/b)B$ is the probability vector with non-negative components of unit sum.

The time to reach an absorbent category is given by $T = Nc$, where c is a column vector with entries equal to 1. The process has to be validated in terms of the Markovian property, which has to be assessed by the corresponding test. If the property is not reached, it is necessary to continue with a model calibration of the stochastic process.

A forecasting using the Markov model is the process to get a measure of the future value of the portfolio in different levels of risk and the expected value of loss given the risk level categories. The procedure is to take the P^n matrix and the exposure values at the observation point, this is the exposure vector by risk levels, to get the final values using a matrix multiplication. The consistency of the results has to be obtained; there are many points to keep in mind for the modeling process, especially that the risk level has been defined by administrative rules more than probabilistic drivers.

This chapter introduced several techniques in data analytics using and not using machine learning. The main message is about types of problems and types of models, each model and each technique are required to review independently according to data available and problem to solve; for instance classification has some techniques, link analysis other, optimization other, etc. The experience in risk analytics is associated with the selection of the techniques that are appropriate for the type of problems and its data to find solutions. There are questions that are above the structure of the models and they are more about the best parameter to use, generalization, capacity to manage samples, manage computational capacity, managing correlations and assumptions that can affect results, and so on. As it has been mentioned in the book on several occasions, the most important is to start with some models and to understand in a better way the problem, the questions to answer, and then to select a short list of algorithms to use to test the results. Factors in using certain models are not only related to accuracy, they are related to capacity to implement and to know what is possible to learn from the model in order to control risk. The issues appear when the models are not doing the work of providing understanding but creating more difficulties to understand the models than the problem itself.

The next chapter is about the issues to work on when risk analytics is in design and implementation of the risk analytics process. This means to review possible bias, errors, updating, controlling data flows, workflows, systems to support actions, etc. that are part of risk analytics. Risk analytics cannot finish when models are created, that is only one subprocess to start, but the full risk analytics process is when the operational information systems are working, it is when AI is doing what is required in the benefit of the creators of the solutions, not when AI algorithms are optimizing solutions without the creator desire. AI is about the intelligence for supporting what humans need to do and to keep human life with better control of risks, and to have better possible results for humans and humans machines interactions.

8 Dealing with Monitoring the Risk Analytics Process

The risk analytics process is intimately related to monitoring risk or the construction of a complete intelligent system to perform the risk management processes. The risk analytics process is not only about assessment but also about monitoring risk and converting risk management into an evolving competitive advantage to keep organizations in good standing and continuous performance improvement. In this chapter the emphasis is on implementation and adoption of the risk analytics processes and all what in the previous chapters of tools and methods have been presented. The review of the concepts in this chapter is related to the understanding of means to embed risk management to strategic planning and the review of possible barriers that are present to maintain a risk analytics system (RAS) properly operating. In this chapter, the main concept to use is risk monitoring. Risk monitoring is one of these crucial aspects to understand how the RAS needs to be designed and supported. Risk monitoring is not only the creation of the awareness of risk events but also the mean of creation of the information and knowledge systems to operationalize risk management processes from data to actions. The RAS includes the following concepts for risk monitoring:

- Monitoring means measure - create knowledge - predict
- Monitoring implies to be in a proactive and reactive position to deal with possible losses.
- Monitoring is a means to improve the analytical capacity of management indicators-measurement systems.
- Monitoring is crucial in the creation of means to analyze and design risk information systems.
- Monitoring includes the entire business, the evaluation of the strategy and business processes.

Brownlee et al. (2020) described what is happening with risk monitoring and motivation to continue building a RAS: "Banking executives continue to evaluate new ways to incorporate artificial intelligence (AI) into the middle and back office to improve efficiency, mitigate risk and reduce cost. Even with these efforts, a Business Insider report estimates the aggregate potential cost savings from AI applications at US$248bn by 2023 in the middle and back office." According to these statements, the first point to study is about barriers and limitations to build a RAS. The next sections will provide an indication of what a RAS requires and what can be limitations for obtaining solutions.

8.1 POSSIBLE BARRIERS TO CREATE A RISK ANALYTICS SYSTEM (RAS)

To achieve the goal of implementing risk analytics there are several steps, techniques, methods, and areas to connect. However, there are hidden aspects that create issues in any implementation and the coordination of all system components and subsystems the same as legacy-inherited systems. In the following paragraphs, there is a presentation of the non-observable issues or barriers that reduce the capacity to create RASs. Risk analytics adoption needs to create the proper organization conditions of people, processes, and technology. The development of data analytics and risk analytics has been with ups and downs, mainly because the expectations and the belief of data science as a magic pill to create solutions. Risk analytics helps to guide the creation of future support decision-making processes, creation of solutions, orientation and

DOI: 10.1201/9780429342899-9

goals definition, and evaluation, but it cannot be the reality itself. Risk analytics as any process is under constraints and uncertainty in implementation. Risk analytics has been limited in the access to data, use of technology, and most important the adoption in organizations. A RAS design helps to organize and maintain a structure that can be updated, improved, and in an ongoing construction to strengthen the risk management and related processes. The evolution of data analytics and related processes have been associated with the methods for solving problems and making decisions.

As Bursk and Chapman (1963) pointed out: "In the years since the mid 1950s a trend toward a new and more scientific approach to the solution of business problems has been developing. It stems from methods first suggested by the advocates of 'operations research.' But it is already apparent that by drawing in depth both on mathematics and on social sciences, and by utilizing intensively the high-speed electronic computer, researchers are beginning to give to the decision-making process a scientific base akin to the established methods which have long provided the bases for research in physics, biology, and chemistry." In several areas and organizations as a whole, the previous description is current, and organizations are in the process of improving the use of better tools, methods, and approaches to enhance the use of available resources.

To reach a balance between intuition and reason for monitoring risk, there is a request of a design of a risk system that is not only involving all steps needed to maintain data that is useful to create knowledge through analytics (people and machines interacting), but also to understand how an organization chart functions in the sense that it can be embedded in operational information systems. Figure 8.6 in Section 8.3 provides more details of the system components. These basic components are represented in a loop of components (Figure 8.1).

The below diagram describing components of the RAS needs the context where people and machine interact. The way to connect hardware-software-people-data-information and knowledge in the RAS requires starting from a holistic view of the risks for the organization digging deeper to

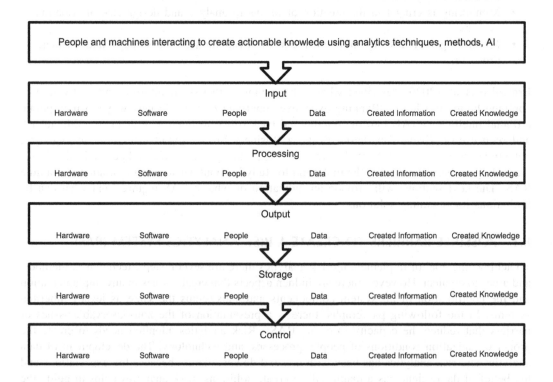

FIGURE 8.1 Summary of the basic components in a RAS.

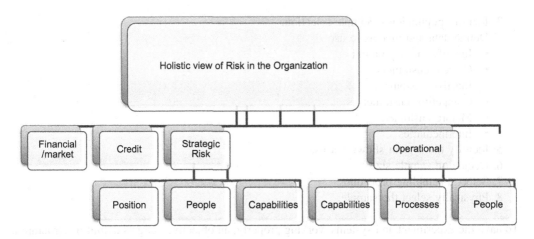

FIGURE 8.2 Holistic view of risk management.

understand the relationships that are generated when information and knowledge are flowing. For example, it is required to clarify the risks are related to position responsibilities, capabilities, processes, and people (Figure 8.2).

8.2 FACTORS AFFECTING THE ORGANIZATIONS' RAS

In the following paragraphs, there is a presentation of the way to connect concepts of the previous chapters and the implementation of a RAS developing plan. The first component in dealing with risk analytics, as was mentioned in Chapter 1 and the previous section, is to have a good understating of potential factors that can affect the organization. A way to put into groups these factors is using the following categories to understand the business first:

1. Sector – environmental analysis factors.
2. Business definition factors (what is the offer, who are my customers, how the offer will be delivered).
3. Factors of business processes.
4. Industry indicators: growth and market share factors.
5. Factors of strategic groups.
6. Strategic and evolutive transformation-digital-intelligence-use of external resources.

Once the business is understood in a general way, the next point is to answer What is the way to formulate objectives? What to measure and how? In the core of ideas of risk analytics, the objectives are based on confidence intervals definition of where potentially an organization's goals can be in the future. The purpose is to identify the main metric and to discover how the variability can be estimated to be closer to a target. Different factors and their relationships can affect the estimation and inference process. The main principle is that in any situation with regular or big data work, the experiment design process has to be well planned and tested through:

1. Definition of objectives-targets – pre-knowledge of the problems and solutions performed in previous studies.
2. Hypotheses definition. The big data access and possibility to use it do not substitute the hypotheses testing process initiatex in several cases with data mining and performed for example using statistical tests or k-fold cross validation.

3. Identify population – Sample selection.
4. Define data and models to use
   - Identify the population
   - Current customers
   - Inactive customers
   - Competitor customers
   - Mature customers
   - Intermediaries
5. Identify the system shows – a list.
6. Decide on sample size.
7. Select a sampling procedure.
8. Physically select the sample.

To have the experiment and systems working properly, an objectives-targets definition structure is required. Goals are associated with several variables and each one has risks that can emerge to connect risk analytics and risk actions for control, such as:

1. Product-based: product use
2. Competition: competitive position
3. Demographics: user profile
4. Profitability: value obtained from the relationship
5. Wealth: customer's potential
6. Conduct: consumer models
7. Customer needs
8. Combination of criteria: using analytical methods
9. Transaction behavior
10. Basic funding
11. Consumer financing
12. Asset management-investment

These variables for the RAS design can be connected though the specificity of the economic sector, the attributes of being strategic or tactical, and risk associated (see Figures 8.3, 8.4, and 8.5).

Using these summaries of relationships of objectives, attributes of business and organization, and strategy lead to defined risks that can affect implementation and generation of value through a RAS. The next section introduces RAS components to figure out the way to assemble what has been presented in previous chapters and will provide actionable tools for organizations dealing with risk.

8.3 DIGGING DEEPER IN RAS COMPONENTS

To supplement what Figure 8.1 indicates and what has been in previous chapters, there is a need to create a more general review of risks, leading the study to a competitive environment through the clarification of the following aspects: Attribute selection and macro-strategy integration, attribute assessment, comparison of attributes, formulation of the micro-strategy, implementation, and control systems. The business environment guides the definition of the RAS components (Figure 8.6) for organizing and connecting key performance indicators and key risk indicators, and data required, as it was introduced models to analyze data, and means to transfer and keep the knowledge generated by the risk analytics process.

These components of the system, after a goal definition, require the alignment to key risk indicators that are part of the key performance indicators of the organization.

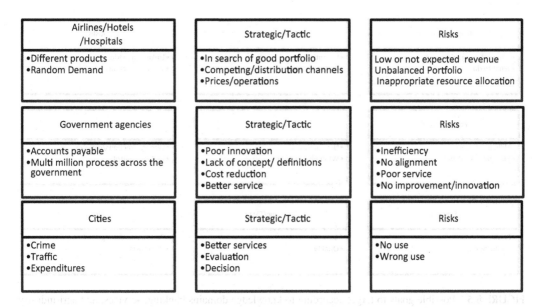

FIGURE 8.3 Possible goals to target according to knowledge domains airlines, government agencies, and cities.

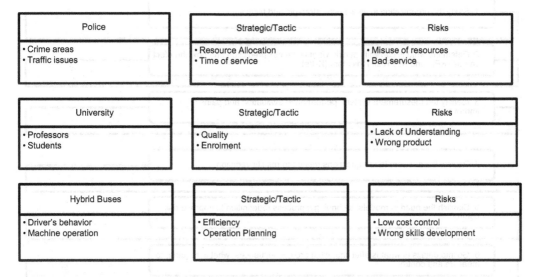

FIGURE 8.4 Possible goals to target according to knowledge domains police department, education, and transportation.

8.4 CREATING A RAS AND THE KEY RISK INDICATORS ANALYSIS

The observation of the potential risks is in connection to strategic and tactical actions the same as the risk indicators and responses that organizations should perform. Table 8.1 and 8.2 present examples of the way to create the chain of KPIs and risk indicators. Key risk indicators (KRIs) can help to guide the creation of metrics through the analytics process, which are going to be monitored and controlled by the RAS system.

In the development of metrics, there are several questions regarding relationships and possible cause-effect. The practice of creating metrics requires a monovariate observation, a multivariate observation, and the way to describe correlations and possibly the influence qualitative model of

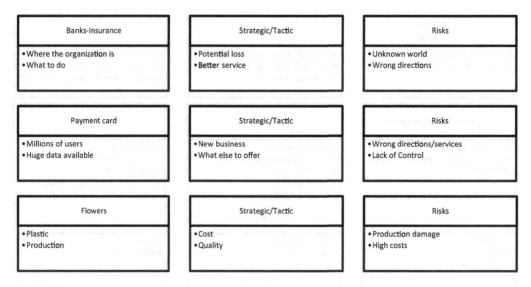

FIGURE 8.5 Possible goals to target according to knowledge domains banking, services, and agri-industry.

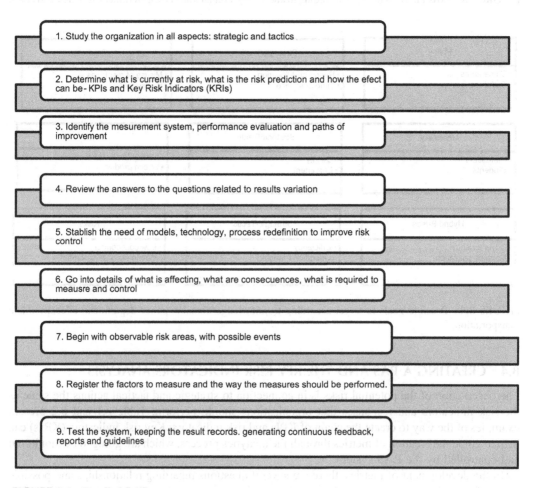

FIGURE 8.6 Detailed RAS components.

TABLE 8.1

Relationship of KPIs and KRIs

KPI: Objective Increase the satisfaction index level of citizens in 2%	Strategic Initiative: Develop programs to educate families for awareness and protection	Potential Risks: Trend of the level of collaboration in the community	Key Risk Indicators: Changes in number of people participating in the program by local crime events	Strategic Response: Development of leaders and closer support to community activities

TABLE 8.2

Application of the Relationship of KPIs and KRIs to Marketing Understanding

Key Performance Indicator	Key Risk Indicator
Net of new customers	Metrics associated with: Complaints without solutions, returns, defects, reviews. Example: Number of customers that did not buy anymore, did not renewed …
Proportion of bad debts to total revenues	Metrics associated with changes in the status of accounts receivables. Example: probability of moving from 30 days payment to 60 days
Market share by products and regions	Many factors can influence

process components that indicate clues of possible cause-effect relationships. In particular, frequencies and severity of risk are the first relationships that can be investigated. In risk analytics, it is possible to have the effects of non-frequent events but with high impact or on the contrary many events that do not represent high impact. One example is to connect customers count with sales and profits generation and study the variation of results that can have effects in each component of frequency and size of the sales of profits. The number of customers can change but it depends on the segment of sales and profit generation. Atomized customers will have a totally different effect from concentrated portfolios when there is a churn trend in the market. The known cause-effect diagrams to identify possible causes for certain outcomes in processes and known as fish diagrams represent the four factors to control: materials, methods, manpower, and machinery. To supplement the description of cause and effect, it is required to divide objectives in a family of factors required for the risk analytics process.

KPIs are part of the performance evaluation system in an organization. One of the aspects to review is the benchmark system to clarify a combination of those KPIs and not only see them in a univariate way but, and more important, to review the combination of them to produce, for example, a gross margin or enterprise goals (Table 8.3).

However, as it was discussed in Chapter 3, the metrics cannot be only univariate, the risk analytics process goes further in identifying that metrics that require evaluation in different dimensions. The dimensions are related to the balanced scorecard where the pillars are financial/benefits, customer/users/beneficiaries, operation/processes, and employees/people. Once the dimensions are identified, the indicators will be grouped and compared to the levels of deviation (risk) that can be accepted regarding a specific target. The deviation is evaluated according to the consequences and, in this step, will appear as appetite, tolerance, and thresholds. The appetite will be the level that is marking a confidence level where the target should be, the tolerance where the risk will have an acceptable impact in organization's performance, and thresholds will be the limits of risk where the risk evaluation will have an expected change (Table 8.4).

TABLE 8.3
Example in the Practice of KPIs for Four Organizations and the Industry

Direct Competitor Comparison	DATA Inc.	ACN	HPQ	MSFT	Industry
Market Cap:	164.44B	60.7B	57.44B	374.01B	850.52M
Employees:	3,79,592	3,23,000	3,02,000	1,28,000	1.95K
QtrlyRevGrowth (yoy):	−0.12	0.05	−0.07	0.07	0.12
Revenue (ttm):	90.15B	30.90B	108.28B	94.78B	697.18M
Gross Margin (ttm):	0.5	0.32	0.24	0.65	0.27
EBITDA (ttm):	23.61B	4.89B	12.94B	33.71B	40.44M
Operating Margin (ttm):	0.21	0.14	0.08	0.3	0.06
Net Income (ttm):	15.64B	3.04B	4.69B	20.00B	N/A
EPS (ttm):	12	4.71	2.51	2.41	0.37
P/E (ttm):	13.92	20.58	12.68	19.14	18.45
PEG (5 YT expected):	2.37	2.06	4.46	2.7	1.62
P/S (ttm):	184	1.97	0.54	3.99	1.02

TABLE 8.4
An Illustration of the Combination of Main Variables to Measure and Related Objectives, Indicators, Dispersion, Appetite, and Tolerance

Quadrant	Objective	KPI current	Target	Dispersion	Appetite m	Appetite M	Tolerance m	Tolerance M	Threshold
financial	Operating Margin Growth	3.95	3.00	0.95	2.09	3.82	1.97	4.98	1
	Profit growth	5.00	3.00	2.00	2.13	4.73	1.96	5.00	1
	Revenue growth	5.00	5.00	0.00	4.04	4.91	3.99	5.00	1
	Stock price growth	5.00	5.00	0.00	2.90	5.00	2.75	5.00	0
operation	Distribution Capacity	3.34	4.00	−0.66	3.28	4.43	3.21	5.00	0
	Price Competiveness	5.00	5.00	0.00	3.52	3.96	3.49	4.24	1
	Cost Competitiveness	5.00	5.00	0.00	3.69	4.12	3.66	4.41	1
	Reduction COGS	5.00	5.00	0.00	3.13	5.00	2.96	5.00	0
	Service time improvement	5.00	2.00	3.00	1.63	4.75	1.42	5.00	1
	New developments	5.00	5.00	0.00	4.04	4.91	3.99	5.00	1
employee	Intellectual Capital Dev.	5.00	5.00	0.00	4.04	4.91	3.99	5.00	1
	Employees development	2.47	3.00	−0.53	2.50	4.00	2.40	5.00	1
	Training by employee	4.63	2.00	2.63	2.13	4.73	1.96	5.00	0
	Education Level	2.98	5.00	−2.02	4.38	5.00	4.32	5.00	1
	Satisfaction level	5.00	5.00	0.00	5.00	5.00	5.00	5.00	0
customer	Product line depth	3.55	4.00	−0.45	1.50	3.00	1.40	4.00	1
	Promotion Effectiveness	5.00	4.50	0.50	3.19	3.62	3.16	3.91	1
	Location	4.91	4.50	0.41	3.52	3.96	3.49	4.24	1
	Service delivery satisf	3.66	4.50	−0.84	3.50	3.50	3.50	3.50	1
	Organization Reputation	5.00	5.00	0.00	2.90	5.00	2.75	5.00	0
	Profit by customer	3.89	5.00	−1.11	2.90	5.00	2.75	5.00	0
	Product satisfaction	4.31	5.00	−0.69	4.38	5.00	4.32	5.00	1
	New customers	5.00	5.00	0.00	2.90	5.00	2.75	5.00	0
	Market share	3.75	4.00	−0.25	1.81	4.86	2.42	5.00	0

A way to determine factors to measure in each dimension is associated with the possibility to connect levels of objectives, understanding the way that those objectives are correlated, and how in several cases a hypothetical diagram showing the variables' relationship can identify effects of decisions to make to achieve defined levels of the objective results. Figure 8.7 shows how the objectives are families of data, models, KRIs, etc. in each of the steps in risk analytics.

Table 8.5 illustrates the identification of KPIs and KRIs in a setting related to smart cities and factors that affect multiple services and their risk in a city. The crucial aspect is to identify the

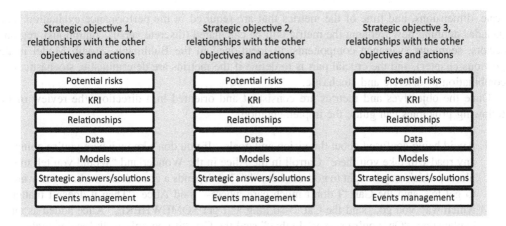

FIGURE 8.7 General structure to develop the RAS core orientation of control.

TABLE 8.5

Example of Application of the KPIs and KRIs Relationship in a Setting of Smart Cities

Perspective vs. Actions in Smart Cities	Crime Control	Accidentality/Traffic signs	Customer Service Requests	Education
		Stakeholders' Perspective		
KPI	Time to respond to inquires	Ratio Pedestrians Volume/accidentality	Ratio calls/emergency level	Ratio expenses/ Graduated Students
KRI	Variability of time for attention	Time to have solutions for traffic signs	Level of cases solved scores changes	Changes in the number of successful student s graduation – Churn analysis
	Variation of appropriate resources	Location – intersections in high probability accidentality	Time for closing cases with solutions	Changes in Expenditure by enrolment
		Financial Resources Management Perspective		
KPI	Reduce operational cost	Investment per sign type	Investment in automation and communication	Support for students
KRI	Level of effectiveness	Changes in a trend in accidents	Goal achievement variation of the solutions	Changes in Number and amounts of benefits
	Level of satisfaction	Level of areas with high accidentality	Cases closed with a good evaluation per dollar invested	Compensation education providers/quality level
		Internal Process Perspective		
KPI	Reduction process steps	Number of cases by dollars invested	Ratio Number cases to dollars of public resources	Number of schools/ number of students/ investment
KRI	Changes in investment/ time of the process	Variation of the ratio cases by dollar	Changes in the ratio cases to dollars	Change in enrolment/ teaching resources
		Trained Public Servant Perspective		
KPI	Hours training per year	Training and incentives	Growth of served cases	Number of m^2 areas for education
KRI	Permeability/retention/ practice of good techniques	Evaluation of accidents by human resources	Number of claims	Changes forecast vs. current

scale, dimensions, and time of the metrics that are required in the performance evaluation. This includes defining how frequent the metric will be calculated (discrete versus continuous), regions, sectors, segments (variance components, as mentioned in the Buhlmann- Straub Model in the previous chapter), and the crucial part is to define if the metrics are deterministic, stochastic, or a combination of discrete and stochastic.

Once the objectives and metrics are consistent and oriented in a direction, the review of the following principles can guide the implementation:

1. Avoid being confused about the vision and goals, "If you don't know where you're going, any road will take you there" Carroll in the Alice in the Wonderland "Would you tell me, please, which way I ought to go from here?" "That depends a good deal on where you want to get to," said the Cat. "I don't much care where–" said Alice. "Then it doesn't matter which way you go," said the Cat. "–so long as I get SOMEWHERE," Alice added as an explanation. "Oh, you're sure to do that," said the Cat, "if you only walk long enough."
2. Avoid strategic traps related to looking for what organization wants to hear or the way that people try to justify previous decisions.
3. Pay attention to avoid hard facts or half truths.
4. Not only to see or ask for bad things, ask why the organization is doing well ...
5. Review continuously the time and market changes.
6. Consider redundancy as a good friend.
7. Start keeping the end in mind to solve problems and identify goals, from the expected results. From the final possible solutions go back to build your processes.
8. Combine different optics of problem and solutions, not only one view, only one kind of people, only one way of thinking.

A RAS is for monitoring risk supports in an organization to deal with known, unknown, and unknowable options to develop projects/decisions and solutions. Maintain a view and distinction among possible futures, desire futures, and feasible futures. Controllable variables to solve problems can be a priority to deep understanding. Figures 8.8 and 8.9 and Table 8.6 help to identify the process of measurement and alignment of risk indicators to actions of the organizations. These steps require clarification of where to go and where to start, decision of what to measure, creating the systems to measure, and being sure that it is possible to measure any indicator. Verify that there is currently data or new data created from the data the risk analytics process, that is able to add value to the raw data. Created data is an outcome of creating knowledge – understanding, finding

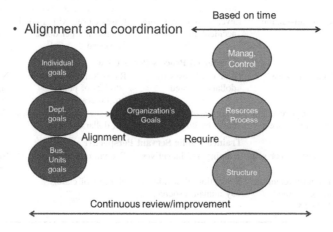

FIGURE 8.8   A representation of alignment of goals as an ongoing process.

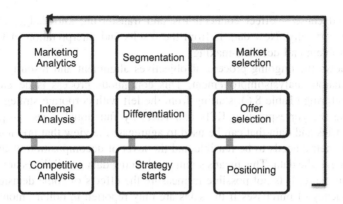

FIGURE 8.9 Application of the sequence of analytics steps in brand name creation – brand equity – strategic risk.

TABLE 8.6

Connecting Strategy and Specific Risk Indicators – Creation of the Control and Monitoring Tree

Hierarchical database structure by objectives, KPIs, KRIs, and alignment with metrics, possibly different metrics use different data and analytics method to calculate and then to incorporate results in the operational information systems. The database will have the capacity to produce reports and data products can be related by the hierarchical level indicated below. The general vector is V={strategy, goal level, objective level, KPI level, KRI level, functional or project KPIs and KRIs}

LEVEL 1 the strategy is the basis, after goal and objectives setting, each objective has its KPIs and each KPI will be related to the functional areas or projects and then each KPI will have associated KRIs				By Functional Area		By Projects of functional areas. It is not required each KRI of functional area to have a related project KRI		Risk Metrics
Strategy	Goal 1	Objective 11	KPI11	KPI11A	KRI11A1	KPI11AA	KRI11AA1	Analytics for creating the metrics and maintain the system
					KRI11A2		KRI11AA2	
					KRI11A3		KRI11AA3	
						KPI11AB	KRI11AB1	
							KRI11AB2	
							KRI11AB3	
						KPI11AC	KRI11AC1	
							KRI11AC2	
							KRI11AC3	
				KPI11B	KRI11B1	KPI11BA	KRI11BA1	
					KRI11B2		KRI11BA2	
					KRI11B3		KRI11BA3	
						KPI11BB	KRI11BB1	
							KRI11BB2	
							KRI11BB3	
						KPI11BC	KRI11BC1	
							KRI11BC2	
							KRI11BC3	
				KPI11C	KRI11C1	KPI11CA	KRI11CA1	
					KRI11C2		KRI11CA2	
					KRI11C3		KRI11CA3	
						KPI11CB	KRI11CB1	
							KRI11CB2	
							KRI11CB3	
						KPI11CC	KRI11CC1	
							KRI11CC2	
							KRI11CC3	

root causes – and cause – effect connectivity, and transferring knowledge, communicating – horizontally and vertically, New data is from the results and interpretation of the results in the context of the problem and decision-making.

Figure 8.8 shows the ongoing process of objectives alignment and resources, keeping a surveillance of variation analysis/improvement. This continuous process is developed as tree for surveillance/monitoring (Table 8.6), starting from the left with corporate strategy/objectives, and moving to define the corresponding KPIs and KRIs by functional areas, projects, and finally assigning the metrics and data that can be used to aggregate the view that previous administrative levels require. A metric needs to be feasible and the level of decomposition of the metrics has to possible according to the data. This means slicing and dicing data possibilities are totally related to the capacity to measure. It is not possible to measure the effects of some decisions at a segment level in the frequency of purchases if the sales are only reported in dollar amounts.

The measurement process helps to reduce barriers of RAS adoption, given the structure of the process itself. The measurement process needs the understanding of business processes and the orientation to creating value and positioning of the organization. Positioning can be based on differentiation and segmentation this means to evaluate possible variation of results based on changes in these specific variables. Strategic risk will then be measured through several metrics and one of it will be based on positioning, brand equity, etc.

Risk analytics implementation requires clarifying how the relationship of the metrics will be to the sources of revenue, profits, or expected results. Figure 8.10 guides the creation based on the financial approach, depending on the area of interest and a tree of metrics that allows the search of data and logic (models) requirements and availability for performing risk analytics. If the profits are the key aspects to evaluate in an organization, a first point to start is to review the sources of

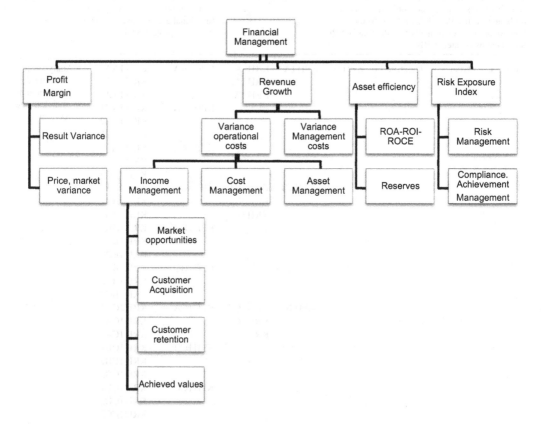

FIGURE 8.10   Creation of metrics: KPI in areas such as finance.

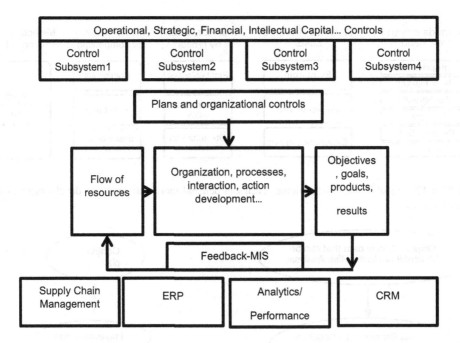

FIGURE 8.11 Control subsystems that help to develop a RAS.

profits. For instance, increasing sales under a certain margin, reducing cost under certain sales levels, managing portfolios of revenue generation, managing portfolios according to expected and desired results in products, regions-markets, promotion, etc. The key point from the risk analytics perspective is the variation analysis of what was expected and what was obtained, identifying causes, defining confidence intervals, and way to perform better to increase the probability of achieving results inside narrower confidence intervals.

Each area of metrics definition, RAS design, and risk analytics work is operating according to control subsystems (Figure 8.11). The control subsystem identification allows the identification of potential areas to monitor risk events and to identify early warning systems. For example, it can be the issues of timing and capacity of answers in online sales based on logistic capacity to deliver, coordination of resources, stock availability, etc. There are areas of operational risk related to operation capacity that can be predefined; the same as it is possible to identify the use of new technologies to manage operational costs of service satisfaction of customers.

A good example of how risk analytics can provide value to the business processes and the way to create metrics is represented by the search of metrics such as revenue generation, where price definition is based on what Figure 8.12 indicates. The decision is to use price policies/differentiation based on multiple portfolios (products, markets, promotion approaches, etc.) or to use revenue optimization according to where the targets will be, volume of customers, high margin, combination of year-round promotion strategies, product strategies, etc.

In summary, a good approach to the RAS analysis and design as it was indicated in the previous illustrations is a sequence going top-down and bottom-up process to create control systems and identify areas of risk monitoring and control. Figure 8.13 represents the sequence from data to control. Everything is based on the development of a plan according to a variety of risks to deal in the organization, the variation of results, metrics to evaluate/assess variation impact, etc. and when it is possible to create as a crucial step to fit a loss function/distribution.

In addition to the RAS development flow showing above, moving up and down for a functional RAS, this is associated with what Figure 8.14 shows in terms how decisions are connected to the link of the decisions-making process. This means the RAS development flow includes the review

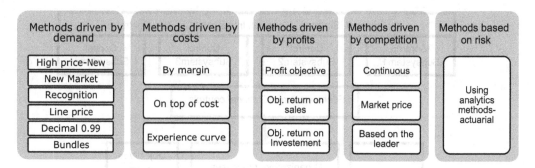

FIGURE 8.12 Possible ways with pricing. Each can demand more data analytics development as it is in actuarial science.

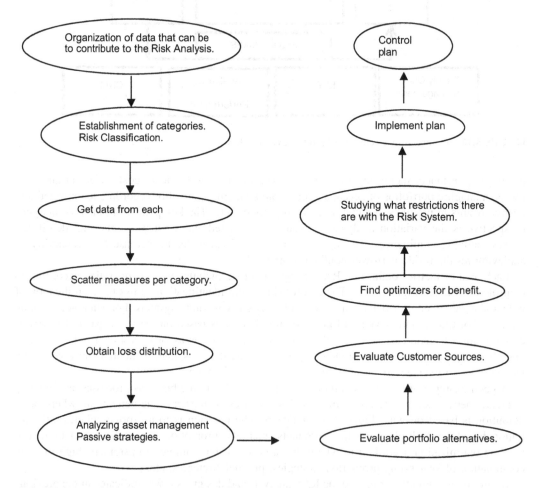

FIGURE 8.13 Moving from data to control and sequential of steps approach.

of how a decision-making process has several dimensions and directions to take. The definition of these dimensions is an outcome of a data analytics process that has impact on risk control. Depending on what dimensions and roads to take a guide to follow a path is identified of how risk metrics should be defined and how data is organized. For example, any component of the business processes can be based on the customer possible settings of prediction. Traditionally, the sequence expected demand and production planning, or distribution/logistic capabilities and a capacity. It is

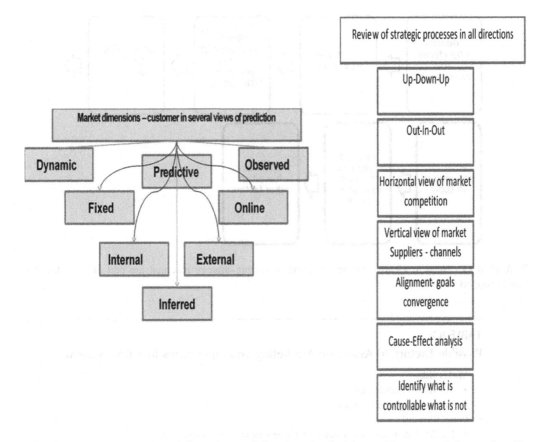

FIGURE 8.14 Decomposition of dimensions and directions that decision-making process brings to the table.

possible that multiple factors affect decisions about customers and those factors can come from the experience online or static or dynamic relationships with the organizations.

At the same time, in a more general approach, Figure 8.15 illustrates all dimensions of analysis of strategic processes that are the input of a RAS design. Figure 8.15 illustrates at the same time a sequence of steps where the control of revenue variations can be part of price changes or additional factors that can influence the customers decisions or margins. These type of approaches in risk analytics can come from regression analysis, considering revenue as a dependent variable and the factors that can affect the revenue generation in a market as explanatory variables.

All of what has been presented in this chapter refers to the fundamentals of analysis and design of a RAS that is the source and support of risk monitoring and control based on risk analytics. The final aspect to review is how risk by risk it is possible to monitor the potential risk impact and what risks have been covered in the RAS stages of development; this means risks that are or not considered. For example, to review different risks and evaluate the level of current knowledge and desire of knowledge that gradually can be created through risk analytics in order to mitigate identified risks. In a general approach, risks are going to appear from possible factors in a market and operation that can be a source of variation of indicators and the fundamental approach is according to Porter's components of competitive strategy. Tables 8.7 and 8.8 show the factors.

And in particular, the relationship to the market development will indicate risk position of the organization that are crucial to monitor. As it was indicated in the risk indicators, review of the benchmarking process is fundamental in risk analytics and in the way that suppliers substitute and portfolio definitions will potentially affect results and require surveillance.

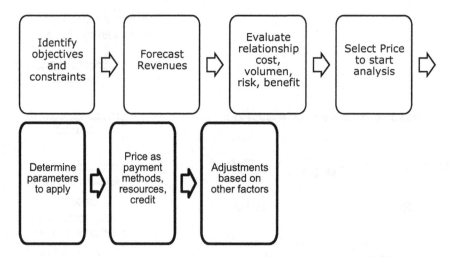

FIGURE 8.15 Need to identify factors affecting marketing-strategy mix that are part of what the RAS should support to control.

TABLE 8.7

Possible Factors to Assess for Marketing and Operations in a RAS System

- Market risks
  - The role of market share
  - Unfamiliarity with the market
- Competitive risks
  - Market share relationships, accumulated experience, and volume cost.
  - The minimum size for viable competition.
  - Changes in market share.
  - The role of competitive strategies and resources.
  - Declination of the added value.
  - Effects of cost structure and capacity utilization.
  - Product lifecycle and competitiveness.
- Financial risks
  - Capital structure
  - Benefits versus cash generation

The risk knowledge based on factors as follows:

Knowledge of the customer's profile	Knowledge of customer potential
Product generation as needed	Adequacy of services
Goodness of communication with the customer	Customer tracking
Information provided	Attention opportunity
Problem-solving capability	Capacity of implementation /adoption plans

Operation

Conditions of business activity	Product development
Customer information system	Control information system
Marketing information system	Executive training
Business training	Remuneration of employees
Building information bases	Production times
Industrial relations	Business atomization
Relations with the government	Utility center development
Customer knowledge	

TABLE 8.8

Possible Factors According to Components of a Competitive Strategy

Suppliers

| Supply relationship management | Supply evaluation system |
| Bargaining capacity | Suppliers follow-up |

Substitutes

Importance scale	Positioning
Quality	Market share
Development capacity	Volume
Offer development	Acceptance

Services

| Before purchasing | After purchasing |
| During the purchase | Offer variety |

In this chapter, it has been reviewed a way to show how the RAS is based on a measurement system and metrics development under the umbrella of KPIs and KRIs. The risk metrics at the end are linked to KRIs. The RAS is associated with the interaction of key performance indicators and the key risk indicators. The principle of metric construction has been based on the variation of key performance indicators considered as the risk that organizations can perceive and take (assess, protect, hedge). The control of variation has been the goal of risk analytics, to identify/monitor factors that can affect the results. At the same time, follow up with the actions that can be taken to manipulate the factors in the direction of reducing or control levels of risk. The process of creating a monitoring system of risk and solutions is then the RAS design bases that will lead the organization to follow the steps to compete in a proper way to be sustainable and mainly adaptable.

The next chapter is about the actions according to the RAS system design. The whole work in risk analytics is about identifying and supporting with evidence where rational changes could have better results, the combination with rational knowledge creation, and what is based on intuition and experience when there is no data. RAS is a socio-technical system that is crucial of the full risk analytics cycle of implementation.

9 Creation of Actions and Value

In the previous chapters, there is a description of components of the RAS and in Chapter 8 the concentration was on surveying components of a RAS under the concept of monitoring risks. Monitoring risks is part of the strategy to be proactive to deal with risk before, in, and after adverse events or for overcoming issues and barriers to develop a RAS to keep adaptive advantages in an organization. In this chapter, there is a presentation of examples mainly in financial markets/institutions related to concepts exposed in previous chapters regarding the structure of the RAS. A RAS is part of a general risk management information system (RMIS) that is connected to operations credit, investment, marketing, operation, etc. and general operations of the organizations.

Bussmann et al., 2021 noted that there are AI models and systems development that require more disclosure of the black boxes of algorithms and methods used in risk management: "... explainable Artificial Intelligence model that can be used in credit risk management and, in particular, in measuring the risks that arise when credit is borrowed employing peer to peer lending platforms. The model applies correlation networks to Shapley values so that Artificial Intelligence predictions are grouped according to the similarity in the underlying explanations." In addition, the article is bringing the point of using a credit peer-to-peer approach in current markets. The main takeaway is to open the eyes in risk analytics about the evolution that RAS needs to have and how new tools to use are connected to what people can do and how to use them, as explained in the previous chapter, relating the RAS design actions aligned to strategy and monitoring market factors affecting variation of expected results of the organization.

The creation of actions in risk analytics is translated to the creation of information systems that contain a data analytics engine to describe, predict, and prescribe the operations in businesses under uncertainty observation. In order to support the risk management processes and to achieve the ERM (enterprise risk management) benefits, a risk management information system (RMIS) is required. Crouhy et al. (2000) identified the requirement of some technology attributes in order to build the RMIS: "The risk management information system needs to be supported by an information technology architecture that is employed in all of the company's information processing." This is further complemented by Crouhy et al. (2000) in the bank setting: "Banks have many business units, which are engaged in different activities and support different products."

The purpose of passing from data to actions requires embedding the analytics workflows in the operational information systems. In risk analytics, there is a need of creating a system that monitors and helps to manage the risk management processes using analytics solutions. The name of this system in this book has been the risk analytics system (RAS) where the design is under principles such as:

- A RAS should be based on accurate and timely data and its processes should be appropriate and fully documented.
- A RAS should be intimately associated with a "profit" goal no necessary economical, but social, or individual, a combination of factors; where an organization would like to be or to achieve (e.g., net claims to premium expectations, events, frequency and severity, time series, etc.). A RAS is about supporting the balanced structure of what the organization requires to operate and generate value, the concept of profit is the outcome of the interaction of employees, customers, suppliers, operations, and so on.
- A RAS should maximize automation while minimizing costs according to organization's risk appetite.

- A RAS should provide simplicity and clarity to the end users.
- A RAS as a sociotechnical system that incorporates advances in technology for data analytics, processing, storing, computing, etc. with human and AI machine interaction.

Components as mentioned in Chapter 8 of the risk analytics system solutions will be at least related to:

- Assess and monitoring risk: Before, in, and after underwriting and direct losses.
- Creating early warning systems, control systems, etc.
- Assign and determine exposure, expected losses, measurement systems-metrics that are possible to compare at different times and apply the analytics tools on the analysis of these metrics (time series, predictive algorithms, etc.) to provide value to the organization.
- Creation of continuous process of metrics evaluation and their control.
- Generation of adaptive systems to compete and to maintain under good performance the organization.

A RAS should assess risk using analytics models that evaluate and classify risk units and transactions according to their risk profile by using analytics techniques. Furthermore, a RAS creates not only a consistent, adequate, and comparable risk classification and differentiation that will be used as an opinion for any cases requiring officer approval; but also, the way to monitor and control risk using a dynamic and continuous system of risk analytics management. Additionally, a RAS uses external models, external data, and information or scores that are aimed at specific segments of the portfolio, e.g., bond ratings and the financial stress score. These scores or models should be aligned based on probabilities of default to manage in-house and external models with metrics with equivalent risk levels. A RAS is part of a knowledge management system applied to risk management, it is in that regard and mentioned before a socio-technical system that not only requires the subsystems of technical/modeling process but also the capacity of humans and machines to interact to transfer and use of the new risk knowledge created by the risk data analytics processes.

There are questions to answer in the RAS definition related to the cost-benefit analysis of risk classification and the limit allocation problem. In the following paragraphs, there is presentation of additional examples of components that a RAS could have and the results that will be used to input operational information systems. The examples are related to stock returns analysis using Monte Carlo Simulation, portfolio decisions, pro-forma financial statements simulation, factors affecting the loss distribution, and contribution of risk analytics.

A RAS should classify risk units by establishing appropriate predictive power to update cut-offs that will be used in the analytic development of risk levels. In addition, a RAS needs to be monitored, calibrated, and validated in a regular basis and its methodology will need to be continuously improved to assure that cut-offs and risk levels are still valid. While assessing risk, a RAS needs to maintain mechanisms to evaluate data and output quality, audit trails, and other rules to preserve the integrity of the system. A RAS should perform surveillance by using the scores yielded by the models and the use of artificial intelligence to discover patterns of behavior of risks and ways that the variance of metrics KPIs and KRIs are kept under discovery of confidence intervals. If the scores go over the predefined threshold, the system should issue an alert. Surveillance should also include the setting of rules regarding data requirement and frequency of data acquisition.

A RAS should assign a statistically based allocation of limits built on the risk classification, size of each risk unit, and the maximum loss acceptable in a portfolio among other factors. A well-defined, robust mechanism to calculate the ideal cut-offs to assign risk levels and allocate limits of acceptable risk is needed. Among other alternatives to calculate limits, if financial information is available, for example a measure of the size and liquidity of the risk unit can be used for evaluating supply chain risk. Another alternative to calculating limits, in the absence of financial information, is the use of historical requested amounts in credit transactions, the average limit used in the past, number of employees, and the number of claims and dollars paid per buyer. The process of defining limits is inherently based on the weighted-loss ratio and the utilized exposure. Such a process has direct implications when analyzing transition matrices for risk migration. In other words, when analyzing risk migration, it is not only important to know how many risk units are going to migrate to worse risk scales but to know what the amount at risk (severity) is of being downgraded and possibly defaulted.

An example of a question to answer with the support of the RAS could be: What is the maximum expected loss in the portfolio that is acceptable? This is a common practice in the general insurance industry. In addition, when financial information is available, different relations can be created based on concepts such as tangible net worth or other size variables; similar to the standards based on the probability of default and the impact on the expected profit or loss. The process of defining limits (acceptable exposure) needs to take into consideration contagion effects and concentration in different sectors, geographical areas, groups, etc. An optimization analysis is required to assign and allocate limits using parent information of the organization, levels of concentration, and so on. This optimization analysis relies on mathematical programming that is associated with goals achievement. The purpose of this analysis is to identify the best combination of variables that will yield an optimal allocation of limits.

A form of analyzing exposure is not only based on limits but also it is based on what the exposure means to the organization. Here it is the example in insurance, in particular in automobile insurance. For many years, the exposure of automobile insurance was based on the car physical attributes, the car value, and the car age, for example. However, the risk exposure of a car in an insurance setting is not because of the physical car on the roads only. The risk can be affected because of attributes of the drivers and attributes of the use of the car. A car in the garage can be of high price and with an elderly owner can be different from a normal car that belongs to a seller in the middle age. The exposure changes will have effects in the definition of pricing. In general, once the exposure to risks is defined, the metrics that are defined will have required adjustments. The exposure will be a component in the metrics that will affect the value to control by defined metrics.

If the problem is defined as the maximization of the credit-granting capacity, the credit-granting capacity constraint is changed for a loss ratio constraint. The RAS is at the same time a means to control the cost of operation and the interaction machine and human capacity. A proper cost-benefit analysis needs to be carried out to determine the model's best risk classification so that results are maximized. Cases processed by a RAS that are correctly classified as "good" save money that would be needed to pay admin expenses such as salaries and benefits. The volume assigned to the officers will affect the result of the cost-benefit analysis.

$$\frac{net\_claims}{exposure} = goal * utilization * premium\_rate$$

where,

$$goal = \frac{net\_Claims}{exposure * utilization * premium\_rate}$$

and,

$$utilization = \frac{volume}{Exposure}$$

A limit allocation problem is seen as the minimization of the weighted-loss ratio or as the max-imization of the credit granting capacity if the risk is credit related. If the problem is defined as the minimization of the weighted-loss ratio, some constraints are:

- Credit-granting capacity
- Total allocated by tool
- Loss ratios defined by segments
- Segment and tool allocation accepted
- Margins
- A RAS share required
- By segment of a RAS-Officer
- Relation premium to loss ratio
- Net loss ratio combination
- Limits used structure
- Segments mixed
- Increments accepted by tools
- Cost of data

A benefit of a RAS with appropriate design is connected with risk classification. Cases processed by a RAS that are incorrectly classified generate other costs, such as information fees, claims, etc., which reduce the benefits due to RAS classification. Matrices of costs can be created and represent the way of initiating the cost assignment in the credit-granting process based on correct or incorrect classifications. A RAS should estimate loss by modeling the probability of default, the loss dis-tribution, and the probable maximum loss, as well as forecasting the dynamics of the portfolio by modeling migration of risk levels. In previous chapters, the components of the RAS description indicates performance measures creation such as:

- Default rates,
- Credit value-at-risk (CVaR) estimation,
- Probabilities of default and expected loss given default,
- Trend analysis,
- Profit and loss forecast for the portfolio,
- Cost-benefit analysis of a RAS approvals vs. officer decisions.

The requirements that Crouhy et al. (2001) propose for a RMIS include managing data globally using distributed database technology. These authors indicate that a "risk management system approach is not simply an aggregate of applications, data, and organisation; instead, it is born out of an IT vision." The architecture for risk management needs to gather the key information that is supplied by different areas, in a data warehouse. The design of the RMIS has to take into account that data is static and dynamic, and to provide an adequate access to all the users. Additionally, it is required to take into consideration the fact that there are different functions in risk management with specific needs, such as the case of trading operations that require systems that support the monitoring of trades, prices, and the decision-making process through models. A summary of attributes and issues of the RMIS is found in Figure 9.1. Crouhy et al. (2001) complemented the above points adding to the RMIS analysis: "The risk management system should be designed to support the transport and integration of risk information from a variety of technology platforms, as well as from multiple internal and ex-ternal legacy systems around the world." Therefore, the RMIS design requirements are technology for integration and the way to address the solutions through "information collection and normal-ization, storage and dimensioning, analytics processing, information sharing and distribution."

Moreover, it is applicable to organizations in general what Caouette et al. (1998) argue indi-cating that a financial institution has to deal with an appropriate risk information management

**Attributes and issues of the Risk
Management System (Levine, 2004)**

Attributes	Issues to analyze
• Flexible architecture	• Volume of data, information, reports
• Ability to deal with different kinds of data, transaction, valuation, static, credit and risk mitigation data, loss, operational	• Technology use, models, reuse, connectivity
• Real time infrastructure and support	• Standards, documents, data, structures
• Query and reporting	• Methods used to solve, to calculate
• Remote access	• Consistency and alignment, validity, integrity
• Technical and control standards	• External information, rating, political, economic conditions
• Application service provider environment	

FIGURE 9.1 RMIS attributes and issues based on Levine (2004).

structure that connects internal and external information in the same was the system connects internal and external users. Data to manage and data to convert into information appears when a business or an individual is looking to satisfy their financial needs. The processes of the risk organization are based on portfolio information, rating agencies, asset-liability control, risk models, default rate analyses, losses, recoveries, credit risk migration, pricing, risk-adjusted returns, credit derivatives and many other variables, indicators and decision support actions, and results (Caouette et al., 1998). Additionally, there is a high volume of external data that is managed because in most cases the credit evaluation, as an example, not only depends on the customer relationship with the lender, but also on the relationships with other organizations and the history that has to be considered in the evaluation.

Thus, the current design of risk management information systems has, as a main challenge for processes and technology in an enterprise risk management (ERM) program, the design of a system aligned with the integral, comprehensive, and strategic view of the organisation (Abrams et al., 2007). This complexity is observed, for example, when the modeling process is looking for aggregation analysis or when each risk organizational section needs to create reports and each one has specific performance measures, problems, and resources that are not clearly connected to the whole organization. ERM comprises attributes of strategic, holistic, and integral views of risk management across the organization, or to say it is risk management of the enterprise risk. Risk management (RM) processes are supported by a risk management system that is associated with people, processes, and technology that require organizing and delivery of risk knowledge-risk analytics outcome to different stakeholders. It has been shown that risk management evolved to ERM and that the processes and risk management information systems are in evolution as well, in order to comply with the new regulations and provide support to the financial institutions.

Lee and Lam (2007) add to the discussion of the risk management system challenges, the problem of architecture design from a current system design: "… IT architecture is divided into separate clusters of IT systems that are owned by individual business units … Each cluster has between 5 to 20 IT systems." This can represent more than 120 IT systems and the bank in the case study, as others have grown with this mix of IT systems that combine different platforms and different technologies. This general IT architecture is related to the issue that RM needs to develop risk management systems architecture given the variety of systems, each one with data designs and processes defined by the specific business line. Some of the general attributes that have issues to solve in a risk management system were presented by Levine (2004) in Figure 9.1 above, which includes the whole spectrum, from data to decisions.

Moreover, the risk management system of the organization needs a specialized functionality regarding the support for different groups interacting in the risk management processes, access to data repositories by different people, integration of resources, and conjoint activities among risk management people in modeling, analytics, and assessment. The functionality needs to consider different users such for example information in the trader life has a factor to consider that is the pressure to make decisions and act rapidly. Risk management not only has a problem with information, but also has more problems with interpretation, people interaction, and communication of meaning areas where the information systems need more development work. In that direction of moving to a system that is with a more integral view in the section there are some suggestions to tackle the system design.

9.1   POSSIBLE BASES OF RAS DESIGN

Crouhy et al. (2001) proposed various particular characteristics of the risk management information system. In a risk management system, functionality enhancement to a risk management information system and to the web channel are more likely to improve the quality of risk control. At the same time, RM activities involve people from different areas and are in charge of different risks, who need to interact, share risk knowledge, and use common technology means in order to perform their work. As mentioned in the introduction of this chapter, a risk analytics system as a knowledge management system (KMS) is a "kind of information system" that supports knowledge management (Alavi and Leidner, 2001) and the concept as a socio-technical system (Lehaney et al., 2004). The RAS is influenced by the quality of people communication, the quality of risk knowledge sharing, and the functionality of the risk knowledge management system and the web channel functionality. Thus, risk control is influenced by people, process, and technology.

Therefore, a RAS should be based on the socio-technical approach (Figure 9.2). This means that based on the results, people and technology are factors for improving risk control and that the ability of people to communicate and share knowledge will complement the improvements of the functionality of the technological components. Massingham (2010) pointed out that risk management "on decision tree methods are ineffective" and this means the need to search for new methods to deal with risk and therefore the need of creating risk management systems and risk

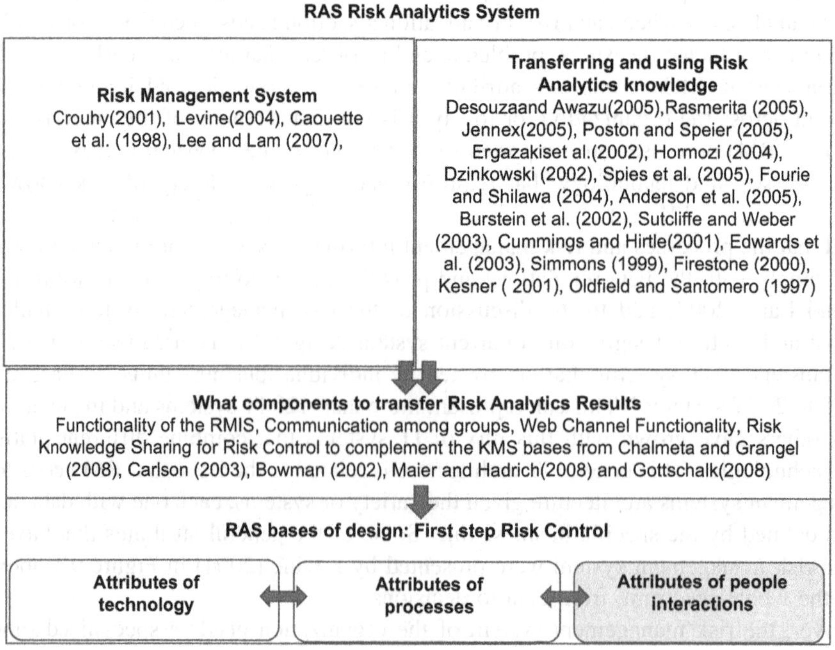

FIGURE 9.2   Bases of RAS with risk control as first step.

analytics systems. The two components that Massingham (2010) proposes are related to the analysis of "environmental uncertainty and cognitive constraints." This author identifies some matrices for risk assessment and risk identification: severity and frequency, which are used in RM practice.

However, Massingham (2010) does not include in the framework the development of the means for improving risk knowledge sharing and collaboration to support risk control. The methods of rational treatment exist in RM and the value of them is in the proper use by risk management staff; and, what is missing is the people, process, and technology integration and development. Gregoriou (2010) indicates the points where RM has been ineffective and, pointing out: "problematic lending practices, the low robustness of the risk management systems to cope with subjective estimates and personal judgement need to be sufficiently robust to be able to compensate the negative extremes." Another point is the correct use of metrics and key indicators. There is room for developing a better means to address the lessons learned: "As a "lesson learned" from the recent financial crisis, it is submitted that in the future, risk metrics must take into consideration what truly is at risk, and what the major risk drivers are and will be."

Gregoriou (2010) continues, saying that there is a "meta risk," referring to the assumptions and to the "failure in quantifying risk appropriately and reflecting the right assumptions." Additionally, he pointed out the need of reviewing "the perfect market hypothesis"; the market is not perfect and there are several anomalies. Finally, Gregoriou (2010) indicates the importance of having a clear and proper evaluation of the results and indicators that are presented by Rating Agencies and Financial Reporting.

Gregoriou's (2010) points indicate the importance of risk judgment and the capacity to create and share risk awareness among the RM staff and the capacity to communicate with others. Regarding the risk awareness, Bhidé (2010) points out: "No single individual has the knowledge to make those adjustments; rather, it is widely dispersed across many individuals ... therefore, individuals who have on-the-spot knowledge must be to figure out what to do." Then the bases of a risk knowledge management system like a RAS are in the creation of capabilities of people and organization not only to keep data alive and models well designed but also to collaborate and to develop the people's judgment trough the proper use of documents, meetings, collaborative activities, models, and multiple sources of data in structured and unstructured formats. Bhidé (2010) continues, saying, "In recent times, though, a new form of centralized control has taken root that is the work of old-fashioned autocrats, committees, or rule books but of statistical models and algorithms. This has been especially true in finance, where risk models have replaced the judgments of thousands of individual bankers and investors, to disastrous effect."

Figure 9.2 represents the elements based on a literature review to identify what people considered as a need of the architecture in a risk management system, additionally the literature indicated the current use of tools, technology, methods in RM and KM in financial institutions, which under this context act independently. It has been identified that means and communication methods among people, knowledge-sharing capabilities, and functionality of a web channel and a risk management information system should be part of the design components of the systems supporting risk management. Chalmeta and Grangel (2008), Carlson (2003), Bowman (2002), Maier and Hadrich (2008), and Gottschalk (2008) provide insights for the KMS design, which are possible to apply to RM and can be summarized as follows: identification of risk knowledge and the structure to organize it, store and retrieve, using technologies for accessing and servicing multiple users with various methods and tools. It should be kept in mind that there are relationships of people to people, people to documents, and people to systems that have to be taken into consideration for the design.

Based on the above points and the research results, Figure 9.3 summarizes the bases of a risk management system: RAS. There is evidence for identifying the attributes for a risk management system that contribute to a better risk control. There is no clear correlation between the KM variables and ERM perceived value; but, the principles of communication, knowledge sharing, and

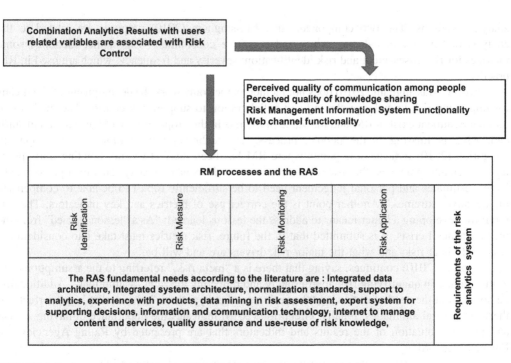

FIGURE 9.3 Summary of the bases of RAS design (first step: risk control).

functionality can be extended enterprise-wide and to provide the bases for system integration, which is one of the main issues in financial intuitions.

Once it is clear what the minimum requirements should be, which were based on the literature review and the research results, it is possible to identify what the answers should be for a system design that support the KM processes. For each KM process, the KM tools, in the context of risk management, are identified from the current practice in financial institutions but with an emphasis placed on KM processes focusing on the RM problems. The evidence of this research shows that financial institutions are doing well in some of the people-oriented items and with these that the design of the RAS has taken some strong steps.

Figure 9.4 summarizes the way that risk analytics processes are linked to a RAS in the sense that the system takes the experience with products, with operations and customer satisfaction to convert them into solutions for the internal and external customers based on the risk knowledge management processes. For instance, risk knowledge creation might be represented by new ways to price products the same as the risks associated with price products, risk knowledge storage and retrieve in the design of a data architecture and means to access this data. Regarding risk knowledge application, it gives the possibility of getting solutions to problems through means of business intelligence, competitive intelligence, expert systems, etc. that might provide insights in risk classification, processes improvement, and customer service. Finally, through structuring risk knowledge transfer and risk knowledge sharing the RM people will be able to organize work with different risk groups and with different views of the problem-solving process.

In a RAS design, the users are expecting to connect concepts such as:

- Information is everywhere we look
- Knowledge is experience
- It is sharing what works and what doesn't
- Use it and reuse it

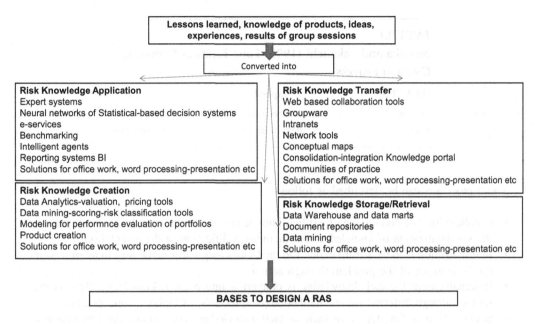

FIGURE 9.4   Using risk analytics process and connecting subsystems of a RAS.

- Make an impact
- Create a place to share, learn
- Ask, tell, brainstorm, collaborate
- Build a community
- Locate, capture, filter, store
- Find answers
- Create value

According to the section a RMS and a RAS are designed to work in synchronized way and a RAS acts as a subsystem of the general RMS. The RAS component of the knowledge management aspects is described in the following section.

9.2   FRAMEWORK FOR THE RISK KNOWLEDGE MANAGEMENT COMPONENT

Risk knowledge understanding to develop a RAS follows the knowledge management principles because of, as it was explained before, the risk analytics process is creating knowledge to be used to mitigate risk. Wiig (1993) indicates: "Knowledge consists of truths and beliefs, perspectives and concepts, judgements and expectations, methodologies and know-how." This view is complemented by other authors that include the concept of reasoning in the definition, such as Beckman (1997): "Knowledge is reasoning about information and data to actively enable performance, problem-solving, decision-making, learning, and teaching."

Additionally, knowledge is not only of one kind. Nonaka and Takeuchi (1995) concentrated on the interaction between two knowledge types: tacit and explicit knowledge. Tacit knowledge is represented by experience, beliefs, and technical skills accumulated in people's minds. Explicit knowledge is the knowledge expressed in documents, data, and other codified forms. The interactions among people correspond to the movements from tacit and explicit knowledge to tacit and explicit knowledge on the individual and organizational level. The dynamic is expressed through the following processes (SECI Model Table 9.1), which contribute to the knowledge creation.

TABLE 9.1

Nonaka and Takeuchi (1995) Four Types of Knowledge Creation Process

FROM\TO	Explicit	Tacit
Explicit	Combination	Internalization
Tacit	Externalization	Socialization

These processes can be described as follows:

- Combination is a conversion of explicit knowledge to explicit knowledge and represents the systematization of knowledge that includes codification or documentation.
- Internalization is to pass from explicit to tacit knowledge; this is the way to learn to work on the solution of the problem through action.
- Externalization: the tacit knowledge is converted into explicit knowledge. This is presented through different means, methodologies, models, metaphors, concepts, etc.
- Socialization is the step from tacit to tacit knowledge. This means the conversion of experience and practice in new experience and practice keeping the bases of human relationships.

Knowledge (Davenport and Prusak, 1998) includes four elements that complement the above SECI model. First, the sources of knowledge are experience, values, context, and information. Second, people are considered the original repository of knowledge from information and experience. Third, processes and procedures act as means to retrieve, describe, and apply knowledge. The fourth element refers to the organization as the place where the knowledge is offered. Thus, knowledge management has various definitions as well, Wiig (1997) defines KM as: "... the systematic, explicit and deliberate building, renewal, and application of knowledge to maximize an enterprise's knowledge–related effectiveness and returns from its knowledge assets." Similarly, Beckman (1997) indicates that: "KM is the formalization of and access to experience, knowledge, and expertise that create new capabilities, enable superior performance, encourage innovation, and enhance customer value." What is common in these two definitions is the methodical access to experience – knowledge in order to develop enterprise capabilities.

Risk knowledge is tacit and explicit, involves people, and the organization processes are the means to put the risk knowledge in practice. Based on these points, risk knowledge is understood as a process of applying expertise and risk knowledge flows. Additionally, the organization is considered the vehicle to risk knowledge creation and where the risk knowledge is processed. In this book, the definition of KM is the management process to maximize the coordination and organization of knowledge, in particular risk knowledge. This KM definition is complemented with the identification of five stages in order to implement KM: Identification of knowledge areas, knowledge mapping or knowledge identification, championship and organizational support, performance evaluation, and implementation. Knowledge includes the processing of information, in the mind of the worker, in order to provide meaning and to achieve a purpose. For instance, the problem-solving process in the business processes is a clear purpose.

The implementation for the risk knowledge management seeks to foster collaboration and partnership, while enabling the organization's resources to capture risk knowledge that is critical to make this risk knowledge available in the most effective and efficient manner possible to those who need it to bring/create value to the organization and protect evolution of organization's performance. Therefore, a RAS provides a bridge within internal users, between internal and

A RAS project is looking for using efficiently and effectively the asset Risk
Knowledge. Connecting people and providing means to use this asset in
the best way (Think in market people offer and buy knowledge we are
trying to create is the Exchange House)

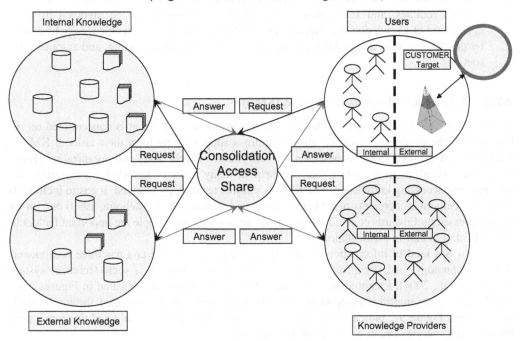

FIGURE 9.5   Connecting users and sources of knowledge: risk knowledge.

external users of risk knowledge that is codified and in the employee's mind. Figure 9.5 illustrates
the dynamic answer-request among the involved entities.

9.2.1   KNOWLEDGE MANAGEMENT PROCESSES

In the RAS design, the knowledge management processes are the core of the system. Models
and their outcomes, data and its organization, risk metrics and risk assessment methods, etc.
are all possible because risk analytics is providing the means to create risk knowledge for
providing organizations – people the capacity and capabilities to deal with uncertainty. Alavi
and Leidner (2001) adopt the definition of knowledge management as a process, with four subprocesses, that identifies and leverages the collective knowledge of the organization in order to
compete (von Krogh, 1998). Equally, Alavi and Leidner (2001) state that KM requires more
than IT; it requires the creation of a means to share knowledge, information processed by
individuals and adapted to be communicated. These processes (Alavi and Leidner, 2001) are
looking to create value from knowledge and the dynamic that individuals and groups have in
the organization in order to achieve "effective organisational knowledge management." The
processes are:

- Knowledge creation: The authors state that organizational knowledge creation involves
  developing new content and replacing the content already in place.
- Knowledge storage and retrieval: This process refers to the reality of the need to
  managing organizational memories; knowledge is created and at the same time forgotten.

- Knowledge transfer: This process takes place "... between individuals, from individuals to explicit sources, from individuals to groups, between groups, across groups and the group to the organisation."
- Knowledge application: This process is associated with competitive advantage development and for that there are three mechanisms to create capabilities: directives, organizational routines, and self-contained task teams. Technology can be involved in the application of knowledge that supports knowledge integration and knowledge application by providing access and updates of directives, organizing, documenting, and automating routines.

9.2.2 KNOWLEDGE MANAGEMENT SYSTEM (KMS)

A RAS in this book is considered a knowledge management system that is concentrated on risk knowledge. The processes described above require a support to perform their tasks: a KMS. A KMS (Alavi & Leidner, 2001) is based on the subsystems of technology and organization. This is to consider an information system that can help in many tasks of knowledge recovering, networking, and accessing knowledge. The KMS is not just technology oriented; it has to include the social and cultural components of KM (Davenport and Prusak, 1998; Malhotra, 1999) or as it has been expressed by Edwards et al. (2003), the KMS technology and people are important factors for the KMS design and implementation.

A KMS is a kind of information system that manages knowledge and has three components: people, technology, and organization structure (in precise terms, it is socio-technical system) (Lehaney et al., 2004). Examples of the basic structure of a KMS are indicated in Figures 9.6 to 9.8. Figure 9.6 exemplifies components of knowledge that can be managed through a portal structure and Figure 9.7 indicates that the different components are a whole and the components should gain synergies because of a unified system design.

A KMS requires a construction by blocks, as is illustrated in Figure 9.8, starting with the analysis and design of tools to manage explicit knowledge and to grow the system structures to support the KM processes that involve better actions and knowledge sharing and collaboration.

Some examples of solutions associated with the specific knowledge process are in Table 9.2.

Because the interaction of humans (Risk Knowledge) and all these components (just to name some examples) is possible through a Web based system plus the integration of Risk Analytics Capabilities

Application Access	Data Sources Access	Shareable Risk Knowledge	Networks	Industry
SAS / Analytics	Moody's S&P	Documents	Data Feeds	Associations
Cognos	Bloomberg / D&B	Virtual work / projects	Mining web	Country/sector portals
Cloud services	Stock E	Experience Repository	Industry Network	Supply chain
Data Management	Stream	Communication	Suppliers	Benchmark
Risk specialized software	Social Media	Risk Units	World OECD	Peer Analysis RMA

FIGURE 9.6 Several components that a KMS could have.

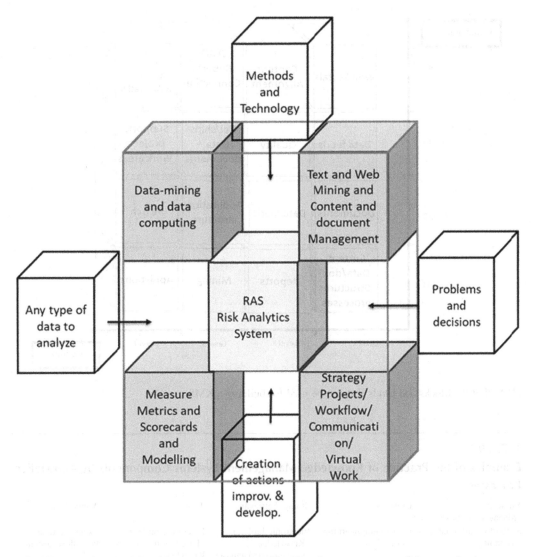

FIGURE 9.7 The principle of integrating and connecting four key components of the organizations.

In summary, a RAS structure can be developed using different technologies; however, the most important component is the capacity to build the bridge between knowledge workers, knowledge, and applications. There are methodologies to implement this, such as:

- Document management systems
- Knowledge maps
- Knowledge creation engines (modeling for risk assessment)
- Communities of practice/storytelling
- Collaboration systems
- Workflow systems
- Business intelligence
- Expert systems
- Competence management
- E-learning systems

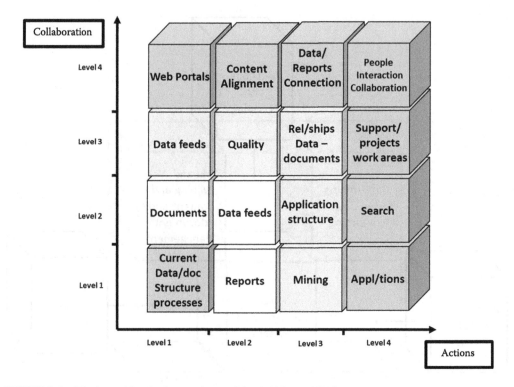

FIGURE 9.8 Blocks and levels that can be used for building a KMS.

TABLE 9.2

Examples of the Practice of Knowledge Management Systems Components by Knowledge Processes

Knowledge Management processes	Creation	Storage/retrieval	Transfer	Application
Supporting information technologies	Data mining/learning tools	Electronic bulletins Knowledge repositories databases	Electronic bulletin Discussion forums Knowledge directories	Expert systems Workflow systems
IT contribution	Combination new sources of knowledge Just-in-time knowledge	Support individual and collective memory Inter-group knowledge access	Extensive internal network More communication channel available Faster access to knowledge sources	Knowledge applied many locations Workflow automation
Platform	Collaboration networks/intranet/ communication technologies	Collaboration networks/intranet/ communication technologies	Collaboration networks/intranet/ communication technologies	Collaboration networks/intranet/ communication technologies

- Customer relationship management
- Corporative portals
- Intellectual capital measurement systems
- Corporate performance evaluation systems
- E-services and products/web services

FIGURE 9.9 Bases of the process to develop a RAS as KMS.

TABLE 9.3

Project control for a RAS

Executive in charge/Sponsor		Core Team:	
Process Owner(s)			
Initiative Lead		Extended Team:	• Other areas that need to participate
Scope Includes:	• Delimit the goals/objectives	Scope Excludes:	• Explicit what not to include
Current state:			
• Description of the conditions before the RAS project starts			
Problem statement and specific questions to answer			

A RAS (KMS) involves the evaluation system of intangible assets (knowledge) and the application process includes the knowledge acquisition or learning processes. The best way to create the RAS (KMS) is using integrated **subsystems that support the KM processes.** The design of RAS can start with a focus on one specific stakeholder's needs and include the explicit knowledge only. However, the framework and method are applicable and repeatable for other areas. The design of the project is based on three main steps (Figure 9.9).

In the case of understanding how to deal with the creation of a RMS to deal with risk knowledge documentation is crucial and the ways to keep a document updated are fundamental attributes to manage in a risk management system. A way to move to the gathering and data processing of data at the beginning is to define your problem, what is the problem that you are trying to solve? The scope of the system starts with a development of a project charter (e.g., see Table 9.3) and the identification of a project sponsor. This step also involves the identification of a project leader and core team that will work to design and implement a RAS. In the system development, the result is very important but the most important is the process definition to achieve goals/solutions in order to improve productivity, efficiency, effectiveness, control risk, solve problems, and preserve a good customer experience. The definition of the problem implies a loop, because, based on the original observation of the current circumstances, the first problem is analyzed. After the voice of the users, the problem identification is clearer, and the formulation of the problem will be more accurate.

A problem statement could include answers to questions such as:

- **What** is the root cause of the risk-related problem?
  - Provide a description of what is happening.
- **How** big (size or magnitude) is the risk-related problem?
  - Provide the metric used to describe it.
- **How** does the organization know there is a risk-related problem?
  - What are the indicators?
- **Where** is the risk-related problem occurring?
  - The process name and location/team where the problem is happening.

- **Who** is involved in the businesses processes?
  - Provide a key stakeholder.
- **When** did the risk-related problem become an issue?
  - Since when has the problem been felt (even if not initially noticed)?
- **How** is this affecting the customers/stakeholders?

These points in the context of the risk knowledge concept include then to answer: Know-what, know-where, know-who as a minimum to start the RAS project. The scope of RAS initiative need to define what to include and exclude. A good way to analyze and to move ahead in the problem definition is observing the "market" of risk knowledge that is in the organization. This means identifying the risk knowledge that is required and identifying the sources of that risk knowledge. This is also the identification of the stakeholders at this stage: which individuals and teams need to either participate or be informed along the way of the system development, implementation, and control; especially those you will need to engage to support the design and implementation of your process and framework. Validate the concepts and to identify the benefits for the organization, resources required, manage the inherit systems, and use of methods/techniques to solve problems.

Internal data includes an assessment of stakeholders' risk knowledge needs and solutions. This step includes assessing the current state of teams' risk knowledge base – what resources (data, models, humans, and machine capacity) are available, where they are stored, who created them or owns them now, what the teams' pain points are with respect to the datedness or accessibility of documents/data etc. It involves assessing the teams' readiness for risk knowledge resources/repository and needs of risk knowledge concepts before a system starts. It is essentially a current-state diagnostic. A diagnostic is according to:

- Voice of the internal customer – this is a tool you can use to gather feedback on the pain points experienced by the content's audience.
- Benchmarking against other groups inside the organization or organizations – what have other teams done with respect to risk knowledge management, what applies to the specific problems, and how to leverage that external risk knowledge.

It is also important to gather information on best practices internally or externally and this is where the a project team met various internal groups, such as:

- Financing
- Functional areas
- Business development
- Electronic document reference management project group
- Record management
- Advisory services
- Account receivables insurance
- Web channel
- Enterprise architecture.

The stakeholder connection with documents can now start. This means to identify how the documents flow or management of the explicit risk knowledge. This step is about developing processes to create or update new content as well as periodically review content that is "alive" in order to keep it fresh and relevant for risk management processes. These processes should be designed by a project team in conjunction with content and business subject matter experts. The main steps to follow are:

- Provide a detailed inventory of all related product information that is available on intranet/networks site (guidelines, notes, documentation, etc.).

- Identify what documents need to be broken down in pieces to match the standard process classification.
- Consolidate all information in each and every related piece. i.e. All relevant product information that should be in the key features section to be merged together in a document.
- In using the standard template, the information should be updated, reduced in point forms, and also as much as possible, put into a table.
- Each piece of content needs to have its owner, update date, and review date. Address the governance and requirements.
- Because documents have been broken down into bite-sized pieces, each section or page can be tagged with an owner and a set of metadata describing the content. This tagging will facilitate the maintenance and searching processes.

Use of metadata (Table 9.4) describes documents through tags that are added into each document properties. On this case, the metadata have been identified as:

TABLE 9.4
Metadata Possible Factors

Name	Activities–processes related
Products	Pieces of product portfolio
Stage	Pre-Underwriting
	Underwriting
	Post-issuance
Step	Perform initial gating
	Risk analysis
	Set parameters
	Request for cover and endorsement
Categories	Business analysis
	Financial analysis
	Advisory analysis
	Eligibility
	Facility structure
	Pricing
	Security/Indemnity analysis
Review date	
Owner	Business, C suit person or both

Document classification is about the way that information will be presented to the users and options to classify and possible relationships of documents. It has to be structured in the way the users are thinking in terms of accessing the information. It has to be meaningful for the users and the categories have to be broad enough to allow flexibility. For instance, a classification can be based on the business process activities already built in the risk management subsystem as the underwriters subsystem, which could be with information organized upon the underwriting process rather than being displayed by product.

The governance framework is a key deliverable of RAS because it insures accountability, sustainability, and integrity within the processes. Here are the benefits:

- Accountability (clear ownership, clear process, clear roles and responsibilities)
- Consistent creation, update, and review of content (formal documented process and timelines)

- Collaborative orientation (built-in validation process, cross-team participation, broader engagement, alignment)
- Sustainability of integrity of the content (acceptance and adherence to the governance process).

A creation of explicit risk analytics knowledge in Figure 9.10 follows a sequence of steps. Everything starts with a map of a current state of the various sources of guidelines changes, i.e., change from underwriting, exceptions, corporate decision, continuous improvement request, etc. A project team identifies various sources of waste, issues in process execution, gaps, and improvement suggestions from the people who are involved daily in this process. Once the current state is identified, the next stage is to map the future state for updating/creation of new content as well as mapping the review process. The goal is to meet simple requirements such as simple process, adequate control, and cover the majority of cases and leverage other activities.

Some experience has indicated that governance of the risk analytics knowledge requires:

- A consultation group to get feedback and have full perspectives on guidelines development (business units/departments).
- Each piece of content has an owner, update date and review date.
- Documentation for the update/creation process.
- A review date can be by periods of 12, 18, or 24 months. The owner needs to judge what frequency is relevant given the likelihood for potential changes of the specific content.
- The owner needs to submit the draft guidelines to a guidelines working group by letting the person in charge know about it and add it to the agenda.
- The content will need to be approved by business manager or manager depending on ownership.

One of the aspects to review in the classification of documents is not only related to the content but also related to the kind of document: finished documents, published documents, document in progress, etc. (Figure 9.11). This classification and the identification of the time span of the document is required to classify, store, and provide access using different tools in the knowledge

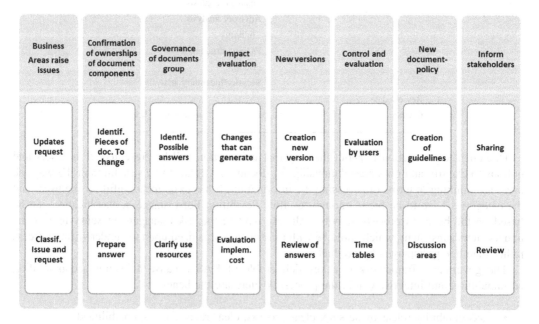

FIGURE 9.10   Process for risk analytics documents creation and update.

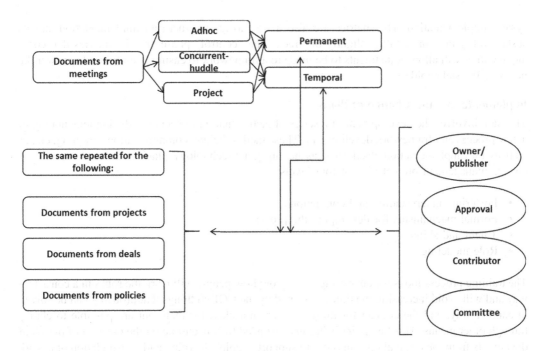

FIGURE 9.11   Basic components of document governance.

management system. The governance developed in this process is limited to the scope of the system functionality design.

Finally, a third step includes a resource assessment to determine the effort of impact on responsible parties to sustain the process and framework. In order to conduct this assessment, it is required to go back to the documents inventory. The inventory can be used to conduct an assessment of size and complexity by document, which determines the effort required to sustain the documentation process and framework. This assessment may take the form of a 3 × 3 matrix (see Table 9.5).

By assigning an effort to each of the nine boxes and tagging documents accordingly, it is possible to calculate the resource flow.

Prototype creation is about creating a functional system model using the intranet/collaboration system based on the analysis made from the voice of customer, the information gathered from the organization's groups, as well as the use of the updated/cleaned content within the scope definition of the system. The goal was to be able to show users the access to the risk management content and make sure that structure was meaningful.

Once the prototype exists, users will provide more clues of what the risk explicit knowledge management metrics could be. The metrics will lead to a measure of the effectiveness of a risk knowledge management implementation and the derived benefits. The metrics chosen should relate back to your problem statement, goals, and objectives and are key to determining the success of a

TABLE 9.5
Bases to Assess the Document Complexity

Size	Complexity – low	Moderate	High
Small			
Medium			
Large			

system implementation. The metrics are also a way to know where an implementation and its sustainability may have fallen slightly off track. The "control" phase and the metrics that come along with it will allow adjustments to be made to a framework to ensure it continues to answer the needs of the stakeholders.

Implementation and Change of Plans

This step involves the development of a series of tactics that will execute in the implementation of a new process and framework development. These tactics include communications, training, etc. as well as the implementation itself such as having your technology platform up and running. A change management project plan of four levels:

- Fostering understanding and conviction
- Formal mechanisms for developing the process
- Talent and skills
- Role modeling

The training process looks for answering a question: how people will learn the robes in a consistent way and will avoid increasing the time consumed by the COE in things that probably can be solved in another way, and the contact for things that are not clear for them but are possible to clarify through other means. This key point is because we need to concentrate on the creation of pieces of documents from the original ones in order to support people's learning and consolidation of a work process across the area.

Lessons Learned and Future Steps

Figures 9.12, 9.13, and 9.14 indicate three main points for further development of the projects to analyze the connectivity of people interactions, activities part of processes, and documents in a detailed way. This is crucial to improve and to introduce the value of the risk knowledge

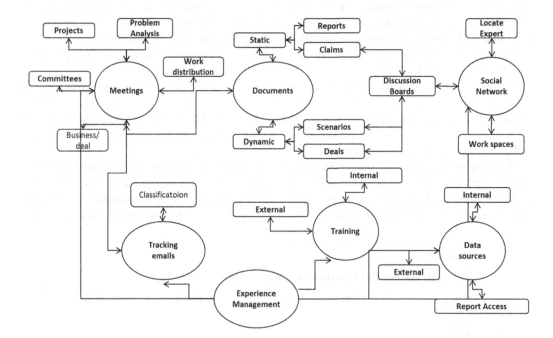

FIGURE 9.12 For future design, example of connections among the components of risk knowledge management.

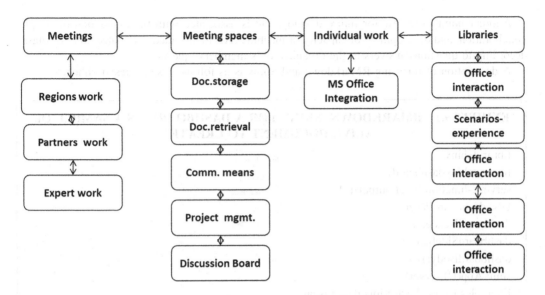

FIGURE 9.13   For future design, example of documents and people interaction.

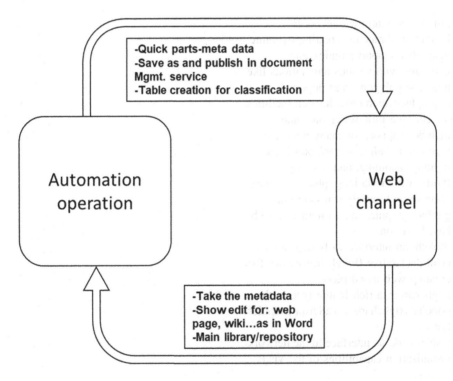

FIGURE 9.14   For future design, the integration of automated office and web channel.

management system. The basic concept is that risk knowledge deposited in documents is alive, documents are pieces of data that require updates, the system should provide the means to update the data, and then to process the data to obtain new knowledge and to disseminate it through the networks to the stakeholders. Documents in general should be created as objected that are data products with three main characteristics: shareable, dynamic, and interactive. The main option for that is to use R or Python to use RMarkdown (or equivalent in Python), Shiny, Plotly, etc.

Another point to review for future development is associated with the interaction of people, collaboration, and development of capacity of machine (AI) to provided automated solutions/tasks according to questions/answers to the organization's members' questions.

A description of for using RMarkdown and Shiny is as follows, using Flesxdashboard:

EXHIBIT 9.1   RMARKDOWN- SHINY FOR A DASHBOARD AS A SAMPLE OF ALIVE DOCUMENT TO CREATE

library(shiny)

library(shinydashboard)

server<-function(input,output){ }

UI<-dashboardPage(

dashboardHeader(),

dashboardSidebar(),

dashboardBody())

shinyApp(UI,server)

Examples to use Javascripts data visualization libraries

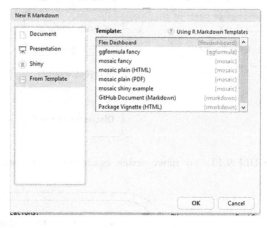

- http://gallery.htmlwidgets.org/
- Leaflet, a library for creating dynamic maps that support panning and zooming, with various annotations like markers, polygons, and popups.
- dygraphs, which provides rich facilities for charting time-series data and includes support for many interactive features including series/point highlighting, zooming, and panning.
- Plotly, which via its ggplotly interface allows you to easily translate your ggplot2 graphics to an interactive web-based version.
- rbokeh, an interface to Bokeh, a powerful declarative Bokeh framework for creating web-based plots.
- Highcharter, a rich R interface to the popular Highcharts JavaScript graphics library.
- visNetwork, an interface to the network visualization capabilities of the vis.js library.

It is possible to have the summary static or dynamic. It is possible to select the layouts and there are options to use components such as gauges. The idea is to get a htmlwidgets framework that can be used in the format.

Finally, the search and implementation of the integration between office automation systems (collaboration systems and operational such as automated office, social networks, web connections, etc.) point as a means to improve capabilities.

A RAS starts concentrated on risk explicit knowledge represented by documents. The system to use and manage documents is based on two pillars: definition of a documentation process and a support through a collaboration systems structure. The steps presented above support the development of a project for any product or area in an organization. The benefits realization and the implementation of the system require the evaluation based on user satisfaction and productivity improvement. A scorecard with the proper metrics is part of the steps to follow in the implementation. Once documents are in the plan of the RAS, other steps are to have simulations and to create portfolios of decisions. The following sections introduce aspects to consider in the process to follow.

9.3   CREATING RISK KNOWLEDGE THROUGH ESTIMATING METRICS USING SIMULATION

The following risk analytics example illustrates how to deal with data and Monte Carlo Simulation as an important component that the RAS should have. In several cases, data is used to estimate probability distributions or to identify statistical metrics and a simulation is required under assumptions and approaches to discover sample points or possible results distribution (Expected – average values). The example takes companies in the same sector and the prices of the stocks during a data window 2013–2016 (the time window can be any Figure 9.15) to analyze a sector and the CO1 organization performance in that sector. A complete analysis should require a review of concepts of adaptive sustainable advantage creation, but in this book the full competitive analysis is out of the scope (Tables 9.6 and 9.7).

The return evaluation used is the $\ln(price_{n+1}/price_n)$.

The behavior of prices helps to understand possible outcomes in the future. The returns distribution can be fitted and using that information a new price can be estimated using the probability (using the inverse of the fitted probability distribution of returns) of having the return value and multiplying by the previous price. In the same way, time series methods will provide price predictions. However, the main point is that models will give a guide according confidence intervals to the possible prices, but the estimation will not be the reality and precision will be just that, "a clue." Models are trying to use the combination of historical data, the assumption of the history will indicate the patterns for the future, and the review of qualitative factors to be closer to the reality, to estimate confidence intervals where the levels of return and price can fall.

The analysis of the data, the fit of the distributions (Figure 9.16), and simulations provide enormous information, mainly in the observation of the values – metrics of VAR and CVAR that are percentile calculations of the loss distribution. The ModelRisk solution offers a complete set of options to understand the VaR analysis, and simulation options. The historic approach is valid, but

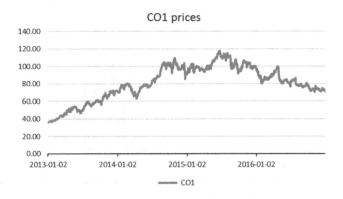

FIGURE 9.15   Stock close prices per day representation for CO1 company.

TABLE 9.6

Extract of the Data of Close Stock Prices

Date	Co1	Co2	Co3	Co4	Co5
2013-01-02	40.55	30.19	150.00	81.45	35.97
2013-01-03	40.83	29.94	147.86	80.94	35.92
2013-01-04	41.04	29.56	145.93	81.30	36.29
2013-01-07	42.87	29.62	146.42	80.88	36.84
2013-01-08	45.71	28.98	144.39	80.54	37.09
2013-01-09	46.17	29.14	144.08	81.01	37.32
2013-01-10	47.74	29.23	143.91	80.23	37.35
2013-01-11	48.15	29.45	143.79	79.45	37.42
2013-01-14	48.83	29.65	143.88	79.41	37.27
2013-01-15	49.70	30.10	143.01	77.73	37.07

TABLE 9.7

Returns Calculations

Date	Co1	LnReturns
2013-01-02	35.97	0.00000
2013-01-03	35.92	−0.00147
2013-01-04	36.29	0.01022
2013-01-07	36.84	0.01520
2013-01-08	37.09	0.00674
2013-01-09	37.32	0.00605
2013-01-10	37.35	0.00090
2013-01-11	37.42	0.00179
2013-01-14	37.27	−0.00398

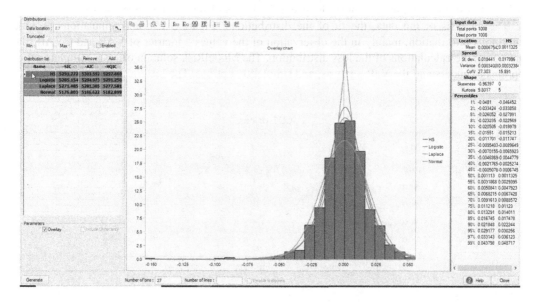

FIGURE 9.16 ModelRisk outcome of the probability distribution fitting process.

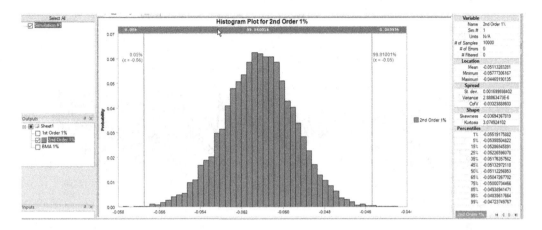

FIGURE 9.17 Dollar amount distribution at 1%.

it does not consider the possible variation of results because of using different samples and it is where the Monte Carlo Simulation adds value.

The user is required to identify the best distribution fit and to consider the option of assuming the parameters are static or random (considering uncertainty). Once the distributions are tested, it is possible to use a function that takes the closest fitted distribution BMA (Bayesian model averaging) in order to create results that take into consideration the randomness of the models. In this example (Figure 9.16), there is a comparison of probability and simulation using the Laplace distribution to test, even though the best indicators were for the HS (hyperbolic secant (μ,σ)) that is similar to the normal distribution with a picked and narrower shape. With static parameters, the VaR at 5% and 1% are −2.97% and −5.12%, respectively; while considering a random parameter, the VAR, 5% and 1% are −2.95% and −5.06%, indicating the means as −2.96% and −5.11%.

Considering the model uncertainty using the BMA for four distributions, HS, Laplace, Logistic and Normal, the results are with uncertainty consideration in the parameters: −2.95%, −4.52% with means −2.95% and −4.52%.

The calculation in dollar amount is to take the original value of capital minus the forecasted value of one day (or number of days of periods of the study) and get the values of the 1 and 5 percentiles of simulated distribution using deterministic, random, and BMA approaches. The CVAR is calculated taking the difference between the original capital minus the forecasted value of one day and then calculate the percentile of the simulated distribution (Figure 9.17).

The estimation of return using three different time series models for one of the companies in a portfolio Co1 shows these results (Table 9.8 and Figure 9.18):

TABLE 9.8

Summary Extract of Time Series Models

Date	GARCH	ARMA	MA1
2017-01-02	0.021444	−0.03516	0.008735
2017-01-03	0.003686	0.004628	0.003562
2017-01-04	0.01498	−0.00996	−0.01613
2017-01-05	−0.00379	−0.00312	0.008646
2017-01-06	−0.02786	0.029741	0.019557
2017-01-07	0.002451	0.022714	0.017428
.	.	.	.
.	.	.	.
.	.	.	.

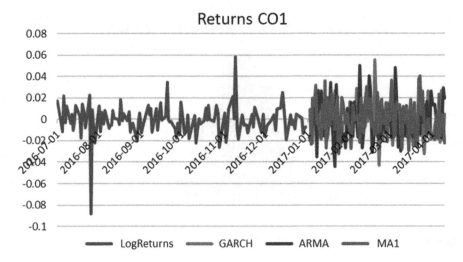

FIGURE 9.18 Represetation of the LogReturns using three different models.

TABLE 9.9
Forecast of Prices and Three Different Models

GARCH	ARMA	MA1
$ 72.60	$ 68.61	$ 71.69
$ 72.87	$ 68.93	$ 71.94
$ 73.97	$ 68.24	$ 70.79
$ 73.69	$ 68.03	$ 71.41
$ 71.67	$ 70.08	$ 72.82
$ 71.84	$ 71.69	$ 74.10
.	.	.
.	.	.
.	.	.

Results in the forecast are represented by Table 9.9 and Figure 9.19.

The main purpose of these examples is to illustrate that if the metrics to use and process used are for all organizations in the subset of companies in a market (for example the ones that are in the same strategic group) this is a way to identify courses of actions according to what is expected to happen. As always in analytics, any model has to be updated with the freshest data available to avoid following static patterns that are evolving and require ongoing review.

9.4 PORTFOLIO DECISIONS

Assume that the behavior of individual organizations is studied as in the previous section. Now the issue is about the combination of companies in portfolios. The evaluation of a portfolio requires correlation involvement in the analysis, requires approaches based on what the goals are, and minimizes variation of maximized returns or any other metric. This section uses as illustration the application of risk analytics techniques to find the optimal allocation of investments through the data of returns and variances. The model used is the Markowitz portfolio optimization model. Table 9.10 indicates LogReturns of five companies in a portfolio.

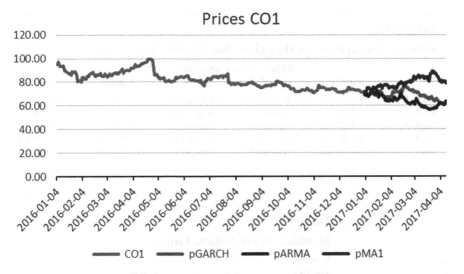

FIGURE 9.19 Illustration of prices forecast.

TABLE 9.10
Extract of Returns of Five Companies

Date	CO2	CO3	CO4	CO5	CO1
2017-01-02	−0.008174185	−0.023223697	−0.003250682	−0.026756281	−0.004337649
2017-01-03	−0.026750214	0.005045519	0.011834901	0.006574435	0.007471638
2017-01-04	−0.00514842	0.010174807	0.004878935	0.005469959	−0.027610212
2017-01-05	0.006423287	0.039322129	−0.003862391	0.005156165	0.015682204
2017-01-06	0.018659933	0.029318917	0.019202468	−0.018590555	−0.001310494
2017-01-07	−0.019543472	0.012408129	−0.002530865	−0.018384888	−0.020620977
2017-01-08	0.024005977	0.004306581	0.020781571	0.026456435	0.011531173
2017-01-09	0.002167372	0.005775268	−0.00663255	0.007155995	0.018628161
2017-01-10	0.012816612	−0.023037055	0.017425745	0.026296072	−0.001313999
2017-01-11	0.021971635	0.015839903	−0.009900648	0.015000239	0.021989549
2017-01-12	−0.02089821	−0.018805748	0.032775761	−0.000450841	0.026084907

The variance-covariance matrix (Table 9.11) is the key input of the model given that the purpose is to minimize the variance under the constrain of an expected return generated by the portfolio.

The return target and the variance-covariance matrix are the input to the minimization of the variance problem. Tables 9.12 to 9.15 indicate the results and Figure 9.20 expresses the efficient frontier that indicates the best return at the level of risk.

To create the efficient frontier requires a combination of expected returns and standard deviation points.

Once individual and portfolio knowledge is flowing through the RAS, an additional step is to connect pro-forma financial statements or operational results based on a combination of variables that are business defined. The next section illustrates this approach of a summary of internal and external analysis.

TABLE 9.11

Variance-Covariance Matrix Calculation for Five Companies

| | Variance/Covariance Matrix | | | | |
	Stock 1	Stock 2	Stock 3	Stock 4	Stock 5
Stock 1	0.067129978	0.0225168	0.0395876	0.0315338	0.0361701
Stock 2	0.022516825	0.0804718	0.0214103	0.0219161	0.011087
Stock 3	0.039587598	0.0214103	0.0954552	0.0346746	0.0438127
Stock 4	0.031533778	0.0219161	0.0346746	0.0549034	0.0272614
Stock 5	0.036170106	0.011087	0.0438127	0.0272614	0.0739789

TABLE 9.12

Identification of Return Target

Variance	0.035858	
Std. Dev.	18.94%	**Target**
Return	30.00%	30.00%

TABLE 9.13

Calculated Expected Returns by Company

	CO2	CO3	CO4	CO5	CO1
Weights	6.97%	30.44%	4.80%	36.67%	21.11%
Expected Return	81.72%	4.07%	30.49%	20.90%	65.99%

TABLE 9.14

Variances and Returns Per Company

Variance	0.002276174	0.0114073	0.0017206	0.013357	0.007097
Return	5.70%	1.24%	1.46%	7.67%	13.93%

TABLE 9.15

Summary of Expected and Variation in Returns

X axis = SD	Y axis = E[r]
St.Dev	E[r]
20.47%	60.00%
18.89%	40.00%
19.40%	50.00%
22.02%	70.00%
24.74%	80.00%
20%	20.00%

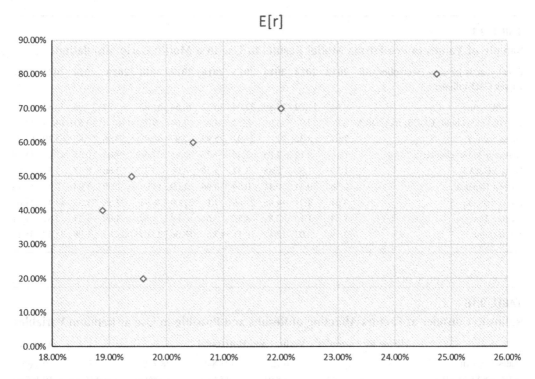

FIGURE 9.20 Efficient frontier representation.

9.5 ANALYZING PRO-FORMA FINANCIAL STATEMENTS

In risk analytics it is important to review what could happen with a project, with the investment of an organization, in valuation of organizations, use multiple portfolios (financial assets, products, markets, promotion), etc. The previous analysis of what is happening with the expected return results is supplemented by the pro-forma financial statement analysis through a Monte Carlo Simulation, in particular, simulations of cash flow or results statement (Tables 9.16, 9.17, 9.18).

TABLE 9.16
Descriptive Variables and Main Values to Analyze

Parameters to Control	Values	Min	Most Likely	Max
Sales Growth	0.4048687			
COGS	0.1918832			
Annual Cost Decrease – Random Variable	0.0199805	0.01	0.02	0.035
R&D %	0.1438996			
Other SGA %	0.1215699			
Other SGA % growth – Random Variable	0.0037284	0	0.00005	0.01
Terminal Growth Rate – Random Variable	0.0170126	0.015	0.02	0.03
Tax Rate	0.1438996			
Interest Expense	0.0269266			
Risk Free	0.025			
Risk Premium	0.055			
Beta – Random Variable	0.0814334	0.07	0.09	0.1
Cost of Equity	0.0294788			

TABLE 9.17

Sample of Values in Pro-Forma Model Results to Use in a Monte Carlo Simulation

Fiscal year is January-December. All values USD Billions	2012	2013	2014	2015	2016	2017	2018	2019	2020	2021	2022
Sales/Revenue	9.61	11.22	24.89	32.04	30.32	40.64	51.83	62.77	71.95	77.83	79.15
Cost of Goods Sold (COGS) incl. D&A	2.6	2.9	3.9	4.12	4.4	7.64	9.75	118	13.53	14.64	14.88
Gross Income	7.01	8.32	21	27.92	25.92	32.99	42.09	50.96	58.42	63.19	64.27
Research & Development	1.76	2.12	2.85	2.95	4.27	5.85	7.46	9.03	10.35	11.2	11.39
Other SG&A	1.33	1.6	2.88	3.32	3.26	4.96	6.32	7.66	8.78	9.5	9.66
Interest Expense	0.36	0.31	0.41	0.69	0.96	1.09	14	1.69	1.94	2.1	2.13
Pretax Income	3.61	4.21	14.86	21.66	17.1	21.09	26.91	32.58	37.35	40.4	41.09
Income Tax	1.04	1.15	2.8	3.55	3.61	3.04	3.87	4.69	5.37	5.81	5.91
Net Income	2.59	3.07	12.1	18.11	13.5	18.06	23.04	27.89	31.98	34.59	35.17

TABLE 9.18

Ratios to Consider as Factors Affecting of Results and Possible to Use as Random Variables

	Items for Formulas – Vertical and Horizontal					Average
Sales Growth		16.75%	121.84%	28.73%	−5.37%	40.49%
COGS/SALES (%)	27.06%	25.85%	15.67%	12.86%	14.51%	19.19%
COGS Trend (% change YOY)		−1.21%	−10.18%	−2.81%	1.65%	−3.14%
Other SGA/SALES	13.84%	14.26%	11.57%	10.36%	10.75%	12.16%
SGA Trend (% change YOY)		0.42%	−2.69%	−1.21%	0.39%	−0.77%
R&D/SALES	18.31%	18.89%	11.45%	9.21%	14.08%	14.39%
R&D Trend(% change YOY)		0.58%	−7.44%	−2.24%	4.88%	−1.06%
Interest Expense	3.75%	2.74%	1.66%	2.15%	3.18%	2.69%
Income Tax	10.82%	10.25%	11.25%	11.08%	11.91%	11.06%

The traditional metrics such as NPV can be consider as deterministic and the discount rates as well. However, in an improved approach to the reality, the discount rates are random and in the NPV is equally random and the study will be centered to the properties of the NPV distribution.

Table 9.18, in particular, indicates horizontal and vertical analysis; this means the evaluation of the rates of change from one time period to another of all items and the ratios among items, which are required to create the spreadsheet model of the cash flow and to identify possible random variables to include in a Monte Carlo Simulation.

The metrics that are important to review in this example are in Table 9.19, which passed from deterministic to stochastic results where the variance and expected values are the indicators to use in a decision-making process. Figure 9.21 shows the probability distribution histogram and accumulated probability function of the NPV, indicating an expected value $153.56.

In the RAS systems and according to the ERM view products, markets and promotion portfolios are fundamental to keep in connection to business simulation and the way that key risk indicators can be reviewed/monitored. One of the issues to keep the appropriate solution in a ERM system is the combination of risks. In the following section, there is a presentation about basics of products and risk combination.

TABLE 9.19

Generation of the Random Value Results of the VPN to Input Them to Study the Probability Distribution

Random Metrics to Study

PV Net Income (6 years)	$ 152.77
Terminal Value	$ 2,869.58
PV of Terminal Value	$ 2,410.54
Total Value	$ 2,563.31

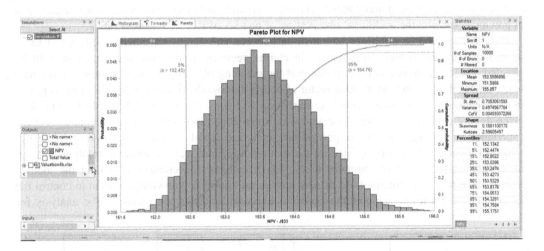

FIGURE 9.21 Probability distribution of the NPV generated by iterations of random variables.

9.6 ABOUT NEW PRODUCTS AS COMBINATION OF RISK

The combination of risks can create levels of risk that can be better for investors or can be dangerous; for example, depending on assumptions such as correlation among products or markets, or other risk factors. The combination of financial assets on what is called a tranche can be the basis for the creation of a new product. Collateralized debt obligations are these types of products. The risk characteristics of the tranches is different according to the definition of the assets combination and a way to obtain the return. A junior tranche is when the condition to default the tranche is that one or only few assets default, a senior tranche is when the condition to default is that all the assets used defaulted. This means the correlation among the assets is crucial to know to understand the behavior of the set of assets. Independence of products reduces the risk; for example, with bonds the analysis is based on correlations-copulas. Copulas are fitted using the information criteria SIC, AIC, and HQIC. The copulas that are used are Normal, Gumbel, Clayton, T, and Frank.

Use ModelRisk once the data has been gathered; the first step is to fit the copula that is, for example, multi-normal/Clayton, or another and to find the best fit according to the best information indicators for all the assets. Then it is to find the probability distribution in including the parameter of the correlation of the copula output. In the case of the tranches, the rule can be for example that after Monte Carlo Simulations the probability of default is calculated using Bernoulli distribution with the parameters of the probability of default for the asset and the copula output. An indicator will say if the asset defaulted of not. In the senior tranches, the condition will be that all the assets will default. This means the indicator of the combination will be equal to the number of assets when 1 represents the default of the asset. And in the case of the junior tranches, the only condition will be that the number of the indicators be greater than 1.

9.7   ABOUT FACTORS AFFECTING A LOSS DISTRIBUTION (LGD)

One of the most important aspects in the creation of risk analytics systems is the creation of methods for understating connections among metrics using previous experience in the analysis, benchmark indicators, and a clarification and simplification of the problem to analyze. This search for metrics connections starts with the identification of relationships among variables, the identification of a way that the analysis can be affected because changes in some indicators or, more important, the potential use of the metrics for predicting a portfolio behavior. Figure 9.22 shows the main links among metrics that are used for portfolio analysis. The core of the analysis is the identification of a loss distribution because from it many statistical indicators can be developed and connected; as mentioned in previous chapters, the traditional observation of metrics of risk such as loss ratios.

Default rates and probabilities of transition between risk stages have been used. All of these metrics are related. If there are changes in claims, recoveries and exposure conditions will be affected and the challenge will be to interpret the meaning of changes and how they can produce new changes in other indicators. One factor affecting the loss distribution is related to the capacity of the organization to recover the loss or to reduce the losses after events. The analysis of the loss given default (LGD) and topics associated with knowledge discovery in the claims and recovery experience at any organization are part of risk analytics. A risk analytics exploratory study presented in this chapter is concentrated on the methodology and ways to discover relationships, on understanding the effect of variables in the LGD analysis, the connection among the metrics already developed, the potential use of new metrics and possible knowledge system to control the LGD, and the means to support the portfolio exposure analysis and control. The analysis for

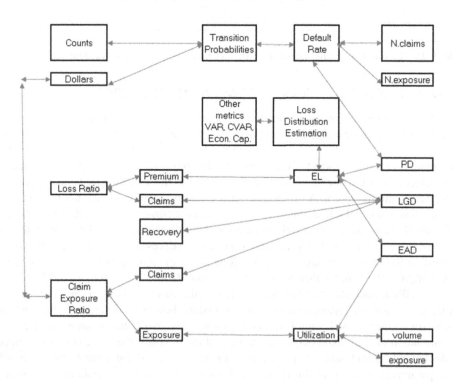

FIGURE 9.22   Metrics relationship.

improving a workflow and processes improvement based on factors identification is not included in this section. The data used includes claims in a credit portfolio in a time period window. The motivation to work more on LGD in risk analytics is expressed in this comment: "Despite its importance in credit risk measurement, LGD estimation is less developed than PD modeling" (Sanders and Allen, 2010) and Engelmann and Rauhmeier (2011) indicate the need to dig deeper to estimate LGD and to understand the application of the numbers in a more precise and complete way given the lack of comprehensive and conclusive studies. The LGD understanding requires an extensive work for better modeling and application. There are many different related problems to address in LGD analysis, from the LGD definition, the kind of risk (credit) analyzed (bonds, loans with and without collateral or seniority) to the segmentation required for the analysis and implementation of solutions/findings.

$$\text{Expected loss (EL)} = \text{Probability of default (PDF)} * \text{Loss given default(LGD)}$$

To calculate the LGD, it is needed to estimate the parameters for the probability distribution function. To calculate the probability of default, there are two alternatives. One is the factor model approach where the probability of default is assumed to depend on a number of variables or factors. The second option is the actuarial approach, to assume that the frequency of default fits a certain distribution, e.g., a Poisson or negative binomial distribution, and the LGD which distribution needs to be estimated.

A good example is when from an individual PD calculation, it is required to jump to the aggregation of default rates based on economic sector, risk levels, or regions where the results can be affected because of the aggregation effect by the dimension studied. For instance, a crucial piece of analysis is the effect that the LGD and the expected losses (ELs) will have in the price and revenue estimation for the organization. The treatment and integration of metrics (Figure 9.22) lead to new metrics as well, such as the probabilities of change of risk status, the analysis of trends in the traditional loss ratio and default rates, the identification of variables affecting groups of obligors in a portfolio, and classification of obligors and segmentation of the portfolio based on bivariate and multivariate analysis. Additionally, there is a clear indication that the segments of portfolio cannot be only based on the regular variables such as economic sector and geographical region, but also the characteristics of the loss distribution and the factors affecting it.

In summary, the analysis of the RAS needs to include the conditions for a design where tasks are performed dynamically; the exposure analysis cannot be performed in isolation if the LGD dynamic is not considered and of course if there is not a clear understanding of how EL is affected or the exposure is moving in the portfolio within risk levels or other risk classifications.

A loss given default analysis looks for improving efficiency and effectiveness in the strategy implementation in an organization. On the one hand, the purpose is to find a better level of productivity, efficiency, and effectiveness very close to marketing and strategy principles to achieve scale and scope economies. Risk analytics encloses principles included in the quality and service management practice that brought the understanding of continuous improvement, the re-engineering methods gave value of thinking based on evidence and without pre-conceptions, the management science/operations research in the "search of the better,". At the same time managing knowledge and leveraging intellectual capital, have provided the understanding of how to achieve goals more intelligently. The original view of systems brought the need of feedback as the definition of systems and organizations and teams identified as systems imply that feedback in any step of risk analytics is required to give a direction to the business actions and to build a learning organization.

On the other hand, the analysis of risk has been in many organizations out of the target of the methodologies that are associated with productivity, in particular to add results to the business value. Risk analytics includes LGD analysis as an end point value provider given the value of correct pricing, underwriting practices, and correct risk analyses in order to improve the sustainability of risk protection programs. The user of LGD analysis, for example, is internal and external. An analysis of

LGD = 1 − RR (Recovery Rate) at the end always has to land in the field of providing better solutions to the customer. To do the best for reducing/controlling the losses will be a way to manage price, underwriting workflow, and post-issuance policies risk control. The implementation of actions for improving LGD needs the aggregation of efforts of many areas. The reason is that several activities are required, such as ongoing measuring processes, analyzing, and creating collaborative work.

LGD analysis contributes to reduce the waiting times for answers/decisions through the development of systems, metrics, and discussion forums based on evidence to decide orientations of the business. From the overproduction point of view, the LGD analysis is the search for integration and a holistic understanding of the severity of risk and the required exposure management. The understanding of LGD contributes to identify duplication of efforts in different areas, the loss of work done, the creation of data, and information sources in the actions to offer less complexity in the processes and overcome the limitations of information interpretation. All of these previous points are associated with many different intellectual activities and people involved that can manage and understand differently the problem(s) and who require alignment in order to deliver reasonable and consistent thoughts for the decision-making process.

LGD in a credit setting, as an example, can be analyzed in at least three ways. The first one is based on the credit instrument/product. The second, related to size of the customers and the third, based on the recovery system. In the first case reviewing credit instruments/products, Table 9.20 is a summary of the results of the studies that presents the recovery rates (Emery et al., 2007; Alman and Ramayana, 2007). Table 9.20 shows what happens with the recovery rate depending on the level of security for recovery actions. What is interesting to observe is that for the senior unsecured loans and bonds the recovery rate should be between 59.65% and 36.85%, respectively. The dispersion is stable in a range 20% to 30% and it could be said not high. Some factors affect the recovery rate. From business processes to the product definition, there are differences such as they appear in bonds and bank loans. Credit rights, country conditions, collateral, credit cycles, sector performance, exporter-buyer experience, etc. are factors that can affect the recovery rate and then the LGD. There is an appetite for improving the accuracy of pricing and to have a better understanding the LGD in the CREDIT portfolio.

Second, the LGD observation based on the size of the customers indicates (Caselli et al., 2008) a LGD in average of 54% and then a recovery rate around 46% (Table 9.21).

However, the dispersion is higher than the one in the instrument classification and the conclusion from Caselli et al. (2008) is that the recovery rates are different because of the differences among the recovery rates across countries and sectors where the customers are. These authors

---

TABLE 9.20

Recovery Rate Based on Prices Just After Default on Bonds and 30 days After Default on Loans. Source Bank Loans: Moody's (Emery et al., 2007) and Bonds (Altman and Ramayana (2007))

Loan/Bond Seniority	Number of Issues	Median (%)	Mean (%)	Standard Dev.(%)
Senior secured loans	260	73.00	69.20	24.60
Senior unsecured loans	48	49.20	51.10	25.20
Senior secured bonds	332	59.08	59.65	27.00
Senior unsecured bonds	1017	45.40	36.85	24.40
Senior subordinated bonds	414	32.79	30.60	24.00
Subordinated bonds	249	31.00	31.17	25.70
Discount bonds	156	19.80	23.90	20.20
Total sample bonds	2168	41.77	37.68	25.56

TABLE 9.21

LGD Rates for Bank Loans Caselli et al. (2008)

Loan Type	Number of Loans	Percent of Total	Mean LGD (%)	Median LGD (%)	Standard Deviation LGD (%)
Small/Medium Business	6,034	51.80	52	52	41
Households	5,615	48.20	55	68	45
Entire sample	11,649	100	54	56	41

broke the samples by sectors and found that for SMEs the average LGD was from 23% to 68% and from household between 15% and 79%. These LGD ranges represent recovery rates between 32% to 77% and 21% to 85%, respectively. The ranges vary widely depending on classification/segmentation suggesting better segmentation analysis for better understanding of LGD.

Third, the LGD observation based on the recovery process is more complex and it has been performed in less rigorous studies. The process analysis has two parts. On the one hand, the studies have shown how the recovery distribution depends on the kind of product or population. The dispersion of results and type of products is wide; for example, Calabrese and Zenga (2010) report for Italian banks a high concentration on zero and 1 (100%), Grunert and Weber (2009) indicate that in German bank loans an average recovery rate of 72% and median 91.8%. Additionally, they say that macro-economic variables do not contribute to the model quality, indicating that exists a negative correlation between recovery and credit worthiness, and that the EAD as significant variable for the recovery rate. Livingstone and Lunt (1992) pointed out that socio-demographic factors have minor influence in personal debt and debt repayment. Loterman et al. (2009) showed that the fit of models was with low with r-squared, between 4% and 43%. Additionally, Chen (2010), in mortgage products, indicated that property location is significant to explain the recovery rate and Qi and Yang (2009) pointed out that the LGD is between 29.2% and 31.7%, for insured and high value mortgages, and additionally, indicating that LGD and loan size are negatively correlated and LGD and age of loan positively correlated. The concept behind this part of the analysis is the collateral value.

On the other hand, the studies show how the recovery rate is affected by the use or not of collection agencies: external or internal. Regarding this aspect of the recovery distribution, Thomas et al. (2012) show that in the recovery process when organizations use a third-party collection organization a 7% of the debt is repaid completely, 16% repaid a fraction, and 77% repaid nothing. Meanwhile, using in-house collection, 30% repaid the whole debt, 60% repaid a fraction, and 10% nothing. Additionally, indicating that models describing the recovery rate, when a third party is involved, have no good fit, and that third party has more mass on zero and in-house more on 100% repaid debt.

As a final point, the review is to investigate with more detail the behavior and LGD relationship of overdues and risk mitigants; in general, to understand the credit experience in a financial organization. For example, the results from Matuszyk et al. (2010), who analyzed the LGD problem for unsecured bank personal loans, opened questions to be answered in a credit portfolio. These authors divided the analysis in two stages: First the classification in two groups, LGD = 0 and LGD > 0. They found that according to the variables used, the classification is based on:

- amount of the loan at opening
- number of months with arrears within the whole life of the loan
- number of months with arrears in the last 12 months

- time at current address
- joint applicant

Additionally, the description of the LGD = 0 model showed that the higher the amount owned the lower the chance of LGD = 0; LGD is more likely to be 0 if there is a joint applicant. But in general, the more the customer was in arrears in the whole life of the loan the higher the chance that LGD = 0. However, those who were in arrears a lot that is, triple the average rate of being in arrears, had a lower chance of paying off everything; the more the customer was in bad arrears recently (in the last 12 months) the more chance that LGD = 0.

For those with LGD > 0, the results show that the older the customer, the lower the loss; if there is a joint applicant, the lower the loss; the higher the application score, the lower the loss; the longer it is from opening the account until default, the lower the loss; the more the customer was in bad arrears recently (in the last 12 months), the lower the loss.

9.8 RISK ANALYTICS CONTRIBUTION TO LGD ANALYSIS

The risk analytics process is not only contributing to organize the 360 degrees analysis of potential losses but also to identify how to move by steps in the discovery of data and its interpretation to support decisions. The problem identification starts with the understanding that machines and human interaction are needed for decision making, none can make appropriate decisions by their own, "Models increased risk exposure instead of limiting it" (The Economist, 2010) or additionally to use only one approach to analyze risk problems is not appropriate: "So chief executives would be foolish to rely solely, or even primarily, on VAR to manage risk" (The Economist, 2010). Probably the most important is that "… the biggest risk lies with us: we overestimate our abilities and underestimate what can go wrong" (Taleb et al., 2009).

Risk analytics contributes to connecting the dots to get understanding of the position the organization's portfolio has in a market reality. However, during the last years, the financial service business has changed dramatically. The organization priorities include the search for strategies to reduce risk or to increase returns. Given the practice of some banks creating special purpose vehicles (SPVs) and structured investment vehicles (SIVs) that were not shown in the balance sheets, the issues of the business results increased. Many different models have been created for understanding LGD. Some are possible to apply to certain organizations and others are not. In particular, for example, there are models that assume continuous pricing. These models have to be reviewed with special care if they are appropriate in certain organizations, introducing a clear in-house approach solution for the risk analytics problem.

The approach through models using bonds and loans can have different results; the same as it could be for an international credit portfolio. In this regard, it is valuable to say that Moody's reviewed that the recovery of senior unsecured bonds is 45.4% and the Altman's result for senior unsecured loans is 49.2% (Hensher and Jones, 2008). The search for a credit recovery rate is a problem to analyze and to position in a correct range of possible values that financial institutions, products, countries, or other factors that can influence the metrics. A significant effort for understanding the PD has been dedicated in financial institutions; however, less attention has been dedicated to the understanding of the LGD or the recovery rates. The LGD parameter for the expected loss calculation needs a better understanding in order to connect the numbers with the operation sustainability and with customer selection and satisfaction. The amount of recoveries on claim payments is an essential part of the claim analysis and pricing processes. The evidence coming from different studies has shown that the higher the PD, the lower the recovery rate; additionally, when collateral values go down, the LGD increases and the frequency of defaults increase because of economic fluctuation up and down.

Risk analytics searches for different approaches for building metrics that contribute to the understanding of the LGD and the estimation of parameters required to create an integrated system for LGD control in order to increase "… the capacity to understand, measure and manage risk conscious that no formula or model can capture every aspect of the risks an insurer faces" (Solvency II) and to be prepared for absorbing the impact of change sources, "… thus reducing the risk of spillover from the financial sector to the real economy" (Basel III). Some important points to keep in mind: the analysis has been performed in the past mainly on the Obligor side but not on the transaction side. LGD is mainly a portfolio transaction analysis. The PD problem has been studied more and it is based on the obligor knowledge, a rating system, has data, it is dichotomous, and a figure as outcome. The LGD can be a number or a distribution, related to human actions (recoveries), where data is scarce, and multiple complex factors involved, such as the standard deviation is very high, problem with the time to define the loss, multiple products, etc.

Therefore, because of the lack of parameter estimation methodology, the changes of the factors affecting the LGD and related topics is better to split the problem of LGD knowledge discovery into some more specific sub-problems. The risk analytics process starts reviewing problems to overcome for performing the analysis:

- Identification of variables/models that describe a percentage of recovery – Process improvement keeping the cause-effect view in the risk portfolio
- Analysis of model risk. In particular, the use of models that were created under assumptions which are not applicable to all kind of businesses
- Estimation of the organization's loss distribution
- Identification of the segments with different behavior associated with the LGD. A different problem is related to the use of data and the variables to consider
- Identification of factors indicating adverse selection or customer risk transfer solutions (e.g., self-insurance)
- Comparison of the impact of expected results in cases of crisis versus no crisis, economic cycles, or compliance processes
- Design and put in operation an enterprise risk knowledge management systems
- Identification of relationship between variables and the design of processes and operations
- Identification of proper cut offs for risk classification not only based on PD but the mix of PD and LGD
- Search for segmentation and portfolio optimization under market and operation restrictions

Based on the previous enumeration, risk analytics can be concentrated on the identification of variables that affect LGD, such as:

- Recovery % estimation and classification variables
- Recovery % according to several variables reviewed independently
  - Common vs. Civil law
  - Macro variables (GDP & inflation)
  - Industry sectors
- Recovery from insolvency
  - Creditors rights in bankruptcy
- Legal uncertainty
  - Days to resolution
  - Recovery forecast errors
- Variables that are required for metrics that supplement the current metrics of the portfolio

And the identification/calculation of the pieces of risk knowledge required to integrate in risk analytics system that supports LGD control. One the most important points to review is the differentiation of the models depending on what kind of data is available. Models can be affected by the availability of data, the same as the variables used. This is applicable to the PD and LGD estimation; for example, the value of non-financial information in SME risk management (Altman et al., 2010), that is in agreement to the PD in-house models that are used at a particular organization.

The literature and practice refer to some kind of models for PD such as structural default prediction models (Moody's KMV Loss Calc) or reduced form models (Kamakura's Risk Manager) (Saunders and Allen, 2010). Kamakura's model has some advantages: one because of easier calculation and second for including additional macro-economic variables. The KMV model is based on the stock price volatility and the stock price. No applicable for private companies; no probability of default is possible to calculate through this method. Kamakura's Risk Manager uses debt and other security prices to describe default probabilities. For the combination of PD and LGD, it is recommended in general to avoid the assumption of the LGD as constant or proportional to the debt value. This includes the firm specific information, industry information, economic environment, and macroeconomic factors. In organizations, there are obligors that are only (1% of the obligors) possible to analyze with models based on security prices. Most of the companies are not public; they are private. The obligors can be around the world and the factors affecting credit in a sector in a country are different from the sector in general worldwide. There is a need for testing other variables, which are significant (e.g., years in business, experience of the CEO, etc.) and evaluate the contribution to the LGD knowledge. Another point to take into consideration is the identification of the PD and LGD correlations. Figures 9.23 and 9.24 are examples of what the literature brings from the analysis of different credit portfolios regarding correlations. However, the point here is that based on the problem identification, the classification of obligors based on the combination of PD and LGD (using EL) as it is shown in Exhibit 9.1 requires the correlations analysis and will provide a different view of what kind of obligors affect in different way the portfolio's performance.

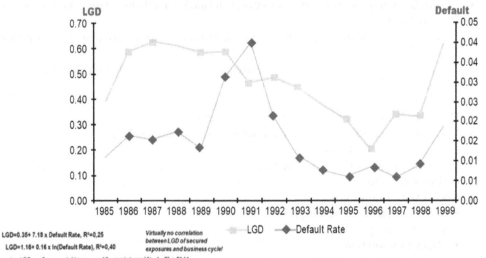

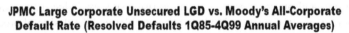

Araten, M., Jacobs Jr., M., & Varshney, P. (2004). Measuring LGD on Commercial Loans: An 18-Year Internal Study. The Journal of the Risk Management Association, 2, 28-35.

FIGURE 9.23 Comparison between LGD and default rates.

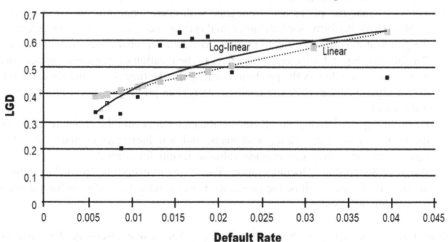

Araten, M., Jacobs Jr., M., & Varshney, P. (2004). Measuring LGD
on Commercial Loans: An 18-Year Internal Study. The Journal of
the Risk Management Association, 2, 28-35.

FIGURE 9.24 Relationship default rate and LGD.

Expected Loss (EL) = Probability of default (PD) ∗ Loss given default (LGD) ∗ EAD

The above expression supports the classification of obligors. To calculate the LGD, it is required to estimate the parameters for the (loss) probability distribution function. To calculate the probability of default, it is assumed to depend on a number of variables or factors. There is an actuarial approach, to assume that the probability of default fits a certain distribution e.g., a Poisson or negative binomial distribution, and any case the LGD distribution needs to be estimated. A way to present the new metric could be like expected loss rate.

Connecting dots, a RAS comprises definitions, data, models, metrics, tests, means for collaboration and means for interpretation, and understanding and evaluation of the portfolio risk. Pieces of the system can be grouped as follows:

- Data integration and organization (management) for risk analytics steps
- Risk analytics processes to describe, predict, and prescriptive of the risk management processes

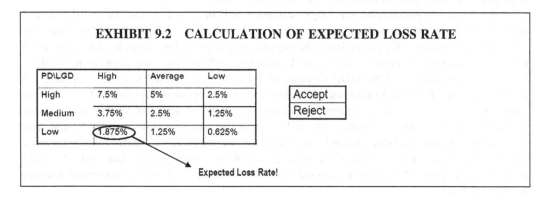

EXHIBIT 9.2 CALCULATION OF EXPECTED LOSS RATE

PD\LGD	High	Average	Low
High	7.5%	5%	2.5%
Medium	3.75%	2.5%	1.25%
Low	1.875%	1.25%	0.625%

Accept
Reject

Expected Loss Rate!

- Risk analytics practice-user-solutions to strategic, managerial, scientific, commercial, and operation actions and plans
- Tools and analytics platforms to integrate with operational information systems
- Portfolio Risk Performance Indicators: In this case, the reference is to create time series of the punctual evaluations of default rates, loss ratios, probabilities of default, etc.
- Portfolio Evolution Indicators: This refers to the creation of transition matrices that show how in count and dollars the portfolio is changing. the time series and the capabilities that the transition matrices (Markov chain property) can provide is very useful for forecasting and control.
- Portfolio Exposure Indicators: Based on the experience and the structure of the portfolio the identification of thresholds, risk maps, and new indicators related to thresholds and business circumstances can provide valuable results for control.
- Pieces of Support and Documentation: This refers to everything related to mitigants and metrics developed to follow the mitigants. For example, the kind of collateral, guaranties, type of seniority, etc.

The analysis of the data uses various methods of knowledge discovery described in the next sections. The analysis used descriptive statistics; the same as statistical and machine learning methods. There are specific characteristics of the data that require special treatment in the analysis. Probably the most important is that the recovery distribution has a "bath tub shape" that means values in zero, values between 0 and 1, and values in 1 are three different groups. These groups affect the loss distribution and suggest the LGD analysis could be separated by LGD = 0, LGD between 0 and 100% and LGD = 100%. Equally, the segments based on results coming up from the outcomes of some multivariate methods suggest better concentration on the LGD behavior analysis through different variables.

9.9   LGD LEARNING PROCESSES

As it was explained in Section 9.7, a factor affecting LGD is the set of credit rights by countries. In this section, there is an example of finding relationships to discover credit rights and their incidence in LGD. The variables used are credit unit profiles, claims data sets, credit rights, law systems, social (religion), and macro-economics. The data, literature review, and results indicate some specific points to observe in order to connect the LGD analysis with the recovery and portfolio analysis process. Additionally, there is a special interest in observing how variables that are related to the risk units basic profile are or not contributing to the explanation of the LGD results, reviewing for example if the organization has lower a recovery rate if creditors have more rights, the difference between common law and civil law systems, or the effect of the original recovery estimation of recoveries and days to resolution of the claims (Djankov et al., 2008) and (Djankov, McLiesh, and Schleifer, Private credit in 129 countries 2007).

In the following paragraphs, the LGD estimation will be based on the review of risk with and without default using multiple risk analytics methodologies. The data variables come from three different groups: Variables from the organization's portfolio, variables from the countries, legal and macroeconomic, and created variables, such as times and dependent variables. Moreover, it has been added GDP Growth in Previous Year, GDP Growth – Average in previous 4 years, Inflation in Previous Year and Inflation Average in Previous 4 Years. For the multivariate analysis some dependent variables were built in addition to the recovery rate (calculation1). One binary variable (recov01) says if the recovery was or not different from zero, another binary variable (ratio01) indication of the recovery is greater than the median (49%) of recovery rate (calculation01) in the group of recoveries greater than zero. A variety of models can guide the decisions around LGD using supervised and unsupervised learning models, such as:

1. Loss given default distribution fitting process
2. Tobit model dependent variable is the recovery rate % recovery/paid (0–100%), clustered by country (control for country)
3. Logistic regression analysis considering different sets of explanatory variables and different dependent variables. Two or three classes (categories) of the dependent variable can be considered: class 1: 0 LGD, class 2: between 0 and 100% LGD, class 3: 100% LGD. For class 2, it is possible to fit a multiple regression model as well.
4. Classification trees were used to identify the groups that provide more information when different constructed dependent variables have been used
5. Clustering was performed with the purpose of using a defined number of groups in order to observe the variables and values that split the groups. These groups should be part of the segmentation for the recovery process.

An illustration of these types of risk analytics models starts by defining the estimate of the loss distribution by jointly modeling the default probabilities and the recovery rates with shared covariates, and analyzing their interdependence (Chava et al., 2011). The recovery or LGD behavior can be described by regressions on explanatory variables that include organizational and business environment variables (macro-economic). The loss distribution could use theoretical distributions for testing; however, the process can be opened to estimate a mixed distribution as well, given the tails of the loss event. In this example, the loss distribution has been analyzed through the full data set and using truncation at the 99th percentile. The procedure that needs to be followed is to identify the probability density function of losses for the general credit portfolio. The definition of loss includes recoveries. Different methodologies to identify the fit approach are used, particularly chi-square and Kolmogorov-Smirnov tests are included in the analysis. Some of the principal descriptive characteristics, including various probability distribution moments, have to be identified and created. Simulation is another method that has been considered but has not been included using the theoretical approach to a compound Poisson distribution.

A typical problem to solve in risk analytics is unbalanced data or insufficient data to solve a problem. The particular illustration ahead indicates some these issues to the analytics process flow. The first result that is important to keep in mind, as it was indicated before, is that there is a concentration of the recovery distribution on the zero value, only 6.4% are values between 0 and 100% recovery. Only 1.62% of the recoveries are 100% recoveries. The 100% and 1 to 100% recovery rate values are below the benchmark results presented before. These are points to review the recovery process and the specificity of the analysis that the risk portfolio requires (Table 9.22).

The portfolio risk performance indicators include the analysis of behavior of the recovery rate; second, an approach to the loss distribution estimation, historical series of default rates and trends by segments, recovery rates through a bivariate view, transition matrices, and comparing products. The first point to include in the analysis is the one related to the loss distribution for the whole portfolio (assuming data known), which shows a 99% lower than $393,000 dollars and a mean of almost $33,000 dollars. This indicates a small size of loss, which is confirmed by the median

TABLE 9.22

Basic Composition of the Portfolio According to the Recovery Rate

% Recovery	Frequency	Distribution
0	20,317	91.98%
100	358	1.62%
0 < RR < 100	1,414	6.40%

located in $5,000 dollars. For the whole portfolio, there is a high standard deviation; a concentration on small values for losses and claims paid; and a difference between median and the mean. The question is if in the groups of recoveries greater than zero, these characteristics are the same. The answer is no (Table 9.23).

Table 9.24 contains information to compare two groups: recoveries greater than zero and the whole portfolio. The figures suggest a loss distribution affected by the high volume of zero recoveries. There is a clear difference between the loss distributions of the two groups. For example, in the group of recoveries greater than zero, the mean of claim paid is almost triple the one of the whole portfolio and the loss means are almost the same.

Another important point is to differentiate the loss and claim paid distributions and at the same time within the two groups of the whole portfolio and the recovery greater than zero. A comparison is based on the ratio of loss to claim paid for each one of the quartiles and the mean. The means ratio shows that the loss is 87.5% of the claim paid for the whole portfolio and a 40.8% when there is a recovery > 0. The review of the loss by claims-paid quartile in the whole portfolio shows higher values of the loss to claim paid ratio in the two lower quartiles. The group of recoveries > 0 (Tables 9.25 and 9.26) has the second and third quartiles with a higher ratio value. Or, in other words, when there is recovery > 0 there is a reduction of the loss to claim paid in the high and small claim paid values. The ratio of the second and third quartiles is almost 50%, and there is a difference of 10 points with the other two quartiles. This suggests that possibly the concentration on recovery work in the quartiles 2 and 3 could bring a good reduction of losses and generate benefits to the portfolio.

For the whole portfolio, there is a concentration on the combination low value of claim paid and low loss; however, there is a high increment of the loss event though the claim paid continues low (Figures 9.25 and 9.26). In the case of the sample with recoveries > 0, the concentration on low values of claims paid and low values of losses is evident. In both sets of data, there are points that follow different patterns and look like outliers. These points should be studied independently to identify the particular behavior. The information and knowledge from descriptive analytics can feed the decision-making process and policies design.

The graphs show the portfolio distribution in terms of claims paid and losses.

General observations in the examined example suggested guides to dig deeper in the understanding of a LGD for example:

- Canada and United States – Less recoveries than rest of the world (ROW).
- ROW common law more recoveries than ROW with civil law.
- Common law countries have more recoveries than civil law system for poor countries.
- Lowest recovery is in the sector of consumer goods.
- More assets figures are related to more recovery.
- Lower recoveries appear in some of the observation years and what the cause could be.
- Common law shows better results in no crisis years.
- More recovery for low risk level.
- Less recovery for med, mod, hi risk levels.
- More recovery is present when GDP growth > 6% in previous year (or average of previous 4 years).
- Less recovery if GDP growth from 0 to 6%.
- Previous years' inflation between 6% and 8% presents the best recovery.
- Previous 4 years' inflation of 4–8% indicate the best recovery.
  - Too low inflation – less recovery
  - Too high inflation – less recovery
- No clear pattern was identified in either mean of recovery or standard deviation of recovery.
- Canada has LEAST days to resolution: HOME COUNTRY ADVANTAGE.

TABLE 9.23

Basic Statistics for the Whole Portfolio and for the Group with Recoveries Greater than Zero

Summary Statistics

Whole Portfolio

Variable	Mean	Std Dev	N	1st Pctl	5th Ptcl	10th pCtl	Lower Quartile	Median	Upper Quartile	90th pCtl	95th pCtl	99th pCtl
Paid Cdn Value	37483.58	356939.1	22096	128.11	391.21	682.1416	1783.87	5547.54	20425.06	61338.98	117922.3	417616.8
loss	32813.38	213183.7	22096	0	272.75512	561.092	1580.21	5019.14	18841.05	57805.03	114476.5	392614.3

Recoveries greater than O

Variable	Mean	Std Dev	N	1st Pctl	5th Ptcl	10th Pctl	Lower Quartile	Median	Upper Quartile	90th pCtl	95th Pctl	99th Pctl
Paid Cdn Value	97915.92	1050655	1772	504.0004	1206.77	2124	4334.18	11497.67	33762.31	84165.65	182784.7	722613.3
loss	39924.95	292048.3	1772	0	0	0	348.3621	4150.3	15980.9	49661.19	96770	503320.8

TABLE 9.24

Comparing the Claims Paid Distribution and the Loss Distribution

Metric Loss to Claim Paid	Mean	Lower Quartile	Median	Upper Quartile	90thPctl	95th Pctl	99th Pctl
Whole portfolio	87.50%	88.60%	90.50%	92.20%	94.20%	97.10%	94.00%
Re c>0	40.80%	8.00%	36.10%	47.30%	59.00%	52.90%	69.70%

TABLE 9.25

Quartiles of the Claims Paid, the Corresponding Loss and Ratio Loss to Claim Paid for Each Quartile for the Whole Portfolio

Quartiles Claims Paid	Paid Cdn Value			loss			Ratio Loss/Claim Paid
	Sum	Mean	Median	Sum	Mean	Median	Using the mean
0	4452176.19	861.99	830.57	4344531	841.15	804.3	97.60%
1	16785083.44	3249.2	3086.43	1.60E+07	3097.96	2957.23	95.30%
2	54099500.17	10472	9688.77	5.10E+07	9851.45	9220.34	94.10%
3	373361417.2	72273	44106.82	3.50E+08	67467.2	41936.18	93.40%

TABLE 9.26

Quartiles of the Claims Paid, the Corresponding Loss and Ratio Loss to Claim Paid for Each Quartile for Recoveries Greater Than Zero

Quartiles Claims Paid	Paid Cdn Value			loss			Ratio Loss/Claim Paid
	Sum	Mean	Median	Sum	Mean	Median	Using the mean
0	1055592	2382.8	2466.03	402216	907.94	545.65	38.10%
1	3283458	7411.9	7222.58	1578704	3563.67	3625.76	48.10%
2	8810359	19888	18552.7	4394890	9920.75	9377.23	49.90%
3	1.6E+08	361981	67608.1	6.40E+07	145307	39736.87	40.10%

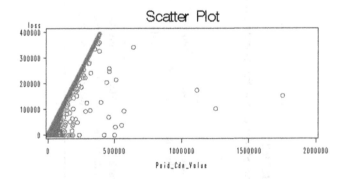

FIGURE 9.25   The whole portfolio distribution of the claims paid.

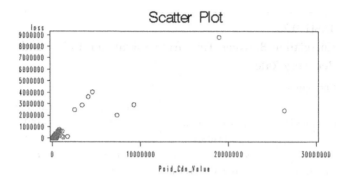

FIGURE 9.26 Only with recovery greater than zero distribution of claims paid.

- ROW has most days to resolution.
- ROW common law has less days to resolution than ROW civil law.
- Conclusion: more uncertainty in ROW civil law.

Other indicators can be created such as:

- Original Estimate of Recovery (%) – Actual Recovery (%)
- Absolute value (Ignore + or −)
- For Canada the forecast error is the smallest and in the ROW civil law is more than ROW common law

Another piece of the analysis is the location of items indicating the highest or lowest recovery rate. Table 9.27 shows this.

This analysis identifies the variables with the highest recovery ratio; for example, the English bankruptcy system, countries with higher income, internal characteristics of the process such as Hi risk level or number of years covered 1 and 6. What is required in additional studies is the identification of some reasons of the specific behavior. For instance, why does the English bankruptcy original system have a better recovery rate? Is it because of a kind of agility steps in

TABLE 9.27
Highest Value of Recovery Rates

Summary	Highest Ratio
poveredyears	1 and 6
yeasrbus	2
bkorigin	English
cr	1 and 4
GlobalArea	CentralAm
Legor	Socialist & English
SupplyChain	Gov & Life
Marketsector	Transp & Infrast
N. invoices	6
Religion	Muslim & Hindu
IGP	High Income
Risk Level	Hig

TABLE 9.28

Correlation Between Time from Submission to Pay and Recovery Rate

Correlations

		dayssubpaid	ratiorecov
dayssubpaid	Pearson Correlation	1	−.093[**]
	Sig. (2-tailed)		.000
	N	1596	1594
ratiorecov	Pearson Correlation	−.093[**]	1
	Sig. (2-tailed)	.000	
	N	1594	1594

Note

[**] Correlation is significant at the 0.01 level (2-tailed).

---

the process? What kind of steps? Are they possible to follow in countries with another kind of system?

The bivariate analysis is performed by correlations and by cross tabulation. The correlation calculations can be a big number because of the high number of possible combination of variables. The correlations were examined in the dataset with recovery rate greater than zero. In this analysis is important to bring to the attention two points that are influencing the recovery process. First, the number of days to payment (submission date to claim payment day) shows significantly that the inverse relation exists as it was expected, the longer the time between submission and payment, the smaller the recovery (Table 9.28).

A second point is the agreement with the credit risk theory that recovery rate has an inverse relationship to the PD. Equally, the number of invoices and the recovery rate have inverse direction. It does not happen with years in business variable that is moving in the same direction as the recovery rate. Regarding the macroeconomic variables, the average inflation of the country appears following the same direction as the recovery rate while the ratio private credit to GDP is not going in the same direction. The significant correlations to the recovery rate appear with number of invoices, the PD, private credit ratio to GDP, and average inflation (Table 9.29).

Are there differences when the global areas and sectors are observed together? The answer is yes. One of the points to bring to the discussion is that the LGD analysis includes the complexity of the relationship between market and region, for example. The generalization of the parameter estimation across the whole portfolio is something to be avoided. Sometimes the parameter, i.e., LGD, can be in general good for all sectors in a region, as it is the case of Central America where in almost all cases the LGD is one of the highest. Moreover, the fluctuation of the LGD can be very high among regions like the case of infrastructure and environment, where in USA the recovery rate is 4.9% and in Africa and Central America can be a two-digit rate (Table 9.30).

A metric and comparison review that is related to LGD is not only based on variables but also by products. Products in the portfolio have different results. The metric loss ratio takes into consideration the loss and the income. In Figure 9.27, the proxy of the loss ratio is exemplified. The differences are certainly appreciable, and it shows the possible different ways to control the loss in case of default. The scope and the data used in this example do not include the evaluation of the specific loss ratio of the risk or specific (endorsements for example) that differentiate the products, this means that the results are based on the aggregation of the attributes of the products.

TABLE 9.29

Variables and Recovery Rate Correlations at 10% Significance Level

Ratio recovered to Claim Paid	Paid Cdn Value	NUMBER OF INVOICES	YRSINBUS	Covered Years	Deduct	Pblended 9808	Pblende 9809	Recovered Cdn Value	OVDSBA MT	pcOgdp	gd pg	gni	avinfl	gdp_gr_a v_123	av infl 1234	Loss
Correlat ion	0.01705	-0.05049	0.11396	-0.00892	-0.00487	-0.06788	-0.0632	0.04744	0.06357	-0.04136	-0.0076	-0.03864	0.05405	0.01912	0.03409	-0.07923
Significance	0.4731	0.0371	0.0002	0.774	0.8377	0.0285	0.0415	0.0459	0.173	0.086	0.7522	0.1086	0.0247	0.4238	0.1538	0.0008
Cases analyzed	1772	1705	1037	1039	1772	1041	1041	1772	461	1724	1726	1726	1726	1752	1752	1772

TABLE 9.30

Recovery Rates Based on Markets

Global Area	Transportation	Resources	Light Manufacturing	Infrastructure and Environment	Info.& ComTechnology	Extractive	Total
AFRICA & THE MIDDLE EAST	3	29	91	24	30	1	178
ASIA & FAR EAST	13	24	57	21	33	4	152
CANADA	75	331	1182	195	111	50	2161
CENTRAL AMERICA & CARIBBEAN	13	63	203	69	44	13	407
EASTERN EUROPE	2	18	47	23	18		108
FORMER SOVIET UNION		6	6	6	5		23
JAPAN, AUSTRALIA NEW ZEALAND	3	11	22	12	13	3	65
SOUTH AMERICA	12	30	90	33	50	10	228
USA	238	530	3320	880	638	75	5682
WESTERN EUROPE	29	93	289	81	116	7	617
Grand Total	388	1135	5307	1344	1058	163	22096
		Ratios based on recovered amount and claim paid					
AFRICA & THE MIDDLE EAST	0.00%	1.10%	7.50%	33.60%	14.30%	0.00%	13.00%
ASIA & FAR EAST	5.20%	0.00%	0.40%	5.40%	1.40%	1.10%	0.96%
CANADA	7.70%	2.00%	2.10%	4.20%	2.10%	2.90%	2.53%
CENTRAL AMERICA & CARIBBEAN	44.50%	5.50%	4.00%	75.90%	6.60%	0.40%	49.40%
EASTERN EUROPE	0.00%	3.40%	4.70%	6.30%	5%	–	4.58%
FORMER SOVIET UNION	–	8.80%	11.50%	7.00%	0.40%	–	10.29%
JAPAN AUSTRALIA NEW ZEALAND	0%	9.70%	0.00%	5.10%	2.30%	0.00%	3.42%
SOUTH AMERICA	7.10%	0.50%	7.20%	8.4%	0.40%	0.20%	280%
USA	27.40%	3.30%	8.60%	4.90%	4.30%	0.40%	8.25%
WESTERN EUROPE	4.40%	1.50%	4.50%	2.50%	3.40%	1.90%	3.37%
Grand Total	22.20%	2.80%	6.80%	41%	3.90%	1.00%	12.46%

FIGURE 9.27 Product loss ratios comparison.

TABLE 9.31

Historical Default Rates by Risk Levels

Ratio	LOW	MOD	MED	HI	PRI	CRI
1998	0.45%	0.74%	1.46%	2.34%	5.18%	
1999	1.23%	1.42%	1.83%	2.05%	3.03%	7.91%
2000	1.39%	1.82%	1.93%	2.10%	2.58%	6.92%
2001	1.43%	2.11%	2.42%	2.00%	5.58%	10.32%
2002	1.02%	2.13%	2.52%	3.00%	1.63%	2.35%
2003	0.75%	1.64%	2.16%	1.86%	5.18%	0.01%
2004	0.62%	0.97%	1.85%	1.32%	1.46%	3.01%
2005	0.42%	0.91%	1.69%	1.59%	2.74%	5.44%
2006	0.40%	0.94%	1.74%	1.84%	0.65%	6.54%
2007	0.40%	1.02%	1.69%	1.91%	2.19%	1.74%
2008	0.56%	1.30%	2.87%	5.13%	6.20%	19.81%
2009	0.64%	1.20%	1.68%	3.16%	4.69%	10.52%

Another aspect of the risk analytics process applied to the relationship $EL = PD * LGD * ED$ is that the calculation of the default rates using variables describing the portfolio behavior when segments are included leads to a better estimator for approaching EL. The use of region or market or combination market and region instead of using just averages of the whole portfolio. First (Table 9.31) is the risk level, second is using supply chain (Tables 9.32 and 9.33). Third is using global area (Table 9.34) and as an example of another variable that can be important it has been used the number of years of bank coverage. Default rates, with the historical presentation, allow the calculation of the variance and mean for describing expected results in the segments of risk levels. The analysis for each risk level requires additionally the historical perspective and the estimation by regression (for instance) of the good estimator of a risk level default rate to predict portfolio behaviors.

The sector and global area default (see Figures 9.28 to 9.31) rates and the years of observation in each case allow the identification of trends. The purpose of the time series generation is to identify the variability and to introduce the possibility to have access to the reasons of this variability through time. Time series of default rates will provide, in the future, a powerful instrument to control the portfolio and to construct better forecasting tools, using the time series models with the best fit. Variance measures include rank, geometric variation, and variance related to the geometric mean. The variance measures themselves have to be studied to identify the random effects and the variance components. Some of the most important concepts associated with the possibility of building time series are the computation of covariance structures and correlation functions.

TABLE 9.32

Historical Default Rates and Supply Chain Classification

Ratios	Mining	Oil & Gas	Knowledge Base	Media & Telecom	Engineering	Environment	Financial Services	Government Services	Power	Tourism	Consumer Goods
1998	1.26%	0.38%	1.43%	1.02%	0.83%	3.33%	0.31%	0.00%	0.68%	0.00%	1.81%
1999	0.81%	0.00%	1.28%	1.53%	1.42%	4.65%	1.03%	0.00%	0.52%	0.00%	2.13%
2000	1%	0.37%	2.11%	1.63%	1.24%	3.19%	0.94%	0.00%	0.27%	1.34%	2.16%
2001	1.78%	0.00%	1.83%	2%	1.59%	1.87%	0.61%	3%	1.05%	2.18%	2.43%
2002	1.12%	0%	1.82%	1.50%	1.45%	0.94%	0.67%	0.00%	1.32%	0.71%	2.45%
2003	0.91%	0.23%	1.16%	1.45%	1.07%	1.38%	0.49%	0.00%	1.07%	5.50%	1.73%
2004	46%	0.32%	1.00%	1.24%	0.78%	0%	0.86%	0.00%	0.55%	0.00%	1.17%
2005	0.27%	0.00%	0.84%	0.89%	0.74%	0.45%	0.18%	0.00%	0.31%	0.56%	1.20%
2006	0.61%	48%	0.61%	0.77%	0.77%	0%	1.30%	0.00%	0.42%	0.01%	1.34%
2007	0.59%	0.21%	0.85%	0.85%	0.74%	0.39%	0.45%	0.00%	0.28%	0.87%	1.31%
2008	1.33%	0.22%	1.22%	1.20%	0.92%	4.25%	0.81%	0.02%	0.93%	1.01%	2.38%
2009	1.01%	0.13%	0.95%	1.19%	0.86%	1.69%	0.57%	0.13%	0.60%	1.14%	1.68%

TABLE 9.33

Historical Default Rates and Supply Chain Classification

Ratios	Life Science	Bulk Agriculture	Fisheries	lumber	Meat	Pulp & Paper	Aerospace	Autos/Trucks	Buses & Specialty Vehicles	Rail	Shipbuilding	Transportation Services
1998	1.00%	0.71%	1.08%	0.70%	3.63%	1.17%	0.00%	1%	1.32%	0.00%	2.25%	1%
1999	1.08%	0.81%	1.17%	1.13%	1.07%	0.83%	0.69%	1.08%	0.00%	0.00%	0.00%	0.64%
2000	1.20%	1.27%	1.53%	121%	1.71%	2.65%	0.62%	1.60%	2.36%	0.00%	1.80%	2.20%
2001	0.64%	0.97%	1.88%	1.31%	1.01%	1.24%	0.58%	1.69%	0.99%	0.00%	4.52%	0.92%
2002	1%	1%	1.46%	1%	1.30%	1%	0.00%	1.41%	0.00%	3%	1.26%	1.33%
2003	0.74%	0.79%	0.66%	1.29%	208%	0.93%	0.00%	0.32%	0.82%	0.00%	1.22%	1.21%
2004	0.77%	0.96%	1.67%	0.93%	1.12%	0.86%	0.00%	1.22%	1.37%	3.01%	0.67%	1.59%
2005	0.65%	0.56%	1.85%	1.03%	0.89%	1.40%	0.49%	0.83%	1.32%	0.00%	0.00%	1.18%
2006	0.27%	0.62%	0.54%	0.94%	1%	0.94%	0%	0.76%	0.86%	0.00%	0.61%	0.61%
2007	0.70%	0.57%	0.90%	0.93%	1.24%	0.98%	0.00%	0.86%	0.84%	0.01%	1.61%	0.73%
2008	0.82%	155%	1.65%	1.45%	1.64%	2%	0.77%	1.45%	1.91%	1.57%	3%	1.55%
2009	0.67%	0.80%	1.31%	1.40%	1.89%	0.93%	0.18%	1.23%	0.73%	0.36%	1.85%	0.95%

TABLE 9.34

Historical Default Rates and Geographical Region

Ratios	1 Central America	2 South America	3 CAN	4 USA	5 Africa Middle East	6 Asia Far East	7_EastEurope_ Former Soviet	8_WestEurope JAP AUST NZ
1998	2.03%	3.23%	1.33%	1.29%	1.19%	1.21%	3.90%	1.00%
1999	1.47%	2.03%	1.77%	1.74%	1.43%	0.82%	2.27%	0.79%
2000	2.82%	1.90%	1.43%	1.93%	2.63%	1.58%	2.47%	0.84%
2001	1%	2.96%	1.97%	2.12%	2.21%	1.25%	2.55%	0.80%
2002	2.37%	2.38%	2.20%	1.94%	1.36%	0.64%	1.14%	0.80%
2003	3.00%	1.25%	1.90%	1.28%	0.85%	0.66%	0.91%	0.55%
2004	0.97%	1.17%	1.29%	1.00%	0.96%	0.97%	1.83%	0.60%
2005	1.08%	0.96%	1.25%	0.91%	1.34%	0.93%	1.19%	0.63%
2006	1.68%	0.74%	1.41%	0.94%	0.83%	0.37%	0.96%	0.67%
2007	1.13%	0.82%	1.30%	1.01%	0.72%	0.63%	1.60%	0.69%
2008	2.24%	1.74%	1.71%	1.67%	2.68%	1.14%	2.21%	1.19%
2009	1.45%	0.99%	1.34%	1.30%	0.90%	0.52%	0.95%	0.77%

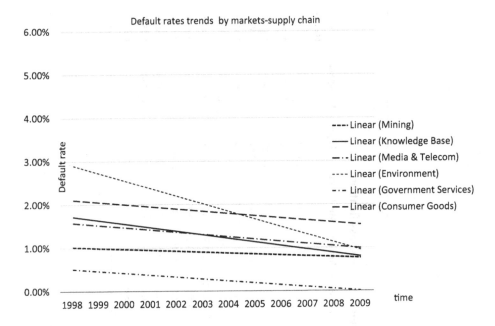

FIGURE 9.28   Default rate trends and markets.

This section has shown the default rates historical data. The trends (outlook) indicate what is happening in general to the specific group in comparison to the others. The models of trend as a first approximation in this review will have a better fit with more data points and in case that the fit be not good the observation of the reasons for the dispersion should be analyzed. The slope of the trend line introduces a concept of "speed of risk" possible to use for comparison among different groups of classification.

In the case of default rates by markets, all the markets trend to reduce the default rate but the speed changes (the slope of the lines) mainly in the case of light manufacture, infrastructure, and the information and communication technology where the slopes are higher (more negative) than

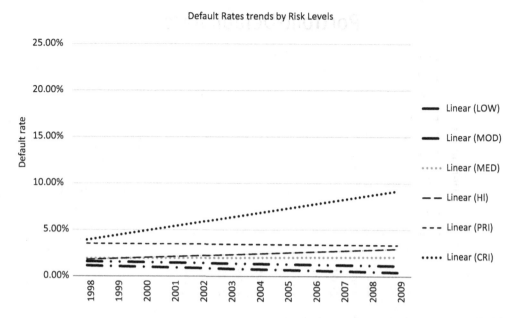

FIGURE 9.29 Default rate trends and risk levels.

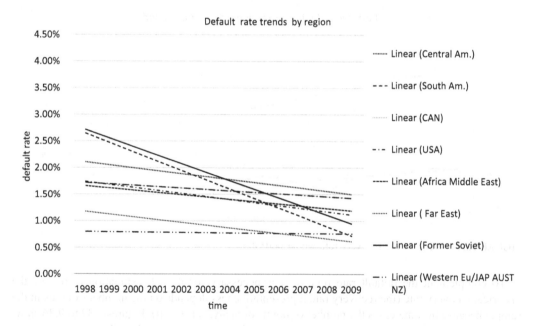

FIGURE 9.30 Default rate trends and geographical regions.

the other markets. These three markets are different from the slopes in resources and extractive, which look more stable along the years. According to the risk levels the situation is that the Med, Hi, and Critical have a positive slope while the others have a negative one with a higher speed of reducing the default rate in the Low risk level. According to the geographical region, South America and East Europe have an accelerated reduction of default rate. The other areas reduce the default rates, except Western Europe and Japan that remain static. The hypothesis that appears at this level is that the combination risk level, region, and sector modify the trends.

Portfolio Default Rate

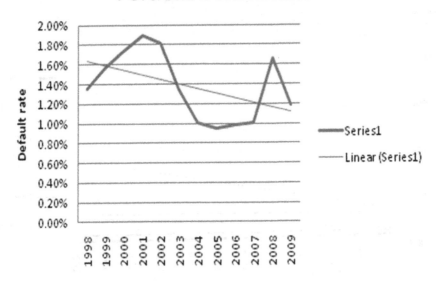

FIGURE 9.31   Portfolio trend of the default rate.

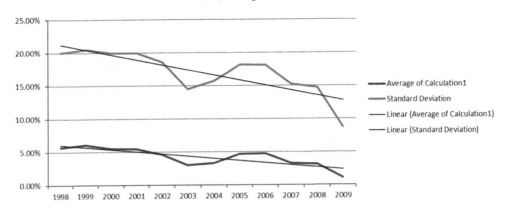

FIGURE 9.32   Trend of the recovery rate whole portfolio.

To complement the default rate review, it is necessary for the EL estimation to review the historical recovery rate (the recovery rate representativeness depends on the number of cases in the sample because in some cases the number of points of analysis is small). Figures 9.32 to 9.36 show the trends of the recovery rate. In most of the cases, there is a trend to reduce the recovery rate, or better increase LGD, value which is in contrast with the trend of the default rates because of the low trend observed. Cases like infrastructure and transportation, the same as Eastern Europe, Central America, South America and Asia, and Far East possibly are with a trend to improve the recovery. The risk levels observed, Low, Mod, Med, and Hi, show for the whole portfolio all decreasing; meanwhile, for those with recovery greater than zero, that Mod and Hi are slightly with trend to better recovery, meanwhile Low and Medium go a trend to reduce the recovery rate.

An additional step to review what is happening with LGD analysis is to move through the transition of periods of recovery and types of losses. The frequency-based transition matrices have four different measures taking as the date basis September 30th 2011. The points of observation

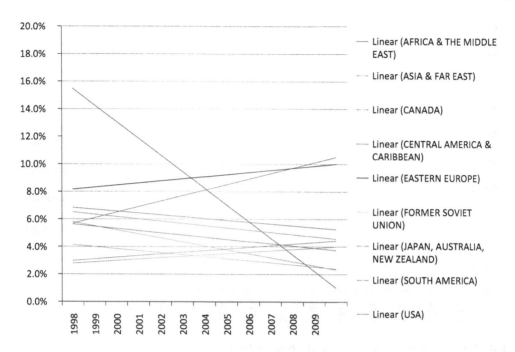

FIGURE 9.33 Recovery rate by region.

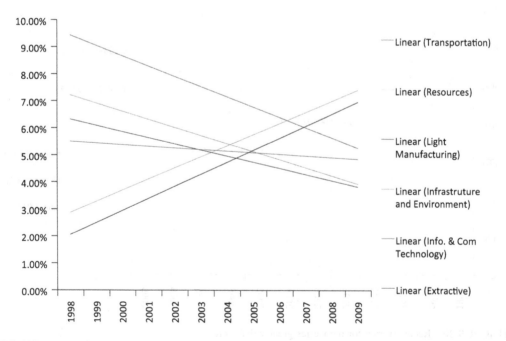

FIGURE 9.34 Recovery rate by market.

were March 31st 2011, June 30th 2011, September 30th 2010, and December 31st 2010. The purpose of transition matrices is to describe the evolution of the portfolio and from it to define means to forecast what is expected for the portfolio. The use is based on what is the exposure that one time the organization has and how this exposure at one risk level will change, evolving to different risk levels, which will have different recovery rates and then different EL.

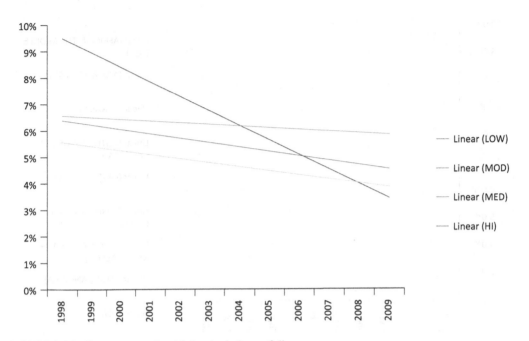

FIGURE 9.35 Recovery rate by risk level whole portfolio.

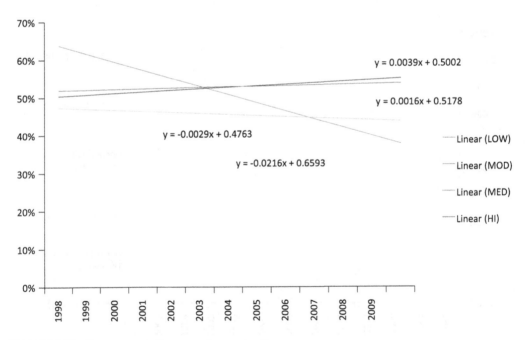

FIGURE 9.36 Recovery rate for recoveries greater than zero.

Tables 9.35 and 9.36 show transition matrices (based on frequencies and dollars) for one-quarter and one-year evolution. In the first one, for example, the total exposure-risk units (in this case, in the tables it is shown the ratio based on counts and dollars but it is possible to identify the dollar amounts of total direct exposure that are changing) in a Low risk level will remain, in a quarter, at the same risk level a 94.85%; meanwhile in one year the figure changes to 75.85%. This means that with an expected recovery rate that is better for Low risk level the EL in one year will

TABLE 9.35
Transition Matrix Counts and Dollars Third Quarter 2011

June 2011 to Sept 2011

Counts	Low	Mod	Med	Hi	pri	CRI
Low	94.85%	1.41%	0.12%	0.13%	0.01%	0.02%
Mod	2.61%	92.48%	0.73%	0.29%	0.03%	0.03%
Med	0.76%	2.30%	91.70%	0.99%	0.00%	0.03%
Hi	0.44%	1.45%	2.86%	89.25%	0.51%	0.17%
pri	0.57%	0.00%	0.00%	6.23%	85.27%	2.83%
CRI	0.00%	0.00%	0.00%	0.00%	3.91%	75.00%

Dollars	Low	Mod	Med	Hi	pri	CRI
Low	95.33%	2.36%	0.34%	0.26%	0.03%	0.02%
Mod	2.80%	93.74%	1.34%	0.42%	0.03%	0.02%
Med	0.79%	2.69%	93.17%	1.49%	0.00%	0.04%
Hi	0.20%	0.56%	4.44%	92.08%	1.35%	0.13%
pri	0.16%	0.00%	0.00%	3.64%	89.13%	4.56%
CRI	0.00%	0.00%	0.00%	0.00%	5.67%	90.34%

TABLE 9.36
Transition Matrix Counts and Dollars Sept 2010-Sept 2011

Sept 2010 to Sept 2011

Counts	Low	Mod	Med	Hi	pri	CRI
Low	75.85%	3.20%	0.78%	0.59%	0.04%	0.06%
Mod	18.79%	55.86%	1.65%	1.01%	0.04%	0.07%
Med	3.31%	27.17%	50.74%	2.03%	0.05%	0.07%
Hi	2.61%	10.11%	15.76%	49.89%	0.85%	0.35%
pri	1.96%	1.40%	3.35%	24.58%	53.07%	6.15%
CRI	0.00%	0.00%	2.24%	12.69%	19.40%	25.37%

Dollars	Low	Mod	Med	Hi	pri	CRI
Low	72.39%	7.78%	2.73%	1.06%	0.09%	0.07%
Mod	11.76%	56.13%	9.36%	1.28%	0.05%	0.16%
Med	3.61%	12.00%	38.26%	5.46%	0.10%	0.05%
Hi	1.92%	3.96%	16.73%	47.98%	1.97%	0.75%
pri	0.68%	0.64%	1.38%	47.74%	50.78%	10.79%
CRI	0.00%	0.00%	0.30%	24.02%	35.77%	26.00%

be reduced if the Low level number of risk units is not compensated accordingly. The differences of the total sum of percentages to 100% represent the exposure that move to one state that in general is called "absorbent" and mainly represented by no more exposure because of claim presented or it is not longer part of the portfolio.

The exposure analysis is the component to complete the model structure EL = PD * LGD * ED. Exposure analysis is more than the calculation of exposure at default. Exposure analysis is a management process where the important aspects to study include: concentration, aggregation, correlation, volume of risks and claims, segments, risk policies compliance, and so on. In the

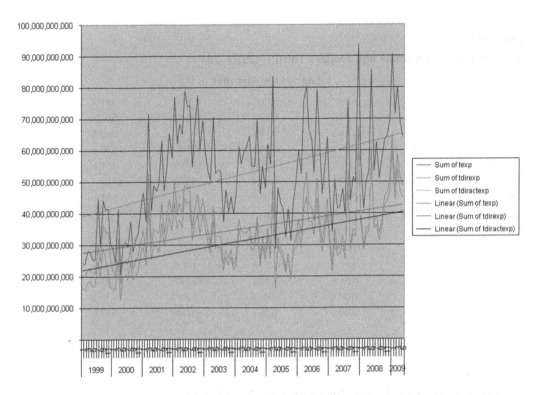

FIGURE 9.37   Trends for differentiation among metrics of exposure.

following, there is an illustration of the combination of factors in exposure analysis. The differentiation of the exposure through time is crucial to develop the outlook indicator and how the total exposure, total direct exposure, and total direct active exposure. These three terms are possible to use when there is exposure based on a direct customer, and there is relationship with an organization parent and there are limits of exposure imposed in some cases used or not by the organization (Figure 9.37).

Another piece of control is the identification of thresholds based on standard deviations. Table 9.37 indicates the case of the risk levels. Through the years (this is connected to the transition matrices as well), the distribution of the risk levels in the total direct exposure can have a different risk share percentage. The point in terms of control is how big the share percentage changes are and which are the means and standard deviations in order to identify a benchmark to turn on lights of analysis for sectors, countries or specific groups of risk units. For example, there are at least three ways to get the thresholds (Table 9.37). One is with the average of the share for the risk level, second with the calculation of the variation of the share, and third, using the standard deviation of the shares or standard deviation of the changes. In particular, a metric that can identify in a better way the fluctuations is the standard deviation of the share changes.

An additional aspect to study in exposure is products related. The point to review is to discover how the portfolio can change from a product to another (see Figure 9.38) or how the companies' portfolio evolves in terms of the risk units-countries-sectors and selected coverage (SC).

The impact of transition of the risk units and exposure or from a product to another has effects in terms of the LGD results. The figures show some changes between CREDIT exposure to selected coverage. The calculation of the effect on the LGD might depend on how efficient/effective the recovery is. In the first approach of data, the transition of CREDIT policies to selected coverage does not affect negatively the loss ratio, but if the transition is to product 1 or to product 2, the loss ratio can be highly different.

TABLE 9.37

Suggested Basis for the Calculation of the Thresholds for Exposure Management

Risk Level/period	Total Portfolio • Exposures									Changes							
	1	2	3	4	5	6	7	Average	Std. dev	1	2	3	4	5	6	Average	Std. Dev
CRITICAL WATCH	3.77%	2.40%	1.72%	0.72%	0.60%	0.60%	0.34%	1.45%	1.30%	-36%	-28%	-58%	-17%	0%	-43%	-30%	20%
PRIORITY WATCH	1.95%	1.55%	1.32%	2.41%	2.41%	2.41%	2.68%	2.11%	0.50%	-20%	-15%	82%	0%	0%	12%	10%	37%
HIGH	12.99%	11.36%	12.28%	11.99%	11.93%	11.93%	15.62%	12.59%	1.40%	-13%	8%	-2%	-1%	0%	31%	4%	15%
MEDIUM	20.38%	21.30%	21.31%	20.75%	21.00%	21.00%	22.33%	21.15%	0.60%	5%	0%	-3%	1%	0%	6%	2%	3%
MODERATE	31.89%	31.85%	32.26%	32.18%	31.16%	31.16%	29.57%	31.44%	0.90%	0%	1%	0%	-3%	0%	-5%	-1%	2%
Low	28.85%	31.34%	30.95%	31.78%	32.84%	32.84%	29.41%	31.14%	1.60%	9%	-1%	3%	3%	0%	-10%	0%	6%
UNX	0.16%	0.19%	0.16%	0.17%	0.07%	0.07%	0.05%	0.12%	0.10%	19%	-16%	5%	-58%	0%	-34%	-14%	28%

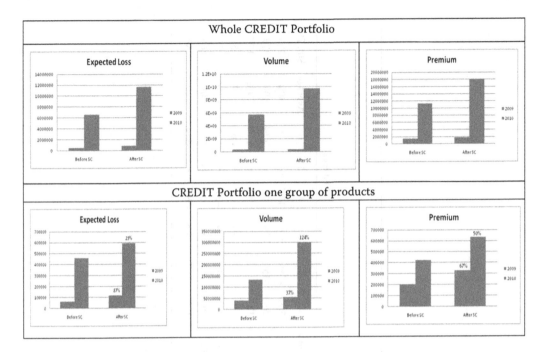

FIGURE 9.38 Observation of an example of transition exposure by products.

9.10 CLASSIFICATION AND LGD

The models used in this part of the analysis follow steps for organizing the learning data sets and development of predictive models. In this way, beginning with identification of segments and variables that are influencing in the LGD estimation, through classification trees, regressions, and clustering. This requires identification of the explicit variables that can modify the dependent variable and provide the opportunity to generate of groups/clusters. The dependent variables used are binary, describing to have or not a recovery greater than zero; another binary variable is describing a recovery greater than a threshold. The threshold can be the median of the recovery ratio. At the end, the purpose is to create a score that identifies the LGD behavior by each one of the obligors or risk units.

The data used and partial results are to illustrate the general procedure to follow and integrating learning techniques. Cluster analysis was performed mainly on the group of recoveries greater than zero. The purpose was to identify the clusters and the variables that define these clusters. Figure 9.39 presents the whole group of cases with recoveries greater than zero. In the search of clusters, the method used is the k-means methodology and with k = 5 looking for easier illustration of the example (remember to use methods explained before to select the appropriate k). Clustering is sensitive to the kind of variables used and if they are possible to measure with interval metrics, the categorical variables are not possible to use. The variables used are a mix of continuous variables between internal and macro-economic variables: No. of invoices, years in business, PD, and eight macroeconomic variables plus the recovery rate.

Using the data for recoveries greater than zero, the main variable to split into groups is the original estimation of recovery. Those with estimation of recovery uses the differentiator the value of years in business. For those with less than 27% estimation of recovery, the variables inflation, number of invoices, and years in business are taken into consideration for grouping. The concentration of sample points is on the clusters 3, 4, and 5 and the original estimation of recovery is less than 27%. The characteristics of the clusters (segments) are as follows:

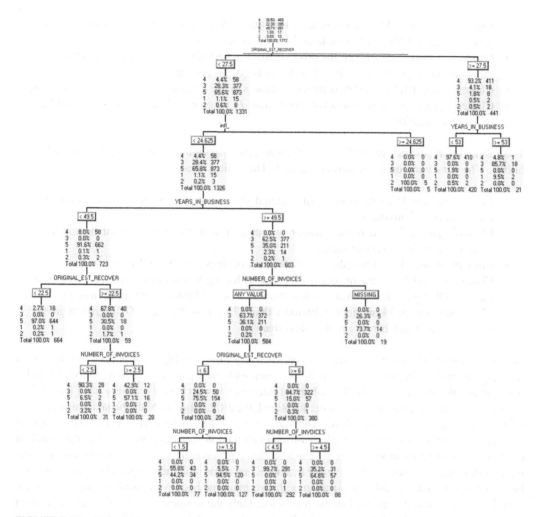

FIGURE 9.39 Clusters for recoveries greater than zero.

- Cluster/Segment 1: 17 members characterized by estimation of recovery less than 27%, inflation less than 24%, with more than 49 years in business and unknown number of invoices.
- Cluster/Segment 2: 10 members characterized by estimation of recovery less than 27% and inflation very high; more than 24%.
- Cluster/Segment 3: 395 members with estimated recovery between 6 and 27%, inflation less than 24%, more than 49 years in business, and number of invoices less than 5.
- Cluster/Segment 4: 469 members characterized by estimated recovery higher than 27% and less than 53 years in business.
- Cluster/Segment 5: 881 members mainly with the characteristics of having estimation less than 22% and less than 49 years in business.

For recovery rate between 0 and 100%, the clusters are different, indicating new knowledge of segments to identify work to do in recovery and loss control. The concentration is on the segments 2 and 4. In this case, the five clusters/segments are:

- Cluster/segment 1: 35 members, characterized by more than 75 invoices, more than 14 years in business, and average inflation in the past four years less than 2%

- Cluster/segment 2: 519 members with less than 5.5 invoices, average inflation last four years less than 3.5%, and more than 37 years in business
- Cluster/segment 3: 1 member, the group is like the first one with the only difference in the inflation that is greater than 2%. This is a case of an outlier.
- Cluster/segment 4: 840 members mainly with less than 74 invoices and 37 years in business.
- Cluster/segment 5: 19 members with more than 74 invoices, 14 years in business, and 2% of average inflation.

The results for recoveries at 100% are indicating new opportunities to define risk control capabilities. The concentration is on cluster 3 and 4. The main characteristics are:

- Cluster/segment 1: 17 members characterized by having more than 16 years in business and more than 7 invoices.
- Cluster/segment 2: 7 members similar to cluster 1 with the difference of having some members with less years in business.
- Cluster/segment 3: 129 members with years in business less than 16.
- Cluster/segment 4: 131 members characterized by having less than 5 invoices, a Gini greater than 27, GDP growth less than 2.8, less than 57 years in business but more than 16.
- Cluster/segment 5: 74 members with more than 47 years in business, GDP growth greater than 2.8%, and number of invoices less than 7.

Now the (Table 9.35) segments have different recovery rates; the highest frequency is the lowest recovery rate and the highest recovery is in the group with the smallest frequency. In the group that does not take the recoveries at 100%, the highest frequency is with lowest recovery rate (Table 9.38).

Once there are segments-groups-cluster identified, the differentiation of the behavior model of the LGD within them is a step to follow. The same exercise has to be performed in the groups of geographical regions, industries etc. Many different methodologies have been used in the search of the description of LGD, models such as: classification/regression trees, multiple regression, logistic regression, neural networks, support vector machines and some other new approaches of regressions. In this presentation a simplified illustration with two main methods were used: classification trees, stepwise regression and stepwise logistic regression. Only the segments of global areas and market sectors were considered and showing the LGD approach through stepwise multiple regression using the whole data and for the recovery rates > 0. The combinations of models, variables, and data sets are many and given the time limitation, only some of the models were evaluated in general in order to identify variables significance for contributing to the changes in the selected variable such as the recovery rate. The formal evaluation-comparison of the models is left for further analysis.

TABLE 9.38

Identification of the Clusters for Two Samples: Recoveries Greater Than Zero Including and Not Including 100% Recovery

Clusters Taking All Recoveries GTO			Cluster Taking Not 100%		
Cluster	Freq	Recovery	Cluster	Freq	Recovery
1	17	54%	1	34	45%
2	10	63%	2	509	44%
3	395	58%	3	1	91%
4	469	55%	4	855	39%
5	881	49%	5	15	40%

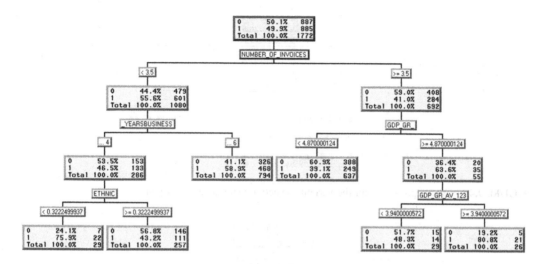

FIGURE 9.40 Dependent variable ratio01 for all records with recovery greater than zero.

Classification trees have two main roles. First, it is a way to identify variables related to the identified clusters and second, the discrimination based on the dependent variable. Two groups were defined below (0) and above (1 including 100%) of the median for the ratio: recovery to paid value. Figure 9.40 indicates in the case of all the recoveries greater than zero that the number of invoices and years in business provide information to discriminate between the two groups. The above ratio median is characterized by a smaller number of invoices (< 3.5) and higher number of years in business (more than 5). The group below the ratio median is characterized by higher number of invoices and lower GDP growth.

In this case, the knowledge of the variables means a way to decide what the groups start with in a process of collection. The point is that based on the model, the higher the effort put on improving the variable when that relationship is positive the higher the contribution to the dependent variable; which means to use this indication as a way to prioritize recovery actions.

In Figure 9.41, the classification is based on the dependent variable with 0 for recovery rate less than median and 1 for recovery higher than median in the group of greater than zero but not 100% recovery. The purpose is to discriminate from those that are fully repaid. There are some

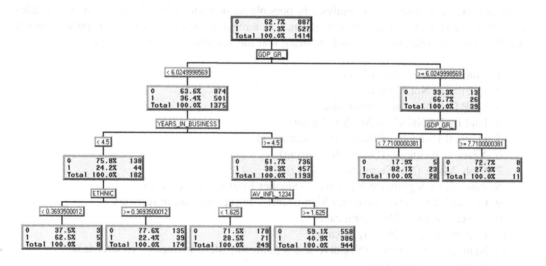

FIGURE 9.41 Dependent variable ratio01 with sample recoveries between 0 and 100%.

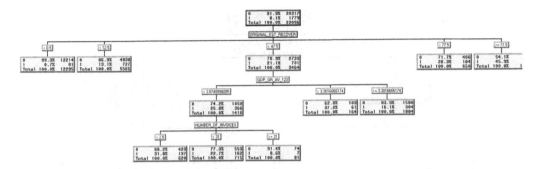

FIGURE 9.42 Whole portfolio and the variable selection using a set of variables.

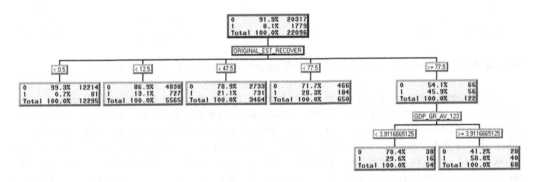

FIGURE 9.43 Whole portfolio and the variable selection using another set of variables.

differences in the node years in business and the use kind of GDP average used. Figure 9.41 indicates that when the whole sample is taken, with 0 as not having recovery and 1 having recovery, the variable that indicates the source of discrimination is only the original estimation of recovery. The higher value of recovery estimation appears affected by the GDP growth of the average for three years, with a higher recovery in those countries with more than 3.9% average GDP growth in three years. Figures 9.46 and 9.47 indicate the changes generated by using different variables to explain the dependent variable (Figures 9.41–9.43).

In a regression process, the analysis is possible to perform using different set of variables according to risk policy decisions. For instance, in a regular transaction without a special sign-off and the whole population, the models indicate that the variables have these results:

1. Common Law – Significant
2. Inflation – Not Significant
3. GDP Growth – Not Significant
4. Paid by BANK C$ – Not Significant
5. Original Estimate of Recovery – Significant
6. Years in Business (Positive Significant)
7. Cash Assets (Not Significant)
8. Asset Size(Significant Negative – (Smaller Firm more recovery)
9. Covered Years (Negative and Significant) – fewer years more recovery
10. Market Sector – Not Significant
11. Overdue Code – Not Significant
12. Number of Invoices – (Negative and Significant) More invoices – recover less
13. Terms – Not Significant

The regression results can be obtained using several combinations of variables and market practice conditions in order to identify the effect of the variables in the target. Taking sectors and global areas as the basis for segmentation (Table 9.36) influences the identification of patterns. Some of the macro-economic variables, such as GDP growth and average inflation, provide guides to determine the recovery ratio value independently of the method used, this means a consistent result. This means that using regression is the same as using the classification tree methodologies and the clustering methods; some variables continue being important for the discrimination: number of invoices and the original estimation of recovery (Table 9.39).

Now, instead of searching for the percent of recovery, the search for the score or probability of having recoveries greater than zero requires reviewing two points: first, the variables that identify probability of having a recovery higher than zero; second, variables that allow the identification of a recovery higher than the median when the recovery is greater than zero (Table 9.40, Figure 9.44).

In the analysis of loss distribution and recovery rate distribution, a first point to understand is that the recovery rate (when it is greater than zero) does not have a unimodal distribution. (Figures 9.45 represents a challenge in the analysis because the generalization of the results can be in danger given the groups.) In this observation, it seems that one group is for those cases that have a recovery rate higher than 70%, another for those between 30% and 70%, and another for those with less than 30%. This differentiation helps as well in the understanding of the selection of one of the dependent variables according to quartiles.

TABLE 9.39
Summary of Stepwise Regressions

Taking the % LGD	Looking for a Possible Estimator		
	Variables Used	All Records	
	Only Those with Recovery >O	All Variables	Models Not Good Fit
All variables	models not good fit. Significant variables original estimate Of recovery avinfl soc ortho		
	Breaking by market sectors		
1	averinflat1234, credit right, original est. recov oecd	number of invoices, aveinfl,	
2	no variable	candumm, gdp gr av 123, lending	
3	number of invoices, original est.recovery	bk dumm	
4	no variable	av infl 1234, ger	
5	muslim, number invoices	av infl 1234, gni, lending	
6	no variable	no variable	
	Breaking by global areas		
1	no variable	no variable	
2	no variable	pblended, lending	
3	number invoices	no variable	
4	gdp gr avg 123	no variable	
5	no variable	infl, eng, av infl 1234, yrsbusiness	
6	no variable	no variable	
7	bk dumm, gni	ger, pblended	
8	no variable	oecd, gdp gr	
9	pblended	no variable	
10	number invoices	gdp gr	

TABLE 9.40

Summary of Logistic Regression; Two Different Dependent Variables

Recovery or Not	Recovery Greater or Not Than 50%
Orig. Estimate.recovery	oeced011 0 vs 1
quickrat_ranges	Orig. Estimate.recovery
Pblended9809	YeCreditnbus
gni	effsale
lending	
igp	

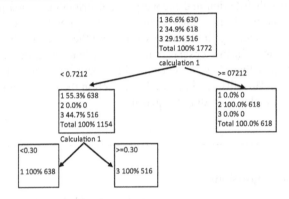

FIGURE 9.44 Basic distribution of three main groups in recovery rate.

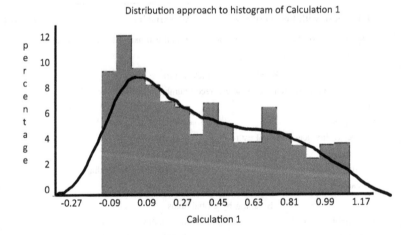

FIGURE 9.45 Histogram and kernel distribution for the recovery rate.

The fit of the loss distribution has been a difficult task for credit institutions. Even some models in the literature are using various distributions in Loss Distribution analysis and given the differences in sample points or data groups the approach to the loss distribution a mixed distribution is used to describe the full loss domain including the tails. When the full data is taken, the 99th percentile is given by a value of $392.000 dollars with a big difference among quartiles, indicating a fast change of frequency from small loss values to big ones.

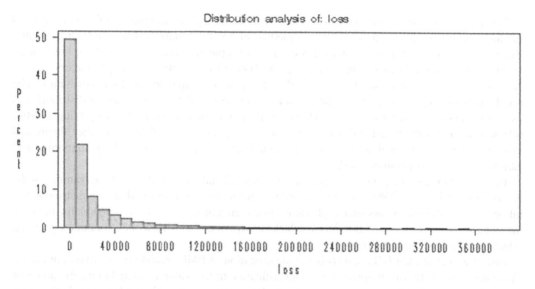

FIGURE 9.46 Histogram for the loss truncated at 99th percentile.

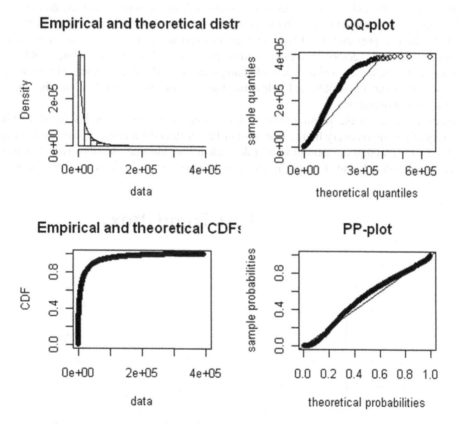

FIGURE 9.47 Example of the fit for the Weibull distribution.

There are points to identify with more care, such as the high concentration of zero values and the loss concentration in values less than a median of $5,000 dollars. Taking the 99th percentile truncated distribution (Figure 9.46), the histogram shows the high concentration of the low values. In Figure 9.47, there is an example of using the Weibull distribution (from parameters scale = 1.2939 * e + 04 and shape = 6.0532 * e – 01) as a good descriptor of the loss distribution. The acceleration of the loss changes can be a description given by the Weibull and the distribution is used sometimes in reliability analysis. However, deeper work is required for supporting a better selection of a model. In general, the fit is not passing the statistical test for other theoretical distributions such as normal, lognormal, exponential, gamma, etc. even though the lognormal and gamma are the most common used.

For the lognormal, the parameters are meanlog 8.6243 and sdlog 1.7032; for the gamma, alpha is 0.002836 and beta is 7361590. Now, another point to keep in mind is that loss distribution is influenced by different factors such high values in a period of time. This is the high value in 2008, the trend of reducing loss and possibly the lack of experience to review the economic cycle that affect the results (Figure 9.48).

One of aspect of the LGD analysis is the identification of PML (probability of maximum loss). There are methods for this purpose and the identification of this value is related to the evolution of the portfolio as well. One approach is using simulation; another directly the loss distribution with observation of the order statistics and another with the identification of exposure changes in the portfolio. Another element of analysis is a risk map that allows comparison with thresholds that should be created using the mean and SD of the previous years. In this example, the emphasis is on the mix between PD and exposure, but in the final result of the future analysis, this kind of map will be complemented by classification maps such as the one shown in the Figure 9.49.

Figure 9.50 is a presentation of the summary of exposure metrics. There is a combination of exposure by economic sectors, by regions, and by products with metrics associated with revenues/ premiums, expected losses, and a review of changes in time. The colors represent how the figures are according to the thresholds and rules that business practice identified for the appropriate performance and operation.

Moreover, based on the identification of the variables and their weights for describing the probability of having recovery higher than zero or higher than the median, it is possible to create a score for LGD. Through the definition of a dependent variable that identifies with 1 if there is a recovery greater than 0 and 0 when the recovery is zero, the regressions provide a score that is

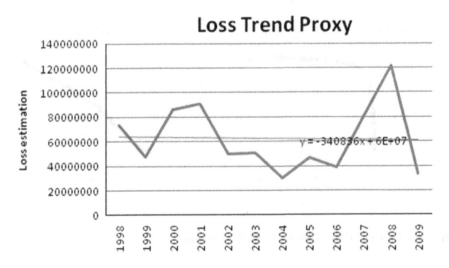

FIGURE 9.48   Trend of the loss.

Grouping	Probability Rank	Exposure by Rank of the Variable Claim Paid Dollar Ranges				
		Low	Med		High	
		<28931	28931-44012	44012-68341	68341-136957	136957+
Low PD	0-0.0022 0.0022-0.0032 0.0032-0.0042 0.0042-0.0055 0.0055-0.0069	13%	5%		21%	
Mod PD	0.0069-0.0090 0.0090-0.0119 0.0119-0.0167	10%	5%		21%	
Med -High PD	0.0167-0.026 0.026+	7%	4%		14%	

FIGURE 9.49 Example of portfolio distribution based on the combination between PD and exposure by categories of claims paid.

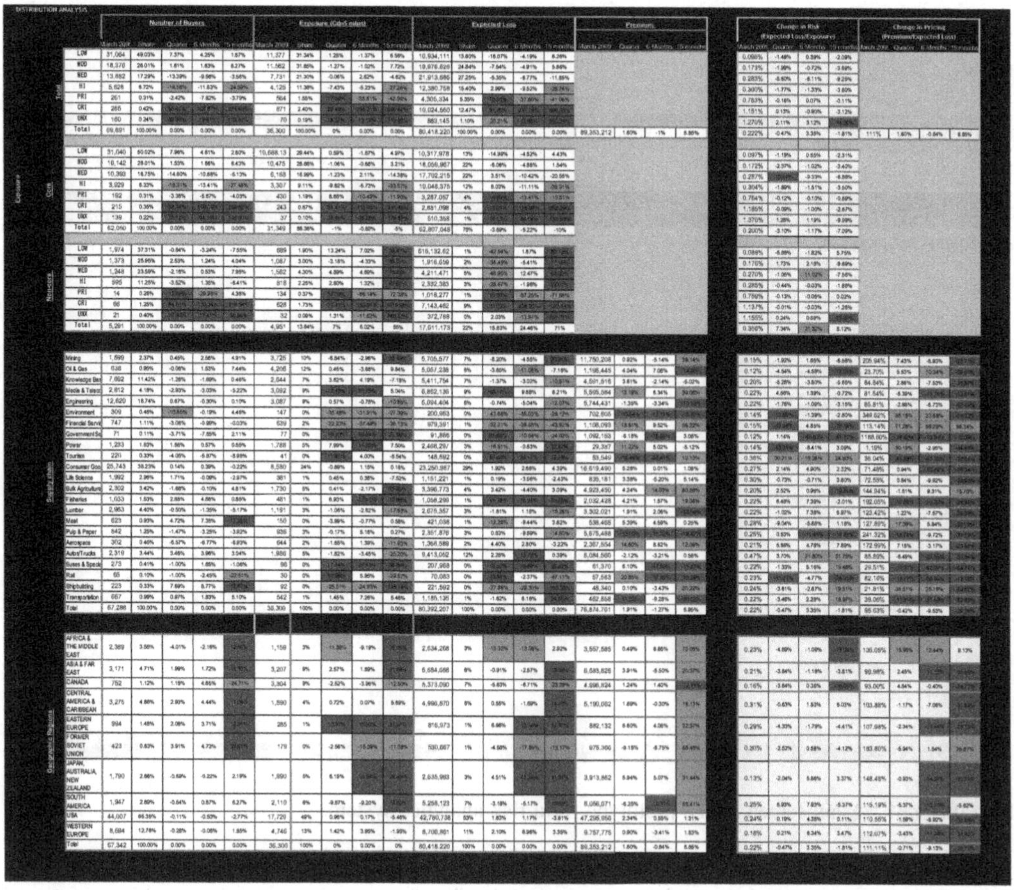

FIGURE 9.50 Tool to create a map of metric results and their comparison with predefined thresholds.

possible to apply to the full population. This score supports the classification of the portfolio obligors based on LGD. With this score plus the PD, it is possible to build a table as the one presented in Table 9.41. The results require a cut-off definition to give a nominal scale for classification. With the first prototype, the values are as follows.

TABLE 9.41

Use of the Classification Based on LGD Score and PD Score (Risk Level)

RankLGD	Low	Mod	Med	Hig	Pri	Cri
0	138	184	421	343	64	26
1	177	322	401	329	5	2
2	300	265	435	249	2	1
3	245	453	331	222	1	2
4	282	392	337	226	4	2
	1142	1616	1925	1369	76	33
0	12.08%	11.39%	21.87%	25.05%	84.21%	78.79%
1	15.50%	19.93%	20.83%	24.03%	6.58%	6.06%
2	26.27%	16.40%	22.60%	18.19%	2.63%	3.03%
3	21.45%	28.03%	17.19%	16.22%	1.32%	6.06%
4	24.69%	24.26%	17.51%	16.51%	5.26%	6.06%

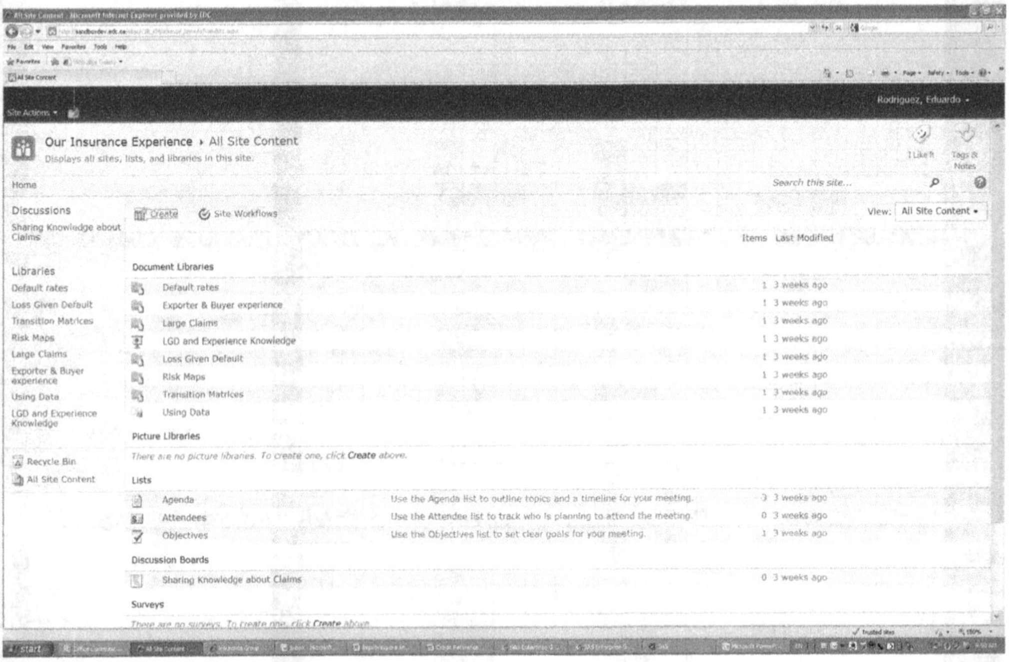

FIGURE 9.51 Main screen of the prototype for a risk analytics system.

The challenge after the metrics are created in the first approach is the creation of a risk knowledge structure that provides access and knowledge mobilization among the stakeholders across the organization. For that purpose, it created a prototype (Figure 9.51) of basic RAS components that provide many great opportunities to improve the understanding of the CREDIT portfolio and support the decision-making process. The structure of the systems is based on the creation of the metrics, the spaces for analysis and discussion of the results, the presentation, and access to different levels of detail.

The recovery rates that the organization has for the whole portfolio are highly affected by the volume of claims with zero recovery. This concentration on zero recovery values is out of the credit benchmark parameters. Additionally, it is clear through the study results and the literature review that the LGD has not to be static. It has to be dynamic, differentiated by segments or business environment conditions. If this is accepted the EL will have changes and the premiums to apply will be potentially modified. The identification of the recovery rates based on credit instruments and the differentiation of the recovery rate based on macroeconomic variables, credit rights, legal systems, etc. lead to ongoing search of the effect of the variables on the LGD results. This point is related to the concept of having more data points that will help to better estimate statistical parameter and model fit.

The process of controlling losses (improvement the recovery) can be improved based on focalizing administrative capacity on segmentation of the portfolio based on the variables that have more influence in the recovery rate behavior. The literature review presented before indicates that the recovery rate improves when there is more in-house work for collection; the same as in the segmentation and the definition of what is needed to do inside the organization and what is not key for improvement. The first estimation of the recovery seems very important and accurate this is an indication that in some cases this work can be supplemented with separating the actions of the external collection vs. internal ones. The problem of LGD control is associated with the construction of indicators that allow the observation of the portfolio changes. The changes should be observed in many different ways. This means using various metrics in order to identify where actions should be taken. The main point to organize is a system that provides the metrics output and allows the exchange of ideas regarding what to do with the results. The purpose is to create a communication and collaboration setting using a knowledge management system for credit risk control. The use of risk analytics systems generates collective discussion (collective intelligence creation) through the interpretation of the figures. This process of creating indicators is not looking to have many it is just a way to build a chain of risk performance indicators that predict potential risk behavior and provide clues for cause-effect identification in different stages of a portfolio.

All that is the outcome of models and process to generate metrics are the input for the RAS operation. A RAS will provide a means to support management and to develop LGD control based on segmentation and differentiation of actions to take according to the variables that describe segments with more influence in the recovery rate. A simplified description of the current process of recovery follows the steps, starting with the analysis of the claim identifying key points, such as, fraud or not, negative outlook of the recovery process, etc. The process of recovery differentiates bankruptcy and the cases when the company is in a complex financial situation (filing Chapter 11) or just when the risk unit disappears. From this analysis, an estimation of recovery appears and the process of recovery through the collection agencies starts.

What the collection agencies do indicate is the value of developing methodologies that segment portfolios to be more effective in the process. The following two examples of the main collection agencies do not show the process of segmentation as the core part in the collection process. First example is collection agencies use demand letters, calls, attorney demands, etc. If time is not working, the case can be closed. In any case, there can be a negotiation process to find a means to repay. Second example is classification of the collections based on age of the delinquency events. There is a combination with amounts (severity) and to find an agreement to pay.

These examples of operations to recovery and the results of the previous sections have some points to take into consideration. The statistics showed something that possibly was expected, that the longer the time of resolution of the claim the smaller the recovery; this is time as a variable that can have a negative impact in the process of recovery. The first point to validate with this observation is the recovery rate of all the claims that are < \$5,000 USD. The recovery is better for those claims lower than \$5,000, but the percentage of claims recovered in this group is less than 50% of the ones that are higher than \$5,000. The threshold of \$5,000 is selected as the median of the whole distribution of claims paid (Table 9.42). This means a segment has significant influence

TABLE 9.42

Review of Recovery Rate of Claims Below and Above 5,000 CAD

Claims	% of Claims Recovered	Recovered Rate
less 5000	4.70%	64%
more 5000	11.10%	49%

TABLE 9.43

Aggregated of Claims Paid and Quartiles for the Whole Population

Claim Paid Quartile	Recovery or Not	N	Sum of Claim Paid	Recovered	Recovery Rate on the Whole Population	Recovery Rate Only on the Recovered Population
0	0	5026	43,07,695			
	1	139	1,44,481	1,07,645	2.40%	74.50%
1	0	4779	1,54,67,741			
	1	387	13,17,342	7,81,019	4.70%	59.30%
2	0	4579	4,77,96,562			
	1	587	63,02,938	32,06,926	5.90%	50.90%
3	0	4536	32,22,09,277			
	1	630	5,11,52,140	2,48,26,005	6.60%	48.50%

on the loss of the portfolio from the number of claims but not in the aggregation of claims. These claims are around 5% of the total claims paid.

Thus, a point to review is the time in the group of claims that provide a higher recovery rate and higher amounts in order to improve efficiency. The proposed process looks for increasing the efforts on time for the third quartile that represents 12% of the total claims paid. Now an increment of 1% in the recovery for the third quartile within those that have 0% recovery represents almost $500,000CAD during the years of analysis. The support of more in-house work, using additional segmentation or collection agency work using a different prioritization schema could guide to more promissory targets of recovery. Table 9.43 shows that the recovery rate increased when the quartiles of claims paid increased, but the recovery rate within the population of the recovered accounts, the % reduced.

A segmentation process (Figure 9.52) works in a very simple way: The variables that have a positive influence in the recovery rate are the priorities to search for recoveries. The groups where the recovery rate can be higher are the priority. The search for a better recovery rate is based not only on the claim paid value but also on the clusters of risk units. The point is an in-house process will deal with the cases that can be the best target with higher recovery rates (Figure 9.53). In particular, years in business is the first variable to take into consideration; for example, the number of invoices. For those where the first estimation of recovery is greater than zero, the way to move is to use claim value or the number of invoices as the first filter, followed by GDP growth and years in business.

Another point to improve the process is to connect the underwriting process with the results. This means to give the opportunity to the underwriter to see the full spectrum of the business not only the production side but the final contribution to the results. The development of the full 360-degree view from underwriting to claims/losses is part of creating the culture of managing the portfolio as a whole. This is related to the connection of risk assessment with the results at the end in the portfolio that different programs and teams have. This is a culture of bottom-line portfolio

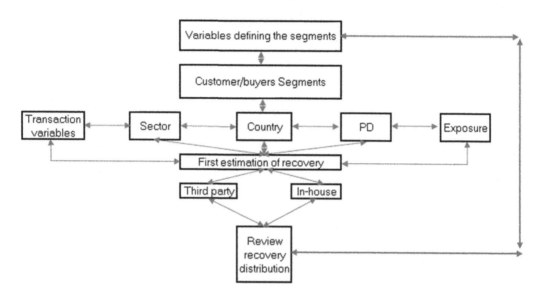

FIGURE 9.52   Proposed recovery workflow based on segmentation.

A decision tree for the recovery process

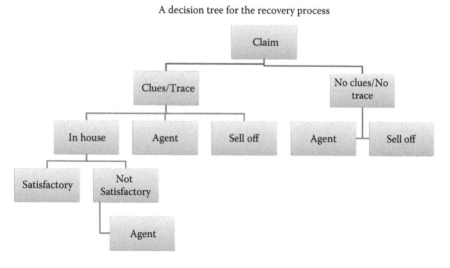

FIGURE 9.53   Basis of the proposed recovery workflow based on segmentation.

analysis. There is a need of continuous analysis based on the combination of methodologies, using the variables such as market sector, geographical region, and risk levels; the same as including the two parameters PD and LGD simultaneously.

In summary, this chapter has presented a general review of components of the RAS, means to deal with documents as explicit risk knowledge, connecting factors of individual and combination of products with not only individual observation of metrics behavior but also of aggregated expected losses, probability of default, losses and recoveries, exposure, and ways to divide the analysis according to factors that defined specific segments of risk. A RAS, is as it was mentioned at the beginning of the book, a socio-technical system that combines the capabilities to delay with data, modeling for specific tasks as pricing, reserves, or prediction-classification, that requires the interaction with people and machines.

References

Abell, D. (1980). *Defining the Business: The Starting Point of Strategic Planning*. Englewood Cliffs, NJ: Prentice Hall.

Abrams, C., Kanel, J. V., Muller, S., Pfitzmann, B., & Ruschka-Taylor, S. (2007). Optimized enterprise risk management. *IBM Systems Journal*, *46*(2), 219–234.

Ackoff, R. (1981). On the use of models in corporate planning. *Strategic Management Journal*, *2*(4), 353–359.

Ackoff, R. (1981). The art and science of mess management. *Interfaces*, *11*(1), 20–26.

Aggaian, S., & Kolm, P. (2017). Financial sentiment analysis using machine learning techniques. *International Journal of Investment Management and Financial Innovations*, *3*(1), 1–9. http://www.aascit.org/journal/ijimfi ISSN: 2381-1196 (Print); ISSN: 2381-120X (Online).

Agresti, A. (1990). *Categorical Data Analysis* (1st ed.). New York: John Wiley.

Alavi, M., & Leidner, D. E. (2001). Review: Knowledge management and knowledge management systems: Conceptual foundations and research issues. *MIS Quarterly*, *25*(1), 107–136. doi:10.2307/3250961

Albrecht, P. (1998). Risk Based Capital Allocation and Risk Adjusted Performance Management in Property/Liability-Insurance: A Risk Theoretical Framework. In ASTIN/AFIR Colloquium 1997, editor, Joint Day-Proceedings (pp. 57–80). Cairns/Australia.

Aleksandrov, A. D., Kolmogorov, A. N., & Lavrent'ev, M. A. (1969). *Mathematics: Its Content, Methods and Meaning*. Boston, MA: MIT Press.

Alpaydin, E. (2014). *Introduction to Machine Learning* (3rd ed.). Boston, MA: MIT Press.

Altman, E. (1968). Financial ratios, discriminant analysis and the prediction of corporate bankruptcy. *Journal of Finance*, *23*(4), 589–609.

Altman, E. I. (2000). Predicting financial distress of companies: Revisiting the Z-score and ZETA® models. Adapted from Altman, E. I. "Financial ratios, discriminant analysis and the prediction of corporate bankruptcy". *Journal of Finance*, September 1968.

Altman, E. I. (2013). Predicting Financial Distress of Companies: Revisiting the Z-Score and ZETA® Models. In A. R. Bell, C. Brooks, & M. Prokopczuk (Eds.), *Handbook of Research Methods and Applications in Empirical Finance* (pp. 428–456). Northampton, MA: Edward Elgar Publishing.

Altman, E. I., & Ramayana, S. (2007). *Default and Returns in the High-Yield Bond Market 2006 in Review and Outlook*. Special Report, NYU Salomon Center, Leonard N. Stern School of Business.

Altman, E. I., Haldeman, R. G., & Narayana, P. (1977). ZETA™ analysis a new model to identify bankruptcy risk of corporations. *Journal of Banking and Finance*, *1*(1), 29–54.

Altman, E. I., Sabato, G., & Wilson, N. (2010). The value of non-financial information in SME risk management. *The Journal of Credit Risk*, *6*(2), 1–33.

Andersen, E. B. (1990). *The Statistical Analysis of Categorical Data* (3rd ed.). Berlin, Heidelberg: Spinger-Verlag.

Anderson, T. W., Fang, K., & Olkin, I. (1994). *Multivariate Analysis and Its Applications*. Hayward, CA: Institute of Mathematical Statistics.

Anthropopoulou, A. (2005). Knowledge sharing: A critical success factor for risk management. In D. Remenyi (Ed.), *Proceedings of 6th European Conference on Knowledge Management*, pp. 26–33. Academic Conferences Limited, Reading, UK, Limerick, Ireland.

AON. (2010). Global Enterprise Risk Management. Available at http://insight.aon.com/?elqPURLPage=4889 Access January 30, 2010.

Apte, C. V., Natarajan, R., Pednault, E., & Tipu, F. A. (2002). A probabilistic estimation framework for predictive modeling analytics. *IBM Systems Journal*, *41*(3), 438–448.

Aven, T. (2003). *Foundations of Risk Analysis*. Chichester, UK: John Wiley & Sons.

Avery, H. (2007). Don't shoot the quant guys! *Euromoney*, *38*(463), 42.

Baesens, B., Mues, C., Martens, D., & Vanthienen, J. (2009). 50 Years of data mining and OR: Upcoming trends and challenges. *The Journal of the Operational Research Society*, *60*(Supplement 1: Milestones in OR), s16–s23.

Baker, M., & Wurgler, J. (2007). Investor sentiment in the stock market. *Journal of Economic Perspectives*, *21*(2), 129–152. doi:10.1257/jep.21.2.129

Banham, R. (2004). Enterprising views of risk management. *Journal of Accountancy*, *197*(6), 65–72.

Bar-Haim, R., Dinur, E., Feldman, R., Fresko, M., & Goldstein, G. (2011, July). Identifying and following expert investors in stock microblogs. In *Proceedings of the Conference on Empirical Methods in Natural Language Processing*, pp. 1310–1319, Edinburgh, Scotland: Association for Computational Linguistics. https://www.aclweb.org/anthology/D11-1121.pdf.

Baranoff, E. (2004). Mapping the evolution of risk management. *Contingencies*, *16*(4), 23–27.

Baranoff, E. (2004a). Risk management a focus on a more holistic approach three years after September 11. *Journal of Insurance Regulation*, *22*(4), 71–81.

Baranoff, E. (2004b). The evolution of risk management. *Contingencies*, *16*(4), 23–27.

Barquin, R. (2001). What is knowledge management? Knowledge and innovation. *Journal of the KMCI*, *1*(2), 127–143. 15 January Basel II: Revised International Capital Framework. http://www.bis.org/publ/bcbsca.htm

Barton, D., & Court, D. (2012, October). Making advanced analytics work for you: A practical guide to capitalizing on big data. *Harvard Business Review*, *90*(10), 78–83.

Basel II and II: Revised International Capital Framework. http://www.bis.org/publ/bcbsca.htm

Basel Committee on Banking Supervision (1999, April). *Credit Risk Modelling: Current Practices and Applications*. Basel.

Bazerman, M. H., & Chugh, D. (2006). Decisions without blinders. *Harvard Business Review*, *84*(1), 88–97 & 133.

Beasley, M., & Frigo, M. (2007). Strategic risk management: Creating and protecting value. *Strategic Finance*, *88*(11), 25–31 & 53.

Beaver, W. (1966). Financial ratios as predictors of failure. *Journal of Accounting Research*, *4*, 71–111.

Beckman, T. (1997). A methodology for knowledge management. In *Proceeding of International Association of Science and technology for development (IASTED) AI and Soft computing Conference*, pp. 29–32, Banff, Canada.

Beinhocker, E. D. (1999). *Robust Adaptive Strategies*. MIT Sloan, Spring.

Beirlant, J., Goegebeur, Y., Verlaak, R., & Vynckier, P. (1998). Burr regression and portfolio segmentation. *Insurance: Mathematics and Economics*, *23*(3), 231–250.

Beleza, J., Esquivel, M. L., & Gaspar, R. M. (2012). Machine learning Vasicek model calibration with gaussian processes. *Communications in Statistics-Simulation and Computation*, *41*(6), 776–786.

Berkowitz, J. (1999). *A Coherent Framework for Stress-Testing*. Washington, D.C.: Federal Reserve Board.

Berry, M., & Linoff, G. (1997). *Data Mining Techniques*. New York, NY: John Wiley & Sons.

Best, O. (1998). *Implementing Value at Risk*. Wiley.

Bhidé, A. (2010). *A Call for Judgment: Sensible Finance for a Dynamic Economy*. Nueva York: Oxford University Press.

Bischoff, H. J. (2008). *Risks in Modern Society*. Dordrecht: Springer.

Biørn, E. (1999). Random coefficients in regression equation systems: The case with unbalanced panel data. *Memorandum* (No. 1999, 27). Department of Economics, University of Oslo.

Blackman, R. (2022). Why you need an AI ethics committee. *Harvard Business Review*, July–August, pp. 119–125.

Bohnert, A., Gatzert, N., Hoyt, R. E., & Lechner, P. (2019). The drivers and value of enterprise risk management: Evidence from ERM ratings. *The European Journal of Finance, Taylor & Francis Journals*, *25*(3), 234–255. doi:10.1080/1351847X.2018.1514314

Bosua, R., & Scheepers, R. (2007). Towards a model to explain knowledge sharing in complex organisational environments. *Knowledge Management Research and Practice*, *5*(2), 93–109.

Bowers, N. L., Gerber, H. U., Hickman, J. C., Jones, D. A., & Nesbitt, C. J. (1997). *Actuarial Mathematics* (2nd ed.). Schaumburg, IL: Society of Actuaries.

Bowling, D., & Rieger, L. (2005). Success factors for implementing enterprise risk management. *Bank Accounting and Finance*, *18*(3), 21–26.

Bowman, B. (2002). Building knowledge management systems. *Information Systems Management*, *19*(3), 32–40.

Bowman, E. (1980). A risk/return paradox for strategic management. *Sloan Management Review*, *21*, 17–31.

Brammer, S., Brooks, C., & Pavelin, S. (2004). *Corporate Reputation and Stock Returns: Are Good Firms Good or Investors?* Faculty of Finance Cass Business School, City University, Available at SSRN: https://ssrn.com/abstract=637122 or doi:10.2139/ssrn.637122

Breiman, L., Friedman, J., Olshen, R., & Stone, C. (1984). *Classification and Regression Trees*. Wadsworth, New York: Chapman and Hall.

Brigo, D., & Mercurio, F. (2006). *Interest Rate Models—Theory and Practice*. Berlin: Springer Verlag.

Brown, B. (2001). Step by step enterprise risk management. *Risk Management*, *48*(9), 43–50.

Brownlee, T., Sommerfeld, J., & Hansen, K. (2020). *Journal of Securities Operations & Custody, 12*(2), 102–115.

Buchanan, L., & O'Connell, A. (2006). A brief history of decision making. *Harvard Business Review, 84*(1), 32–41 & 132.

Buehler, K., Freeman, A., & Hulme, R. (2008). The new arsenal of risk management. *Harvard Business Review*, September.

Buehler, K., Freeman, A., & Hulme, R. (2008b). Owning the right risks. *Harvard Business Review, 86*(9), 102–110.

Bursk, E., & Chapman, J. (Eds.). (1963). *New Decision–Making Tools for Managers: Mathematical Programming as an Aid in the Solving of Business Problems*. New York, NY: The New American Library.

Burstein, F. V., Zyngier, S., & Rateb, Z. (2002, September 24–25). Knowledge management in the financial services sector: Understandings and trends in Australia. In *Proceedings of the 3rd European Conference on Knowledge Management (ECKM2002)*, pp. 113–125. Trinity College Dublin, Ireland, MCIL.

Bussmann, N., Giudici, P., Marinelli, D., & Papenbrock, J. (2021). Explainable machine learning in credit risk management. *Computational Economics (2021), 57*, 203–216.

Butcher, P. R., & Steltz, D. G. (2001). Is your loan loss reserve adequate? *The RMA Journal, 2*, 32–36.

Cacoullos, T. (1973). *Discriminant Analysis and Applications*. New York: Academic Press.

Cady, F. (2017). *The Data Science Handbook* (1st ed.). New York, NY: John Wiley & Sons, Inc.

Calabrese, R. (2010, June 16–18). Regression for recovery rates with both continuous and discrete characteristics. In *Proceedings of the 45th Scientific Meeting of the Italian Statistical Society (SIS)*. University of Padua, Italy.

Calabrese, R. (2014). Predicting bank loan recovery rates with a mixed continuous-discrete model. *Applied Stochastic Models in Business and Industry, 30*(2), 99–114. https://onlinelibrary.wiley.com/doi/10.1002/asmb.1932

Calabrese, R., & Zenga, M. (2010). Bank loan recovery rates: Measuring and nonparametric density estimation. *Journal of Banking and Finance, 34*(5), 903–911.

Caldwell, J., & Ram, Y. (1999). *Mathematical Models Case Studies*. New York, NY: Springer.

Cao, L. (2021). AI in finance: Challenges, techniques and opportunities. *1*(1), (June 2021), 40. doi:10.1145/nnnnnnn.nnnnnnn.

Caouette, J. B., Altman, E. I., Narayanan, P., & Nimmo, R. (2008). *Managing Credit Risk: The Great Challenge for the Global Financial Markets* (2nd ed.). Hoboken, New Jersey: John Wiley & Sons, Inc.

Carnap, R. (1966). *An Introduction to the Philosophy of Science*. New York, NY: Basic Books Inc.

Cascio, W. F. (2007). Evidence-based management and the marketplace for ideas. *Academy of Management Journal, 50*(5), 1009–1012.

Caselli, S., Gatti, S., & Querci, F. (2008). The sensitivity of the loss given default rate to systematic risk: New empirical evidence on bank loans. *Journal of Financial Services Research, 34*(1), 1–34.

Catasus, B., & Grojer, J. (2003). Intangibles and credit decisions: Results from an experiment. *European Accounting Review, 12*(2), 327–355.

Chalmeta, R., & Grangel, R. (2008). Methodology for the implementation of knowledge management systems. *Journal of the American Society for Information Science and Technology, 59*(5), 742–755.

Chamberlain, G. (1984). Panel Data. In Z. Griliches, & M. D. Intriligator (Eds.), *Handbook of Econometrics* (1st ed., Volume II). North Holland: Elsevier Science Publishers BV, Imprint.

Chapman, P., Clinton, J., Kerber, R., Khabaza, T., Reinartz, T., Shearer, C., & Wirth, R. (2000). CRISP-DM 1.0 Step-by-step data mining guide The CRISP-DM consortium.

Chaudhry, A. (2004). *CRM: Making it Simple for the Banking Industry* (Paper 180). SAS Institute-SUGI 29.

Chava, S., Stefanescu, C., & Turnbull, S. (2011). Modeling the loss distribution. *Management Science, 57*(7), 1267–1287.

Chen, H., Chiang, R. H. L., & Storey, V. C. (2012). Business intelligence and analytics: From big data to big impact. *MIS Quarterly, 36*(4), 1165–1188.

Chen, L. (2010). A structural analysis of Chinese mortgage law. *Essays in Honour of C G van der Merwe (2011) Lexisnexis*, 395–412. Available at SSRN: https://ssrn.com/abstract=1681942

Chisar-Molnar, A. (2007). Characteristics of risk management information systems and an example of a STARS solution. *Strategic Management, 12*(3–4), 71–73. http://www.rmmag.com/MGTemplate.cfm?Section=RMMagazine&template=Magazine/DisplayMagazines.cfm&AID=1690&ShowArticle=1

Choo, C. W. (1998). *Knowing Organization*. New York, NY: Oxford University Press.

Christensen, R. (1990). *Log-linear Models and Logistic Regression*. New York, NY: Springer Verlag.

Cincera, M. (1999). Imputation and missing data, Belgian Federal Office for science, technical and cultural affairs, 8 rue de la science, B-1000 Brussels and Université Libre de Bruxelles.

Crouhy, M., Galai, D., & Mark, R. (2001). *Risk Management*. New York: McGraw Hill.

Cumming, C., & Hirtle, B. (2001). The challenges of risk management in diversified financial companies. *Federal Reserve Bank of New York Economic Policy Review, 4*(3), 1–17.

Curtis, J. (2022). Technology and skill trends in the actuarial profession. *Society of Actuaries*, August Issue 26.

Dahchour, M., & Dionne, G. (2000). *Pricing of Automobile Insurance Under Asymmetric Information, a study on Panel Data* (pp. 01–06). Ecole des Hauts Etudes Commerciales. Working paper 2002.

Dalkir, K. (2005). *Knowledge Management in Theory and Practice*. Boston, MA: Elseiver.

Daniell, M. (2000). Strategy and volatility: Risk and global strategic challenge. *Balance Sheet*, 8(4), 24–36.

Dannenburg, D. (1995). Crossed classification credibility models. *Transactions of the 25th International Congress of Actuaries*, 4, 1–35.

Dash Wu, D. (2020). Data intelligence and risk analytics. *Industrial Management & Data Systems*, 120(2), 249–252. doi:10.1108/IMDS-02-2020-606

Davenport, T. (2006). Competing on Analytics. *Harvard Business Review*, 1, 99–107.

Davenport, T. (2009). Make Better Decisions. *Harvard Business Review*, 87(11), 117–123.

Davenport, T. (2010). How to make better decisions and get better results. *Harvard Business Review*, 2, 87(11), 117–118, 120–123, & 134.

Davenport, T., & Harris, J. (2007). *Competing on Analytics: The New Science of Winning*. Boston, MA: Harvard Business School Press.

Davenport, T., & Prusak, L. (1998). *Working Knowledge: How Organizations Manage What They Know*. Boston, MA: Harvard Business School Press.

Davenport, T., De Long, D., & Beers, M. (1998). Successful knowledge management projects. *Sloan Management Review*, 39(2), 43–56.

David, F. (1999). *Strategic Management: Concepts And Cases* (13th ed.). Upper Saddle River, NJ: Prentice Hall.

Degagne, C., Leandri, C., & Puchley, T. (2004). Linking knowledge and risk management controlling the information flood. *Business*, January, PricewaterhowseCoopers. www.pwc.com/extweb/newcoth.nsf

Delanty, G. (1997). *Beyond Constructivism and Realism*. Buckingham, England: Open University Press.

Delanty, G. (2002). *Beyond Constructivism and realism*. Buckingham, England: Open University Press.

Desai, P. S., Kalra, A., & Murthi, B. P. S. (2008). When old is gold: The role of business longevity in risky situations. *Journal of Marketing*, 72(1), 95–107. doi:10.1509/jmkg.72.1.095

Deloitte Insights Blockchain A technical Primer (2019).

Dickinson, G. (2001). Enterprise risk management: Its origins and conceptual foundation. *The Geneva Papers on Risk and Insurance*, 26(3), 360–366.

Djankov, S., McLiesh, C., & Schleifer, A. (2007). Private credit in 129 countries. *Journal of Financial Economics*, 84(2), 299–329. doi:10.1016/j.jfineco.2006.03.004

Djankov, S., Hart, O., McLiesh, C., & Schleifer, A. (2008). Debt Enforcement Around the World. *Journal of Political Economy*, 16(6), 1105–1149. The University of Chicago.

Doherty, N. (2000). *Integrated Risk Management: Techniques and Strategies for Managing Corporate Risk*. New York, NY: McGraw-Hill Inc.

Dua, D., & Graff, C. (2019). *UCI Machine Learning Repository*. Irvine, CA: University of California, School of Information and Computer Science. http://archive.ics.uci.edu/ml

Dunham, M. (2003). *Data Mining Introductory and Advanced Topics*. Upper Saddle River, NJ: Prentice Hall.

Dzinkowski, R. (2002). Knowledge management in Financial Services. *FT Mastering Management*. http://www.ftmastering.com/mmo/mmo10_2.htm

Dzinkowski, R. (2002). Knowledge for all: Knowledge sharing at the world bank. *Financial Times Mastering Management Online, June*. Retrieved November 11, 2008 from http://www.ftmastering.com/mmo

D'Vari, R., Yalamanchili, K., & Bai, D. (2003, September 26–30). Application of quantitative credit risk models in fixed income portfolio management. State Street Research and Management, The 3rd International Workshop on, Computational Intelligence in Economics and, Finance (CIEF'2003).

Earl, M. (2000). Evolving the e-business. *Business Strategy Review*, 11(2), 33–38.

Earl, M. (2001). Knowledge management strategies: Towards a taxonomy. *Journal of Management Information Systems*, 18(2), 215–233.

Edwards, J. S. (2009). Business Processes and Knowledge Management. In M. Khosrow-Pour (Ed.), *Encyclopedia of Information Science and Technology* (2nd ed., Vol. I, pp. 471–476). Hershey, PA: IGI Global.

Edwards, J. S., & Rodriguez, E. (2019). Remedies against bias in analytics systems. *Journal of Business Analytics*, 2(1), 74–87. doi:10.1080/2573234X.2019.1633890

Edwards, J. S., Collier, P., & Shaw, D. (2002). *Making a Journey in Knowledge Management*. Aston Business School Research Institute.

Edwards, J. S., Handzic, M., Carlsson, S., & Nissen, M. (2003). Knowledge management research and practice: Vision and directions. *Knowledge Management Research and Practice*, 1(1), 49–60.

Electronic Textbook STATSOFT, Discriminant Function Analysis, © Copyright StatSoft, Inc. (1984–2002). STATISTICA is a trademark of StatSoft, Inc., 2300 East 14th Street, Tulsa, OK 74104. http://www.statsoftinc.com/textbook/stdiscan.html#classification

Emery, K., Cantor, R., Keisman, K., & Ou, S. (2007). Moody's Ultimate Recovery Database: Special comment. Moody's Investor Service, April.

Engelberg, J. E., & Parsons, C. A. (2011). The causal impact of media in financial markets. *The Journal of Finance, 66*(1), 67–97.

Engelmann, B., & Rauhmeier, R. (Eds.). (2011). *The Basel II Risk Parameters: Estimation, Validation, Stress Testing - with Applications to Loan Risk Management* (2nd ed.). Berlin Heidelberg: Springer-Verlag.

Engle, R. F., & Ng, V. K. (1993). Measuring and testing the impact of news on volatility. *The Journal of Finance, 48*(5), 1749–1778.

Eppler, M. J. (2008). Knowledge Communication. In M. E. Jennex (Ed.), *Knowledge Management: Concepts, Methodologies, Tools, and Applications.* (pp. 324–335). Hershey, PA: IGI Global.

Erdem, Cumhur, Üniversitesi, Gaziosmanpaşa, Ve, İktisadi, & Fakültesi, İdari. (2008, January 1). Factors Affecting the Probability of Credit Card Default and the Intention of Card Use in Turkey. *International Research Journal of Finance and Economics ISSN, 18*, 1450–2887.

Esser, J. (2021). *The Secret of Adaptable Organizations Is Trust.* Harvard Business Review, March.

Fairchild, A. (2002, January). Knowledge management metrics via a balanced scorecard methodology. In *Proceedings of the 35th International Conference on System Sciences*, Vol. 8. doi:10.1109/HICSS. 2002.994356

Fairchild, A. M. (2002). Knowledge management metrics via a balanced scorecard methodology. In *Proceedings of the 35th Annual Hawaii International Conference on System Sciences*, pp. 3173–3180. doi:10.1109/HICSS.2002.994356

Falkenstein, E. G., Boral, A., & Carty, L. V. (2000). *RiskCALCTM for Private Companies: Moody's Default Model, Rating Methodology.* New York, NY: Moody's Investors Service - Global Credit Research, Special Comment. doi:10.2139/ssrn.236011

Fayyad, U., Piatetsky-Shapiro, G., & Smyth, P. (1996). From data mining to knowledge discovery in databases (A survey). *AI Magazine, 17*(3), 37–54.

Feldman, R., Rosenfeld, B., Bar-Haim, R., & Fresko, M. (2011, August 9–11). The stock sonar - sentiment analysis of stocks based on a hybrid approach. In *Proceedings of the Twenty-Third Conference on Innovative Applications of Artificial Intelligence*, pp. 1642–1647, San Francisco, CA: Association for the Advancement of Artificial Intelligence.

Ferguson, C., & Pemberton, M. (2000). Knowledge management a selective guide of resources. *The Information Management Journal, 34*(3), 42–46.

Fiegenbaum, A., & Thomas, H. (1988). Attitudes toward risk and the risk-return paradox: Prospect theory explanation. *Academy of Management Journal, 31*(1), 85–106.

Foster, D. (1985). *The Philosophical Scientists.* New York, NY: Barnes & Noble Books.

Fourie, L., & Shilawa, J. (2004). The value of concept maps for Knowledge Management in the banking and insurance industry: A German case study. In *Proceedings of the First International Conference on Concept Mapping*, Pamplona, Spain: Open Text Actuarial Community.

Francis, S., & Paladino, B. (2008). Enterprise risk management: A best practice approach. *Journal of Corporate Accounting & Finance, 19*(3), 19–33.

Frees, E. (1998). *Risk Management and Insurance Department.* Class notes, Madison, WI: University of Wisconsin.

Frees, E. (2004). *Longitudinal and Panel Data: Analysis and Applications for the Social Sciences.* Cambridge, UK: Cambridge University Press.

Frees, E. (2020). Loss Data Analytics. ewfrees.github.io

Frees, E. W., Young, V. R., & Luo, Y. (2001). Case studies using panel data models. *North American Actuarial Journal, 5*(4), 24–42.

Frigo, D., & Mercurio, F. (2006). *Interest Rate Models – Theory and Practice: With Smile, Inflation and Credit*(2nd ed.). Heildelberg: Springer.

Froot, K. A., Scharfstein, D. S., & Stein, J. C. (1994). A framework for risk management. *Harvard Business Review, 72*(6), 91–102.

Galindo, J., & Tamayo, P. (2000). Credit risk assessment using statistical and machine learning: Basic methodology and risk modeling applications. *Computational Economics, 15*(1–2), 107–143. doi:10.1023/A:1008699112516

Galloway, D., & Funston, R. (2000). The challenges of enterprise risk management. *Balance Sheet, 8*(8), 22–25. doi:10.1108/EUM0000000005390

Garcia, D. (2013). Sentiment during recessions. *Journal of Finance, 68*(3), 1267–1300.

Garson, G. D. (2009). PA 765 Statnotes: An Online Textbook, Quantitative Research in Public Administration, North Carolina State University, Raleigh, North Carolina 27695. https://faculty.chass.ncsu.edu/garson/PA765/index.htm. http://www2.chass.ncsu.edu/garson/pa765/index.htm

Goldratt, E. M., & Cox, J. (1986). *The Goal*. Aldershot, Hants: Gower.

Goodfellow, I. J., Bengio, Y., & Courville, A. (2016). *Deep Learning*. MIT Press.

Goovaerts, M. J., de Vylder, F., & Haezendonck, J. (1984). *Insurance Premiums: Theory and Applications*. Amsterdam, North-Holland: Elsevier Science Pub. Co.

Goulet, V. (1998). Principles and application of credibility theory. *Journal of Actuarial Practice*, 6(1–2), 5–62.

Gourieroux, C. (1999). The econometrics of risk classification in insurance. *The Geneva Papers on Risk and Insurance Theory*, 24, 119–137.

Greenacre, M. J. (1984). *Theory and Application of Correspondence Analysis*. New York: Academic Press.

Gregoriou, G. N., Hübner, G., & Kooli, M. (2009). Performance and persistence of commodity trading advisors: Further evidence. doi:10.1002/fut.20441

Griliches, Z., & Intriligator, M. D. (Eds). (1984). *Handbook of Econometrics* (1st ed., Volume 2). North Holland, https://www.elsevier.com/books/handbook-of-econometrics/griliches/978-0-444-86186-3

Grunert, J., & Weber, M. (2009). Recovery rates of commercial lending: Empirical evidence for German companies. *Journal of Banking & Finance*, 33(3), 505–513.

Guimon, J. (2005). Intellectual capital reporting and credit risk analysis. *Journal of Intellectual capital*, 6(1), 28–42, doi:10.1108/14691930510574645

Gupton, G. M. (2000, November). *Bank Loan Loss Given Default*. New York, NY: Moody's Investors Service – Global Credit Research, Special Comment.

Hagiu, A., & Julian Wright, J. (2020). *When Data Creates Competitive Advantage And When It Doesn't*. Harvard Business Review, February.

Hair, J. F., Black, B., Babin, B. J., & Anderson, R. E. (2010). *Multivariate Data Analysis: A Global Perspective* (7th ed.). London: Pearson Education, Inc.

Hammond, J. S., Keeney, R. L., & Raiffa, H. (2006). The hidden traps in decision making. *Harvard Business Review*, 1, 118–126.

Hartigan, J. A., & Wong, M. A. (1979). Algorithm AS 136: A K-means clustering algorithm. *Journal of the Royal Statistical Society. Series C (Applied Statistics)*, 28, 100–108. doi:10.2307/2346830

Hayward, M. L. A. (2002). When do firms learn from their acquisition experience? Evidence from 1990–1995. *Strategic Management Journal*, 23(1), 21–39.

Helliwell, J. F., Layard, R., Sachs, J. D., Aknin, L. B., De Neve, J.-E., & Wang, S. (Eds.). (2022). *World Happiness Report 2023* (11th ed.). Sustainable Development Solutions Network.

Hensher, D. A., & Jones, S. (2008). Forecasting corporate bankruptcy: Optimizing the performance of the mixed logit model. *Abacus*, 43(3), 241–264.

Herrity, J. V. (1999). *Measuring Private Firm Default Risk*. New York, NY: Moody's Investors Service – Global Credit Research, Special Comment.

Hillestad, C. (2007). An analysis of financial ratios for the Oslo stock exchange. *Economic Bulletin*, 78, 115–131.

Hoffman, D. L., & Franke, G. R. (1986). Correspondence analysis: Graphical representation of categorical data in marketing research. *Journal of Marketing Research*, 23(3), 213–227.

Hormozi, A., & Giles, S. (2004). Data mining a competitive weapon for banking and retail industries. *Information Systems Management*, 21(2), 62–71.

Horton-Bentley, A. (2006). The new best practice: Unifying banking across lines of business. *KMworld Best practices in Financial Services*, 9, S10–S11.

Howell, D. (1997). *Statistical Methods for Psychology* (7th ed.). Belmont, CA: Cengage Wadsworth. (Duxbury Press Wadsworth Publishing Co.).

Hubbard, D. W. (2009). *The Failure of Risk Management: Why It's Broken and How to Fix It*. Hoboken, NJ: John Wiley & Sons, Inc.

Hunter, J., & Isachenkova, N. (2002). *A Panel Analysis of UK Industrial Company Failure* (Working Paper No. 228). Cambridge, United Kingdom: ESRC Centre for Business Research, University of Cambridge.

Höchstöttera, M., Nazemia, A., & Racheva, S. (2011). Reflection on recovery and loss given default. *What Is and What Is Amiss*. https://statistik.ets.kit.edu/download/Michigan2011.pdf

Iansiti, M., & Lakhani, K. R. (2020). In the AGE of AI how machine intelligence changes the rules of business. *HBR*, Jan-Feb.

Ignatius, A. (2010). Editorial. *Harvard Business Review*, 88(6), 14.

Ipe, M. (2003). Knowledge sharing in organizations: A conceptual framework. *Human Resource Review*, 2(4), 337–359.

Isachenkova, N., & Hunter, J. (2002). *A Panel Analysis of UK Industrial Company Failure* (Working Papers No. 228). Cambridge, United Kingdom: ESRC Centre for Business Research, University of Cambridge.

James, L. (1997). *Applying Generalized Linear Models*. New York, NJ: Springer.

Jia, D., & Wu, Zh. (2022). Application of machine learning in enterprise risk management. *Hindawi Security and Communication Networks, 2022*, Article ID 4323150, 12. doi:10.1155/2022/4323150

Jobson, J. D. (1992). *Applied Multivariate Data Analysis, Volume II: Categorical and Multivariate Methods* (1st ed.). New York, NY: Springer-Verlag.

Johansson, T., & Kumbaro, J. (2011). *Predicting Corporate Default – An Assessment of the Z-Scor Model on the U.S. Market 2007–2010* (LUP Student Papers). Lund, Sweden: Lund University Libraries. Retrieved from http://lup.lub.lu.se/luur/download?func=downloadFile&recordOId=2061526&fileOId=2436268

Johnson, D. (1997). The triangular distribution as a proxy for the beta distribution in risk analysis. *Journal of the Royal Statistical Society. Series D (The Statistician), 46*(3), 387–398. *JSTOR.* www.jstor.org/stable/2988573 Accessed 2 Sept. 2021.

Johnson, L., Neave, E., & Pazderka, B. (2002). Knowledge, innovation and share value. *International Journal of Management Reviews, 4*(2), 101–134.

Johnson, R. A., & Wichern, D. W. (1998). *Applied Multivariate Statistical Analysis* (4th ed.). New York, NY: Prentice Hall.

Jones, R. (2003). Measuring the benefits of knowledge management at the FSA. *Journal of Information Science Journal, 29*(6), 475–487.

Jorion, P. (2007). *Value at Risk: The New Benchmark for Managing Financial Risk* (3rd ed.). New York: McGraw-Hill.

Jucaityte, I., & Virvilaite, R. (2007). Integrated model of brand valuation. *Economics and Management, 12*, 376–383.

Julibert, S. (2008). Employee attitudes to information sharing: A case study at the European Central Bank. *Records Management Journal, 18*(3), 194–204.

Kaplan, R., & Norton, D. (1999). The balanced scorecard: Measures that drive performance. *Harvard Business Review*, July.

Karlin, S., & Taylor, H. (1998). *An Introduction to Stochastic Modeling*. Orlando, FL: Harcourt Publishers Ltd.

Kazemian, S., Zhao, S., & Penn, G. (2016). Evaluating sentiment analysis in the context of securities trading. In *Proceedings of the 54th Annual Meeting of the Association for Computational Linguistics* (Volume 1: Long Papers). In *ACL* (pp. 2094–2103). Berlin, Germany. https://www.aclweb.org/anthology/P16-1197.pdf

Keenan, S. C. (1999). *Predicting Default Rates: A Forecasting Model For Moody's Issuer-Based Default Rates* (Special Comment, August). New York, NY: Moody's Investors Service – Global Credit Research.

Keith, L. (2006). Knowledge Sharing Barriers. In D. Schwartz (Ed.), *The Encyclopedia of Knowledge Management* (pp. 499–506). Hershey, PA: Idea Group Reference Global.

Kimball, R. (2000). Failures in risk management. *New England Economic Review, January/February*, 3–12.

King, W. (2006a). Knowledge Sharing. In D. Schwartz (Ed.), *The Encyclopedia of Knowledge Management* (pp. 493–498). Hershey, PA: Idea Group Reference Global.

King, W. (2006b). Knowledge Transfer. In D. Schwartz (Ed.), *The Encyclopedia of Knowledge Management* (pp. 538–543). Hershey, PA: Idea Group Reference Global.

Klugman, S. A., Panjer, H. H., & Willmot, G. E. (1998). *Loss Models: From Data to Decisions*. New York, NY: John Wiley & Sons.

Klugman, S. A., Panjer, H. H., & Willmot, G. E. (2019). *Loss Models: From Data to Decision* (5th ed.). New York, NY: John Wiley & Sons. https://www.wiley.com/en-us/exportProduct/pdf/9781119523789

Kocagil, A. E., Reyngold, A., Stein, R. M., & Ibarra, E. (2002). *Moody's RiskCalc™ Model For Privately-Held U.S. Banks, Rating Methodology*. New York, NY: Moody's Investors Service - Global Credit Research.

Krause, S. K., Natarajan, H., & Gradstein, H. L. (2017). *Distributed Ledger Technology (DLT) and Blockchain (English)*. FinTech note, no. 1 Washington, D.C.: World Bank Group. http://documents.worldbank.org/curated/en/177911513714062215/Distributed-Ledger-Technology-DLT-and-blockchain

Kubo, I., Saka, A. & Pan, S.-L. (2001). Behind the scenes of knowledge sharing in a Japanese Bank. *Human Resource Development International, 4*(4), 465–485.

Kuss, O. (2002). How to use SAS for logistic regression with correlated data. *SUGI-SAS, 27*, Paper 267-27.

Lachembruch, P. A. (1975). *Discriminant Analysis*. New York: Hafner Press.

Ladley, J. (2016, July 28). Mastering and managing data understanding. *Turning Data Into Insight. CIO.* Retrieved at https://www.cio.com/article/3097501/analytics/mastering-and-managing-data-understanding.html

Lam, J. (2000, March 25). *Enterprise-Wide Risk Management and the Role of the Chief Risk Officer*. [White paper], ERisk.com.

Lam, J. (2001). The CRO is here to stay. *Risk Management, 48*(4), 16–22.

Lam, J. (2003). *Enterprise Risk Management*. Hoboken, NJ: John Wiley & Sons.

Lamb, C. M. (2001). Creating a collaborative environment. *Information Outlook, 5*(5), 22–25.

Lane, M. (2000, June). Default rates: Declaration year versus event year method, RACS, internal document.

Larose, D. T., & Larose, C. D. (Eds.). (2014). *Discovering Knowledge in Data: An Introduction to Data Mining* (2nd ed.). Somerset, NJ: John Wiley & Sons, Inc.

Laudon, K., & Laudon, J. (2004). *Management Information Systems: Managing the Digital Firm*. New York, NY: Prentice Hall.

Lee, S., & Lam, W. (2007). Application Integration: Pilot Project to Implement a Financial Portfolio System in a Korean Bank. In W. Lam, & V. Shankararaman (Eds.), *Enterprise Architecture and Integration: Methods, Implementation and Technologies* (pp. 273–283). Hershey, PA: IGI Global. doi:10.4018/978-1-59140-887-1.ch016

Lehaney, B., Clarke, S., Coakes, E., & Jack, G. (2004). *Beyond Knowledge Management*. Hershey, PA: Idea Group Publishing.

Lemaire, J. (1985). *Automobile Insurance*. Hingham, MA: Kluwer-Nijhoff Publising.

Leo, M., Sharma, S., & Maddulety, K. (2019). Machine learning in banking risk management: A literature review. *Risks, 7*(1), 29. doi:10.3390/risks7010029

Leonard, D. (1998). *Wellsprings of Knowledge*. Boston, MA: Harvard Business School Press.

Levine, R. (2004). Risk management systems: Understanding the need. *Information System Management, Spring*, 31–37.

Liao, S.-H., Chang, J.-C., Cheng, S.-C., & Kuo, C.-M. (2004). Employee relationship and knowledge sharing: A case study of a Taiwanese finance and securities firm. *Knowledge Management Research & Practice, 2*(1), 24–34.

Liebenberg, A., & Hoyt, R. (2003). The determinants of enterprise risk management: Evidence from the appointment of chief risk officers. *Risk Management and Insurance Review, 6*(1), 37–52.

Lim, L., & Dallimore, P. (2002). To the public-listed companies, from the investment community. *Journal of Intellectual Capital, 3*(3), 262–276.

Lim, T. S., Loh, W. Y., & Shih, Y. S. (2000). A comparison of prediction accuracy, complexity, and training time of thirty-three old and new classification algorithms. *Machine Learning, 40*(3), 203–228. doi:10.1023/A:1007608224229

Lindsey, J. K. (1997). *Applying Generalized Linear Models* (1st ed.). New York, NY: Springer-Verlag.

Liu, B. (2012). *Sentiment Analysis and Opinion Mining*. San Rafael, CA: Morgan & Claypool Publishers.

Liu, B. (2012, May). *Sentiment Analysis and Opinion Mining*. Morgan & Claypool Publishers.

Livingstone, S. M., & Lunt, P. K. (1992). Predicting personal debt and debt repayment: Psychological, social and economic determinants. *Journal of Economic Psychology, 13*(1), 111–134.

Loh, W., & Shih, Y. (1997). Split selection methods for classification trees. *Statistica Sinica, 7*(4), 815–840.

Loterman, G., Brown, I., Martens, D., Mues, C., & Baesens, B. (2009). *Benchmarking State-Of-The-Art Regression Algorithms For Loss Given Default Modelling*. CRC 2009.

Loterman, G., Brown, I., Martens, D., Mues, C., & Baesens, B. (2012). Benchmarking regression algorithms for loss given default modelling. *International Journal of Forecasting, 28*(1), 161–170.

Loughran, T., & Mcdonald, B. (2011). When is a liability not a liability? Textual analysis, dictionaries, and 10-Ks. *Journal of Finance, 66*(1), 35–65.

Lunt, P. K., & Livingstone, S. M. (1992). *Mass Consumption and Personal Identity: Economic Experience*. Buckingham, U.K.: Open University Press. ISBN 0-335-09671-9.

Luo, L., Xing, A., Pan, F. Y., Wang, J., Zhao, T., Yu, N. Z., & He, Q. (2018). Beyond polarity: Interpretable financial sentiment analysis with hierarchical query-driven attention. In *Proceedings of the Twenty-Seventh International Joint Conference on Artificial Intelligence (IJCAI-18)*, pp. 4244–4250. doi:10.24963/ijcai.2018/590

Maier, R., & Hadrich, T. (2008). Knowledge management systems, in knowledge management: Concepts, methodologies, tools, and applications, IGI. doi:10.4018/978-1-59904-933-5.ch046

Maier, R., & Remus, U. (2003). Implementing process-oriented knowledge management strategies. *Journal of Knowledge Management, 7*(4), 62–74.

Malchow-Moller, N., & Svarer, M. (2002). *Estimation of the Multinomial Logit Model with Random Effects*. Discussion Paper No 2002-16. Denmark: Centre for Economic and Business Research (CEBR).

Malchow-Møller, N., & Svarer, M. (2003). Estimation of the multinomial logit model with random effects. *Applied Economics Letters, 10*, 389–392.

Malhotra, Y. (1999). *Beyond Hi-tech hidebound Knowledge Management: Strategic Information System for the New World of Business* (Working Paper). Brint Research Institute.

Markey, R. (2020). Are you undervaluing your customers? *Harvard Business Review*, 43–50.

Marshall, C., Prusak, L., & Shpilberg, D. (1996). Financial risk and need for superior knowledge management. *California Management Review*, *38*(3), 77–101.

Marzban, C. (2003). A comment on the ROC curve and the area under it as performance measures. Center for Analysis and Prediction of Storms, University of Oklahoma, Norman, OK 73019 and Department of Statistics, University of Washington, Seattle, WA 98195. http://faculty.washington.edu/marzban//roc.pdf

Mashrur, A., Luo, W., Zaidi, N. A., & Robles-Kelly, A. (2020). Machine learning for financial risk management: A survey. *IEEE Access, Digital Object Identifier*, *8*, 203203–203223. doi:10.1109/ACCESS.2020.3036322

Massingham, P. (2010). Knowledge risk management: A framework. *Journal of Knowledge Management*, *14*, 464–485.

Matuszyk, A., Mues, C., & Thomas, L. C. (2010). Modelling LGD for unsecured personal loans: Decision tree approach. *Journal of the Operational Research Society*, *61*(3), Special Issue, 393–398.

Mayer-Schönberger, V., & Ramge, T. (2022). *The Data Boom Is Here—It's Just Not Evenly Distributed* (pp. 7–9). MIT Sloan Management School, Spring.

McCarthy, M., & Flynn, T. (2004). *Risk from the CEO and Board Perspective*. New York, NY: McGraw Hill.

McClenahan, C. L. (2014). *"Ratemaking", Chapter of Foundations of Casualty Actuarial Science*. New York, NY: Casualty Actuarial Society.

McClernon, J. (2003). Proving the value of KM during a transformation program at ANZ. *Knowledge Management Review*, *6*(4), 77–101.

McDonald, R. (2022). Package 'derivmkts', version 0.2.5, R-Cran repository, MIT + file LICENSE.

McKibben, D. (2004). Banks evolve in their approach to enterprise risk management. *Gartner G2 Report*, 1–10.

McKinnell, C. (2006). Knowledge Sharing Between Individuals. In D. Schwartz (Ed.), *The Encyclopedia of Knowledge Management. Idea Group Reference* (pp. 507–514).

McKinsey Global Institute. (2018). Report Smart Cities.

McNamara, G., & Bromiley, P. (1997). Decision making in an organizational setting: Cognitive and organizational influences on risk assessment in commercial lending. *Academy of Management Journal*, *40*(5), 1063–1088.

McNamara, G., Luce, R., & Tompson, G. (2002). Examining the effect of complexity in strategic group knowledge structures on firm performance. *Strategic Management Journal*, *23*(2), 153–170. Retrieved August 2, 2021, from http://www.jstor.org/stable/3094439

McNeil, A. J., Frey, R., & Embrechts, P. (2005). *Quantitative Risk Management: Concepts, Techniques, and Tools*. Princeton University Press.

Mendenhall, W., Ott, L., & Scheaffer, R. L. (1971). *Elementary Survey Sampling*. Belmont, CA: Wadsworth Publishing. Co.

Meulbroek, L. (2002). The promise and challenge of integrated risk management. *Risk Management and Insurance Review*, *5*(1), 55–66.

Meulbroek, L. K. (2002). Integrated risk management for the firm: A senior manager's guide. *Harvard Business School Working Paper*, No. 02-046, March.

Michele, C. (1999). Rapporteur's report for the parallel session on imputation and missing data. *ULB Institutional Repository 2013/913*. ULB – Universite Libre de Bruxelles.

Miller, K., & Bromiley, P. (1990). Strategic risk and corporate performance: An analysis of alternative risk measures. *Academy of Management Journal*, *33*(4), 756–779.

Mitchell, V. (2006). Knowledge integration and information technology project performance. *MIS Quarterly*, *30*(4), 919–939.

Mizik, N., & Jacobson, R. (2008). The financial value impact of perceptual brand attributes. *Journal of Marketing Research*, *XLV*, 15–32.

Mladenic, D., Lavrač, N., Bohanec, M., & Moyle, S. (Eds.). (2003). *Data Mining and Decision Support: Integration and Collaboration*. Boston, MA: Kluwer Academic Publishers.

Moody's Investors Service - Global Credit Research (2004). *Default & Recovery Rates of Corporate Bond Issuers: A Statistical Review of Moody's Ratings Performance, 1920–2002. Special Comment*. New York, NY: Author.

Moro, S., Laureano, R. M., & Cortez, P. (2011, October). Using data mining for bank direct marketing: an application of the CRISP-DM methodology. In P. Novais et al. (Eds.), *Proceedings of the European Simulation and Modelling Conference – ESM'2011*, pp. 117–121, Guimaraes, Portugal: EUROSIS.

Moro, S., Cortez, P. & Rita, P. (2014). A data-driven approach to predict the success of bank telemarketing. *Decision Support Systems, 62*(3), 22–31.

Mosterin, J. (1978). La Estructura de los Conceptos Científicos, Investigación y Ciencia, Enero.

Motameni, R., & Shahrokhi, M. (1998). Brand equity valuation: A global perspective. *Journal of Product & Brand Management, 7*(4), 275–290.

Mulligan, E., & Hasti, R. (2005). Explanations determine the impact of information on financial investment judgements. *Journal of Behavioral Decision Making, 18*(2), pp. 145–156.

NIST/SEMATECH e-Handbook of Statistical Methods (2003, October). http://www.itl.nist.gov/div898/handbook/

Nonaka, I. (1994). A dynamic theory of organizational knowledge creation. *Organizations Science, 5*(1), 14–37.

Nonaka, I., & Takeuchi, H. (1995). *The Knowledge-Creating Company: How Japanese Companies Creates the Dynamics of Innovation.* New York, NY: Oxford University Press.

Nonaka, I., & Toyama, R. (2003). The knowledge-creating theory revisited: Knowledge creation as a synthesizing process. *Knowledge Management Research and Practice, 1*(1), 2–10.

Nopp, C., & Hanbury, A. (2015). Detecting risks in the banking system by sentiment analysis. *Proceedings of the EMNLP 2015*, pp. 591–600, Lisbon, Portugal: The Association for Computational Linguistics.

Oldfield, G., & Santomero, A. (1997). Risk management in financial institutions. *Sloan Management Review, 39*(1), 33–47.

OECD (2018). Blockchain Primer Secretary-General of the OECD.

OECD (2021). Artificial Intelligence, Machine Learning and Big Data in Finance: Opportunities, Challenges, and Implications for Policy Makers. https://www.oecd.org/finance/artificial-intelligence-machine-learningbig-data-in-finance.htm

Oliver, K. (2002). How to use SAS for logistic regression with correlated data. Paper 261-27, SUGI 27, SAS.

Ong, M. (Ed.). (2002). *Credit Rating: Methodologies, Rational and Default Risk.* London: Risk Books.

Ong, M. (Ed.). (2005). *Risk Management: A Modern Perspective.* Burlington, MA: Academic Press/Elsevier.

Orerler, E., & Taspmar, D. (2006). Utility function and risk taking: An experiment. *The journal of American Academy of Business, 9*(2), 167–174.

O'Dell, C., & Grayson, C. J. (2004). Identifying and Transferring Internal Best Practices. In C. W. Holsapple (Eds.), *Handbook on Knowledge Management 1. International Handbooks on Information Systems* (vol 1). Berlin, Heidelberg: Springer. doi:10.1007/978-3-540-24746-3_31

Pang, B., Lee, L., & Vaithyanathan, S. (2002). Thumbs up?: Sentiment classification using machine learning techniques. In *Proceedings of ACL.*

Pang, B., Lee, L., & Vaithyanathan, S. (2002). Thumbs up? Sentiment classification using machine learning techniques. In *Proceedings of the 2002 Conference on Empirical Methods in Natural Language Processing (EMNLP 2002)*, pp. 79–86. Association for Computational Linguistics. https://www.aclweb.org/anthology/W02-1011.pdf

Pang, B., Lee, L., & Vaithyanathan, S. (2002, July). Thumbs up?: Sentiment classification using machine learning techniques. In *Proceedings of the Conference on Empirical Methods in Natural Language Processing (EMNLP)*, pp. 79–86.

Panjer, H., Boyle, P., Cox, S., Gerber, H., & Mueller, H. (Eds.). (1998). *Financial Economics: With Applications to Investments, Insurance and Pensions*, Society of Actuaries.

Patton, J. (2007). Metrics for knowledge-based project organizations. *SAM Advanced Management Journal, 72*, 33.

Peavy, J. W., & Edgar, S. M. (1984). An expanded commercial paper rating scale classification of industrial issuers. *Journal of Business Finance & Accounting, 11*(3), 397–407.

Perrin, T. (2008). Embedding ERM: A tough nut to crack. http://www.towersperrin.com/tp/getwebcachedoc?webc=GBR/2009/200901/2008_Global_ERM_Survey_12809.pdf

Peterson, J. (2006). Ready for ERM. *ABA Banking Journal*, January, 19–23.

Pfeffer, J., & Sutton, R. (2006). Evidence-based management. *Harvard Business Review*, January 63–74.

Phaltankar, A., Ahsan, J., Harrison, M., & Nedov, L. (2020). MongoDB Fundamentals.

Philippe, J. (2007). *Value at Risk: The New Benchmark for Managing Financial Risk* (3rd ed.). New York, NY: McGraw-Hill.

Pinches, G. E., & Mingo, K. A. (1973). A multivariate analysis of industrial bond ratings. *Journal of Finance, 28*(1), 1–18.

Pindick, R. S., & Rubenfield, D. L. (1998). *Econometrics Models and Economic Forecasts* (4th ed.). Boston, MA: Irwin/McGraw-Hill. https://trove.nla.gov.au/work/2169631

Pinheiro, J. C., & Bates, D. M. (1998). *LME and NLME: Mixed-Effects Methods and Classes for S and S-PLUS, 3.0.* Madison, WI: Lucent technologies, Bell labs and University of Wisconsin.

PriceWaterHouse (2008). *How are Companies Practicing Value Trough ERM*. Retrieved at http://www.pwc.com/en_GX/gx/insurance/pdf/erm_survey.pdf

Puri, M. L., & Sen, P. K. (1993). *Nonparametric Methods in Multivariate Analysis*. Malabar, FL: Krieger Publishing.

Qi, M., & Yang, X. L. (2009). Loss given default of high loan-to-value residential mortgages. *Journal of Banking & Finance, Elsevier, 33*(5), 788–799.

Quinlan, J. R. (1987, Dec). Simplifying decision trees. *Int J Man-Machine Studies, 27*, 221–234.

Raiffa, H. (1968). *Decision Analysis Introductory Lectures on Choices Under Uncertainty*. Reading, MA: Addison-Wesley Reading.

Rao, A., & Marie, A. (2007). Current practices of enterprise risk management in Dubai. *Management Accounting Quarterly, 8*(3).

Rao, M. (2005). *Knowledge Management Tools and Techniques*. Amsterdam: Elsevier.

Reeves, M., & Deimler, M. (2011). Adaptability: The new competitive advantage. *Harvard Business Review*, July–August.

Rekabsaz, N., Lupu, M., Baklanov, A., Dür, A., Andersson, L., & Hanbury, A. (2017). Volatility prediction using financial disclosures sentiments with word embedding-based IR models. *Proceedings of the 55th Annual Meeting of the Association for Computational Linguistics* (Volume 1: Long Papers). In *ACL* (pp. 1712–1721). Vancouver, Canada: https://www.aclweb.org/anthology/P17-1157.pdf

Rodriguez, E. (2006). Application of knowledge management to enterprise risk management: Country Risk Knowledge (CORK). In J. S. Edwards (Ed.), *Proceedings of 3rd Knowledge Management Aston Conference*, pp. 190–202. Birmingham: The OR Society.

Rodriguez, E. (2008a). A bottom-up strategy for a KM implementation at EDC Export Development Canada. In J. Liebowitz (Ed.), *Making Cents out of Knowledge Management*. Lanham, MD: Scarecrow Press Inc.

Rodriguez, E. (2017). *Analytics Process: Strategic and Tactical Steps* (Editor, ISBN 978-1-4987-8464-1). CRC Press.

Rodriguez, E., & Edwards, J. S. (2007). Knowledge management applied to enterprise risk management: Is there any value in using KM for ERM? In D. Remenyi (Ed.), *Proceedings of 8th European Conference on Knowledge Management*, pp. 813–820. Academic Conferences Limited, Reading, UK, Limerick, Ireland.

Rodriguez, E., & Edwards, J. S. (2008a). Risk and knowledge relationships: An investment point of view. In D. Remenyi (Ed.), *Proceedings of 9th European Conference on Knowledge Management*, pp. 731–742. Academic Conferences Limited, Reading, UK, Limerick, Ireland.

Rodriguez, E., & Edwards, J. S. (2008b). Before and After Modelling. Risk Knowledge Management is Required. *ERM Symposium 2008 Casualty Actuarial Society – PRMIA*. Schaumberg, IL: Society of Actuaries.

Rollett, H. (2003). *Knowledge Management: Process and Technologies*. Boston, MA: Kluwer Academic Publishers.

Ross, S. (1997). *Introduction to Probability Models*. New York, NY: Academic Press.

Rud, O. P. (2001). *Data Mining Cookbook: Modeling Data for Marketing, Risk, and Customer Relationship Management*. New York, NY: John Wiley and Sons.

Samoff, J., & Stromquist, N. (2001). Managing knowledge and storing wisdom? New forms of foreign aid? *Development and Change, 32*(4), 631–656.

SAS Institute (Ed.). (1999). *SAS User's Guide: Version 8* (Volume 2). Cary, NC: SAS Institute Incorporated.

SAS Publishing (1999). *SAS Users guide Version 8*. Cary, NC: Author.

Saunders, A., & Allen, L. (2010). *Credit Risk Management In and Out of the Financial Crisis: New Approaches to Value at Risk and Other Paradigms* (3rd ed.), Hoboken, NJ: John Wiley & Sons, Inc.

Sax, J., & Andersen, T. J. (2019). Making risk management strategic: Integrating enterprise risk management with strategic planning. *European Management Review, 16*(3), 719–740.

Saxena, R., & Srinivasan, A. (2013). Business Analytics (127th ed.). *International Series in Operations Research & Management Science*. New York: Springer Science+Business Media.

Schoonjans, F. (2003). MEDCalc© Manual, Version 7.2.0.2 - © 2003 - Last modified: 23 August 2003. http://www.medcalc.be/manual/roccurves.php

Schwartz, J. (1980). Mathematics as a tool for economic understanding. In L. A. Steen (Ed.), *Mathematics Today*. New York: First Vintage Books.

Sharman, R. (2002). Enterprise risk management – the KPMG approach. *The British Journal of Administrative Management*, May/June, 26–28.

Shaw, J. (2005). Managing all your enterprise's risks. *Risk Management, 52*(9), 22–30.

Sheikh, N. (2013). *Implementing Analytics: A Blueprint for Design, Development, and Adoption*. Elsevier Science.

Sheldon, R. (2014). *Introduction to Probability Models* (11th ed.). Oxford, Kidlington: Academic Press.

Simon, H. A. (1977). *The New Science of Management Decision.* Englewood Cliffs, NJ: Prentice-Hall.

Simoneou, L. (2006). Enterprise search: The foundation for risk management. *KMWorld*, November 1.

Simons, R. (1999). How risky is your company. *Harvard Business Review, 77*(3), 85–94.

Singh, T., & Premarajan, R. (2007). Antecedents to knowledge transfer: Trust and culture. *South Asian Journal of Management, 14*(1), 93–104.

Smith, H., & McKeen, J. (2003). Developments in practice VIII: Enterprise content management. *Communications of the Association for Information Systems,* 11, 647–659.

Smithson, C. W., & Hayt, G. (2001). The state of the art in credit portfolio modeling. *The RMA Journal, 3,* 34–38.

Sobehart, J., Stein, R., Mikityanskaya, V., & Li, L. (2002). *Moody's Public Firm Risk Model: A Hybrid Approach To Modeling Short Term Default Risk, Rating Methodology.* New York, NY: Moody's Investors Service - Global Credit Research.

Sobehart, J. R., Keenan, S. C., & Stein, R. (2002). *Benchmarking Quantitative Default Risk Models: A Validation Methodology.* Special Comment, New York, NY: Moody's Investors Service - Global Credit Research.

Spedding, L. S., & Rose, A. (2007). *Business Risk Management Handbook: A Sustainable Approach.* Amsterdam: Elsevier.

Standard and Poor's (2001, September 7th). Criteria Topics, Corporate Ratings Criteria, Parent/Subsidiary Rating Links. 98–101.

Standard and Poor's (2003). Ratings performance 2002: Default, transition, recovery, and spreads. *Research from Standard & Poor's Risk Solutions.* https://www4.stat.ncsu.edu/~bloomfld/RatingsPerformance.pdf

Steenakers, A., & Goovaerts, M. J. (1989). A credit Scoring model for personal loans. *Insurance. Mathematics and Economics, 8*(1), 31–34.

Stein, E., & Zwass, V. (1995). Actualizing organizational memory with information systems. *Information Systems Research, 6*(2), 85–117.

Stein, R. M. (2007). Benchmarking default prediction models: Pitfalls and remedies in model validation. *Journal of Risk Model Validation, 1*(1), Spring, 77–113.

Steven, A. (1999). *Information Systems: A Management Perspective.* Reading, MA: Addison Wesley.

Stevens, C. (2003). Enterprise resource planning. *Information System Management,* Summer, 61–67.

Stroinsky, K. J., & Currie, I. D. (1989). Selection of variables for automobile insurance rating. *Insurance, Mathematics and Economics, 8*(1), 35–46.

Stulz, R. M. (1996). Rethinking risk management Bank of America. *Journal of Applied Corporate Finance, 9*(3), 8–25.

Sutcliffe, K., & Weber, K. (2003). The high cost of accurate knowledge. *Harvard Business Review, 81*(5), 74–82.

Swan, J., Newell, S., Scarbrough, H., & Hislop, D. (1999). Knowledge management and innovation: Networks and networking. *Journal of Knowledge Management, 3*(4), 262–275.

Taboada, M., Brooke, J., Tofiloski, M., Voll, K., & Manfred Stede, M. (2011). Lexicon-based methods for sentiment analysis. *Computational Linguistics, 37*(2), 267–307.

Taleb, N. N., Goldstein, D. G., Mark, W., & Spitznagel, M. W. (2009). The six mistakes executives make in risk management. *Harvard Business Review,* October.

Te'eni, D. (2006). Organisational Communication. In D. Schwartz (Ed.), *Encyclopedia of Knowledge Management* (pp. 734–740). Online Publisher: Idea Group Reference.

The Energy & Power Risk Management Glossary - Energy & Power Risk Management (2001, 3rd ed.). Risk Waters Group, Robin Lancaster Managing Editor, Published by Energy & Power Risk Management Risk Publications© Financial Engineering Ltd, London, 1999. http://www.riskwaters.com/guides/engloss/eprmglosc.htm

Thomas, L. C., Edelman, D. B., & Crook, J. N. (2002). *Credit Scoring and Its Applications.* Philadelphia, PA: Society for Industrial and Applied Mathematics (SIAM).

Thomas, L. C., Matuszyk, A., & Moore, A. (2012). Comparing debt characteristics and LGD models for different collections policies. *International Journal of Forecasting, Elsevier, 28*(1), 196–203.

Traykov, M., Trencheva, M., Todorin, I., Mavrevski, R., Stoilov, A., & Trenchev, I. (2015, June 10–14). Risk analysis with R language. In *Preceding of Sixth International Scientific Conference – FMNS2015 South-West University,* pp. 137–146. Faculty of Mathematics and Natural Sciences.

Turing, A. M. (1950). Computing machinery and intelligence. *Mind, 59,* 433–460.

Uzzi, B., & Lancaster, R. (2001). Social capital and the cost of business loan contracting. Proceedings, Federal Reserve Bank of Chicago, issue April. 237–260.

Uzzi, B., & Lancaster, R. (2003). Relational embeddedness and learning: The case of bank loan managers and their clients. *Management Science, 49*(4), 383–399.

Vach, W. (1994). *Logistic Regression with Missing Values in the Covariates*. New York, NY: Springer-Verlag.

Van Greuning, H., & Bratanovic, S. (2003). *Analyzing and Managing Banking Risk: Framework for Assessing Corporate Governance and Financial Risk* (2nd ed.). Washington, D.C. The World Bank.

Van Liebergen, B. (2017). Machine learning: A revolution in risk management and compliance? *Journal of Financial Transformation, Capco Institute, 45*, 60–67.

Vincent, G. (1998). Principles and application of credibility theory. *Journal of Actuarial Practice, 6*, 5–62.

Von Krogh, G. (1998). Care in knowledge creation. *California Management Review, 40*(3), 133–153.

Vose, D. (2000). *Risk Analysis – A Quantitative Guide*. John Wiley & Sons.

Waldvogel, A., & Whelan, N. (2008). Towards better financial risk learning. *Journal of Risk Management in Financial Institutions, 1*(4), 382–393.

Wang, C. J., Tsai, M. F., Liu, T., & Chang, C. T. (2013). Financial sentiment analysis for risk prediction. In *Proceedings of the Sixth International Joint Conference on Natural Language Processing*, pp. 802–808, Nagoya, Japan: Asian Federation of Natural Language Processing. https://www.aclweb.org/anthology/I13-1097.pdf

Warren, B. (2002). What is missing from the RMIS design? Why enterprise risk management is not working. (No RMIS, No ERM). *Risk Management, 49*(10), 30–34.

Weick, K. (2001). *Making Sense of the Organization*. Malden: Basil Blackwell.

Wenger, E. C., & Snyder, W. M. (2000). Communities of practice: The organizational frontier. *Harvard Business Review, 78*(1), 139–145.

Whalen, T., & Samaddar, S. (2003). Problem Solving: a Knowledge Management Process. In C. Holsapple (Ed.), *Handbook on Knowledge Management*. New York: Springer.

Wiener, N. (1961). *Cybernetics*. Cambridge, Massachusetts: MIT Press.

Wiig, K. (1993). *Knowledge Management Foundations: Thinking about Thinking. How People and Organizations Create, Represent and Use Knowledge*. Arlington: Schema Press.

Wiig, K. (1997). Knowledge management: Where did it come from and where will it go? *Expert Systems with Applications, Pergamon Press Elsevier, 13*(1), 1–14.

Wilkinson, M. (1983). Estimating probable maximum loss with order statistics. *Proceedings of Casualty Actuarial Society, LXX*, 133–134.

Williams, R., Walker, J., & Dorofee, A. (1997, June). Putting risk management into practice. *IEEE Software, 14*(3), 75–82.

Wolfinger, R. D. (1999). *Fitting Nonlinear Mixed Models with the New NL Mixed Procedure* (Paper 287). Cary, NC: SAS Institute Inc.

Wong, A., Carducci, B., & White, A. (2006). Asset disposition effect: The impact of price patterns and selected personal characteristics. *Journal of Asset Management, 7*(3), 291–300.

Wu, A. (2005). The integration between balanced scorecard and intellectual capital. *Journal of Intellectual Capital, 6*(5), 267–284.

Wurtz, D., Setz, T., Chalabi, Y., Lam, L., & Ellis, A. (2015). Basic R for Finance, Rmetrics Association and Finance Online GmbH, Zurich.

Yeh, I. C., & Lien, C. H. (2009). The comparisons of data mining techniques for the predictive accuracy of probability of default of credit card clients. *Expert Systems with Applications, 36*(2), 2473–2480.

Zachman, J. A. (1997). Enterprise architecture the issue of the century. *Database Programming and Design, 10*(3), 44–53.

Zack, M. (1999b). Developing a knowledge strategy. *California Management Review, 41*(3), 125–145.

Zhang, A., Lipton, Z. C., Li, M., & Smola, A. J. (2022). Dive into Deep Learning. https://d2l.ai/index.html

Zhang, W., & Skiena, S. (2010). Trading strategies to exploit blog and news sentiment. *Proceedings of the 4th International AAAI Conference on Weblogs and Social Media*, pp. 375–378, Washington, DC: Association for the Advancement of Artificial Intelligence.

Zhang, Z. (2009). Recovery Rates and Macroeconomic Conditions: The Role of Loan Covenants. (January 10, 2009). AFA 2010 Atlanta Meetings Paper, Available at SSRN: https://ssrn.com/abstract=1346163 or http://dx.doi.org/10.2139/ssrn.1346163

Zieba, M., Tomczak, S. K., & Tomczak, J. M. (2016). Ensemble boosted trees with synthetic features generation in application to bankruptcy prediction. *Expert Systems with Applications, 58*, 93–101.

Index

Printed in the United States
by Baker & Taylor Publisher Services

Printed in the United States
by Baker & Taylor Publisher Services